TOLSTOY'S LETTERS
VOLUME II

TOLSTOY'S LETTERS

VOLUME II
1880–1910

selected, edited and translated by

R. F. Christian

UNIVERSITY OF LONDON
THE ATHLONE PRESS
1978

Published by
THE ATHLONE PRESS
UNIVERSITY OF LONDON
at 4 *Gower Street, London* WC1

Distributed by
Tiptree Book Services Ltd
Tiptree, Essex

Selection, English translation and editorial matter
© *R. F. Christian* 1978

British Library Cataloguing in Publication Data
Tolstoy, Leo, *Count*
　Tolstoy's letters
　I. Christian, Reginald Frank
　891.7'6'3　　PG3379

ISBN 0 485 11170 5 *two-volume set*
ISBN 0 485 71172 9 *volume two*

Printed in Great Britain by
WESTERN PRINTING SERVICES LTD
Bristol

CONTENTS

VOLUME I

Preface		v
The Letters		
I	1828–1851, Letters 1–9	1
II	1852–1855, Letters 10–33	19
III	1856–1862, Letters 34–112	55
IV	1863–1869, Letters 113–152	175
V	1870–1879, Letters 153–252	223

VOLUME II

VI	1880–1886, Letters 253–306	337
VII	1887–1894, Letters 307–402	411
VIII	1895–1902, Letters 403–494	513
IX	1903–1910, Letters 495–608	627
Index		719

VI
1880–1886

Tolstoy's *A Confession*, completed in 1882 but not allowed to be published in Russia, is the best introduction to the spiritual struggle he was to wage for the remaining thirty years of his life and which was to have such profound repercussions on his art. For the next few years he published no more fiction, but wrote *A Criticism of Dogmatic Theology* and *A Translation and Harmony of the Four Gospels*, both eventually published abroad. In 1881 Tolstoy wrote to the new Tsar, asking him to pardon the assassins of Alexander II, but to no effect. In 1882 he took part in a three-day Moscow census and made his acquaintance at first hand with the Moscow slums. His article *On the Moscow Census* was published the same year, when he also began work on the social treatise *What Then Must We Do?*, which grew out of the same experiences of urban squalor and destitution. In 1884 some fragments of *The Decembrists* were published; in 1885 several popular tales including the well-known *Where Love is, God is*, and in 1886 the powerful and harrowing story *The Death of Ivan Ilich*.

In 1882 Tolstoy reluctantly bought a town house in Moscow where his wife wished to move for the sake of the children's education. There he began to study Hebrew, and there, in the following year, he first met Vladimir Chertkov (see Letter 276), who was to play an important part in the rest of his life, and with whose cooperation he established the publishing house *The Intermediary*, to provide the people with edifying and morally improving literature. Tolstoy's hardening beliefs began to be reflected in his refusal to do jury service, his adoption (though not at first completely) of vegetarianism, his renunciation of blood sports and alcohol and his attempts (at first unsuccessful) to give up smoking. He also took up cobbling as a sign of his determination to live a simple and useful life.

Relations between Tolstoy and his wife seriously deteriorated during these years, and in 1884 Tolstoy made his first attempt to leave home. In a long letter to his wife the following year (see Letter 297) he set out the reasons, as he saw them, for their estrangement; meanwhile two more children were born, and his wife also found time to bring out a collected edition of his works in 1884.

Tolstoy's travels at this time were largely confined to a journey to the Crimea with his old friend Prince Urusov (1885), and a walk of some 130 miles from Moscow to Yasnaya Polyana (1886), which he completed in five days.

253. To N. N. STRAKHOV

Yasnaya Polyana, 4 May 1880

I received your books yesterday,[1] dear Nikolay Nikolaich. I think they are just what I need. I'm very grateful to you. Turgenev has only just left us today. I haven't sat down to work for three days and I feel quite a different man—very much at ease. The weather and the spring are wonderful. Come and see us as soon as possible.

I had many interesting conversations with Turgenev. Up to now, if you will forgive me for the presumption, it's always been my experience, thank goodness, that people have said: 'What's Tolstoy doing, working away at some nonsense or other? He ought to be told to stop that nonsense.' And every time it's been the case that the people giving advice have felt ashamed and frightened on their own behalf. I think it was the same with Turgenev too. I found it both painful and comforting to be with him. And we parted amicably. So come as soon as possible. How glad I shall be.

If you are writing, I shan't disturb you. We shall only go out for walks and eat sour milk.

L. Tolstoy

254. To N. N. STRAKHOV

Yasnaya Polyana, 26(?) September 1880

Dear Nikolay Nikolaich,

I've been asking you for a long time to scold me and now you really have scolded me in your last letter, although with considerable reservations and compliments; but I'm grateful to you even for that. I will only say by way of justification that I don't understand the life in Moscow of those people who themselves don't understand it. But the life of the majority—peasants, pilgrims and others who understand their own life—I do understand and am terribly fond of.

I'm still continuing to work on the same thing, and, I think, not unprofitably.[1] I was unwell the other day and read *The House of the Dead*.[2] I'd forgotten a lot, and reread it, and I don't know a better book in all modern literature, Pushkin included. Not the tone, but the point of view is astonishing—sincere, natural and Christian. A good, edifying book. I enjoyed myself all day yesterday, as I haven't enjoyed myself for a long time. If you see Dostoyevsky, tell him I love him.

Goodbye; write, and above all, more venomously; you are such an expert at it. I have a new graduate student, a philologist[3]—a good, clever young man. I was

---

[253] 1. A German edition of the New Testament, Dahl's *Proverbs of the Russian People*, and Sadovnikov's *Riddles of the Russian People*.

[254] 1. *A Translation and Harmony of the Four Gospels*.

2. Dostoyevsky's *Notes from the House of the Dead*.

3. I. M. Ivakin who helped Tolstoy in his work on translating the Gospels.

telling him something very incoherently about your new article today, and I was very glad to see his surprise and enthusiasm.

                                                              Yours,
                                                        L. Tolstoy

255. To N. N. STRAKHOV

Yasnaya Polyana, 28(?) December 1880

I don't deserve letters like your last two, dear Nikolay Nikolaich, especially as I haven't written to you for a long time with that same heartfelt joy which they afford me.

Please write in more detail about your illness. I simply don't know what's the matter with you. I thought from your last letter that you were better. You don't like being in the doctor's hands yourself, so don't overdo it. The temptation is great—there are many doctors, and they are friends. If I lived in town I would probably go to the doctor's; but as it is I don't, and it makes no difference. I'm glad that your article is growing, and I understand this, and desire it so, and I beg you to work more on serious things, and not on trifles such as translations, especially that trashiest of trash, Goethe's *Faust*. Fet reminded me of it.[1]

Oh yes, and I also received something else from you—your introduction to Schopenhauer—the last page is splendid.[2] But I simply don't understand the 4 roots, and I'm afraid Schopenhauer didn't understand them either when he wrote it as a boy, and later on, when he was grown up, he didn't want to disown it.[3]

Judging from your letters you are very well at heart. That surprises me—in Petersburg. When I get a letter from you I terribly want to see you. Let's hope that if we are alive and well, you will come to see us at Shrovetide. I would come to see you if you lived somewhere alone; but Petersburg is, for me, something terrible and vile—quite repulsive to my feelings, if not my thoughts. I would look forward to seeing you, and would adjust my work in order to be more free.

All is very well with us. Every day I'm astonished at my happiness. Work is going smoothly.[4] I would say I am half way through. And everything becomes brighter and brighter as the work goes on. I embrace you.

                                                     Yours,
                                                L. Tolstoy

I praise your introduction to Schopenhauer, but I don't agree that pessimism is the basic feature of the religious temperament.

If you should happen to be able to get hold of a book about Philo,[5] or his works,

[255] 1. Fet was translating *Faust* at the time. Tolstoy's comment here is not typical of the many positive things he said about *Faust* at different times.
2. The last page is critical of Schopenhauer's pessimism.
3. A reference to Schopenhauer's earliest work *Über die vierfache Wurzel des Satzes vom sureichenden Grunde* (1813).
4. *A Translation and Harmony of the Four Gospels*.
5. Philo of Alexandria, a Jewish philosopher writing just after the time of Christ, whose main object of inquiry was a reconciliation of the Old Testament with Greek philosophy.

255. To N. N. Strakhov

without any trouble—the sort of book which would give a clear idea about him—please get it and send it to me.

256. To N. N. STRAKHOV

Yasnaya Polyana, 5–10(?) February 1881

I have just received your letter, dear Nikolay Nikolaich, and I hasten to reply to it.

Of course, quote my letter.[1]

How I should like to be able to say all I feel about Dostoyevsky. In describing your feeling, you expressed part of mine. I never saw the man and never had any direct relations with him, and suddenly when he died I realised that he was the very closest, dearest and most necessary man for me. I was a writer, and all writers are vain and envious—I at least was that sort of writer. But it never occurred to me to measure myself against him, never. Everything that he did (every good and real thing that he did) was such that the more he did it, the happier I was. Art arouses envy in me, and so does intelligence, but the things of the heart arouse only joy. I always considered him my friend, and I never thought otherwise than that we should meet, and that it was my fault that we hadn't managed to do so yet. And suddenly during dinner—I was late, and dining alone—I read that he was dead. Some support gave way under me. I was overcome; but then it became clear how precious he was to me, and I cried and am still crying.

The other day, before his death, I read *The Insulted and Injured*, and was moved by it.

I knew instinctively that the feeling at the funeral was genuine, however much the papers played it up.

What do you say to my wife's letter? I don't need the book at the moment.[2] I'm very grateful to you. I embrace you most cordially and send my love to you.

Yours,
L. Tolstoy

[Postscript omitted]

257. To THE EMPEROR ALEXANDER III

This is a rough draft of a letter which Tolstoy sent to Alexander III; the final copy undoubtedly underwent changes and refinements, but there is no record of them.

Alexander II was assassinated in Petersburg on 1 March 1881, by a group of six members of the revolutionary party The People's Will. The assassination itself and the trial and impending execution of the conspirators so preyed on Tolstoy's mind that, as he wrote many years later, he lay down in his study one day after dinner,

[256] 1. Letter 254, in which Tolstoy referred to *Notes from the House of the Dead*.
2. The book about Philo (see Letter 255).

257. To The Emperor Alexander III

fell asleep and dreamed vividly that he was both the executioner and the victim in the punishment of the assassins. As soon as he woke up, he began to write the following letter.

Tolstoy first tried to forward the letter through Pobedonostsev to Alexander III, but after reading it Pobedonostsev returned it to Strakhov, Tolstoy's emissary. It ultimately reached the Tsar through other channels and an informal reply was conveyed to Tolstoy saying that, as the criminals had directed their attack not against Alexander III but against his father, Alexander III did not feel that he had the right to pardon them. Pobedonostsev replied in a brief letter written three months later, saying that for him Christ was a man of strength and truth who healed the sick, while for Tolstoy he was a sick man who himself needed healing. The assassins, who included a General's daughter, Sofya Perovskaya, were executed on 3 April 1881.

Yasnaya Polyana, 8–15 March 1881

Your Imperial Majesty,

I, an insignificant, unqualified, poor, weak man, am writing a letter to the Russian Emperor and advising him what he should do in the most complex, difficult circumstances which have ever existed. I feel how strange, improper and impudent this is, and yet I am writing. I think to myself: if you write this letter, it will be of no use, and it will either not be read or it will be read and found to be harmful, and you will be punished for it. This is all that can happen. And there will be nothing for you to regret about it. But if you don't write this letter and learn afterwards that no one had told the Tsar what you meant to say, and that the Tsar thought and said to himself afterwards when it was too late to change anything: if only someone had told me then! If this happens, you will for ever regret not having written what you thought. And therefore I am writing to Your Majesty to say what I think.

I am writing from the depths of the country and I know nothing for certain. What I know, I know from newspapers and from rumours, and I may therefore be writing unnecessary nonsense about something which may not be so at all; if so, pray forgive my presumption, and believe me when I say that I am not writing because I think highly of myself, but only because I am already so much to blame towards everybody that I am afraid of being even more to blame through not doing what I can and ought to do.

(I am not going to write in the tone in which people usually write letters to emperors—with flourishes of false and servile eloquence which only obscure both feeling and thought. I shall write simply as man to man. My genuine feeling of respect for you, as a man and as a Tsar, will be more evident without these adornments.)

Your father, the Russian Tsar, a kind old man who had accomplished much good and had always wished people well, was inhumanly mutilated and killed—not by personal enemies, but by enemies of the existing order of things. He was killed in the name of the supposed greater good of mankind. You have taken his place, and have before you those enemies who poisoned your father's life and caused his death.

257. To The Emperor Alexander III

They are your enemies because you occupy your father's place and, for the sake of the illusory general good which they seek, they are bound to wish to kill you too.

In your soul there must be a feeling of vengeance towards these people as the murderers of your father, and a feeling of terror at the obligation which you have had to take upon yourself. It is impossible to imagine a more terrifying situation—more terrifying because it is impossible to imagine a stronger temptation to do evil. Enemies of the fatherland and of the people, despicable rascals, godless creatures who have ruined the tranquillity and the lives of the millions of people who are your subjects—they are also your father's murderers. What else is there to do but to cleanse the Russian soil of this infection, and to crush them like vile serpents? This is not required of me by my personal feelings, nor even by a desire to avenge my father's death; it is required of me by my duty, it is expected of me by the whole of Russia.

The whole terrifying nature of your situation lies in this temptation. Whoever we may be—Tsars or shepherds—we are all men, enlightened by Christ's teaching.

I am not speaking of your obligations as a Tsar. Before the obligations of a Tsar there are the obligations of a man, and they must form the basis of the obligations of a Tsar and must coincide with them.

God will not ask you to fulfil the obligations of a Tsar; he will not ask you to fulfil a Tsar's obligations, but he will ask you to fulfil human obligations. Your situation is terrifying and for that reason alone Christ's teaching is necessary in order to guide us in those fearful moments of temptation which fall to the lot of men. To your lot has fallen the most terrifying of temptations. But however terrible it is, Christ's teaching overcomes it, and all the snares of temptation which encompass you will vanish like dust for a man who fulfils the will of God. Matt. 5, 43: Ye have heard that it hath been said, Thou shalt love thy neighbour, and hate thine enemy. But I say unto you, Love your enemies...do good to them that hate you—That ye may be the children of your Father which is in heaven. Matt. 5, 38: Ye have heard that it hath been said, An eye for an eye, and a tooth for a tooth: But I say unto you, That ye shall resist not evil. Matt. 18, 20: I say not unto thee, Until 7 times: but, Until 70 times 7. Do not hate your enemy, but do good to him, do not resist evil, do not cease to forgive. This is said to man and any man can fulfil it. And no considerations, whether the Tsar's or the state's, may break these commandments. Matt. 5, 19: Whosoever therefore shall break one of these least commandments, and shall teach men so, he shall be called the least in the kingdom of heaven: but whosoever shall do and teach *them*, the same shall be called great in the kingdom of heaven. Matt. 7, 24: Therefore, whosoever heareth these sayings of mine, and doeth them, I will liken him unto a wise man, which built his house upon a rock: And the rain descended, and the floods came, and the winds blew and beat upon that house; and it fell not: for it was founded upon a rock. And everyone hearing...[1]

I know how far the world in which we live is from those divine truths which are

[257] 1. There is a gap in the text here.

expressed in the teaching of Christ, and which live in our hearts—but the truth is the truth, and it lives in our hearts and calls forth our admiration and the desire to draw near to it. I know that I, an insignificant, worthless man whose temptations are 1,000 times weaker than those which have fallen on you, have given in not to truth and goodness, but to temptation, and that it is impertinent and mad of me, having done evil to man, to require of you a spiritual strength which has no precedent; to require that you, the Russian Tsar, under pressure from all who surround you, and being a loving son, should after a murder forgive the murderers and return them good for evil; but I cannot help wishing this, nor can I help seeing that your every step in the direction of forgiveness is a step towards good; or that every step in the direction of punishment is a step towards evil. And so, just as in quiet moments when I experience no temptation, I hope and wish with all my heart and soul to choose the path of love and goodness for myself, so I now wish it for you, and cannot help hoping that you will strive to be as perfect as your father is in heaven and to do the greatest thing in the world and overcome temptation; that you, the Tsar, will set the world the greatest example of the fulfilment of Christ's teaching—that you will return good for evil.

Return good for evil, resist not evil, forgive everyone.

This and this alone needs to be done; this is the will of God. Whether one has or does not have the strength to do this is another question. But we must wish for this alone, we must strive towards this alone, we must consider this alone to be good and must know that all considerations to the contrary are temptations and seductions—*all considerations to the contrary, all* are groundless, unsound and unenlightened.

But, apart from the fact that every man can and must be guided in his life by nothing other than these expressions of God's will, the fulfilment of these divine commandments is at the same time the most sensible course of action for your own life and for the lives of your people. Truth and goodness are always truth and goodness on earth as well as in heaven. To forgive these terrible transgressors of human and divine laws and to return them good for evil will seem to many people, at best, idealism or madness, and to many others an ill-intentioned act. These latter will say: 'What is needed is not to forgive, but to purge the corruption, to put out the fire.' But if one challenges those who say this to prove their opinions, both madness and ill-intent will be found to be on their side.

About 20 years ago a nest of people was formed—mostly young people—who hated the existing order of things and the government. These people imagined a different order of things, or even no order at all, and by every godless, inhuman means—by fires, robberies, murders—tried to destroy the existing system of society. For 20 years people have been fighting against this nest. Like a beehive,[2] it constantly brings forth new workers and to this day the nest has not only not been destroyed, but has been growing bigger, and these people have gone so far as to commit the most terrible acts of cruelty and audacity which upset the course of the life of the state. People who tried to fight this plague with superficial, external

2. The text is corrupt, and the reading is a conjectured one.

257. To The Emperor Alexander III

remedies, employed two types of remedy: the one, that of directly cutting away what was diseased and rotten by harsh punishments; the other, that of allowing the disease to run its course while regulating it. The latter were the liberal measures intended to satisfy the discontented forces and to diminish pressure from the harmful ones. For people who look at the matter from a material point of view, there are no other ways—either firm measures of excision or liberal weakness. Wherever any people gathered to discuss what needed to be done in the present circumstances, and whoever they were—friends in a drawing room, members of a committee, meetings of representatives—if they talked about what should be done in order to excise the evil, they would never go beyond these two views on the subject: either excision—harshness, executions, exiles, the police, tightening of the censorship etc., or liberal indulgence—freedom, a moderate relaxation of penal measures, even representative government, a constitution, an assembly. People can say a great deal more that is new with regard to the details of the one or the other manner of action: many people from one and the same camp will be in disagreement over many things and will argue, but neither the one nor the other will abandon their positions—some will look to the remedy of the forcible excision of evil, others will look to the remedy of giving an outlet to, and not curbing the growing unrest. Some people will treat the illness by firm remedies against the illness itself; other people will not treat the illness, but will attempt to place the organism in the most advantageous and most hygienic conditions, in the hope that the illness will go of its own accord. It is very possible that both will say much that is new in detail, but they will not say anything new, because both systems have been tried and both have not only failed to cure the sick man, but have had no effect at all. The illness continues to the present day, gradually growing worse. And therefore I think that one should not without more ado call the application of God's will to political affairs a day-dream or madness. If we regard the fulfilment of God's will, that holiest of holies, as a remedy against everyday, worldly evil, then we must not look on it disdainfully once it has become evident that all worldly wisdom has not helped and cannot help. They treated the sick man with strong remedies and then they stopped giving him strong remedies and allowed his organism to function freely, but neither system has helped: the sick man is getting sicker. There remains yet another remedy—a remedy about which the doctors are completely ignorant, a strange remedy. Why not try it? This remedy has one primary and inalienable advantage over the others and that is that the others have been used with no success while this one has never been used.

People have tried in the name of the state's need to secure the good of the masses, to restrict freedom, to exile and to execute; they have tried in the name of the same need to secure the good of the masses, to give freedom, and the result was just the same. Why not try in the name of God only to fulfil His law, without thinking about either the state or the good of the masses. There can be no evil in the name of God and the fulfilling of His law.

The second advantage of a new remedy—also an indubitable one—is that the other two remedies were bad in themselves: the first consisted in force and executions (no matter how justified they may have appeared, everyone knew that they

257. To The Emperor Alexander III

were evil) and the second consisted in a not entirely honest connivance at freedom. The government gave this freedom with one hand and held it back with the other. The application of both these remedies, however useful they may have seemed to the state, was not a good thing for those who applied them. But the new remedy is such that it is not only natural to man's soul, but it also brings supreme joy and happiness to man's soul. Forgiveness and the returning of good for evil are good in themselves. Therefore the application of the two old remedies must be repugnant to the Christian soul and must leave behind a feeling of regret, while forgiveness brings supreme joy to the one who practises it.

The third advantage which Christian forgiveness has over repression or the artificial direction of harmful elements relates to the present moment and has special importance. Your own condition and that of Russia now is like the condition of a sick man going through a crisis. One false step, or the application of an unnecessary or harmful remedy can destroy the sick man for ever. In the same way, a single action now in one sense or the other: whether avenging evil by cruel executions or convening representatives—may seal our future. Now, in these 2 weeks when the criminals are being tried and sentenced, a step will be taken which will select one of 3 paths at the crossroads before us: the path of suppressing evil by evil, the path of liberal indulgence (both paths already tried and leading nowhere), or a new path—the path of Christian fulfilment of God's will by the Tsar, as a man.

Sire! As a result of some fatal, terrible misunderstandings a terrible hatred against your father flared up in the souls of the revolutionaries—a hatred which led them to commit a terrible murder. This hatred can be buried with him. The revolutionaries could—although unjustly—have blamed him for the death of dozens of their comrades. But you are pure in the eyes of all Russia and in their eyes. There is no blood on your hands. You are the innocent victim of your position. You are pure and innocent in your own eyes and in the eyes of God. But you stand at the crossroads. A few days more, and if those people triumph who say and think that Christian truths are only for conversation, and that in the life of the state blood must flow and death must reign, then you will pass for ever from that blessed state of purity and life in God, and will enter on the dark path of the needs of the state which justify everything, even the transgression of God's law for man.

If you do not forgive, but execute the criminals, you will only have uprooted 3 or 4 individuals from among hundreds and, evil begetting evil, 30 or 40 will grow up in place of these 3 or 4, and you will have lost for ever the moment which alone is worth more than a whole lifetime—the moment when you could have fulfilled God's will but did not do so; you will leave for ever the crossroads where you could have chosen good instead of evil, and will be forever entangled in evil deeds called the interests of the state. Mat. 5, 25.

Forgive; return good for evil, and from among hundreds of evil-doers, dozens will come over—not to you and not to them (that is not important) but will come over from the devil to God, and thousands, even millions of hearts will tremble with

257. To The Emperor Alexander III

joy and emotion at the sight of this example of goodness from the throne at such a terrible moment for the son of a murdered father.

Sire! If you were to do this, to summon these people, to give them money and to send them away somewhere to America, and were to write a manifesto headed by the words: 'but I say unto you, love your enemies',—I don't know about others but I, a poor loyal subject, would be your dog and your slave. I would weep with emotion as I am weeping now, every time I heard your name. But what am I saying —'I don't know about others?' I know that at these words goodness and love would flow across Russia in a torrent. The truths of Christ are alive in the hearts of man, and they only are alive, and we love others only in the name of these truths.

And you, the Tsar, would proclaim this truth, not in word but in deed. But perhaps this is only a dream and nothing can be done about it. Perhaps, even though it is true that (1) there is more probability of success with actions not yet tried than with actions which have been tried and proved useless, and (2) that such an action is undoubtedly good for the one who performs it, and (3) that you now stand at the crossroads and that this is the only moment when you can act according to God's law, and that if you allow this moment to escape you can never bring it back —perhaps all this is true, but it will be said that it is impossible. If you did this you would ruin the state.

But let us suppose that people are used to thinking that divine truths are truths only for the spiritual world and are not applicable to the earthly one; let us suppose that doctors say: we do not accept your remedy because, although it has not been tried and it is not harmful in itself and it is true that there is a crisis now, we know that it is no use and can do nothing except harm. They will say: Christian forgiveness and returning good for evil are all right for each man, but not for the state. The application of these truths to the government of the state will ruin the state.

Sire! This is a lie, a most evil, most perfidious lie, to say that the fulfilment of God's law will ruin people. If this is the law of God for man, then it is always and everywhere the law of God, and there can be no other law to express His will. And there are no more blasphemous words than to say: God's law is no good. In that case it is not God's law. But let us suppose that we forget that God's law is above all other laws and we forget that it is always applicable. Very well: God's law is not applicable and if we fulfil it, the evil will become even worse. If the criminals are forgiven, if they are all released from prison and from exile, the result will be an even worse evil. But why should this be? Who said so? How do you prove it? By your own cowardice. You have no other proof. Moreover, you have no right to reject anybody else's remedy because everyone knows that yours are no good.

People will say: if you release all the criminals, there will be a massacre, because when a few are released, there are minor disorders, so when a great many are released, there will be major disorders. They reason in this way and speak of revolutionaries as if they were bandits or a gang which had joined together and would be finished once they were caught. But it is not like that at all: it is not their number which is important, nor is it important to destroy or exile a few more of them, but it is important to destroy this ferment, and replace it by a different ferment. What are revolutionaries? They are people who hate the existing order of things, find it evil, and envisage the foundations of a future, better order of things. One cannot fight them by killing and destroying them. It is not their number which is important but their ideas. To fight against them one must fight spiritually. Their ideal is a general sufficiency, equality, and freedom. To fight against them, one must oppose their ideal with another ideal which will be superior to, and will include their ideal. The French, the English, and the Germans are fighting them now, and also without success.

There is only one ideal which can be opposed to them. It is the one from which they have themselves proceeded, without understanding it and blaspheming it, one which includes their ideal—the ideal of love, forgiveness and the returning of good for evil. Only one word of forgiveness and Christian love, spoken and fulfilled from the height of the throne, and the path of Christian rule which is there for you to tread, can destroy the evil gnawing away at Russia.

As wax before fire, every revolutionary struggle will melt away before the Tsar-man who fulfils the law of Christ.

258. To K. P. POBEDONOSTSEV

Konstantin Petrovich Pobedonostsev (1827–1906), Chief Procurator of the Holy Synod of the Russian Orthodox Church from 1880 to 1895 and one of the most influential advisors to Alexander III and Nicholas II. He was a graduate of the Institute of Jurisprudence, and from 1860 to 1865 was a professor of law at the University of Moscow, as well as acting as private tutor to the children of Alexander II and the future Alexander III. In 1868 he became a Senator and in 1872 a member of the Council of State, where he served until his appointment to the Holy Synod in 1880. His correspondence with Dostoyevsky about *The Brothers Karamazov* is of particular interest to students of Russian literature.

Always deeply conservative in his political and religious convictions, Pobedonostsev became increasingly associated in later life with the more reactionary policies of the period. His personal influence on the last two tsars was enormous. During his Procuratorship the Orthodox Church became more identified with the secular powers than ever before. Persecution of religious sectarians reached its height and censorship was tightened to an unprecedented degree.

Tolstoy addressed the following request to Pobedonostsev in the knowledge that in 1875 he had been responsible for gaining the release from prison of A. K. Malikov (see Letter 226, note 5). However, he counted in vain on Pobedonostsev's humanitarian and Christian principles to support his proposal to pardon the assassins of Alexander II, for he was one of the most intransigent supporters of capital punishment, and of repression generally, as the solution to the revolutionary problem.

258. To K. P. Pobedonostsev

Yasnaya Polyana, 15(?) March 1881

Dear Konstantin Petrovich,

I know you to be a Christian, and without mentioning everything I know about you, that is sufficient for me to be bold enough to approach you with an important and difficult request, namely to hand on to the Emperor a letter written by me about the recent terrible events.[1]

It is not presumptuousness which impelled me to such a bold act, but only the thought, or more accurately the feeling which gives me no rest, that I shall be to blame towards myself and towards God if nobody tells the Tsar what I think, and that these thoughts will leave at least some trace in the Tsar's soul; and that I could have done this but did not do so. You are close both to the Emperor and to the upper circles; you know all that has been said and is being said about the present situation. For the love of God, take the trouble to read my letter, and if you find there is nothing in it which has not been said, please destroy the letter and forgive me for the trouble I have caused you. But if you find that there is something new in my letter which might attract the Emperor's attention, please hand it or send it to him.

Forgive me for my boldness in approaching you and believe the feelings of true respect and devotion with which I have the honour to be your obedient servant,

Count Lev Tolstoy

259. To N. N. STRAKHOV

Yasnaya Polyana, 15(?) March 1881

Dear Nikolay Nikolayevich,

The registered letter which you will receive is a letter from me to the Emperor.[1] I don't know whether I'm doing right or wrong, but I was so obsessively worried by the thought that I owe it to my conscience to write and tell the Emperor what I think that I worried all week—I wrote a letter, revised it, and now I'm sending it off. My plan is this: if you are well, and are willing and able to do so, pass on personally or, if you like, send to Pobedonostsev the letter to the Emperor and the letter I have enclosed with it. If you see Pobedonostsev, tell him that it is awkward for me to write, and that if it should be possible to pass on this letter or the thoughts it contains without naming me, that is what I should like most of all; of course, that is only if there is no danger in presenting the letter. If there is any danger, then of course please pass it on in my name.

The letter has not turned out well. At first I wrote it more simply, and although it was longer it came more from the heart, as my family say and as I know myself, but then people who are familiar with the proprieties struck a lot out—the whole tone of cordiality disappeared and I had to resort to logic and for that reason it

[258] 1. See Letter 257.
[259] 1 Letter 257.

turned out to be dry and even unpleasant. But come what may. I know you will help me, and I thank you in advance and embrace you.

Yours,
Tolstoy

260. To N. N. STRAKHOV

Yasnaya Polyana, 26(?) May 1881

Dear Nikolay Nikolayevich,

I only received and read your third and fourth articles yesterday. I liked these two very much, but, if you will forgive me, precisely because they refute the first ones.[1] In the first article you put the question like this: some evil men turned up in the midst of a good, well-ordered society, hunted down a good Tsar for 20 years and killed him. What are these evil men like? In the 2nd article you expose all the faults of these evil men. But in my opinion the question has been wrongly put. There are no evil men, but there was and is a conflict between two principles, and in analysing the conflict from a moral point of view you may discuss which of the two sides had departed further from the good and the truth, but you must not forget about the conflict. Only the person who is involved in the conflict himself may forget it. But you just discuss. A second reproach is that in order to discuss a subject you need a clear, firm platform from whose height the subject can be discussed. But you take 'the people' as your platform. I must say that this word has recently become as repulsive to me as the words 'church', 'culture', 'progress', etc. What is the meaning of the people, nationalism,[2] the national outlook? It is nothing but my own opinion, plus my assumption that this opinion of mine is shared by the majority of Russian people. Aksakov,[3] for instance, is naively convinced that autocracy and Orthodoxy are the people's ideals. He doesn't notice that autocracy of a certain nature is nothing but a certain, completely external form in which the Russian people lived for actually a short period of time. But you need to ask him how a form, and a bad one at that, and one moreover which had patently revealed its insolvency, can be an ideal? You need to ask him that. How can the external religious form of the Graeco-Russo-Josephan dogmas of the *creed*—and a very insolent and very bad form at that—be the ideal of the people? You need to ask him that. It's so stupid, you know, that one is ashamed to object. I shall assert that I know Strakhov and his ideals because I know that he goes to the library every day and wears a black hat and a grey overcoat; and that therefore Strakhov's ideals are going to the library and a grey overcoat and Strakhovism. Two accidental and quite external

[260] 1. Strakhov's *Letters about Nihilism* were published in the Slavophile newspaper *Russia*, edited by I. S. Aksakov. The first two letters sharply criticised the Populist revolutionaries. The third and fourth also criticised the ruling classes and the moral state of society.

2. *Narodnost*.

3. I. S. Aksakov (1823–86), a leading Slavophile publicist of the post-reform period, and a fervent believer in Pan-Slavism as a guiding principle in Russia's foreign policy. Aksakov was considered second only to Herzen as a political journalist.

260. To N. N. Strakhov

forms—autocracy and Orthodoxy—plus nationalism which means nothing at all—are presented as ideals. Strakhov's ideals are going to the library and a grey overcoat and Strakhovism. To say I know the people's ideals would be a very bold thing to do, but nobody is forbidden to say it. It can be said, but you need to say clearly and definitely what you think they consist of, and to express genuinely moral ideals and not pancakes at Shrovetide or Orthodoxy, and not a fur hat or autocracy.[4]

The mistake in your article is almost the same. You condemn in the name of the people's ideals, and you don't state them at all in your first two articles, and you state them indistinctly for other people (though they are clear to me) in your last articles. In the last articles you judge from a Christian eminence and there the people have nothing to do with it. And this is the one point of view from which it is possible to judge. The people have nothing to do with it. If the people, whoever they are, fit in with the point of view I consider the true one, so much the better; if they don't, so much the worse for the people. Once you have adopted this point of view, the result is the complete opposite of what was said in the previous articles. Then there were evil men; but now these same evil men turn out to be the only people who are believers—mistakenly—but nevertheless the only ones who believe and sacrifice the life of the flesh for the heavenly, i.e. the eternal life.

Dear Nikolay Nikolaich, a rich man doesn't need to steal, or an old man to lie—I have too short a time to live not to tell the whole truth frankly to people I love and respect, like you. Examine what I say and if it isn't true, tell me, but if it is true, then be just as truthful to me when you have the opportunity. Your silence weighs heavily on me. I value and shall never cease to value friendly relations with you.

What are you doing in the summer? Yasnaya Polyana, as always, opens her loving arms to you. I hope that if you travel, you will not miss us out and will stay with us—the longer, the happier for us all.

I go on living as of old, and grow nearer to death with less and less doubt. I am still working and see no end to my work.

I embrace you most cordially,

Yours,
L. Tolstoy

261. To N. N. STRAKHOV

[Not Sent]

Yasnaya Polyana, 1–5(?) June 1881

Dear Nikolay Nikolayevich,

I always get very sad when I suddenly run into a blind alley with a man like yourself, when we have always understood each other before. And so I was sad when I got your letter.

I told you that I didn't like your letters[1] because your point of view is wrong;

4. The 'fur hat' may be a reference to 'Monomakh's hat' and hence autocracy.
[261] 1. *Letters about Nihilism.*

261. To N. N. Strakhov

failing to see that the latest evil which made such an impression on you was the result of a conflict, you discuss that evil. You say in reply: 'I don't want to hear about any conflict or any convictions if they lead to this, etc.' But if you discuss the matter, you are bound to listen. I see that a 100-year-old Chumak has been most brutally murdered by colonists, and a fine young man colled Osinsky has been hanged in Kiev.[2] I have no right to condemn these colonists or the people who hanged Osinsky if I am not willing to hear about any conflict. Only if I am willing to hear shall I discover that the Chumak had murdered 60 people and that Osinsky was a revolutionary and wrote proclamations. The murder of the Tsar made a particularly strong impression on you, and the people you call nihilists are particularly repulsive to you. Both feelings are very natural, but in order to discuss the subject you must stand above these feelings, and you haven't done so. And that is why I didn't like your letters. If I assumed, because you mention the people and because you condemn this murder particularly strongly, pointing out why it is more important than all the other murders in the midst of which we live—if I assumed that you consider the present Russian system of government to be very good, then I did so in order to find some explanation for the mistake you make in not being willing to hear about any conflict, while at the same time discussing one of the results of the conflict. Your point of view is very, very familiar to me (it is very common now and I am very much out of sympathy with it). 'Nihilists' is a name given to some terrible creatures with a barely human image. You carry out an examination of these creatures, and as a result of your examinations it turns out that even when they sacrifice their lives for a spiritual end they are not doing good, but acting unconsciously and badly, according to some kind of psychological laws.

I can't share this view and I consider it bad. Man is always good, and if he acts badly it is necessary to look for the source of the evil in the temptations which lure him into evil, and not in the bad qualities of pride or ignorance. And there is no need to go far in order to discover the temptations which lure revolutionaries into murder. An overcrowded Siberia, prisons, wars, the gallows, the poverty of the people, the blasphemy, greed and cruelty of the authorities—these are not excuses, but the real causes of temptation.

This is what I think. I'm very sorry that I simply don't agree with you, but please don't forget that it is not I who am discussing the evil which is done: you are discussing it, and I merely expressed my opinion, or rather not an opinion but an explanation why I didn't like your letters. I only desire one thing, namely never to judge without hearing about these things.

What a pity you won't be coming in summer. It's a pity for me, and a great pity for you. Sitting in Petersburg in summer must be awful, particularly if you are still sick. Perhaps you can still make arrangements. How good it would be. Please don't be angry with me or think that I don't read you carefully. I embrace you.

Yours,
L. Tolstoy

2. V. A. Osinsky (1853–79), a Populist and organiser of terrorist activities, executed in 1879.

262. To I. S. TURGENEV

Yasnaya Polyana, 26–7(?) June 1881

I would very much like to visit you, dear Ivan Sergeyevich. I felt more at ease with you at our last meeting than ever before. And however strange it is to say it, I feel that only now after all the ups and downs of our acquaintanceship have I really become friends with you and that now we shall become closer and closer friends.

My pilgrimage was a great success.[1] I could count up some 5 years of my life which I would exchange for those 10 days. I would come to visit you now, but something has happened to me since my return which has never happened before—a gumboil, which hasn't let me eat or sleep for 6 days. I got up today for the first time and feel as weak as after typhus. On Tuesday my wife is going to Moscow and I'm staying here to look after the house. When she returns, i.e. between 5 and 20 July, I very much want to come and visit you.[2] I shall be very glad to renew my acquaintance with Yakov Petrovich;[3] give him my regards. Our family all thank you for remembering them, and I press your hand in friendship.

Tolstoy

263. To COUNTESS S. A. TOLSTAYA

farm on the Mocha, 31 July 1881

[35 lines omitted]...Now about ourselves. Seryozha is quite well and is in good spirits now; he shoots ducks and goes riding and walking. The melons are not yet ripe. This is how we live: we get up about 7, and all drink tea together, i.e. myself, Seryozha, Vasily Ivanovich, Kostya, Mitya, Liza and Alexey Alexeyevich for the most part.[1] Lizaveta Alexandrovna is busy all the time with the dinner and the washing and the oil and with Masha, and rarely comes to the table. I walk about three versts, drink kumys and try to write (without success, it's true), then I walk or ride to the other farm where the herd is, or to the reaping, or to Ivan Dmitriyevich's farm or somewhere or other. Walking and riding in the village is most pleasant. I come back too late for dinner—at 12—and often have nothing to eat until evening. In the evening I go out riding again on my own or with Seryozha or Kostya, and we all have supper together again in the evening at about 9. Sometimes I have tea in the afternoon or after supper. Everyone likes it except me. Seryozha doesn't drink any kumys at all. I drink it with relish in large quantities, 12 cupfuls at a time, but I didn't drink any this morning. He worries and irritates me a lot. But as for the thing that interests you most, the good of my health, I can say that the

[262] 1. A pilgrimage to the Optina Monastery with his manservant Arbuzov and a teacher from the local school.
2. Tolstoy spent two days with Turgenev at Spasskoye in July.
3. The poet Polonsky (1819–98), who was staying with Turgenev at the time.

[263] 1. Tolstoy spent a month on his Samara estate in July and August 1881 with his son Seryozha, the Alexeyevs, Bibikov, and the children of A. K. Malikov.

kumys is doing, and has done me good and is cheering me up. The question is whether it's necessary or not. Our repas are very monotonous—substantial but not elegant. Roast and boiled mutton, cutlets, sometimes with peas, excellent carp, curds, porridge and cheese cakes...[46 lines omitted]

264. To V. I. ALEXEYEV

Vasily Ivanovich Alexeyev (1848–1919) had emigrated to America in 1875 with a small group of people in order to found an agricultural commune. The experiment failed and he returned to Russia in 1877 and took a post at Yasnaya Polyana as tutor to Tolstoy's son, Sergey. Despite his avowed atheism, he was well liked by Tolstoy, who frequently discussed social and religious problems with him. He eventually left Yasnaya Polyana in 1881, partly as a result of Sofya Andreyevna's hostility towards him.

Moscow, 15–30(?) November 1881

Thank you, dear Vasily Ivanovich, for your letter.

I think about you constantly and love you very much. You are dissatisfied with yourself, but what can I say about myself? It's very hard for me in Moscow. I've been living here for more than two months and it's still just as hard.[1] I see now that I knew about all the evil and the mass of temptations among which people live, but I didn't believe them and couldn't imagine them, just as you knew from geography that Kansas exists, but only got to know it when you arrived there. And the mass of evil overwhelms me, depresses me and makes me incredulous. It's astonishing, but how is it nobody sees it?

Perhaps I needed this in order to find my own path in life more clearly. At first one of two courses suggested itself: either to lose heart, give way to despair and suffer passively; or else to become reconciled to evil, to stupefy oneself with whist, empty talk and vanity. But fortunately I can't do the latter, and the former is too painful, and I looked for a solution. One solution suggested itself—to preach orally and in print, but vainglory, pride, and perhaps self-deception lie that way and I was afraid of it. Another solution was to do good to people; but here the huge number of unfortunate people overwhelmed me. It's not like the country, where small groups form naturally. The only solution I can see is to live well—to turn one's good side to everyone. But I still can't do this, as you can. I think of you when I break down in the attempt. I can't often be like that—I'm hot-tempered, angry, irritable and dissatisfied with myself. But there are people like that here and, thank God, I have got to know two of them. Orlov is one; the other, more important one is Nikolay Fyodorovich Fyodorov.[2] He's the Librarian of the Rumyantsev

[264] 1. In autumn 1881 Tolstoy reluctantly moved to a town house in Moscow, for the sake of the children's education.
2. The illegitimate son of Prince Gagarin and a peasant girl, Fyodorov taught in primary schools before becoming Librarian of the Rumyantsev Library. He was abnormally ascetic, and

264. To V. I. Alexeyev

Library. You remember, I told you about him. He has drawn up a plan for the common good of all mankind, which has as its object the resurrection of all people in the flesh. In the first place, it isn't as mad as it seems. (Don't be afraid, I don't share, and never have shared his views, but I understand them in such a way as to feel able to defend these views against any other belief which has an external object). In the second place, and most important, he is, thanks to this belief, the purest type of Christian in his way of life. When I talk to him about fulfilling Christ's teaching he says: yes, of course, and I know he fulfils it. He is 60 years old, a pauper who gives everything away and is always cheerful and gentle. Orlov, who has suffered—he spent 2 years in prison over the Nechayev[3] affair and is ill—is also an ascetic in his way of life, feeds 9 people and lives a good life. He's a teacher in a railway school.

Solovyov is here. But he's all head. I've been to Syutayev's[4] again. He's also a Christian in deed as well. Orlov and Fyodorov have read my *Short Exposition*[5] and we think alike. So do Syutayev and I, in everything down to the smallest details. So things would seem fine. Moreover, I'm writing stories in which I want to express my thoughts. Things would seem fine, but there is simply no peace and quiet. Festivities, indifference, proprieties, and the habitual presence of evil and deceit oppress me. I stay at home and try to work in the mornings—it's not going well—and at 2 or 3 o'clock I go across the Moscow river to saw wood. When I have the strength and the desire to climb the hill, it refreshes me and gives me new strength—you see real life and plunge into it at least sporadically and come out refreshed. But sometimes I don't go out. About 3 weeks ago I grew weak and stopped going for walks, and I completely lost heart—bad temper and depression. In the evenings I stay at home and am overwhelmed by guests. Though the talk may be interesting, it's futile and I want to shut myself off from it now.

Please write more often. Kiss Lizaveta Alexandrovna, Liza and Kolya for me.[6] Liza wrote a splendid letter; she and Lizaveta Alexandrovna may feel bored, but how I envy your life.

I've read this letter through and I see that it's terribly incoherent, but I'm afraid I shan't be able to write any better and I'm sending it off.

I'll certainly write better another time.

---

completely indifferent to money and status. He shared many of Tolstoy's anarchical and co-operative ideals, but his belief in the resurrection of all people in the flesh was quite alien to Tolstoy.

3. The organiser of several revolutionary student circles, he was responsible for the murder of a group member suspected of disloyalty, an incident which attracted widespread attention and gave Dostoyevsky a theme for his novel *The Devils*.

4. V. K. Syutayev (1819–92), a sectarian peasant who lived according to Christian anarchist principles. He and his sons gave up their business in Moscow, renounced the state and the Orthodox Church, and lived on their own commune. His life and ideals made a profound impression on Tolstoy who regarded him as one of his main teachers.

5. *A Short Exposition of the Gospels.*

6. Lizaveta Alexandrovna, the wife of V. I. Alexeyev; Liza, the daughter of A. K. Malikov, who was living with the Alexeyevs at the time; Kolya, Alexeyev's son.

265. To COUNTESS S. A. TOLSTAYA

Yasnaya Polyana, 4 March 1882
Thursday, 9 p.m.

No news from me here about myself. I sleep little and for that reason I can't work. I'm better today in the sense that I ate better, with a good appetite. I sit all by myself—reading and playing patience. The weather is poor. It's thawing and windy, and there's a droning noise day and night. I'm doing some splendid reading. I want to collect all the articles from the *Revue*[1] to do with philosophy and religion; they will make a wonderful collection of religious and philosophical trends of thought over 20 years. When I get tired of this reading, I take up the *Revue Étrangère* for 1834 and read the stories in it—also very interesting. They didn't get your letter in Tula yesterday—they probably didn't know how to ask for it. On the other hand, I got your letter at Kozlovka. I was very glad to get it. Don't worry about me, and above all don't blame yourself. 'Forgive us our trespasses, as we forgive them that trespass…' Once a man forgives others, he is right himself. And you forgive in your letter, and are not angry with anyone. And I've ceased to reproach you a long time ago.[2] I only felt like that at first. I don't know why I was so downcast. Perhaps my age, perhaps ill health and haemorrhoids; anyway I've nothing to complain about. Life in Moscow gave me a great deal, made my work clearer to me, if there is still some for me to do, and brought me nearer to you than before. What will you write today? You don't write about yourself—how your health is. Please don't be restrained in your letters, but let yourself go, as the spirit moves your heart.

I walked along the main road towards the big bridge before dinner today, and was angry with Tolstaya[3] the whole time. People are driving to Tula now and you can hardly get to Kozlovka by sledge. There's some water in low-lying places, but there isn't much of either water or snow, and it's possible to drive everywhere.

How are the big children? Are they behaving badly? I'm sure they are behaving badly, and you're cross. It's fun to behave badly, even to nobody in particular, simply to do what isn't allowed. Only angels don't get cross. How is Misha?

I was thinking about the big children today. They probably think that parents like us aren't too good at all, and ought to be a lot better, and that when they are grown up they will be a lot better themselves. It's like jam pancakes—they think they're the most commonplace things and couldn't be worse—but they don't know that having jam pancakes is as good as winning 200,000. And for that reason it's a completely false idea that they ought to behave less badly towards a good mother than a bad one. The wish to behave badly is just the same whether she is good or bad; but it's safer to behave badly towards a good mother than a bad one, and for that reason they behave badly more often.

[265] 1. *Revue des deux mondes.*
2. About difficulties caused by the move to Moscow, which Tolstoy disliked so much that he had temporarily returned to Yasnaya Polyana without his family.
3. Alexandra Tolstaya, who preached Christianity to him while continuing to live a privileged life at Court.

265. To Countess S. A. Tolstaya

How is my brother Sergey? Will he be staying long? I'd like to see him.

Goodbye, darling. If we are still alive we'll see each other soon and love each other as we do now. I came back again with the firm intention to say as little as possible. But it's impossible. I shan't be telling a lie if I say that my nerves are bad. This irritation lingers on.

What news of the people sentenced?[4] I can't get them out of my head or my heart. It torments me, and a most painful feeling of indignation wells up in me.

266. To N. N. STRAKHOV

Yasnaya Polyana, 12(?) March 1882

Dear Nikolay Nikolayevich,

I'm sorry not to have replied to you for so long, sorry because I know my reply about your book[1] is of interest to you and my silence is painful. I read it as soon as I received it. I was delighted with the articles on Herzen, pleased with the article on Mill but not pleased with the ones on the commune and Renan.[2] The positivists say that what people think about and have always thought about is nonsense, and that one shouldn't think about it. They haven't the right to say this, and they get out of the difficulty by denying there is one. That's wrong. You do the same, only worse. You reject not what people think, but what they do. You say they do absurd things. The problem is to understand why they do them.

I didn't like this about your book. Forgive me—not for the truth, but for the truthfulness.

I am terribly tired and weak. The whole winter has passed idly. What people need in my opinion most of all turns out to be needed by nobody. I sometimes wish I were dead. My death will be useful for my cause. But if I don't die, it is evidently the will of the Father. And by constantly surrendering to that will you are not oppressed by life and not afraid of death. Write about yourself. I'm always glad to get your letters. And write and tell me what you hear about the people sentenced.[3]

267. To S. A. VENGEROV

Semyon Afanasyevich Vengerov (1855–1920), literary historian, bibliographer, professor at the University of Petersburg and a prolific writer on Russian literature.

4. A reference to the death penalty imposed on ten of the defendants in 'The Trial of the Twenty'.

[266] 1. Strakhov's book, *The Struggle with the West in Our Literature: Historical and Critical Essays*; this was a collection of articles which had previously appeared separately.

2. The essay on Herzen rated him highly as a writer, and examined his attitudes towards political questions in the European and Russian context. The essay on Mill was devoted to the question of female equality. The essay about the Paris Commune condemned revolution, while the article about Renan was concerned with Renan's élitist interpretation of history, and sharply criticised revolutionary France. 3. 'The Trial of the Twenty'.

His works include six volumes of an unfinished *Critical-Biographical Dictionary of Russian Writers and Scholars* (1886–1904). He first corresponded with Tolstoy in 1882 when he was editor of the monthly journal *Foundations*, and invited Tolstoy to contribute an article to it.

Yasnaya Polyana, end of March 1882

Semyon Afanasyevich,

I can't do anything in time for the April number. Nor can I publish part in advance. For one reason or another I may not manage to get it done—and it will be unpleasant both for you and for me. But I would very much like to publish an article of mine in your journal,[1] and to support the journal if that will support it, because I very much like its courageous and forthright nature.

I wish you two things above all: restraint, adroitness and the art of speaking the truth in such a way that you aren't closed down. Have you such a clever person? If so, hold on to him.

And the second—and more important—thing is not to get angry or to attack people more than is required by their evil influence on society. I haven't noticed this with you yet—but it is the Achilles heel of all journals. And the interests of your journal are so important that God forbid that you should descend to personal provocation.

I am particularly sympathetic towards the financial side of your business.[2] Buy wisdom, but do not sell it (Ecclesiastes). There is something particularly repulsive about the sale of mental labour. If wisdom is for sale, it surely isn't wisdom.

My article, so far as it is written, will be difficult to get past the censors. However much I want to say all I think, I leave it to you—*a master of censorship*—to discard anything that might be dangerous for the journal.

If I can, I'll send it to you soon; send it to me in proof form so that I can correct it and revise it.

268. To COUNTESS S. A. TOLSTAYA

Yasnaya Polyana, 8 April 1882

I got home safely.[1] The room was heated; I drank tea with Marya Afanasyevna, talked about Alexey and his legacy—Semyon Stepanovich died three days before him[2]—and went to sleep. I went out this morning at 11 o'clock, and was intoxicated by the freshness of the morning. It was warm and dry, the paths shone here

[267] 1. Tolstoy had in mind an article on the census in Moscow in 1882, which he never finished.
2. Those who worked for the journal received no fixed salary, but proceeds from the sales were to be equally distributed among them.
[268] 1. Tolstoy had returned to Yasnaya Polyana after a few days in Moscow, attending to business affairs.
2. A. S. Orekhov, Tolstoy's manservant for more than thirty years, had just died, having only just received an inheritance from his brother who had died three days previously.

268. To Countess S. A. Tolstaya

and there, the grass was coming up everywhere in blades or in clumps from under the leaves and the straw; the lilac was in bud; the birds were no longer singing at random, but were talking to each other; and in the quiet, round the corners of the houses and all round the dung heap, the bees were buzzing. I saddled a horse and rode round to Bibikov's for corn...[12 lines omitted]...I read in the afternoon, and then walked round the bee-garden and the bathing place. Everywhere there was grass, birds and lungwort; no policemen, pavements, cabmen or smells—it was very good. So good, that I felt very sorry for you, and I think you and the children ought to leave earlier, and I'll stay on with the boys. Everywhere is equally good or bad for me, with my thoughts, and the town can't have any influence on my health, but it can have a great influence on yours and the children's. I had dinner—finished up the luxuries which you sent and Marya Afanasyevna had kept—and then had just settled down with a book when the sun began to set beautifully behind the wood, and I rushed off to load a gun and saddle a horse, and rode away past Mitrofan's hut. The birds were flying a long way away and there weren't many of them and I didn't fire a shot, but thought a lot about religion as usual and listened to the thrushes, the grouse, the mice on the dry leaves, the dogs barking beyond the forest, the gunshots near and far, an eagle owl—even Bulka barked at it—and the singing in Grumant. The moon rose on the right from behind the clouds; I waited till the stars were visible and rode home. And here I am just back and writing to you...[6 lines omitted]

269. To I. S. TURGENEV

Moscow, beginning of May 1882

Dear Ivan Sergeich,

The news of your illness which Grigorovich told me about and which people have been writing about since, distressed me very much when I believed that it was serious. I felt how much I loved you. I felt that if you died before me, I should be very grieved. The latest news in the papers is encouraging. Perhaps it's all the lies and suspiciousness of the doctors once more, and we shall see each other again at Yasnaya or Spasskoye. God grant we shall.

The first moment I believed—wrongly I hope—that you were dangerously ill, I even thought of going to Paris to see you. Write or get someone to write with definite news and in detail about your illness.[1] I shall be very grateful. I want to know for certain.

I embrace you, my dear, old, and beloved friend.

Yours,
Tolstoy

[269] 1. Turgenev replied that his illness was not serious and that he was recuperating (in fact he was very ill and died the following year). The letter encouraged Tolstoy to continue writing, while saying that 'his own song was sung'.

270. To V. I. ALEXEYEV

Moscow, 7–15(?) November 1882

My dear Vasily Ivanovich,

I had just dreamed about you and intended to write to you when I received your letter. I often miss you, but am glad that things are well with you. Never think that they aren't. Your lot is a very, very happy one. Of course, happiness is always within oneself; but as for external conditions—one may live in very hard conditions, in the thick of temptations, or in average ones, or in very easy ones, and you live in almost the easiest ones. God never granted me such conditions. I often envy you. I envy you affectionately, but I still envy you. I was sorry about your brother. From your description I understood him completely, and understood him particularly well because the type is familiar to me—one of my dead brothers was a little the same, and Fet's brother who disappeared in America was exactly the same. A very weak mind, great sensuality and a saintly heart. And it's all tied together with a knot that can't be undone—and life snaps. There's nothing to be done in this case, and generally speaking there's nothing to be done for another man. One can only avoid sinning oneself against such a man. Tuchkov[1] is in the Kursk province; I've asked to get his address and I'll either write to him myself, or send you his address.

We have had illnesses in the family, but now all is well and more or less back to normal. Seryozha is studying hard, and believes in the university. Tanya is half good, half serious, half clever—she gets better rather than worse. Ilyusha is lazy; he's growing up and his soul is still crushed by organic processes. Lyova and Masha seem to me better. They haven't picked up my coarseness as the older ones have, and I think they are growing up in better conditions, and are therefore more sensitive and kind than the older ones. The little ones—wonderful children—are well.

I'm quite calm, but sad—often because of the exultant, self-assured madness of the life of the people around me. I often don't understand why it has been granted to me to see their madness so clearly, and they are completely incapable of understanding their own madness and their own errors; and we just stand opposite each other without understanding each other, being astonished, and condemning each other. Only they are legion, and I am one. They seem to be happy and I seem to be sad.

All this time I've been studying Hebrew very intensively, and have almost learned it; I can read and understand it now. I'm taught by a local Rabbi—Minor— a very good and clever person. I've learned a great deal, thanks to these studies. But the main thing is, I'm very busy. My health is weak and I very often wish I were dead; but I know this is an evil wish—it's the second temptation. Evidently I haven't overcome it yet.

Kiss your wife Liza, Liza Malikova and Kolya for me. I love them all very much. And kiss Bibikov. I got his letter and the accounts and am glad to think that I shall soon see him.

[270] 1. A Samara landowner whom Alexeyev wished to approach about the sale of some land.

270. To V. I. Alexeyev

Goodbye, my dear; God grant you what I feel in my good moments—you know what it is—there is nothing better than it.

Your friend,
L. Tolstoy

271. To M. A. ENGELHARDT

Mikhail Alexandrovich Engelhardt (1861–1915), a young journalist who left the University of Petersburg without completing his studies, and was exiled in 1881 to his father's estate in the Smolensk Province for his part in student disorders. In 1882 he wrote a reply to an article by Vladimir Solovyov ('About the Church and the Schism', published in *Russia*) and sent it to Ivan Aksakov, the editor of that journal. Engelhardt's opinions were hostile to the Orthodox Church, and Aksakov refused to publish the article, but sent it to Solovyov, who corresponded with Engelhardt about the issues raised. The latter also sent a copy of his article to Tolstoy in the hope of finding support for his views, and Tolstoy replied, but his letter has not survived. Engelhardt wrote him a second letter, enclosing his correspondence with Aksakov, and this prompted a very long reply of nearly 5,000 words. The letter is mainly to do with the question of non-resistance to evil, although Tolstoy also touched upon property and the exercise of authority. The following extracts from the letter illustrate Tolstoy's understanding of the Christian attitude to violence, the essential message of the Sermon on the Mount and his own awareness of his failure to live up to his beliefs.

Moscow, 20(?) December 1882–20(?) January 1883

...If a mother is beating her child before my eyes, what should I do? You must understand that the question is what ought I to do, i.e. what is good and reasonable, and not what my first reaction to this would be. The first reaction to a personal insult is to avenge it, but the question is: is this reasonable? And it is exactly the same question whether it is reasonable to use force against a mother who is beating a child. If a mother beats her child, what causes me pain and what do I consider evil about it? That the child feels pain, or that the mother feels the torments of malice instead of the joy of love? I think that the evil is in both things. A man on his own can do no evil. Evil is lack of communication between people. Therefore, if I want to act, I may only do so with the object of getting rid of this lack of communication and restoring communication between the mother and child. How should I go about it? Exert force on the mother? I shouldn't get rid of the lack of communication between her and the child (a sin), but would only introduce a new sin, lack of communication between her and me. What is possible then? One thing is to put myself in the child's place—this would not be unreasonable. What Dostoyevsky writes, and what is very repugnant to me, has been said to me by metropolitans and by monks namely that one may fight, and that it is an act of defence to lay down one's life for one's brethren, but I have always replied: to defend by interposing

271. To M. A. Engelhardt

one's body, yes, but to fire on people from guns is not defence but murder. Consider carefully the teachings of the Gospel and you will see that the very short third commandment (Matt. 5, 38–9) not to resist evil, i.e. not to repay evil by evil, is—I won't say the main—but actually the final link in the whole teaching, the very one which pseudo-Christian teachings have assiduously avoided and still avoid, and the very proposition, the failure to recognise which lies at the base of everything which you so justly hate...

...It is said in Deuteronomy: love God and love your neighbour as yourself, but the application of this principle according to Deuteronomy consisted of circumcision, the sabbath and criminal law. The importance of Christianity is the indication of the possibility and the happiness of fulfilling the law of love. In the Sermon on the Mount Christ defined very clearly how, for one's own happiness and that of all people, it is necessary and possible to fulfil this law. In the Sermon on the Mount, but for which Christ's teaching would not exist—everyone agrees about this—in which Christ addressed himself not to wise men but to the illiterate and the uncouth, in a sermon which is furnished with an introduction that 'whosoever shall break one of these least commandments' (Matt. 5, 17–20) and a conclusion that one should not speak but fulfil (Matt. 7, 21–7)—everything is said in this sermon, and 5 commandments are given about how to fulfil the teaching. The Sermon on the Mount expounds the simplest, easiest, most understandable rules for loving God, one's neighbour, and life, without the recognition and fulfilment of which it is impossible to speak of Christianity. And no matter how strange it is to say this after 1800 years, it was my lot to discover these rules as if they were something new. Only when I understood these rules—only then did I understand the significance of Christ's teachings. These rules embrace the whole life of each man and of all mankind so amazingly that a man only need imagine fulfilling these rules on earth, and the Kingdom of Truth would come on earth. Then take each of these rules separately and apply them to yourself, and you will see that this inconceivably blissful and tremendous result follows from fulfilling the simplest, most natural, easiest and most pleasant rules to fulfil. You may think: is it necessary to add anything to these rules to achieve the Kingdom of Truth? Nothing is needed. You may think: is it possible to reject one of the rules and not destroy the Kingdom of Truth? Impossible. If I knew nothing of Christ's teaching apart from these 5 rules, I would be just as much a Christian as I am now: (1) Do not be angry. (2) Do not fornicate. (3) Do not swear. (4) Do not judge. (5) Do not make war. This is what the essence of Christ's teaching is for me.

This clear expression of Christ's teaching was hidden from people, and therefore mankind constantly deviated from it in two extreme directions. Some people, seeing in Christ's teaching a teaching about the salvation of the soul for a crudely imagined eternal life, withdrew from the world and concerned themselves only with what they needed to do for themselves—how to perfect themselves in solitude—which would have been laughable had it not been pitiful. These people—and there were many of them—expended terrible efforts on what was impossible and stupid —doing good for themselves in solitude, without other people. Others, on the

271. To M. A. Engelhardt

other hand, who didn't believe in a future life, lived—the best of them—only for other people, but didn't know and didn't want to know what they needed for themselves and in what name they wanted to do good for others or what kind of good. It seems to me that the one is impossible without the other; a man cannot do good to himself or his soul, as religious ascetics—the best of them—do, without acting for others and with others; and a man cannot do good to people, as politicians without faith have done and still do, without knowing what he himself needs and in what name he is acting. I love people of the first category, but I hate their teaching with all my soul, and I love people of the second category very much, and I hate their teaching too. Only that teaching contains the truth which points to activity—life—which satisfies the needs of the soul, and which at the same time is constant activity for the good of others. Such is the teaching of Christ...

...There are two objections or questions which I imagine you are bound to put. The first is that if you submit, as I say, to the Zulu[1] and to the police chief, and give away to an evil man everything he wants to take, if you don't participate in government institutions, courts, schools and universities, if you don't acknowledge your own property, then you will drop to the lowest rung on the social ladder, you will be crushed and trampled on, you will be a beggar and a tramp, and the light which is in you will go out in vain, no one will even see it—and therefore would it not be better to maintain yourself at a certain level of freedom from want, with the possibility of education and of communication with the largest circle of people—the press? It seems so in fact, but it only seems so. And it seems so because our comforts of life, our education and all the apparent joys which it provides us are precious to us, and in saying this we act against our conscience. This is wrong, because no matter on how low a rung a man stands, he will always be with other people, and therefore be in a position to do good to them. Whether university professors are better and more important than inhabitants of doss houses for the Christian cause is a problem which no one can solve. My own feeling and the example of Jesus speak in favour of beggars. Only beggars can be evangelists, i.e. teach us a reasonable life. I can reason admirably and be sincere, but no one will ever believe me as long as they see that I live in mansions and get through in a day with my family the cost of a year's food for a poor family. And, as for our apparent education, it's time to stop talking about it as a good. It completely ruins 99 out of 100 men, but it can't in any way add anything to a man. You probably know about Syutayev. Here you have an illiterate peasant, and his influence on people, on our intelligentsia, is greater and more significant than all the Russian scholars and writers, the Pushkins, Belinskys and all, from Tredyakovsky to our day. So you have nothing at all to lose. And if a man leaves his home, his father and mother, his brothers, wife and children, he will find 100 times more homes and fathers here in this world and eternal life as well. Many who are first shall be last (Matt. 10, 29).[2]

Now for the second question which stems directly and inevitably from this one.

[271] 1. An omitted passage raises the question of what one would do if a Zulu were about to roast one's children.
2. In fact Matthew 19, 30.

Well, Lev Nikolayevich, you preach very well, but how do you fulfil the commandments?...I reply that I am a vile creature and deserve blame and contempt for not fulfilling them, but at the same time I say not so much in justification as in explanation of my inconsistency: look at my former life and at my present one, and you will see that I try to fulfil them. I haven't fulfilled even 1/1000th part, it's true, and I'm to blame for this, but I haven't done so, not because I didn't want to, but because I didn't know how to. Teach me how to escape from the snares of temptation which have encompassed me, help me and I will fulfil them, but even without help I want and hope to fulfil them. Accuse me—I do this myself—but accuse *me* and not the path I follow, and which I show to those who ask me where it is in my opinion. If I know the road home and walk along it drunk, staggering from side to side, does that make the path I follow the wrong one? If it is the wrong one—show me another; if I lose my way and stagger—help me, support me in the real path, as I am ready to support you, and don't make me lose my way, don't rejoice that I have lost my way, don't shout with delight: 'There he is! He says he's going home, but he's falling into a swamp.' No, don't rejoice at that, but help me and support me...

272. To N. N. STRAKHOV

Moscow, 5 December 1883

Dear Nikolay Nikolayevich,

I was only just beginning to bemoan the fact that I hadn't had any news from you for a long time when I got your book[1] and letter, and the books. I'm very grateful to you for them all and for the Hebrew Bible which I was glad to get some time ago, and which I thought I had already thanked you for. How much do I owe you? When shall we see each other? Will you be coming to Moscow? I have read your book. Your letter made a very sad impression on me and disappointed me. But I fully understand you, and, unfortunately, almost believe you. It seems to me that you have been the victim of a false and erroneous attitude—not on your part but on everybody's part—towards Dostoyevsky—an exaggeration of his importance, an exaggeration to fit a pattern, the elevation into a prophet and saint of a man who died in the very feverish process of an inner struggle between good and evil. He is touching and interesting, but one cannot set on a pedestal for the edification of posterity a man who was all struggle. From your book I learned for the first time the full measure of his mind. He is remarkably clever and genuine, and I still regret that I didn't know him. I have also read Pressensé's book,[2] but all his learning is spoilt by a blemish.

There are horses which are beauties: a trotter might be worth 1,000 roubles, and suddenly it develops a flaw, and—beautiful and strong as it is—it's almost worthless. The longer I live the more I value horses without a flaw. You say you became

[272] 1. *The Biography, Letters, and Extracts from the Notebooks of F. M. Dostoyevsky.*
2. A French Protestant theologian whose works had been warmly recommended to Tolstoy by Strakhov.

272. To N. N. Strakhov

reconciled with Turgenev. I grew very fond of him too, and mainly because he didn't have a flaw, and a sturdy little steed without a flaw will get you there, while you might get nowhere on a trotter, and it may even land you in a ditch. Both Pressensé and Dostoyevsky have flaws. All the learning of the one and all the brain and heart of the other were of no avail. Surely Turgenev will outlive Dostoyevsky, and not because of his artistry but because he is without flaws. I embrace you most cordially. Oh yes, an unfortunate thing happened to me which affects you as well. I went for a week to the country in the middle of October and on my return home from the station I dropped a case out of the sledge. The case contained books and manuscripts, and proofs. One book which was lost was yours; the first volume of Griesbach. All advertisements have led to nothing. I hope to find a copy in the second-hand bookshops. I know you will forgive me, but I'm so ashamed and annoyed to be without a book which I always need.

Lev Tolstoy

273. To A. N. PYPIN

Alexander Nikolayevich Pypin (1833–1904), a distinguished historian of Russian literature and society, and a member of the Academy of Sciences. A cousin of N. G. Chernyshevsky, he was influenced by the ideas of Chernyshevsky and Belinsky, but never became a political radical. He was a man of immense learning, and a prolific writer who published more than 1,200 works on the history of Russian, Slavonic and European literature, the history of social thought, ethnography, palaeography and folklore. His best-known works include *A History of Russian Literature*, *A History of Russian Ethnography* and *A History of Slavonic Literatures*. He made a special attempt to study Slavonic folklore in its entirety, and to further the relatively neglected study of ancient Russian literature. His general theory of literary development placed the literary work in its social and historical context, and he had many affinities with Western European cultural historians of his day.

Moscow, 10 January 1884

Alexander Nikolayevich,

I am very glad of the opportunity to enter into personal relations with you. I have known you for a long time and respect you. I shall hand over Turgenev's letters to you with pleasure.[1] I'm afraid I shall not be able to find many. I'm very careless. I shall be going to the country about Shrovetide and will send you what I can find. I have no secrets, i.e. nothing to hide from other people. So do what you like with the letters.

I am sending you one letter now which my sister gave me here. I think it will be very interesting to you. My sister, Countess Marya Nikolayevna Tolstaya (Moscow, Metropole Hotel) was friendly with Turgenev; he got to like me through my

[273] 1. Pypin had asked for Turgenev's letters to Tolstoy in connection with a literary biography of Turgenev which he was planning to write.

273. To A. N. Pypin

letters, made her acquaintance before we became acquainted and wrote to her. Apply to her. Apart from this letter she must have other interesting ones.

I sympathise very much with your work, and am very interested in it. I am not writing anything about Turgenev because I have too much to say about him, and all in one connection. I always loved him, but only after his death did I appreciate him properly. I am sure that you see Turgenev's importance where I see it too, and so I am very glad about your work. I cannot, however, refrain from saying what I think about him. The chief thing about him is his *truthfulness*.—In my opinion in every literary work (including works of art) there are three factors: (1) who, and what sort of man is speaking? (2) how?—is he speaking well or badly? and (3) is he saying what he thinks and absolutely what he thinks and feels? Various combinations of these three factors define for me all the works of human thought. Turgenev was a fine man (not very profound, very weak, but a good and kind man) who always expressed well *the very thing* that he thought and felt. These three factors rarely come together so propitiously, and nothing more can be asked of a man, and therefore Turgenev's influence on our literature was very good and fruitful. He lived and searched and expressed in his works what he found—everything he found. He didn't use his talent (the ability to portray well) in order to conceal his soul, as people have done and do, but in order to turn it fully to the light. He had nothing to fear. In my opinion there are three phases in his life and works: (1) belief in beauty (a woman's love—art). This is expressed in very many of his things; (2) doubt about this and doubt about everything. This is expressed both touchingly and charmingly in *Enough*; and (3) an unformulated belief in the good—love and self-sacrifice—which guided him in his life and works—unformulated, as though deliberately, for fear of profaning it (he says himself somewhere that only the unconscious is strong and effective in him) and expressed through all his self-sacrificing characters and most clearly and charmingly of all in *Don Quixote*, where the paradoxical nature and peculiarity of the form liberated him from his feeling of shyness at his role of preacher of the good. There is a lot more I would like to say about him. I very much regretted that I was prevented from speaking about him.[2]

Today is the first day that I haven't been busy with the proofs of what I am publishing.[3] I took the last of it to the printers yesterday. I can't imagine what the censors will do. It can't be passed in my view. Nor in their view either, I think. I press your hand in friendship.

L. Tolstoy

2. Tolstoy had been invited to speak about Turgenev at a meeting of the Society of Lovers of Russian Literature to be held in his memory on 23 October 1883. The lecture was banned by the censor.
3. *What I Believe.*

274. To COUNTESS S. A. TOLSTAYA

Moscow, 29 January 1884
Sunday

I'm writing earlier than usual—7 o'clock in the evening—because I've moved house; Bibikov came and invited me to his house for the night, to which I agreed. I'm afraid there will be a smell of fumes. This morning I read *Macbeth* with great care—a farcical play written by a clever actor with a good memory who has read a lot of clever books—an improved *Robber Churkin*.[1] Then I went out with my skis and gun; I got as far as Grumant, and from there along the forest road in the Tula direction and across the forest to the inn and back along the main road. A drunken peasant picked me up, kissed me and Bulka, and said that I was his father. The kindest, most perfect and dearest creature in the world is a drunken—not too drunken—peasant. I had some splendid thoughts on the way. You can't imagine my pleasant feeling of freedom after finishing my work. I've stopped feeling like une machine a écrire. I too keep thinking and worrying about the older children. I got your short letter today. Tomorrow morning I'm returning to Yasnaya.

L.T.

275. To N. N. GAY senior

Nikolay Nikolayevich Gay (1831–94), a distinguished Russian artist, studied in Kiev, Petersburg and abroad, and became widely known on his return to Russia for his painting *The Last Supper* and other pictures based on scenes from the Gospels and from Russian history. In later life he was deeply influenced by Tolstoy's religious and ethical views, which profoundly affected his way of life and the content of his art. Tolstoy once said of him: 'If I am not in the room, Nikolay Nikolayevich can answer you: he will say the same thing as me.' He frequently visited the Tolstoys in Moscow, and illustrated Tolstoy's story *What Men Live By*. Both men had the greatest respect for the other, as artist and human being. Their considerable correspondence has been published as a separate volume in the Soviet Union.

Moscow, 2–3(?) March 1884

Dear Nikolay Nikolayevich,

I was very glad to get your letter. Our life goes on in the same old way with the only difference that I don't have the concentrated work to do which I had when you were here, and as a result I can put up more calmly with the foolish life which goes on all round me. I am busy with another task which I'll tell you about later—

[274] 1. A contemporary novel concerned with the exploits of a thief and murderer named Churkin in the late 1870s.

one which doesn't require such concentration.[1] My book,[2] instead of being burnt as it should have been according to the laws, was taken to Petersburg, and copies have been examined there by the authorities. I'm very glad about this. Perhaps someone will understand it. About your portrait[3]—I have only heard from a visitor from Petersburg that it is hanging in a special room with Kramskoy's portrait of Maykov and that the doors into the room are shut and not many people go in there. I haven't heard any opinions yet.

I understand what you have painted. It's true that figuratively speaking we are living through the period, not of Christ's preaching or his resurrection, but the period of the crucifixion. I won't believe for anything that He was resurrected in the body, but I shall never lose the belief that He will be resurrected in His teaching. Death is birth, and we have lived to see the death of His teaching, therefore birth is already close at hand. Cordial greetings to Anna Petrovna from me and all of us. I rarely have to write these words so truthfully. Give your granddaughter a kiss from me.

Yours,
L. Tolstoy

276. To V. G. CHERTKOV

Vladimir Grigoryevich Chertkov (1854–1936), Tolstoy's most famous and dedicated disciple, was profoundly influenced by his religious and ethical ideas, and was responsible for publishing abroad and popularising many of his works which were banned by the censor. He was the dominant figure in Tolstoy's life after 1883.

Until his own spiritual crisis in the late 1870s, Chertkov's life had followed a course common to most young aristocrats of the period. His family was very rich, highly placed, and connected with the Royal Family. Chertkov was privately educated; as a boy he knew the future Alexander III, and as a young man entered the Horse Guards Regiment where he soon became an officer. As an officer he was from time to time assigned to duty in military hospitals, where political prisoners as well as soldiers were treated; this experience seems to have brought on a crisis of conscience which was to some extent resolved by a study of the Bible and Christianity. In 1881 he resigned from the Guards and retired to his mother's estate in the Voronezh district where he devoted himself to improving the life of the peasants by building libraries and trade schools. He simplified his manner of life while continuing to develop his views on government, education, and the application of Christian teachings to all aspects of life. Through friends of Tolstoy's, whom Chertkov also knew, he learned at this time that his ideas were very similar to Tolstoy's own.

[275] 1. Reading and translating Chinese philosophy. It was at this time that he first thought of compiling a selection of the thoughts of religious philosophers which later grew into *A Circle of Reading*.
   2. *What I Believe*.
   3. Gay's portrait of Tolstoy at work in his study in Moscow in January 1884, and exhibited in the same year. It is now in the Tretyakov Gallery in Moscow.

276. To V. G. Chertkov

Chertkov's meeting with Tolstoy in 1883 was fortuitous: they were both travelling on the Moscow to Petersburg train. Their friendship quickly developed, and in 1884 Chertkov was encouraged by Tolstoy to set up a publishing firm, *The Intermediary*, designed to produce edifying booklets and illustrations for the masses at a nominal cost. Tolstoy actively assisted Chertkov both by writing stories himself, and by suggesting suitable works for publication. At the same time Chertkov, independently of *The Intermediary*, also printed and disseminated Tolstoy's censored writings, and translated several of them into English for publication abroad.

After 1889 Chertkov became increasingly involved in Tolstoy's daily life as he undertook to organise and preserve all his papers (letters, private writings, forbidden works and works in progress, etc.). It was this activity which led to the ever-increasing conflict between him and Tolstoy's family, especially Sofya Andreyevna.

Chertkov's publicist activity on behalf of persecuted sectarians and conscientious objectors to military service led to his being exiled in 1897. He and his family were allowed to settle in England, and he spent nearly eleven years there in all. While in England, and more particularly in Christchurch, Hampshire, he continued his publishing and publicist activities. He founded the so-called Free Age Press which issued in English more than sixty volumes of works by Tolstoy and authors of kindred views. He also started a Russian journal *The Free Word*, with information about Tolstoy and his followers, material about religious persecution in Russia and abroad, and articles on Christian anarchism among other subjects. His excellent command of English made him much sought after as a public speaker, and he lectured in many parts of England on Tolstoy's moral and religious ideas.

After the 1905 Russian revolution Chertkov was able to return to Russia on occasions and he eventually left England for good in 1908. For the next two years he worked closely with Tolstoy and was with him when he died at the railway station at Astapovo in 1910.

A more negative side to Chertkov's activity was revealed by the part he played in Tolstoy's strained family life, especially by his conflict with Sofya Andreyevna over Tolstoy's will and personal papers. Several people who observed the worsening family situation in the last years of Tolstoy's life—Aylmer Maude and Valentin Bulgakov, Tolstoy's secretary—although sympathetic to Tolstoy's ideas themselves, felt that Chertkov's interference in family affairs was unjustified and was a strong contributory factor in a continuing series of family crises. Under Chertkov's influence, Tolstoy amended a clause to his will stating that all his papers—personal and otherwise—were to go to Chertkov after his death, to be published or disposed of as his associate saw fit. This led to lengthy legal battles after 1910. Chertkov seems to have aroused animosity in some Tolstoyans by his dictatorial methods, and Tolstoy himself had occasion early in their friendship to criticise him for considering religious conversion as an end in itself.

After Tolstoy's death, Chertkov continued to play an important part in editing and introducing his works and writing about him, and for a number of years edited a journal called *The Voice of Tolstoy and Unity*. In 1928 he was appointed general editor of the Jubilee edition of Tolstoy's works in ninety volumes, a position he continued to hold until his death in 1936.

The letter translated below is the fifth in the correspondence between the two men, a correspondence which extended to nearly a thousand letters in all.

Moscow, 4–6 March 1884

Dear Vladimir Grigoryevich,

Thank you for writing to me. Any letter of yours disturbs me. I'll tell you my feeling when I get your letters: I'm frightened and alarmed in case you should break your neck. And not because I don't trust your strength, or that I don't value you highly; not because you have climbed up terribly high in my opinion (where you need to be), but because I think you are insecure there. I say this because I love you very much and because the work you are doing on this bell-tower is very dear to me. I want to give advice and am frightened of interfering. One thing I can't help saying in reply to your last letter but one. You ought to get married—i.e. I think you will be safer high up there if you tie this rope round you. I was alarmed by the words in your last letter but one: '*I have had a lot to drink and I have depraved thoughts.*' I know you deliberately exaggerate what is shameful, and in this respect I always make you an example for myself; but this is frightening. Another thing— I'm afraid you are carried away by proselytism—by conversion as an end in itself. Conversion is only effective and is only accomplished when it is the consequence (almost unconscious) of one's own consolidation and therefore improvement. It seems so to me and so it was with me. Please don't blame me for teaching you—I say what I feel, and it turns out badly...[15 lines omitted]

277. To V. G. CHERTKOV

Moscow, 27 March 1884

...[1] I shall write about myself: I would like to say that I'm happy and cheerful, but I can't. I'm not unhappy—far from it—and I've not become feeble yet—still further from it. But I feel miserable. I have no work which can completely absorb me and make me work like a madman in the knowledge that it is my own concern, and so I am sensitive to the life around me and to my own life, and this life is repulsive.

I went for a walk yesterday night.[2] On the way back I saw some tussle going on in the *Deviche Pole*[3] and heard a policeman shouting: 'Take them away, Kasim.' I asked what was going on. They had picked up some prostitutes from Protochny Street: three were taken away but one who was drunk dropped behind. I waited. A yardman with a lantern caught up with her: she was a girl of the same build as my

---

[277] 1. The following translates an excerpt made by Chertkov from a letter that Tolstoy asked him to destroy, but which has survived in this form.
2. Both incidents here are also described in chapter 24 of *What Then Must We Do?*
3. Literally 'Maidens Field', a suburban area of Moscow not far from Tolstoy's home.

277. To V. G. Chertkov

13-year-old Masha, in a filthy torn dress, with a hoarse, drunken voice; she wouldn't move and lit a cigarette. 'I'll give it you, you bitch's whelp', the policeman shouted. I looked at her snub-nosed, grey, old, coarse face. I asked how old she was: she said '16'. Then they took her away. (Oh yes, I asked if she had a father and mother; she said she had a mother.) They took her away, and I didn't take her home, didn't give her a meal, didn't do anything at all for her—but I grew fond of her. They took her away to the police station to sit in jail till morning, and then to the doctor's to be examined. I went off to my clean and comfortable bed to sleep and read a book (and eat and drink figs and water). What did it all mean? In the morning I decided to go and see her. I went to the police station but they had already taken her away. A police officer answered my questions incredulously and explained what they did with people like that. It's a normal thing for them. When I said I was surprised at her youth he said *there are many younger*.

This same morning a certain lieutenant Ivanov, who does some copying for me, came round. He has lost his way, but he's a fine man. He spends the nights in a doss house. He came to me in great agitation. 'A terrible thing has happened in our place. A laundry woman lived in our room. She's 22. She couldn't work and had nothing to pay for the night's lodgings. The landlady turned her out. She was ill and hadn't had a square meal for a long time. She wouldn't go away. A policeman was summoned. He took her away. "Where can I go", she said. He said: "You can die where you like, but you can't live without any money." And he sat her down in a church porch. In the evening she had nowhere to go and she went back to the landlady, but before she could reach the apartment she fell down at the gates and died.' I walked there from the police station. There was a coffin in the cellar, and in the coffin a barely clothed woman with a stiff leg bent at the knee. Wax candles were burning. A deacon was reading a sort of requiem. I had gone out of curiosity. I'm ashamed to write this, ashamed to live. At home a dish of sturgeon, the fifth course, was found not to be fresh. My talk about all this with my own people was greeted with bewilderment—why talk about it if you can't put it right? That's when I prayed: 'God, teach me how to exist, how to live, so that my life should not be loathsome to me.' I'm waiting for Him to teach me...

278. To V. G. CHERTKOV

Yasnaya Polyana, 24 July 1884

My dear, good friend, Vladimir Grigoryevich,

I was just reproaching myself for the fact that I hadn't written to you for a long time or replied to your last letters with your mother's reply when I received your last two letters: one about my writing for the people and about loving one's neighbour *as oneself*, the other with excerpts from Matthew Arnold's book[1] and with 2 questions: on the help received through prayer from an external God, and on whether it is good to give up abstract reading and 'simplify oneself' intellectually...

[278] 1. *Literature and Dogma*.

278. To V. G. Chertkov

[62 lines omitted, in which Tolstoy writes about his attempts to live sincerely according to Christian teachings and questions the true Christianity of those believers whose faith makes them reject people with different beliefs.]

But I was wrong to be distracted by arguments which convince nobody. One can't talk to a blind man about flowers, still less argue about them. Recently when I was reading the Salvation Army articles[2] I explained to myself their activities and their spiritual condition, and my own attitude towards them. I remember you explained to me the path by which they come to Christ: (1) fear of everlasting torments (2) hope of escape from them (3) the teaching of redemption (4) belief in this teaching and its salvation. This path is very strange to me. Since childhood I have never believed in the torments of hell and I know a good proportion of people who can't believe in them. I also know people who do believe in them—mostly women. This 2nd category of people (it seems to me that their characteristic feature is coldness of heart) are little able to know the joy of love and so are led to love—by fear. You know how people drive a herd of cattle to the water to drink. Some—the energetic ones—run to the water themselves from thirst; others have to be driven. It seems to me that this Salvation Army and its teaching fulfil this task—a task previously fulfilled by the church (but the church is obsolete and has compromised itself). This teaching drives people to the spring of living water—and it can do nothing more. It leads people who have gone away from Christ back to Him again. And it is good that they [the Salvation Army] should do so and nothing more can be asked of them. The man who comes to the spring of living water and who is thirsty will find out himself what to do with the water and how to drink it. They are mistaken only in insisting that the water ought to be drunk precisely in this way and not any other, and precisely in this position. And this mistake is particularly harmful to them because they have never thought and never think about the method of drinking the water, but they adopt an old, well-worn tradition which has been proved in practice to be inappropriate. My attitude to them is awfully strange. By my searchings and sufferings and above all, of course, by God's mercy I was brought to this spring; I was dying and I came to life again; I live by this water alone, and suddenly people come to the same spring. I welcome them with enthusiasm and with love, and suddenly instead of the simple kindness —I won't say love—which I expected to find, I find condemnation, rejection and a sermon to the effect that I ought, before drinking, to go through all those psychological processes, foreign to my nature, which they have gone through, renounce the awareness of life and happiness which the water of life gives me, and admit that I do it only for fear of the herdsmen who drove me to the watering-place. I'm not saying that they or anybody else ought to take my path. It's not a question of how one arrives, but where. But if we have come to Christ and want to live by Him alone, we shall not quarrel.

Your first question was about outside help from God. Who will deny that all that is good in me is done by God alone? But the question whether He is outside me

---

2. Chertkov had sent them to him. He was on a short visit to England when this letter was written.

278. To V. G. Chertkov

is a dangerous one. I can't say anything about it. He is everything, I am not everything, therefore He is outside me. But I only know Him through what is divine in me, therefore He is always in me and outside me. But this is dangerous and, I'm afraid, blasphemous metaphysics. As for the question of prayer and help through prayer. This question has been occupying me recently too. Almost every day now I feel the need to pray, to ask God's help. This need is natural (to us, at least, accustomed to it from childhood); perhaps natural to all people, as I think. To feel one's weakness and to seek help from without, i.e. not simply by struggling against evil but seeking methods by which evil might be overcome—is called to pray. To pray doesn't mean to use methods which deliver us from evil; but among the methods which deliver us from evil is the act which we call prayer. The special thing about prayer compared with all other methods is that it is a method pleasing to God. If this is right, then first of all the question arises why must prayer, i.e. an act pleasing to God and saving me from evil, be expressed only through words or obeisances and other things of short duration, as is usually understood. Why can't prayer be expressed through prolonged actions of the arms and legs (is the journeying of pilgrims prayer by the legs)? If I go and work a whole day or a week for a widow, will that be prayer? Yes, I think so. Secondly, prayer is a request to grant some wish, inner or outer. For example, I ask that my children shouldn't die or that I should be rid of my vice, weakness. But why should I turn to such a great and incomprehensible God with the sort of requests which can be fulfilled by His manifestations on earth—people united in fulfilling His will—the church in the true meaning of the word? And I came to the conclusion that prayer to God is superstition, i.e. self-deceit. All the things I prayed and pray for—all these requests can be fulfilled by people and by me. I am weak, I am evil, I have a vice (this is not an illustration but the truth; I have a terrible vice) which I am struggling against. I want to pray and I pray in words; but isn't it better for me to broaden my understanding of prayer; isn't it better for me to seek the cause of this vice and find a divine activity, not of an hour's duration, but of days and months, a 'prayerful' activity which could counteract this vice? I have been trying to find it for myself. I am sensual and I lead an idle, well-fed life, and I pray. Isn't it better for me to change my godless life, work for others, do less to satisfy my body—marry, if I'm not married—and the result will be that all my life will be a prayer, and this prayer will surely be granted. Moreover, the very need for prayer—the request for direct help from a living creature—is satisfied in the most simple, unsupernatural way. I am weak and evil, and I know in what respect, and I suffer. I reveal my weakness to another person and I ask him to help me with advice, sometimes directly with his presence or by his standing in my way. This I have done. But you will say, can prayer directed to God be a bad thing? Of course not. I not only don't consider it bad, but I pray myself from former habit, although I don't consider it important. It is only important to fulfil all that God requires of me, and for which He gave me the tools. And so if I had the means of saving myself with the aid of certain actions, or with the aid of other people, and I did nothing about it, but prayed to God, I would feel that I had done wrong.

278. To V. G. Chertkov

I can't break off, there is so much I want to say. I'll tell you something that happened to me and which I haven't told anybody yet. I fell into temptation of the flesh. I suffered terribly, struggled, and felt my own powerlessness. I prayed and still felt I was powerless—that I would fall at the first opportunity. Finally I performed a most loathsome act; I made an appointment with a woman, and went to keep it. The same day I should have had a lesson with my 2nd son. I walked past his window into the garden, and suddenly—something that had never happened before—he hailed me and reminded me that it was his lesson that day. I came to my senses and didn't keep the appointment. Clearly it can be said that God saved me. And He really did save me. But did the temptation pass after that? No, it remained, and I again felt that I would certainly fall. I then confessed to the teacher who was living with us and told him not to leave me at a certain time, and to help me. He was a good man. He understood me and looked after me like a child. Then later I took measures to have the woman moved elsewhere and I saved myself from sin, not in thought but in the flesh, and I know that that was right. Well, was it prayer that saved me? You know, a person who indeed loves God ought not to pray to Him. If I love God, then I consider Him to be loving and good. If He loves me, He will save me and do everything I need, just as He made (if He did make) my son look out of the window. What am I to ask Him for? It's like a child asking for soup, when his mother isn't giving it to him because she's blowing on the spoon.

One other thing. On one occasion this year I was lying in bed beside my wife. She wasn't asleep, nor was I, and I suffered painfully from the awareness of my own loneliness in the family because of my beliefs, and the fact that they all in my eyes see the truth but turn away from it. I suffered both for them and for myself, and because there was no hope of seeing...[3] I don't remember how, but being sad and miserable, and feeling that tears were in my eyes, I began to pray to God to touch my wife's heart. She fell asleep; I heard her quiet breathing and suddenly it occurred to me: I suffer because my wife doesn't share my convictions. When I speak with her under the influence of vexation at her rebuffing me, I often speak coldly, even in an unfriendly manner; not only have I never entreated her with tears to believe in the truth, but I have never even expressed to her all my thoughts lovingly and gently; yet there she is lying beside me, and I say nothing to her, and what ought to be said to her I say to God.

Goodbye, dear friend. Write more often. When will you come?

To the second question—should one simplify oneself intellectually—I would say that one should wish to do so, but that it is impossible for us to achieve this without going to the end of the intellectual path in order to find out all its snares. This path is not long. Man is not alone. We all help one another in this.

One more thing about prayer, and the main one: remember what Jesus said to the woman from Samaria: people should worship God in spirit and in truth—the accurate translation of truth is 'deeds'.[4] This is one of the texts which, as Arnold says, should take pride of place.

3. There is a gap in the text here.
4. In translating the Gospels Tolstoy had rendered John 4, 24 as 'they that worship him must

279. To V. G. CHERTKOV

Yasnaya Polyana, 13–15 August 1884

[9 lines omitted]
P.S. I have read *The Ground Ash*[1] too. It's very good. I'm very interested in your impression of the English. It's unfortunately very true that they are not free.[2]

280. To V. G. CHERTKOV

Moscow, 7 November 1884

[24 lines omitted]...I would terribly much like to live with you. I want to see whether you are always in that tense state you are in when I see you.[1] You can't be like that at home (although judging from your letters you are usually short of time). Do you know, I once wrote about Peter I, and there was one good thing I wrote. It was the explanation of Peter's character and of all his evil deeds by the fact that he was constantly terribly busy—ships, working at a lathe, travelling, issuing decrees, etc. It's a truism that idleness is the mother of vice; but not everyone knows that feverish, hasty activity is the habitual handmaid of discontent with oneself and especially with other people. I would wish you more calmness and idleness, more good-natured, kindly and indulgent calmness and idleness. I would like to live with you and, if we are still alive, I *shall* live with you. Never cease to love me, as I love you...[12 lines omitted]

281. To COUNTESS S. A. TOLSTAYA

Yasnaya Polyana, 13 December 1884

[9 lines omitted]...I got up early this morning and sat down to work early, and I worked for about 5 hours on end and scribbled over a lot of paper, but whether there is any sense or not in my scribbling I don't know. No, that's not true—I know there is, and for that reason my heart is at ease. How completely different would be the lives of all people and how much happier they would be if they made

---

worship him in spirit and *in deeds*', and commented that spirit and truth together would be a pleonasm.

[279] 1. *The Ground Ash: A Public School Story* (1874), a novel by H. W. Pulley which Chertkov had sent to Tolstoy from England. It is the story of a young boy who attempts to lead a Christian life in a society which does not practise what it preaches, and who eventually dies from nervous exhaustion.

2. Chertkov had written that he was happy to be returning to Russia because the English seemed to be far less free as individuals, despite the political oppression under which Russians lived.

[280] 1. Tolstoy's early correspondence with Chertkov shows much concern for his personal life, which at the time was in a considerable state of turmoil. He advised him several times to marry, and occasionally complained of his apparent lack of affection for Tolstoy.

it their objective to *make* something which doesn't exist and which is good and necessary, and not pleasure. There is no real pleasure except what follows from making something. One can make pencils and boots and bread and children, i.e. people, and the thoughts which nourish these people. Without making something there can be no real pleasure, i.e. pleasure unmixed with fear, suffering, pangs of conscience or shame; and the more important the thing made, the greater the pleasure. This is so for us, for adults and old people; for children and young people the place of making something is taken for the most part by the acquiring of knowledge or skill. This happens with the old too. But with the old there's more of making and less of acquiring knowledge and skill, and with the young it's the other way round. But when in place of this you have the search for pleasure, and the taste for making things and acquiring knowledge and skill is lost, it's no longer a joke—it's fatal...[42 lines omitted]

282. To L. L. TOLSTOY

Lev Lvovich Tolstoy (1869–1945), Tolstoy's third son, was principally an author and journalist who inevitably suffered by comparison with his illustrious father. He was educated at a well-known classical grammar school in Moscow, and briefly at the University of Moscow, from 1889 to 1891, first as a medical student and then in the philological faculty. His first story, a children's story, was published in 1891; the great majority of his later stories were in the same *genre*, and often autobiographical. In 1900 he published a story entitled *The Chopin Prelude* which was intended as a rebuttal of his father's *The Kreutzer Sonata*. His literary output also included many plays, articles about his father, and a memoir of the difficult last years of his parents' marriage, *The Truth About My Father* (Prague, 1923; English translation, New York, 1924). He worked on the editorial boards of many journals. During 1908–9 he took up the study of sculpture and went to Paris to work with August Rodin.

Although L. L. Tolstoy never entirely sympathised with his father's philosophy, he participated in several of his social undertakings, especially in the famine relief in Samara in 1891–3 and in 1899. In 1905 he was a member of the basically conservative and constitutionalist Octobrist Party.

He travelled widely throughout the world before 1918, and after emigrating he lived for various periods in Sweden (his wife, whom he married in 1896, was the daughter of a Swedish doctor), America, Italy and France. He died in Sweden in 1945.

exact date and place unknown, 1884

My dear Lyova,

Mama said to me that you said that I said I would be very upset if you pass your exam, or some such thing—in a word, something that meant that I was encouraging you not to take exams and not to study. There's a misunderstanding here. I

282. To L. L. Tolstoy

couldn't have said that. A grammar school boy came in to see me and asked whether he should leave school and insisted that he wanted to leave. I advised him not to. My opinion is that a person need never change his outward condition, but must constantly endeavour to change his inner state, i.e. constantly become better. (And 'better' means more useful and agreeable to others.) And also that when there is a change in the inner state, the outward state will change of its own accord, i.e. if you had in mind some occupation more useful to others than the grammar school and you had already started it and knew it to be good and if you couldn't abandon it, then you could give up the grammar school. But since (unfortunately) you have no other occupation, or even a notion of any other occupation except your own plaisir, the grammar school is the best place for you. Firstly it satisfies the demands mama makes, and secondly it gives you work and at least some knowledge which might be useful to others. In order to do the thing I consider the chief and only thing in life—to make oneself as good as possible and to serve others—any situation will suffice: you can do it in Moscow, in a grammar school, in a palace or in the country. To do this—to become better—there are many exercises, of which one consists of finishing something you have begun and not giving it up when it seems difficult. To give up something you have begun from conviction, and to do so from weakness and feebleness, are two different things. But you have no convictions, and although it seems to you that you know everything, you don't even know what convictions are or what my convictions are, although you think you know all this very well. But it's too early yet; the thing is that I'm very glad for you, and shall be very glad to see you. And I shall be even more glad if at least in a small way, on occasions and especially now when you are alone, you will try to be better and to think about yourself and to work on yourself. Goodbye.

283. To COUNTESS A. A. TOLSTAYA

exact date and place unknown, 1884

[25 lines omitted]...You now say that I am acting the teacher. This is unfair. The whole purport of my writings is that I am expressing my *own*, my own personal faith, and not only do I not say that there is no salvation apart from my faith, but I recognise that any faith is good if it is sincere and unites us without fail in acts of love. I only say what I believe and what I don't believe, and why I don't believe. I am often surprised by the annoyance my profession of faith causes. Why don't Protestantism, Unitarianism or Mohammedanism cause the same annoyance?

I would be very glad if you and I were of the same faith; but if you are of a different faith, I understand how it has come about that you are of a different faith, and our difference cannot annoy me. But to be annoyed with me is particularly cruel. Look a little at my life. All the former joys of my life—I have been deprived of them all. All the comforts of life—riches, honours, fame—all these things I lack. My friends, even my family, turn away from me. Some people—liberals and aesthetes—think me mad or feeble-minded like Gogol; others—revolutionaries

and radicals—think me a mystic or a gas bag; government people think me a pernicious revolutionary; Orthodox people think me the devil. I confess this hurts me, and not because it's offensive; what hurts is that the thing which constitutes the main aim and happiness of my life—loving relations with people—is destroyed; it is even harder when everyone turns on you with bitterness and reproaches. And so please regard me as a good Mohammedan, and then all will be splendid...
[2 lines omitted]

284. To COUNTESS S. A. TOLSTAYA

Yasnaya Polyana, 2 February 1885

I got your last letter this morning—Friday. It's rather better, perhaps, and so am I; anyway it made me long for you less. I've spent the whole day at home, reading, writing and sitting quietly thinking. In the evening I walked to the village to call on Nikolay Yermilin to appeal to his conscience about the debt he is repudiating, and to call on Kostyushka, and Ganya the thief. She is an unhappy creature, persecuted by people and therefore embittered—she lives alone with 3 children.

There were many more impressions of poverty and suffering. I am always seeing them everywhere, but they are easier to see in the country. You can see them *all* here from start to finish. And you can see both the cause and the remedy. And I like it, or rather not so much like it as feel happy, when I can clearly see my own position among other people.

From what you wrote about Garshin[1] I'm not sorry I didn't see him. Generally speaking I'm under such pressure to see people in Moscow that the fewer there are the better. It always seems to me that they don't need me at all.

I'm reading Eliot's *Felix Holt*.[2] It's a splendid book. I had read it before, but at a time when I was very stupid, and I had completely forgotten it. It's a thing which needs to be translated, if it hasn't been translated. It would be a job for Tanya. I haven't finished it yet, and I'm afraid the ending will spoil it. My brother Seryozha gave it to me. Tell him that it's all true what he told me about the book—it has everything. This is the second time that I've written from the country and praised books that he has recommended.[3]

I have in front of me a note from a widow who came to see me today. She has no house and no land—her husband was a soldier in the Grumant barracks. She was left a widow at 32, with 8 children—the eldest one 11. When I began to take notes it took me a long time to understand her—it turned out that one was a twin. The lieutenant gave her a corner for the winter.

[284] 1. V. M. Garshin (1855–88), the author of *Four Days* and *The Red Flower*. Highly strung, nervously morbid and abnormally conscience-stricken, he took his own life in 1888. He had called at Tolstoy's Moscow home in January 1885, and later came to Yasnaya Polyana where he collaborated briefly with Tolstoy on *The Intermediary*.

2. Tolstoy read the novel in English (and spells Eliot with a double 'l' in the original).

3. The first work recommended by Sergey Tolstoy was *Tristesses et sourires* (1884) by Gustave Droz.

284. To Countess S. A. Tolstaya

I'm going to Tula tomorrow and will try to do all I can for her.

I'm taking this letter to Kozlovka—I'll open yours with trepidation. How is your health? Judging from your letters you are not at all well. How is Misha and the whole household?

Yesterday I regretted our temporary lack of affection. The result of this lack of affection is uncertainty about our mutual wishes. I told you that if you wanted me to return, to write to me and I would come at once, and not from any constraint, but with sincere joy that I could do for you what you wanted me to. But you don't write anything, or only something vague.

Goodbye, darling. I kiss you and the children.

L.

[Postscript omitted]

285. To COUNTESS S. A. TOLSTAYA

Simeiz, 15 March 1885

I'm writing in the knowledge that my letters will all reach you haphazardly, and not in the right order. It's now the evening of Friday the 15th; I've just moved into Maltsov's house.[1] He was expecting me, it turns out, and had made preparations, and had even gone to Sevastopol to meet us, but we missed each other. He's a remarkably cheerful and lively old man, not antipathetic and not stupid, but very spoilt by power.

From Baydar (the station), where I sent you a letter yesterday, I walked uphill to the famous Baydar gates; Urusov drove there. I had a guide with me, a Russian boy living in a Tatar village. His mother is a widow, and he has some job or other to support himself; but his backwardness is astonishing. He has never been to church and he gets 'Our Father' all the wrong way round. He's 17.

The valley which I walked through was charming and deserted; the birds were singing, you could smell the violets and the sun was burning hot. The prince reached the gates before me. One is meant to admire everything at the gates, and they were built for that reason. But a mist happened to get up and we could see nothing. It was cold, damp and dark; broken cliffs jutted out, and the road wound uphill. Urusov started to gasp for breath because of the mist and got needlessly worried, and had words with the driver. We got there safely in the dark. I put up at a hotel—it was beautiful. It was a moonlit night, cypresses covered the slopes like black columns, fountains gurgled everywhere and down below—the 'incessant sound' of the blue sea. The bad thing was that there were children in the next room —3 and 1½ years old; one of them was given quinine and he cried miserably, saying 'it's bitter', and then suddenly he cheered up again, while close to the house

---

[285] 1. Tolstoy had gone to Simeiz in the Crimea with Prince Urusov who needed a change of climate for his health. The wealthy industrialist, Sergey Maltsov, had a luxurious house there, where Tolstoy stayed briefly, and took the opportunity to visit Belbek where he had fought in the Crimean War.

cats were starting up a serenade. There's an enormous number of cats here. I woke up at 5, drank some coffee and walked 4 versts to Alupka. There's a very good stony road—olive trees, vines, almond trees and the deep blue sea. I sent you a telegram, had a drink of tea in a Turk's hut and went home. I went for a walk with Urusov up and down his favourite places on the cliffs and along the shore. It was so hot that I could hardly restrain myself from bathing. Before our walk we had a table d'hôte lunch: a teacher, two doctors and a wealthy merchant with a dying wife. The children were theirs. Then I wanted to go to sleep, but the cats continued their serenade. Urusov came, and he and I went to Maltsov's, had a table d'hôte dinner, then had a drink of tea and now I'm in bed. I'm very tired and sunburnt, and my thoughts are disjointed i.e. I've got out of the rut of work. I still think about the English milord, however.[2] I'll try to write tomorrow. There are still no letters from you—I'm very anxious.

The good thing about it here is that apart from the warmth and the beauty it is rich—there are no beggars. Wages are good. Those who want to live well ought to start living here or in the south generally. Urusov and I sat for a long time on the shore under the cliff. It's lonely, beautiful and majestic, and there is nothing here made by people. Then I thought of Moscow and your worries and all the pursuits and entertainments of Moscow. It's incredible that people can ruin their lives so. Till tomorrow. I embrace you and kiss the children.

286. To I. Y. REPIN

Ilya Yefimovich Repin (1844–1930) is, with Kramskoy, Russia's best-known painter in the realist *genre*. He was closely associated with the 'Wanderers', a group of thirteen artists who had seceded from the Academy of Art in 1863 from a dissatisfaction with academic tradition and a desire to bring art to the people (their name is derived from their practice of taking travelling exhibitions round the countryside). He studied at one time under Kramskoy, but was never a fully committed member of the group. Repin was primarily a portrait-painter, although his two best-known paintings, *The Volga Boatmen* and *They Did Not Expect Him*, are 'narrative' works, and were intended to expose social injustices.

Repin met Tolstoy in 1880, and later visited the family frequently in Moscow and at Yasnaya Polyana. In the early 1890s he gave painting lessons to Tatyana Tolstaya. Repin painted several portraits of Tolstoy, of which the best known are: Tolstoy writing in his study, Tolstoy sitting with an open book and Tolstoy ploughing and harrowing. He also did many informal sketches of Tolstoy's family, illustrated several of his post-1880 stories, and did other illustrations for *The Intermediary*.

2. A humorous name given to the stories for the people which Tolstoy was planning to write (he wrote one the following day) taken from the title of a cheap popular novel *The Story of the Adventures of the English Milord George*...

286. To I. Y. Repin

Moscow, 1 April 1885

I went to the exhibition[1] the day before yesterday and meant to write to you at once but didn't manage to. This is actually what I meant to write, just as it was said to me: Repin is splendid, really splendid. There is something lively, forceful, bold and to the point about him. I could say a lot to you in words, but I don't want to philosophise in a letter. We used to have a haemorrhoidal, half-witted old woman dependant living with us,[2] and you know the Karamazov father—your Ivan[3] is for me a combination of Karamazov and this old dependant, and he is just the very ugly and pathetic, yes, pathetic murderer that people like that must be; and the true beauty in death of his son—it's good, very good; and the artist wanted to say something important and said it fully and clearly, and moreover, so skilfully that the skill doesn't show. Goodbye, and may God help you to penetrate deeper and deeper still.

287. To L. Y. OBOLENSKY

Leonid Yegorovich Obolensky (1845–1906), a landowner and a versatile writer (poetry, literary criticism, journalism and philosophy), spent the years 1866–73 in exile following the assassination attempt on Alexander II in 1866. He was acquainted with Tolstoy and to a certain extent shared his ideas, but as the following letter shows, not in the absolute sense required by Tolstoy. He wrote several articles about Tolstoy, later collected in a book entitled *L. N. Tolstoy: His Philosophical and Moral Ideas* (1887). He is not to be confused with Tolstoy's son-in-law, Prince Obolensky.

[Not sent]

Moscow, 5–10 April 1885

Leonid Yegorovich,

I don't agree at all with your letter.[1] Not only do I not agree, but to tell you the truth it distressed me. You try to vindicate yourself in it. For 40 years I have worked on myself in order to produce from the fog of philosophical views and religious feelings some clear and definite views on the phenomena of life—my own very intimate daily life—in order to know what is good and what is bad. But you want to assure me that it is far more profitable to let in the fog again from which I have spent 40 years in escaping—the fog of philosophy and love generally, of high-flown Christian love, so that I should once more fail to see the difference between good and evil and calmly take advantage of the labours of other people,

[286] 1. The XIII 'Wanderers' Exhibition in Moscow.
    2. N. P. Okhotnitskaya.
    3. *Ivan the Terrible and his son, 16 November 1582*, depicting the father's murder of his son.
[287] 1. The letter has not survived.

eat people's flesh and blood, and console myself with high-flown words. No, this is no good. If Christian teaching and love (which I hate, because it has become a pharisaical word) leads to people calmly smoking cigarettes and going to concerts and theatres and arguing about Spencer and Hegel, then the devil take such teaching and love. I would rather accept bourgeois morality; at least it lacks pharisaism. That's the worst thing of all. Forgive me for my outspokenness.

L. Tolstoy

288. To V. G. CHERTKOV

Moscow, 2 May 1885

I got both your letters and the parcels, dear friend, and I rejoice that your work is progressing. But rejoice not that the spirits are subject unto you, but try to have your names written in heaven.[1] I can't repeat this to myself often enough.

Repin gave me great joy. I couldn't tear myself away from his picture and was deeply moved.[2] And how many other people will be deeply moved. I'll try to have it reproduced as well as possible. I'm sending you a rough draft of my story.[3] Excuse the scribblings. I'll send it to the printers to set up tomorrow. Likewise the cobbler.[4] There are no pictures, though, for the incendiary.[5] Can we not commission somebody in Moscow? I had an idea today for doing pictures of heroes with legends to them. I have two. One is a doctor who sucked out diphtheria poison and died. The other is a teacher in Tula who perished in a fire after dragging children out of his school. I'll collect information about them and, God willing, will write the texts and commission pictures and portraits. Give some thought to these pictures of heroes and heroines. There are a lot of them, thank God. And they need to be collected and made famous as an example to us. God gave me this idea today, and I'm terribly glad about it. I think it has much to offer. I wrote a letter to Gribovsky today, but didn't send it.[6] I can't write a personal letter to a stranger. But he inspires in me such a feeling of respect and love that I'm afraid of spoiling it by words, without experiencing it. If you see Repin, tell him that I always loved him, but that his figure of Christ bound me to him more closely than before. I only have to call to mind the face and hand, and tears come to my eyes. Kalmykova has been, and read what she had revised and added.[7] This book will be the best of all,

[288] 1. A paraphrase of Luke 10, 20.
2. Repin had adapted a painting by the French painter Bouguereau, *The Scourging of Christ* for printing in *The Intermediary* (the original had not been passed by the censor).
3. *A Spark Neglected Burns the House.*
4. *Where Love is, God is.*
5. The story in note 3.
6. A boy of eighteen who had just left school and had written to Tolstoy to describe his evolution from an atheist to a 'Tolstoyan'—an entirely fabricated story, with many melodramatic details. A meeting was arranged, and Gribovsky took advantage of it to publish articles based on Tolstoy's alleged confidences to him, using material from *A Confession.*
7. A. Kalmykova was preparing a book on Socrates for *The Intermediary* which was edited in its final version by Tolstoy.

288. To V. G. Chertkov

i.e. the most important of all. Goodbye, dear friend; write to me more often. I am well. The life of Tikhon is poor; it has no content.[8]

Half of M. Arnold's thoughts are my own. I rejoice to read him. If possible, get a copy to him in England of *Ma religion*.[9]

L.T.

289. To PRINCE L. D. URUSOV

Prince Leonid Dmitriyevich Urusov (d. 1885) served in the Ministry of Foreign Affairs and later in the Ministry of Internal Affairs. In 1875 he became vice-governor of Tula and shortly afterwards met Tolstoy. He was profoundly attracted by Tolstoy's views and the two men became close friends. They visited each other frequently in the 1880s and when Urusov had to go south to the Crimea on account of his health Tolstoy accompanied him. His death, so soon after their journeying together, was a great blow to Tolstoy.

Yasnaya Polyana, 22 May 1885

I got your letter before leaving Moscow and didn't have time to reply. The extracts you copy out from Feuerbach are wonderfully good and forceful. How strange that Feuerbach is known only as a negator. I meant to copy out some extracts from M. Arnold for you, but I shan't have time today. He will give you great pleasure because he insists particularly on destroying the concept of God as something external, 'a magnified man',[1] as he puts it. He finds in the Jewish teachings the concept of God not as a person, but as an 'eternal power, not ourselves, which makes for righteousness'.[1] Don't be afraid of the words 'not ourselves'. He only means by them that the Jews recognised a common law, common to all that exists and to man, which demands order for the world and *righteousness* for man, and leads to it. And that only on condition that he observes this law does man obtain the good. And this law, and nothing else, he calls God, and asserts that this is what the Jews also meant by God. This concept, he says, became distorted, and Christ restored it, offering a method for finding this God and 'a secret',[1] as he calls it, for fulfilling the law's commands. The method is 'inwardness',[1] i.e. the recognition of the source of everything in oneself, and the secret of fulfilling the law is to renounce life in order to win true life. I would like this to please you as much as it does me. It's 5 days since we moved to the country. Only the two eldest children are in Moscow. I'm rather miserable in the country. The wrongness of our life—the slavery of the poor which is so clear to me and which we take advantage of so naively, makes me especially miserable. I don't know why, but I often recall: 'he that endureth to the

---

8. A re-telling for *The Intermediary* of *The Life of Tikhon Zadonsky*, a model for Father Zosima in *The Brothers Karamazov*.

9. Chertkov sent Matthew Arnold the French translation of *What I Believe*.

[289] 1. These words appear in English in the original.

end shall be saved'. And although I shouldn't, I still wait for something to save me from the jarring discord between my life and my consciousness...[8 lines omitted]

290. To V. G. CHERTKOV

Yasnaya Polyana, 1–2 June 1885

[13 lines omitted]...What you write to me about my writings is not only not disagreeable to me, but is helpful and convincing. I feel I am convinced by your arguments. But—there is a 'but'—I'm still drawn to philosophising;[1] and not from vanity, I know for sure, but, as it were, to break with the falsehood amid which I lived with my companions in falsehood. If you are going to be led away from the hotel where you are staying in order to be executed for telling the truth, you would do better, in spite of the gravity of what awaits you, not to forget to cancel the dinner you have been invited to, and to pay the proprietor and the laundry-woman, and to settle accounts with everybody so that no one will be offended. And so I feel that I need to settle accounts with my world—of artists and scholars—and to explain that I am not doing what they expect me to do, and why. You will think this is a lame excuse. Perhaps it is. But it's my last one. Before I got your letter I spoke to Gribovsky who was here and whom I liked very much (if he survives, this man will serve God well), and I said that this article of mine[2] was the last one (as I wish and hope) which is addressed to my own circle of lost souls. (There will still be *The Death of Ivan Ilich*, if I'm still alive; I promised to finish that for my wife for her new edition, but this article only relates to our circle in its form (the way it starts); in content it relates to everyone). Your remark that it would be better to call it *What Must I Do?* is a fair one, and I shall take advantage of it. There is irascibility and pride in it too; but I must finish it off. It's difficult writing in the country, though. I long to mow and chop wood, which I am in fact doing. My arms ache, but my heart is at ease...[52 lines omitted]

291. To V. G. CHERTKOV

Yasnaya Polyana, 6–7 June 1885

In my last letter I wrote that I was feeling well; but now, as I reply to your 2nd letter from England which I got yesterday, I'm feeling unwell. My written work is at a standstill, my physical work is virtually pointless, i.e. not forced on me by necessity, I have virtually no relations with people round about me, beggars come and I give them coppers and they go away, and before my eyes there is a systematic corruption of the children going on all round me in the family, a hanging of

---

[290] 1. Perhaps a reference to Chertkov's concern that Tolstoy's preoccupation with the theoretical question 'what must we do?' might distract his attention from more important spiritual problems, and from writing stories for the masses.
2. *What Then Must We Do?*

291. To V. G. Chertkov

millstones round their necks. Of course I'm to blame, but I don't want to pretend to you, or to display a composure which I haven't got. I'm not afraid of death; I even desire it. But that's bad too; it means that I've lost the thread given me by God for guidance in this life, and for full satisfaction. I'm confused, I want to die, I make plans to run away or even to take advantage of my position and turn all this life upside down. All this only shows that I am weak and evil, but I want to blame other people and to see in my own position something exceptionally miserable. I've been very miserable for 6 days or so now, but my one comfort is that I feel it is only a temporary state; I'm miserable, but I'm not in despair; I know I shall find the thread I have lost, that God has not forsaken me, that I am not alone. But at moments like these, you feel the lack of intimate living people—the commune or the church which the Pashkovites[1] and the Orthodox have. How good it would be now if I could place my difficulties before a court of people who believe in the same faith, and do whatever they tell me. There are times when you pull hard and feel the strength within you, but there are times when you want, if not to rest, then to put yourself in the hands of other people you trust, for them to guide you. All this will pass. If I'm still alive, I shall write and tell you how and when it passes. I got a letter from Obolensky yesterday, together with the letter from you. He asks about Sibiryakov,[2] is looking for a position and some means of livelihood, and calls the situation he is in, and which I have been passionately longing for for 10 years now, a hopeless one. When I feel sorry for myself, I say to myself; shall I have to die without having spent at least one year outside that immoral madhouse in which I'm compelled to suffer every hour; without having spent at least one year in a sensible, human way, i.e. not in a manor house in the country, but in a peasant hut among working people, working together with them as far as my strength and abilities allow, exchanging jobs with them, feeding and clothing myself as they do, and boldly and shamelessly telling everyone Christ's truth, as I know it. I want to be frank with you and I tell you everything, and that is what I think when I feel sorry for myself; but then immediately I revise my judgement, as I do now. Such a desire is a desire for external blessings for oneself—just the same as the desire for palaces and riches and fame—and therefore it doesn't come from God. This desire to set the horizontal and vertical arms of the cross at right angles[3] is a dissatisfaction with the conditions in which God has put me, a failure to do what I was sent to do. But the point is that I am in a complicated and difficult position now as an envoy, and I sometimes don't know how best to do the will of Him who sent me. I shall wait for elucidation. He has never refused it and has always given it in good time.

L.T.

[291] 1. Followers of the Russian evangelist, V. A. Pashkov (Chertkov's uncle), in turn a follower of Lord Radstock.

2. The son of a wealthy Siberian merchant who came under the influence of Tolstoy's ideas and gave away land and money to communes and village schools. He also gave financial support to *The Intermediary*.

3. One interpretation of the cross as a symbol is that the longer, vertical bar represents God's will, and the shorter, horizontal bar symbolises man's. Tolstoy's metaphor implies working at cross-purposes with the divine will.

292. To V. G. CHERTKOV

Yasnaya Polyana, 11 October 1885

I got your 2nd letter, dear friend, before I had time to reply to your first. I was very glad about your interest in the project—the pictures, I mean.[1] I'll try my best as long as I'm alive; I'll start work in a few days. Get someone to look for subjects in the *Russian Readers*,[2] or have a look yourself. I think something can be found there. Frey[3] has been staying with me for 4 days now; he's a very interesting, very clever, sincere, and—most important—a good man. He talked a great deal about positivism, and I began to talk about it too, but then restrained myself. It was too painful for him to hear anything that could destroy his faith. He lives by it, and faith is good. Although he distracted me from my work, I don't regret it: he told me a lot of new things about American life—transported me entirely into that life which is alien to us—and moreover I hope he will be very useful for our journal.[4] I asked him to write about 3 things for us: (1) the technology of the simplest methods used in the most ordinary jobs—axes, saws, carts, etc. (he promised this part, but if he won't do it, we shall all have to look for somebody to run this section); (2) hygiene—what to eat, how to eat, how to dress, how to take advantage of fresh air, how to sleep—all this with particular reference to those unfortunate people who perish in towns, not so much from shortages, as from the inability to use what they have, and from ignorance of what they need (he promised this and it will be necessary to insist that he does it); and (3) his own memoirs about how he, a landowner and an educated officer, went to America as a labourer, how he encountered misfortune there, how he learned to live and work there for 17 years, and how people live there. This would be splendid. And it seems to me that he can do this, and he has promised me to do it.

All my folk left for Moscow today, and I am staying here on my own for an indefinite time. I feel that it won't be possible to spend the whole winter like this. However, I'm not looking ahead at all. How glad I am that vegetarianism has been of benefit to you. It can't be otherwise. Are your relations with the peasants continuing? Like all good things they must be enjoyable, wholesome and useful. Thanks to Feinermann[5] I drop in of an evening at the school where adults meet to listen to reading, and there are very interesting conversations. I was very glad about the success of my story, more than glad—I was deeply moved. *Sofron*[6] is having an astonishing success here and touches people's hearts. Please forgive me if I'm

---

[292] 1. A new publishing project for *The Intermediary*: a series of illustrated books, with text by Tolstoy and illustrations by leading artists including Repin.

2. Chertkov had suggested choosing the texts for the illustrated *Intermediary* series from the *Russian Readers* (published 1874) which contained stories and material by Tolstoy designed to teach children to read.

3. William Frey. See Letter 300.

4. A journal for the people, which Tolstoy was planning at the time, but which never materialised.

5. Isaac Feinermann, a young Jewish teacher who was attracted by Tolstoy's ideas and came to Yasnaya Polyana to teach at the school for peasants.

6. *Uncle Sofron*, a story by V. I. Savikhin, published by *The Intermediary*.

292. To V. G. Chertkov

wrong, but it seems to me that you took away with you both the stories you write about: the one from Zola and the fairy tale.[7] I've looked for them and can't find them. I'm sorry about Urusov,[8] but, between ourselves, external events can cause me neither grief nor joy...Goodbye, dear friend. God grant that you may keep on along the same road.

L.T.

293. To COUNTESS S. A. TOLSTAYA

Yasnaya Polyana, 17 October 1885

I heard from Tanya and Ilyusha yesterday, and today they brought me your letter and telegram. You must have received a letter from me since writing, perhaps even two—I don't remember. I see from everything that you are very agitated, and this makes me very sad; i.e. I feel for you and it hurts me. I would like to help you, but you know yourself that I can't do so, and the fact that I say I can't isn't an excuse. All those things—or at least the majority of them—which disturb you, namely; the children's schooling, their progress, money matters, book matters even—all those things seem to me unnecessary and superfluous. Please don't give way to a feeling of annoyance and a desire to reproach me—you surely know this is not due to my capriciousness or laziness, in order to save myself trouble, but to other reasons which I don't consider bad, and therefore—however much I like to try to improve myself—I cannot wish to do so in this respect. If, as you have sometimes put it, you think I go to extremes, you will see, if you look carefully at my motives, that there can be no extremes in what guides me, because if you admit that it is necessary to stop somewhere on a good road, it is better not to take it at all. The nearer to one's destination, the less possible it is to stop and the harder you need to run. You know, I look at life, both my own and the family's, in this way and not any other, not out of caprice, but because I have come to this view of life through life's sufferings, and not only do I not conceal the reason why I look at it in this way and not any other, but I express it as far as I am able in my writings. I write all this only so that you shouldn't bear that feeling of ill will towards me which, I'm afraid, is latent in you. If I'm mistaken, please forgive me; if not, root out your annoyance with me for remaining here and not coming to Moscow yet. My presence in Moscow in the family is virtually useless: the conventionality of life there paralyses me and the life there is repulsive to me, again for the same general reasons to do with my view of life which I cannot change, and I can do less work there. We apparently didn't agree about why and for how long I should remain here, and I would like nothing to be left unagreed. I remained because I feel better here; there I am not needed at all. For how long? You know I don't make any plans. As long as there is life and work I go on living. I know one thing, that for my own peace of mind and therefore happiness I need to have loving relations with you, and so this

7. A re-telling of Zola's *L'Assommoir* by M. K. Tsebrikova, and a fairy-tale by the same author, *The Weaver and the Baker*.
8. L. D. Urusov died on 23 September 1885.

condition is paramount. If I see that you are not well without me, or that separation from all of you is hard for me to bear and work comes to a stop, then I shall come. All will be clear there, if only there is love and harmony.

Publish *Two Old Men*,[1] only leave out in the last paragraph the words: 'not in Jerusalem and not with the saints'. I will certainly have a portrait done.[2] I'm quite well and cheerful. I never go anywhere, never see anyone, work a lot both with my hands and my 'head' like the devil,[3] get up early while it's still dark and go to bed early. Goodbye; I kiss you and the children. Write about all the children—the little ones too.

294. To T. L. TOLSTAYA

Tatyana Lvovna Tolstaya (1864–1950), Tolstoy's eldest daughter, was educated at home and later, during the 1880s and 1890s, studied painting seriously in Moscow, attending an art school and taking lessons from Repin. She did several accomplished portraits of members of her family and family friends such as Nikolay Strakhov. She also assisted for a while with the work of *The Intermediary*, and published some children's stories from the early 1890s onwards. In 1899 she married Mikhail Sergeyevich Sukhotin, a widower. After 1918 she was Caretaker of the Yasnaya Polyana Museum; in 1922 she organised a painting school in Moscow, and from 1923 to 1925 she was Director of the Tolstoy Museum in Moscow.

She wrote several memoirs about her father including *Friends and Guests at Yasnaya Polyana* (Moscow, 1923) and *About My Father's Death and the Reasons for his Leaving Home* (Paris, 1928). There is an English edition of her diaries from her girlhood to her father's death, *The Tolstoy Home: Diaries* (London, 1950).

Tatyana Tolstaya emigrated to France in 1925 and later established a Tolstoy Museum in Rome, where she died in 1950.

Yasnaya Polyana, 18 October 1885

Well done Tanya. Thank you, dear, for the letter. Write more often and I'll collect your stamps for you. I already have a collection. But now to be serious.

For the first time you have spoken out clearly and said that your views on things have changed. That is my *only* dream and my greatest possible joy which I daren't hope for—namely to find brothers and sisters in my family, and not what I have seen so far—estrangement and deliberate opposition—in which I see partly contempt—not for me but for the truth—and partly fear of something. It's a great pity. One day soon death will come. Why should I carry away to the grave nothing

[293] 1. Tolstoy's story *Two Old Men* was published with the deletion of these words in a new edition of Tolstoy's works which Sofya Andreyevna was bringing out.
2. Tolstoy's portrait was needed for the new edition and was included.
3. A quotation from Tolstoy's story, *The Tale of Ivan the Fool*, where the suggestion is made that one can earn more by working 'with the head' than with the hands.

294. To T. L. Tolstaya

but a feeling—towards my own family—of deliberate equivocation, and of greater estrangement from them than from those outside the family? I'm very afraid for you, not for your weakness but for your propensity for yawning, and I would like to help you. I am helped by my undoubted conviction that there is nothing more important in the world for you or for all of us than our actions and the habits formed by them. For me, for example, it's far more important that I should get up early and break the habit of tobacco than to have all my external wishes fulfilled; For Auntie Tanya, from whom I have had a letter saying she needs money, money, money, it's far more important that she should, I won't say break the habit of swearing, but refrain once from swearing, than that she should receive the fortune of a Rothschild; and one last example as a special treat—it's more important that you should do your own room and make your own soup (it would be good if you organised this and pushed to one side everything that interfered with it, especially people's opinions), than that you should marry well or badly. Perhaps you agree only too well with this, or perhaps you don't agree at all, but I'm always astonished by this absurdity: a man considers his own actions from which his whole life stems to be mere trifles, while the things which cannot change his inner life he considers very important. An awareness of the importance of what is important and the triviality of what is trivial can be a great help against all sorts of temptations...[7 lines omitted]...In any sort of life, especially town life, there is one salvation—work and more work. I can see you; you will say that's no consolation. But the thing is, you don't need to be consoled, but to keep on going where you are going, whether you like it or not, and it's only a question of marcher droit. And when you keep going straight ahead, pleasant things, even very pleasant things will happen. I say this from experience. I feel it now. I'm living very well. I see nobody except Alexander Petrovich[1] whose resources are very limited, and if I believed in happiness, i.e. if I thought it necessary to take note of it and wish for it, I would say I was happy. I don't notice how the days pass, I don't think what will come of my work, but I think I am doing what is necessary and what is required of me by the being that sent me to live here. Separation from the family here at the moment is no greater than it always is when we are all together. Even then I often feel more lonely. Now I think of you very, very often, think of you and feel you better. I haven't been to the school once. The more alone I am the busier I am. I have had letters from Auntie Tanya and Chertkov. I have a spare copy of *What Then Must We Do?*, and I'll send it you tomorrow, although you might have got one from mama. Then again, why don't you take up some work to do with publishing editions for the people? I'm reading *Bleak House* bit by bit at the moment—it's very good—and I've been thinking about *Oliver Twist*. Just imagine if you had read them at school.

Please tell me what Stakhovich means.[2] What makes you think he wants to

[294] 1. Tolstoy's copyist.
    2. A member of a wealthy landowning class and a friend of the Tolstoys from childhood. He was a frequent visitor to Yasnaya Polyana and often took part in play readings there. See Letter 553.

marry you? And why, if he does, doesn't he propose? Tell me frankly what you think about it. In his relations towards us there is much that is similar to my relations to Mama's family. Mama is Auntie Tanya, Lyova is Styopa, etc.[3] There is no need to pay money to the doctor because of your finger,[4] but it would be good if you settled down and learned how to make soup. I was chopping wood today, and 3 peasant boys led by Ivan Pavlich came up and stopped in front of me. I asked then what they wanted, and they hummed and hawed, and Ivan Pavlich gave me a bit of paper: 'I've written a story', he said, 'about a poor peasant.' The story is ironical, but there are two very good details in it. The sleeves of the peasant's sheepskin coat were torn at the elbows, and his toes were sticking out of his boots, but when he started to dance, the sleeves began to flap like a kite's wings, and his toes peeped out from his boots like young nightingales out of a nest. Don't think that the two sheets I'm writing on means that I tore up and didn't send something I had written; no, it's only economy of paper, and I'm writing at random, and although I feel I'm writing very badly, I'll send it as it is. When I got your letter at Kozlovka yesterday I thought about you so nicely and spoke to you in thought, but now I've lost the tone and the result is pedantic and disconnected. You can have a splendid life on earth—you have many powers, physical, mental and spiritual—only you must guard them. And people love you—ladies as you say—and I can believe it; love you simply for what you are. Well, goodbye, my darling. Write.

L.T.

295. To M. Y. SALTYKOV-SHCHEDRIN

Mikhail Yevgrafovich Saltykov-Shchedrin (1826–89), was Russia's best-known satirical writer. 'Semi-novelist and semi-journalist' to quote D. S. Mirsky, his writings attacked hypocrisy and stupidity in all social classes, but most vehemently in the provincial bureaucracy. A civil servant himself, he was exiled to Vyatka in 1848 as a consequence of the radical tone of his first two stories, but he was able to continue in the civil service in exile, and even rose to a relatively important position. He was allowed to return to Petersburg in 1856, where he met Tolstoy as a member of the *Contemporary* circle. Saltykov-Shchedrin's reputation with the Russian reading public was made in the early, reforming years of Alexander II's reign when his type of satirical, journalistic fiction was particularly suited to the times. In 1868 he was obliged to leave the civil service in which he held a senior post in one of the provinces, and he joined Nekrasov as co-editor of the *Notes of the Fatherland*, the successor to *The Contemporary* which had been suppressed in 1866. In the late 1860s he was regarded as the chief spokesman for the radical intelligentsia and in the 1880s, when *Notes of the Fatherland* was suppressed (a year before this letter

---

3. In Tolstoy's courtship of Sofya Andreyevna, her sister and brother had encouraged the match, as presumably Tatyana's mother and brother were encouraging her to marry Stakhovich.

4. Tatyana had dislocated her finger and was seeing the doctor about it.

295. To M. Y. Saltykov-Shchedrin

from Tolstoy), he was considered the last representative of the type of crusading journalism which characterised the reform era.

Saltykov-Shchedrin's two major novels are *The History of a Town* (1869–70) and *The Golovlyov Family* (1875–80), a particularly pessimistic and morbidly satirical work.

Saltykov-Shchedrin and Tolstoy were never more than literary acquaintances, and their correspondence is slight, confined to Saltykov-Shchedrin's attempts in 1878 and 1883 to persuade Tolstoy to publish in *Notes of the Fatherland*, and the following letter of 1885 in which Tolstoy attempts to persuade Saltykov-Shchedrin to contribute to *The Intermediary*. In general, Tolstoy did not seem to rate Saltykov-Shchedrin's work very highly; the following letter is one of the few instances in which he expressed himself positively about his talent (although many years later, on hearing a reading from *The Golovlyov Family*, he was enthusiastic about it).

The material which Tolstoy solicits in this letter was never published in *The Intermediary*. Saltykov-Shchedrin submitted two stories to Chertkov in 1885, and five more in 1887, but each time they were rejected as 'unsuited' to the spirit of the journal.

Moscow, 1–3(?) December 1885

I was very glad of the opportunity, dear Mikhail Yevgrafovich, to express to you, if only in a somewhat official form, my sincere feelings of respect and love, but at the same time I learned about your ill-health; sadly I began to look out for news in the papers and then I learned from them and from friends that you were better. That's splendid, only don't trust the doctors and don't ruin yourself with their treatment.

I'm writing to you about a matter of business: perhaps you have heard of the firm *The Intermediary* and of Chertkov. This letter will be delivered to you by V. G. Chertkov, and he will tell you the details of the business which might interest you. My business is as follows: since you and I have been writing, the reading public has changed enormously, and views about the reading public have also changed. Previously it was the journals which had the largest and most valuable public—about 20,000—and the greater part of them were honest and serious readers, but now the position is that the quality of the intelligent readers has declined very much—they read more to help their digestion—and a new and enormous circle of readers has arisen, which needs to be counted in hundreds of thousands, practically millions. The issues of *The Intermediary* which Chertkov will show you were sold out in six months, at a hundred thousand copies each, and the demand for them is still increasing. I would say about myself that when I correct the proofs of my writings for our circle I am relaxed and composed, but when I write something which will be read in a year's time by millions of people, and read in the way they read, with the utmost attention to detail, I am overcome by doubt and faintheartedness. However, that's not the point. The point is that I think, as I recall many, many things from your old and new writings, that if you could picture to yourself this imaginary reader and address him, and if you were willing to do so, you could write a splendid thing, or things, and would find the same sort of pleasure in them as a craftsman finds in displaying his craftsmanship to true connoisseurs. If I were to tell you all I think about what you could actually do in this genre, you would in my opinion take it as flattery, in spite of the fact that you don't consider me a devious person. You have everything that is necessary—concise, powerful and authentic language, a characteristic which you alone have retained, not humour, but something which produces a happy laugh, and—as for content—a love of, and therefore a knowledge of the true interests of the life of the people. In these publications there is no special trend, but several trends are excluded. But I have no need to say this. We put it this way: we publish everything which does not contradict Christian teaching; you perhaps put it rather differently, but you have always acted in the same spirit and for that reason you are dear to me, and your work would be dear to me, because you would always go on acting in the same way. You can provide millions of readers with valuable and necessary food of the sort which nobody can give except yourself.

L.T.

296. To V. G. CHERTKOV

[Not sent]

Moscow, 9–15 December 1885

I am sorely heavy at heart, and there is nobody I wish to share this heaviness with as much as you, dear friend, because it seems to me that nobody loves the good that there is in me as much as you. Of course it's all my weakness, my remoteness from God—some physical condition even—but I'm living what may be the last hours of my life and living them badly, in despair and in anger with those around me. There are some things I do which are not what God wants, but I seek and do not find, and all the time I feel the same melancholy, despair, and worst of all, anger and the wish to die. I haven't been writing these last few days, and I'm still not writing, and that is why I look around me and judge myself and am horrified.

All this animal life—and not just animal, but an animal life coupled with isolation from all people and pride—goes on getting worse and worse, and I see how the souls of God's children enter the mill one after another, and one after another put on and fasten millstones round their necks and perish. I see that I, with my own faith and my own expression of it in word and deed, am pushed to one side and acquire for them the meaning of some unpleasant, anomalous phenomenon like maggots in beehives which the bees can't kill and so smear with honey so that they shouldn't be in the way, and barbarous life goes triumphantly on along its ever worsening path. The children are *studying* at grammar schools—the younger ones actually study the same things at home, as well as scripture which they will later need at school. They overeat and amuse themselves by buying with money the fruits of the labours of other people for their own pleasure, and they are more and more convinced, the more they have of them, that this is right. They don't read what I

296. To V. G. Chertkov

write about this, and don't listen to what I say, or else answer angrily as soon as they understand where my talk is leading, and either don't see or try not to see. The other day subscriptions were taken out and books sold on terms which were very harsh for the book merchants and very profitable for the seller.[1] I would go downstairs and meet a customer who would look at me as though I were a fraud, writing against property and then, under my wife's name, squeezing as much money as possible out of people for my writings. Oh, if only somebody could really point out in the papers clearly and truly and venomously (a pity for him, but an excellent thing for us) the baseness of it all. Yesterday I was asked to sign a paper saying that I, *by virtue of the lands owned by me*, make over to my son the right to vote to elect an assembly of the gentry. Why do I allow it? Why do I do it? I simply don't know what I should do at all. I live in the family, and I never see anybody who isn't always rushing off somewhere and isn't to some extent angry as a result of this rushing about and, moreover, convinced that this rushing about is not only necessary, but also as natural as breathing. And if you begin to speak, then the person—if he isn't angry and doesn't start talking such illogical nonsense that you need to redefine every word in every sentence—even if he isn't angry, he looks at his watch and at the door, wondering whether the grumbling of a peevish old man with a one-track mind who doesn't understand the young will soon be over. If I begin to talk to my wife or my eldest son, the result is malice, plain malice, against which I am weak and which infects me as well. But what is it better for me to do? To put up with it and to lie, as I lie now with my whole life—sitting at the table, lying in bed, allowing the sale of my works, signing papers about voting rights, allowing peasants to be punished and persecuted for stealing my property, on my authority? Or to make a complete break—and give way to anger? For without anger I cannot, and don't know how to make a complete break and free myself from lies. I pray to God—that is I seek from God a way towards a solution—and find none. Sometimes I actually ask God how I should act. I always ask like this when I'm faced with a choice of doing one thing or another. I say to myself, if I were dying now, how should I act? And I always feel when I vividly imagine myself departing this life, that the most important thing is to depart this life without leaving behind any malice, but only love, and then I'm inclined to agree to everything so as not to cause anger. And the main thing is that I then become quite indifferent to people's opinions. But afterwards, when I look round at the results of this, and at the lies in which I live, and when I'm weak at heart, I feel a revulsion towards myself and ill will towards the people who put me in this position. A slender consolation to me in the family are the girls. They love me for what deserves to be loved, and they love that too. There is still a bit of it in Lyovochka, but the older he gets the less there is. I've just been talking to him. He kept looking at the door—he needs something from school. Why am I writing this to you? I just want to, because I know you love me, and I love you. Don't show this letter to other people.[2] If it is *absolutely clear* to

[296] 1. A reference to his wife's new (sixth) edition of his collected works.
2. Although this letter was not sent, Tolstoy referred to it briefly in his next letter, and promised to show it to Chertkov sometime in the future.

you what it is better for me to do, write and tell me. But to me at least it seems terribly difficult to decide. One solution is to live every minute of one's life with God, doing His will, not one's own, and then these problems won't arise. But you lose this support, this real life, for a time, as I have just lost it, and you struggle desperately like a fish out of water. Well, that's all. I don't know whether I shall send this letter. If I don't send it, I'll show it to you when we meet.

I wrote this two days ago. I couldn't stand it yesterday and began to speak out, and got angry, which only resulted in them seeing and hearing nothing and putting it all down to my anger. I've been crying all day on my own and can't stop myself.

297. To COUNTESS S. A. TOLSTAYA

From September 1885 to February 1886 Tolstoy was busy correcting the proofs of *What Then Must We Do?* Because of this, he delayed his own move to Moscow when the family went there in early October. Only on 1 November 1885 did he leave Yasnaya Polyana to join his wife and children in Moscow—and continue work on the proofs. As in previous years, he was very unhappy and dissatisfied in Moscow, feeling more keenly than ever his moral and spiritual estrangement from his family. His wife was well aware of his unhappiness, and according to her, he told her of his wish to live apart from the family.

Sometime between 15 and 18 December this letter to Sofya Andreyevna was written in an attempt to clarify an ambiguous situation which both Tolstoy and his wife felt to be unbearable. Tolstoy then left for the estate of Tatyana Kuzminskaya, leaving the letter behind for his wife. According to Marya Tolstaya, Sofya Andreyevna became very distraught on reading the letter, and insisted on reading it aloud to the family. On the margin she wrote: 'A letter from Lev Nikolayevich to his wife, neither given nor sent to her'.

Moscow, 15–18 December 1885

For the last 7 or 8 years all our conversations have ended after many painful torments in the same way, at least on my side. I said: there can be no agreement and no loving life between us until you come to what I have come to, I said, either from love for me, or from an instinctive sense given to all of us, or from conviction, and we can go along together. I said: until *you* come to me; I didn't say: until I come to you, because that is impossible for me. It is impossible because the things you live by are the very things I have only just escaped from, as from a horrible and monstrous thing which nearly brought me to suicide. I can't go back to the things I lived by, the things in which I found perdition, and which I acknowledged to be the greatest evil and misfortune. But you can try to come to something you haven't yet known, something which has always been considered best by everyone and which finds a response in your own conscience—I mean in general terms a life devoted to God and to other people, and not to one's own pleasures (I'm not

297. To Countess S. A. Tolstaya

speaking about your life, but about the children's lives) or to one's own ambition. All our quarrels in recent years have always ended in one and the same way. Surely it's worth thinking why that is so. And if you think sincerely and, above all, calmly, it will be clear to you why that is so. You publish my works so assiduously, you went to so much trouble in Petersburg, and you hotly defended my articles which were banned. But what was written in those articles? This is what I wrote in the first of them, *A Confession*, written in 1879, but expressing thoughts and feelings which I had lived with for a couple of years before that, and consequently not far short of 10 years ago. I wasn't writing it for the public; I wasn't writing what I had gone through and what I had come to for the sake of talk or fine words, but, as you know, I came to the point I did sincerely, and with the intention of doing what I said. This is what I wrote: pages 56, 57, 58, and 59, the places marked...[1]

You surely know that I didn't write all this for stylistic effect, but that it was what I had come to in trying to save myself from despair. (For goodness sake don't say this is madness, and that you can't keep up with all these fantasies, etc. Please don't say this, so that we shan't digress from the subject. The subject at the moment is *me*—I'll speak about you later—and I want you to imagine me in the actual condition I am now in, and in which I live and shall die, straining every effort to speak nothing but the truth before God.) Well then, it's not far short of 10 years since the quarrels between us would all end with me saying that we shouldn't be friends again until we came to the same view of life; since then my life has taken a completely different turn from before, and not only in my thoughts (in my heart of hearts I always inclined this way), and it has gone, and continues to go further and further in the same direction, both in my thoughts, which I elucidate more and more for myself and express as clearly and accurately as I can, and also in my actions which express more and more closely what I believe in. At this point, in order to speak about myself, I am bound to speak about your attitude to my changing faith and life. I shan't speak about you in order to blame you—I don't blame you, and I think I understand your motives and I see nothing bad in them, but I am bound to say what happened, so that the outcome can be understood; and so, my darling, for the sake of all that is holy, listen calmly to what I'm going to say. I am not blaming you for anything, nor can I, nor do I wish to; on the contrary, I want you to be united with me and to love me, and so I can't wish to cause you pain; but in order to explain my position I am bound to speak about the unfortunate misunderstandings which led to our being united but disunited, and to this state which is agonising for both of us.

For goodness sake contain yourself and read this calmly, putting aside all thoughts of yourself for the time being. Later on I'll talk about you, about your feelings and your situation, but just now it's necessary for you to understand your relationship to me, to understand me and my life, such as it is, and not as you would

---

[297] 1. In the 1884 edition of *A Confession* these pages correspond to the end of chapter 10 and the beginning of chapter 11, and especially to Tolstoy's remarks that the life of his own class had lost all meaning for him, while that of the working class had assumed real importance.

297. To Countess S. A. Tolstaya

like it to be. What I say to you about my position in the family being a constant unhappiness to me is an undoubted fact; I know it as well as one knows toothache. Perhaps I'm to blame, but it's a fact, and if it hurts you to know that I'm unhappy (I know it does hurt you), one oughtn't to deny the pain or say that one is to blame, but one should rather think how to get rid of the pain—the pain which hurts me and makes you and the whole family suffer. This pain is due to the fact that I came to the conclusion nearly 10 years ago that my only salvation, and that of any man in this life, is to live not for oneself but for others, and that the life of our class is entirely arranged for the sake of living for oneself and is entirely based on pride, cruelty, violence and evil, and that therefore a man in our circles who wants to live a good life, to live with a clear conscience, to live joyfully, has no need to look for any difficult and remote feats to accomplish, but needs to act this very minute, to work hour by hour and day by day in order to change this life and to go from bad to good; this alone constitutes the happiness and virtue of people of our circle, but you and the whole family are not moving towards changing this life, but, as the family grows and the selfishness of its members increases, towards aggravating its bad sides. That is the cause of the pain. How can it be cured? Should I renounce my faith? You know that's impossible. If I said by word of mouth that I renounce it, nobody, even you, would believe it, any more than if I said that 2×2 is not 4. But what should I do? Profess this faith in words and books, and do something different in actual fact? Again, even you can't advise me to do that. Should I forget? Impossible. But what should I do? The point is that the subject which occupies me and to which, perhaps, I have been called, is the business of moral teaching. And the business of moral teaching differs from all others in that it can't be changed, it can't remain mere words, it can't be binding for one person and not binding for another. If conscience and reason demand a thing, and it is clear to me what conscience and reason demand, I can't fail to do what conscience and reason demand and be at ease—I can't look at people, bound to me by ties of love and knowing what reason and conscience demand and not doing it, without suffering.

Whichever way I turn I can't help suffering, living the life we live! And neither you nor anybody else can say that the reason for my suffering is false. You know yourself that if I die tomorrow, other people will say what I have been saying; the very conscience of people will speak, and will go on speaking until people do, or at least begin to do what it demands. And so in order to put an end to our discord and unhappiness, you can't extract the cause of my suffering from me because it isn't me, but something present in the conscience of all people, present in you also. Therefore it remains to examine another possibility: can we not put an end to the suffering which I experience and pass on to you? I said that I was saved from despair by coming to see the truth. This may seem a very proud assertion for people who say, like Pilate: 'What is truth?', but in this case it isn't pride at all. Man cannot live without knowing the truth. But I want to say that I'm prepared, in spite of the fact that all wise men and saintly people in the world are on my side, and that you yourself acknowledge what I acknowledge to be the truth—I'm

297. To Countess S. A. Tolstaya

prepared to assume that what I lived and live by is not the truth, but only my infatuation, and that I was possessed with the idea that I know the truth and can't cease to believe in it and live for it, and that I can't be cured of my madness. I'm prepared to assume all this, and in that case you are left with the same situation: since it is impossible to tear out from me what I live by and restore me to my former state, how are you to put an end to those sufferings, mine and yours, which derive from my incurable madness?

Whether you regard my vice as truth or madness (it's all the same), there is only one remedy for it: to look hard at this view, examine it and understand it. But by an unhappy chance of which I have spoken, not only has this never been done by you, or by the children after you, but you have all become accustomed to fear it. You have evolved for yourself a means of forgetting, of not seeing, of not understanding, of not recognising the existence of this view, or of regarding it as you would regard interesting ideas, and not as a key to understanding a man.

It so happened that when a spiritual revolution was taking place inside me and my inner life had changed, you ascribed no significance or importance to it, and paid no heed to what was going on inside me, succumbing by an unhappy chance to the general opinion that a literary artist like Gogol should write works of art, and not think about his life or improve it, and that all that is a kind of folly or mental illness; and in succumbing to this mood, you immediately took up a hostile attitude to what for me was salvation from despair and a return to life.

It so happened that all my activity on this new path, everything that sustained me on it, began to seem to you harmful and dangerous for me and for the children. So as not to come back to this later, I'll mention here the relationship of my view of life to the family and the children, to counter the false objection that my view of life might be good for me, but not applicable to the children. There are various views of life—personal views: one man considers that in order to be happy it's necessary to be a scholar, others—an artist, others again—a rich man or a nobleman. These are all personal views, but my view was a religious and moral view, which tells what a man must be in order to fulfil God's will and in order that he and all other people might be happy. The religious view may be wrong, and then it needs to be refuted, or simply not accepted; but one mustn't say against the religious view, as people do and you sometimes do, that it's good for you, but is it good for the children? My view is that I and my life have no importance or rights, but I value my view, not for my own sake, but for the happiness of other people; and of other people, my children are nearest to me. And so what I consider good, I consider so, not for myself, but for others, and particularly for my children. It so happened that owing to an unfortunate misunderstanding, you didn't try to understand what was for me a fundamental revolution which changed my life, but actually took, not exactly a hostile attitude to it, but regarded it as a morbid and abnormal phenomenon, and from worthy motives wanted to save me and other people from this infatuation of mine; since when you have pulled with particular energy in exactly the opposite direction to which my new life was drawing me. All that was precious and important to me became repulsive to you; both our charming, peaceful,

297. To Countess S. A. Tolstaya

modest country life and the people who were part of it like Vasily Ivanovich,[2] whom I know you esteem, but whom you then considered an enemy, sustaining, in your opinion, a false, morbid and unnatural mood in me and the children. And then you began to treat me as though I were mentally ill, which I felt very keenly. Even before this, you had been resolute and determined, but now this determination increased still more as it does with people looking after a patient, when it's recognised that he is mentally ill. Darling, remember these recent years of our life in the country when on the one hand I worked as I had never worked before and will never in my life work again on the Gospels (whatever the results of this work, I know that I put into it all the spiritual strength given me by God), and on the other hand began to put into practice what had been revealed to me from the Gospel teaching: I renounced my property, began to give what people asked of me, renounced ambition for myself and for the children, knowing (what I knew 30 years ago, but what had been stifled in me by ambition) that what you were arranging for them in the form of a refined education with French and English tutors and governesses, music etc., was the temptation of the love of fame and of exalting oneself above others, a millstone which we were putting round their necks. Rememder that time and the attitude you took to my work and to my new life. All this seemed to you a one-sided, sorry infatuation, and the results of this infatuation seemed to you even dangerous for the children. I fear to say so, and I don't insist on it, but in addition to all this was your early marriage, your tiredness after your duties as a mother and your ignorance of society, which you imagined to be something fascinating; and with still more determination and energy, and shutting your eyes completely to what was going on in me and to those things in whose name I became what I did become, you pulled in the reverse, the opposite direction: sending the children to grammar schools, bringing out your daughter, making friends in society, organising a respectable environment. You believed your own feeling and the general opinion that my new life was an infatuation, a sort of mental illness, and you didn't try to understand its meaning, but began to act with a determination unusual even for you, and with even greater freedom, such that everything you did: the move to Moscow, the organisation of life there, and the education of the children, was so alien to me that I could no longer have any voice in it, because it was all going on in a field of activity I regarded as evil.[3] What we did in the country on the basis of mutual concessions had meaning and significance for me, because of the very simplicity of life, and particularly because it was 20 years old; but the new arrangements, which are opposed to all my ideas about life, could have no meaning for me beyond trying to put up with them in the best and calmest way possible. This new Moscow life has been agony for me, the like of which I have never experienced in all my life. Not only did I suffer at every step and at every moment from the incompatibility of my own life and my family's and the sight of luxury, dissipation and poverty which I felt myself party to—not only

2. V. I. Alexeyev. Tolstoy is referring to Alexeyev's support for his decision to write to Alexander III, and to Sofya Andreyevna's public rebuke of Alexeyev.
3. The reading of this phrase is unclear in the original.

297. To Countess S. A. Tolstaya

did I suffer, but I became vile and demented, and took a direct and conscious part in that dissipation, eating, drinking, playing cards, bragging, feeling remorse and being disgusted with myself. My one salvation was writing, and I buried myself in it, without finding peace.

It was no better in the country. The same disregard of me, not only by you but by our children too as they grew up, who were naturally inclined to adopt a view of me, which indulged their tastes and weaknesses, as a kind and not particularly dangerous mental patient, with whom one mustn't talk about the things that made him mad. Life passed me by. Sometimes you appealed to me—and you were wrong to do so—to take part in this life; you made demands on me, and reproached me for not bothering about money matters and the upbringing of the children, as though I could bother about money matters and the increase or preservation of my fortune, in order to increase or preserve the very evil from which in my view my children were coming to grief—or could bother about their upbringing, the aim of which was pride, separation from other people, worldly education and diplomas—the very things I knew to be the ruin of people. You and the children as they grew up moved further and further in one direction, and I in another. So the years went by—one, two—five years. The children grew up, we drifted further and further apart, and my situation became more false and difficult. I went along with people who had taken the wrong road and were lost, in the hope of making them turn round; sometimes I was silent, sometimes I tried to persuade them to stop and turn back, sometimes I gave in to them, sometimes I got angry and stopped them. But the further I went, the worse it was. Now inertia has set in—people carry on, because they have started and are used to it, and my exhortations only irritate them. But I feel no better as a result, and sometimes, such as now, I grow desperate and ask my conscience and reason how to act, and can find no answer. There are three choices: (1) to use my authority: to give up my property to those it belongs to—the workers, anybody, in order to save the young ones from temptation and ruin; but I should resort to force, I should arouse malice and anger, I should arouse the same desires, only they wouldn't be satisfied, which is even worse; (2) to leave the family—but if I abandoned them entirely it would mean destroying my influence, which, although it seems to me ineffectual, may perhaps be effective and able to do something—and I should leave my wife and myself to live apart and break God's commandment; (3) to continue to live as I have lived, developing in myself the strength to fight against evil, lovingly and gently. This is what I do, but I don't achieve lovingness and gentleness, and I suffer twice over from life and from remorse. Is this really necessary? Is it necessary to live in these agonising conditions until death? It isn't far away now. And it will be hard for me to die with a reproach for all the useless burden of the last years of my life, which I can scarcely rid myself of before I die, and for you to see me off with the doubt whether you could have avoided causing me the uniquely painful sufferings I have experienced in life. I'm afraid that these words will cause you sorrow, and that your sorrow will turn to anger.

Imagine if I were to come across your diary in which you express your inner-

297. To Countess S. A. Tolstaya

most thoughts and feelings and all your motives for this or that action of yours, imagine with what interest I should read it all. But all my works, which have been nothing more or less than my life, have been, and are of so little interest to you that when you come across them you read them out of curiosity, like works of literature; while the children are not even interested in reading them at all. You think that I am one thing and my writing is another. But my writing is the whole of me. In life I have not been able to express my views fully; in life I make concessions to the necessity of living together in the family. I live, and in my soul I deny that life; but this life which is not mine you consider to be my life, while my life which is expressed in my writings you consider to be words which have no reality. All our disagreement has been caused by the fateful mistake 8 years ago whereby you regarded the revolution which had taken place in me—the revolution which brought me from a region of dreams and shadows to real life—as something unnatural, fortuitous, temporary, fantastic, one-sided, which there was no need to study and understand, but which you need to struggle against with all your might. For 8 years you struggled, and the result of this struggle is that I suffer more than ever, but not only do I not give up the views I have adopted, but I keep on going in the same direction and gasp for breath in the struggle, and cause you to suffer too through my own suffering.

What are we to do about it? It's strange to answer, because the answer is the simplest one: we must do what should have been done from the very beginning, what people do when they encounter any obstacle in life: find out where the obstacle comes from, and having found out, destroy it, or having recognised it to be insurmountable, bow down to it.

You attribute what has happened to everything except this one thing, that you are the unwitting, unintentional cause of my sufferings.

People are out driving and they pass a suffering, dying creature lying on the ground covered in blood. They feel sorry and want to help, but they don't want to stop. Why not try and stop?

You look for the cause: look for the remedy. The children can stop overeating (vegetarianism). I shall be happy and cheerful (despite rebuffs and malicious attacks). The children can do their rooms, stop going to the theatre, feel sorry for the peasants, start reading serious books—I shall be happy and cheerful, and all my illnesses will disappear instantaneously. But no, you obstinately and deliberately refuse.

A struggle to the death is going on between us. Either God's works, or not God's works. And since God is within you...[4]

---

4. The letter breaks off here. It was written hastily and under great stress, and in translating it it has been necessary to smooth over some of the rough passages where careless syntax or the omission of words make a literal translation very difficult. I have tried to render the sense faithfully while 'improving' the style in places in the interests of readability.

298. To V. G. CHERTKOV

Moscow, 22 February 1886

I haven't gone to the country. The day after you left I began to feel unwell, and I didn't go out for two days—I'm feeling better today, Saturday. I'm writing to tell you, so as not to miss any of your letters. If and when I leave, I'll let you know. I got Obolensky's story from him. It's not good. It's all unreal—these things couldn't happen—and it makes a disagreeable impression, and will make the same impression, I think, on the peasants. I've been doing nothing except reading and thinking. Dickens interests me more and more.[1] I've asked Orlov to do a version of *A Tale of Two Cities*. I'll ask Ozmidov to do *Little Dorrit*. *Our Mutual Friend* is charming. Only one needs to take as much liberty as possible with the original: to put divine truth above the writer's authority. I would have tackled *Our Mutual Friend*, but there's something else I want to do. But it would be a good thing if one of us could do it.

Did you have a good journey, and how are you? You seemed sad at our last meeting. Perhaps I was in low spirits (as I was) and just thought so, or perhaps you really were sad.

Orlov has been here recently and has begun to write a publisher's foreword to *What Then Must We Do?* for Sofya Andreyevna.[2] He's also written a fine article pointing out the difference between my views and those of the socialists and the revolutionaries. 'They want to reform the world, while he wants to save souls.' The foreword is not likely to come out, but the article is good. I got a very nice letter from Mrs Maximovich, asking for unpublished articles. This morning I want to finish writing a tale about *The Godson*.[3]

299. To V. G. CHERTKOV

Moscow, March 1886

No, Vladimir Grigoryevich, *Yulianiya Lazarevskaya*[1] is no use at all. I say it advisedly. If I see Nekrasova, I'll tell her so.

All Lives of saints, once they are translated into plain language, strike one at

---

[298] 1. Dickens was always one of Tolstoy's favourite authors. In *What is Art?* several of his works are quoted as examples of the highest art. The three novels mentioned in this letter were intended to be adapted for publication in *The Intermediary* but nothing came of the plan.

2. Sofya Andreyevna was then busy bringing out the first edition of this work. The publisher's foreword mentioned here was not published, for unknown reasons.

3. This story was based on a folk-tale. It was not published in *The Intermediary* as planned, due to increasing difficulties with the censor over the general publishing activities of the firm, but appeared in the journal *Books of the Week*.

[299] 1. *The Life of St Yulianiya Lazarevskaya*, written by her son in the seventeenth century, was rewritten for publication in *The Intermediary* but never published, by Y. S. Nekrasova, a historian of Russian literature and a member of the editorial board of a number of literary journals.

once by their artificiality. They can only be read in Slavonic or in an ancient language. And hence they can deceive.

L.T.

300. To W. FREY

William Frey (1839–88), the assumed name of a well-to-do Russian of Estonian extraction, who had emigrated to America in 1868 to found an agricultural community on communist lines. He was a highly educated man, and later became a fervent adherent of Comte's positivism to which he adapted his own ideas to postulate a new 'religion of humanity'. In 1884 he left America for England, where he first became acquainted with Tolstoy's ideas and on returning to Russia in 1885 wrote a long letter to Tolstoy expounding his own beliefs. Tolstoy replied with an invitation to visit Yasnaya Polyana, where Frey stayed from 7–12 October (see Letter 292). Frey did not convert Tolstoy to positivism, but he did persuade him to become a vegetarian. Tolstoy always retained a high opinion of Frey as a thinker, an idealist, and a man.

Moscow, 1–31(?) March 1886

All our misunderstanding[1] is based on the fact that when you speak about religion, you don't at all understand by it what was understood by Confucius, Lao-Tzu, Buddha or Christ. Religion for you is something to be invented, or at least thought out—the sort of thing which should have a good influence on people, tally with science, and unite and embrace everything, warming people's hearts, encouraging them to do good, but not interfering with their lives. But I understand religion (and I flatter myself with the hope that I am not the only one) in quite a different way. Religion is the awareness of those truths which are common and comprehensible to all people in all situations at all times, and are as indisputable as $2 \times 2 = 4$. The business of religion is to find and express these truths, and when the truth has been expressed, it inevitably changes people's lives. And therefore what you call a scheme, is certainly not somebody's arbitrary assertion, but the expression of laws which are always immutable and felt by everyone. Religion is like geometry. There has always been a relationship between the side adjacent and the hypotenuse, and people have known that there was one; but when Pythagoras pointed it out and proved it, it became common property. And to say that a scheme of morals is bad because it excludes other schemes is like saying that the theorem of the relationship between the side adjacent and the hypotenuse is bad because it violates other false assumptions. One cannot impugn Christ's scheme (as you call it) or truth (as I call it) on the grounds that it does not fit in with the invented religion of humanity and excludes other schemes (according to you) or

[300] 1. After Frey had visited Tolstoy at Yasnaya Polyana, he wrote him a long letter containing a defence of positivism. Tolstoy annotated Frey's letter and sent the above reply in explanation of their failure to understand each other.

300. To W. Frey

lies (according to me), but you must impugn it by proving outright that it is not the truth. Religion is not made up of a collection of words which can have a good influence on people; religion is made up of simple, very obvious, clear indisputable moral truths which stand out from the chaos of false and deceitful opinions, and such are the truths of Christ. If I had found these truths in Katkov,[2] I would have been obliged to recognise them at once. This failure of yours to comprehend what I, and all religious people, consider to be religion, and your wish to put in its place a particular form of propaganda, is the basis of our misunderstanding.

301. To COUNTESS S. A. TOLSTAYA

Yasnaya Polyana, 4 May 1886

I'm writing in the morning so as not to have to hurry in the evening. I saw my guests off yesterday[1] and was very glad to be left on my own. It rained the whole day. I went for a walk in the wood—I didn't find any mushrooms, but I picked a lot of violets. A lot of peasants came to the house. There has always been poverty, but these last years it has been getting worse, and this year it has reached terrifying proportions and is alarming the rich whether they like it or not. It's impossible even to eat porridge or have a roll and tea in peace when you know that right by you there are people you know—children like Chilikin's children at Telyatinki or Tanya's nurse Matryona—going to bed without any bread, which they ask for and which isn't there. And there are many such people. Not to mention the seed oats, the lack of which makes the people worry about the future, i.e. makes it plain to them that if the fields are not sown and are given over to some other purpose, there will be nothing to look forward to in the future either, except the sale of that crop and the begging bowl. One can shut one's eyes to it, as one can shut one's eyes to a man tumbling over a precipice, but that doesn't change the situation. People complained about poverty before, but only occasionally, and there were few of them; but now it's one general moan. On the roads, in the pub, in church and round the houses everyone is talking about the same thing—need. You ask: what can we do, how can we help?[2] We can help by giving seeds and bread to those who ask for it, but it's not really help, it's a drop in the ocean, and besides, this help is self-defeating. If I give to one or 3, why not to 20, or 1,000 or a million? Obviously I can't give to all, even by giving everything away. But what can we do? How can we help? Only in one way—by living a good life. Evil doesn't all come from the rich robbing the poor. That's a small part of the cause.

2. M. N. Katkov.

[301] 1. Anna Dieterichs (who married Chertkov in the autumn of 1886) and Olga Ozmidova, both adherents of Tolstoyan ideas.

2. In her letter of 5 May Sofya Andreyevna had argued against Tolstoy's attitude towards the growing famine, i.e. that help offered to individuals is inadequate and self-defeating, because the need is so large and the reasons for it lie so deep. Instead, she had promised him all the money she could raise from the sale of his books, and urged him to use these funds entirely for famine relief.

The cause is that all people, rich, middle and poor, live like animals, each for himself, each treading on the other. This is what causes distress and poverty. The only escape from it is to introduce into one's own life, and so into the lives of other people, respect for all people, love for them, concern for others and the greatest possible renunciation of the self and one's egotistical pleasures. I'm not making suggestions to you or preaching; I'm only writing what I think—thinking aloud to you.

I know and you know—everyone knows—that human evil can be overcome by human beings, and that this alone is their task and the point of life. People will work and are working for this; why then shouldn't we work for the same thing?

I could go on writing to you about this, but I somehow think that when you read this you will have some harsh words to say, and my hand won't let me write any more. The weather today is wonderful and warm. I want to heat the house for tonight, and tomorrow to open it to the sun. Already today warm air is circulating upstairs, and I don't notice the damp much. I remember before you left that you said something about the master key. Did you give it me or not? If not, send it to me; if so, write and tell me. If it's lost I'll order a new key. The house has been scrubbed out, and if it stays like this it will be possible to travel in about 4 days. Only how are things with you? How is the young children's cough? Has Kolechka arrived?[3] Goodbye, dear. I dreamed about you today that you were hurting me. That means the opposite. May it be so. I kiss you and the children. How good that Ilya and Lyova are sitting with you. That's how it should be. More in a group. Has Masha stopped crying? Has Tanya stopped hiring a horse at 5 roubles an hour? 5 roubles would give children bread for a month instead of crusts. I'm afraid they don't understand that in Moscow. I look forward to having you all here very soon. Thank you for the apples and oranges (more than I need). You have been very concerned for me generally. But I'm quite well. Whatever I look for is there. You have laid in everything.

I got your letter. There was no need to attack the girls.[4] They are very muddled, but good and pure. I heard about Orlov[5] this year too. It's very sad.

302. To A. N. OSTROVSKY

Alexander Nikolayevich Ostrovsky (1823–86), a well-known dramatist of the mid-nineteenth century, highly prolific and enormously popular in his day. His plays are still frequently produced in the Soviet Union, although hardly known abroad. He took as his subject for the most part the Russian merchant classes and the petty bureaucracy in Moscow and the provinces, and he introduced the colloquial language of

3. Nikolay Gay junior.
4. Sofya Andreyevna had made some harsh comments about Anna Dieterichs and Olga Ozmidova and their intentions towards Chertkov in her last letter.
5. Vladimir Orlov had recently begun to drink heavily and to behave badly towards his family.

302. To A. N. Ostrovsky

these classes to the stage. Tolstoy often commented in his diaries and letters on Ostrovsky's plays, and he was particularly fond of *Poverty is No Crime*. His acquaintance with Ostrovsky dated from the mid-1850s, which may account for the fact that he uses the familiar second person singular form of address in this letter, which he very rarely does with other correspondents. Only four of his letters to Ostrovsky have survived.

Yasnaya Polyana, 22(?) May 1886

My dear Alexander Nikolayevich,

This letter will be handed to you by my friend Vladimir Grigoryevich Chertkov who publishes cheap books for the people. Perhaps you know our editions and our programme, but if not, Chertkov will tell you. Our aim is to publish what is accessible, comprehensible and necessary to all, and not to a small circle of people, and has a moral content in accord with the spirit of Christ's teaching. Of all Russian writers nobody comes closer to these requirements than you, and so we are asking you to allow us to publish your works in our edition, and to write for this edition if God should so move your heart. Negotiate with Chertkov about all the details—details about what to publish and how, and many other things if you accept (which I implore you to do, and am almost certain that you will). I know from experience how your works are read, listened to and remembered by the people, and so I would like to help you now as quickly as possible to become in reality what you undoubtedly are—a universal writer in the very broadest sense.

I kiss you as a friend and wish you peace of mind and good health.[1]

Lev Tolstoy

303. To V. G. CHERTKOV

Yasnaya Polyana, 27–8 May 1886

I got your letter, dear friend, and was very glad of it. Mine, I suppose, won't find you in Petersburg. We are well here. I continue to work a little—more with my hands now than with my head, since I'm more attracted to that sort of work. Besides, there have been many guests. We have had Ozmidov,[1] Gribovsky and Marya Alexandrovna Schmidt,[2] and Sosnovsky is here now.[3] I was very glad to

[302] 1. Chertkov did not hand the letter directly to Ostrovsky, but sent it via a mutual friend. Ostrovsky died suddenly on 2 June 1886 before he was able to contribute anything new to *The Intermediary*, but he gave permission for two of his older plays to be published by Chertkov.

[303] 1. Nikolay Lukich Ozmidov (1843–1908), a Tolstoyan who trained as an agronomist and at one time owned a dairy farm near Moscow and a dairy shop in Moscow. He became acquainted with Tolstoy in the early 1880s, gave up his own commercial activity and devoted himself to Tolstoy's publishing activities, first as a copyist and distributor of Tolstoy's forbidden works, then as a collaborator on *The Intermediary*. In 1886 he organised an agricultural colony along Tolstoyan lines in the Caucasus; both his daughter and M. A. Schmidt were members. Later he changed his views and left the Tolstoyan circle altogether.

2. Marya Alexandrovna Schmidt (1844–1911), a Tolstoyan, a former *dame de classe* in the

303. To V. G. Chertkov

see Ozmidov. And I got on very well with him. I'm also glad that the prejudice against him in my family has been overcome. Gribovsky is very young. This is the main thing to remember about him, as well as the fact that the first awakening of his spiritual activity was revolutionary—scientific, as it's called. What a terrible plague this is! The same is true to a far greater degree with Sosnovsky. We often delude ourselves by thinking that when we meet revolutionaries, we stand close by their side. No state—no state; no property—no property; no inequality—no inequality; and much else. It seems we're just the same. But not only is there a big difference; there are no people further apart from us. For a Christian there is no state, but for them it is necessary to destroy the state; for a Christian there is no property, but they destroy property. It's just like two ends of a ring that hasn't been joined up. The ends are adjacent, but they are further apart from each other than all the other parts of the ring are. You have to go right round the ring in order to join up the ends.

Sosnovsky and Feinermann interrupted me as I was writing this letter. They came from the country (Sosnovsky had spent 2 days with Feinermann) and we had a very good talk. Incidentally I read to Sosnovsky what I'm writing about him. I liked him very much. There's a lot of goodness in him. He's just leaving now. If you have copied out the beginning of the story about the peasant and the boy[4] (from my papers: it's in a very messy state), send it to me. I was thinking about it today. Perhaps I shall manage to finish it. I'm busy now not only with the Buddha, but with Brahmanism, Confucius and Lao-Tzu. Perhaps nothing will come of it, but perhaps something will—which I won't write about because you can't say anything in a letter. There are heaps of guests here today—young people, Seryozha, Kuzminsky—inundating us with frivolities and temptations for the children, and the children succumb, while I struggle, not against the temptations, but against anger at those who introduce them. I hope God will help. At moments

St Nicholas Institute for Girls in Petersburg. She first came to Yasnaya Polyana in 1885 seeking a copy of Tolstoy's translation of the Four Gospels (not available because of the censorship) in order to become acquainted with his religious and moral ideas. Thereafter, she remained at Yasnaya Polyana, devoting herself to the task of simplifying her life in accordance with Tolstoyan principles, taking part in all tasks offered, and making firm friends with the Tolstoy girls.

In 1886 she joined a Tolstoyan colony headed by N. L. Ozmidov in the Caucasus. When this venture failed, she and a friend (another former *dame de classe*) settled on a particularly desolate part of the Crimean shore where they continued to spend their days in manual labour. After the death of her companion in 1893, Marya Schmidt moved to a small hut on the property of Tatyana Tolstaya. Tolstoy later praised her as the woman with the highest moral convictions and qualities of any he had ever met.

3. Mikhail Ivanovich Sosnovsky (1863–1925), the son of a teacher, and a member of the revolutionary terrorist organisation 'The People's Will'. He studied at the University of Petersburg. In 1885–7, the time of his friendship with Tolstoy, he belonged to a Petersburg terrorist group. In 1887 he was arrested in the aftermath of the assassination attempt on Alexander III and exiled to southern Siberia. In 1917 he was a member of the Socialist Revolutionary party in Turkestan.

4. A reference to a short work which had been laid aside, unfinished, in 1882, beginning with the words 'In a village there lived a righteous man, and he was called Nikolay...' Chertkov had taken it for recopying. It was never completed.

303. To V. G. Chertkov

like this I think with special affection about you and all who are near to me. Write more often, dear friend. Give my regards to your mother. Sosnovsky asked me to send his warm regards. All my family remember you with love.

304. To N. N. MIKLUKHO-MAKLAY

Nikolay Nikolayevich Miklukho-Maklay (1846–88), a well-known explorer, geographer and anthropologist. The son of an engineer, he was expelled from the University of Petersburg for alleged participation in student unrest, then went abroad to Heidelberg, Leipzig and Jena, where he studied comparative animal anatomy. His first voyage, to the Canary Islands and Morocco, was made as an assistant to the zoologist E. Häckel. Miklukho-Maklay believed that social and cultural characteristics of groups are determined by their social and natural environment. To test this theory he obtained the support of the Imperial Geographical Society to make a voyage to the Pacific in order to study the Papuan tribes of New Guinea. In 1871 he visited the north-east coast of New Guinea, now known as the 'Maklay Coast', and spent fifteen months there; in 1874 he visited the south-west of the island, and in 1876-7 he again visited the Maklay Coast (results of this expedition are given in an article in the Yasnaya Polyana library, undoubtedly one of two sent to Tolstoy with the letter referred to below). The purpose of his trips to New Guinea (there was a fourth in 1883) was not limited to research: he sought to introduce simple tools and domestic animals to the Papuan tribes, and to halt the colonisation drive being carried out at that time by the English. Miklukho-Maklay believed strongly in the unity and equality of all racial types, regardless of cultural differences. Another of his firm beliefs, on which he based his relations with the tribesmen, and which was of special interest to Tolstoy, was that violence was futile and self-defeating, and that only persuasion and moral example would yield positive results.

Yasnaya Polyana, 25 September 1886

Dear Nikolay Nikolayevich,

I'm very grateful to you for sending your brochures.[1] I read them through with pleasure and found something of what interests me in them. What interests me in your work—not only interests, but moves me and rouses my admiration—is that as far as I know you were the first to prove indisputably, on the basis of experience, that man is man everywhere—i.e. a good, friendly creature, with whom one can and should enter into association only with truth and goodness, not guns and vodka. And you proved this by an exploit of true courage, which is so rarely encountered in our society that the people of our society don't even understand it. I imagine your work as follows. People have lived for so long under the delusions of violence, that both those who use violence and their victims are naively

[304] 1. Two brochures containing the results of his voyages to New Guinea.

convinced that this monstrous relationship between people, not only between cannibals and Christians, but between Christians themselves, is a perfectly normal one. And suddenly one man, on the pretext of scientific research (please forgive me for the frank expression of my views) turns up on his own in the midst of the most terrible savages, armed only with reason instead of bullets and bayonets, and argues that all that ugly violence in which our world lives is only old, outmoded humbug,[2] which people who want to live rationally ought to have got rid of long ago. It is this which moves me and makes me admire your work, and for this reason I particularly wish to see you and communicate with you. I would like to say this to you: if your collections are very important, more important than anything that has so far been collected in the world, even so, all your collections and all your scientific observations are nothing in comparison with the observations about the properties of man which you made after dwelling in the midst of savages, associating with them and influencing them by reason alone; and so for the sake of all that is holy, give an account in the greatest detail and with your customary strict truthfulness of all your relationships, man to man, which you had with the people there. I don't know what contribution will be made by your collections and discoveries to the science which you serve, but your experience of associating with savages will mark an epoch in the science which I serve—the science of how people should live with each other. Write this story and you will render a good and great service to mankind. If I were you, I would describe all your adventures in detail, leaving out everything except your relations with people. Please forgive me for the incoherence of this letter. I am ill and am writing in bed and in continual pain. Write to me, and don't object to my attacks on scientific observations—I take those words back—but reply to what is important.[3] It would be good if you could come and see us.

Yours truly,
L. Tolstoy

305. To F. F. TISHCHENKO

Fyodor Fyodorovich Tishchenko (1858–?), a minor writer and native of the Kharkov province. Tishchenko began publishing in 1886, and Tolstoy's first letter to him is dated 11 February 1886, in reply to a letter and a story (*The Sinner*) which the latter had sent to him. The letter translated here is the third in their correspondence, and concerns another story, *The Unfortunate Ones*. Tishchenko did not meet Tolstoy until 1894, but later visited him frequently and wrote two memoirs about him: *How Count Tolstoy Teaches Writing* (1903) and *L. N. Tolstoy: Reminiscences and Characteristics* (1916).

2. 'Humbug' is in English in the original.
3. Miklukho-Maklay's reply was favourable and said that Tolstoy's letter would have a considerable influence on the content of the book about his voyages, and that he would include much which he had previously decided to discard.

305. To F. F. Tishchenko

Moscow, 12(?) December 1886

Fyodor Fyodorovich,

I have just got your letter, and I hasten to reply to it in order to express to you more clearly what I wrote immediately after reading your story.[1] The story as far as the pistol (the pistol is unnatural) is good both in language and content. You can see the life of the people being described, and this life is interesting and moving; the passage in the first brackets is particularly good, but with the pistol begins cold invention, not only uninteresting but exceptionally boring. You can't see people's lives, but you can see that the author is relating something that never happened; you can also see that he himself finds it boring to bother with this trifling matter. Cross out everything from the pistol and continue the way you began—live the lives of the people described, describe in images their inner feelings, and the characters themselves will do what they must do according to their natures, i.e. a dénouement resulting from the nature and situation of the characters will invent itself and materialise of its own accord, especially as the characters are splendidly drawn. But instead of that you neglect the inner progress of your character's feelings and describe what nobody needs to know and what is not relevant, and describe it superficially, without any interest in the new characters. You are wrong to think that this will be an entertainment for the reader. Better to play knucklebones or cards; they will provide more entertainment. Forgive me, dear friend, for writing to you so outspokenly. I want to stave you off from a frivolous attitude to art. It is a great thing, and cannot be undertaken for fun or for purposes outside art. But you are capable of mastering art, in order to serve people by means of it.

You could end the story with the murder of the general,[2] or the murder of the shop-assistant and the wife's return to her husband, or with the death of either of them, as the story might have ended in real life, and you could bring to it all the truth and illumination which comes from its author's view of life. If you had to bring in the general and the shopkeeper, you should have brought them in at the beginning, and in describing the events to do with them, you should have described them too with the same love and detailed description of their inner impulses, as Katerina and Semyon are described, otherwise it will be like a picture with a caption saying 'this is a man'. You describe Karpinsky at length, but he is still not alive.

However, I am wrong to write all this to you. If, as I understand you, you have talent, you must feel all this yourself. If not, then what is blunt can never be sharpened. This is how I understand you: you have a sensitive, artistic nature, but your view of life is wrong. For example you look on writing as a means of liveli-

[305] 1. *The Unfortunate Ones*. Tolstoy had written a short note on the preceding day, 11 December, giving his first reaction to the story and offering to print it in *The Intermediary* if Tishchenko rewrote the ending. Tishchenko later did so, but asked for it to be published in a journal which could afford to pay higher rates. It was published first of all in *The Herald of Europe*, under the title *The Orphan Semyon and his Wife* and appeared later in *The Intermediary*.

2. In the first version of the story, the action culminated with a murder, but Tishchenko, under the influence of Tolstoy's letters, substituted for it the reconciliation of the husband and wife. However, in a collected edition of his works published in 1903, he reverted to his original ending, discarding the revisions as 'tendentious'.

hood. That is a terrible mistake. It means subordinating a higher condition to a lower one. If you think about what writing will give you, it will give you nothing. If you don't think about it, it will give you far more than you can expect.

Please accept all my outspoken words with the same love with which they are written.

L.T.

Please approach Obolensky about the money for *The Sinner*.[3] I did as you wished and passed on to him both the manuscript and your letter, and can do nothing more apart from reminding him, which I shall do.

I'm sending the manuscript back in the hope that you will follow my advice.

306. To THE YOUNG LADIES OF TIFLIS

This letter was written in reply to a letter from several women students in Tiflis who wished to know how they could make the best use of their knowledge and energies for the common good. These young women had been doing socially useful work in accordance, as they thought, with Tolstoyan principles, when an article by Tolstoy appeared entitled *The Labour of Men and Women* in which he agued that a woman's social usefulness was best fulfilled in motherhood. Several of the women wrote to Tolstoy for clarification and received this answer.

Moscow, 17 December 1886

You ask for a task to do. Apart from the task common to all of us—to try to reduce the labour used by others to support our lives, by cutting down our requirements and doing with our own hands what we can do for ourselves and others—there is another task for those who have acquired knowledge: to share that knowledge and give it back to the people[1] who brought us up. And this is a task I have set myself.

In Moscow there are publishers of popular books, primers, arithmetic books, histories, calendars, pictures and stories. All these are sold in enormous quantities of copies, regardless of the quality of the content, and only because buyers are accustomed to them and there are skilful sellers. One of these publishers, Sytin, is a friend of mine, a good man who wishes to improve the content of these books as much as possible.

The task I suggest to you is the following: take one or several of these books—a primer, a calendar or a novel (work particularly needs to be done on stories—they are bad, and there are a great many of them about)—read it through and correct it, or revise it completely. If you correct the misprints and the nonsense you find

3. The first story which Tishchenko sent to Tolstoy. It was published in the journal *Russian Wealth*, 1886, under a pseudonym.
[306] 1. *Narod*.

306. To The Young Ladies of Tiflis

there—historical and geographical mistakes and nonsense—then that in itself will be a service, because however bad a book is, it will be sold just the same. The service will be that less rubbish and nonsense will be communicated to the people. If as well as this you also cut out stupid or immoral passages, and replace them by other ones without destroying the meaning, that will be better still. And if, under the same title and using the same plot, you compose your own story or novel with a wholesome content, that will be very good indeed. The same thing applies to calendars, primers, arithmetic books, histories and pictures.

And so if this work appeals to you, choose the kind at which you think you can work best, and write to me. I will send you several books.

I would very much like you to agree to my proposal. The work is undoubtedly useful. The extent of its usefulness will depend on the love you put into it.

Yours,
Lev Tolstoy

VII
1887–1894

The main event outside Yasnaya Polyana which impinged on Tolstoy's life during this period was undoubtedly the serious famine which affected large areas of European Russia in 1891 and 1892. For the greater part of two years he devoted much time and energy, with the active assistance of his wife and family, to the alleviation of suffering in the regions to the south of Tula and Ryazan, organising relief programmes, soliciting contributions of food, clothing and money (not without qualms of conscience), opening 'soup kitchens' and generally alerting public opinion in Russia and abroad to his country's serious economic plight. Working towards a common cause did something to improve the uneasy relations between Tolstoy, his wife and his growing sons at this period (a thirteenth and last child was born to the Tolstoys in 1888 when he was already sixty and Sonya forty-four), but the growing influence of Chertkov in Tolstoy's life was a constant source of domestic friction which Sonya was never really able to overcome. In 1891 Tolstoy publicly renounced the copyright of all his works published after 1881, much to his wife's annoyance. He finally gave up meat, spirits and tobacco, spent more and more of his time in the country, and turned his energies increasingly towards agricultural tasks when he was not either reading or writing.

His major literary work during these years was the notorious *Kreutzer Sonata*, banned by the censors but allowed to be included in Tolstoy's *Collected Works*, thanks to Sonya's personal intercession with the Tsar. His new play *The Fruits of Enlightment* was given its first production at the Maly Theatre in Moscow in 1892. *The Kingdom of God is Within You*, his powerful statement of the case for non-resistance and against patriotism and war, was completed and sent abroad for translation and publication in 1893, while the articles *Why Do Men Stupefy Themselves?*, *The First Step* (advocating vegetarianism), *Christianity and Patriotism* and his preface to some of Maupassant's stories were all written in the course of these few restless and extremely strenuous years.

307. To V. G. CHERTKOV

Moscow, 19–21 January 1887

Petrov only received the drama today.¹ I haven't yet received your valuable parcel of manuscripts,² but I'm very much looking forward to them. All you say gladdens me. What I see around me gladdens me equally. There's a lot of work to do collaborating with Petrov. What did Potekhin say about his stories *In the Commune* and *The Sick Woman*?³ Is he going to let the people have them, i.e. *The Intermediary* or Sytin?⁴ I've asked my wife to let them have *Polikushka*,⁵ and I'll now ask every writer what he can give. We must ask Grigorovich, and choose what is most suitable. But I think the main thing is to let them have all famous works by Germans, Frenchmen and Englishmen which have run into many editions and particularly translations, and I'm doing something about this, but the harvest is plenteous, and the labourers are few: Voltaire, Rousseau, Bernardin de St Pierre, Lessing's *Nathan der Weise*, Schiller's *Die Raüber*, *The Vicar of Wakefield*, *Gulliver*, *Don Quixote*, Silvio Pellico, Franklin's *Autobiography*, Plutarch and much else.

Semyonov has just brought me a story—not bad, but he will need to revise it.⁶

This week Sytin promised to put me in touch with the publishers. I shall tell them that everything of mine that Sytin publishes belongs to nobody and can be republished by anybody. If they want to have a certificate to that effect, I'll give them a note about it. *The Intermediary* will need to do the same.

I've been to Ostrovskaya's, but she told me nothing.⁷ Won't it be necessary to ask her brother-in-law, the Minister? I'm looking forward to seeing Pavel Ivanovich.⁸

L.T.

308. To V. G. CHERTKOV

Moscow, 13 February 1887

I sent you the *Primer* via Petrov. I smiled a lot—I won't say laughed—when I read

[307] 1. Petrov worked for *The Intermediary* publishing house. The drama referred to is Tolstoy's *The Power of Darkness*.

2. Manuscripts of three of Tolstoy's works and two of Leskov's.

3. Only *The Sick Woman* was published by *The Intermediary*.

4. I. D. Sytin (1851–1935), the publisher responsible for printing and distributing the *Intermediary* publications.

5. First published by Tolstoy in 1863, and therefore now belonging to his wife under their copyright agreement. She did not agree to the request, and the story only became public property after Tolstoy's death.

6. S. T. Semyonov, a peasant writer of whom Tolstoy thought highly. He later wrote an introduction to a collection of Semyonov's stories published in 1894. The story mentioned here is *Into the City*, published by *The Intermediary* in 1887.

7. As Ostrovsky had died before he could reply to Tolstoy's request to republish some of his plays, Tolstoy visited his widow, who later granted the necessary permission.

8. Biryukov. See Letter 309.

your ironical reproaches about my surprises.¹ I won't give you any more surprises like that, although I thought this one was admirably prepared. But the main thing is that the *Primer* is a very, very desirable thing. I think that if it gets past the censors (and I can't think of any reason why it shouldn't), it will become the favourite, the only *Primer* for the Russian people. If that happens, it will mean a very important change in the first (very powerful) impressions a child receives when he starts to learn: instead of the bewildering fog of the Scriptures, and incomprehensible prayers, there will be lucidity, holiness of feeling and joy. May God help you. Thank you for taking my remarks in a loving spirit—perhaps they will be of use to you; your strictness as regards truthfulness has long been of use to me and helped me. Why don't you write about yourself and your spiritual condition? From your last two letters and their tone I sense a weakening of your love. God grant that I'm mistaken. Write and tell me if you are well. I don't want to take Mikhaylov's story away from Tanya—she has started it. Ivanov needs to work and to learn to take a strict attitude towards himself and his own work. (I'm writing this for him).² He sent me a comedy which was painful to read. It's terribly bad, obviously there's a complete lack of self-criticism in him. He needs to learn to restrain his thoughts so that they can be worked over; so that out of 1,000 thoughts only one may be chosen, and then this one thought may eventually find, out of 1,000 possible places, the one place appropriate to it. This and much else like it comprises the inner work of a writer which precedes the writing itself—work which he, Ivanov, doesn't know about or doesn't do, writing down on paper what he ought to do in his head. Don't be angry, dear friend, but think a little and apply it to yourself;³ perhaps it is true and perhaps this is just what you need. The Pythagoreans had to be silent for 5 years, and you should be silent for a while too.⁴

        By stirring up the springs you will cloud them.
        Drink of them, and be silent. (Tyutchev)⁵

[10 lines omitted]

309. To P. I. BIRYUKOV

Pavel Ivanovich Biryukov (1860–1931), who was introduced by Chertkov to Tolstoy towards the end of 1884, ranks second after Chertkov in the circle of 'Tolstoyans' who worked closely with Tolstoy. Like Chertkov, he was a personal

---

[308] 1. What Tolstoy had termed a 'surprise' in his previous letter to Chertkov was his decision to send his *Primer* direct to the censor and not first of all to Chertkov, who believed himself better able to handle censorship problems.
   2. A reference to N. N. Ivanov's play *Sin*. Tolstoy did not write a separate letter to Ivanov, but intended the criticism to be passed on by Chertkov.
   3. The direct address is meant for Ivanov.
   4. The Greek philosopher Pythagoras founded a religious group who, like Tolstoy, sought for moral perfection and practised vegetarianism.
   5. A quotation from *Silentium*.

309. To P. I. Biryukov

friend of Tolstoy as well as a collaborator, carried on a voluminous correspondence with him, and wrote a great deal about his life and ideas.

Biryukov had been educated first in the aristocratic *Corps de Pages*, and later in the Naval Academy in Petersburg, from which he graduated in 1884. By this time he had already sailed round the world and accompanied one of the Grand Dukes on a voyage to Palestine. Even before entering the Academy, however, he had come to view war as immoral, and being deeply religious by nature he had subjected his own beliefs to close scrutiny and had arrived at conclusions basically similar to Tolstoy's before the two men met.

Biryukov was one of the founders of *The Intermediary*. He continued to work closely with Chertkov, a fellow-founder, and was responsible for the day-to-day management of *The Intermediary* until 1888, when he returned to the family estate in the Kostroma district, in order to farm the land and to live a simple life. In 1891 he resumed active work on behalf of Tolstoy, and went abroad to arrange publication of *The Translation and Harmony of the Four Gospels* in Geneva. He returned to Russia in 1892 and helped Tolstoy with his famine relief work until 1893. He continued working on the staff of *The Intermediary* until 1897 when he was exiled as the result of the publication of a polemical article about the Dukhobors. He was allowed to leave Russia in the following year and began a long period of publishing work abroad, first in Essex with Chertkov, and then in Switzerland where he began to publish the journal *Free Thought*. At the beginning of the 1900s he began the work for which he is best known, the four-volume *Life of Tolstoy* (1906–23). He returned to Russia in 1907, but continued to travel abroad frequently. In 1927 he left for Canada to live amongst the Dukhobors. He died in Switzerland in 1931.

Biryukov's *Life of Tolstoy* was the first attempt at a comprehensive biography of Tolstoy and was a reliable and much-used source for all later biographies (both Aylmer Maude and Romain Rolland acknowledged their indebtedness to it). There are numerous shorter writings by Biryukov on Tolstoy's ideas, projects, and life, of which a few were originally published in English during his period of exile in Britain. He also edited and annotated two major editions of Tolstoy's *Collected Works* in 1912 and 1913.

Moscow, 1 March 1887

My dear Pavel Ivanovich,

Lyova was telling me that he overtook you, and you were smiling. I was terribly glad. What were you smiling at? I'm sending a letter to you. I had already sent the book before getting your note. I got the statement from Chertkov today.[1] It's fine. But it would be good to try and find company. Kolechka will write to Ertel, but can anyone else be found as well? It would be good if I were not the only one.

Chertkov writes about Savikhin.[2] The language of his poem and the imagery are

[309] 1. The statement in *Russian News* on 7 March 1887, that all Tolstoy's works published in *The Intermediary* could be republished without payment.

2. V. I. Savikhin-Ivanov, a working-class author. The reference is to his poem in blank verse *Two Neighbours* which was published in *The Intermediary* after some corrections suggested by Tolstoy had been made.

excellent. The verse is good in places, but it wouldn't do any harm to make it still smoother and better; but the content is not only not good—there simply isn't any. The content is only an imitation of what doesn't need imitating in Nekrasov, i.e. an exaggeration of the people's poverty and a despairing attitude towards it, arousing only indignation against somebody. Why did the gentleman in glasses go there? What is he doing? And above all, what does he live on? There can't be any sympathy for him, because there is something mysterious and secretive about him. But there is bound to be sympathy for the peasants, and you get angry at the fact that the author treats them with contempt, while treating with respect what only arouses bewilderment and suspicion. It's a long time since I've seen so clearly in any work how impossible it is for a person to write without drawing a definite line for himself between good and evil. The talent my be great, but there will be no work of art. Apart from surface talent, a writer who is an artist needs two things: firstly, to know thoroughly what should be; and secondly, to believe in what should be, sufficiently to depict what should be as though it already is, as though I were living in the midst of it. With artists who are incomplete—immature— there is the one, but not the other. Savikhin has the ability to see what should be, as though it already is. But he doesn't know what should be. With others it's the reverse. The majority of untalented works belong to the 2nd category; the majority of so-called works of art belong to the first. People feel that it's impossible to write what *is*—that that wouldn't be art; but they don't know what should be, and start to write what has been (historical art—Surikov's picture),[3] or else write not what should be, but what pleases them or their circle. Both are bad. The first is the failing of Ivanov,[4] the second of Savikhin. Mix the two together—the result will be a great artist. But even without mixing them together, each can become a good brainworker, i.e. writer, by developing what is lacking in him. That's what I think. You decide, since you know Savikhin, whether it's possible to show him this, for his own good, without upsetting him. I meant to go to the country. But I felt ashamed. Where could I go to get away from myself and from people? And so I stayed behind. The time will come when, if need be and if I do what I should, I may be useful even here. Goodbye. I embrace you and all our friends.

L.T.

310. To P. M. SVOBODIN

Pavel Matveyevich Svobodin (1850–92), an actor at the Alexandriinsky Theatre in Petersburg and a writer. He had written to Tolstoy to ask for advice about the appearance and manner of speech of the peasant Akim in Tolstoy's *The Power of Darkness*, a part he was to play at the Alexandriinsky Theatre.

3. *The Boyarynya Morozova*, on a seventeenth-century theme, by the historical painter Vasily Surikov, one of the so-called 'Wanderers' group.

4. N. N. Ivanov, a minor author of short stories and poems who worked for *The Intermediary* and wrote his reminiscences of Tolstoy in 1886.

310. To P. M. Svobodin

Moscow, 5 March 1887

Pavel Matveyevich,

As I see him, Akim[1] has light brown hair; he is not at all grey and not bald; the hair on his head can even curl a little, and his beard is sparse.

He talks with a stutter, phrases suddenly burst out, then a stutter again, and 'I mean' and 'you know'…[1 line omitted][2] There is no need, I think, to mumble. He walks firmly; I imagine him in bast shoes, with turned-out feet. His actions—movements—are punctilious, only God didn't give him the gift of fluent *speech*.

Great attentiveness, careful listening to everything said, especially to him, and approval of everything good that is said; but restlessness and strong disapproval of anything bad that is said. In the 3rd act he must suffer physically at the sight of his son's disgraceful behaviour.

One should exploit the contrast between his comic, incoherent babbling and the ardent, and at times solemn delivery of the words which *issue forth* from him. In the 5th act he should put up a resistance, loathing the sight of the wedding, and then begin to understand what is going on, then go into raptures over his son's action and before the end of the act safeguard even physically—by spreading out his arms and forestalling disturbers—safeguard from interference the repentance being solemnly enacted. Your letter moved me. I wish you success.

Lev Tolstoy

311. To F. F. TISHCHENKO

Moscow, 18 April 1887

Fyodor Fyodorovich,

I got your story[1] and read it through. You want my frank opinion. These are its shortcomings. It's very long drawn out, especially the description of Semyon's state of mind after his wife's infidelity. The scene in front of the mirror is long and artificial. But the upheavals going on in Semyon's soul are not sufficiently clear: first malice, then despair, then composure, and finally the resolve to have his wife back. All this needs to be brought about through the events, and not just described. You do try to make these upheavals coincide with events, but not always successfully.

---

[310] 1. Akim, the only 'positive' character in the play, is the father of Nikita, the central figure, whose unbridled sensuality leads to a series of murders—first the husband of a peasant woman who returns Nikita's passion and wants to live with him, then an illegitimate child of his liaison with the woman's sixteen-year-old daughter. At the end of the play, Nikita makes a public confession of his crimes at the wedding of the girl he had seduced, and asks his father for forgiveness. Akim willingly gives it and embraces his son as the wedding guests advance in a menacing fashion towards Nikita.

2. Two sentences are omitted here on the pronunciation of *tae*, the spoken version of *t.e.* (i.e. in English)—rendered here by 'I mean'.

[311] 1. A revised version of *The Unfortunate Ones*, now re-entitled *The Orphan Semyon and His Wife*. (See Letter 305, note 1.)

The scene with the eau-de-cologne is too long. Then you make the mistake of repeating various things. This weakens the impression; for example you twice mention throwing away money and breaking the accordion. Then Semyon was evidently not at first intended for the ending which now exists. These are all the shortcomings, which I have carefully tried to remember. Apart from them there is occasional incorrectness of language. But it's not worth speaking about that. And I won't reproach you for it. I like what is called incorrectness, that is to say, what is characteristic.

Now the merits. It's remarkably truthful. That's a great and important quality. And the most important thing is the sincerity in the last splendid scene with the child. Generally speaking, the story is good. And I think you have the particular qualities which a writer needs.

One important thing that I think you have or may have, judging by this story, is inner content. Without it there's no point in taking up writing. A writer needs two things: to know *what should be* in people and between people, and to believe in what should be, and to love it sufficiently to see before one what should be, and what deviates from it.

I am sending your story by this post to Chertkov in Petersburg and to *The Intermediary*. I am asking him to publish the story in a journal, as you wish, or straightaway in *The Intermediary*, but in such a way that you may receive a fee for it.

Settle this with him by letter. Probably he will write to you first. He is my close friend, and relations with him can only be pleasant for you.

Write and tell me how you are. Why are you in the Akhtyrka district now, and how are your family and children?

May God help you,

Yours affectionately,
Lev Tolstoy

Chertkov's address is: Vladimir Grigoryevich Chertkov, Petersburg, 32 Millionnaya. You can empower Chertkov to make any necessary cuts. Cuts can only improve the work, especially the ones Chertkov will make.

312. To F. A. ZHELTOV

Fyodor Alexeyevich Zheltov (1859–?), a member of the Molokan sect, a writer and an acquaintance of Tolstoy. He first wrote to Tolstoy in 1887, to ask his opinion about the purpose of literature, and wrote again in October 1895 for advice on the education of children (see Letter 418).

Moscow, 21(?) April 1887

...[1] I think that a man who writes has only one task: to communicate to other people

---

[312] 1. The beginning of the letter is missing.

312. To F. A. Zheltov

those thoughts and beliefs which have made his own life joyful. Only the understanding and application to himself and the varying circumstances of his life of the Gospel truth makes life joyful, truly joyful.

Only this can and should be written in all possible forms: as reasoned statements, as parables and as stories. One thing only is dangerous: to write only as a result of reasoning, and not of the kind of feeling which can encompass the whole of a man's being. The main thing is not to be in a hurry to write, not to grudge correcting and revising the same thing 10 or 20 times, not to write a lot and not, for heaven's sake, to make of writing a means of livelihood or of winning importance in people's eyes. It's just as bad and harmful in my opinion to write immoral things, as to write edifying works coldly, without believing in what you teach or without having a passionate desire to pass on to people what it is that gives you happiness.

I can't express briefly what I consider necessary for writing, otherwise than by pointing to my recent stories for the people and the introduction to *The Flower Garden*[2] in which I tried to express what the business of poetic writing consists of. I'm very glad that you wish to write, firstly because you are a peasant, and secondly because you are free from the false teaching of the Church which conceals from people the meaning of Christ's teaching.

I have read your articles.[3] The best from the point of view of content is the one about the journey and the dream; but this article has a literary, feuilleton-like character which I find unpleasant, and not much content. The dream might have been one episode in a complete whole, but it doesn't have much meaning on its own. The article about the festival is cold and also has a literary character. By literary character I mean that it's addressed to the newspaper reader, the educated reader. What is desirable and what I advise you to do is something different: the imaginary reader for whom you are writing should not be a man of letters, an editor, a civil servant, a student etc., but a 50-year-old literate peasant. That is the reader I always have before me now, and I advise you to do the same. You won't show off your style or your phrases before a reader like that; you won't say empty and superfluous things, but will speak clearly, succinctly and pithily. Read the story *The Partition*, written by a peasant, and *Uncle Sofron*.[4] Both stories move people because they speak about the vital interests of people, and these interests are dearer than their authors' interests.

If you want to send me what you write for publication in *The Intermediary*, send it to Tula.

Your affectionate brother

You are able to write, it seems to me, both because you have a command of language, and particularly because, from your childhood years, you have imbibed Christ's teaching in its moral significance, as is evident from your letter.

---

2. An anthology published by *The Intermediary*, for which Tolstoy wrote an introduction in 1886.
3. Two stories entitled *A Village Festival* and *The Quagmire*.
4. A story by V. I. Savikhin which was very popular with peasant readers.

313. To N. N. GAY senior

Yasnaya Polyana, 14 May 1887

[4 lines omitted]...P. I. Biryukov came to see me a week ago, and has been staying until our family arrived, but now they have arrived, and he wants to leave soon—tomorrow. I thought about him and introduced him because he and I said something about you which is very important, namely: all real artists are only artists because they have something to write, know how to write, and have the ability to write, while at the same time reading and looking at and criticising themselves most severely. I fear you have too much of this ability, and it prevents you from doing for people what they need. I'm talking about the Gospel pictures.[1] Nobody except you knows the content of the pictures which are in your heart; nobody except you can express them so sincerely, and nobody can paint them like you. Suppose some of them will be on a lower level than the best. Suppose they won't be finished to perfection. Nevertheless, those on the very lowest level will be a great and important acquisition for true art and for the one and only true business of life. I imagined all this particularly vividly when I received the beautiful print of *The Last Supper* made for Marya Alexandrovna. (Sofya Andreyevna had 10 of them done without your permission. You will surely give it.) I know it's impossible to advise and explain to an artist what to do. They have their own private way of working. But I was terribly sorry to think that the wonderful job you have begun won't be completed. I was dragged off to the exhibition;[2] I think there is nothing to compare with pictures as works, not of the hands, but of the human soul. How did your talks with Tretyakov end? I'll be glad when your pictures are there. I'm still picking over my article;[3] I think it's necessary, but God knows. I want to finish it as soon as possible, to free myself for other work which is crowding in on it...[9 lines omitted]

314. To A. P. ZALYUBOVSKY

Zalyubovsky was the nephew of N. L. Ozmidov (see Letter 303, note 1) and was twenty-four at the time of writing.

Yasnaya Polyana, 30 or 31 May 1887

[21 lines omitted]...Every man who is grown up and wants to live a good life must certainly marry, but he must certainly not marry *for love* but *from calculation*—only understanding these two words in precisely the opposite way to which they are normally understood—i.e. marry without sensual love, but from the calculation, not of where to live or what to live on (everybody lives), but from the calculation

---

[313] 1. Gay was working at the time on *Christ in the Garden of Gethsemane* and *The Last Supper*.
2. The XIV Wanderers' Exhibition.   3. *On Life*.

314. To A. P. Zalyubovsky

of how probable it is that your future wife will help you, and not prevent you from living a humane life. Goodbye for the present.

315. To V. G. CHERTKOV

Yasnaya Polyana, 20 June 1887

[47 lines omitted]...I would like to write a fairy story like this.[1] There was a tsar, and nothing ever went right for him, and he went to ask some wise men why he wasn't successful. One wise man said: because he didn't know the right time to do things. Another said: because he didn't know the man most necessary to him. A third said: because he didn't know what task was the most valuable of all tasks. And the tsar sent someone to ask these wise men and others: what time is the most important, what man is the most necessary, and what task is the most valuable. And nobody could answer the riddle. And the tsar kept thinking about it and asking everybody. And then a young girl answered the riddle for him. She said that the most important time of all is the present, because there is no other time exactly like it. And the most necessary man of all is the one you are now dealing with, because he is the only man you actually know. And the most valuable task of all is to do good to this man, because this is the only task that will certainly be of advantage to you.

This thought of mine doesn't solve the problem of money for me, but it puts it in its proper place...[10 lines omitted]

316. To M. A. NOVOSYOLOV

Mikhail Alexandrovich Novosyolov (1864–?) was a teacher in a Moscow grammar school when he wrote his first letter to Tolstoy in October 1886, asking certain questions about the teaching of history. His second letter, in March 1887, criticised Tolstoy for inconsistencies between his beliefs and his way of life. In the late 1880s he organised an agricultural community along Tolstoyan lines in the Tver district. At one time he was also associated with the hectographing of some of Tolstoy's forbidden works, and for his participation in the distribution of *Nicholas Stick* (a savage criticism of Nicholas I) he was imprisoned for a short period. He also helped Tolstoy in 1891–2 during the Samara famine relief. He later returned to the Orthodox Church.

[315] 1. Tolstoy is replying to two letters from Chertkov, complaining about his inability to decide what would be the best thing for him to do to relieve the guilt he felt at benefiting from the physical labour of those who worked on his mother's estate. He could not fully justify his work for *The Intermediary*, which was largely mechanical, and he felt that his first concern should be to return the money to those from whom it had been unjustly extorted. At the same time he was afraid that it would be unfair to his colleagues to abandon his work with *The Intermediary*, and in any case, such an act might not lead to anything more useful on his part. He therefore turned to Tolstoy for advice, which was given in the form of this fairy-tale.

317. To Romain Rolland

Yasnaya Polyana, August 1887

I got your letter, my dear Mikhail Alexandrovich, and was very glad that you are checking my translation of the Gospels. I already agreed beforehand, in general, with the corrections of passages which are too far removed from previous translations and which were artfully translated, and I agree with particular cases such as 'On the Sabbath and the conversation with the woman of Samaria'. I don't agree about the expulsion from the temple. Why not, would take too long to say in writing—we'll talk about it when we meet. Generally speaking I don't think there are any bad mistakes in my translation (I asked the advice of a philologist, a connoisseur and a shrewd critic), but there must be many places such as the ones you indicated where the meaning is strained and the translation artificial. This happened because I wanted as far as possible to depolarise, like a magnet, words of an ecclesiastical interpretation which had acquired an uncharacteristic polarity. To correct them would be a useful task.

I have worked a lot all summer on a book about life—I've started printing it. My health gets weaker, but life gets stronger and seemingly brighter. How are you? Give your esteemed grandfather a brotherly kiss from me.

Yours affectionately,
Lev Tolstoy

317. To ROMAIN ROLLAND

Romain Rolland (1868–1944), later famous as a novelist, musical biographer and historian, and a biographer of Tolstoy, wrote to Tolstoy while a seventeen-year-old student at the Ecole Normale in Paris. His first letter went unanswered, but undaunted, he wrote again (16 April 1887), eliciting this famous reply from Tolstoy expounding his beliefs on the relationship between physical and intellectual labour. In the *Introduction* to his *Vie de Tolstoi* Rolland has described how he had first been captivated by Tolstoy's early novels, and how his literary idol's later ideas, which he knew only incompletely, had come as a revelation to him. Burning with the desire to find the answers to the moral questions troubling him, he wrote to Tolstoy for an explanation of, among other things, his seemingly negative attitude towards art. Not to know 'the moral essence of things' was for him, Rolland said, 'not to live'.

Romain Rolland's studies of Tolstoy include: 'Tolstoï', in *La Revue de Paris* (1911, no. 4), *Vie de Tolstoi* (Paris, 1911), and 'Tolstoi, l'esprit libre', in *Les Tablettes* (1917, no. 9).

Yasnaya Polyana, 3(?) October 1887

Cher frère!

J'ai reçu votre première lettre. Elle m'a touché le coeur. Je l'ai lue les larmes aux yeux. J'avais l'intention d'y répondre, mais je n'en ai pas eu le temps, d'autant plus,

317. To Romain Rolland

qu'outre la difficulté que j'éprouve à écrire en français, il m'aurait fallu écrire très longuement pour répondre à vos questions, dont la plupart sont basées sur un malentendu.

Aux questions que vous faites: pourquoi le travail manuel s'impose à nous comme l'une des conditions essentielles du vrai bonheur? Faut-il se priver volontairement de l'activité intellectuelle, des sciences et des arts, qui vous paraissent incompatibles avec le travail manuel?

A ces questions j'ai répondu comme je l'ai pu dans le livre intitulé *Que faire?* qui, à ce qu'on m'a dit, a été traduit en français. Je n'ai jamais envisagé le travail manuel comme un principe, mais comme l'application la plus simple et naturelle du principe moral, celle qui se présente la première à tout homme sincère.

Le travail manuel dans notre société dépravée (la société des gens dits civilisés) s'impose à nous uniquement par la raison que le défaut principal de cette société a été, et est jusqu'à présent, celui de se libérer de ce travail et de profiter, sans lui rendre la pareille, du travail des classes pauvres, ignorantes et malheureuses, qui sont esclaves, comme les esclaves du vieux monde.

La première preuve de la sincérité des gens de cette société, qui professent des principes chrétiens, philosophiques ou humanitaires, est de tâcher de sortir autant que possible de cette contradiction.

Le moyen le plus simple et qui est toujours sous main y parvenir est le travail manuel qui commence par les soins de sa propre personne. Je ne croirai jamais à la sincérité des convictions chrétiennes, philosophiques ou humanitaires d'une personne qui fait vider son pot de chambre par une servante.

La formule morale la plus simple et courte c'est de se faire servir par les autres aussi peu que possible, et de servir les autres autant que possible. D'exiger des autres le moins possible et de leur donner le plus possible.

Cette formule, qui donne à notre existence un sens raisonnable, et le bonheur qui s'en suit, résout en même temps toutes les difficultés, de même que celle qui se pose devant vous: la part qui doit être faite à l'activité intellectuelle—la science, l'art?

Suivant ce principe, je ne suis heureux et content que quand, en agissant, j'ai la ferme conviction d'être utile aux autres. (Le contentement de ceux pour lesquels j'agis est un extra, un surcroît de bonheur sur lequel je ne compte pas, et qui ne peut influer sur le choix de mes actions). Ma ferme conviction que ce que je fais n'est ni une chose inutile, ni un mal, mais un bien pour les autres, est à cause de cela la condition principale de mon bonheur.

Et c'est cela qui pousse involontairement un homme moral et sincère à préférer aux travaux scientifiques et artistiques le travail manuel: l'ouvrage que j'écris, pour lequel j'ai besoin du travail des imprimeurs; la symphonie que je compose, pour laquelle j'ai besoin des musiciens; les expériences que je fais, pour lesquels j'ai besoin de ceux qui font les instruments de nos laboratoires; le tableau que je peins pour lequel j'ai besoin de ceux qui font les couleurs et la toile;—tous ces travaux peuvent être des choses très utiles aux autres, mais ils peuvent être aussi (comme ils le sont pour la plupart) des choses complètement inutiles et même nuisibles. Et

317. To Romain Rolland

voilà que pendant que je fais toutes ces choses dont l'utilité est fort douteuse, et pour produire lesquelles je dois encore faire travailler les autres, j'ai devant et autour de moi des choses à faire sans fin, et qui toutes sont indubitablement utiles aux autres, et pour produire lesquelles je n'ai besoin de personne: un fardeau à porter, pour celui qui est fatigué; un champ à labourer pour son propriétaire qui est malade; une blessure à panser; mais sans parler de ces milliers de choses à faire qui nous entourent, qui n'ont besoin de l'aide de personne, qui produisent un contentement immédiat dans ceux pour le bien desquels vous les faites:—planter un arbre, élever un veau, nettoyer un puits—sont des actions indubitablement utiles aux autres, et qui ne peuvent ne pas être préférées par un homme sincère aux occupations douteuses qui, dans notre monde, sont prêchées comme la vocation la plus haute et la plus noble de l'homme.

La vocation d'un prophète est une vocation haute et noble. Mais nous savons ce que sont les prêtres qui se croient prophètes, uniquement parce que c'est leur avantage, et qu'ils ont la possibilité de se faire passer pour tels.

Un prophète n'est pas celui qui reçoit l'éducation d'un prophète, mais celui qui a la conviction intime de ce qu'il est et doit, et ne peut ne pas être. Cette conviction est rare, et ne peut être éprouvée que par les sacrifices qu'un homme fait à sa vocation.

De même pour la vraie science et l'art véritable. Un Lully[1] qui, à ses risques et périls, quitte le service de la cuisine pour jouer du violon, par les sacrifices qu'il fait, fait preuve de sa vocation. Mais l'élève d'un conservatoire, un étudiant, dont le seul devoir est d'étudier ce qu'on leur enseigne, ne sont même pas en état de faire preuve de leur vocation; ils profitent simplement d'une position qui leur paraît avantageuse.

Le travail manuel est un devoir et un bonheur pour tous; l'activité intellectuelle est une activité exceptionnelle, qui ne devient un devoir et un bonheur que pour ceux qui ont cette vocation. La vocation ne peut être connue et prouvée que par le sacrifice que fait le savant ou l'artiste de son repos et de son bien-être pour suivre sa vocation. Un homme qui continue à remplier son devoir, celui de soutenir sa vie par le travail de ses mains, et, malgré cela, prend sur les heures de son repos et de son sommeil pour penser et produire dans la sphère intellectuelle, fait preuve de sa vocation. Celui qui se libère du devoir moral de chaque homme, et, sous le prétexte de son goût pour les sciences et les arts, s'arrange une vie de parasite, ne produira jamais que de la fausse science et du faux art.

Les produits de la vraie science et du vrai art sont les produits du sacrifice, mais pas de certains avantages matériels.

Mais que deviennent les sciences et les arts? Que de fois j'ai entendu cette question, faite par des gens qui ne se souciaient ni des sciences, ni des arts, et n'avaient même pas une idée un peu claire de ce que c'était que les sciences et les arts! On dirait que ces gens n'ont rien tant à coeur que le bien de l'humanité qui,

---

[317] 1. Jean Baptiste Lully, the seventeenth-century French composer, had worked as a boy in the kitchen of an aristocratic household until his skill as a violinist caught the attention of Louis XIV, who made him the leader of his court orchestra.

317. To Romain Rolland

d'après leur croyance, ne peut être produit que par le développement de ce qu'ils appellent des sciences et des arts.

Mais comment se trouve-t-il qu'il y ait des gens assez fous pour contester l'utilité des sciences et des arts? Il y a des ouvriers manuels, des ouvriers agriculteurs. Personne ne s'est jamais avisé de contester leur utilité; et jamais ouvrier ne se mettra en tête de prouver l'utilité de son travail. Il produit; son produit est nécessaire et un bien pour les autres. On en profite et personne ne doute de son utilité. Et encore moins, personne ne la prouve.

Les ouvriers des arts et des sciences sont dans les memes conditions. Comment se trouve-t-il qu'il y ait des gens qui s'efforcent de tout leur pouvoir de prouver leur utilité?

La raison est que les véritables ouvriers des sciences et des arts ne s'arrogent aucuns droits; ils donnent les produits de leur travail; ces produits sont utiles, et ils n'ont aucun besoin de droits et de preuves à leurs droits. Mais la grande majorité de ceux qui se disent savants et artistes savent fort bien que ce qu'ils produisent ne vaut pas ce qu'ils consomment, et ce n'est qu'à cause de cela qu'ils se donnent tant de peines, comme les prêtres de tous les temps, de prouver que leur activité est indispensable au bien de l'humanité.

La science véritable et l'art véritable ont toujours existé et existeront toujours comme tous les autres modes de l'activité humaine, et il est impossible et inutile de les contester ou de les prouver.

Le faux rôle que jouent dans notre société les sciences et les arts provient de ce que les gens soi-disant civilisés, ayant à leur tête les savants et les artistes, sont une caste privilégiée comme les prêtres. Et cette caste a tous les défauts de toutes les castes. Elle a le défaut de dégrader et de rabaisser le principe en vertu duquel elle s'organise. Au lieu d'une vraie religion—une fausse. Au lieu d'une vraie science—une fausse. De même pour l'art. Elle a le défaut de peser sur les masses, et, pardessus cela, de les priver de ce qu'on prétend propager. Et le plus grand défaut, celui de la contradiction constante du principe qu'ils professent avec leur manière d'agir.

En exceptant ceux qui soutiennent le principe inepte de la science pour la science et de l'art pour l'art, les partisans de la civilisation sont obligés d'affirmer que la science et l'art sont un grand bien pour l'humanité.

En quoi consiste ce bien? Quels sont les signes par lesquels on puisse distinguer le bien du mal? Les partisans de la science et de l'art ont gardé de répondre à ces questions. Ils prétendent même que la définition du bien et du beau est impossible. 'Le bien en général, disent-ils, le bien, le beau, ne peut être défini.' Mais ils mentent. De tout temps, l'humanité n'a pas fait autre chose dans son progrès que de définir le bien et le beau. Le bien est défini depuis des siècles. Mais cette définition ne leur convient pas; elle démasque la futilité, si ce n'est les effets nuisibles, contraires au bien et au beau, de ce qu'ils appellent leurs sciences et leurs arts. Le bien et le beau est défini depuis des siècles. Les Brahmanes, les sages des Bouddhistes, les sages des Chinois, des Hébreux, des Egyptiens, les stoïciens grecs l'ont défini, et l'évangile l'a défini de la manière la plus précise. Tout ce qui réunit les hommes est le bien et

317. To Romain Rolland

le beau,—tout ce qui les sépare est le mal et le laid. Tout le monde connaît cette formule. Elle est écrite dans notre coeur.

Le bien et le beau pour l'humanité est ce qui unit les hommes. Et bien, si les partisans des sciences et des arts avaient en effet pour motif le bien de l'humanité, ils n'auraient pas ignoré le bien de l'homme, et, ne l'ignorant pas, ils n'auraient cultivé que les sciences et les arts qui mènent à ce but. Il n'y aurait pas de sciences juridiques, de science militaire, de science d'économie politique, ni de finances, qui n'ont d'autre but que le bien-être de certaines nations au détriment des autres. Si le bien avait été, en effet, le critérium de la science et des arts, jamais les recherches des sciences positives, complètement futiles par rapport au veritable bien de l'humanité, n'auraient acquis l'importance qu'elles ont, ni surtout les produits de nos arts, bons pour tout au plus à désennuyer les oisifs.

La sagesse humaine ne consiste point dans le savoir de choses. Et il y a une infinité de choses qu'on peut savoir. Et connaître le plus de choses possibles ne constitue pas la sagesse. La sagesse humaine consiste à connaître l'ordre des choses qu'il est bon de savoir, consiste à savoir ranger ses connaissances d'après leur importance.

Or, de toutes les sciences que l'homme peut et doit savoir, la principale, c'est la science de vivre de manière à faire le moins de mal et le plus de bien possible, et de tous les arts, celui de savoir éviter le mal et produire le bien avec le moins d'efforts possible. Et voilà qu'il se trouve que parmi tous les arts et les sciences qui prétendent servir au bien de l'humanité—la première des sciences et le premier des arts par leur importance non seulement n'existent pas, mais sont exclus de la liste des sciences et des arts.

Ce qu'on appelle dans notre monde les sciences et les arts ne sont qu'un immense *humbug*, une grande superstition dans laquelle nous tombons ordinairement dès que nous nous affranchissons de la vieille superstition de l'église. Pour voir clair la route que nous devons suivre, il faut commencer par le commencement,—il faut rélever le capuchon qui me tient chaud, mais qui me couvre la vue. La tentation est grande. Nous naissons,—ou bien par le travail, ou plutôt par une certaine adresse intellectuelle, nous nous hissons sur les marches de l'échelle, et nous nous trouvons parmi les privilégiés, les prêtres de la civilisation, de la *Kultur*, comme disent les allemands, et il faut comme pour un prêtre brahmane ou catholique, beaucoup de sincérité et un grand amour du vrai et du bien pour mettre en doute les principes qui vous donnent cette position avantageuse. Mais pour un homme serieux qui, comme vous, se pose la question de la vie,—il n'y a pas de choix. Pour commencer à voir clair, il faut qu'il s'affranchisse de la superstition dans laquelle il se trouve, quoiqu'elle lui soit avantageuse. C'est une condition *sine qua non*. It est inutile de discuter avec un homme qui tient à une certaine croyance, ne fut-ce que sur un seul point.

Si le champ du raisonnement n'est pas complètement libre, il aura beau discuter, il aura beau raisonner, il n'approchera pas d'un pas de la vérité. Son point fixe arrêtera tous les raisonnements et les faussera tous. Il y a la foi religieuse, il y a la foi de notre civilisation. Elles sont tout à fait analogues. Un catholique se dit: 'je

317. To Romain Rolland

puis raisonner, mais pas au delà de ce que m'enseigne notre Ecriture et notre tradition, qui possèdent la vérité entière, immuable'; un croyant de la civilisation dit: 'mon raisonnement s'arrête devant les données de la civilisation:—la science et l'art. Notre science, c'est la totalité du vrai savoir de l'homme. Si elle ne possède pas encore toute la vérité, elle la possédera. Notre art avec ses traditions classiques est le seul art véritable.' Les catholiques disent: 'il existe hors de l'homme une chose en soi, comme disent les allemands: c'est l'église'. Les gens de notre monde disent: 'il existe hors de l'homme une choise en soi: la civilisation'. Il nous est facile de voir les fautes de raisonnement des superstitions réligieuses, parce que nous ne les partageons pas. Mais un croyant réligieux, un catholique même, est pleinement convaincu qu'il n'y a qu'une seule vraie religion, la sienne; et il lui paraît même que la vérité de sa religion se prouve par le raisonnement. De même pour nous—les croyants de la civilisation: nous sommes pleinement convaincus qu'il n'existe qu'une seule vraie civilisation—la nôtre, et il nous est presque impossible de voir le manque de logique de tous nos raisonnements, qui ne tendent qu'à prouver que de tous les âges et de tous les peuples, il n'y a que notre âge et les quelques millions d'hommes, habitant la peninsule qu'on appelle l'Europe, qui se trouvent en possession de la vraie civilisation, qui se compose de vraies sciences et de vrais arts.

Pour connaître la vérité de la vie qui est tellement simple, il ne faut pas quelque chose de positif:—une philosophie, une science profonde;—il ne faut qu'une qualité négative:—ne pas avoir de superstition.

Il faut se mettre dans l'état d'un enfant ou d'un Descartes, se dire:—Je ne sais rien, je ne crois rien, et ne veux pas autre chose que de connaître la vérité de la vie, que je suis obligé de vivre.

Et la réponse est toute donnée depuis des siècles, et est simple et claire.

Mon sentiment intérieur me dit qu'il me faut le bien, le bonheur pour moi, pour moi seul. La raison me dit: tous les hommes, tous les êtres désirent la même chose. Tous les êtres qui sont comme moi à la recherche de leur bonheur individuel vont m'écraser:—c'est clair. Je ne peux pas posséder le bonheur que je désire; mais la recherche du bonheur—c'est ma vie. Ne pouvant posséder le bonheur, ne pas y tendre—c'est ne pas vivre.

Je ne peux donc pas vivre?

Le raisonnement me dit que dans l'ordre du monde où tous les êtres ne désirent que leur bien à eux, moi, un être désirant la même chose, ne peux avoir de bien. Je ne peux vivre. Mais malgré ce raisonnement si clair, nous vivons et nous cherchons le bonheur, le bien. Nous nous disons: je n'aurais pu avoir le bien, être heureux, que dans le cas où tous les autres êtres m'aimeraient plus qu'ils ne s'aiment eux-mêmes. C'est une chose impossible; mais malgré cela, nous vivons tous; et toute notre activité, notre recherche de la fortune, de la gloire, du pouvoir, ne sont que des tentatives de se faire aimer par les autres plus qu'ils ne s'aiment eux-mêmes. La fortune, la gloire, le pouvoir nous donnent des semblants de cet état de choses; et nous sommes presque contents, nous oublions par moments que ce n'est qu'un semblant, mais non la réalité. Tous les êtres s'aiment eux-mêmes plus qu'ils ne nous aiment et le bonheur est impossible. Il y a des gens (et leur nombre augmente de jour en jour) qui, ne pouvant résoudre cette difficulté, se brûlent la cervelle en se disant que la vie n'est qu'une tromperie.

Et cependant, la solution du problème est plus que simple, et s'impose de soi-même. Je ne peux être heureux que s'il existe dans ce monde un ordre tel que tous les êtres aiment les autres plus qu'ils ne s'aiment eux-mêmes.

Le monde entier serait heureux si les êtres ne s'aimaient pas eux-mêmes, mais aimaient les autres.

Je suis un être humain, et la raison me donne la loi du bonheur de tous les êtres. Il faut que je suive la loi de ma raison—que j'aime les autres plus que je m'aime moi-même.

L'homme n'a qu'à faire ce raisonnement pour que la vie se présente à lui tout d'un coup sous un tout autre aspect qu'elle ne se présentait auparavant. Les êtres se détruisent; mais les êtres s'aiment et s'entr'aident. La vie n'est pas soutenue par la destruction, mais par la réciprocité des êtres qui se traduit dans mon coeur par le sentiment de l'amour. Depuis que j'ai pu entre-voir la marche du monde, je vois que ce n'est que le principe de la réciprocité que produit le progrès de l'humanité. Toute l'histoire n'est autre chose que la conception de plus en plus claire et l'application de cet unique principe de la solidarité de tous les êtres. Le raisonnement se trouve corroboré par l'expérience de l'histoire et par l'expérience personnelle.

Mais outre le raisonnement l'homme trouve la preuve la plus convaincante de la vérité de ce raisonnement dans son sentiment intime. Le plus grand bonheur que l'homme connaisse, l'état le plus libre, le plus heureux, est celui de l'abnégation et de l'amour. La raison découvre à l'homme la seule voie du bonheur possible, et le sentiment l'y pousse.

Si les idées que je tâche de vous communiquer ne vous paraissent pas claires, ne les jugez pas trop sévèrement. J'espère que vous les lirez un jour exposées d'une manière plus claire et precise.

J'ai voulu vous donner seulement une idée de ma manière de voir.

Léon Tolstoi

318. To P. I. BIRYUKOV

Yasnaya Polyana, 5 October 1887

I'll just add a word. I'm expecting a letter from you. I'm writing something which I don't think I told you about.[1] My brother-in-law Stepan has been tormenting us, and I've been trying very hard to help him. I don't know whether I've succeeded. I've been very much occupied again recently with Gogol's correspondence with his friends.[2] What a wonderful thing! 40 years ago it was said, and said admirably, what

[318] 1. *The Kreutzer Sonata*.
2. Gogol's *Selected Passages from Correspondence with Friends* was his attempt to preach his strongly Orthodox and conservative beliefs to readers whom he thought had misunderstood his works. There was, in fact, very little real correspondence with friends in the book—the letters were a pretext for essays on edifying topics. The publication of the work in 1847 created a literary scandal and was strongly criticised by Westerners and Slavophiles alike.

318. To P. I. Biryukov

literature ought to be. Vulgar people didn't understand, and for 40 years our Pascal has been hiding under a bushel. I even thought of publishing select passages from the correspondence in *The Intermediary*.[3] I've marked the places to omit.[4] I embrace you.

319. To N. Y. GROT

Nikolay Yakovlevich Grot (1852–99), a distinguished professor of Philosophy at the University of Moscow. In 1888 he became President of the Moscow Psychological Society, and he was the founder-editor of the journal *Problems of Philosophy and Psychology*. He argued against logic as a separate field of philosophical inquiry, and proposed the assimilation of logic to the field of psychology. Grot became acquainted with Tolstoy in 1885, and at the time the following letter was written he was engaged in editing the manuscript of Tolstoy's philosophical work *On Life*.

Yasnaya Polyana, 13(?) October 1887

I have only just received your registered letter from Tula, dear Nikolay Yakovlevich. I'm very grateful for the correction you made:[1] the thought remains the same, but it is expressed with more moderation, which is always better.

You take me at my word. I don't know Aristotle in the sense that I haven't read his works in the original, but I have read an exposition of his views many, many times, and I have never been drawn to reading him.[2] Moreover, having read and gone most carefully into the meaning and associations of his teaching (as also with the majority of philosophical, bookish teaching), I am able to pass an examination in them no more than a week after reading them—and then I forget about them completely (for which, I confess, I thank God). But that is not my experience with people who seem to me to be not bookmen, but sages; I can't forget them, for which I thank God even more. It's very possible that this is a personal peculiarity of mine, connected with the wrongness of my ideas; but this is the peculiarity of all of us who have no professional relationship with philosophy. It seems to me that in this distinction there are advantages and disadvantages for both of us. We lose sight of the general associations of human thought which are always clear to you who know a lot, but you, on the other hand, are inclined to confuse the tributaries and random channels of thought with the fundamental main stream. So contact between

---

3. Extracts were published by *The Intermediary* in 1888 in a book about Gogol edited by Tolstoy and A. I. Orlov, *N. V. Gogol: 1809–1852*.

4. There is a marked copy of the *Correspondence with Friends* in the Yasnaya Polyana library.

[319] 1. In his letter of 4 October 1887 Grot suggested certain modifications to Tolstoy's very strongly worded criticism of Aristotle and his 'worthless teachings'.

2. Grot in a later letter (10 October) had turned Tolstoy's own criticism of those who condemn the teachings of Christ and Lao-Tzu without having read their works back on Tolstoy himself who, Grot suggested, had not read Aristotle and yet was ready to condemn his ideas.

319. To N. Y. Grot

people like you and me which you so readily call for is very useful to both parties. And I am very, very grateful to you for your hard work and for your completely justified remarks.

I've been unwell these last few days and so I've been reading, and I read through for the first time Kant's *Critique of Practical Reason*—and felt a joyful admiration. It seems to me that in your work on free will,[3] having pointed out the foolish definitions of freedom by modern people, you were wrong to leave out Kant's definition, which cannot be ignored. The singling out of free will as the only thing in itself comprehensible to us, from his critique of all the rest of knowledge, is the consummation of all his philosophical work, as he himself says. If his definition of freedom is wrong, then all his work on the critique of knowledge on which all modern philosophy is based is wrong. Surely you can't say: nous avons changé tout ça.[4] And so it seems to me that in order to expound a new definition of free will it is necessary to show either that Kant's is unsatisfactory, or that you don't accept it.

From your last letter which you wrote from the country about the fact that proof of free will must be built on proofs of the incorrectness of all denials of it, I concluded that you essentially recognise Kant's definition, although you feel the need to expound it anew in accordance with the objections and misunderstandings which have arisen since Kant. Have you read, or is it a long time since you read, *The Critique of Practical Reason*?

I wrote to P. I. Biryukov, asking him to pass on to you some requests of mine about publishing, but since he may not be in Moscow for some time, I'll repeat them. There is an 'introduction' printed in small type; I wrote on it that it should be published as an appendix at the end of the book, but then I had doubts whether it wouldn't be better to leave it as an introduction. Please read this introduction and decide whether to leave it as an introduction or to relegate it to an appendix.[5] In its favour is the fact that it directs the reader to the main sense of the book; against it is its bad tone. The scales are balanced absolutely equally with me, so let your opinion weight them down on one side or the other—i.e. you decide. I also asked for the proofs to be sent to me here of the chapters after number 20 or thereabouts (the ones after the proofs I last returned). This will probably be done by P. I. Biryukov when he arrives, but I shan't reach that chapter before he does arrive, so there will be no need for you to bother. I'm very, very grateful. All our family send their regards.

Yours,
L. Tolstoy

Write to me at Kozlovka. Letters take a long time from Tula, especially registered ones.

3. Grot had read a paper, 'On Free Will', to the Moscow Psychological Society on 25 February 1887. Tolstoy had been present.
4. A quotation from the Molière comedy, *Le médecin malgré lui*.
5. The Introduction was left as such.

320. To V. G. CHERTKOV

Yasnaya Polyana, 16 October 1887

[38 lines omitted][1]...There is a view about medicine which is ascribed to me, namely that medicine is evil and that one should escape from its clutches and in no case make use of it: this view is wrong. There is another view that a man dies and suffers, not because that is natural for him, but only because the doctor was late or made a mistake or couldn't find a drug, or because medicine hasn't yet had time to invent what it's about to invent any moment. This view unfortunately is very widespread (especially among doctors) and it's very false and harmful. The body sometimes suffers from the first error, but the soul always suffers from the second. A reasonable attitude towards medical help for us unscholarly people (and even for the scholarly too) will always be of this nature: I shan't look for any help in advance against the threat of death and suffering, (because if I do so, all my life will be spent on it and I shall still fail to obtain it), but I shall make use of those means of protecting myself against death and suffering which are contrived by people especially engaged in this work, and which intrude on my life whether I like it or not, but only within the limits of what is confirmed by the evident nature of its effectiveness for me, by experience, and by its availability and convenience of acquisition; i.e. those means, the use of which does not offend against my moral demands. There are, of course, constant dilemmas here, and the solution to them lies in the soul of each individual. May God help you, dear friends...[5 lines omitted]

321. To N. N. STRAKHOV

Yasnaya Polyana, 16 October 1887

Dear Nikolay Nikolayevich,

I am greatly excited. I've been unwell with a cold these last few days, and not being able to write, I've been reading, and I read through Kant's *Critique of Practical Reason* for the first time. Please tell me: have your read it? When? And did it impress you?

Some 25 years ago I believed that talented dauber Schopenhauer (I recently read his Russian biography and also read *The Critique of Pure Reason* which is nothing but a polemic with Hume, and an introduction to the exposition of his basic views in *The Critique of Practical Reason*)—and I simply believed that the old man had talked nonsense, and that his centre of gravity was negation. I lived for 20 years

[320] 1. Chertkov's last letter had raised the question of what medical measures should be used to make his wife's approaching childbirth easier. Chloroform and anaesthetic gas had been suggested, but he and his wife had doubts. Tolstoy replies in the first paragraph (omitted here) that to bring a midwife or doctor in to help with the birth was one thing, and quite permissible, but to tamper with nature by the use of anaesthetics was another: 'God gives childbirth, God gives strength, too.' He adds that for the mother to breastfeed the baby is important also—important psychologically for the mother and physically for the baby.

with that conviction, and nothing made me think of looking in the book itself. You know, such an attitude to Kant is just like taking the woods round a building for the building itself. Is it my own mistake or a general one? I think it's a general mistake. I made a point of looking up Weber's[1] history of philosophy which I happened to have and saw that Mr Weber doesn't approve of the basic position which Kant came to, namely that our freedom, bounded by moral laws, is a thing in itself (i.e. life itself), and only sees in it a pretext for the lucubrations of Fichte, Schelling and Hegel, and sees all Kant's merits in *The Critique of Pure Reason*, i.e. he doesn't see the temple built on the clearing at all, but only sees the clearing, which is very suitable for gymnastic exercises. Grot, a doctor of philosophy, writes a paper about free will, quotes some Ribots[2] and others whose definitions are a tilting-yard of nonsense and contradictions, and ignores Kant's definition, and we listen and talk, discovering an already discovered America. Unless there is a revival of the sciences and the arts in our world by separating the pearls from the dung, we shall simply drown in the cess-pool of our ignorance which comes from too many books and too much undigested learning...[17 lines and postscript omitted]

322. To N. L. OZMIDOV

Yasnaya Polyana, 20 October 1887

I got your long letter about a fortnight ago, dear brother Nikolay Lukich, and was very glad to get it. I was going to reply today, and in order to reply sensibly I read it through again and did as you wished—looked as carefully as I could at the meaning of the important things. I agree with you about everything[1]—about the important things without reservations, and about the details with only this reservation that if we—you and I and anybody else who agree about fundamentals and what is reasonable—were to agree about details, there would be no point in one of us living, he may as well die—we would only duplicate one another and be unable to produce anything real for ourselves or to give to others. Such agreement would be false, as false as would be the agreement of everybody about what a horse looks like when one person looks at it from in front and another from behind: one would say that it has a big tail over a hole, and the other would say it has a little tail over two eyes. If we know what a horse is like, we shan't deny that everybody who sees one and the same horse may see different sides of it. When I first read your letter, I wanted to object to the most essential thing, your divisions of the law to which man is subject, but now on reading it through carefully I won't do so. You know, it's like

[321] 1. Georg Weber (1808–88), German historian and philosopher.
2. Théodule Ribot (1839–1916), French psychologist and philosopher, author of several major works on experimental psychology and psychopathology, and founder of the important *Revue philosophique de la France et de l'étranger*.
[322] 1. Ozmidov had sent Tolstoy an article of his own which (according to Biryukov) was a compilation of Tolstoy's own ideas about Christianity (the article has not survived). His last letter expressed complete agreement with Tolstoy on all fundamental issues, but had asked Tolstoy to question any passages in the article over which there might be disagreement.

322. To N. L. Ozmidov

denying that a water-melon, when cut lengthwise or across, isn't the same water-melon. If all the parts make up a whole complete water-melon, then, however it has been cut, it's still a water-melon. The thing is that it should be complete and whole. And I see that yours is just as whole and has the same seeds and everything. Only your division is an unusual, unnatural one for me, whereas a different division—of the same thing—is normal and natural and seems simpler. If it's true that the same thing can be cut from different sides without destroying the wholeness of it all, then that can only be a matter for joy. There are minds which are akin in character to one type, and those which are akin to another. And however a man begins to cut (I mean to think), whatever side he begins from, he will find people before him who did the same thing and achieved their aim, making his work easier for him...
[43 lines omitted]

323. To I. L. TOLSTOY

Ilya Lvovich Tolstoy (1866–1933), Tolstoy's second son (for a character sketch of him at the age of seven by his father, see Letter 173). He studied at the Polivanov School in Moscow, but left early to join the army, much to his father's distress. In 1888 he gave up military service to marry Sofya Nikolayevna Filosofova (the following letter was written while they were contemplating marriage), and he and his wife settled on the estate of Grinyovka, close to Yasnaya Polyana. Tolstoy often spoke angrily about his son's way of life, which he saw as that of a typical unquestioning landowner content to live off the labour of those who served him, but other sources say that Ilya and his wife tried to live as simply as possible on their estate, and that he was by no means indifferent to his father's precepts. He did in fact assist him in the Samara famine relief work of 1891–2.

After many changes of employment (he served in several posts in the civil service) and a determined attempt to make a living as a journalist, Ilya went to America in 1916. There were several reasons for this: the failure of his newspaper *The New Russia*, a cooperative venture; the termination of his contract as a journalist (after a protracted illness) for the newpaper *The Russian Word* (he had served as their war correspondent in the Balkans, where he came at last to sympathise with his father's views on war); and in addition the breakdown of his marriage. In 1917, after the February Revolution, he returned briefly to Russia (incidentally bringing a letter from President Roosevelt to the Chairman of the Council of Ministers) but left again permanently after he and his wife had been divorced.

In America he began a new, and at first very successful, career as a journalist. He wrote a syndicated column commenting on the course of the Russian revolution and on Russo-American relations. He also lectured widely on his father's life, works and ideas, and for a while was very happy in his new country. But this did not last. Later correspondence shows his deep distaste for American life—its standardisation, worship of money, and (in his eyes) total lack of culture. His discontent was

323. To I. L. Tolstoy

aggravated by his increasing difficulty in finding suitable employment. In the late 1920s he worked as a consultant on films based on his father's novels *Anna Karenina* and *Resurrection*, but he had no control over the final scripts and considered both films travesties of the originals (*Anna Karenina*, re-entitled *Love*, ended with Anna marrying Vronsky and living happily ever after.)

In his last years he had little employment apart from occasional lecturing about his father, and he died in poverty in a New York hospital in 1933.

Ilya Tolstoy wrote several articles and memoirs about his father: 'Who is to Blame?' in *The Life and Death of L. N. Tolstoy* (1911); 'Selections from Reminiscences about my Father' in *Lev Tolstoy and the Famine* (1912) and *My Reminiscences* (Moscow, 1914). He also published a story, *One Scoundrel Less*, under the pseudonym of Ilya Dubrovsky.

Yasnaya Polyana, October 1887

We got your letter to Tanya, my dear Ilya, and I see you are still going ahead in the direction of the goal which is your objective, and I wanted to write to you and to her (because you probably tell her everything) to say what I think about it. I think about it a lot, with joy and fear alike.

This is what I think: to marry in order to enjoy oneself more will never work. To put marriage—union with the person you love—as your main aim, replacing everything else, is a big mistake. And it's obvious if you think about it. The aim is marriage. Well, you get married, and then what? If you have no other aim in life before marriage, then later on it will be terribly difficult, almost impossible for the two of you, to find one. It's almost certain that if you have no common aim before marriage, nothing will bring you together afterwards, and you will always be falling out. Marriage only brings happiness when there is a single aim—people meet on the road and say, 'Let's walk on together'; 'yes, let's'; and offer one another their hands—and not when people are attracted to one another and then both turn off the road in different directions. In the first case it will be like this:

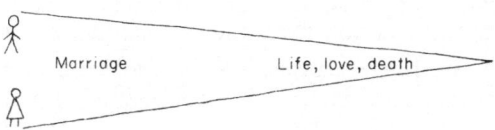

In the second, like this:

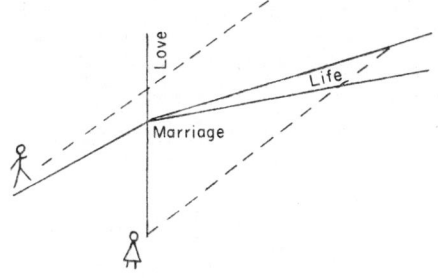

323. To I. L. Tolstoy

I say all this because the idea many people have that life is a vale of tears is just as false as the idea which the great majority have, and to which youth, health and wealth incline you, that life is a place of entertainment. Life is a place of service, where one sometimes has occasion to put up with a lot that is hard, but more often to experience a great many joys. Only there can only be real joys when people themselves understand their life as service: have a definite aim in life outside themselves and their own personal happiness. Usually married people forget this completely. Marriage and the birth of children offer so many joyful things to look forward to that it seems that these things actually constitute life itself, but this is a dangerous delusion. If parents live and produce children without having any aim in life, they only put off the question of the aim of life and the punishment to which people are subjected when they live without knowing why—they only put it off, but they can't avoid it, because they will have to bring up and guide children and there will be nothing to guide them by. And then parents lose their human qualities and the happiness linked with them, and become pedigree cattle. So I say: people intending to marry because their life *seems* to them to be full, need more than ever to think and make clear to themselves what each of them is living for. And in order to make this clear, it's necessary to think, and to think hard about the conditions you live in and about your past, to estimate what you consider to be important and unimportant in life and to find out what you believe in—i.e. what you consider the invariable, indisputable truth, and what you will be guided by in life. And not only find out and make clear to yourself, but experience in practice and put into operation in your own life, because until you do what you believe in, you don't know whether you believe it or not. I know what you believe, and that belief, or those sides of it which are expressed in your actions, you need now more than at any other time to make clear to yourself by putting it into operation. Your belief is that good consists of loving people and being loved by them. To attain this, I know three activities which I constantly practise, which cannot be practised often enough, and which are particularly necessary to you just now. The first—in order to be able to love people and be loved by them it is necessary to train oneself to require as little as possible from them, because if I require a lot and am deprived of many things, I'm inclined not to love but to reproach—this involves a lot of work. The second —in order to love people, not by word but by deed, it is necessary to teach oneself to do something useful for them. This involves even more work, especially for you at your age when it's natural for a person to be studying. The third—in order to love people and be loved by them, it is necessary to learn gentleness, humility and the art of enduring unpleasant people and unpleasant things, and if it's impossible not to offend somebody, to be able to choose the least offence. And this involves the most work of all, and work which is non-stop, from waking up to going to sleep. And it's the most joyful sort of work, because day after day you can rejoice at your progress in it, and apart from that you gain the reward—insignificant at first but very joyful—of people's love.

And so I advise you, both of you, to think and to live as lovingly as possible, because only in this way will you find out whether you are really going along the same road and whether or not it's good for you to give one another your hands; and then if you are sincere, you will make your own future. Your aim in life should not be the joy of marriage, but that of bringing more love and truth into the world through your life. Then after that—marriage, in order to help one another to attain this aim.

Les extrêmes se touchent. The most egotistical and nasty life is the life of two people united in order to enjoy life, and the highest vocation is that of people who live in order to serve God by bringing good into the world, and uniting with each other for that purpose. Don't be confused—one is right and one is wrong. Why should man not choose what is higher? But once having chosen what is higher, it's necessary to put all one's heart and soul into it, not just a little bit of oneself; a little bit is no use. Well, I'm tired of writing, though there's more I wanted to say. I kiss you.

324. To P. I. BIRYUKOV

Moscow, 20 November 1887

[16 lines omitted]...I was talking to you about 'Christian Science', a teaching which has recently sprung up in America. They sympathise with my views very much, and write to me and send me books and brochures. There is a lot in this teaching which is far more important than I thought at first. Their weak side, which is made worse by their women, is the idea that you can cure illnesses spiritually, and this is silly, but their basic idea—beautifully expressed—which I gave to my niece[1] to translate, is as follows: illnesses and sin are just like motion and heat: the one passes into the other. Illnesses for the most part are the consequences of sin, and in order to be rid of them you must be rid of the sin—delusion. And when you live in a state of delusion, you must know that you are living in a state of illness which, if it hasn't yet appeared, inevitably will appear. It is also important that every person subjected to illness bears the responsibility for the delusions of others—ancestors and contemporaries—and that everyone living in a state of delusion brings illness and sufferings to others—descendants and contemporaries. And that everyone living free from illness is obliged to these others—both their ancestors and the good people of today—and that everyone who frees himself from delusions not only heals himself (you can't heal one person only), but also his descendants and contemporaries.

Novosyolov also brought me Simon's book on China (in Russian translation).[2] Get hold of it and read it without fail. Reading it gave me great delight, and you, particularly you, will find reading it useful and enjoyable for the way agriculture is described in it, and indeed the whole way of life of the Chinese. This is a book which must, absolutely must, be summarised for *The Intermediary*...[8 lines omitted]

[324] 1. V. S. Tolstaya, the daughter of Tolstoy's elder brother Sergey.
2. The Russian translation of a study of Chinese life *La cité chinoise* by a French consul in China. Extracts from it were published by *The Intermediary* in 1889 as *How the Chinese Live*.

325. To I. Y. REPIN

Moscow, 1–2 February 1888

My dear Ilya Yefimovich,

How glad I am that the various old cats—some other people's—which ran between us, have disappeared, and that there are no shadows falling across our friendship.[1] Essentially, for my part and, I'm sure, for yours too, there has been, and there can be no change in the feelings of respect and love which we used to have for one another. The head of a woman with no nose on the vignette about syphilis reminded me particularly vividly of you.[2] It makes a terrible impression. And here I am with a request to make of you, a piece of advice, and a suggestion. I've been editing some books on drunkenness. There are two by a Dr Alexeyev (which will be coming out any day), another is with the censor, and a third is being reprinted, and I keep thinking about a booklet on the same subject myself. It just occurred to me that you could draw two things: one picture with vignettes, depicting all forms and conditions of drunkenness, and another small one for the cover of a book I'm writing,[3] as well as a third to do for all books published by us on drunkenness. Choose the subjects of all three yourself, but make them as terrible, powerful and directly relevant to the subject as your picture on syphilis.

I haven't been well recently, and because of that it's taking me a long time to finish my article on drunkenness, and I want to get it up by the roots. It's a subject of enormous importance. Give me encouragement. I sketched out long ago the story about the Beethoven sonata I told you about,[4] and about which I remember your promise. But that will come later. What are you doing? How are you? Probably working hard. After all you are not one of the talented ones, but one of the 'hard workers'. My daughter and I often repeat this saying of yours about yourself. Your strength is that you sincerely believe this, as you should.

Our union against drunkenness,[5] in spite of its indeterminate shape, is expanding and embracing more people, i.e. it's having an effect.

Yours most affectionately,
L. Tolstoy

[325] 1. A reference to their disagreement over Repin's recent portrait of Tolstoy in the fields at Yasnaya Polyana, which Repin had wanted to have reproduced for publication against the wishes of Tolstoy and his wife. Tolstoy, however, later changed his mind, and gave permission for the painting to be lithographed.

2. Drawn by Repin for the cover of a book by V. K. Trutovskaya, *The Evil Disease, or Syphilis*. The original is in the Tolstoy Museum in Moscow.

3. This and the 'article on drunkenness' mentioned in the next paragraph is either an unfinished article *To Young People* or the article which appeared in 1888 entitled *Time to Come to Our Senses*.

4. *The Kreutzer Sonata*.

5. The Union against Drunkenness was founded on Tolstoy's initiative on 9 December 1887. It soon numbered more than one hundred and fifty members who were pledged (1) not to drink spirits themselves, (2) not to buy or serve spirits to others, and (3) to spread word of the harmful effects of drink.

326. To N. N. GAY senior

Moscow, 13 February 1888

Thank you for cheering me up with your letter and the good news that you are hard at work. May God help you. It's high time! I say this to myself rather than to you. At the same time I know that one can't force oneself to work when one is accustomed to working at a certain depth of consciousness, and can't reach it. But then what joy it is when one does reach it. I'm in that position now. I've started a mass of things, all of them things I love, but I can't dive down there, I keep coming up to the surface. All is well with us—very well in fact. My wife is expecting a baby in due course—in another month.[1] Ilya is marrying Filosofova on 28 February (you probably know her: a wonderful, simple, healthy, pure girl), and is quite beside himself, as people in love always are. Life has come to a stop for him and everything is in the future. I see a lot of people, good people, and their company is a joy to me. Everyone is looking forward to Kolechka coming and is sad that he's not here. Everyone, because everyone loves him especially warmly and dearly. Obolensky, my niece's husband, died suddenly here a few days ago.[2] All this is as it should be and is good. He was a very good man—simple and kind. He has left a widow with 7 children—poor, and with many debts—but even this is good, and arouses a lot of kindness in people. I can't see anything bad here at all, but only a variety of material for the finest thing which it lies in our power to make of it. Lately I've been reading Herzen a lot, and still am, and I often think about you. What a wonderful writer. Our Russian life for the last 20 years would have been different if this writer hadn't been hidden from the young generation. As it is, a very important organ was violently wrenched out of the organism of Russian society. Give my love to Anna Petrovna (I'm glad that she's better now), and to your young and very young ones. Could you draw a picture about drunkenness? I need two—one big one, and also a vignette for all publications on this subject entitled *Time to Come to Our Senses*. Well, goodbye for now. I kiss you, as a brother.

What are you going to bring to the exhibition?

Yours affectionately,
L. Tolstoy

327. To S. T. SEMYONOV

Yasnaya Polyana, 2 June 1888

[15 lines omitted]...I don't know about you, but I don't experience the same satisfaction in any other activity as I do in agricultural work (I especially like mowing, and even more so ploughing), and mainly because in any other activity you need and want people's approval, but not in this one. In writing, in any skill,

---

[326] 1. Tolstoy's last child, Ivan, (Vanichka), was born on 31 March 1888. He died in 1895.
2. L. D. Obolensky, who was married to the daughter of Tolstoy's sister, Marya Tolstaya.

327. To S. T. Semyonov

even in hunting, you need and enjoy people's approval, but in agricultural labour nothing is necessary except the product of labour and the awareness of time spent well, profitably, morally and in accordance with God's law...[10 lines omitted]

328. To V. G. CHERTKOV and N. N. IVANOV

Yasnaya Polyana, 20–8 September 1888

I meant to write to you today when I got your letter asking about a copy of *On Life* for Ertel. I've only got one copy and I'll gladly send it today to Ertel, a very nice man, but unfortunately, so it seems to me, a man who is interested, like many others, in the most fundamental problems of life, not in order to solve them for themselves so as to live, but in order to expound both the problems and their (various) solutions for other people. Sometimes, I confess, I prefer those who hate and revile the truth to those who sympathise with it, but not in order to follow it... [120 lines omitted]

329. To R. SAILLENS

Ruben Saillens, a French pastor in Toulouse and the author of several stories (published in a collection, *Récits et allégories*, 1888) had written to Tolstoy on 26 September accusing him of plagiarising one of his works, *Le père Martin*. Saillens had recently come across a volume of Tolstoy's latest stories containing *Where Love is, God is*, and had recognised it as substantially his own. He informed Tolstoy of the date and place of publication of *Le père Martin* and asked for an explanation.

Yasnaya Polyana, (?) October 1888

Monsieur.

Je suis vraiment désolé de vous avoir causé de la peine et je vous prie de me pardonner ma faute, qui est bien involontaire, comme vous allez voir. Il parait en Russie une feuille mensuelle très peu répandue: le Rabochie, c'est à dire: L'Ouvrier.[1] Un de mes amis[2] me donna le numéro de ce journal dans lequel se trouvait une traduction et une adaption à la vie russe de votre récit *le père Martin*, sans nom d'auteur, en me proposant de profiter de ce récit pour en faire un conte populaire. Le récit me plut beaucoup; je ne fis que changer un peu le style et ajouter quelques scènes et le remis à mon ami pour le publier sans mon nom, comme cela était convenu non seulement pour *le père Martin* mais même pour les récits, qui étaient de moi. Pour la séconde édition l'éditeur me pria de lui accorder le droit de mettre

---

[329] 1. A monthly publication of the Pashkovites, a Russian evangelical sect founded by V. A. Pashkov, Chertkov's uncle. The issue in question was no. 1, 1884; the name of the author was not included in the Russian translation done for the *Russian Worker*.

2. Chertkov.

mon nom aux récits qu'il avait reçus de moi. J'y consentis sans penser que parmi ces récits dont huit étaient de moi le récit *Martin* ne l'était pas. Mais comme il avait été refait par moi, l'éditeur y mit mon nom comme aux autres. Dans l'une des éditions redigées par moi je fis ajouter au titre: *Là où est l'amour, là est Dieu* la parenthèse: *emprunté de l'anglais*, l'ami qui m'avait donné le journal m'ayant dit que le récit était d'un auteur anglais. Mais dans mes oeuvres complètes on a omis la parenthèse et le traducteur a fait la même faute. C'est ainsi, monsieur, qu'à mon grant regret je me suis rendu coupable envers vous d'un plagiat involontaire, et c'est avec le plus grand plaisir que je constate ici par cette lettre que le récit; *Là où est l'amour, là est Dieu* n'est qu'une traduction et une adaption aux moeurs russes de votre admirable récit Martin.[3]

Je vous prie, Monsieur, d'excuser ma négligence et de recevoir l'assurance de mes sentiments fraternels.

Léon Tolstoi

330. To N. V. MIKHAYLOV

Nikolay Vasilyevich Mikhaylov, a Kharkov student, had written to Tolstoy on 11 February 1889, asking his advice on 'what to read and how to read'.

Moscow, 16 February 1889

Nikolay Vasilyevich,

I would be very happy if I could answer your very important question—the most important one to do with mental and spiritual development—in such a way as to be satisfied with the answer myself. But so far, in spite of the fact that I have long felt the need to answer this question, I am not yet able to do so. But I have thought a great deal about it and shall therefore try to pass on to you, if only briefly, the most important things.

The first general rule is: don't do what the majority does—don't read what is modern, taking that to mean all that has appeared in the last half century. You are bound to find out which modern things are really significant at all; it will be drummed into your ears, in school, in literature, in conversation. But to waste time on the study of what is modern is unprofitable and dangerous, firstly because the importance of everything modern which is seen at close quarters is always bound to be exaggerated; secondly because it nearly always turns out that what is modern —unsifted by the criticism of centuries and seeming very important—turns out in 10 years' time to be an inflated thing which everyone has forgotten. Read the ancients. Of the ancients, read above all the teachers of life, the founders of religious teachings. The ideas of people which are the basis of beliefs and the guiding principles of life of millions and millions of people are the most necessary and the most important ideas. Such are the teachings of Confucius and Mencius. I don't

---

3. *Where Love is, God is* was first published in *The Intermediary* in 1885.

330. To N. V. Mikhaylov

know if there are any good Russian translations, but there is a good book in French, *Les livres sacrés de l'Orient* by Pauthier, then there is the teaching of the Brahmins and the Buddha. There are also the Vedas and a book by a German scholar (I've forgotten his name) on Buddhism, translated into Russian about five years ago, and there are excellent books by Max Müller in French and English. Then there is the same Max Müller on Zend-Avesta—the teaching of the Persians. Then Lao-Tzu in French by St Julien.[1] Then the teaching of the Stoics, Marcus Aurelius, and especially Epictetus and Seneca. Then the teaching of the Hebrew prophets, especially Isaiah, then the Gospels. A man who wants to lay the stable foundations of a true education must read and get to know and understand the teachings by which mankind has lived and still lives. Of these teachings, the ones that are particularly accessible because of the clarity of the books themselves are: Confucius, Mencius, the Buddha, the Stoics, the Prophets and the Gospels. I would advise you to read these books, as I advise you to read the four Gospels—the most important of these books, the most recent, and the one on which we were brought up—in this way: read them if possible in the original, i.e. the 4 Gospels in Greek. As you read them, first strike out the passages in which Christ is spoken about, leaving the ones in which Christ speaks himself. Then divide up Christ's words themselves, marking off all that is incomprehensible, unclear, contradictory, or even seemingly so, leaving the passages which are absolutely clear. You must read these passages over and over again, trying to unite them into one whole, and then, having mastered this whole, having mastered the spirit of the teaching, read through the unclear passages again, trying to understand them too, but in no way forcing the sense; better to leave in something incomprehensible than to make strained interpretations. The religious books of other peoples should be read in the same way. From all this a single whole outlook on the world will be evolved. This is the foundation of everything. After that it is possible and not without profit to read the philosophers too (i.e. the compilers of philosophical theories), the Platos, Aristotles, Descartes, Leibnitzes, Kants etc., and to read the historians and the poets. Only when the teaching about life is clear can the reading of philosophers, poets and historians be profitable and necessary, to illuminate reality. This is all my general advice in reply to your question; a specific answer ought to be directly contained in a list of books and a division of them according to the degree of their importance. I have wanted to do this for a long time and if I don't die very soon I'll try and do what I can.

In indicating what to read I mentioned French, English and German books to you. Perhaps you don't know all these languages; perhaps you don't even know a single one, as is often the case with young people leaving school. If so, study modern languages during your university course. Whatever faculty you are in, we all know that students have almost nothing to do, particularly in the Law, Philology and Natural Science Faculties. And so I advise you first of all to fashion for yourself a tool for reading—to acquire a knowledge of languages. This is the most

[330] 1. *Lao Tseu...Le livre de la voie et de la vertu* (Paris, 1841).

humane knowledge. Nothing does so much to help unity among people as this knowledge.

Well, I have said what I can.

I wish you all the best.

Yours affectionately,
L. Tolstoy

331. To E. ROD

Eduard Rod (1857–1910), Swiss novelist, critic and literary historian. His early novels were much influenced by the social and literary theories of Zola, but his later writings were in an entirely different vein, being devoted to the analysis of spiritual conditions or the exploration of general moral problems, e.g. *La course à la Mort* (Paris, 1885) and *Le Sens de la Vie* (Paris, 1889).

Moscow, 22 February 1889

Cher confrère.

Je suis très reconnaissant à Mr Pagès de la bonne idée qu'il a eu de vous envoyer mon livre,[1] grâce à quoi j'ai reçu le votre.[2] Ne connaissant pas même de nom l'auteur, j'ai commencé à le feuilleter, mais bien vite la sincérité et la force de l'expression de même que l'importance du sujet m'ont gagnés, j'ai lu et relu le livre surtout à certains endroits. Sans parler de la peinture des sentiments intimes du mariage et de la paternité, deux endroits surtout m'ont frappé: celui où vous parlez de la guerre—c'est un endroit admirable et que j'ai relu plusieurs fois à haute voix—et sur le fléau de notre civilisation que vous nommez dilettantisme. J'ai rarement lu quelque chose de plus fort comme analyse de l'état mental d'une grande partie de notre société, mais je vous avouerai franchement, cher confrère, que la conclusion est une chute et n'est pas en rapport avec la hauteur de cet endroit et de plusieurs autres du livre. La conclusion à mon avis, n'est qu'une manière de se tirer tant bien que mal des problèmes si franchement et si nettement posés dans le livre. Le pessimisme m'a toujours paru, celui de Schopenhauer, par exemple, non seulement un sophisme, mais une sottise, et qui plus est une sottise de mauvais genre. Un pessimiste que met son opinion sur le monde et prêche sa doctrine à des hommes qui se trouvent très bien dans la vie, ressemble à un homme reçu en bonne société, qui a le mauvais goût de déranger le plaisir des autres par l'expression de son ennui, qui ne prouve qu'il n'est pas au niveau de la société dans laquelle il se trouve. J'ai toujours envie de dire à un pessimiste: 'si le monde n'est pas à ton gré, ne fais pas parade de ton mécontentement et quitte le et ne dérange pas les autres'. Au fond votre livre m'a procuré l'un des sentiments les plus agréables que je connaisse—celui de rencontrer un compagnon inattendu, energique

---

[331] 1. *What Then Must We Do?* in a French translation.
2. *Le Sens de la Vie.*

331. To E. Rod

dans la voie que je suis. Vous aurez beau dire et avoir écrit sur Léopardi[3] jeune ou vieux, riche ou pauvre—bien vigoureux ou faible de corps—je suis convaincu que vous trouverez, si vous ne l'avez fait déjà, la vraie réponse au titre de votre livre.

332. To G. A. RUSANOV

Gavriil Andreyevich Rusanov (1845–1907), a landowner in the province of Voronezh, a graduate of the University of Moscow and a member of various district courts until 1887 when he was disabled by illness. Always a keen admirer of Tolstoy's fiction, he decided after reading *A Confession* to visit him to discuss various moral and religious problems raised by the book, and their friendship dates from Rusanov's visit to Yasnaya Polyana in 1883. Tolstoy respected and trusted Rusanov's aesthetic sensibility and frequently discussed literature with him. Most of their correspondence was on the subject of literature—Tolstoy's, and that of other writers. Rusanov was an invalid for the last twenty years of his life, hence Tolstoy's suggestion that Rusanov's wife should take down his letters. He declared in his will that it was due to Tolstoy that he became a Christian.

Moscow, 12 March 1889

The other day I received from Chertkov the letter you wrote to him,[1] dear Gavrilo Andreyevich. He knew it would give me pleasure. If it is difficult for you to write, ask your dear wife to write to me about yourself, herself and your children. I am very well; I can say sincerely that the longer I live, the better I feel; and this improvement, i.e. this increase in the joy of life, is in accordance with the law which governs the falling of bodies—in inverse proportion to the square of the distance from death. I want to write a lot, but I'm not writing anything just yet. There are not the former incentives of vanity and profit which used to goad me on and therefore (I know how jealous you are on my account, but I can't help saying what I think), produced immature and feeble works. But why write? If I were a legislator, I would pass a law to prevent any writer from daring to publish his works in his own lifetime.

It's a strange thing—the books I always carry about with me, and which I would like to have always, are the unwritten books: The Prophets, the Gospels, Beal's Buddha, Confucius, Mencius, Lao-Tzu, Marcus Aurelius, Socrates, Epictetus, Pascal. Nevertheless I sometimes want to write, and, can you imagine, it's usually a novel actually—a broad, free one like *Anna Karenina* which could include without any strain everything that seemed comprehensible to me, from a new, unusual and useful angle. The rumour about a story has its foundations.[2] A couple of years ago I did indeed write a story in rough draft on the theme of sexual love, but so

3. Count Giacomo Leopardi (1798–1837), Italian poet renowned for his pessimistic and despairing philosophy of life.

[332] 1. To ask what Tolstoy's literary plans were.
2. *The Kreutzer Sonata*.

carelessly and unsatisfactorily that I shan't revise it, and if I were to take up the idea again I would start writing from the beginning. There is nobody to whom I write and tell so much about my literary works and dreams as I am now doing to you, because I know there is nobody who has such a warm regard for this side of my life as you have.

Karamzin said somewhere that the important thing is not to write *A History of the Russian State* but to live well.[3] This can't be repeated often enough to writers. I'm convinced from experience how good it is not to write. There is no avoiding it, the job of each one of us is simply to fulfil the will of Him who sent us. And the will of Him who sent us is that we should be perfect, even as our heavenly father, and only by this means, i.e. by our approach towards perfection, can we influence other people—the watering can must be filled to the brim for it to pour—and this influence will work through our life and through the oral and written word, in so far as this word will be a part and a consequence of our life, and in so far as the mouth will speak out of the fullness of the heart. I kiss you and your wife and children.

Yours affectionately,
L. Tolstoy

333. To COUNTESS S. A. TOLSTAYA

Spasskoye,[1] 29 March 1889

I got an even sadder letter from you yesterday, my dear. I see you are suffering physically and morally and I grieve for you: I can't be joyful and contented when I know you're unhappy. However hard I try to raise my spirits, a letter like that makes me gloomy and despondent. You enumerate all the things I don't sympathise with, but you forget the one thing that includes all the others, and with which I not only never cease to sympathise, but which forms one of the main interests of my life—your whole life, what you sympathise with, i.e. what you live by. And since I can't take any other view except this that the main thing is the spiritual life, I never cease to sympathise with your spiritual life, to rejoice at its manifestation and to grieve at its decline, and I not only always hope, but am convinced that it will manifest itself in you more and more vigorously, and will deliver you from your sufferings and give you the happiness which you sometimes seem not to believe in but which I constantly experience, and the more keenly, the nearer I approach my physical end.

Were it not for the thought that you are feeling unwell, it would be splendid for me here. Urusov is the kindest possible hôte: I feel I'm no burden to him, and I feel fine myself. I get up at 8, and write and write till 12[2] (very badly, I think, but still I

---

3. A paraphrase of a passage in a letter to A. I. Turgenev.

[333] 1. The estate of Prince Urusov who had served with Tolstoy in the Crimea. Tolstoy spent a week there in March with Biryukov and visited the Knop factory mentioned in the letter.

2. The play *The Fruits of Enlightenment*.

333. To Countess S. A. Tolstaya

write). We have lunch and then I go for a walk. Yesterday I walked more than 10 versts to the enormous factory which used to belong to Lepeshkin, where, you remember, there was a riot which Petya and Perfilyev put down.[3] 3,000 women grow ugly and perish there so that Knop should have cheap cotton goods and fat profits. Today I walked more than 3 versts to a village in the Vladimir province. The road went through an old wood. It was very nice. The larks have come back, but there's still a great deal of snow. The starlings in the starling-house right in front of my window continually display their art: they can sound like orioles, quails, corncrakes, even frogs, but they haven't a sound of their own. I call them professors, only they are nicer than professors. I kiss you fondly and *all* the children too. Thank Tanya for her open letter. I won't refuse a sealed one either. Don't despair, Tanya. The prince sends his regards. Please write more often; there are other deliveries as well as those on regular days.

334. To N. N. GAY senior

Moscow, 21 April 1889

[12 lines omitted]...I've been waiting for your picture and now I've seen it. There's a remarkable illustration of what art is at the present exhibition: your picture and Repin's.[1] With Repin's you get the impression of a man stopping an execution in Christ's name, i.e. doing a very remarkable and important thing. With yours you get the impression of Christ with his disciples not only being transformed, riding into Jerusalem, being crucified and rising again, but also living just as we live, thinking, feeling and suffering morning, noon and night. With Repin, what he wanted to say is said in such a narrow and cramped way that it could have been said much more accurately in words. It's said, and nothing more. He prevented an execution—all right, he prevented it. But what happened next? But not only that— since the content is not artistic, not new, not precious to the author, even that isn't said properly. The whole picture lacks focus, and all the figures sprawl. But with you, what needed to be done has been done. I knew the study, I'd heard about the picture, but when I saw it I was deeply moved. The picture does what it needs to— it reveals the whole world of Christ's life apart from the familiar moments, and shows him to be as everyone can imagine him to be, according to their own spiritual powers. My only reproach is—why does John, who is looking for something in the dark, stand so near to Christ? I liked the figure of Christ better when it was apart from the others. It's a real picture, i.e. it gives what art ought to give. And how glad I am that it got through to everyone, even those to whom its meaning is most alien.

I've been staying for 3 weeks with Urusov. He's a general, a very old friend, a mathematician and a theologian, but a good person. I did a little writing there in

---

3. Petya Behrs, Sonya's brother, and V. S. Perfilyev, Governor of Moscow.

[334] 1. Gay's picture *The Last Supper*, and Repin's *Saint Nicholas Saves Three Men Unjustly Condemned to Death in Myra in Lycia*.

solitude.² Here I've dried up again. I've started writing an article about art, among other things, but I can't finish it.³ It's not what I need to write at all. But I do need to write. There's something I can see that no one else can see except me. At least I think so. It's the same with you too. And before one dies it's necessary to do something to make others see it too. And this doesn't prevent one living a clean and honest life, i.e. not living off someone else, but the one thing encourages the other. I kiss you, Anna Petrovna and Kolechka and his family.

I don't know when I'll be at Yasnaya. I live here because my departure would cause pain and irritation. But living here is good. I've many friends, their number is increasing, and we all grow together. It gladdens me very much.

335. To N. N. STRAKHOV

Yasnaya Polyana, 28 May 1889

A request, dear Nikolay Nikolayevich. What is there on art, and on the history of this concept? Art in the broad sense, but also plastic art in particular. Is there a history and theory of art other than Kugler's,¹ and if you have one, could you bring it, please? And please help me in general with the work I've begun. Before saying my own say, I need to know how the quintessence of educated people regard this matter. Is there such a Catechism? I hope you will understand me and help me, and in particular that you will soon gladden us with a visit.

L. Tolstoy

336. To V. I. ALEXEYEV

Yasnaya Polyana, 22 August 1889

Thank you, my dear Vasily Ivanovich, for having written about yourself and your life. I often think of you and always with much love. You say that you seem to be complaining about life. No, you are not complaining, but you are dissatisfied—not with life but with yourself in it—as I always am dissatisfied in my good moments. And you are always dissatisfied because you are always striving towards something better, and are always shifting your foot from one rung to another. And may God help you. Just recently I had a visit from a former naval officer, Rugin, a friend and now the life companion of Biryukov's, and he told me about the Alyokhins' commune in the Dorogobuzh district of the Smolensk province.¹ 15 people live there—8 men and 7 women—admirably, industriously, abstemiously—potatoes,

2. *The Fruits of Enlightenment.*
3. Tolstoy had resumed work on his article *On Art*, begun in the early 1880s.

[335] 1. F. T. Kugler's *Handbuch der Kunstgeschichte*, translated into Russian in 1872.

[336] 1. Three Alyokhin brothers of a wealthy merchant family in Kursk founded a commune in the Smolensk province in spring 1889, which lasted for about two years. One of them later worked with Tolstoy on famine relief. See Letter 358.

336. To V. I. Alexeyev

peas, skimmed milk on occasions, tea twice a week—purely and lovingly; they help the poor people round about, but there is one thing not quite right, and that is that some of them think and say that there's no other life for a Christian except in a commune, and that in any other life, yours and mine, for example, we take part in cannibalism—we make 30 copecks and devour a rouble. I like this—I like the clear demonstration of a sin which we are so inclined to forget—but in answer to it and in connection with my thinking about you, the following imaginary story occurred to me, which I'd like to write if I have the strength and the time.[2] A young man enters an educational institution and devotes himself to science; but before long, after seeing the futility and wrongness of the scientists' leisure time and good living, gives it up and joins the revolution; but after getting to know the pride, cruelty and exclusiveness of the revolutionaries, gives them up and joins the people. The superstitions of the people and the egoism of their struggle for existence repel him. Perhaps he turns for a time to Orthodoxy, goes into a monastery—finds hypocrisy. He joins a commune—also finds it not the thing—leaves it. Then he becomes friends with a woman who attracts him particularly because she seems to share his aspirations—becomes friends, has children, finds in her something quite different from what he expected, and goes through agonies with her. She abandons him. He's left alone and lives with a friend, not knowing what to do or how to live, but, as always, loving people everywhere round about him and helping them, and then he dies. As he's dying he says to himself: 'I'm a failure, I'm an empty, worthless man, I'm no use at all, I've never finished anything I started, I'm not needed by anybody, I haven't even managed to capture anybody's affections.' And smiting himself on the chest he says: 'I'm an empty, worthless man; oh God, have mercy on me, a sinner.' I think all is well for him, and I would like to be him. Such a man will be saved, even outside a community.

I am well. Of my children, only Masha is close to me in spirit. The others, poor things, are only oppressed by the fact that I'm always around, reminding them of what their conscience demands of them. But we live amicably...[16 lines omitted]

337. To V. V. MAYNOV

Vladimir Vladimirovich Maynov (1871–?) writer, journalist, Esperanto scholar and translator.

Yasnaya Polyana, 13 September 1889

I have read carefully through the international language textbook you sent[1] and I find that this language fully satisfies the requirements of an international European language (Europe and its colonies, including America). It is still too far away to think of a world language including India, China and Africa. I consider this matter

---

2. It was never written.
[337] 1. A textbook of Esperanto, invented in 1887 by Dr Zamenhof.

—the mastery by Europeans of a single language—to be a matter of prime importance, and so I thank you very much for sending me the book, and I shall try my best to propagate this language, and especially the belief in the necessity for it.

L. Tolstoy

I don't know Volapük,[2] or how this language is related to it, i.e. what are the advantages of the one over the other.

338. To P. I. BIRYUKOV

Yasnaya Polyana, 27 September 1889

I got another letter from you, dear friend, but I think one of yours must have gone astray, and one of mine in which I wrote to you incidentally about Alexeyev's article.[1] I asked you to send it to me. I'll certainly read it and send it to Sytin. I'm sure in advance that it's good of its kind. This is how our life is: my wife and I, the two Mashas, the two boys, Vanichka, Sasha and Miss Kate are at home now. Tanya and Seryozha have gone off to the Paris exhibition. I'm truly sorry for her.[2] You know, it's like giving an ailing invalid stronger and stronger stimulants. But she's very nice and kind. Lyova is in the medical faculty in Moscow and pretends not to be afraid of the fact that there are human bones under his table. He's also nice and kind. Ilya went away today. The boys had been staying with him, and he brought them back and stayed a couple of days here hunting. He's quite asleep and dreams about carriages, horses, hunting and farming. It's an astonishing thing how everyone lives inside his own atmosphere, carries it about everywhere with him and jealously guards against anyone destroying it. It's impossible to penetrate this atmosphere; he directs all his spiritual resources simply to guarding it, so that he should not be naked without it. There *are* naked people, and they are the good ones. My wife and I live well enough. She is gentler; I sometimes think she wants to be gentler; but she has terribly strong superstitions. Or rather not superstitions, but inertia. Besides, spiritual force has little influence on her, and doesn't move her —only the lowest physical forces. Besides, I've caused her a lot of confusion and harm. I look at it this way: if I can give her anything that can make her life easier, I consider it necessary to give it (this has rarely, if ever, happened up to now); if she repulses me and makes life troublesome, I say to myself: here's something for you to do, go and show her how much you believe in what you preach. And this is also rare; I hardly ever do it. But still, things are going better. She always speaks of you with the desire to alienate Masha from you.[3] I keep correcting, changing and adding

---

2. The first 'international language', invented in 1880 by an Austrian priest, the Rev. F. Schleyer, but superseded by the grammatically much simpler Esperanto.

[338] 1. *On Drunkenness*.
2. Presumably a reference to her friend Mikhail Olsufyev's recent declaration that he did not wish to marry her.
3. Tolstoy's daughter Masha and Biryukov had become close friends through their work together, and were contemplating marriage. The marriage was opposed by Sofya Andreyevna and never took place.

338. To P. I. Biryukov

to *The Kreutzer Sonata*. But I write little and lethargically. I write a lot of letters and saw and hew wood. Both Mashas are very good. They live an inner life, i.e. a true one. My Masha teaches the children in the mornings, writes letters for me and does copying, and reads and wants to study English, French and German. Everyone loves her, and she is happy everywhere. We don't say anything to her about you and marriage, but of course we remember you and talk about you. Let her live her own life. I'm always afraid of influencing her in any direction at all. I know one thing, that I've never seen any attempt by her to compromise or relax the demands on herself. Popov is with Alyokhin, I got a letter from him the other day.[4] He's content with his life. Invite him over. But if you are on your own, it's very good like that. I kiss you.

Yours affectionately,
L.T.

339. To N. N. STRAKHOV

Yasnaya Polyana, 17 November 1889

Thank you, Nikolay Nikolayevich (I'm so muddled over various epithets in addressing you that I decided today not to use any) for your letter. I valued your opinion very much and received a far more indulgent criticism than I expected.[1] In artistic respects I know it's beneath criticism: it was the product of two devices, and the two devices are incompatible with each other, and that's the reason for the shocking things you heard. But still, I'm leaving it as it is, and I don't regret it. It's not from laziness, but I can't correct it: I don't regret it because I know for certain that what is written there, so far from being useless, is probably very useful to people and is in part new. To write something artistic—which I don't promise not to—I'd have to write it all over again, and at once...[7 lines omitted]

340. To V. G. CHERTKOV

Yasnaya Polyana, 31(?) December 1889

I got your letter. There's a great deal of truth in what you say to me, and I'm always glad of advice from you.[1] I asked Stakhovich to call on you, and to say that I would very much like to see yours and Ivan Ivanovich's notes on my story. I'll certainly make use of them. I know Berkeley, and his outlook is very near to mine. I finished reading Minsky's book *By the Light of Conscience* today.[2] It's a wonderful

---

4. Y. I. Popov. See Letter 356.

[339] 1. Strakhov had just attended a private reading of the yet unpublished *Kreutzer Sonata* in Petersburg given by Anatoly Koni, and made a detailed criticism of it in a letter to Tolstoy of 6 November 1889. The criticisms, however, were about the form, not about the content.

[340] 1. Chertkov's letter contained criticisms of *The Kreutzer Sonata*, especially of some passages which seemed inappropriate to the narrator's character and situation.

2. N. M. Minsky, pseudonym of the poet N. M. Vilenkin (1855–1937). He began to publish

book. The first part is exceptionally powerful, and there are a lot of passages which are remarkable for their power, sincerity and beauty of expression. Besides, I feel the affinity of his views with mine. But the ending about meons is a terribly stupid thing. It would be good for you and Ivan Ivanovich to get to know Minsky if he's in Petersburg. He's a well-known and excellent poet. There are some wonderful things by him. I think it would be possible to help him. Of course, the first and foremost thing is respect and love for him, which he deserves not only as a man like any other, but as a man with a warm heart and a profound mind. He's probably terribly proud.

His mistake, like that of all verbose and empty philosophy, is that he argues about what the world is and what its beginning was etc., when there is as little need to know this as to know how many buttons there are on your yardman's waistcoat; the only thing one needs to know is—how should I live? It's not necessary to know whether I have free will or not, but only to use the force which I'm conscious of as free will. He and others will say that for this purpose it's necessary to know first of all with the help of Aristotle, Kant and Minsky what this world is and what I am. But this is untrue; it's a cunning and crafty sophism of a lazy slave, like the boy who was praised to me for being able to spell, but when I asked him to spell the word paw, said what sort of paw, a dog's or a wolf's? It's not given to us to know what the world is or ourselves in it, even if we devote half our life to the study of everything written about it; but we always know what we need to do, as soon as we want to know. Aristotle and a peasant and all of us have to do one thing or another immediately, and there's no time to wait till I find out what the world is (even if it were possible to find out): and for that reason we are all given the possibility of knowing what we have to do, both in our conscience and in the clear, comprehensible and indisputable teaching of the truth—for me, the teaching of Christ. From this aspect I would like to help him; I would like to direct his attention to this aspect. For he's a man of exceptional strength. Regards to Ivan Ivanovich, Galya and all friends.

L. Tolstoy

Write and tell me all you can find out about Minsky.

341. To A. I. ERTEL

Alexander Ivanovich Ertel (1855–1908), a Populist writer, at one time arrested and imprisoned for alleged revolutionary sympathies, but in later life more interested in

in the 1870s and his poetry was at first well received by the Populists, but in the 1880s his philosophical views veered towards mysticism (he also wrote an article sometimes considered to be the first programme of the 'decadent' movement in Russia), and his book *By the Light of Conscience* was written under the dual influence of mysticism and Tolstoyan ideas. Part of his philosophical system was based on the concept of *meonism* (Plato's μὴ ὄν—the non-existent), and this is what Tolstoy is alluding to in his letter. He emigrated after the 1905 Revolution, and lived in Berlin, London and Paris. His many translations include *The Iliad*, and works by Byron, Shelley, Verlaine and Flaubert.

341. To A. I. Ertel

religious and spiritual problems (and in Tolstoy's attitude towards them). His great admiration for Tolstoy's work was reciprocated, and after Ertel's death in 1908, Tolstoy wrote an introduction to his best-known novel *The Gardenins*. Tolstoy often praised Ertel's excellent Russian, and tried to recruit his services for *The Intermediary*, where some of his stories were published. Their acquaintance dated from 1885 when Ertel wrote and asked if he could visit him, and they corresponded from time to time (three of Tolstoy's letters and eight of Ertel's have survived). At one time Ertel worked as a factor on the Chertkov estates.

Yasnaya Polyana, 15 January 1890

Alexander Ivanovich,

I can't tell you anything about Napoleon.[1] No, I haven't changed my opinion, and I would even say I value it very much. You won't find any bright sides; it's impossible to find them until all the dark and terrible sides this person presents have been exhausted. The most valuable material is *Mémorial de Sainte-Hélène*.[2] And his doctor's memoirs about him.[3] However much they exaggerate his greatness, this pathetic fat figure with a paunch and a hat, loafing around an island and living only on the memories of his former quasi-greatness, is pathetic and nasty. I was always terribly agitated reading about this, and I very much regret that I didn't have to touch on this period of his life. The last years of his life when he plays at greatness and sees himself that it's no good—the period when he is shown to be a complete moral bankrupt, and his death—all this should be a very big and important part of his biography.

About my story—it was sent off to Storozhenko yesterday.[4] He wants to try to get it past the censors with cuts. We are now copying it out for the translators. When the time comes I'll order a copy for you. May God help you. The works you have undertaken are good, both the Buddha[5] and Napoleon, as I recall. Oh, what a truly popular book could be written—and by *you*. Well, goodbye. All the family send you their regards.

L. Tolstoy

[341] 1. Ertel was writing an essay about Napoleon (which was never finished) for *The Intermediary*.

2. A work written by Emmanuel Las Cases, a writer who accompanied Napoleon to exile on St Hélène. *Mémorial de Ste Hélène* (1823) is composed mainly of recollections in exile, and enjoyed a huge success at the time of its publication. Tolstoy had read it in 1857 and had used its material in *War and Peace*.

3. Barry O'Meara, one of Napoleon's doctors in exile, had written *Napoleon in Exile, or a Voice from Ste Hélène*. (London, 1822).

4. *The Kreutzer Sonata* had been sent to N. I. Storozhenko for publication in an anthology in memory of S. A. Yuryev. However, the story was not passed by the censor, and not published.

5. Ertel was also writing an essay on the life and teaching of the Buddha, which was never completed.

342. To V. G. CHERTKOV

Yasnaya Polyana, 15 January 1890

I haven't written to you for a long time, so I don't even remember what letter I didn't answer. The main thing I remember is your notes on my story.[1] Everything is completely true, I agree with everything, but although I've started writing an afterword, I probably won't finish it, and so the passage about the ideal of mankind being not fertility but the fulfilling of the law for achieving the Kingdom of Heaven, which coincides with purity and continence, will have to be left as it is. It's difficult for me now to work on it. I simply can't do it, and misunderstandings[2] can't be avoided. Only yesterday Storozhenko, the editor of the Yuryev anthology,[3] was here, and read it and didn't understand a thing. He sees in it pessimism, and I couldn't explain it to him. I'll have to be reconciled to this. There's a lot that I not only want to write now, but am writing, and it's all artistic. Please don't tell anybody, I don't even speak about it at home. Recently the comedy which was performed at home[4] has so taken hold of me that I've been working on it continually over 10 days, improving it and embellishing it from an artistic point of view. The result is still a very insignificant and feeble work, but the thing is that it made me see what a soul-degrading occupation art is. A man may die at any time, and all of a sudden he jots down anxiously a phrase which is appropriate to a particular person and is funny; and he's glad to have found it. Generally speaking I felt ashamed, but I think I've finished now. My wife has made a copy of the last version of *The Kreutzer Sonata* and given it to Storozhenko, and he will attend to it. Masha is putting all the changes into your copy, and we'll send it to you so that you can give it to dear Hansen.[5]

After America the country which is most sympathetic to me is Denmark. What a wonderful letter I got from there from a schoolteacher. My wife will send a copy to Vogüé[6] as well; his wife has asked to translate it; and my daughter Tanya is writing one for Hapgood.[7] So let them translate it; it will probably come out afterwards in Russian. My health has now improved, i.e. my stomach doesn't ache much. How

---

[342] 1. *The Kreutzer Sonata*, in his letter of 25 December 1889.

2. In English in the original.

3. See Letter 341, note 4.

4. *The Fruits of Enlightenment*.

5. P. G. Hansen translated several of Tolstoy's works, including *The Kreutzer Sonata*, into Danish.

6. Vicomte Melchior de Vogüé (1848–1910), French novelist, literary critic and translator, and a member of the French Academy. Among his numerous works on Russian literature, the best known and most influential was his pioneering study *Le Roman russe* (1886). His wife did not translate *The Kreutzer Sonata*—the first French translation was done by I. Galperin-Kaminsky.

7. Isabel Florence Hapgood (1850–1928), an American writer and translator, most of whose numerous publications were devoted to Russian literature, music and religion. She translated Tolstoy's *Childhood, Boyhood and Youth, Sevastopol Stories, On Life, What Then Must We Do?* and *The Kreutzer Sonata*, and works by Turgenev, Gogol, Leskov and Gorky. She has left an account of her visit to Yasnaya Polyana in 1891. Tolstoy turned to her when seeking support and publicity for Gay's painting *What is Truth?*, on display in America, and she also helped him materially by raising money in America for the victims of the Russian famine.

are Galya and you? Are you just as thin? We all love Yaroshenko,[8] and of course would be very glad to see him. But I'm always afraid when a man travels so far for a meeting, and I feel that my conversation won't pay his fare to the first station, especially in my present low spirits, when one is thinking about artistic details.

L.T.

343. To S. L. TOLSTOY

Sergey Lvovich Tolstoy (1863–1947), Tolstoy's eldest son, seems in many ways to have led the most balanced and successful life of all Tolstoy's sons (see Letter 173 for an early opinion about him by his father). Although he took a first degree in chemistry at the University of Moscow, he had always shown a marked aptitude for music, and he also studied the piano and musical theory and composition at the Moscow Conservatory.

For several years after graduating, he worked in various administrative capacities for the government, but later devoted himself to farming, first at the Tolstoys' Samara estate and then on his own estate of Nikolskoye-Vyazemskoye which he had inherited from his father when Tolstoy disposed of all his property. In 1895 he married Marya Rachinskaya, who died of tuberculosis five years later. In 1906 he remarried; his second wife, Marya Zubova, died in 1939. He had a son by his first wife.

Sergey never entirely subscribed to his father's social and philosophical ideas (his scientific training imparted to him a touch of scepticism, and his father more than once reproached him for his 'Darwinism'). As he said in his memoirs: '...although we didn't differ very much in our outlook, I never could accept his criticism of the function of pure reason, of scientific thinking'. Nevertheless, he assisted his father in some of his activities, particularly in connection with the resettlement of the Dukhobors in Canada, in preparation for which he spent a short while in England in 1898.

Apart from assisting in the organisation of museums and archives devoted to his father, writing about him and acting as a consultant in any project concerned with his father's life, Sergey was an accomplished composer, musical ethnographer, teacher and performer. His pronounced interest in, and knowledge of national music can be seen from a short list of his published compositions: *Twenty-Seven Scottish Songs*, *Two Belgian Songs*, *Hindu Songs and Dances* and settings of poems by Pushkin, A. K. Tolstoy, Fet and Tyutchev. His publications also include the articles 'L. Tolstoy and P. Tchaikovsky' and 'Music in the Life of L. N. Tolstoy'. In the years after 1917 he gave many public concerts and lectures and from 1928 to 1929 he lectured on musical ethnography at the Moscow Conservatory.

Sergey wrote a number of other articles about his father, and a full-length book, discovered posthumously, which expands these earlier essays (translated into

---

8. N. A. Yaroshenko (1846–98), an artist whose work was known to Tolstoy, and who wished to meet him. He had modelled one of his paintings on Chertkov's wife.

343. To S. L. Tolstoy

English as *Tolstoy Remembered by His Son*, London, 1961). He also prepared his mother's diaries for publication, a delicate task, and provided an introductory essay which attempted to explain the well-known family tensions in the last years of his father's life. He acted as consultant on the definitive edition of his father's works, the Jubilee edition (for which he also edited the story *Two Hussars*) and he played a large part in organising and maintaining the Yasnaya Polyana Museum. Despite the loss of a leg in an accident and the gradual loss of his sight and hearing in his last years, Sergey remained active and alert until his death in 1947. He was the only one of Tolstoy's children who never left Russia.

Yasnaya Polyana, 8 March 1890

Don't think, Seryozha, that I'm treating you ironically, as you say. If I joked with Sasha Kuzminsky, it *was* only a joke.[1] I try to remember and I do remember my youth, and I hope, and am almost sure even, that you are doing, and have done, fewer stupid things than I, even relatively speaking, i.e. in proportion to the time and the conditions in which I lived and in which your are living. One thing that used to make me cross with you before (before; it isn't so now), was the fact that you, so sensible and apparently practical in acquiring scientific and practical knowledge, always able to take advantage of things done by people before you, not having invented logarithms yourself, and other things which were invented long ago, and knowing where to turn for this knowledge—that you should wish to try to understand with your own mind and experience the most important knowledge of all, namely what is good and bad, and therefore how to live, and not take advantage of what has been explained and proved long ago, indisputably and more clearly than any geometrical theorem.

For example, you've discovered that it's absolutely necessary to be occupied, and you seek an occupation for yourself, but you don't really know what actually you need to be occupied with: the bank, prisons, farming or local government. And that's not all: why not music, why not literature, why not a factory, why not travel etc.? It's obvious that the proposition that it's necessary to be occupied has no sense or meaning unless you've decided what it's necessary to be occupied with. And this was decided a long, long time ago by people who occupied themselves with these questions. It's necessary to be occupied (au risque de te déplaire I must repeat what has long since been refuted in your opinion)—to be occupied above all in our privileged situation with getting off the backs of the people we're sitting on, and before doing anything which in your opinion is useful for the people, to stop troubling them with demands to satisfy your own life's whims, i.e. above all to do what is necessary for yourself. Then there will be no doubts about what to do, and life will be peaceful and joyful. The only possible exception to this is when someone has an exceptional vocation. But what is an exceptional vocation can never be

[343] 1. Tolstoy had made a sarcastic remark to Kuzminsky about Sergey's participation in a conference on prison reform to the effect that he and his friend thought a long time about which new tavern to go to and decided in the end to go to the conference instead. Sergey heard about it and took offence.

343. To S. L. Tolstoy

determined by the person who has or hasn't that vocation, but only by other people who will demand that in such a case a man should devote himself to that vocation of his which brings profit and joy to others.

Please, don't argue with me, my dear, I'm not writing for the sake of an argument, but in case it might be of some help to you. Try and consider what I say in the same way as people try to solve equations in a serious manner, i.e. by assuming in advance that x (and x here is your situation) may be a positive or negative quantity, or may be zero, and not by deciding in advance that x is a positive quantity and then thinking up various tricks to solve the equation so that x should be a positive quantity.

You know, the mistake is that we who are the descendants of oppressors and tyrants and who belong to their circle want, without changing our situation and without recognising its criminal nature, to find at once the sort of occupation by which we might redeem all our past and present sins. It's necessary once and for all to recognise one's situation, and that isn't difficult. But having understood that, it's obvious that before thinking about the benefit to the people (and to people), it's necessary to stop being a party to their oppression by means of the ownership of land, bureaucracy, trading etc. And that leaves one thing: to take as little as possible of the products of people's labour and to work as much as possible oneself. And this rule, however tedious I'm afraid it is to you, is such that it's applicable to the most complex and involved situation we often find ourselves in. In any situation it's possible to strive towards this and to realise it more and more. It's impossible to define one's situation from without, on the surface. It's absolutely necessary to do so from within, from the centre, i.e. not to try and decide where it's best for me to serve or live, but to try and decide what I am, what I live by, what my relations are to people and what my rights and duties towards them are. Well, goodbye now. I kiss you.

See that you read this letter in the same loving way that I have written it.[2]

344. To N. P. WAGNER

Nikolay Petrovich Wagner (1829–1907), a professor of Zoology at the University of Petersburg, an occasional writer of *belles-lettres* (under the pseudonym of 'Kot-Murlyka') and a believer in spiritualism. He was an old friend of Tolstoy's. This letter is in response to Professor Wagner's letter to Tolstoy of 13 March 1890, written after he had attended a reading of Tolstoy's satirical play on spiritualism, *The Fruits of Enlightenment*, at the Russian Literary Society. Wagner felt that Tolstoy had based the character of the professor in the play, an adherent of spiritualism, on himself and on another Petersburg professor, Alexander Butlerov, the distinguished chemist.

2. Sergey replied that he appreciated his father's opinion, however harsh, and admitted that his way of life left something to be desired.

344. To N. P. Wagner

Yasnaya Polyana, 25 March 1890

Dear and truly respected Nikolay Petrovich,*

Your letter aroused the very feelings which you probably wanted to arouse by it—feelings of regret, remorse almost, and grief that I caused distress, although unwittingly, to a man I love and respect, and above all love and gratitude to you for your loving attitude towards a man who has caused you pain. Please forgive me first of all and then hear me out. By way of justification I would say the following: (1) that this comedy had been written by me a long time ago in rough and discarded; it saw the light of day unexpectedly; my daughters asked me if they could perform it, I began to revise it without thinking it would get any further than our house and in the end it was widely circulated. This is a feeble justification, but still it is one: if I had really thought of it for publication, it's very possible that I wouldn't have published it as it is. (2) I never thought of you or Butlerov when I was writing the comedy. All that I knew of Butlerov inspired my respect, and I've already told you of the feelings I have for you. The professor[1] is a personification of a constantly encountered and comic contradiction: the profession of strict scientific methods and of the most fantastic formulations and assertions. (3)—And most important—is my loathing, which increases with the years and which I don't disavow, for all superstitions, among which I reckon spiritualism. The more I look at people's lives the more convinced I am that the main obstacle to getting things done, or rather a delaying factor, is the various superstitions which have grown on to the true teaching from different sides, and are preventing it from getting through to people's souls. Superstitions are the spoonful of tar which ruins the barrel of honey, and it's impossible not to hate them or at least not to make fun of them. I recently visited the Optina Monastery and saw people there burning with true love for God and mankind, and at the same time considering it necessary to stand for several hours a day in church, take communion, and give and receive blessings, thereby paralysing the active power of life in themselves. I can't help hating these superstitions. I see how for some people these superstitions substitute the form for the essence, for others are an instrument of disunity, and for others again a means of repelling them from the true teaching. It's the same with any superstition, with any spoonful of tar. And the reason is that truth is common to all, universal, the property of all mankind, while superstitions are egotistical. Superstitions are particular forms, agreeable and convenient for particular people in particular situations. As soon as a man is in a different situation, other people's superstitions repel him and his superstitions repel them. Such in my opinion are the superstitions of all churches and such too are those of spiritualism. It seems to me that people who are followers of a particular kind of private teaching ought to learn to separate the truth common to all from what they alone, these particular people, consider to be the truth. If that were so, if they didn't consider that communion, or the origin of the holy spirit, or the existence of spirits were just as indisputable truths as the law of humility, unselfishness, or the purity of love, if they were to dissolve their

[344] 1. Professor Krugosvetlov, a character in *The Fruits of Enlightenment*.

344. To N. P. Wagner

spoonful of tar in a special vessel without infecting the whole barrel, it would be possible not to hate these private teachings. Then it would be possible to agree over those enormous areas which are common to all people, and not to touch on those areas which are distorted in such varied and fanciful ways in so many different creeds. I thought this particularly keenly when I read or heard about your work, deeply sympathetic to me, in the name of the principle of humanity which you mention in your letter. I constantly experience these feelings when I receive, as I have done recently, from America, a great many spiritualist publications and journals, many of which, for example *World's Advance Thought*, are filled with the highest Christian spirit.

This is my confession to you: please forgive me once again if in making it I have expressed myself too harshly anywhere. I will say, as children say: forgive me, it will be the first and last time; the last time because having once spoken my mind, I shall never speak to you about spiritualism again, and if you don't deprive me of friendship and communication with you, I shall only communicate with you about those areas where there is agreement between us. It seems to me that this is possible, and I hope that the circumstance which was the cause of this correspondence will not be the instrument of disunity, but on the contrary of rapprochement between us.

Yours truly and affectionately,
L. Tolstoy

* Forgive me if I have got your patronymic wrong. I could have found it out in town, but there is nowhere to do so in the country.

345. To W. L. KANTOR

William L. Kantor (Chaim-Wolf Kantor, 1866–?) had written to Tolstoy on 30 March 1890 to state his agreement with the doctrine of non-resistance to evil. In the same year Kantor emigrated to America, hence his anglicised name here.

In the first part of Tolstoy's reply, omitted here, Tolstoy wrote that non-resistance to evil does not mean indifference in the face of evil, but only that the use of physical force is morally wrong and counter-productive, and that the force of goodness is the best and most successful 'weapon' in the struggle against evil.

Yasnaya Polyana, 9 April 1890

[36 lines omitted]...There is only one thing you are wrong about, and that is that you are timid about following up your argument on the question of mad people. It's impossible to admit the slightest compromise over an idea. Compromise will inevitably come in practice (as you rightly say), and therefore it's all the less possible to admit compromise in theory. If I want to draw a line as near as possible to a mathematically straight line, I mustn't for one moment admit that a straight line might not be the shortest distance between two points. If I admit that a madman may be locked up, I ought to admit too that he ought to be killed. Why should he go on suffering? Take for example a mad dog. Even that oughtn't to be locked up or killed. If I admit that one may lock up a very mad person, then it will turn out to be possible and necessary for somebody to lock up a person who is just a little mad, and then you and me. Don't be afraid, as you have been frightened, of reasoning along these lines. If people may be locked up, the result will be the violence from which the world now suffers—there are 100,000 prisoners in Russia; but if they may not, what will be so terrible about it? The fact that a madman might kill me or you, or my daughter or your mother? But what is so terrible about that? We all can, and we all have to die. But we don't all have to do evil. But in the first place, madmen rarely kill; and then if they do, surely the object which needs to be pitied and helped is not me—a madman can only kill me—but the madman himself —most likely deformed and suffering; he needs to be helped, he needs to be thought about. If people were to refuse, for their own safety, to lock up and kill these madmen and so-called criminals, they could concern themselves with seeing that more madmen and criminals are not created...[25 lines omitted]

346. To D. A. KHILKOV

Prince Dmitry Alexandrovich Khilkov (1858–1914), a former Guards Officer and wealthy landowner who gave up his career and most of his estates to work on the land as a peasant and to live on Tolstoyan lines. Because of his anti-clerical opinions, however, he was exiled to the Caucasus. While in exile he lived among the Dukhobors, and later played a major role in organising their emigration to Canada. A second term of exile (brought about by the Dukhobors' refusal to do military service in 1895 which the police wrongly attributed to Khilkov's influence) was commuted to exile abroad; he chose to go to England and lived in the Purleigh Colony in Essex. Khilkov later modified his Tolstoyan attitudes and adopted a more active stance towards social reform. In later years he said to Tolstoy, summarising their points of agreement and disagreement: 'I admit that we all of us have to die, and that our work on earth should be to fulfil the will of God, as each of us understands that will. But why not admit that they should devote themselves to replacing the present government of Russia by a better one?' He eventually returned to Orthodoxy, joined the army in 1914 as a volunteer, and was killed in the fighting in Galicia.

The first fifty lines of this letter expound Tolstoy's belief that Christianity in its true form is a purely internal, personal religion, an ideal towards which men strive, and not the fulfilment of certain ritual practices. In contrast Judaism emphasises the observance of certain external rites, and Islam also demands public ritual observance from its adherents. A Christian, however, cannot be identified as such by any outward and visible signs, but only by the surrender of his life to others and to God.

346. To D. A. Khilkov

Yasnaya Polyana, 9 April 1890

[50 lines omitted]...Man is not a lake but a river, and furthermore, a river which dries up in places, as in the steppes. The river is sometimes broad, sometimes deep, sometimes shallow; sometimes it is only mud, sometimes it is dirty, sometimes clean, sometimes fast, sometimes still; but it is always the same river. So it is with man; sometimes he is near to Christ, sometimes to a swine. This must be known. And when you know it, it is easier to move in the direction of Christ and away from the swine. But if you imagine that you are a Christian and therefore almost a saint, you will never understand where man ends and the swine begins. There is a Christian teaching, there is a Christian ideal, but there is not, and cannot be, a Christian... [10 lines omitted]

347. To V. G. CHERTKOV

Yasnaya Polyana, 23 May 1890

[18 lines omitted]...I'm very sorry that I can't send you my diaries. I wasn't thinking when I wrote before. Not to mention the fact that it would upset my attitude to what I write, I can't send them without causing unpleasantness to my wife or keeping secrets from her. That I can't do. In order to make amends for my broken promise, I'll copy out extracts for you, as I have started doing, and send them. This will amount to 1/12 part or thereabouts. But the diaries won't be destroyed. They are hidden, and the people at home—my wife and daughters—know about them. Nothing of God's can be destroyed. So I believe...[10 lines omitted]

348. To F. B. GETZ

Faivel-Meyer Bentzelovich Getz (1853–?), a journalist, teacher and newspaper correspondent. He visited Yasnaya Polyana in May 1890, but not finding Tolstoy at home, left several books for him on the Jewish question. He expected to see him at a later date, but Tolstoy's health prevented this. On 20 May he wrote to Tolstoy, who sent the following reply. In a later letter to Getz, (30 June 1890), he admitted, in the light of certain objections made by Getz, that the high moral standards which he believed were required of all Jews by their faith were in fact only found in those few who were capable of making exceptional spiritual demands on themselves.

Yasnaya Polyana, 25–6 May 1890

Mr Faivel Getz,

I read all the books you left for me at the time, and I have now read your letter.

Firstly you ascribe to my (and everybody's) word an importance a hundred times more than it has; secondly you unwittingly transfer to me in your imagination all the passionate desire to improve the material position of the Jews and to

348. To F. B. Getz

express indignation at the persecutions endured by them and which you yourself experience.

I regret the constraints to which Jews are subjected; I consider them not only unjust and cruel, but also senseless; but this subject doesn't occupy my feelings and thoughts exclusively or in preference to others. There are many subjects which disturb me more than this, and for that reason I couldn't write anything on this subject which could move people.

I think this about the Jewish question, and a reading of your articles about Jewish ethics confirmed it still more, that the moral teaching of the Jews and the practice of their lives is incomparably higher than the moral teaching and practice of the life of our quasi-Christian society which recognises from Christian teaching only the theories of repentance and redemption invented by theologians, which release them from any moral obligations, and that therefore Judaism, which adheres to the moral principles it professes, has the advantage, in everything that constitutes the aims of our society's aspirations, over quasi-Christian people who have no moral principles, and that this is the cause of envy, hatred and persecutions.[1]

I think therefore that these persecutions will not cease, just as in America the persecutions of better, cheaper and more industrious workers than the Americans —the Chinese—will not cease. The Americans know very well that in persecuting the Chinese, they are departing from the basic principles of freedom and equality which they profess; but the matter concerns their own skins, and they trample underfoot the principles they profess in words. It's just the same with us, with this difference that we don't even profess principles of freedom and equality, and so have nothing to trample underfoot.

In their ability to achieve what constitutes the aim of the aspirations of the majority, the Jews are undoubtedly superior to the quasi-Christians, and so far as is possible the quasi-Christians will always stand in their way. They are doing so, and will do so, and will only cease to do so when they assimilate the true Christian principles of life which leave far behind the archaic, outmoded Jewish principles of morality—the very ones in whose name the present persecutions are carried out, since it is said that *the beggars of your own town always take precedence over the beggars of someone else's town* and *if anyone is on the point of killing you, forestall him and kill him first* etc.[2]

I very much regret that my illness has caused you so much trouble, and has deprived me of the chance to make your acquaintance. Please don't be angry with me if the content of my letter doesn't meet your expectations, and try and put yourself in my position and see that I can't take any other attitude towards this question.

Please write to me and tell me what to do with the books you left with me.

I am still weak and unwell, but if you found it necessary to see me I could receive you. I think, however, that our meeting wouldn't alter my attitude to the question which interests you.

[348] 1. Tolstoy modified his opinion in a later letter, and also expressed his opposition to Jewish messianism.   2. Quotations from the Talmud.

348. To F. B. Getz

Once again, in asking you to evoke kind feelings towards me, I remain with respect, and the desire for your peace and quiet,

L. Tolstoy

349. To P. M. TRETYAKOV

Pavel Mikhaylovich Tretyakov (1832–98), a wealthy Moscow merchant, art collector and joint founder, with his brother, of the Tretyakov Art Gallery in Moscow. In 1869 he requested a portrait of Tolstoy for his gallery. At the time Tolstoy refused, but in 1873 he changed his mind after a renewed request from Tretyakov to sit for Kramskoy. Tolstoy's first letter to Tretyakov, an undated one, is tentatively attributed to the late 1870s and their first meeting also took place about then. Their total extant correspondence, which extended to the mid-1890s, amounts to seventeen letters, nearly all concerned with art.

Yasnaya Polyana, 11 June 1890

Pavel Mikhaylovich,

Yesterday I saw Gay's picture *What is Truth?* I am now writing to America to my friends there about this picture.[1] It's being taken there in a few days' time. I have seen it, and I no longer need it. Those Russians who have seen it have also seen it, and no longer need it either, and those who won't see it if, as is very probable, it remains abroad, won't see it, just as Americans wouldn't see it if it were to remain in Russia. I don't recognise patriotism in any respect, least of all in education. It makes no difference where light is shed, so long as it is shed. And so I am writing to you about this picture, not because I want the picture to remain in Russia for my sake or for Russia's, but I am writing only for your sake.

It's an astonishing thing: you have devoted your life to collecting works of art—painting—and have collected them all, one after another, in order not to overlook among a thousand worthless canvases the one for whose sake all the others were worth collecting. You collected a heap of dung in order not to miss a pearl.

[349] 1. The Gay painting, *What is Truth?* (showing a solid Pontius Pilate and a fiery-eyed Christ in conversation) holds a special place in the Tolstoy–Tretyakov correspondence. The painting had been shown at the XVIII Wanderers' Exhibition in 1890 but because of the uproar it caused, had been banned from further showings in Russia. Tolstoy, always a firm believer in Gay's talent and vision (Tretyakov was rather indifferent to Gay) had been especially struck by the philosophical implications of this painting and made efforts to have it shown elsewhere. He wrote to George Kennan (see Letter 355), Isabel Hapgood and others, and the painting was shown in Germany and America, but it did not excite any great interest and the tour was a financial failure. He also tried to persuade Tretyakov to buy the painting, the subject of this letter. Tretyakov took Tolstoy's advice and acquired *What is Truth?*, not because he was entirely convinced that it represented a new epoch in Christian art, as Tolstoy claimed, but because he thought it did have some value and might be impossible to acquire later. His letter to Tolstoy on 18 June 1890 shows that he was swayed by Tolstoy's arguments about the painting, but he also defended the collection he had built up, and which Tolstoy attacked in this letter, as a comprehensive collection of all trends in Russian art, valuable for this reason if no other, and selected according to his personal taste which was by no means infallible.

351. To A. V. Zhirkevich

And when there is an obvious pearl lying there in the middle of the dung, you pick up everything else except for it.

This is simply incomprehensible to me. Forgive me if I have offended you, and try to correct your mistake if you can see it, so as not to ruin all your many years' work. But if you think I am mistaken in considering this picture as constituting an epoch in Christian art, i.e. our true art, then please explain my mistake to me.

But please don't be angry with me, and believe me that this letter has been dictated by love and respect for you. Nobody knows about the content of my letter.

Yours affectionately,
L. Tolstoy

350. To V. G. CHERTKOV

Yasnaya Polyana, 11 June 1890

[25 lines omitted]...One thing I can say is that while I was ill and weak I was spiritually stronger. Now I'm recovering physically, my body is beginning to oppress me again and I'm sorry my illness is over. Do you remember the story about the monk who died and was resurrected so that he could be reconciled with his brother? (They felt sorry for him in the other world, and allowed him to be resurrected so that he could be reconciled.) After his resurrection he told people how good, clean, joyful, easy and bright it was there, and how he had been suddenly taken from those clean, joyful, bright places and led to a stinking, rotten pit and told to get into it. With fear and loathing he obeyed and got into it. This pit was his body. And now I feel that I, having already begun to climb out, and having got my head and shoulders out of the pit, am sinking in again and beginning to choke, thanks to medical treatment, kumys and physical idleness. I don't know about you young people, but I, who have already lived my life, don't think so much as feel that I want to be free of the worms...[8 lines omitted]

351. To A. V. ZHIRKEVICH

Alexander Vladimirovich Zhirkevich (1857–1927), a military lawyer, archaeologist, and aspiring poet. He sent Tolstoy a long poem, *Pictures of Childhood*, for his comments, together with some favourable observations on his work from Goncharov and Repin, but Tolstoy's reply was not encouraging.

Yasnaya Polyana, 30 June 1890

[15 lines omitted]...You should only write when you feel within you some completely new and important content, clear to you but unintelligible to others, and when the need to express this content gives you no peace.

In order to express this content in the clearest possible way, a writer will use all

351. To A. V. Zhirkevich

possible methods, and will free himself from all restrictions which hinder the accurate transmission of the content, and he will not fetter or confine himself with the obligation to express this content in a definite metre and with a definite repetition of assonances at fixed intervals.

A man thinks in words as Max Müller says—without words there is no thought, and I absolutely agree with that. Thought is the force which moves my life and that of all mankind. And therefore not to treat thought seriously is a great sin, and 'verbicide'[1] is no less a sin than 'homicide'.[1]

I said that in my opinion you don't have *what is called* talent, and I meant by that that in this book you don't have the sparkle and the wealth of imagery which are considered necessary for a writer, and are called talent, but which I don't consider necessary for a writer.

In my opinion a writer only needs sincerity and a seriousness of approach to his subject...[6 lines omitted]

352. To P. M. TRETYAKOV

Yasnaya Polyana, 30 June 1890

Thank you for your kind letter, my dear Pavel Mikhaylovich.

What do I mean by the words: 'Gay's picture will constitute an epoch in the history of Christian art'? I mean the following. Catholic art primarily depicted the saints, the Madonna, and Christ as God. That was so until recently, when people began to make attempts to depict Him as a historical person.

But to depict as a historical person, a person who was recognised for centuries and who is now recognised by millions of people to be God, is awkward: awkward, because such depiction provokes argument. And argument destroys the impression made by art. I see many various attempts to get out of this difficulty. Some people have simply argued passionately: such are, in our country, Vereshchagin's pictures,[1] and even Gay's *Resurrection*.[2] Others have tried to treat these subjects as historical—in our country Ivanov, Kramskoy and once again Gay's *Last Supper*.[3] Others again have tried to ignore any argument and have simply taken a subject as

---

[351] 1. In English in the original.

[352] 1. V. V. Vereshchagin (1842–1904); his best-known paintings depict battle-scenes and Biblical subjects. He had written a famous and controversial article *On Progress in Art* which accused contemporary artists of copying or continuing without innovation the work of the old masters.

2. *The Heralds of the Resurrection* (1867, painted in Florence during Gay's early period, and markedly 'realistic' (i.e. lacking the philosophical quality which Tolstoy admired so much in *What is Truth?*).

3. A. A. Ivanov (1806–58); Tolstoy is thinking of his painting *The Appearance of Christ to the People* (completed in 1857).

I. N. Kramskoy (1837–87), a reference to his *Christ in the Wilderness* (1872).

The Last Supper (1863), another of Gay's early 'realistic' works, which caused an upheaval in academic circles when it was first shown, because of its departure from iconographical traditions.

being known to everyone, and have only bothered about beauty (Doré, Polenov).[4] And still it wasn't right.

Then again there were attempts to bring Christ as God down from heaven, and from the pedestal of a historical person on to the soil of ordinary everyday life, giving to this everyday life a somewhat mystical illumination. Such are Gay's *Mercy*,[5] and the French artists: Christ in the form of a priest, barefoot, among children etc. And it still wasn't right. Then Gay took the most simple motif, and one that is intelligible now that he has taken it: Christ and his teaching in conflict with the teaching of the world not just in words but both in words and deeds, i.e. the motif which then constituted and still constitutes the main importance of the phenomenon of Christ, an importance which is not disputable, but something about which churchmen who regard Him as God, and historians who regard Him as an important person in history and Christians who regard His practical teaching as the main thing about Him cannot help but agree.

The picture depicts with complete historical accuracy the moment when Christ, after being led, tormented, beaten and dragged from one jail to another and from one official to another, is brought before the governor, a very kindly fellow who is not concerned with Christ or the Jews, still less with any truth explained to him, an acquaintance of all the scholars and philosophers of Rome, by this ragamuffin; his only concern is not to be at fault in the eyes of a superior official. Christ sees before him a deluded man bloated with fat, but he decides not to spurn him just because of his appearance, and so begins to express to him the essence of his teaching. But the governor is not concerned with this. He says: what is truth? and goes away. And Christ looks sorrowfully at this impenetrable man.

That was the situation then, and that is the situation which is always and everywhere repeated thousands and millions of times between the teaching of the truth and the representatives of this world. And this is expressed in the picture. And this is true historically and is true today, and therefore grips the heart of everybody who has a heart. This attitude, then, to Christianity constitutes an epoch in art, because there can be a whole host of pictures of the same kind. And there will be.

Goodbye for now. Yours affectionately,

L. Tolstoy

353. To L. P. NIKIFOROV

Lev Pavlovich Nikiforov (1848–1917), the son of a wealthy landowner, educated at Moscow and Petersburg universities, and in his younger days a 'populist' and an acquaintance of the notorious revolutionary conspirator, Nechayev. Nikiforov was

4. Gustave Doré (1832–83), who did a well-known cycle of Biblical illustrations and works on Biblical themes.

V. D. Polenov (1844–1927), a painter of mainly historical subjects and landscapes, but also of a few scenes from the life of Christ.

5. This painting was done in 1879–80 and later destroyed by Gay himself as a result of a religious crisis.

353. To L. P. Nikiforov

imprisoned and exiled after the 'Nechayev affair' in 1869, but was allowed to return home in 1876 and eventually received permission to live in Moscow in 1884, when he first made the acquaintance of Tolstoy. He worked for many years as a translator and was employed for a time by *The Intermediary*, for which he translated works by Ruskin, Maupassant and Mazzini. He wrote a short biography of Tolstoy and also some reminiscences about him.

Yasnaya Polyana, 21–2 July 1890

I have just received your letter, dear Lev Pavlovich, and I'm very grateful to you for having written to me about your difficulty, not to say misfortune.[1] I would very much like to be of help to you and I'm sending you what I have thought of, namely: (1) An English novel *Donovan* by Edna Lyall.[2] It isn't new—about 5 years old—but almost certainly hasn't been translated, although it very much deserves to be: a novel with a serious religious content. I think Gaydeburov will publish it in *The Week*, despite a certain danger with regard to censorship, and I'll gladly write to him about it.[3] There's another novel by the same author which is a continuation of it: *We Two*. If the one is any use I'll send the other. (2) A little book by a very original and courageous poet, Walt Whitman.[4] He's very well known in Europe, but hardly known at all in our country. And an article about him with a selection of his poems in translation would, I think, be accepted by any journal (*Russian Thought*, I'm sure—I can write to them as well). The poetry isn't difficult to translate since there is no metre or rhyme in the original. (3) Drummond's *The Greatest Thing in the World*,[5] a small article about love, a splendid one and one which has had a great success in Europe. Only I don't know what journal to send it to.[6] (4) A novel by Howells,[7] the best, and very remarkable American novelist, with a good, modern content and beautifully written. This ought to be accepted gladly by any journal if it hasn't been translated. I'm also sending you a good story in manuscript by Hawthorne and another by Theuriet.[8] Both would do for a feuilleton or for *The Intermediary*.

Is there any other way in which I can be of use? It occurs to me that in our big and luxuriously living family there is so much we don't need that I would like to

[353] 1. Nikiforov had written to say that he had lost his home and all his possessions in a fire (including two books about Ruskin lent by Tolstoy) and to ask Tolstoy for translating work.

2. Edna Lyall, pseudonym of the English authoress Ada Ellen Bayly. Her novel *Donovan* (which Tolstoy misspells as Donavan in the original) appeared in 1882.

3. Gaydeburov, the editor of the liberal newspaper *The Week*, refused to publish it on the grounds that he had too much translated material already.

4. *Leaves of Grass*. The Yasnaya Polyana library contains a copy of an 1887 British edition.

5. A brochure by the English theologian and scientist Henry Drummond published in 1889.

6. A note was made in the margin here by Tatyana Tolstaya saying that on reconsideration her father did not approve of the book and was not sending it.

7. William Dean Howells (Tolstoy misspells his name as 'Howels' in the original), the American journalist, novelist and literary critic. According to Isabel Hapgood, the book Tolstoy probably meant is the novel *The Undiscovered Country* (1880). The Yasnaya Polyana library contains another of Howells' works, *The Rise of Silas Lapham* (1885).

8. Nathaniel Hawthorne, the American author. It is not known to which work Tolstoy was referring.

André Theuriet, a French novelist and dramatist; his main theme was provincial family life.

share it if you would let me send it to you and if you would mention what you need most of all, also the age and height of your children. I go on as before, dissatisfied with the outward forms of my life, and trying to improve my inner life. My health is good, and I'm writing a little. I was always very glad to see you, and now more so than ever.

Yours affectionately,
L. Tolstoy

How I envy the way your life has turned out. May God help you. Please don't replace my books.

354. To B. N. CHICHERIN

Yasnaya Polyana, 31 July 1890

I have just got your pamphlets, dear friend, and having glanced at your reminiscences of Krivtsov,[1] I couldn't tear myself away from it and read it right through; so remarkably well, simply, naturally and pithily is it written. The one thing I regretted was that nothing was said about a very important thing: relations with the serfs. The question inevitably arises: what supported all this refinement of life and how? Was there the same moral refinement—the same sensitivity—in relations with the serfs? I'm sure that these relations must have been better than with some other people, but I'd like to know. I absolutely agree with the conclusion, contrary to my expectations, and I was particularly struck by the truth of the idea about the pernicious effect on society of the development of journalism in our time, the end of the XIX century, under XV century forms of government.

Not for nothing did Herzen say how terrible Genghis Khan would have been with telegraph offices, railways and journalism.[2] This is exactly what has happened now in our country. And it's precisely with journalism that this incongruity is most noticeable. My son[3] took the pamphlet on chemistry away to read.[4] He has been making a special study of chemistry and writing a dissertation on atomic theories. I'll also read it and try to understand it. I very much regret that you had such a bad summer. I hope that when you are completely fit you will call in and see us when you are passing. My wife thanks you for remembering her. Please give my regards to your wife.

Yours affectionately,
L. Tolstoy

I am completely fit, as are all the family.

[354] 1. Chicherin had sent Tolstoy an offprint of his article which originally appeared in *Russian Archives*, 'From my Reminiscences: About the Diary of N. I. Krivtsov'. Krivtsov (1791–1849) had fought at Borodino and was the brother of a Decembrist.
    2. Herzen wrote this in his article 'A Letter to the Emperor Alexander II'.
    3. Sergey Tolstoy.
    4. Another of Chicherin's articles, 'Le système des éléments chimiques'.

355. To GEORGE KENNAN

George Kennan (1845–1924), the American journalist, writer and traveller, was born in Ohio and became a military telegraph operator during the Civil War. In 1865 he was sent by the Western Union to Siberia to survey a telegraph route; from 1866 to 1868 he supervised the construction of the Siberian part of the telegraph line laid by the Russo-American Telegraph Company. His consuming interest in Russia and Russian life dates from this period. After completing his work, he remained in Russia to travel and explore the eastern Caucasus and Dagestan. On his return to America he lectured on Russia and worked for the Associated Press until 1885, when he returned to Russia, commissioned by *The Century Illustrated Monthly Magazine* to gather material for a series of articles on the Siberian exile system. That he was allowed to do so was no doubt due to his favourable attitude towards the Russian government's internal policy; his stated intention at the outset of the inquiry was to vindicate the exile system. His travel for this study was extensive, lasting approximately two years and taking him to all the mines and prisons in Central Siberia; he also had wide contact with provincial officials, the police, and exiles living in towns and settlements. His two-volume study incorporating the *Century* articles (*Siberia and the Exile System*, New York, 1891) gives a many-sided picture of the life of exiles and is, contrary to the initial intention, a devastating condemnation of the exile system and, by extension, of the repressive policies of the government at every level. Some material from it was used by Tolstoy when writing *Resurrection*.

On returning to America Kennan resumed his career as a journalist, reporting from Cuba and Martinique and, during the Russo-Japanese War, from the Far East. His other books on Russia are *Tent Life in Siberia* (1870) and *A Russian Comedy of Errors* (1915).

Kennan met Tolstoy in 1887 when he called at Yasnaya Polyana at the request of a political exile he had met in Siberia. His account of the visit is not entirely favourable; he mentions that Tolstoy did not appear interested in a discussion of the injustices of the system, saying that while he felt pity for the prisoners and exiles, their methods which relied on physical force to combat evil could only have harmful results for themselves and others. Only one other letter in their correspondence is extant, from Kennan to Tolstoy.

Yasnaya Polyana, 8 August 1890

My dear mister Kennan,[1]

Despite the English greeting, I am boldly writing to you in Russian, certain that with your excellent knowledge of Russian you will have no difficulty in understanding me.

I don't remember whether I answered your last letter. If not, I hope you are not angry with me for it.

[355] 1. These words appear in English in the original.

355. To George Kennan

Ever since I got to know you, I have been in spiritual contact with you many, many times when reading your excellent articles in *The Century* which I've succeeded in getting without deletions.[2] I haven't yet read the latest articles, but I hope to get them. I've been reminded of you lately by your articles about the Siberian horrors which caused such a stir throughout Europe. Some of these articles have reached me uncensored in Stead's journal—I don't recall which: *Pall Mall Budget* or *Review of Reviews*.[3]

I am very, very grateful to you, as is every Russian person now living, for publicising the horrors which have been perpetrated under the present government.

You have undoubtedly heard the terrible story of the hanging in Penza of two peasants out of the 7 sentenced to death for the murder of an estate-manager who had murdered one of them.[4] This was in the newspapers, and even in the light given it by these organs of the government, aroused terrible indignation and revulsion, especially among us Russians educated in the knowledge that the death penalty does not exist in our legislation. I remember how often I was proud of this as a young man, but now, since the present reign, the death penalty has received full recognition, and that without a trial, or rather with a semblance of one.

There's no point in talking about the horrors perpetrated on political prisoners. We know nothing here. We only know that thousands of people undergo the dreadful agonies of solitary confinement, forced labour and death, and that all this is hidden from everyone except those participating in these cruelties.

I've spoken a lot about what interests you and what cannot fail to interest me: but the purpose of my letter is as follows.

At the Petersburg Wanderers' Exhibition this winter a picture by Nikolay Gay was shown of Christ before Pilate, entitled *What is Truth?*, John 18, 38. To say nothing of the fact that the picture was painted by a great master (a professor at the Academy), and one well-known for his pictures—of which the most remarkable is 'The Last Supper'—this one, apart from its masterly technique, caught the special attention of everyone by the strength of expression of its basic idea and by the novelty and sincerity of its approach to the subject. As Swift, I think, so rightly said: 'we usually find that to be the best fruit which the birds have been picking at',[5] and this picture has provoked terrible attacks and the indignation of all the people in the Church and the Government—to such an extent that on the Tsar's orders it has been taken down from the Exhibition and forbidden to be shown.

Now a certain lawyer, Ilin (I don't know him) has decided to take this picture to

2. *The Century Illustrated Monthly Magazine*. Kennan's articles were not published without deletions in Russia until 1906, owing to the unfavourable nature of his observations on the exile system.

3. The *Review of Reviews*, founded by William Thomas Stead, contained several of Kennan's articles in 1890.

4. This incident took place in 1887 on the estate of N. A. Tuchkova-Ogaryova; the case was tried in Penza by a division of the Kazan military court. Thirty peasants were tried and fourteen of these condemned to death, but as the result of an appeal the sentence was only carried out on two, while the rest were exiled.

5. A quotation from *Gulliver's Travels*, in English in the original.

355. To George Kennan

America at his own cost and risk,[6] and yesterday I received a letter saying that the picture had gone. The purpose of my letter is to draw your attention to this picture which, in my opinion, constitutes an epoch in the history of Christian art, and if it produces the same impression on you as it did on me—as I'm almost certain it will—to ask you to help the American public to understand it—to interpret it.

The meaning of the painting, in my view, is as follows: in the historical sense, it expresses the moment when Jesus, after a sleepless night during which he has been bound and led from place to place and beaten, is brought before Pilate. Pilate is a Roman governor, similar to our Siberian governors whom you know; he lives only for the interests of his mother country and, of course, reacts with contempt and a certain disgust to these disturbances—religious disturbances to boot—among the coarse, superstitious people whom he governs.

At this point a conversation occurs (John 18, 33–8) in which the good-natured governor tries to lower himself en bon prince to the barbarous interests of his subjects and, as is natural to important people, he has formed an idea of what he is going to ask and he himself speaks first, without any interest in the answers; with a smile of condescension, I imagine, he keeps saying: 'So you are a king?' Jesus is exhausted and one look at this well-groomed, self-satisfied figure, dulled by his luxurious life, is sufficient to understand the gulf which divides them, and how impossible or enormously difficult it is for Pilate to understand his teaching. But Jesus remembers that even Pilate is a man and a brother, a lost one, but still a brother, and that he doesn't have the right not to reveal to him the truth which he reveals to people, and he begins to speak (37). But Pilate stops him at the word *truth*. What can a ragged beggar, a mere youth, tell him, the friend and companion of Roman poets and philosophers—about truth? He's not interested in listening to all the rubbish which this little Jew might tell him, and it is even rather disagreeable that this vagrant can imagine he can instruct a Roman dignitary; so he stops him immediately, and points out to him that people more intelligent, more learned, more refined than himself and his Jews have thought about the word and the concept *truth* and have decided long ago that it's impossible to know what truth is, and that *truth* is an empty word. Having said 'What is truth?' and turned on his heel, the good-natured and self-satisfied governor leaves the room. And Jesus feels sorry for the man and is terrified because of the gulf of lies which separates him and people like him from the truth, and this is expressed on his face.

The virtue of this picture, in my opinion, is that it is truthful (realistic, as they say now) in the most authentic meaning of this word. This Christ is not the sort of person who it would be pleasant to look at, but he is precisely what a man should be who has been tortured all night and is going to be led out to be tortured again. And Pilate is what a governor should be now in...[7] and in Massachusetts.

This picture marks an epoch in Christian art because it establishes a new treat-

6. P. M. Tretyakov, the famous collector (see Letter 349), had bought the painting in June, at Tolstoy's suggestion, but both he and Gay agreed to Ilin's proposal to exhibit it abroad. Tretyakov donated 2,000 roubles towards expenses, but the showings in Germany and America were a financial failure and Ilin was forced to borrow money from Gay.

7. These dots occur in the original.

ment of Christian subjects. It is not a treatment of Christian subjects as historical events, such as many people have attempted, always unsuccessfully, because Napoleon's abdication or Elizabeth's death represents something important owing to the importance of the persons depicted; but Christ at the time that he was doing His work was not only not important, He wasn't even noticed, and therefore pictures of His life will never be historical pictures. The treatment of Christ as God has produced many pictures whose supreme perfection is already far behind us. Contemporary art can no longer treat Christ in this way. And now in our time people are attempting to depict the moral significance of Christ's life and teaching. These attempts have been unsuccessful until now. But Gay has found a moment in Christ's life which is important for all of us now and which is repeated everywhere throughout the world—in the struggle of the moral, rational consciousness of a man making himself manifest in the humdrum realms of life, with the traditions of a refined, good-natured and self-confident force crushing this consciousness. Such moments are many, and the impression created by the depiction of such moments is very strong and fruitful.

See how I've been chattering on.

Yours truly respectfully and affectionately.

356. To Y. I. POPOV

Yevgeny Ivanovich Popov (1864–1938), a friend of Tolstoy's, a staunch Tolstoyan and a collaborator on *The Intermediary*. He was the author of a number of books and articles on agriculture and educational methods. Later he and Tatyana became emotionally attached to each other and Tolstoy strongly disapproved of the relationship (see Letter 395).

Yasnaya Polyana, 16 September 1890

[55 lines omitted]...A man ought not to set himself the task of chastity, but only the approach towards chastity. Strictly speaking there can be no such thing as a chaste full-blooded man. A full-blooded man can only strive towards chastity, just because he is not chaste, but lustful. If man were not lustful, there would be no chastity and no conception of it for him. The mistake is to set oneself the task of chastity (the outward state of chastity) and not the striving towards chastity, the inner recognition, at all times and in all conditions of life, of the advantage of chastity over dissoluteness, the advantage of greater purity over lesser. This mistake is very important. For a man who has set himself the outward state of chastity as his task, a retreat from this outward state, a fall, destroys everything and halts the possibility of work and living; for a man who has set himself the task of striving towards chastity, there is no fall, no halting of his work; and temptations and a fall cannot halt the striving towards chastity, but often actually intensify it...
[24 lines omitted]

357. To L. L. TOLSTOY

Yasnaya Polyana, 30 November 1890

I didn't reply to you at once, my dear, because I've been to Krapivna,[1] and since my return there's been a lot of bother and ill health.[2] Mama is rather unwell, and Misha very—a sort of typhus—and Borel too;[3] and I've been unwell myself for 2 days and my head aches. Don't publish the article and don't write either.[4] If stupid and false opinions are disagreeable, the best way to ensure there are as few of them as possible is not to reply, as I've always done and consider it necessary to do. Besides, to reply means to go against the system I've long since adopted. Now the stories. If I were Tsertelev, I wouldn't have published it either.[5] The main thing is, there are two faults: the hero is uninteresting and unsympathetic, while the author treats him sympathetically, and the other one is that the student's speech has an unpleasant effect and his homily is unnatural. The hero is unsympathetic because he's a gentleman's son, and it isn't obvious for what cause he's exerting himself—apparently only for himself. And for that reason his indignation is feeble, and doesn't grip the reader.

You have, I think, something called talent, something very ordinary and not valuable, i.e. the ability to see, observe and transmit, but so far in these two stories there is no sign of a genuine inner need to express yourself, or else you haven't found a sincere and genuine form of expression.

In both stories you take on something beyond your strength and beyond your age, something too big. I won't try to defend my opinion, I'll only try to express what I think as best I can. Try to take a less broad and obvious subject, and try to work it up in depth, something in which you can express more feeling that is simple, childlike, youthful, and personally experienced. I'm writing so as not to delay any longer, but my head is aching. I could express it more clearly another time. We can talk about it again; we'll still be alive.

I kiss you.

358. To A. V. ALYOKHIN

Arkady Vasilyevich Alyokhin (1854–1918), the son of a wealthy merchant and a

[357] 1. Tolstoy had gone to Krapivna where the Tula district court was to try four Yasnaya Polyana peasants accused of killing another peasant, a horse-thief. By his testimony Tolstoy hoped to reduce their sentence and he was successful.
2. The text is corrupt and the sense has been paraphrased.
3. M. Borel, a French tutor to the boys, Andrey and Mikhail.
4. Lev Lvovich had written an article protesting against the recently published memoirs of a man who had studied with his father at the University of Kazan, V. N. Nazaryev (*Life and People of the Past*), which evidently included some false material about Tolstoy. The article was never published.
5. Lev Lvovich had written a story, *Love*, which was eventually published over the name L. Lvov in *Books of the Week* (March 1891). It had been rejected by Dmitry Tsertelev, editor of *The Russian Survey*.

358. To A. V. Alyokhin

graduate of a famous Russian agricultural academy. He first met Tolstoy in 1889, and in the same year he and his two brothers started a Tolstoyan commune in the Smolensk province which lasted for about two years. During the famine years of 1892–3 he assisted Tolstoy in his relief work. He subsequently modified his Tolstoyan ideas and served in the provincial administration, eventually becoming mayor of Kursk.

Yasnaya Polyana, 2 December 1890

I've thought and am still thinking about your letter, and I'd very much like to be of service to you, but so far I haven't arrived at any definite plan. I'll tell you all I think.

An objective exposition would be most unprofitable.[1] It's chosen for the most part by people who need to hide something; but you, on the contrary, need to reveal your inner self. The more sincerely and intimately, the better and more necessary (sincerity is usually equated with self-condemnation: don't fall into that error; you are only completely sincere when you abuse and condemn, *and* applaud yourself). The first form—of very intimate confession—is the best, but this form has its drawbacks; you often lapse into introspection and rummage about in your soul, and the result is coldness, abstraction and lack of interest. I think you need to take as the leading thread of the whole story your own inner spiritual life—your growth—but to describe it in the most simple and ordinary images and events—in the form of a diary if you like—in which you can dwell on what will attract attention. I imagine it like this: 1 February—own solitary spiritual activity;[2] brief mention of friends and work. 2, 3, 4, and 5 February—nothing particular, everything as usual. 6th—arrival or departure of NN: description of his character; my relations with him. 7th—work on the threshing-floor or with the cattle; my attitude to it and that of my friends. 8th—some peasants come and talk. 9th—talk with friends; conflict. Solitary inner activity. Food, hardships, joys, children; inner activity again.

This isn't very clear, I'm afraid, but the main thing is, I'd like you to describe both the material of life upon which you have to work, and the work itself. The main thing is inner, spiritual activity—and to show, not the finished activity but the actual process of it. There's no need to aim at a general theme, not even, for example, whether life in a commune is desirable or not, but only to express your attitude to the life which is led, and the various phases of that attitude. Don't be afraid of details, don't be afraid to offend your friends; write what you feel and give the most detailed descriptions—again, not general ones, but ones taken from the course of life. Write with the thought that it will be read after my death and the impression made won't affect me, but that I'm writing only to serve God and to tell my brethren what I've managed to find out, and what they don't know, and what they need to know.

Don't spare your labour, write as it comes, at length, and then revise it, and

[358] 1. Presumably of his attitude to life and his religious views (Alyokhin's letter has not survived).
2. The Russian *rabota* in a spiritual context has been translated as 'activity' rather than 'work'.

358. To A. V. Alyokhin

above all shorten it. In the business of writing, gold is only obtained, in my experience, by sifting.

Write in the sort of language (this is very desirable, if possible) that a peasant with a certificate of literacy can understand.

I'll do some more thinking. If I can think of anything better, I'll write. And you write too.

Yours affectionately,
L.T.

[Postscript omitted]

359. To N. S. LESKOV

Nikolay Semyonovich Leskov (1831–95), novelist and short-story writer, with an exceptionally rich and idiomatic command of the Russian language. He came of a family of minor gentry, but was orphaned at the age of sixteen, and was forced to take employment, first as a provincial civil servant and then as a steward on a large estate.

His first novels in the 1860s were political; he took a strongly anti-radical stand and was branded an arch-conservative for the rest of his career by the liberal and radical press. (The press almost entirely neglected his work in his lifetime, although he was popular with the reading public.) At the same time, Leskov was writing short stories about dark and morbid passions in provincial settings, such as *A Lady Macbeth of the Mtsensk District* (1865), of more enduring literary value. In the late 1860s and early 1870s he wrote a trilogy of 'chronicles' about the imaginary town of Stargorod which includes his best-known work, *Cathedral Folk* (1872), a novel about the provincial clergy. Other novels and stories followed, many with a religious background, and in the early eighties he came under the spell of Tolstoy's moral and religious ideas. He felt that the author of *War and Peace*, whose philosophy of history had formed the subject of an article he had written in 1869 ('The Heroes of the War of 1812 According to Count Tolstoy') was pursuing aims which were common to both of them. However, although Leskov followed the development of Tolstoy's thought with great interest and approval, he cannot be termed 'a Tolstoyan'. Even his last short stories on early Christian life retain his individual stamp and differ much from Tolstoy's in form and content. Leskov wrote a series of articles on Tolstoy's peasant tales and his story *The Death of Ivan Ilich* in 1886. Their first meeting took place in Moscow in 1887, arranged by Chertkov, and their surviving correspondence runs to more than 60 letters from the period 1887–94.

Yasnaya Polyana, 3 December 1890

I got your last letter, dear Nikolay Semyonovich, and the issue of *The Review* with your story in it.[1] I started to read it, and very much liked the tone and the un-

[359] 1. *The Hour of God's Will*, a story on a theme suggested by Tolstoy.

common mastery of language but...then your particular shortcoming emerged which it would seem so easy to correct and which is in itself a virtue and not a shortcoming—exubérance of images, colours and characteristic expressions which intoxicates you and distracts you. There is much that is superfluous and out of proportion, but the verve and tone are marvellous. The tale is still very good, but it's annoying that, had it not been for an excess of talent, it would have been better still.

Your intention of coming to see us with Goltsev[2] can afford us nothing but great pleasure at any time.

Gay was still here when your last letter arrived, and he and I laughed together at your description. But laughter apart, it's a very interesting and significant thing. We'll talk about it when we meet.

Goodbye.

Yours affectionately,
L. Tolstoy

360. To N. N. STRAKHOV

Yasnaya Polyana, 7 January 1891

It seems I'm to blame, dear Nikolay Nikolayevich, for not answering your last good letter. I'm very busy. All the strength I have I put into the work I'm busy with and which is progressing a little—it's reached the phase where regularly each day you take up what is already done, look through it, correct the most recent part and move a little bit forward or else revise the earlier part for the 10th or 20th time; but you can already see that the foundation is laid and will stand firm. You do this in the morning, then have a rest and go for a walk, then there's the family and visitors, and then reading.

A propos of reading, I'm reading a book which makes me think of you constantly, and I keep wanting to share my impressions with you: it's Renan's book *L'avenir de la science*.[1] I don't regret having sent for it. I've read a third, and in my opinion Renan never wrote anything cleverer: it all sparkles with intelligence and subtle, true and profound remarks about the most important things, about science, philosophy, philology as he understands it, and religion. In the foreword he disparages himself in a condescending way, but in the 1848 volume (I think he revised it a lot in 1890) he refers ironically, contemptuously and remarkably cleverly to people who judge things in the way he does in the foreword; so understand it how you like, but be sure we're full of intelligence, which is the one thing which needs to be proved. Generally speaking the formulation of the question 'what is science?' is false, and there's a lack of seriousness of heart, i.e. it doesn't matter to him at all; he's just the same sort of eunuch, with his moral testicles cut off, as all

2. A lawyer and journalist, who became editor of *Russian Thought* in 1885.

[360] 1. Ernest Renan's *L'avenir de la science. Pensées de 1848*, one of his first works, but not published until 1890. The main theme, arising from a consideration of the 1848 revolution, is the need for a scientific history of religion to take its place alongside the other sciences.

360. To N. N. Strakhov

the scholars of our time; but on the other hand he's got a lucid mind and he's remarkably clever. For example, isn't it a delightful argument that for ancient people miracles were not supernatural, but were natural phenomena, as they are for the people today? But what is the state of mind of a man with a scientific view of the world who wants to force the miracles of the ancient world to fit into this view?

Your letter isn't to hand, and so perhaps there's something I haven't replied to; if so, forgive me. I kiss you.

Lev Tolstoy

361. To N. N. STRAKHOV

Yasnaya Polyana, 25 January 1891

Thank you for your letter, dear Nikolay Nikolayevich. I won't answer it yet, but I have a request to make: if it won't present any special difficulties and you are well, please fulfil it as soon as possible. Together with my other work, I've started to, or rather I'm continuing to write about art, *but not about art only*, but about art and science, and I need a current and recognised definition of *science*. If there are several, so much the better. It can be an indirect one, as long as it's authoritative. Is it possible there isn't one, as with religion? Probably. I make so bold as to ask you to copy out a definition or definitions and send them to me. If there should happen to be a similar definition of art which you know about, send that also, although I don't particularly need it. I embrace you.

L. Tolstoy

362. To HAMILTON CAMPBELL

Hamilton Campbell, a minister of the Free Church of Scotland. Born in Argyllshire, he studied at the University of Glasgow and at Trinity College, Glasgow. He wrote to Tolstoy on 28 January 1891 N.S., asking for a clarification of certain points of Tolstoy's religious beliefs for a paper which he was preparing to read at a theosophical society meeting.

[Original in English]

Yasnaya Polyana, 27 January–6 February 1891

Dear Sir,

I am very glad to avail myself of the opportunity of answering your questions sensibly.

1. Do I accept the miraculous element in the gospel narratives?

I think that to accept or to believe the miracles of the gospel is a complete impossibility for a sane person in our times. We cannot believe the miracles not because we wish, or we do not wish to believe in them but because such narratives, having a certain meaning for people of the 4th century, have none for us. If Christ in body ascended the sky, he is ascending it still and never will reach the seat at the right hand of his father. And the same stands for all the miracles of the gospel. I think that the faith in the miracle excludes the faith in the teaching. If Christ could make all men healthy and rich (if he could make wine out of water, he could make all men rich) he should have done it instead of teaching men how to be blessed without health and riches. Those who accept the miracles, accept them only because they do not want to accept the teaching.

2. The divinity of Christ?

The chief meaning of the definition of God is that He is a being different from man, above him, and therefore if I say that man is God, I say a contradiction, just as if I said: spirit (the definition of which is something that is not matter)—spirit is matter. Christ being God is a belief that can be kept only by people who do not want to accept his teaching. If Christ is man the chief purport of his advent is his teaching, and if I accept Christ as teacher I must follow his doctrine, but if he is God his teaching is only a little part of his significance. The chief thing is the story of his relation to the Father, the punishment of innocent people, the atonement, the sacraments, the church, the pope and so on, but not his teaching, which cannot be accepted by the clergy because it destroys at once their position and shows that their vocation is only a pretence to feed at the cost of the people.

3. About personal immortality?

I think that in this life internal experience shows us that the less we live our personal life, the more we feel sure of immortality, and the reverse, so that by analogy we must think that immortality must coincide with complete renunciation of self. I said all I thought about this matter in the last chapters of my book 'On Life'.

4. I not only believe that a life founded on the laws of Jesus, as they are expressed in the sermon on the mount, is to be realised very soon, but I am convinced that it is the sole escape of our Christian humanity from the total destruction, and that we are come just now to such a crisis that we will be obliged to accept those laws as our rule. Moreover I think that as it is plain that if everybody would follow the laws of Jesus, the Kingdom of God would have been come, so it is the duty of all of us to live so now, as if those laws were ruling in our world, and therefore it is said thus: 'The Kingdom of God is within you.'

My letters get often lost. You would oblige me very much to tell me that you have received my letter.

Yours truly,
Leo Tolstoy

363. To N. N. STRAKHOV

Yasnaya Polyana, 6 February 1891

Thank you very much, dear Nikolay Nikolayevich, for your prompt and detailed reply.[1] It's almost what I need. Very vague definitions. I have also had several from

[363] 1. A reply to a request for some current definitions of science. See Letter 361.

363. To N. N. Strakhov

other quarters—from encyclopaedias—and Grot sent me his own, and they are all almost equally imprecise. How long have I wanted to express all I think about this! It seems quite clear, but it still won't come out sufficiently briefly and precisely. It's too long to write about, but I'd like to talk to you about it: in fact I'd like answers to these questions: (1) Does science, whose distinguishing feature is the strict verification of its propositions—criticism—apply this criticism to those propositions on the basis of which certain knowledge and information is separated off from the whole infinite quantity of knowledge transmitted by people from generation to generation? (2) Can those features which constitute the special nature of scientific knowledge according to existing definition, be applied to knowledge of any kind—the most worthless and even harmful? (3) Is the distinguishing property of science the special nature of its content, not its form? (4) If there is any knowledge which is separated off by its content from all other knowledge as being especially important and meriting the special respect which is characteristically ascribed to science, is true art also distinguished by this same content from art which is not true?...[16 lines omitted]

364. To N. N. STRAKHOV

Yasnaya Polyana, 25 March 1891

I haven't had news of you for a long time, dear Nikolay Nikolayevich. I thank you—I always have to thank you, and not you me, which must make you glad—for Spencer's book.[1] Only it's wasted on me. I'd quite forgotten the effect Spencer makes on me, but in trying to read this pamphlet through I felt many times what I used to feel: not boredom, but depression, dejection and the physical impossibility of reading a single page more. However, I didn't need it just now, since I've put off my article on science and art again—it was distracting me from another, and in my opinion more important matter. And besides, I'd taken it up again not from any inner craving, but because of various pressing circumstances of which one was the fact that people don't argue with me now, but write me off as an enemy of science and art, a thing which seemed to me offensive, since I've been occupied all my life only with the things of which they call me an enemy, considering them to be the most important thing in a man's life. I sent for Diderot[2] and have been reading him recently and thinking about you. Do you remember his *De l'interprétation de la nature*—the first paragraphs as far as VII, and further on too, particularly the place where he speaks about the interest in mathematics in his time, and of how the natural sciences will take its place and how they too will reach their limit. And how their limit is the useful. All this and much else struck me by its truth and novelty.

[364] 1. Herbert Spencer, *Principles of Biology* (1864–7), which Strakhov had sent for Tolstoy's essay on science and art.
 2. The Yasnaya Polyana library contains a copy of Diderot's *Oeuvres choisies. Edition du centenaire. 30 juillet 1884* (Paris, 1884). The essay mentioned, 'De l'interprétation de la nature', contains Tolstoy's markings on sections to do with the development of science and society's attitude towards it.

365. To N. N. Strakhov

If you don't remember, or haven't read it—which can't be the case, but if it were I should be very glad, as I would earn your gratitude thereby—read it or reread it. Another thing—I had a visit the other day from an American, the editor of the New York Herald, and from talking to him and from quotations I've come across, I began to be interested in Thomas Paine's *Age of Reason*[3] and not only wanted to read it but to acquire it. If you come across it and it isn't expensive, buy it on my account—and I would also like to get Schopenhauer's *Parerga und Paralipomena*.[4] Could I ask you to buy it for me if you see it when you are out for a walk, but please don't give it me as a present, but get the money from Sofya Andreyevna who will be in Petersburg in a few days, I think, to my great regret, to petition for the publication of Volume XIII.[5] You can't imagine what a misunderstanding there has been about it—first tragic and now comic: Sofya Andreyevna is petitioning for the publication of this volume, apparently for my sake, while everything to do with its publication is merely unpleasant to me—previously very much so, now only slightly, but still unpleasant: unpleasant because extracts of articles appear with cuts, unpleasant because my works are for sale, unpleasant just because they are coming out now in the vulgar form of a complete edition. I keep writing about myself, but I can't even ask about you, because if I ask about the main thing in your life, writing, I shall be asking about myself.[6] Is the work successful? That's important. I know from my own experience that only when you think it's successful are you not ashamed of living. Well, goodbye for now; I embrace you.

L. Tolstoy

[Postscript omitted]

365. To N. N. STRAKHOV

Yasnaya Polyana, 7 April 1891

I have read your article,[1] dear Nikolay Nikolayevich, and, I must admit, it wasn't what I expected. You understand that it's embarrassing for me to speak about it, and I don't say this out of false modesty, but I found it unpleasant to read about the exaggerated importance you attach to my work. It would be wrong if I were to say that in my own thoughts—vague, indeterminate and breaking loose without my consent—I don't sometimes elevate myself to that height, but on the other hand I often demean myself in my own thoughts, and always with pleasure, to the lowest depths as well, so that the balance is held somewhere in the middle. And therefore I

---

3. Tolstoy misspells this as 'Paene' in the original.
4. There are two German editions of it in the Yasnaya Polyana library.
5. *The Kreutzer Sonata*, when first published in 1889, had created a scandal in Government and Church circles, and the Orthodox clergy had succeeded in having it banned. After a personal interview with Alexander III, Sofya Andreyevna (justifying her intervention as Tolstoy's publisher, not his wife) obtained permission to print it in volume XIII of Tolstoy's *Collected Works*, not to be sold separately.
6. Strakhov was writing an article about Tolstoy at the time.

[365] 1. Talks about L. N. Tolstoy published in *Problems of Philosophy and Psychology*, 1891.

365. To N. N. Strakhov

find it unpleasant to read. But leaving that aside, your article impressed me by its sincerity, love, and deep understanding of that Christian spirit which you ascribe to me. Moreover, when the censorship conditions under which you wrote are taken into account, one is astonished at the mastery of exposition. But all the same, if you will forgive me, I shall be glad if it's banned.

In any case this article of yours has brought me still closer to you over the most fundamental things.

What are you doing now?

Sofya Andreyevna will bring me a live record of you. I'm still working on my article a little at a time, doggedly, sometimes cheerfully, but more often despondently, and I want to, but don't dare to write something artistic. I sometimes think I don't want to, and I sometimes think that I probably can't. Well, goodbye for now; I kiss you.

L. Tolstoy

[Postscript omitted]

366. To V. G. CHERTKOV

Yasnaya Polyana, 15 April 1891

[18 lines omitted]...My wife returned from Petersburg yesterday, where she saw the Emperor and spoke to him about me and my writings—completely in vain. He promised her to allow *The Kreutzer Sonata* to be published, which doesn't please me at all. There was something nasty about *The Kreutzer Sonata*. Any mention of it is terribly offensive to me. There was something bad about the motives which guided me in writing it, such bitterness has it caused. I can even see what was bad. I'll try not to let this happen again if I manage to finish anything...[2 lines omitted]

367. To O. A. BARSHEVA and M. A. SCHMIDT

Olga Alexeyevna Barsheva (1844–93) and Marya Alexandrovna Schmidt (1843–1911), schoolgirl companions, who subsequently became close friends and disciples of Tolstoy.

Yasnaya Polyana, 22 May 1891

[8 lines omitted]...Masha (since she is not here now and won't read this letter) is a great joy to me. I see she is firmly treading the path on which there can be no evil, but only the joy of greater and greater nearness to God. Whatever happens to her, whatever thing might infatuate her (I deliberately allow this possibility, of which there is no likelihood), she will never leave this path which leads to the light, through all possible trials and temptations of this life. She is always dissatisfied with herself, never thinks up justifications for herself and her life, but constantly makes higher and higher demands on herself and becomes better and better without noticing it.

Everything is just the same in our family. Your favourite, Marya Alexandrovna—Ilya—is much to be pitied; he is infatuated by the luxurious and idle life of a landowner, feels in the depth of his heart that it's not good, and tries to forget himself and not think. I talk to him when I can, but 'nobody will come to me except through the Father'. The paths which all lead to one and the same place are infinitely various, and I believe he will get there. The closest of all to me after Masha is Lyova. He's at the university; he transferred from the medical to the philological faculty, but now wants to go back to the medical. The dangerous thing is that he has written 2 stories, one for children, *Montecristo* for *The Spring*—a good one—the other, also quite good in its idea, for the supplement to *The Week*, entitled *Love* and signed Lvov. He is making progress and is alive. What will happen I don't know, but I'm always glad to share his company...[25 lines omitted]

368. To A. N. DUNAYEV

Alexander Nikiforovich Dunayev (1850–1920), a friend of Tolstoy's and a director of a Moscow bank.

Yasnaya Polyana, 21(?) June 1891

Thank you for your long and good letter, dear Alexander Nikiforovich.

The other day Alyokhin, Khokhlov and I walked to the Butkeviches' and called in to see Bulygin,[1] and I brought away the same impression as you did from the visit—a good one. Everywhere there is the same open or latent, obdurate struggle against obstinate women. What can be more harmful and stupid for women than the fashionable talk about the equality of the sexes, even of the superiority of women to men. For a person with a Christian outlook there can of course be no question of affording any rights exclusively to a man or of not respecting and loving a woman like any other person; but to assert that a woman has the same spiritual powers as a man, especially that a woman can be guided in the same way by reason—can trust it in the same way as a man—means to ask of a woman what she can't give (I'm not speaking about exceptions, but about the average woman and the average man), and to stir up anger against her, based on the supposition that she doesn't wish to do what she is unable to do, her reason lacking the categorical imperative to do it. I have suffered and sinned a lot because of this delusion, and so I know how dangerous it is.

Semyonov is writing me a letter about his story.[2] It seems I gave it to you to

[368] 1. M. V. Bulygin, a close friend of Tolstoy and a former guards officer who owned a small farm in the Tula province. The others were all Tolstoyans.

2. *The Butuzov Brothers* by S. T. Semyonov, a peasant writer whom Tolstoy had encouraged in his literary career. At the time, Semyonov was still a Tolstoyan, although later he modified his ideas considerably.

368. To A. N. Dunayev

offer to *The Russian Review*. If that's the case, do so and send a reply, and if it's unsuccessful, send the article to Gorbunov who's with me now and will be with you in a few days.

How glad I am that the girl you write about found at least something of use in my writings. Goodbye.

Yours affectionately,
L. Tolstoy

369. To N. S. LESKOV

Yasnaya Polyana, 4 July 1891

I was very glad to get news from you, dear Nikolay Semyonovich, and glad that you are calm and cheerful, although sick. As long as the power of the spirit works unceasingly, let the body behave as it can and will.

I would very much like to be able to express clearly what I think and feel with regard to the question you ask me about the famine. I think and feel something very definite about this subject, namely: there is a famine in some places (not with us, but in some districts near us—the Yefremovsky, Yepifensky and Bogoroditsky districts) and it will get worse, but famine, i.e. a greater shortage of bread than usual among those people who need it, although there is plenty of it among those who don't need it, can certainly not be averted by collecting and borrowing money, and buying bread and giving it to those who need it, because it's all a question of distributing the bread people have. If this bread which people had and still have, or the land or the money which there is, has been distributed in such a way that people have been left hungry, it's hard to think that the bread or the money which will be given now will be better distributed. The money which will be collected and given afresh will only provide a fresh temptation. When you feed hens and chickens, if the old hens and cocks make trouble—if they pick up the food more quickly and drive off the weak ones—it's not likely that by giving more food the hungry ones can be satisfied. You have to imagine in this case that the cocks and hens who drive the others off are insatiable. Since you can't kill the cocks and hens which drive the others off, it's all a question of teaching them to share with the weak ones. Until this happens, there will always be famine. There always has been, and there has never ceased to be—famine of the body, famine of the mind, famine of the soul.

I think that it's necessary to use all one's powers in order to counteract—starting with oneself of course—what it is that produces this famine. But to take from the government or to appeal for donations, i.e. to collect more of the mammon of unrighteousness and to increase the quantity of food without changing its distribution, is not, I think, necessary, and will produce nothing but sin. There are a whole host of people willing to do this sort of work—those who always live without concerning themselves at all about the people, and often even hating and despising them, and who are suddenly seized with concern for their lesser brethren —and let them do it. Their motives are vanity, ambition or fear that the people might become embittered. But I think that good deeds ought not to be done suddenly on the occasion of a famine, but that whoever does good, did it yesterday and the day before, and will do it tomorrow and the day after, and during a famine and not during a famine. And therefore the one thing needed against famine is for people to do as many good deeds as possible—so let's try, since we are people, to do so yesterday, today and always. And a good deed consists not in feeding the hungry with bread, but in loving both the hungry and the well-fed. And it's more important to love than to feed, because it's possible to feed and not to love, i.e. to do evil to people, but it's impossible to love and not to feed. I'm not writing this so much to you, as to those people with whom one is continually having to talk and who assert that to collect money or to obtain it and hand it round is a good deed, not realising that a good deed is only a deed of love, and a deed of love is always a deed of sacrifice. And so if you ask what should you do, I would reply: awaken in people love for one another; not love on the occasion of a famine, but love always and everywhere; but I think the most effective remedy against the famine is to write something which might touch the hearts of the rich. Write whatever God inclines your heart to write, and I should be glad if God were to bid me to write likewise.

I kiss you.

Yours affectionately,
L. Tolstoy

370. To COUNTESS A. A. TOLSTAYA

Yasnaya Polyana, 29–31 August 1891

Thanks for your greetings,[1] my dear, and for remembering me. This is always very pleasant for me, particularly when coming from people whom I love as dearly as you. And how good your wishes are! If only the smallest part of them were to come true! What you wish for me is exactly what I strive for: to be at least to some extent loving and useful to people. I haven't read Eckermann's conversations[2] and was thinking about them only the other day. I don't like Goethe at all. I don't like his self-confident paganism. Thank you very much too for the pencils (I have a weakness for them), and for the cards, and for the books.

I'm returning the books to you. There isn't much about Damien,[3] but still I was glad to read it. But I didn't like Gordon,[4] and didn't go on with it. I

[370] 1. On Tolstoy's birthday—28 August.

2. Johann Eckermann (1792–1854), a German writer and poet who was a constant companion to Goethe from 1823 until his death. He prepared a forty-volume edition of Goethe's works for publication (1839–40), and published a book recording Goethe's conversations which Tolstoy read in 1897 and found 'quite interesting'.

3. Father Joseph Damien (1841–89), a Belgian priest at Honolulu. In 1873 he went to a leper colony on the island of Molokai, where he spent the rest of his life tending the sick. He contracted leprosy in 1885.

4. General Charles George Gordon (1833–85) served in the Crimea, China and Equatorial Africa, and from 1877 to 1880 was Governor-General of the Sudan. He was killed in 1885 at Khartoum by the rebel forces of the Mahdi. His Chinese diaries, Khartoum journals and several volumes of his letters have been published. He was a devoutly religious man, and a devoted student of the Bible.

370. To Countess A. A. Tolstaya

can't reconcile myself to a Christian general. It's rather like dry water...[12 lines omitted]

L. Tolstoy

371. To N. N. GAY junior

Nikolay Nikolayevich Gay junior (1857–1940), the eldest son of the artist, left the University of Moscow without completing his course, in order to simplify his way of life and work on the land. He married a peasant woman, and, after meeting Tolstoy in 1884, discovered that his views and beliefs were very close to his own. He lived for a while with the Tolstoys, helping Sofya Andreyevna with the distribution of her husband's works, and later assisted Tolstoy in his famine relief work. Eventually he renounced his 'Tolstoyanism' and emigrated to Switzerland.

Yasnaya Polyana, 12(?) September 1891

[16 lines omitted]...What a wonderful thing work is! You know, we think we work in order to eat, or to clothe ourselves, or to be of service to people or to be praised, but that's not true: we all work in order to escape from ourselves into work. And to escape from ourselves is a happiness and a blessing. Of course it's more enjoyable to escape into work whose usefulness you believe in, and which you probably won't derive advantage from yourself...[19 lines omitted]

372. To P. G. HANSEN

Peter Hansen (1846–1930), born in Copenhagen; he became acquainted with Russia, like George Kennan, while working in Siberia for a telegraph company. He taught in an electrical institute in Petersburg and translated contemporary literature: Goncharov and Tolstoy into Danish, and Ibsen, Brandes and Kierkegaard into Russian. He also translated articles on Scandinavian literature for Russian journals.

Yasnaya Polyana, 14 September 1891

Dear Peter Gotfridovich,

I had forgotten your name and patronymic, but thanks to Masha I've remembered it. I got both your letters and I thank you for them, and for the articles and portraits.[1] I haven't yet received the parcel from Tula. I read Björnson's *The New System* back in summer.[2] A very good and interesting work. I also read in English

---

[372] 1. Hansen had sent Tolstoy the final versions of his translations of *The Fruits of Enlightenment* and *The Kreutzer Sonata*, and also of *Hedda Gabler*, which he said had been influenced by the theme of *The Kreutzer Sonata*. He also included two extracts of a short work by the Norwegian writer B. Björnson. The portraits referred to are probably of Scandinavian writers.

2. Tolstoy read it in a Russian translation.

his novel which is translated under the title *In God's Way*.³ It's also good. He is true to himself in everything, sincerely loves what is good and therefore has something to say and says it powerfully. Everything he writes I read and like, and I like him as well. But I can't say the same about Ibsen. His dramas, all of which I've also read, and his poem *Brand*⁴ which I had the patience to get through, are all made up, false, and even very badly written in the sense that all the characters are not truthful and not consistent. His reputation in Europe only proves the terrible poverty of creative strength in Europe. What a difference with Kierkegaard and Björnson; although they differ in their genres of writing, they both have the most important qualities of a writer—sincerity, warmth, and seriousness. What they think and say, they think and say seriously.

Kierkegaard's articles which you write about were here, I know, but so far Masha and I haven't been able to find them. We'll go on looking. But if they don't turn up, tell me, will it be a great nuisance to you? I am sent a lot of manuscripts, and there's no proper system here and they often get lost.

I've been working for a long time on rather a big work which, of course, will be passed on to you for translation by Chertkov.⁵ Judging by his letter, he has this in mind. Apart from that, I've written a short article entitled *The First Stage* which is now with Chertkov. It's being published in a collection he is editing, and he'll also pass it on to you as soon as he possibly can.⁶

Give my regards to your wife. I'm very sorry you weren't able to come and see me. I remember your visit with pleasure.

Yours affectionately,
L. Tolstoy

373. To THE EDITORS OF 'THE RUSSIAN GAZETTE' AND 'NEW TIMES'

Yasnaya Polyana, 16 September 1891

Dear Sirs,

As a result of frequently received requests for permission to publish, translate and perform my works on the stage, I ask you to insert in your newspaper the following statement of mine.

I grant to all who so desire the right to publish free of charge, in Russia and abroad, in Russian and in translation,¹ and similarly to perform on the stage,² all

3. Translated by E. Carmichael (London, 1890).
4. The Russian word *poema* can be applied to prose and drama as well as to narrative poetry.
5. *The Kingdom of God is Within You*.
6. The article *The First Stage* was translated into Danish by Hansen in 1891 and was included in the collection *The First Step* which appeared two years later.

[373] 1. As far as translation was concerned, there was no need for such a statement. Russia did not adhere to any international copyright agreement, and it was therefore open to anybody to translate Tolstoy's work, although certain translators had been specially chosen by Tolstoy, and given permission to do authorised versions.

2. The Imperial Theatres had a special obligation to pay an author whose work they

373. To The Editors of 'The Russian Gazette' and 'New Times'

those of my works which have been written by me since 1881 and printed in volume XII of my complete works (1886) edition, and in volume XIII published in the present year, 1891, and similarly all my works which have not been published in Russia and which may come out again after the present day.

Lev Tolstoy

374. To M. M. LEDERLE

Mikhail Mikhaylovich Lederle (1857–1908), a Petersburg publisher, bookseller and minor author, and a member of the Petersburg Committee on Literacy. He did not know Tolstoy personally, but had written to him and many other famous people to ask for a list of the hundred books which had had the greatest influence on their lives.

Yasnaya Polyana, 25 October 1891

Mikhail Mikhaylovich,

I asked my daughter to reply to your first letter. To your recent letter enclosing a copy of the list which Marakuyev had, I shall try to reply a little better myself.[1]

I am very grateful to you for sending this copy; this list was compiled from notes made by me on a list of the 100 best books published in *The Pall Mall Gazette*,[2] and this list is no use, firstly because it only names authors, without specifying actual works by these often very prolific and uneven authors, and secondly because the best books can be the best or not the best, according to the age, education and character of the people for whom they are selected. Generally speaking, having thought more seriously about the matter, I have come to the conclusion that the plan for compiling a list of the 100 absolutely best books is unrealisable, and that the project I thoughtlessly undertook by marking books on Stead's list was a frivolous one.

But your first question, applied to each individual person about the books which have had the greatest influence on him, is in my opinion of genuine interest, and conscientious replies to it can lead to interesting conclusions.

performed at least a minimal fee and if the fee was refused it was applied to 'the improvement of the Imperial Ballet'. Tolstoy could not approve of this—he had a special dislike for ballet—and so Sofya Andreyevna in future accepted the fee, which was used for various charitable purposes.

[374] 1. On receiving Lederle's first letter of 1 June, Tolstoy instructed his daughter Tatyana to get Vladimir Marakuyev (for whom Tolstoy had made such a list in 1889) to forward this old list to Lederle. In early September Lederle wrote again, this time to Tatyana, enclosing a copy of the Marakuyev list for Tolstoy's approval and permission to publish. Tolstoy decided to revise the list and sent the above letter to Lederle.

Because Tolstoy referred to the list as 'unfinished' (Lederle had asked for 100 titles, and this list includes only about 50) Lederle decided to wait for Tolstoy's promised additions before publishing it. Tolstoy never completed it, and Lederle's book, *The Opinions of Russians on the Best Books to Read* (Petersburg, 1895) came out without it.

2. *The Pall Mall Gazette*, an influential English journal published by Thomas Stead. The list referred to here was compiled by the naturalist John Lubbock and published in the *Gazette* in early 1889.

374. To M. M. Lederle

This letter which I am now copying out I wrote about three weeks ago, and at the same time I began to compile a list of books which had made a strong impression on me, defining the extent of the impression by four [sic] degrees which I denoted by the words 'enormous', 'very great' and 'great'. I subdivided the list according to ages, thus: (1) childhood to 14, (2) 14 to 20, (3) 20 to 35, (4) 35 to 50 and (5) 50 to 63. I partly compiled this list, in which I recalled up to 50 various works which had made a strong impression on me, but I saw that it was very incomplete since I couldn't recall everything, and I was recalling and inserting things one at a time. The conclusion from all this is as follows: I can't fulfil your wish to compile a list of a hundred books, and I'm very sorry about it; but I'll try to supplement the list of books I am writing about which made an impression on me, and send it to you.

Lev Tolstoy.

I am sending the list I began, but didn't finish, for your consideration, but not for publication, since it is still far from complete.[3]

WORKS WHICH MADE AN IMPRESSION

Childhood to the age of 14 or so

The story of Joseph from the Bible	Enormous
Tales from *The Thousand and One Nights*: the 40 Thieves, Prince Qamr-al-Zamān	Great
The Little Black Hen by Pogorelsky	V. great
Russian *byliny*: Dobrynya Nikitich, Ilya Muromets, Alyosha Popovich. Folk Tales	Enormous
Pushkin's poems: *Napoleon*	Great

Age 14 to 20

Matthew's Gospel: Sermon on the Mount	Enormous
Sterne's *Sentimental Journey*[4]	V. great
Rousseau: *Confession* [sic]	Enormous
Emile	Enormous
Nouvelle Héloise	V. great
Pushkin's *Yevgeny Onegin*	V. great
Schiller's *Die Räuber*	V. great
Gogol's *Overcoat, The Two Ivans, Nevsky Prospect*	Great
Viy	Enormous
Dead Souls	V. great
Turgenev's *A Sportsman's Sketches*	V. great
Druzhinin's *Polinka Sachs*	V. great
Grigorovich's *The Hapless Anton*	V. great
Dickens' *David Copperfield*	Enormous
Lermontov's *A Hero of our Time. Taman*	V. great
Prescott's *Conquest of Mexico*	Great

3. This list, which was attached separately to the body of the letter, is not extant in its entirety; only the last division ('Age 50 to 63') still exists. The list printed here was taken from a copy made by Masha, with Tolstoy's corrections.   4. Misspelt by Tolstoy as 'Stern'.

374. To M. M. Lederle

Age 20 to 35

Goethe. *Hermann und Dorothea*	V. great
Victor Hugo. *Notre Dame de Paris*	V. great
Tyutchev's poems	Great
Koltsov's poems	Great
The Odyssey and *The Iliad* (read in Russian)	Great
Fet's poems	Great
Plato's *Phaedo* and *Symposium* (in Cousin's translation)	Great

Age 35 to 50

The Odyssey and *The Iliad* (in Greek)	V. great
The *byliny*	V. great
Xenophon's *Anabasis*	V. great
Victor Hugo. *Les Misérables*	Enormous
Mrs Wood. Novels	Great
George Eliot. Novels[5]	Great
Trollope, Novels	Great

Age 50 to 63

All the Gospels in Greek	Enormous
Book of Genesis (in Hebrew)	V. great
Henry George. *Progress and Poverty*	V. great
Parker. Discourse on religious subject[6]	Great
Robertson's sermons[7]	Great
Feuerbach (I forget the title; work on Christianity)[8]	Great
Pascal's *Pensées*	Enormous
Epictetus	Enormous
Confucius and Mencius	V. great
On the Buddha. Well-known Frenchman (I forget)[9]	Enormous
Lao-Tzu. Julien[10]	Enormous

375. To COUNTESS S. A. TOLSTAYA

Begichevka, 2 November 1891

We haven't received any letters yet, my dear, and I'm worried about you. I hope we shall get one tomorrow, with good news from you. Our work here is very

---

5. Misspelt by Tolstoy as 'George Elliot'.
6. *A Discourse of Matters Pertaining to Religion* (1852) by Theodore Parker, an American renegade Unitarian minister and emancipationist.
7. *Sermons Preached at Trinity Chapel, Brighton* (London, 1855) by Frederick William Robertson.
8. Tolstoy had in mind Feuerbach's *Das Wesen des Christentums* (1841).
9. *Lalita Vistara*, translated by Philippe-Edouard Foucaux.
10. S. Julien's *Lao Tseu...Le Livre de la voie et de la vertu* (Paris, 1841).

375. To Countess S. A. Tolstaya

enjoyable, if one can call work caused by people's misfortune enjoyable.[1] Three kitchens are open and working. It's touching to see how little is needed to help, and especially to arouse kind feelings. I visited two of them today while they were getting ready for, and having dinner. Each has about 30 people. Among them are a priest's widow and a deaconess. I observed today that you get very used to sufferings, and are not surprised by great hardship and suffering because you see worse round about. And the person who suffers sees it too. Our girls are all very busy and useful and feel it. We aren't expanding our work so as not to exceed our means, but if anyone wished to be useful to people, there's a wide field here. And it's so easy and simple. The setting up of the kitchens, for which we are indebted to Ivan Ivanovich,[2] is a wonderful thing. The people take to them as to something native and familiar, and look on it all as something that must be so and can't be otherwise. I'll describe it to you in more detail another time. Ivan Ivanovich is very nice to us all. He's warm-hearted, clever and serious. We all like him more and more. We live well. Too comfortably and luxuriously. Pisarev was here yesterday, and his wife is due to come today. Tomorrow Tanya wanted to go and see her. Natasha[3] is very nice, energetic and serious. Bogoyavlensky has been twice. I've written the article.[4] I read it to Pisarev and Rayevsky and they approved of it, and I think it might be useful. There's no eloquence in it, and no place for it, but there's something, as it were, necessary and disturbing to everybody. Send it as soon as possible to *The Russian Gazette*, and if they offer any money for it, take it—the more the better—for our kitchens. If they send something, all right; if they don't, that's all right too. We don't need money, but if they send some, a use will be found for it.

I'm afraid as I write this. I'm afraid that this money and any other that is sent might distract us and involve us in work which is beyond our powers. People are needed most of all. Write in detail about yourself, your health and the children. I kiss you, my dear, and the children. The girls will probably add something.

Ask Alexey Mitrofanovich[5] (whom I thank for his good letter) to look through

[375] 1. Although Tolstoy was in principle opposed to famine relief, he was unable to ignore the terrible suffering in the famine-stricken areas when in autumn 1891 his friend and neighbour Ivan Ivanovich Rayevsky (a local zemstvo official), who had already been attempting to relieve the starving peasants in the Tula area, asked Tolstoy to come with him on a tour of the villages to see for himself what was happening. They went together to Begichevka, a village about one hundred miles south-east of Yasnaya Polyana where the Rayevsky's estate was situated, and Tolstoy, appalled at the degree of suffering, immediately applied himself in earnest to the relief programme. He suggested setting up eating centres, and this was done, with the aid of charitable contributions received in response to his letters and articles in the press and fees from the sale of these articles (an exception to his principle of refusing payment for his writing). Tolstoy never altogether overcame his objections to the work he was doing, but he stayed on and off in Begichevka until the successful harvest of 1893. Most of the Tolstoy family helped at one time or another, and many of his friends and followers: Natalya Filosofova, the sister of Ilya Tolstoy's wife, who opened food kitchens in the villages, and R. A. Pisarev, a Tula landowner and a member of the local zemstvo. Rayevsky himself died in November 1891 from pneumonia contracted as a result of his work in the famine area.

2. Rayevsky.   3. Filosofova.   4. *A Terrible Question*.

5. A. M. Novikov, who taught the Tolstoy children in 1889–90 and later worked with Tolstoy on famine relief. He eventually became a professor in the medical faculty at the University of Tashkent after the revolution. He left some reminiscences of Tolstoy.

375. To Countess S. A. Tolstaya

the article and correct the punctuation and the expressions where they may be incorrect, under your supervision; the proofs you will probably look through yourself. Regards to M. Borel.

Well, goodbye for now.

376. To T. FISHER UNWIN

T. Fisher Unwin (1848–1935), the London publisher and a member of the committee collecting money for famine relief in Russia, had written to Tolstoy to ask how and where to send the money, and requesting Tolstoy to act as an intermediary in distributing it.

Begichevka, 4 November 1891

Dear Sir,[1]

I am very touched by the sympathy expressed by the English people at the disaster which has now overtaken Russia. It is a great joy to me to see that the brotherhood of people is not an empty word, but a fact.

My answer to the practical side of your question is as follows: the institutions which are working best to combat the year's famine are undoubtedly the zemstvos, and so any help which is forwarded to them will be well used for the cause and quite expedient. I am now living on the borders of two provinces, Tula and Ryazan, and I am trying to the best of my ability to help the peasantry of this district, and I maintain very close relations with the zemstvos of both these provinces. One of my sons[2] is working for the same purpose in the eastern provinces, of which Samara is in the worst condition. If the money collected in England does not exceed the sum needed for the provinces in which my son and I are now working, I can undertake, with the aid of the zemstvos, to use it in the best way I can. If the sum collected in England exceeds these limits, I shall be very glad to direct your help to those leaders of the zemstvos in other provinces who are people who can be completely trusted, and who will be quite ready to give a public account of such money. The method of help which I have chosen, although it does not exclude other methods, is the organisation of meals for the peasant population.

I hope to write an article on the details of our work[3]—an article which, if translated into English, will give your public an idea of the state of affairs and the means being used to combat the disaster of the present year.

Yours sincerely,
Lev Tolstoy

[376] 1. This letter was printed in three London newspapers on 14 January 1892, and translated back into Russian by *The Russian Gazette*. My translation is based on the Russian text.
2. Lev Lvovich Tolstoy.
3. *On the Means for Helping the Famine-Stricken Population* (published in 1892).

377. To I. B. FEINERMANN

Isaac Borisovich Feinermann (1863–1925), a Jew from the Ukraine, who was strongly influenced by Tolstoy's ideas and came to live near Yasnaya Polyana in 1885. He became a convert to Orthodoxy in order to teach at the Yasnaya Polyana school, but his position as a teacher was not confirmed by the authorities, and for some time he lived and worked with a local peasant family, in great poverty. He was eventually obliged to return to the Ukraine where he worked as a joiner, but in later years his views changed and he qualified as a dentist as well as practising journalism under the pseudonym of Teneromo. He wrote extensively about Tolstoy and his relations with him, but his writings are generally regarded as unreliable, and he was apt to attribute to Tolstoy his own opinions and ideas.

Begichevka, 23(?) November 1891

Thank you, dear Isaac Borisovich, for letting me have news of you. I was very, very glad to hear about you all and how you are living. I am living abominably. I don't myself know how I was dragged into this work of feeding the starving, this abominable work, because it isn't for me to feed those by whom I'm fed. But I was dragged in, with the result that I now find myself distributing the vomit sicked up by the rich. I feel this is abominable and disgusting, but I can't stand aside; not that I don't consider it necessary—I consider I ought to stand aside—but I haven't the strength.

I began by writing an article on the famine, in which I expressed my main idea that it was all the result of our sin in separating ourselves from our brothers and enslaving them, and that our only salvation, our only way of putting things right, was repentance: i.e. changing our lives, destroying the wall between us and the people, returning to them what we have stolen, and drawing nearer to them and uniting with them as the involuntary consequence of renouncing the privileges conferred by violence. This article, which I sent to *Problems of Psychology*, has caused Grot a lot of trouble for the last month, and is still doing so. It's been toned down, passed by the censors and then banned, with the result that it still hasn't appeared. The thoughts prompted by the article made me come and live among the starving, and then my wife wrote a letter asking for donations, and without my noticing it I've become a distributor of other people's vomit, and at the same time entered into certain relations which put me under an obligation to the local people.

The disaster here is serious and keeps getting worse, but the help is increasing at a slower rate than the disaster, and therefore having once got into this position it's impossible for me to stand aside. This is what we do: we buy bread and other food, and in the huts of the poorest householders we organise—no, not organise, because the householders do it all themselves—but simply provide the means, i.e. the provisions for the kitchens, and the hungry are fed—the weak, the old, the young and sometimes the middle-aged as well. There is much that is bad about it, and much that is good, i.e. not in the sense of our work, but in the sense of the manifestation of good feelings. The other day a well-to-do peasant from Kaluga offered

377. To I. B. Feinermann

to send 80 horses from a famine area to the Masalsky district for the winter. They would be fed there during winter and sent back in spring. The Kaluga peasants made the offer and the local peasants rounded up all 80 horses in one day and are prepared to send them off, putting their trust in their unknown, unseen brothers.

Well, goodbye for now. Give my fraternal greetings to all your companions, whether known to me or not. Write more fully about yourself.

L.T.

[Postscript omitted]

378. To D. A. KHILKOV

Begichevka, 7 February 1892

You ask me about the Buddhist concept 'karma'. This is what I was thinking recently:

When we are asleep, we live just as we do when we are awake. Pascal says, I think, that if we were to see ourselves asleep constantly in one and the same situation, but in different ones when awake, we would consider sleep to be reality, and reality sleep. That's not quite true. Reality differs from sleep principally in that it's more actual, more real. So I would say this:

If we didn't know a life more real than sleep, we would certainly consider sleep to be life and never doubt that it isn't real life. Isn't all our life now, from birth to death, with all its dreams,[1] also in its turn a sleep which we take for real life, and in the reality of which we don't doubt, only because we don't know another, more real life? I not only think so, but am convinced that it's so.

Just as dreams in this life are states during which we live by impressions, feelings and thoughts of a previous life and gather strength for a subsequent life, so all our present life is a state during which we live by the 'karma' of a previous, more real life and during which we gather strength and earn karma for a subsequent one—that more real life from which we have come.

Just as we experience thousands of dreams in this life of ours, so is this life one of thousands of such lives which we enter into from the more real, actual, true life from which we come when we enter this life, and to which we return when we die. Our life is one of the dreams of that truer life. But even that truer life is only one of the dreams of another, even truer life and so on to infinity, to the one last true life, the life of God.

Birth and the appearance of one's first notions of the world is a falling asleep and a most sweet sleep; death is an awakening.

An early death means a man has been woken up before he has had a good sleep; a late death means he has had a good sleep and was sleeping lightly and woke up by himself. Suicide is a nightmare which is abruptly ended by recalling that you are asleep, and you make an effort and wake up.

[378] 1. I have consistently translated *sny* (the plural of *son*, 'sleep') as 'dreams', although Tolstoy may sometimes have meant merely the periods when one is asleep.

A man who lives by this life alone, with no presentiment of another one—that is deep sleep; the deepest sleep of all, with no dreams, is a semi-animal state. To feel what is going on round you when you are asleep, to sleep lightly, to be ready at any moment to wake up—that is to be aware, if only dimly, of the other life from which you have come and to which you are going.

When asleep, a man is always an egoist, and lives alone without the partnership of others and without contact with them. In the life which we call reality there is a semblance of love of one's neighbour. But in the life we came from and to which we are going the relationship is much closer, and love is no longer something to be desired, but something real. And in the ultimate life for which even that life is a dream, relationship and love are greater still. And in our sleep we already feel what may be and will be. The basis of it all is within us and penetrates all our dreams.

I would like you to understand me. I'm not making it up to amuse myself. I believe in it, see it and know it for certain, and when I die I shall rejoice that I am waking up to that more real world of love.

I got Drozhzhin's last letter.[2] I'm terribly sorry for him. I think he needs to be more cheerful.

Yours affectionately,
Tolstoy

379. To D. A. KHILKOV

Begichevka, 25 April 1892

[8 lines omitted]...You make observations about the life of the Dukhobors,[1] and they are depressing, but I can't help making similar observations about the life of the local peasants. It's difficult to imagine the situation of any Christians—albeit in name only, but still people among whom the teaching of Christ has been preached and apparently accepted—who are more savage and more remote from Christ than the local population. Their interests are: food, clothes, and housing, improving these things and getting more money. They are all struggling, some at the top, others at the bottom, but their aspirations are all the same—they all hypnotise and infect one another with their greed, and all burn with one desire and strive in one direction, and you can only breathe freely at the sight of children, madmen and drunkards. It's particularly noticeable in the present famine situation and in the work we do. It seems to me that it can't go on like this and that there must be a revolution. Perhaps it seems so to me because there is a revolution coming in my own life—the revolution of death—which will surely come soon...[50 lines omitted]

2. Y. N. Drozhzhin, a school-teacher and a conscientious objector who was in a disciplinary division of the army in Kharkov. He had written a short description of his daily life there in his letter to Tolstoy. He died in 1894 in prison, and Tolstoy later wrote a preface to a memorial article on him by Y. I. Popov.

[379] 1. Khilkov was living in exile among the Dukhobors in the Caucasus at the time.

380. To S. A. TOLSTAYA

Begichevka, 16 May 1892

[28 lines omitted]...How glad I shall be to meet our new teacher. Vegetarianism, as long as it doesn't have health as its object, is always associated with high moral views on life. This is immodest, but I'm writing it for his benefit, not for yours or mine...[4 lines omitted]

381. To D. A. KHILKOV

Yasnaya Polyana, 24–9 May 1892

[21 lines omitted]...Love cannot lead to like-mindedness, just as like-mindedness cannot lead to love. Truth and love are two independent aspects of God...[31 lines omitted]

...Christianity, like any truth, has this peculiarity that if it is not accepted in its entirety, it may as well not be accepted at all. Isn't this what James meant? This is the root of almost all, indeed all the perversions of Christianity. Some single feature, for example equality, brotherhood, humility or non-violence, is disregarded, and the whole teaching loses its meaning. And in order to re-establish the meaning, artificial supports, theories, miracles etc. are invented...[42 lines omitted]

382. To N. N. STRAKHOV

Yasnaya Polyana, 3 September 1892

Dear Nikolay Nikolayevich,

I got your wonderful letter[1]—and both agreed and disagreed with it. I disagreed because your letter is the best confirmation of my words and disproves its content.

In this letter you do just what I advised you, and the consequences are that you both convince me and move me. No, I stick to my own opinion. You say Dostoyevsky described himself in his heroes, imagining that all people are like that. Well then! The result is that even in these exceptional characters, not only we who are his kinsmen, but foreigners also, recognise themselves and their own souls. The deeper one dips in, the more one finds what is common to all, familiar and dear. Not only in works of art, but also in scientific, philosophical works, however hard a man tries to be objective, whether he is Kant or Spinoza, we see—I see—only the soul, the mind, the character of the writer.

I also got your pamphlet from *The Russian Herald*,[2] and liked it very much. It's

---

[382] 1. Strakhov's letter of 29 August 1892 in which he discusses an article by Rozanov about a recently published book of his and defends himself against Rozanov's allegation that he does not carry his thoughts through to their conclusion for fear of exposing too much of himself to his readers. Strakhov contrasts himself with Dostoyevsky and Rousseau in not considering his own personality to be of wide interest, and prefers to discuss 'general, objective questions'.
2. *The Course and Nature of Modern Natural Science.*

so brief and so full of content. I know you won't change now, and I'm not thinking about that; but even in your manner of writing there's something which expresses the essence of your character. I seem to have got confused. Goodbye for now, I kiss you. I'm still living the same old life. I keep working just the same and keep approahcing the end without reaching it.

Please write. We're going for a short time to Begichevka in a few days.

Yours affectionately,
L. Tolstoy

383. To D. A. KHILKOV

Begichevka, 13 February 1893

[7 lines omitted]...I've been thinking and talking about you a lot, especially with two Quakers[1] who have come to Russia to help to relieve the position of all who have suffered for their faith, and to visit them. I won't write about them, because I'm sure they have already visited you by now. I particularly liked Bellows. I had an interesting conversation when he was here with a Baptist, Fast, who was travelling with him. Their doctrine is a fine one; they have Barclay's book.[2] I'll send it you from Moscow. I'm only sorry that they tie themselves down to a belief in certain church dogmas such as the resurrection and the divinity of Christ, and particularly sorry that they haven't drawn the inescapable conclusion of the denial of the state which follows from their position of non-resistance...[4 lines omitted]

384. To D. A. KHILKOV

Yasnaya Polyana, 15 May 1893

[8 lines omitted]...It's a surprising thing that what you write at the end of your letter about so-called free will formed the main idea of the ending of my work, which represented the conclusion of the book from one aspect. I regard it in the same way as you do. God willing, you will be able to read it in my book,[1] but I'll try to say it briefly.

Truth is being revealed more and more to people all the time, and the nature of people's lives is such that they all arrive at the truth—are illuminated by it whether they like it or not. Man's freedom consists only in willingly and joyfully recognising the truth that has been revealed to him, or else being drawn towards it against

[383] 1. Two English Quakers, John Bellows (see Letter 479) and Joseph Neave, called on Tolstoy in Moscow in December 1892 *en route* for the Caucasus to investigate the position of the Dukhobors as a result of the publicity given to their cause in England by Tolstoy's writings. He gave them a letter to take to Prince D. A. Khilkov.

2. Robert Barclay (1648–90), a Quaker writer of Scottish origin. His major work, to which Tolstoy is probably referring, is *An Apology for the True Christian Divinity* (1678) which defines the Quaker movement in relation to the major Western religions as a religion based on 'the inner light'. This book is still one of the most popular expositions of Quaker beliefs.

[384] 1. *The Kingdom of God is Within You*, which Tolstoy was correcting at the time.

384. To D. A. Khilkov

his will by other people who have accepted it. All man's actions depend on recognising truth, a higher or lower degree of truth. (A man does what he does only because he considers it to be the truth, or because he is so used to having considered it the truth before that he can't break with it.) But people think that they are free in their actions. People are not free in their actions, but in what causes them, in sticking rigidly to what they previously recognised as the truth, or in recognising a higher degree of truth which has been revealed to them. From the side it might seem that an engine driver is free to move the wheels of the tender backwards and forwards, while he is only free to control the steam. And just as movement inevitably follows the action of the steam, so do actions inevitably follow the recognition of truth. (Of course I'm speaking about genuine recognition of truth from within, not externally.)

This, briefly, is what I say in the book, and you see it's just the same as what you are saying.

From this it follows that for genuine progress in life, external, feverish activity is not only not necessary, but is actually harmful. Activity is only necessary to verify whether my conclusions are correct, and furthermore it is an inevitable condition of truth. Doing nothing, without the amusements provided by the work of other people, is a very hard state to endure unless it's filled up by inner work; but if one is removed from conditions of luxury and other people's work there's no reason to fear this idleness. A million times more harm has probably been done and is being done to mankind by love of work than by idleness.

I was reading Zola's speech to the students in *The Russian Gazette* yesterday,[2] directed against the tendency, becoming apparent among them, towards mysticism, as he calls the religious trends among modern French youth: Desjardins, Lavisse, Aulard and others.[3] To counter it he recommends science and work, without explaining what we should call and recognise as science, and what, especially, as work. Work, le travail, is the only idol of people wishing to free themselves from the demands of Christianity which are being made on all sides, and people so need and so wish to be befogged that they don't even see all the obvious stupidity of preaching *science*, without defining what ought to be called science, or *work*, without defining what it ought to consist of. Do you know Lao-Tzu? He has some wonderful things to say precisely about this higher virtue adduced by him which consists in non agir. [4 lines of parenthesis omitted]

Lao-Tzu derives all the evil in the world directly from agir, from people's concern for their own and other people's apparent good. And however strange it is, one can't help agreeing with it: our famine is the result of our being too concerned about feeding: we have ploughed everything up; our illnesses the result of our

---

2. Zola's speech was printed in a newspaper article from a Paris correspondent entitled 'Zola and the Students'. Tolstoy wrote the article *Non-Action* in reply.

3. 'Aulard' misspelt as 'Olard' in the original. Tolstoy misinterpreted what was written in the article about Zola's attitude towards F. V. A. Aulard, a historian, with whom Zola expressed agreement, while opposing the ideas of Paul Desjardins, a writer and professor of rhetoric, and Ernest Lavisse, a historian.

worrying too much about health—hence our state of enervation; the insecurity and danger of our lives the result of our worrying too much about safety—hence our governments, police forces, armies; the reason for our slavery is that we worry about freedom—hence our obligations to take part in governing; the reason for our ignorance is that we worry about enlightenment—hence our church's preaching of lies and superstition.

I already have Christ's revelation, and so I'm not content just with Lao-Tzu's revelation of the truth, but I can't help seeing all the depth and truthfulness of this truth we have forgotten. And we mustn't forget what we too often forget, that it's impossible to begin to do good without ceasing to do evil which is the direct opposite of that good; impossible for a landowner to help the starving people; impossible for a judge, tsar, ruler or military man to oppose murders and violence; I won't speak about a superstitious Orthodox believer opposing superstitions etc. We are all so immersed in evil, so accustomed to it, that the point of equilibrium at which there won't yet be good, but where there won't be evil either, is for all of us the nearest landmark on the path to the ideal which we ought to try to reach for the time being. But the strange thing is that people who are immersed up to their ears in evil imagine that they are saints, and so make not the slightest effort to escape from evil...[53 lines omitted]

385. To N. N. STRAKHOV

Begichevka, 13 July 1893

I got your letter, dear Nikolay Nikolayevich, and was very glad to get it since I've been longing for news about you for ages. As you see, we're at Begichevka, where we shall be until the 20th, and after that at Yasnaya, where we shall be very glad to see you as always. You like the Slavophile circle,[1] but I wouldn't like them at all, especially if Rozanov[2] is the best of them. His articles in *Problems*...and *The Russian Review* seem very repulsive to me. He writes about everything in a superficial, bombastic, ill-considered, falsely excited, self-satisfied, retrograde manner. It's very nasty. You'll do a good turn if you introduce some free thinking.[3] But best of all would be to persuade them to stick to their inspecting.[4] As it is, to use thoughts and words in order to oppose the truth is completely inappropriate. Recently in the face of death I've acquired such an aversion, generally, to lying and hypocrisy that I can't stand them calmly, even in very small doses. And there's much of both, very refined, in Slavophilism.

[385] 1. A Slavophile circle in Petersburg to which Strakhov had recently been introduced.
2. V. V. Rozanov (1856–1919), at the time a journalist for *The New Times*, a conservative newspaper, and the liberal paper *The Russian Word* (for which he wrote under a pseudonym). He was a fervent admirer of Dostoyevsky, and had been married to Dostoyevsky's mistress, Polina Suslova. He was already establishing himself as a leading figure in the Decadent movement.
3. Strakhov had boasted of being the free-thinker in the group.
4. The head of the group was T. I. Filippov, a government inspector.

385. To N. N. Strakhov

Have you read Milyukov's article on the Slavophiles?[5] I read part of it, and liked what I read. But what I've written about the Slavophiles wasn't written under the impression of it, but probably because I'm out of sorts, for which you'll forgive me. Here we are finishing our stupid work which has been going on for two years, and as always when you do work like this you become sad, and unable to understand how people of our circle can live calmly, knowing that they have ruined and are completing the ruin of a whole people, how, having sucked out of them all they can and sucking out the last remnants now, can argue about God, the good, justice, science and art. I've finished my article. It's being translated. I'm already looking at it from the side and can see its defects, and I know it will leave no mark (while I was writing it, I thought it would change the whole world). I've now written, and am just correcting an article on a speech of Zola's to some students and an excellent letter about it by Dumas in *Gaulois*. I'll send it to the *Revue de Famille*. But now I want to write about the situation of the people, and sum up what these two years have revealed.[6] Goodbye for now; I kiss you. We are all well except Lyova. He is still on the kumys cure, but still sick.

Yours affectionately,
L. Tolstoy

386. To V. V. STASOV

Yasnaya Polyana, 31 August 1893

Vladimir Vasilyevich, I was very glad to get your letter. I entirely agree with what you say, that people's attitude to animals is cruel and ought not to be so, and that the time has come or is coming when the majority of people should be aware of it, and when this awareness that it's cruel and unnecessary and stupid to cause pain to animals should become public opinion, and be transmitted through literature, art and education.

To what you say, I have the following qualifications, additions, and observations to make: (1) The fact that Christ never preached mercy to animals, hence his journey on an ass (which is of no interest, incidentally) doesn't contradict his teaching. Christ preached love, the state of love in general, and from his teaching about love we can't help also deducing love of animals, whose turn hadn't yet come in his time. (2) The fact that a Brahmin hardly ever drives bullocks—since, not allowing himself to kill animals, he probably doesn't allow himself to cause them pain. In the Buddhist legend of Sakyamuni there is, as you know, a story about a stadium in which Sakyamuni views the sufferings of animals with horror. (3) The fact that the idea that man shouldn't cause animals pain is beginning to spread. In England there is a humanitarian league[1] with this aim: it fights against hunting, bloodsports, steeplechasing, vivisection, slaughterhouses and all forms of cruelty to

---

5. 'The Decline of Slavophilism' (*Problems of Philosophy and Psychology*, 1893) by P. N. Milyukov (1859–1943), cultural historian, politician and Foreign Minister in the Provisional Government.

6. *A Final Report on Help for the Famine-Stricken* (1893).

[386] 1. This appears in English as 'humanitarian ligue' in the original.

animals. (4) The fact that I'm convinced that the future of agriculture is no longer with work done by animal power or the breeding of special strains of animals, but with machines operated by steam or electricity, and the manual power of agriculture which produces a lot in a small space, as the suburban maraîchers near Paris and London prove. (5) And most important, the fact that the desired freedom from dependence on animals can be achieved in two ways and from two directions: (a) by overcoming the forces of nature by studying them and (b) by limiting one's desires by moderation, restraint and hard work. The first step towards freeing oneself from dependence on animals is not to feed on them, and not to travel by them, but to go on foot. And every one of us ought to start this now. Otherwise, if we go on eating meat and travelling by animal and using all the thousands of products of the animal kingdom we shall multiply our desires (and they are growing endlessly) in the expectation that science will replace everything for us with its artificial products, and our desires will grow so fast that science will never keep up with them.

Do you agree with this? Goodbye. I would be very glad to have a talk with you about it all.

L. Tolstoy

387. To COUNTESS S. A. TOLSTAYA

Yasnaya Polyana, 20 October 1893

I've been waiting for news about Lyova, about his decision and Zakharin's.[1] I meant to write to him yesterday, but I was so listless and I read so much in the evening that I let the chance go. I was engrossed in reading Potapenko's story in *The Northern Herald*[2]—it's astonishing! An 18-year-old boy finds out that his father has a mistress and his mother a lover, is very angry about it and expresses his feelings. And it turns out that by doing so he destroyed the happiness of the whole family and acted badly. Terrible. I haven't read anything so disgraceful for a long time. The terrible thing is that all these writers—the Potapenkos and the Chekhovs, the Zolas and the Maupassants—don't even know what is good and what is bad: for the most part they consider what is bad to be good, and under the guise of art, entertain the public with it and corrupt them. This story was for me the coup de grâce, making clear what I had vaguely felt for a long time. There were some interesting things in it too about madness and criminality. I wrote a lot yesterday —all about religion—and then had too much to eat for lunch and was listless all evening...[11 lines omitted]

[387] 1. An eminent Moscow specialist who had been consulted about Lev Lvovich's continual bad health.
2. *A Family Story*.

388. To L. P. NIKIFOROV

Yasnaya Polyana, 3 November 1893

Dear Lev Pavlovich,

I haven't received your translations yet.¹ When I do, I shall certainly look through them as I did the previous ones. It doesn't matter which of the novels is first; they both deserve translating. *Mont-Oriol* is actually the better.²

I fully understand that you don't like the opinion that a writer needs to be judged by his writings, and not by what he does. This opinion offends me too. But as I told you at the time, my only comment is that writing is the writer's business, as Pushkin aptly said, i.e. if a good blacksmith or worker drinks a lot, I ought to take his work into account and not compare him to an idle drunkard. If Rousseau was weak and sent his children to a foundling home and much else besides, nevertheless what he did as a writer was good, and he can't be compared to an idle profligate. As for a man needing to strive with all his might to do and perform what he says, this goes without saying, since this is the basis of human life. I would even say that if a man doesn't strive with all his might to do what he says, he will never be good at saying what ought to be done, he will never infect others.

You and I can't disagree about this.

We shall spend a couple more weeks in the country—it's very nice here—and then we shall see you in Moscow.

Yours affectionately,
L.T.

389. To N. N. GAY senior

Yasnaya Polyana, 5 November 1893

I was glad to get your letter, my dear Nikolay Nikolayevich, and glad to know you are satisfied with your latest idea for the picture.¹ I'm sure it will be good. I like the robber shaking with fever (I've known about and expected this for a long time) and I like the moment itself. If only Christ were not exceptional, even exceptionally unattractive, as he was in your last picture.² And if only you could satisfy the demands of the artistic crowd by your technique. If there is to be an exhibition and a big picture, you need to take this into account. You will forgive me if what I say is wrong, but I can't help saying what I think. It seems to me that there's a terrible waste of very valuable material in your pictures and the work your pictures do, rather like, if you'll forgive the comparison, the baking of white bread from best quality flour, which the gentry like, and throwing away the bran which contains

---

[388] 1. Of Maupassant, some of whose works were being translated by Nikiforov at Tolstoy's suggestion. Tolstoy helped with the editing and proof-reading, and wrote a preface.

2. Nikiforov had asked Tolstoy which work to translate first: *Mont-Oriol, Pierre et Jean* or *Sur l'eau*.

[389] 1. *The Crucifixion* (1892–4).   2. *The Verdict of the Sanhedrin.*

the very tasty and nourishing part. You told me about your first idea for the picture —and it has probably been painted now—namely that Christ's death on the cross overcomes the robber. I liked this very much, for its clarity, pictorial quality and the expression of Christ's majesty through the impression made by him on the robber. In the same way Homer, in order to describe Helen's beauty, says that when she came in, the elders were amazed by her beauty and stood up.³ Later you depicted it differently again. All these were pictures of important content. It was the same too, as far as I know, with your Judas.⁴ All these studies are very nourishing bran, and it is all lost in order to make bread for the gentry. I shall be the first to rejoice at your picture as it is now and to be moved by it, but I still regret all those ones which have been left by the wayside and which now at least nobody but you can paint. I constantly regret that you have abandoned your plan for a series of Gospel pictures.⁵ Perhaps it's difficult to finish them, to bring them to a certain necessary stage of technical perfection—that I don't know—but I do know that you ought to elaborate everything you have thought and felt and seen with your artistic, Christian vision: that is your plain duty, your service to God. *Dixi*. If I'm mistaken, forgive me. I received an astonishing piece of news from Khilkov today.⁶ His mother travelled up with a police officer from Tiflis, and took his children away from him by sovereign decree, and took them home with her, first to the Kharkov province and then to Petersburg. 'If they have persecuted me, they will also persecute you.'⁷ But it's sad for the mother and for all those who are party to this sin. Give my dear friends Kolechka and family and Ruban and his family a kiss from me. Write and tell me what you are thinking and doing, and what the state of the picture is. Goodbye; I embrace you. Masha also sends greetings to your family.

L.T.

390. To G. A. RUSANOV

Moscow, 27(?) November and 3 December 1893

[23 lines omitted]...You write to me about yourself, and I must pay you back in the same coin, because I know you are just as interested in the details of my life as I

3. Tolstoy is evidently recalling this scene from Apollon Maykov's poem based on the Iliad, *The Elders of Ilium were Seated*. In Homer the scene is not quite as Tolstoy describes it.
4. Reference to a painting known variously as *Judas, Conscience*, or *The Traitor*, finished in 1892 and displayed in the XX Wanderers' Exhibition that year.
5. Gay had been planning and making preliminary sketches for a series of illustrations to the Gospels since 1886; Tolstoy had taken particular interest in this project.
6. In October Khilkov's mother, the Princess Khilkova, in the absence of her son who was living in exile, forcibly took his children away from his common-law wife. Khilkov's anti-Orthodox religious beliefs did not permit a church wedding or baptism of the children—which, according to Russian law, made the children subject to removal from their parents. Tolstoy wrote first to Princess Khilkova but, receiving an intransigent reply, he then wrote a letter to Alexander III in early January 1894 when Khilkov's wife was in Moscow, petitioning for her children's return. He received no reply and the children were never returned to their parents.
7. John 15, 20.

390. To G. A. Rusanov

am in yours. Writing absorbs all my life now. I write in the morning from 9 till 12, sometimes till 1, then have lunch and a rest, then go for a walk or chop wood, although my strength is getting less now, then I have dinner and after dinner I translate Amiel[1] with Masha (such a nice French writer—now dead—a native of Geneva)—it will be published in *The Northern Herald*—or else Lao-Tzu with Popov, then letters or visitors. But in terms of vital energy expended on it, all this relates to the morning's work in the proportion of 1 to 10. All my life is concentrated in the morning's writing. I'm now writing about Toulon and the hypnotic power of patriotism;[2] I think I've finished. Next on the list is a foreword to Maupassant, written in rough, a foreword to Amiel, an afterword to *The Kingdom of God*, also nearly written, and an article on art. Then I shall be able to get down to something artistic—begun and not begun—which particularly attracts me. You confessed your weaknesses to me, and I'll confess mine to you: I have often thought, and still think: if I were to be put in prison and given paper and pen, how glad I should be to write something artistic. Of course, it's like your dreams about travelling—just as unfeasible and vain. You, more than anybody else, attract me to artistic work, not by your advice to me, but by showing me in your own person how it can have a good and beneficial effect...[4 lines omitted]

391. To A. D. ZUTPHEN

A. D. Zutphen, a Dutch medical student, had written to Tolstoy to ask how he managed to live on only 18 centimes' worth of food a day, according to a newspaper report.

Yasnaya Polyana, 8/20 February 1894

Monsieur,

Voici les réponses que je puis faire à vos questions: Ma nourriture principale consiste dans un gruau d'avoine que je prends chaud deux fois par jour avec du pain de froment (graham bread). Excepté cela je dîne d'une soupe aux choux ou aux pommes de terre, d'un gruau de blé de sarrazin ou bien de pommes de terre cuites ou frites à l'huile de tournesol ou de moutarde et d'une compote aux pruneaux et aux pommes. Le dîner, que je prends avec ma famille, peut être remplacé, comme j'en ai fait l'épreuve, par le gruau d'avoine, qui forme ma nourriture

[390] 1. Henri Frédéric Amiel (1821–81), Swiss philosopher and writer. His best-known work and the one from which Tolstoy was translating excerpts was the massive *Fragments d'un journal intime* (published posthumously in 1883), a highly introspective and analytical work.

2. Toulon, the French naval station on the Mediterranean where the Russian fleet called in on a widely publicised official visit in October 1893; a Franco-Russian defence pact was then in process of negotiation. Among other things Tolstoy's article attacked the view that one can ensure peace by preparing for war, and exposed the strong *revanchiste* sentiment in France at recapturing Alsace-Lorraine. The article, eventually called *Christianity and Patriotism*, was sent abroad by Tolstoy for translation and publication in England, France and Germany. In Russia, of course, the article was banned, but it was published in Russian in Geneva (1895).

principale. Ma santé n'a non seulement pas souffert, mais s'est sensiblement améliorée depuis que j'ai abandonné la lait, le beurre et les oeufs, ainsi que le sucre, le thé et le café.

Léon Tolstoy

392. To I. A. BUNIN

Ivan Alexeyevich Bunin (1870–1953) who emigrated to France after the Revolution and subsequently won the Nobel Prize for literature, was in 1894 a little-known writer with one collection of poems to his name. For a brief period in 1893–4 he considered himself a Tolstoyan. In 1893 he visited several Tolstoyan colonies in the Kharkov province, and in January 1894 he went to Moscow in order to meet Tolstoy, but was disappointed with the brevity of his talk with him—hence Tolstoy's apology in this letter. As a result of his enthusiasm for Tolstoyan ideas, Bunin considered leaving his job as a librarian in Poltava and working in an administrative capacity for *The Intermediary*. However, his interest in 'Tolstoyanism' was short-lived—although he retained his admiration for Tolstoy's fiction to the end of his life. His controversial book, *The Liberation of Tolstoy*, was published in France in 1937. The surviving correspondence between the two men is limited to a handful of letters between 1893 and 1901.

Moscow, 23 February 1894

I was very glad to get your letter, Ivan Alexeyevich. I was especially glad because our meeting in Moscow was very brief, and I was afraid that I hadn't treated you with sufficient consideration.

Don't expect anything from life: there can be nothing better than what you now have, and no more serious and important moment than the one you are now experiencing, because it is a real one and the only one within your power. Don't think, either, of a different and more desirable form of life: they are all alike. The best one is only the one which requires the greatest exercise of spiritual power. I think that this exercise of the spiritual power of love is very necessary for you in order to maintain good relations with your wife and, at the same time, to make continual progress in thought and deed in the cause of Christian perfection and service to God.

Drozhzhin's death and the taking away of Khilkov's children are two important events which call us all to make greater moral demands on ourselves, and to free ourselves more and more from any solidarity with the power which does such deeds.

Yours affectionately,
L. Tolstoy

393. To L. L. and T. L. TOLSTOY[1]

Moscow, 12 March 1894

[54 lines omitted]...Yanzhul[2] was insulted by the students on 19 February; they asked him not to lecture, but he started to do so, and they shouted him down. It was all the work of students from outside—final-year medical students—as with Brunetière in Paris.[3] Yanzhul isn't to blame, but the students are disgusting. I called on Yanzhul to pay him a visite de condoléance, which touched him very much. Uncle Seryozha is here, and I'll go and see him now while we're still alive, and give him the chance to pour out his dissatisfaction with Christianity and then go home and admit that yes, of course...

A propos of my foreword to Maupassant, I got some books on aesthetics from Storozhenko's, and have read a lot about the subject and learned a lot. Knight's book in English, *Philosophy of the Beautiful*,[4] is excellent, and there is very much that is good in Guyau's books[5] (I've forgotten how he's spelt). His two books *L'art au point de vue sociologique*, and another one I can't remember, contain much that is good. I hadn't read them before. If there is no full and, more important, no lucid theory in them—evolution confuses him—there is on the other hand much that stimulates one to think in the right direction.

I'm glad, Tanya, that you got back from the theatre you went to with Richet.[6] He's a good man, but still he's a Frenchman, and a bit 'kopke'.[7] In fact he's generally very 'kopke'. I think that Schroeder and Rod[8] are far more serious and clever than he is. Problems of the theory of art worry me incessantly. Obviously, it's all still vague in my mind. And there's no point in just saying any old thing. It's necessary to read the history of aesthetics in order to see how much has been said about it which is clever and true, but very vague. And now everything reminds me about the subject and stimulates thought; yesterday's party at the Behrs' and your visit to the Louvre, which tormented me. After a rubbishy quartet of Tchaikovsky's yesterday I had a talk with the cellist—a student at the conservatoire

[393] 1. In January 1894 Lev Lvovich, who had been ill for some time, went to Paris to consult specialists. A month later he sent an urgent telegram to his sister Tatyana asking her to come to Paris and take him home as he was unfit to travel alone. Tatyana left at once, and stayed in Paris for some weeks, looking after her brother, visiting the specialists, the art galleries and the shops, and going to the theatre with young men who knew her father.

2. I. I. Yanzhul, Professor of Financial Law at the University of Moscow, had refused to cancel his lectures in honour of the emancipation of the serfs on 19 February. Those students who attended his lectures that day shouted him down.

3. Professor of Literature at the Ecole Normale in Paris.

4. William Angus Knight, *The Philosophy of the Beautiful* (London 1893–5). Tolstoy used this book when examining theories of aesthetics in *What is Art?*

5. Marie Jean Guyau, French philosopher and poet, author of *Les problèmes de l'aesthétique contemporaine* (Paris, 1884) and *L'art au point de vue sociologique* (Paris, 1889).

6. Charles Richet, physiologist and psychologist; he had visited Russia in 1891 and called at Yasnaya Polyana.

7. A nonsense-word having a special significance among the Tolstoy family; its meaning is not known.

8. F. Schroeder, French journalist and author of *Tolstoyanism*; Edouard Rod, Swiss novelist and literary critic (see Letter 331).

394. To N. N. Gay senior

and a very good player. And then they began to sing. So as not to disturb the singing, we went into another room at the back, and I was maintaining heatedly to him that modern music had taken the wrong road, when suddenly something interrupted my thoughts, took a hold of me, drew me towards it and demanded obedience. They had started to sing in the other room—a charming baritone, Baburin, a student at the conservatoire, and a young girl Rig—the duet *La ci darem la mano*.[9] I stopped talking and began to listen and rejoice and smile at something. What a dreadful power it has! It's just the same with your Louvre. Just as people were put to death for witchcraft, i.e. for a mysterious evil influence, and were praised and glorified for prayer, a mysterious good influence, so it should be with art too. It's no joking matter, but a terrible power. But it appears that people only want the bad influence. And amazing things were said about your story, Lyova, in *The Russian Gazette*[10]—disapprovingly—because it's passive perfection, or something of the sort. And Gay's picture has been taken down because it's butchery, because it destroys pleasure. There's something to think about. You must begin at the beginning.

Well, goodbye and good night, my dears; I'm going to Uncle Seryozha's.

This letter is about everything—like the ones young ladies write.

394. To N. N. GAY senior

Moscow, 14 March 1894

I ought to have answered you long ago, dear friend, but your letter was moved from my desk and I answered other letters but not yours, one of the closest to my heart.[1]

The fact that your picture has been taken down, and the fact that it has been talked about is very good and instructive. Especially so the words 'it's butchery'. These words tell everything: one has to represent an execution, this very execution now reproduced, in such a way that it should be as nice to look at as a bunch of flowers. The fate of Christianity is astonishing! It's been made a domestic, pocket-sized affair, it's been rendered harmless, and people have accepted it in that form, and not only accepted it but grown used to it and settled down comfortably to it. And suddenly it starts to expand in all its enormous importance, terrifying them and shattering all their orderly regime.

Not only the teaching (there's no need to speak about that) but the very story of Christ's life and death suddenly acquires its true, accusatory importance, and the people are terrified and shun it. The taking down of your picture is a triumph for

9. An aria from Mozart's *Don Giovanni*.
10. Lev's story *The Age of Majority* (*The Northern Herald*, 1894, no. 2) was unfavourably reviewed in *The Russian Gazette* (3 March 1894).

[394] 1. Gay's letter of 8 March 1894, telling Tolstoy that his picture *The Crucifixion* had been taken down from the Wanderers' Exhibition due to official displeasure. The words 'it's butchery' have been variously attributed to Alexander III and to the President of the Academy of Arts.

394. To N. N. Gay senior

you. When I first saw it I was sure it would be taken down, and now, as I vividly imagine to myself an ordinary exhibition with their majesties and their highnesses and ladies and landscapes and nature mortes, it's funny even to think of it being there at all. I didn't fully understand the Emperor's words to the effect, I think, that religion is religion, and why paint something unpleasant.

What are the artists saying? Who is saying what? What are you doing yourself? Will you be coming to see us soon? Everything is as usual with us. I kiss you. The news about the Stundists[2] is good. I haven't had time yet to write to Kolechka.

L. Tolstoy

395. To T. L. TOLSTAYA

Moscow, 22(?) March 1894

My dear, darling, very dearest Tanya, for God's sake take my words to heart in a loving and serious way, and think carefully about them. If I'm mistaken anywhere and have exaggerated, reject what is irrelevant, but don't cross it all out mentally; take to heart what is true in what I'm going to say. After this introduction I'll start by saying that I'm in agony from morning till evening, and at night when I wake up, and the longer it is since I found out, the worse my torments are. N.N. has just left me.[1] For two days we've been seeing each other, but only with others present; we've been cold, and I've avoided a tête à tête, avoided an agonising, humiliating conversation for me, a vile, proud man, thinking as I looked at him: NN is a petite brebis de Dieu—but in vain. Now we have had this agonising conversation. It was the same thing all the time: acknowledgment on his part that he had felt for a long time that it was bad, and on my part suffering at what he was saying. Before telling you how our conversation ended I'll tell you what I now think about it all with a clear mind. It's all à lang fea [*sic*]—the longer it lasts the more it astonishes me. When I first got to know about it, I didn't realise all the awfulness of the situation, as is usually the case when you get to know about some awful disaster, but the longer it has lasted, the clearer has the significance of it all become. The matter is simple, clear, and, to put it crudely, amounts to this: you have entered into exceptionally close relations—relations only entered into by people who are deeply in love, relations which never remain static but always develop, becoming stronger and more intimate and leading to lawful or unlawful marriage—with a man who is despised and hated even by all your closest relations, a man with a not very good past, a man who doesn't have the main attributes of manliness which arouse real love in a woman, and a man who is married. Masha told me that you regard him as unmarried. That is wrong. The fact that he is married imparts a special pungency to the evil feeling that is latent. And then, can it be right for you to be above these considerations about his marriage when, in the eyes of the world, you cannot be above society and its conventions.

2. A Baptist sect.
[395] 1. Y. I. Popov, now in love with Tatyana. Popov was separated from his wife, and Tolstoy viewed Tatyana's growing attachment to him with alarm.

These relations are so close, and the man's personality such, that you can't help but be ashamed even to admit to them now. You can't help but be ashamed of your letters and your appeal to him. And when I remember what you were like when I saw you near him in Dolgy Street, the blood rushes to my heart from a strange mixed feeling of pity for you, and shame for you and for me. It's an incomprehensible, diabolical delusion. He retracts everything, i.e. he admits the justice of my opinion; he agrees to everything, and I have asked him not to write to you (I hope you won't write to him), not to see you, and to tell me everything that concerns you. As it was, he wanted to write to you to tell you not to write, and so on indefinitely. I advise you to burn all diaries and letters, to look on this episode as an example of how craftily the devil can ensnare us, and to be on your guard against him in future. Life is great, and you have much that is good ahead of you. Why ruin it? You told me to ask his permission to read his diaries. I forgot to ask, and I don't feel like asking, because I don't feel like reading them, I don't feel like suffering once again the agonising pain of pity for you, such a pure, serene, cheerful and honourable woman, or of seeing you wallowing in this slime of vague, insincere, deceitful and downright evil feelings. However, I shall ask him—we parted amicably—and he will probably let me read them, and I'll do so. And I'm sure that reading them will explain to me the path you have taken. Well, forgive me, darling, and don't punish me for the outspokenness of this letter by not trusting me in future. For God's sake, always be just as open with me. I'm ready to suffer 100 times more (and what sufferings! it's not just words), as long as I don't lose you. I kiss you, my dear Tanya, very tenderly, and I ask you to forgive me if I have offended you.

396. To N. S. LESKOV

Yasnaya Polyana, 14 May 1894

Nikolay Semyonovich,

I have recently had to use conventional epithets in letters so obviously untruthfully that I have decided once and for all not to use any at all, and so I shall not now put in front of your name one of those epithets expressing sympathy and respect which I could address to you with complete sincerity.

What I wrote about inventions being repugnant to me oughtn't to be applied to other people, but only applies to me, and only at a certain time and in a certain mood, the mood in which I wrote to you at the time.[1] Moreover there are inventions and inventions. Inventions which lead nowhere can be repugnant. This was never so with you before, and even less so now than ever. And so in reply to your question[2] I say that I only wish for your activity to continue, although this wish doesn't exclude another one, natural to us all, for ourselves and therefore for

---

[396] 1. In an earlier letter to Leskov, Tolstoy had complained that he was unable to continue a story (*Who is Right?*) which was only invention, and bore no relation to real life.
    2. Leskov had asked Tolstoy for his advice on what he should write.

396. To N. S. Leskov

people we love, that they, and therefore their work, should constantly improve right until their death, and should become more and more important and necessary to people and more acceptable to God. It's always frightening when I say this about myself, close as I am to death, because I feel more and more that I'm taking all sorts of rubbish out of my bag, imagining that people need it, and suddenly it will turn out that I've forgotten to shake out the most important and necessary thing that has got stuck in a corner. And the bag which has served its purpose will be thrown into the dung, and the one good thing in it will perish to no avail. For God's sake don't think that this is false humility. The likes of us who enjoy public fame can most easily fall into this error; you are sure that what people praise in you is the very thing that God needs, while what God really needs will be left to rot.

This is frightening for all of us old people, and for you as well, I think. And so we are awestruck in the face of death, and need to grope about carefully in every corner. And we still have a lot left there that is good.

Goodbye for now. I want this letter to reach you in Petersburg—and in good physical and mental condition.

Lev Tolstoy

397. To D. A. KHILKOV

Yasnaya Polyana, 14(?) May 1894

[18 lines omitted]...You write about your wife's plan to go abroad and petition from there.[1] I think this is impracticable, expensive and, most important, will lead nowhere. It seems to me that the likes of us will fare just as badly, or just as well, abroad, with the Germans, French, Italians or English, as we would in Russia. Their distance from Christianity is just as great as ours, though in a different direction. And so I'm glad when you say you don't wish to go abroad. Your relations with your wife, like all relations between husbands and wives generally speaking in our time (in our time particularly, I think. I don't like to talk about the peculiarities of our time, but there is something peculiar about relations between husbands and wives, between men and women, in all Christian countries, among rich and poor alike)—your relations, then, with your wife, it seems to me, have been ruined by the spirit, not merely of recalcitrance, but of hostility, of women towards men, of irritability, of the wish to show they are no worse than men and can do everything men can do, and at the same time the absence of a moral, religious feeling which has been replaced in women, when it was there, by a maternal feeling. I think that women are completely equal to men, but as soon as they get married and become mothers, there is a natural division of labour between the married couple. Maternal feelings absorb so much spiritual energy that there isn't enough of it left for moral leadership, and the leadership passes naturally to the husband. This has always been so as long as we've known the world. But now, when after the abuse of this natural order of things, the leadership of men has been

[397] 1. To recover her children. See Letter 389, note 6.

asserted by crude violence, and women have been liberated by Christianity and, furthermore, exasperated by all sorts of stupidities about equal rights (which they don't need and which no reasonable man wants to deprive them of), women have ceased to obey men out of fear and haven't yet begun—not to obey, but to offer men the leadership in life—out of the awareness that it is better that way, and we have begun to get the confusion and disorganisation of life which is noticeable in all strata of society and under all sorts of conditions...[32 lines omitted]

398. To P. M. TRETYAKOV

Yasnaya Polyana, 7–14 June 1894

Pavel Mikhaylovich,

5 days have already gone by since I learnt about Gay's death, and I still can't come to my senses. This man combined for me two beings, three even: (1) one of the dearest, purest and finest men I ever knew, (2) a friend who loved and was loved tenderly not only by me, but by all my family, old and young, and (3) one of the greatest artists, I don't say of Russia, but of the whole world. It's about this third aspect of Gay's importance that I wanted to convey my thoughts to you. Please don't think my friendship has blinded me: firstly, I'm sufficiently old and experienced to be able to distinguish feelings from criticism, and secondly there's no reason for me to ascribe to him, out of friendship, such a great importance in art: it would be enough for me to extol him as a man, which I do, and which is far more important. If I'm mistaken, then I'm not mistaken out of friendship, but because I have a false conception of art. According to the conception I have of art, Gay is, among modern artists I know, both Russian and foreign, just like a Mont Blanc among ant-hills. I'm afraid this comparison will seem strange and incorrect to you, but if you adopt my point of view you will agree with me. In art, apart from sincerity—i.e. the fact that an artist shouldn't pretend to like what he doesn't like and believe what he doesn't believe, as many ostensibly religious painters now pretend—apart from this feature which Gay had in the highest degree, there are two sides to art: form-technique, and content-thought. Form-technique has been evolved in our time to great perfection, and an enormous number of masters of technique have recently appeared, now that teaching has become more accessible to the masses, and more will appear in time; but people with a mastery of content, i.e. of artistic ideas, i.e. of the shedding of new light on important problems of life—such people have become fewer and fewer as technique which satisfied immature dilettantes has improved, and have recently become so few that not only all our exhibitions but also foreign *salons* are full, either of pictures which strive after outward effects, or landscapes, portraits, nonsensical genre-painting and invented historical or religious pictures like those of Uhde, Béraud or our own Vasnetsov.[1]

[398] 1. Fritz Uhde, a contemporary German painter, and Jean Béraud, a Russian-born French artist, both painted subjects from the Gospels in which Christ was portrayed in an ordinary, realistic manner. Vasnetsov, one of the 'Wanderers' group, is perhaps best known for his

398. To P. M. Tretyakov

There are no pictures of sincere heart-felt content. But Gay is the main force when it comes to sincerity, and to content which is significant, very clear and accessible to all. It is said that his technique is weak, but that isn't true. Technique always seems poor in a picture which is full of content, especially for those who don't understand the content. And that has constantly happened with Gay. The ordinary public demands icons of Christ to which it can pray, but he gives it the living Christ, and the result is disappointment and dissatisfaction, as though a man was expecting to have a drink of wine, and people poured some water into his mouth, and the man spat out the water, although water is better and more health-giving than wine. I have been to your gallery three times this winter, and every time I couldn't help stopping in front of *What is Truth?* quite independently of my friendship with Gay, and forgetting that it was his picture. This same winter I have had two clever and educated peasant visitors, so-called Molokans, one from Samara and the other from Tambov. I advised them to go round to your gallery, and both of them, despite the fact that I told them nothing about Gay's picture and both of them went at different times—both of them were most of all impressed by Gay's picture *What is Truth?*

I'm telling you my opinion in order to advise you to acquire all that is left of Gay's work, so that your gallery, i.e. the Russian national gallery, should not be deprived of the works of the very best painter in the history of Russian painting.

I'm very sorry not to have seen you this winter. I wish you all the best.

Yours affectionately,
L. Tolstoy

399. To M. L. TOLSTAYA

Marya Lvovna Tolstaya (1871–1906), Tolstoy's second daughter. While still a girl she was strongly attracted by her father's ideals, and remained very close to him in spirit. A convert to vegetarianism, she shared his love of country life and hard work, and his concern for the underprivileged. She taught the local peasant children, nursed the sick and assisted her father in innumerable ways, copying his manuscripts and letters, working in the fields and helping him during the famine relief campaigns. She even wore shoes made by him, and out of respect for his views on the private ownership of land, refused to accept her share of the estate when he divided it up among his family in 1891. It was a great sadness to Tolstoy when she eventually decided to marry the penniless and somewhat indolent Prince Obolensky and was forced to reclaim her portion of the inheritance which her mother had prudently put aside for her. Her married life proved happier than her father had feared, despite a series of miscarriages (from which her elder sister Tatyana also suffered). In 1901 she and her husband accompanied Tolstoy and his wife to the Crimea where she was a great help to him in his illness and convales-

---

paintings on Russian historical and folk-lore themes, and for his decoration of the interior of St Vladimir Cathedral in Kiev.

cence. Her death at the early age of 35 was a grievous blow to him, for not only was she his favourite child, but, as Sofya Andreyevna wrote, 'of all our family she loved Lev the most'.

Yasnaya Polyana, 30 August 1894

Masha dear, here is a letter from Leonila Fominichna[1] which Velikanov brought— a good and wise one, as usual. Do reply to it. Did Tanya send on to you the letter from your Zinovyev? I was glad to read your letter. A state of prayer is a great happiness.

After a cold night the sky, obscured by light clouds, is still and warm today, but you can feel the freshness of the night, and the grass and the leaves are bright green. It's quiet in the woods; only the shrieking of hawks. The fields are deserted. Winter crops are coming through on ploughland bare of grass like thick green stubble, in places coloured, in places completely green. Cobwebs are beginning to appear. Underfoot there are leaves and mushrooms, and the stillness is such that any sound is frightening. I went out to look for saffron milk-caps and found none, but I felt happy all the time. Sometimes there would be a flood of good, lucid coherent thoughts (once I seemed to see the whole of my present work, the catechism),[2] and at other times none at all, only a happy feeling of gratitude.

We talked to Tanya about Ovsyannikovo,[3] and I very much want to arrange things for her there so that the money for the land should go to serve the community à la Henry George. We're on friendly terms with everybody, and we often think about you. I kiss you both. Andryusha, it seems, has weakened. Misha has apparently come to his senses.

400. To COUNTESS S. A. TOLSTAYA

Yasnaya Polyana, 15 September 1894

Masha wants to go to Kozlovka, so here I am writing to tell you that in spite of the cold and the rain, everything is quite all right: the children, big and small, are perfectly well; now—after lunch—they are going mushrooming. Masha assures me that she saw a lot of mushrooms yesterday among the fir trees near Poruchik, but nanny denies it. They are going all the same and are very happy. Sasha and Vanichka have just been on the floor looking at a map of the world, and trying to find out where Patagonia is, where Captain Grant's children went,[1] and Korea, where I told them there was a war on. Yesterday evening I was unwell, and felt cold, and I went upstairs and started to play Haydn with Miss Welsh[2] to get warm. I did

[399] 1. L. F. Annenkova, a Kursk landowner.
   2. *Christian Teaching*, as it was eventually called.
   3. Tatyana's property, which she agreed to rent, and to reinvest the money in accordance with the 'Henry George system', as understood by her father.

[400] 1. In Jules Verne's novel *Les enfants du capitaine Grant*.
   2. Hannah Welsh, an English governess and music teacher at Yasnaya Polyana during the summer months from 1894 to 1900.

400. To Countess S. A. Tolstaya

get warm, but I think it was unpleasant to listen to. I feel very fit today and have been writing very well.

Masha couldn't sleep until 2 o'clock yesterday, for fear of a rat which was scrambling about under the bed. And there was one under Miss Welsh's sheet. And I found a dead mouse in the middle of the room. Yesterday j'ai passé un mauvais quart d'heure. A student from Kharkov turned up in the evening in uniform; he had come on foot from Tula in the rain where, according to him, he was stranded and unable to travel on to Kharkov—he was travelling from Petersburg—and he asked me to give him 10 roubles. I was probably 10 times more harrassed than he was, hesitating whether to give anything or not, and in the end I did, and I felt angry and ashamed. All last night I dreamed my usual dream that I was doing military service as a cadet, this time in the uhlans, and my uniform was dirty and everything was wrong and everyone was laughing at me. And I dreamed about Andryusha on a bicycle. I thought about him and Misha. They have a great many worldly goods: because of that there is no time or inclination to bother about spiritual ones. A peasant came to ask me to intercede on behalf of his soldier brother who is to be tried in Tula on Saturday for letting a prisoner escape. I'll go to Tula, probably tomorrow, and the day after tomorrow Tanya and I want to go to Pirogovo. I don't know about her, but I'll go one day and come back the next. She also says only for one day, or two at the most. The house is heated here and there, and is warm. I haven't found out about the bricks yet, but I'll go to Tula today and get someone to find out from the architect. Well, that's all. I kiss you all.

401. To V. G. CHERTKOV

Yasnaya Polyana, 19 October 1894

My dear Vladimir Grigoryevich,

My diary for 1884 has just come into my hands in Masha's room[1] (she's going to send you a box of papers tomorrow, and was getting them out for some reason). Reading it aroused in me a very painful feeling of shame, remorse and fear for the grief which a reading of these diaries may cause to the people about whom such bad and cruel things are said in many places. It's unpleasant—more than unpleasant, it's painful—that these diaries have been read by people other than you—even by the person who copied them—painful because everything that was written in them was written under the impression of the moment, and was often terribly cruel and unjust, and furthermore because they speak about the sort of intimate relations

---

[401] 1. Tolstoy had given Chertkov his diary for 1884 ten years previously, and Chertkov had copied it out in full, keeping the original under lock and key elsewhere and retaining copies for himself. When seriously ill in the summer of 1894, he gave these copies to Masha Tolstaya for safe-keeping. Masha read the diary, which contained some very harsh comments about her mother and her brothers. When Tolstoy discovered this, he wrote this letter to Chertkov, asking to have the original returned and all copies destroyed. Chertkov's reply asked for a reprieve until winter when he could personally retrieve the original which was locked up in an inaccessible place in a friend's home in Petersburg.

which it was vile and odious of me to record, and still more odious to allow anyone except myself to read. You will surely understand me and agree with me, and help me to destroy everything that has been copied, and leave the original with me; if I don't destroy it, at least it will be together with all my other recent diaries, from which it will be obvious how I wrote them and how I changed my views of the people I wrote about. As it is, I am horrified at the thought of the use which enemies may make of words and expressions in this diary directed against people mentioned there. I don't know whether Masha will send you the box tomorrow; I would advise her not to send it, at least not the diary. I see that everything has already been copied out of it, and so you no longer need it. But if she does send it, please destroy it. Forgive me if you find my letter unpleasant. But enter into my situation, put yourself in my position with love, and you will see that I must do this.

My two daughters and I are living here now, the three of us together. I'm still busy with the same thing. I'll write and tell you shortly what suffering this writing has caused me.[2] I shan't have time for anything today apart from saying that I got your last letter and that I constantly think about you and love you. It's good that your work is progressing—perhaps is already finished.

The Emperor's illness moves me very much. I'm very sorry for him. I'm afraid that it's hard for him to die and I hope God will find him and he will find the way to God, despite all the obstacles which the conditions of his life have placed between him and God.

Tolstoy

I've extracted the diary and am keeping it here. When you send the original which I suppose you have, I'll destroy this copy. Please don't let anybody copy the diaries you have, but copy out thoughts of a general nature and send the diaries to me. How many exercise books do you have?—I've changed my mind again: I'm sending you the diary but please destroy it.

402. To ERNEST CROSBY

Ernest Crosby (1856–1906), an American social reformer and Tolstoyan. He was trained as a lawyer and served in the New York State Assembly and later as a judge in the International Court in Egypt. He resigned his post after becoming acquainted with Tolstoy's religious and ethical works, and returned to America in order to live in accordance with his beliefs. In 1891 Crosby had written to Tolstoy expressing agreement with his principles, and before returning to America he visited him at Yasnaya Polyana in May 1894. Tolstoy suggested to him that he should collaborate with Henry George over tax reform, which he subsequently did, as well as working for pacifism and arranging for an American edition of *Resurrection*.

Crosby's numerous writings on Tolstoy include an article on his 1894 visit, 'Two Days with Count Tolstoy', and a book, *Tolstoy and His Message* (1903).

2. *Christian Teaching*.

402. To Ernest Crosby

Tolstoy wrote an introductory essay for Crosby's book *Shakespeare's Attitude toward the Working Class* (1902).

[Original in English]

Moscow, 24 November 1894

Dear Mr Crosby,

I write to you this letter only to tell you that Mr Vladimir Tchertkoff, of whom I am sure, you have heard from me, and who will address you on behalf of some literary matters, i.e. about publications of some translations of my writings, is a very dear friend of mine, and you will oblige me in helping him in his work.

From a letter that I received from a contributor to the 'Labour Prophet',[1] I guess that you have communicated my opinion about his paper to the editor. I thank you for it, because I appreciate very much his work and I wish him to know it.

Henry George has sent me all his books. I know some of them, but some others, as the 'Perplexed Philosopher' and others, were new to me.[2] The more I know of him, the more I esteem him, and am astonished at the indifference of the civilized world to his work.

If the new Tsar were to ask me what I would advise him to do, I would say to him: use your autocratic power to abolish the land property in Russia and to introduce the single tax system; and then give up your power and the people a liberal constitution.

I write this to you, because I know that you are one of the coworkers of H. George, and that you hold his ideas.

I wish you success in your work.

Yours truly,
Leo Tolstoy

[402] 1. *The Labour Prophet. The Organ of the Labour Church*, edited by John Trevor and published in Manchester.

2. Henry George (see Letter 423) had sent three of his books with an American journalist, V. N. MacGachan, who visited Yasnaya Polyana in August 1894: *The Perplexed Philosopher*, *The Irish Land Question* and *Protection or Free Trade*. The first is a study of Herbert Spencer and the land question.

VIII
1895–1902

The end of the nineteenth century saw the publication of three outstanding works by Tolstoy: the short story *Master and Man*, the stimulating, irritating and iconoclastic *What is Art?*, and the last of his three major novels, *Resurrection*. For a man in his late sixties and early seventies this was a remarkable achievement, especially when set against the background of a family life, unsettled by Tolstoy's absurd jealousy of his wife's platonic friendship with the composer Taneyev, his stern disapproval of his sons' dissipated behaviour, and his concern that his daughters were actually showing signs of wanting to get married.

Tolstoy's public activity was channelled almost exclusively into the campaign on behalf of the Dukhobors, victims of religious persecution in the south of Russia, most of whom were eventually resettled in Canada largely as a result of his efforts and of the financial proceeds of *Father Sergey* and *Resurrection*. In his seventieth year he was busy organising aid for the starving peasants of the Tula province. Three years later he was excommunicated from the Orthodox Church for his heretical beliefs and writings, and retaliated with *A Reply to the Holy Synod's Edict*. Shortly afterwards he became seriously ill, and was persuaded to move to the Black Sea coast of the Crimea to the luxurious house of the wealthy Countess Panina. He and his wife spent nearly a year there until he was well enough to return to Yasnaya Polyana in the summer of 1902. Despite his serious illness, he continued to work as and when he could, his most important essay being *What is Religion?* At the same time he wrote a long letter to the Tsar on the evils of autocracy and coercion, and appealed to him to abolish the private ownership of land. His correspondence increased rather than diminished with the advance of old age, and his energy remained formidable (he was still strong enough for horse-riding, bicycling and tennis), but from the time of his return from the Crimea there was always a doctor living in the house, despite his well-known dislike of the medical profession. He published no more works of fiction in his lifetime, but his posthumous publications show that his creative energy had by no means dried up, and in 1902 he was still busy working on his novel *Hadji Murat* and his last play *The Light Shineth in Darkness*.

403. To N. N. STRAKHOV

Moscow, 27–8 January 1895

Dear Nikolay Nikolayevich,

Thank you very much for sending the book.[1] I'll certainly read what you indicate and probably read it all. I'm sending some heavily corrected proofs to you.[2] Please don't let them be printed in a messy condition. I ought to look over them again after you. I'm also writing to Gurevich to ask for some more to be sent. If you will be kind enough to look through them once again and correct anything wrong, I shall be very grateful. I don't like the story. And I sense disapproval in your opinion. Please write everything you have to say about the story as harshly as you like, as though it were not to me. I want to know whether my talent has declined or not. And if it has, it will grieve and surprise me as little as the fact that I can't run as well now as I could 40 years ago.

Well, goodbye for now. I kiss you.

L. Tolstoy

[Postscript omitted]

404. To N. N. STRAKHOV

Moscow, 14 February 1895

[19 lines omitted; only postscript translated]

Tear off and burn what I write on this sheet, namely this: my story[1] has caused a great deal of unhappiness. Sofya Andreyevna was very upset that I gave it to *The Northern Herald* for nothing, and added to this she had an almost crazy fit of jealousy towards Gurevich (which has no semblance of a foundation). This coincided with women's troubles, and we have all suffered some dreadful days. She was near to suicide, and it's now only the second day since she regained control of herself and came to her senses. As a result, she has published an announcement that the story will come out in her edition,[2] and as a result has written to you to ask Gurevich for a fee, and to give it to the writers' fund.

I'm writing to you as an old friend to explain my position, and to ask you to put in a word of explanation somewhere for the fact that the story is being published simultaneously in her edition and in *The Intermediary*. I think that this is fair, and thus prevents the exclusive use of the story by *The Northern Herald* for nothing. If you write to me about this, write in such a way that it won't be seen that I have written to you.

[403] 1. Strakhov's new book, *Philosophical Essays*.
2. Proofs of *Master and Man*, to be published in *The Northern Herald*, edited by L. Y. Gurevich.

[404] 1. *Master and Man*.
2. The story eventually came out in three editions in March 1895: *The Northern Herald*, volume XIV of Tolstoy's *Collected Works* published by Sofya Andreyevna, and *The Intermediary*.

405. To D. A. KHILKOV

Moscow, 12 March 1895

[53 lines omitted]...Recently, for the last couple of weeks, I have written nothing. I want to finish the catechism,[1] but the further I get into it, the shorter, clearer, more accessible and more incontrovertible I want it to be. And this is very difficult, and I'm afraid I've taken on a task beyond my powers. I also want to finish some artistic works which I've begun. They all seem necessary to me. I counted them up only today and it turns out that there are 9 altogether.[2] Obviously I shall never finish them. I've also been occupied recently with compiling a programme of publications for what we call *The International Intermediary*. We aim to publish in Switzerland, in one format and under one title, various books and pamphlets in 4 languages—Russian, German, French and English—in the cheapest possible way, which (1) elucidate the meaning of life, (2) indicate the lack of correspondence between the forms of life and its meaning and (3) indicate means of establishing such a correspondence, not by revolution or by the state, but by every individual person changing his own life. I've been prompted to do this mainly by the fact that in recent times, to my great joy, groups of people have been springing up, not only in Russia but in various parts of Europe, who are in complete agreement with our views and with one another, although they all look at things from their own particular aspect. Such are Kenworthy and Morrison[3] and their circle in England, Schmitt and the Religion des Geistes association in Budapest,[4] Grunsky in Stuttgart,[5] Järnefelt in Finland[6] and a circle of doctors in Hungary—Makovitsky[7] who

---

[405] 1. *Christian Teaching* (begun the previous year, much revised and not finished until 1896).
 2. List from Tolstoy's diary, 12 March (some of these titles only denote plans for the future):
  (a) Koni's story (i.e. *Resurrection*)
  (b) *Who is Right?*
  (c) *Father Sergey*
  (d) *The Devil in Hell* (i.e. *The Destruction of Hell and its Rebuilding*)
  (e) *The Coupon* (i.e. *The False Coupon*)
  (f) *The Diary of a Mother*
  (g) *Alexander I* (i.e. *The Posthumous Memoirs of Fyodor Kuzmich*)
  (h) a play (i.e. *The Light Shineth in Darkness*)
  (i) *The Settlers and the Bashkirs*
 3. John Kenworthy, see Letter 420; John Morrison Davidson, see Letter 462.
 4. Eugen Heinrich Schmitt, an Austrian writer who shared many of Tolstoy's ethical beliefs and hoped to systematise them; he considered himself an anarchist, but Tolstoy had certain reservations about his ideas. In 1894–5 he published the journal *Religion des Geistes* in Budapest, for which he solicited Tolstoy's participation. He translated some of Tolstoy's articles into German and corresponded with him from 1894 to 1910. He also wrote a book *Leo Tolstoi und seine Bedeutung für unsere Kultur* (1901).
 5. Karl Grunsky, editor of the journal *Neues Leben* in Stuttgart.
 6. Arvid Järnefelt. See Letter 538.
 7. Dushan Petrovich Makovitsky—a Hungarian Slovak doctor, educated at the University of Prague, and a dedicated Tolstoyan. He was Tolstoy's personal doctor and lived at Yasnaya Polyana from 1904 to 1910. During this period he opened a surgery for peasants on the estate and in neighbouring villages. He took copious notes on Tolstoy's conversations which served as the basis for a later book, *Yasnaya Polyana Diary* (Moscow, 1922). He accompanied Tolstoy to Astapovo in 1910. In 1921 he returned to Hungary after marrying a Yasnaya Polyana peasant girl, and died there in 1922.

405. To D. A. Khilkov

was here and Škarvan[8] who recently refused to do military service and was put in a lunatic asylum for it. What do you think of such a publication? What do you think generally? I miss having contact with you. Give my regards to Tsetsiliya Vladimirovna. How is she? I would also like to know about her state of mind and way of life. Goodbye for now.

Always yours affectionately,
L. Tolstoy

406. To COUNTESS A. A. TOLSTAYA

Moscow, 31 March 1895

Sonya began writing this letter the day before yesterday, but didn't finish it, and yesterday she fell ill with influenza and is still feeling unwell today, and asked me to finish it. And I'm very glad to do so, my dear, beloved old friend. Sonya's physical condition is apparently not dangerous or serious; but her mental anguish is very serious, although I think that not only is it not dangerous, but that it's even beneficial and joyful, like a confinement, like being born to a spiritual life. Her grief is very great. She used to take refuge from everything in life that was painful, incomprehensible and vaguely worrying to her, in her love, her passionate and reciprocated love, for this boy who was truly exceptionally endowed, both spiritually and emotionally.[1] (He was one of those children who are prematurely sent by God into a world not yet ready for them, one of those ahead of their time, like swallows arriving too early and freezing to death.) And suddenly he was taken away from her, and, notwithstanding her motherhood, it was as though nothing was left to her in this worldly life. And in spite of herself, she has been brought to the necessity of raising herself to another, spiritual world in which she hasn't lived before. And it's amazing how motherhood has kept her pure and alive to the perception of spiritual truths. She astonishes me by her spiritual purity—particularly her humility. She is still seeking, but so sincerely and with all her heart, that I'm sure she will find. What is good about her is the fact that she is obedient to the will of God, and only asks Him to teach her how to live without the being in whom she invested the whole power of her love; and so far she doesn't know how to do so. This loss was painful to me, but I don't feel it nearly as much as Sonya, firstly because I had and have another life, a spiritual one, and secondly because Sonya's grief prevents me from seeing my own deprivation, and because I see that something great is taking place in her soul, and I feel sorry for her and am troubled by her condition. Generally speaking, I can say that I'm well.

These past days Sonya has been fasting in preparation for communion, together with the children and Sasha, who prays in a touchingly earnest way, fasts and reads the Gospels. Poor thing, she was very painfully afflicted by this death. But I

---

8. Albert Škarvan, a Slovak friend of Dushan Makovitsky. See Letter 546.

[406] 1. Tolstoy's youngest son Ivan (Vanyushka) died on 23 February, a month before his seventh birthday.

think it's good. She took communion today, but Sonya couldn't as she was ill. Yesterday she went to confession to a very intelligent priest, Father Valentin (my sister Masha's friend and confessor), who put it well to Sonya that mothers who have lost their children always turn to God initially, but then return again to the cares of the world and again move away from God, and he warned her against this. I don't think this will happen in her case.

How glad I am that your health is better or is getting better. Perhaps, God willing, we shall see each other again. I'd like that very much.

How many times before have I asked myself, as many people ask: why do children die? And I've never found an answer. Recently, without thinking of children at all, but thinking of my own life and human life in general, I became convinced that the only task of every person's life is to increase the love within him, and by increasing the love within him to infect others with it and increase the love in them. And now that life itself has posed me the question: why did this little boy live and die without having lived through even a tenth part of a normal person's life?—the universal answer for all people that I've arrived at, without thinking of children at all, not only fits this death, but is confirmed as correct by what has happened to all of us. He lived to increase the love within him, to grow in love, since this was required by Him who sent him, and to infect all of us around him with this same love, so that when departing this life to join Him who is love, he could leave behind in us the love that had grown in him and unite us with it. We have none of us ever felt as close to each other as we do now, and I have never felt either in Sonya or in myself such a need for love and such an aversion towards all disunity and evil. I have never loved Sonya as much as I do now. And I feel good because of it.

Goodbye, my dear, beloved friend, and forgive me for always writing about myself and my family. Write us a line about yourself. Sonya and I and all the children kiss you.

L. Tolstoy

407. To V. G. CHERTKOV

Moscow, 26 April 1895

[22 lines omitted]...As I wrote to you, I am doing nothing; reading, making a few notes and learning to ride a bicycle. The treatment is continuing. Both things—the bicycle and the treatment—trouble my conscience, but the treatment more so. I wanted to give it up, but Sonya asked me, and I don't know whether I'm doing it only for her sake. The bicycle doesn't trouble me, despite the reproaches, very useful ones, of Yevgeny Ivanovich, firstly because I'm not wasting any money on it and secondly because, when I'm carting water, I always feel glad when people see me, but when they see me on a bicycle I feel ashamed...[17 lines omitted]

408. To T. M. BONDAREV

Timofey Mikhaylovich Bondarev (1820–98), a peasant, a religious sectarian and the author of a book *The Triumph of the Farmer, or Hard Work and Slothfulness* which Tolstoy admired for the clarity of its ideas about land-ownership and manual labour, and for which he wrote a preface.

Yasnaya Polyana, 19–26 August 1895

[12 lines omitted]...Everywhere abroad where *enlightened* peoples live, the land has been taken away from the farmers and is owned by those who don't work on it. Only among savage, *unenlightened* people is the land considered to be God's property and owned by those who work on it. That's why it's necessary to show people that what they consider enlightenment is not enlightenment but obfuscation, and that as long as they own land and buy and sell it, they are worse than any savages, idolators or brigands. This is what I want to show people as clearly as possible before I die. And this is what I'm writing about now...[8 lines omitted]

409. To N. V. STASOVA

Nadezhda Vasilyevna Stasova (1822–95), sister of Tolstoy's old friend, the art and literary critic V. V. Stasov. As an active member of a society which sought to obtain greater rights for women in higher education and which was planning to establish reading rooms and libraries in Petersburg, she wrote to Tolstoy hoping to obtain his approval and practical advice.

Yasnaya Polyana, 4 September 1895

Please forgive me, Nadezhda Vasilyevna, if you find what I'm going to say to you about your society unpleasant. I have never seen anything real come of a society with a charter and royal approval etc., and so I don't think anything will come of your society either. The fact that many very harmful and deeply rooted prejudices against women and their work exist is absolutely true, and it's even more true that it's necessary to fight against them. But I don't think that a society in Petersburg which will establish reading rooms and premises for women is the way to fight them. I am not disturbed by the fact that a woman gets a lower salary than a man: prices are determined by the cost of labour. And if the government gives a man more than a woman, it's not that it gives the woman too little, but that it gives the man too much. I am disturbed by the fact that the woman who carries, feeds and brings up young children has the additional burden laid on her of kitchen work, cooking at the stove, washing the dishes, doing the laundry, making clothes, and washing tables, floors and windows. Why is all this terribly heavy burden laid solely on the woman? There are times when the peasant, the factory worker, the civil servant or any man at all has nothing to do, but he'll lie down and smoke and leave it to the woman—often pregnant, or ill, or with children—(and the woman submits)—to cook at the stove or bear the terrible burden of doing the laundry or looking after a sick child at night. And all this because of the superstition that it's somehow a woman's work.

This is a terrible evil and the cause of innumerable illnesses of unhappy women, premature old age, death or the stupefaction of the women and their children.

This is what one needs to fight against by word and deed and example.

Forgive me for giving a different answer, perhaps, from the one you wanted.

Yours truly,
L. Tolstoy

410. To L. L. TOLSTOY

Yasnaya Polyana, 4 September 1895

I haven't written to you for a long time, Lyova, and I would like to talk to you, although there's nothing particular to write about and probably mama, in her masterly way, has described to you all our external affairs. With regard to your questions about what you should do—Sweden or the Isle of Wight—I have no opinion. Your illness will disappear, in my opinion, not as a result of treatment or doctors or even the climate, but because the time will come for it to disappear, as with all illnesses which do disappear. If you have to choose, I would advise you to choose what is simpler, less worry and expense, and involves you less in an atmosphere of people undergoing treatment. All health resorts have this failing that everybody in them is occupied with his own ailments, and you can't help learning to ascribe to health or ill-health more importance than it deserves. You don't write anything about your inner life. What are you thinking, reading and writing? No doubt the time since we saw each other has been filled up with something. I can't boast about anything myself during that time. I've been working on my story[1] continuously, and I don't think it was worth spending the time on it. I have been heartily sick of it recently,[2] the more so since, standing as I do at the edge of the grave, I have, I think, many thoughts which are more serious and necessary to people. But it's started and I want to finish it, but the time drags on.

Chekhov has been staying with us and I liked him.[3] He is very gifted and he has a kind heart, no doubt, but so far he has no definite point of view.

[410] 1. *Resurrection*.

2. At the beginning of September Tolstoy felt very dissatisfied with *Resurrection*, and wanted either to rewrite it entirely or abandon it. On 22 September he saw new possibilities in the story, but continued to have difficulty in writing throughout September and October; only in November did he find a new beginning (starting with Katyusha Maslova instead of Nekhlyudov) which enabled him to go on.

3. Chekhov stayed at Yasnaya Polyana on 8 and 9 August. Tolstoy gave him a draft of *Resurrection* to read and comment on. Having had some contact with courts and prisoners (on Sakhalin), Chekhov praised the truthfulness and accuracy of the draft, but remarked that prisoners sent to forced labour camps had longer sentences than the two and a half years which Tolstoy had given Maslova in this draft.

410. To L. L. Tolstoy

Andryusha distresses us.[4] He disappears into the village and is, I think in love with a peasant girl—not having an affair, but in love—they say it's Akulka Makarycheva. Things have been better recently, at least in the sense that he doesn't get angry, and talks to us gently, although he doesn't tell us what attracts him in the village. He tried to give up smoking and promised not to drink. He doesn't keep it, but it's good that he wants to. Mama is very distressed, but I hope that it's an infatuation which will pass when it has gone full circle...[15 lines omitted]

411. To M. O. MENSHIKOV

Mikhail Osipovich Menshikov (1859–1919), a journalist who was working at the time for the newspaper *The Week* and who spent a few days at Yasnaya Polyana in 1895. He subsequently turned against Tolstoy and attacked him on several occasions in print.

Yasnaya Polyana, 8 September 1895

Dear Mikhail Osipovich,

I learned from your letter that our difference of opinion is far greater than I thought.[1] I very much regret this, but I don't despair of removing it. You say that the intervention of reason doesn't contribute to the good, and that goodness depends on the practice of the good and the conditions in which people are placed. This is the very root of our difference of opinion. Firstly, reason and intelligence—Vernunft and Verstand—are two completely different attributes, and it's necessary to distinguish between them. Bismarck and people like him have a lot of intelligence, but no reason. Intelligence is the ability to understand and grasp the worldly conditions of life, but reason is the divine power of the soul which reveals to it its attitude to the world and to God. Reason is not only not the same thing as intelligence, but is the opposite of it: reason releases a man from the temptations (deceits) which intelligence puts in his way. This is the main activity of reason: by removing temptations, reason releases the essence of the human soul—love—and enables it to manifest itself. In childhood there are few temptations, and so the essence of the soul—love—is more evident in children, but *temptations are bound to come into the world*,[2] and so they do, and a return to love is only possible through the removal of temptations, and the removal of temptations is only achieved through the activity of reason. This is the fundamental idea of the Christian teach-

---

4. See Letter 415.

[411] 1. Tolstoy's letter is part of a correspondence concerning his story *Master and Man*. Menshikov had written an article about the story ('Have We Lost the Road?') which badly misinterpreted the doctrine of non-resistance to evil which served as the theme of the story. L. P. Nikiforov had seen the article and had written a refutation of it ('Where is the Road?'), first sending it to Tolstoy, who then wrote to Menshikov, trying to clarify his ideas. This is his second letter to Menshikov about the question.

2. Probably a reference to Matthew 18, 7 ('for it must needs be that offences come').

411. To M. O. Menshikov

ing, and I have tried to express it in all my writings as well as I could. That's the first point. Secondly, if goodness—love—has only increased, as you say, as a result of inherited characteristics, environment, the conditions in which a man finds himself, the practice of love—also independent of his will—then all our arguments about goodness would be completely useless. If my heredity is not good, my environment not good and the practice of my life not good, then not only do I not need any arguments about what goodness is, but, on the contrary, I need the sort of arguments which would represent my badness as goodness. And so it often happens. If there is no free activity of the reason to remove temptations in people, and thereby release in them the divine essence of their life—love; if every man is the product of the conditions surrounding him and the causes preceding him, then there is neither good nor evil, neither morality nor immorality, and there is no point in our thinking and talking and writing letters and articles, but we should *take life as it comes*, as the saying has it. If my heredity and environment are bad, I shall be bad; if they are good, I shall be good. I don't think that is so. I think that every man possesses a free, creative, divine power (For as the Father hath life in himself, so hath he given to the Son to have life in himself—John 5, 26), And this power is reason. The more this power increases, the more the essence of a man's life—love—is released within him, and the more closely is man united with other beings and with God. The aim of the life of each individual man and of all mankind is this greater and greater unity of people with each other, with the whole world and with God, which is only brought about by reason. And so the activity of reason is the highest activity of man. The Christian teaching which I profess consists in recognising this activity as life itself. That is why I can't agree with you, not only that one can and must prefer spontaneous, unreasoning goodness which constitutes the physiological attribute of certain creatures to the reasonable activity of people consciously striving to follow the dictates of reason, but I cannot even compare the two.

The goodness of a dove is not a virtue. And a dove is no more virtuous than a wolf, or the gentle Slav more virtuous than the vindictive Circassian. Virtue and the degrees of it only begin when reasonable activity begins.

I shall be very upset if my arguments don't remove our difference of opinion. But I can't agree with you, because to do so I would have to renounce all I have lived by these past 15 years, and what I live by now and what I intend to die with.

I'm sending Nikiforov's article. I meant to tone down those passages in it where he, in the heat of the argument, ascribes to you thoughts which you probably never had, but I shan't manage to do so, there's no time. It would be good if you could do it. He gave me carte blanche to change the article and I hand it on to you. It's desirable because it isn't a question of who got the better of whom in the argument, but of making the truth as clear as possible.

I press your hand in friendship.

Yours affectionately,
L. Tolstoy

[Postscript omitted]

412. To THE EDITOR OF 'THE TIMES'

Yasnaya Polyana, 10 September 1895

Dear Sir,

I am sending for publication in your newspaper a note about the persecutions to which the Caucasian sectarians, the Dukhobors have been subjected this summer.[1] There is only one way to help the persecuted, and more particularly the persecutors who know not what they do—publicity—the presentation of the case before the court of public opinion which, having expressed its disapproval of the persecutors and its sympathy for the persecuted, will restrain the former from their cruel acts, often only perpetrated out of darkness and ignorance, and keep up the spirits of the latter and give them comfort in their sufferings.

The censorship in Russia will not pass my article and so I turn to you with the request to publish it in your paper. This note was composed by a friend of mine who travelled to the spot to collect accurate information about the events that had taken place, and so the information supplied by him can be trusted.

The fact that the information communicated in this note has been obtained from one side only—the persecuted—and that the other side has not been consulted, does not lessen the reliability of what is being said. The persecuted had no reason to conceal what they were doing; they proclaim it to the whole world; but the persecutors cannot help being ashamed of the measures they have taken against the persecuted, and so will try to conceal their doings by every means. While there might have been exaggerations in the stories of the Dukhobors, we deliberately excluded everything that seemed so to us. The most important things mentioned in this note are authentic and beyond doubt, namely that the Dukhobors have been cruelly tortured in various places on numerous occasions, that a large number of them have been put in prison, and that more than 450 families have been completely ruined and driven out of their homes only because they were not willing to act contrary to their religious beliefs. All this is undoubtedly authentic, because it has been pub-

---

[412] 1. In 1895, having learned of the renewed persecution of the Dukhobors, Tolstoy asked Biryukov to go to the Caucasus to investigate the situation and to collect material for a study of the Dukhobors—in particular to find out whether their way of life was actually as close to Tolstoyan ideals as it seemed. The result of this visit is the article *Persecution of Christians in Russia in 1895*, a laudatory report on Dukhobor beliefs and practices, which could not be published in Russia. Tolstoy's letter was printed in *The Times* on 23 October 1895, in an English translation by Kenworthy and Rapoport, as an introduction to Biryukov's article which appeared on the same page. It was also the subject of an editorial in the same issue.

Biryukov's information, however, was far from complete, as Aylmer Maude tells us. The Dukhobor sect had already been split for many years over the question of the recognition of P. Verigin as its leader. Biryukov, not knowing of the various internal dissensions, only visited one area of settlement, that of the most loyal Verigin followers, and consequently received a false impression of their beliefs and way of life. What could not be told to an outsider such as Biryukov by a truly believing Dukhobor was that they considered their leader to be a reincarnation of God. What Biryukov saw—and what the Dukhobors represented themselves as practising—was Christian 'anarchism', but what in fact existed was a rigidly authoritarian social and religious structure imposed by an autocratic leader. Tolstoy never had a chance to discover this for himself because he never visited any of the Dukhobor settlements.

lished in many Russian newspapers and has provoked no denial on the part of the government.

I have expressed separately the thoughts aroused in me by these events, and if you wish, I can send them to you for publication after this note has appeared.[2]

413. To N. N. STRAKHOV

Yasnaya Polyana, 5 October 1895

[10 lines omitted]...My writing has become terribly complicated and I'm sick of it[1]—it's worthless, vulgar, and above all offensive to write for the good-for-nothing parasitic intelligentsia, from whom nothing but vanity has ever come or will ever come.

I've been unwell and so I read the latest volume of *Problems of Philosophy*. How scholarly, clever and empty it all is.

Goodbye. I kiss you.

Yours affectionately,
L. Tolstoy

But there's no point in talking about the journals—everything in them is empty, brazen and false.

An American visitor came today and said that America is just like Russia only without the peasant. He meant to win me over by this. But I thought: I would have died of grief and despair long ago if it hadn't been for the peasant.

414. To T. L. TOLSTAYA

Yasnaya Polyana, 5 October 1895

It's dull without you, my dear daughters. I keep expecting one of you to come and start saying silly things; and it would be nice and comforting if you did. Our life here is better, jollier and happier without the pressure of dentists and Kartsev's apples of all varieties. Masha's last letter was good but sad. It's very autumnal here and I find it pleasant, although I haven't done any work today, only written letters and been reading the Gospels with great pleasure in Italian. You notice every word and learn a new language. It's pleasant too that there are no outsiders. Andrey is as tormenting as ever. Nightly absences or else the accordion, and a thin, sickly face and listless eyes. Shall we really have to witness the ruin of Misha as well? It's awful; if only I could hurry up and die. I shall have to soon, anyway. I've been playing duets with mama. I kiss you.

2. *The Times* omitted the last paragraph of Tolstoy's letter.
[413] 1. *Resurrection*.

415. To A. L. TOLSTOY

Tolstoy's fourth son, Andrey (1877–1916), was not yet eighteen when the following letter was written. He never completed his secondary education, spent most of his time with gipsies, and led a profligate life. The plans for marriage mentioned in the letter came to nothing. In 1899 he married Countess Olga Dieterichs, Chertkov's sister-in-law, but the marriage did not last. He later married the former wife of the governor of Tula (see Letter 547). Andrey joined the army as a volunteer in 1896, fought in the Russo-Japanese War, and was a member of the 'Black Hundred' organisation, a right-wing, anti-Semitic group which indulged in terrorist acts. Maude records that Andrey 'grieved his father in various ways'. He later held various administrative posts in Tambov and Petersburg, and died during the First World War at the age of thirty-eight.

Yasnaya Polyana, 16(?) October 1895

Andryusha,

Although I promised not to approach you any more, but to wait until you approached me for advice (and I'm still waiting for this), I'm writing to you all the same—firstly, because your situation torments me too much and I think about it incessantly; secondly, because there is a misapprehension about your understanding of the words I said to you, and it must be corrected so that neither you nor others will be misled; and thirdly, because I hope that a letter will be easier for you to read and understand properly than any words. I earnestly beg you to read attentively and think carefully about what I write.

The misapprehension which I'm talking about consists of your taking my words that in my opinion it's exactly the same whether one marries a princess or a peasant girl (I even consider a peasant girl better than a princess) to mean my agreement to your marriage to Akulina Makarova[1] in the state in which you now are. I not only cannot agree to this, but would consider my agreement or even my indifference to such an action on your part the greatest of sins against yourself, against the girl, and, most important, against God. I told you then that it's always possible and even necessary to marry if a young man feels that he can't live purely without a wife, or if he's so much in love that he loses his peace of mind and the ability to do anything, but that marriage and acquaintance with Bibikov and the Bergers[2] and drinking vodka with them and the peasants and playing the accordion have nothing in common with marriage. On the contrary, such a frame of mind and such a way of passing the time and, most important, the continual stupefying of oneself with vodka show that a man certainly can't marry while he's in such a state. In order to go shopping, to go out hunting, or to write a letter, a man must be in a sober, clear-headed state; but in order to marry, to do the most important thing in life which is only done once, one must be all the more clear-headed, and get rid of

[415] 1. A peasant girl from the village of Yasnaya Polyana.
2. V. A. Bibikov, the son of Tolstoy's old neighbour and acquaintance A. N. Bibikov; the Berger brothers—one of them later became manager of Andrey's estate of Taptykovo.

everything which might cloud one's judgement or distract one's attention. But you, on the contrary, ever since you wanted to get married, have continually done your best to stupefy yourself by every means—tobacco, vodka, the accordion, every kind of distraction which prevents you from remaining alone and at peace with your thoughts for a single minute. Thus this state of yours shows that you not only haven't thought out the significance of this action which you wish to perform, but on the contrary you don't want to think about it, you want to force yourself to forget its significance, and it also shows that it's not a question of marriage, but of an unnatural state of excitement which you are in and which you must try by all means to overcome, because such artificial excitement won't stop with marriage but will grow and grow and lead you to ruin. Therefore, I not only can't agree to your marriage now, but, on the contrary, I would consider it the most decisive step to ruin, after which a return to a good life would hardly be possible. Your marriage now in all probability would mean that—in a week's time or perhaps even earlier— you would find yourself not only with an unloved wife, but with a hated, repulsive wife round your neck (as always happens as a result of purely sensual intimacy), and in the hands of your wife's coarse and greedy parents who won't let you out of their clutches with the fortune you will have. Because of the habit you have adopted of drowning all unpleasantness in vodka, with the help of those same relatives with whom you drink even now, drunkenness will take complete control of you, and it's terrible to think of the unhappy situation which you will surely be in in two or three or at the most 5 years, i.e. in those years when you should begin to live a family life, if it's so necessary for you to marry.

And so I repeat to you what I said when I said that it's all the same whether one marries a princess or a peasant girl, namely that before thinking about any marriage at all you must calm down and get back to a normal state in which you can associate with those who are close to you, can think calmly, can refrain from offending those closest to you and, most important, can work, can do some job or other and live like that not for a week or a month but at least for a year or two. To do this, the main thing necessary is for you to stop drinking vodka, and *in order to stop drinking it—to stop associating with people who drink it.* God has given man an immortal soul and for the guidance of this soul—reason. And now man has thought up a means to stifle his reason so that his soul is left without guidance. Vodka does this, and for that reason it is not only a dreadful sin, but a dreadful deception, because a soul without guidance always leads man into a situation where he suffers terribly. You are already beginning to suffer, and I'm sure that you suffer, and suffer greatly, because you are torturing your mother (I know you have a good heart and love her) and you are suffering from the awareness of your fall which you want to conceal from yourself. Don't try to conceal it but admit it to yourself, repent before God and with His help begin a new life, and set yourself as the main aim in it your own improvement, your moral self-perfection. To attain this goal, I advise four things: (1) most important, abstinence from everything which clouds the reason, especially any alcohol; (2) association with people higher than yourself in education, intelligence, social position, even fortune, and not with those lower than yourself; (3) an

415. To A. L. Tolstoy

outward change in the conditions of your life—go away somewhere from those conditions in with you have lived badly, and don't remain in them; and, (4) abstain from amusements and distractions and don't fear boredom to begin with. This is so that you can find a job to do, start doing it, and get to like it. The devil ensnares us by wiles and we need wiles to struggle against him. These four rules are such wiles: they destroy his intrigues. However, if you want to live well, you will discover for yourself what you need. Where is a will is a way.³ If only you could understand who you are. If only you could understand that you are a son of God whom God in His love sent into the world so that you could do work that is pleasing to Him there, and that for this purpose He gave you reason and love which will certainly give you happiness, if only you develop them and don't stifle them.

Yours affectionately,
L. Tolstoy

416. To M. A. SOPOTSKO

Mikhail Arkadyevich Sopotsko (1869–?), a former medical student and follower of Tolstoy, had been expelled from the University of Moscow in 1890 for taking part in a student demonstration. After serving a prison sentence, he worked with Tolstoy during the famine years 1892–3 but was again arrested and exiled. He subsequently reversed his views, wrote several virulent articles attacking Tolstoy and Tolstoyanism, and became a member of the 'Black Hundred' organisation 'Union of the Russian People'. He emigrated in 1917. At least fifteen of Tolstoy's letters to him have survived.

Yasnaya Polyana, 28 October 1895

[10 lines omitted]…I won't answer your questions, or rather interrogation, about writing, because they are all empty questions. The one thing I can say to you and advise you is to try as hard as you can not to be a writer, or only to be one when you can no longer help being one. Just as in speech the spoken word is silver and the unspoken one gold, so in writing—I would say that the written word is tin, and the unwritten one gold. But you actually want to be a writer, to develop, as you say, your writing ability. God save you from that. Try and do this: say to yourself that you will not show what you write to anybody, and will only allow it to be published after your death, and then write. If you write on this condition, it will be real. It's real when I write primarily in order to clarify my own thoughts, to see whether I am thinking correctly, just as an inventor of a machine makes a model to find out whether he has made a mistake. It's just as obvious from the word as from the model whether a person is writing for himself, for the purpose of clarifying his own thoughts. This is the terrible difference between two kinds of writing: they stand side by side and seem to be very little different from each other (this is so with

3. The words are in English in the original.

all important things—there is the thing itself, made by God, and its likeness made by the devil to deceive people)—two kinds of writing apparently alike, but between them there is a gulf, a direct contradiction: one kind is legitimate and divine— writing written by a man in order to clarify his own thoughts—and in that case the stern judge inside one is dissatisfied until the thoughts are brought to the greatest possible clarity, and this judge assiduously rejects everything that could obscure or confuse the idea, even words, expressions or turns of speech. The other sort is diabolical, often completely like the first externally—writing written in order to obscure and confuse the truth for oneself and others, and in that case the more art, cunning, embellishments, erudition, foreign words, quotations and proverbs the better. A man only writes in the first way when a thought arises in him and apparently assumes a certain form but requires clarification, and this happens rarely: and this sort of writing is difficult, often agonising, and gives no peace and rest; but you can always write in the second way when you sit at a desk and take up a pen, especially when life is so organised that there is nothing to do apart from that, and the stoves are lit and meals and clothes are attended to by slaves; and I firmly persuaded myself that my diabolical writing which corrupted people was very useful. This is the writing which fills our, and everyone's newspapers and journals of every possible trend, and which I hate with all my soul because it is the devil's most powerful weapon. God save us from that. And so try as hard as you can *not to be a writer*, and unlearn what you have already learned of this kind of writing...[40 lines omitted]

417. To M. L. TOLSTOY

Mikhail Lvovich Tolstoy (1879–1944)—Tolstoy's youngest son to survive childhood. He volunteered for army service in the late 1890s and was a source of considerable anxiety to his father, especially before his marriage in 1901. After Tolstoy's death he emigrated to France where he lived until 1935. He eventually moved to Morocco and died there in 1944.

Yasnaya Polyana, 27–30 October 1895

Misha,

The long letter I wrote to you is too serious, lengthy and generalised, i.e. it might seem uninteresting to you now, and so I'm not sending it to you,[1] but I want to say what is most important and, I think, necessary to you, and necessary at this very time.

Your situation is bad because you are living without any religious or moral

---

[417] 1. A letter of 16–19 October which is not translated here, as it covers similar ground in an even more ponderous manner. Mikhail Tolstoy was sixteen at the time and like his brother Andrey had found a girl in the village of Yasnaya Polyana whom he thought he loved and wanted to marry.

417. To M. L. Tolstoy

principles; you don't believe in Orthodox-aristocratic or bourgeois rules of social propriety—and quite rightly so, because these rules won't last long in our time—but you don't have any other ones. And what is worst of all is that other religious and moral principles which are natural and proper to people of our time—principles by which all the best people in the world live—are hidden from you by the very fact that they are right in front of you, so that you don't see them, as one doesn't see an object which is close to one's eyes. It seems to you that everything I profess and preach is something which, though not bad, is ill-defined, vague and inapplicable. I don't think you've even glanced once at any of my books except the novels, but nevertheless I profess and preach what I profess and preach only because I consider it the most precise, clear, applicable and necessary guide for the behaviour of just such young people as yourself.

So you live without any guiding principle, except the instinct for good, under the influence of your lusts which have been inflated to terrible proportions by your luxurious and idle life. But one can't live this way, because the instinct for good is always stifled by lusts, and this type of life inevitably leads to dreadful sufferings and to the ruin of what is most precious in man—his soul, his reason. This type of life leads to ruin because, if life's happiness lies in the satisfaction of one's lusts, then as they are satisfied, one's pleasure decreases and decreases, and one must arouse newer and stronger lusts in order to obtain the same pleasure. And this increase in one's lusts always inevitably leads to the two strongest ones: women and vodka. And there lies true ruin. You will probably think a bit and say that you don't lust after women, but that you are in love. I don't know which is better: sin with a woman or being in love, as you think of it. Both are bad. If being in love is to be pure and lofty, it's necessary for both lovers to be on an equally high level of spiritual development; apart from that, being in love has a beneficial influence when, in order to attain reciprocity from the object of one's love, great efforts and achievements are needed on the part of the one who is in love, and not when, as in your case, nothing except the accordion and honey cakes is needed to attain reciprocity and, to place yourself on an equal level with the object of your love you don't have to raise yourself to her, but to lower yourself; such being in love is nothing else but hidden lust, magnified by the charm of the primitive life of the people.

The consequences of your present relationship with a peasant girl can only be these: at the worst, that you will marry without a church wedding before reaching full maturity, i.e. before the age of 21–25, and after living that way for a while and becoming coarse in mind and conscience with the aid of what is always at your service, especially in that way of life—vodka—you will separate from her, and realising that you have thereby committed a crime, you will seek forgetfulness of this crime in similar relationships with other girls, and again in vodka. This is the worst and most probable consequence—one which will complete the ruin of your soul and body.

Less bad, is that before the age of 25, i.e. before full maturity, you will marry a peasant girl in the proper way, with a church wedding, and as a consequence of

417. To M. L. Tolstoy

your immaturity and lack of firmness, you will not only fail to raise her to a higher moral level but, on the contrary, will yourself fall to the level of coarseness and immorality in which she has lived and will continue to live. Recognising your fall, you will drink or debauch yourself so as to forget, or else abandon her altogether. That is the second outcome. The third outcome, less bad again, is that you will spend the best, most energetic and most important years of your life for the development of character and habits—years in which the main progress is made in moral development and in which the foundations of one's whole life are laid—you will spend these years in an enervating, stupefying, immobilising state of being in love (which in essence is only lust disguised by the imagination) and will then wake up, having realised that you have irretrievably lost the best years of your life, weakened your best powers through acquiring the fatal habit of stupefying yourself, and lost irretrievably the possibility of future family happiness. This is the best outcome. But even this is terrible, and it is awful for me to foresee this for you. What you are probably dreaming about vaguely, without forming a clear picture of how it will come about, namely that you will marry the object of your love and will live a good life, is as improbable as winning with one ticket in a million. For this to happen it's necessary, firstly, that you should marry no earlier than the age of 21, consequently no sooner than in 5 years' time, or even 8 or 10 years; to take the average, let's say in 7 years; secondly, that in these 7 years you should stop learning to play the accordion and to dance, and should inure yourself to every form of abstinence and hard work and, in addition, should not only not sink lower in mental and moral development, but should raise and consolidate yourself so as to raise your wife in this respect too; thirdly, that you and she should live for these 7 years chastely, without ceasing to work on yourselves.

However hard this may be, and however remote from your present course in life, it is possible, and if you want to try to accomplish it, I shall only rejoice and assist you with all my strength. Only you need to begin by doing just the exact opposite of what you are doing now: to restrain yourself in everything, to work on yourself constantly, making yourself work hard either for other people or for your own perfection, and not for your own pleasure as you do now.

The need to get married is only legitimate in a man who is fully mature, and then a meeting with a woman may cause you to fall in love, i.e. to feel an exclusive love for that woman; then this feeling is natural, although even then you mustn't stimulate this feeling as you are doing, but struggle against it. At your age this is just simply over-indulgence, caused by your luxurious, idle and unprincipled life, and by the wish to imitate. Therefore what is most important, what is necessary for you now, is for you to come to your senses, to take a look at yourself and at the lives of other people, and ask yourself: what are you living for?[2] And what do you want of yourself?

To say to yourself what the animal in you prompts—that you want as much satisfaction and pleasure as possible for yourself—and that this is the goal and the

---

2. A lengthy section of the letter was deleted at this point, on Tolstoy's instructions, when his manuscript version was being copied out.

417. To M. L. Tolstoy

meaning of your life, is simply impossible for a person who hasn't yet entirely stupefied himself, who hasn't become a complete swine; it's impossible because in our rich way of life (this is our advantage) we quickly come to the end of these pleasures and see what they are leading us to—sweetmeats, rides, bicycles, theatres, etc.; they all become tiresome and one thing remains: a woman's love, in no matter what form, and vodka. Both one and the other fundamentally ruin a man's soul. You will say: why is man given this desire for a woman's love, stronger than any other, if he ought not to desire it? It is given to us, as you know, for the continuation of the species and certainly not for pleasure. Pleasure only accompanies this feeling when it isn't made the goal of life. Pleasure comes as a reward only to the man who doesn't seek it or make it the goal of his life. When a man makes it his goal in life, the absolute opposite always happens, he destroys life: you get debauchery, illness, onanism, or that stupefying state of being in love which you have succumbed to and its inevitable consequence; the crippling of body and soul and the incapacity for any type of enjoyment. Vodka, tobacco and other means of stupefaction such as the accordion invariably accompany this frame of mind because, by befogging the reason, they hide from a man the falseness of his goal. This goal is false, firstly, because its attainment destroys our lives and souls and bodies and, secondly, because this goal is a short distance away and can be attained. So, you marry the object of your love—and then what?—particularly since the object of your love grows old and inevitable disenchantment sets in.

And so the question, why are you living and what do you want of yourself, must certainly not be answered: for pleasure; but one must inevitably establish another goal in life, one which, firstly, will not ruin the life and soul and body given to you and, secondly, can always be attained but never fully attained, so that you can always strive towards it while you are living, and constantly get nearer to it. There is only one such goal towards which every man is involuntarily drawn, and which is natural, not only to you at 16 but to me at 67, and satisfies me as equally as it can satisfy you, and its attainment cannot be impeded by anything. I don't want to say it, I would like you yourself to name this goal—you will surely guess that the only important and joyful thing in which no one can ever hinder us and which can never be entirely finished so that there should be nothing more to do—is one thing only: one's own spiritual and moral perfection. As a blindfolded man is guided on his path by being pushed by people from all sides where he shouldn't go, and is only left with one direction to go in, so all our lusts which end in disenchantment and unhappiness push us all from all sides and leave open to us only the one path of moral perfection—moral, not physical and not mental—because there may be conditions in which I can't be strong and agile (if I'm a cripple), there may be conditions in which I can't develop mentally (if I live in a backwater, if I'm mentally slow), but moral perfection is always and everywhere possible for everyone, and the joy which comes from making progress is enormous, as you will find out if only you try it. And not only does striving and making progress bring about spiritual joy in life, but in such a life it usually happens that worldly joys also come just when one isn't seeking them, when one doesn't set

417. To M. L. Tolstoy

them as a goal—it usually happens that both worldly and higher joys come of their own accord to such a man.

Therefore, this is what I advise you to do: first of all, come to your senses, take a look at yourself—this means, once you have seen the falseness of your life, having serious doubts about yourself, acknowledging the one goal of life which is natural to man and trying to live for this goal. Try it for yourself and then you will find out whether it's true. And if you begin to do this, don't give in to the one most common temptation which most frequently scares off beginners. This temptation consists in the fact that having once begun the inner work of perfecting himself, a person of our circle finds himself in such senseless conditions, so far removed from moral perfection, and with such bad and false habits, that he has so much work to do that he gives up, and wants to abandon it all and do nothing. A moral life must be one in which a person doesn't take advantage of the labours of other people, in which he doesn't make the poor work for his own whims, in which he himself must work for others: but we live by devouring the labours of thousands of people and giving them nothing. What are we to do? We must change everything, temptation says, and when the time comes I'll do so, but at present I must live like everyone else. There lies the deception. It's just like a man stopping ploughing because the field he has to plough is too large. A man only needs to begin work to see that the further the work progresses, the more joyful it is. So it is with our lives too. If my goal is perfection, how can I stop working now because there is too much to do? Do whatever comes to hand first: decrease your demands for work for yourself and increase your work for others: carry and clean what you can carry and clean yourself, travel on foot instead of riding, do a service for another person, rather than for yourself. And the further this work progresses, the more joyful it will be. You must do what you can now, and not despise small things. To put it off means to deceive yourself. This is one thing I advise you, if you are to try to live not for animal pleasure, but for moral perfection. Another very important thing which I also advise you is to remember that reason is the instrument given us in order to know the good, and therefore in order that we may perfect ourselves and see the ideal of good towards which we should strive, we should try to protect our reason with all our strength, not to destroy its growth, but to increase its content by absorbing in our reason all that has been accomplished by the reason of people who have lived before us, i.e. to associate with the most reasonable people, both living and dead, through the ideas expressed in their writings. If we don't yet have an inclination to do this, then at least don't let us do that terrible thing which is now being done more and more by all of us— i.e. don't stupefy ourselves, don't kill our reason with strong food which is unnatural to man, and with stupefying drinks and smoking.

Reason is the highest spiritual force in man, it's a small particle of God in us and therefore every attempt to stifle it is a most terrible sin, which doesn't pass without consequence.

One more piece of advice, and a very important one, is that if you begin such a life and try to live for moral perfection and then for some reason you weaken, or

417. To M. L. Tolstoy

get distracted, and return again to those bad habits which you've already adopted—don't despair and don't give it up as a bad job, but realise that such falls and turnings back are natural to any progress, and that the only person who doesn't fall is the one who doesn't strive towards anything, but only lives an animal life. Fall a thousand times and get up a thousand times and if you don't despair, you will make constant progress and, as I've already said, apart from the very great spiritual joy of life, all the worldly joys of life which you wanted before will also be added unto you and will be increased an hundred-fold, as Christ promised.

Goodbye. May God help you. He who is in you and in me and outside us. This letter is directed both at Andryusha and at Mitya.[3] It would be a great joy to me if it helped either of you to free yourselves from the temptations which are drowning you, and at least to see the true road, in order to get on to it.

L. Tolstoy

418. To F. A. ZHELTOV

Moscow, 18 December 1895

Dear Fyodor Alexeyevich,

As soon as I got your letter I meant to reply to you at once, since I have very definite ideas about the question which interests you, but I have been delayed up to now, partly by ill health and partly by the turmoil of life and my occupations. I have thought a great deal about education. There are questions in which you arrive at doubtful conclusions and there are questions in which the conclusions you arrive at are final, and you feel unable to alter them or to add anything to them: such are the conclusions I arrived at about education. They are as follows. Education is a difficult and complicated affair only as long as we wish to educate our children, or anyone at all, without educating ourselves. But if we understand that we can only educate others through ourselves, by educating ourselves, then the question of education lapses, and we are left only with the question of living: how ought one to live oneself? I know of no process of educating children which does not include educating oneself too. How should children be clothed, fed, put to bed or taught? The same way as you should be. If a father and mother dress, eat and sleep in moderation, and work and study, their children will do the same. I would offer two rules for education: not just to live well oneself but to work on oneself, constantly striving to be better, and to conceal nothing of your life from your children. It's better that children should know their parents' weak sides than that they should feel that their parents have a life concealed from them and one that they show to them. All the difficulties of education stem from the fact that parents, while not ridding themselves of their failings and not even regarding them as failings, but justifying them to themselves, still want to see their children without these failings. This is the whole difficulty and the root of all conflict with children. Children are far more morally perceptive than adults and often, without showing

3. Andrey Tolstoy and Dmitry Dyakov.

it or even being aware of it, see not only their parents' failings but also the worst of all failings—their parents' hypocrisy—and lose respect for them and interest in all their homilies. The hypocrisy of parents over their children's education is a very common phenomenon, and children are sensitive and notice it at once, and turn away and become corrupt. Truth is the first, main condition of the effectiveness of spiritual influence, and therefore is the first condition of education. And in order not to be afraid to show one's children the whole truth of one's life, it is necessary to make one's life good, or at least less bad. And so the education of others includes the education of oneself also, and nothing else is necessary.

Yours affectionately,
L. Tolstoy

419. To N. N. STRAKHOV

Yasnaya Polyana, middle of January 1896

[24 lines omitted]...The other day, in order to verify my opinion about Shakespeare,[1] I went to see *King Lear* and *Hamlet*, and if I had any doubts at all about the justice of my dislike of Shakespeare, that doubt vanished completely. What a crude, immoral, vulgar and senseless work Hamlet is. The whole thing is based on pagan vengeance; the only aim is to gather together as many effects as possible; there is no rhyme or reason about it. The author was so concerned with the effects that he didn't even bother to give the main person any character, and everybody decided that it was a brilliant portrayal of a characterless man. I never understood so clearly the utter helplessness of the crowd in making judgements, and how they can deceive themselves...[4 lines omitted]

420. To JOHN KENWORTHY

John Coleman Kenworthy, an English lay preacher, writer, and ardent Tolstoyan. Until 1893 he pursued a business career, but after becoming acquainted with Tolstoy's religious and ethical writings (an influence on his life only approached by that of Ruskin's ideas), he gave up business and moved to London's East End in order to make a study of the social and economic conditions of the life of the urban poor. His book *The Anatomy of Misery* (London, 1893) was the outcome of this experience. Kenworthy sent Tolstoy a copy of this book in 1894, and Tolstoy was so impressed with it that he arranged for it to be translated into Russian, and started a correspondence with him. (Tolstoy also wrote an introduction for the third

---

[419] 1. In a letter written to Sofya Andreyevna a year and a half earlier, Tolstoy expressed a similarly negative opinion of Shakespeare after reading *Julius Caesar*, adding that, given the time, he would like to write an article on Shakespeare's plays 'to save people the necessity of pretending that they like them'. This article was written in 1903–4 (*On Shakespeare and the Drama*). At the very end of 1895 Tolstoy had been reading *Romeo and Juliet* and *Othello* and found them equally distasteful and badly constructed.

420. To John Kenworthy

edition in English.) In 1895 Kenworthy went to Russia in order to meet Tolstoy, and visited him several times at his Moscow home.

Kenworthy's main work in England was now carried on at the Croydon Brotherhood Church which was the centre of a small cooperative community. When Chertkov was exiled in 1896 over the Dukhobor affair, he went to Croydon. The Purleigh Colony, a Tolstoyan community which grew up after Chertkov's arrival, can be considered an offshoot of Kenworthy's Croydon nucleus—although the Croydon group was never an entirely Tolstoyan venture. Chertkov's Free Age Press was likewise an offshoot of Kenworthy's Brotherhood Publishing Co.

Kenworthy's relations with Tolstoy's personal friends and followers were often strained. He fell out with Chertkov in England, and also quarrelled with Aylmer Maude over the English translation of Tolstoy's works. Kenworthy was under the impression (based on the following letter from Tolstoy) that he enjoyed the exclusive right to make the first English translations of Tolstoy's future works, and this caused considerable unpleasantness when the Maudes were given the task of translating *Resurrection*. To make matters worse, Tolstoy was unable to remember having written this letter to Kenworthy. Kenworthy's translations were seriously marred by the fact that he knew very little Russian, and his intransigence over the question of publishing rights led to increasing emotional instability. At the time of Kenworthy's second visit to Tolstoy (in May 1900) Chertkov warned Tolstoy of his condition. Soon after his return to England he became so aggressive towards other Tolstoyans that Tolstoy severed relations with him, and in later life he became mentally deranged.

Kenworthy's writings on Tolstoy include *Tolstoy: His Teaching and Influence in England* (1901) and *Tolstoy: His Life and Works* (1902), a badly informed study of Tolstoy's ideas and milieu and a vindication of Kenworthy's own relations with Tolstoy and some of his followers.

[Original in English]

Moscow, 4 February 1896

My dear Friend,

Sympathising with all my heart with the aims of your Brotherhood Publishing Co., I intend to put at your disposition the first translation of all my writings as yet unpublished, as well as forthcoming. Should you find it in any way expedient, as for instance in order to secure for them a wider circulation, to offer the first publication of any of my works to one of the English periodical papers or magazines, and should any pecuniary profit therefrom ensue, I would desire it to be devoted to the work of your Brotherhood Publishing Company.

As for the further right of publishing my works (i.e. after this the first appearance in English, which I intend placing at your disposal), they are to become public property in accordance with a statement I have formerly made public and now desire to confirm.

Yours truly,
Leo Tolstoy

421. To M. M. KHOLEVINSKAYA

Nikolskoye-Gorushki, end of February 1896

Marya Mikhaylovna Kholevinskaya (1858–?), a Tula doctor, arrested in 1893 for distributing Tolstoy's banned works. Tolstoy felt personally responsible and tried to secure her release by writing to the Minister of Internal Affairs. He received no reply, but Marya Kholevinskaya was subsequently released without charges being pressed. In 1896 her rooms were searched and a visiting card of Tolstoy's discovered, with instructions to give a copy of *What I Believe* to a certain person. This was the pretext for her letter to Tolstoy's daughter.

Dear Marya Mikhaylovna,

I have just read your letter to Tanya, and I can't express to you how much it distressed me. I am the cause of everything, but they leave me alone, while they torment as they choose—I think they do it deliberately—the people for whom it is most difficult to endure their moral tortures. And now they have chosen you. I want to try and write to Petersburg and say that if they want to counteract the damage I do, they ought to direct their activity against me, and me alone. The main thing, I think, in cases of this sort is not to let them misconstrue their role, and not to allow them to appear in the role of accusers and oneself in the role of accused, or, what is worst of all, of a person admitting guilt and wishing to conceal it. I argue this theoretically—it's very possible that I shouldn't be able to maintain my position in practice—but theoretically I still consider that one mustn't forget one's position of accuser and denouncer of the very thing in consequence of which they are using violence against us. They can confiscate and burn books, move people from place to place and put them in prison, but they cannot judge, because they are themselves being judged, and the conscience of all mankind as well as their own is judging them. And so the only thing we can say to them is not to explain our behaviour, but to point out to them their evil and dishonest activity and to give them the good advice to abandon it as quickly as possible. If I can consider myself guilty, it is only of one thing, namely that while knowing the truth, I am disseminating it too feebly and only in a confined circle. If an official found out that some peasants had taken a decision to go and cut down telegraph poles without knowing their liability for doing so, the official would probably consider himself obliged to warn the peasants of this liability, and would consider himself entirely to blame if he didn't disclose to the peasants the superior law which he knew. In just the same way, we who know the superior law whereby people who are the instruments of violence are liable to enormous responsibility before God and other people—we cannot be guilty of disclosing this responsibility, but can only be guilty of knowing the truth and not communicating it to people. The conclusion of your letter in which you say, if only one could remember the account which will have to be rendered to God, gave me great joy. If only we could remember that all our life is a fulfilment of the ministry entrusted to us, there would be nothing to fear, and all would be easy. In order to have the support of a granite rock you only need to stand on it squarely. May God who lives in you help you. I kiss you as a brother.

L. Tolstoy

422. To M. V. ALYOKHIN

Mitrofan Vasilyevich Alyokhin (1857–1935), a landscape painter and one of three brothers who were all Tolstoyans. At this time he was working as a market gardener and bee-keeper and was concerned about the question of ownership of land.

Moscow, 20 March 1896

[15 lines omitted]...I am bound to say that I think that, just as with marriage, it is better for a man to remain chaste, but once marriage has taken place a man should stick to that marriage, and try to make it as chaste as possible, so also with land: it is better to be unsullied by property, but, given an established link with the land by means of property, one should hold on to that land (as long as it only satisfies modest needs), and make the use of it as unexclusive as possible, i.e. not defend it by direct violence, legal proceedings or the threat of violence. I think you have chosen the better part, and if it fell to my lot to live again and live freely, I would try to live by working on the land, but without having ties with the land. All this is an ideal conception of what one should strive towards in my opinion, but the life of family people, once they have found themselves with land, can only remotely approach that ideal; and therefore, as a man who has remained free, be indulgent towards us, don't judge us harshly, don't say that if we haven't done everything we have done nothing, but take into account the greater or lesser approach to the ideal, those tiny little steps, but steps nevertheless, which people take when their feet are bound...[10 lines omitted]

423. To HENRY GEORGE

Henry George (1839–97), a distinguished American economist and the author, among other works, of the influential *Progress and Poverty* (1879) and *Social Problems* (1884). He was fundamentally opposed on moral grounds to the private ownership of land and advocated a tax system (the Single Tax) whereby landlords would continue to retain nominal ownership, but would effectively be transformed into land agents. Tolstoy was a fervent admirer of George's writings and did much to popularise them in Russia by expounding them in his own writings, in letters to friends and in private conversation.

424. To L. L. Tolstoy

[Original in English]

Moscow, 27 March/8 April 1896

Dear Sir,

The reception of your letter[1] gave me a great joy, for it is a long time that I know you and love you. Though the paths we go by are different, I do not think that we differ in the foundation of our thoughts.

I was very glad to see you mention twice in your letter the life to come.

There is nothing that widens so much the horizon, that gives such a firm support or such a clear view of things, as the consciousness that although it is but in this life that we have the possibility and the duty to act, nevertheless this is not the whole of life, but that bit of it only which is open to our understanding.

I shall wait with great impatience for the appearance of your new book, which will contain the so much needed criticism of the orthodox political economy.[2] The reading of every one of your books makes clear to me things which were not so before, and confirms me more and more in the truth and practicability of your system. Still more do I rejoice at the thought that I may possibly see you.

My summer I invariably spend in the country near Tula.

With sincere affection,
I am truly your friend,
Leon Tolstoy

424. To L. L. TOLSTOY

Moscow, 5 April 1896

I've been waiting for a letter from you, dear Lyova, in answer to mine, but then I decided to write to you without waiting, and now I've received your good letter. I'm very pleased about your marriage. I've no definite grounds for this, just a general feeling which makes me happier, and pleased that it's actually Dora Westerlund you will be marrying. Everything I know about her pleases me—the fact that she is Swedish, the fact that she is young, and especially the fact that you are very much in love with one another. As I wrote to you, I can't help being of the opinion, as Paul said, that it's better not to marry if you can, in order to serve God with all your strength. But if you can't, you should marry and hand on what you haven't finished yourself to the children you bring into the world. And if you marry, you should only marry when you simply can't help marrying. From all I can see, this is the case with you and Dora, and it's good when people are attracted to one another by the irresistible force of their whole being.

I'm an old man and you are young, and I would like to give you advice at such

---

[423] 1. A letter from Henry George dated 3 March 1896 (15 March N.S.) in which he expressed his appreciation of Tolstoy's support for his 'Single Tax' system, and suggested that he and Tolstoy might meet during a visit he hoped to make to Europe. They never did meet, as George died in 1897.

2. *The Science of Political Economy*. Out of five projected volumes only two were completed before the author's death; the remaining three were prepared for publication on the basis of the rough drafts.

424. To L. L. Tolstoy

an important time of life. But it's difficult to give advice when people are far apart from each other in outlook. Intellectually I know you agree, and want to agree with me, but with your whole being you are remote, and she, because of her age, is still more remote. And so I would like to give the sort of advice where this difference won't be felt, and in which there won't be any demands which seem difficult. I have such advice, and I would like to give it to you in spite of the fact that it will probably be contrary to the advice given to you by practical (that is very unpractical) people. My advice is for you both to fetter your freedom as little as possible, not to undertake anything, not to make promises, not to arrange a definite form of life for yourselves but to garder ses coudes franches. You are so young that you still need to find out what you are, who you are, and what you are capable of, and therefore to learn in every way possible, to try to explain life to yourselves and to learn to live better without thinking of a form of life. This form will take shape of its own accord. Shake hands with your dear father-in-law to be and his wife and kiss Dora from me.

I'm well, although I feel I have aged. I'm still working happily on the statement of my beliefs. I make excursions into other works, but this is the main one. I devote my best powers to it.

Goodbye. I kiss you.

L.T.

425. To S. N. TOLSTOY

Moscow, 19 April 1896

I haven't seen you for a long time, and I often remember you and think of you. I was terribly hurt to learn that you had written me a letter and not sent it. Verochka[1] wrote and said so. Even if it was only objections and refutations, it's still very important and valuable to me. You have been unwell, but our illness —old age—never ends. Perhaps you changed your mind about something in particular? How are you now? How is Grisha?[2] Has he calmed down?

Our busy, mad life goes on just the same. The only time in life when I'm alive is the morning hours when I'm alone, otherwise it's one long rush. It's even worse now with the coronation and spring. I went out of town on my bicycle yesterday and saw people ploughing and heard the larks, and smelt the smell of ploughed land. And I very much wanted a different life from the one I lead. Yesterday evening I went to the theatre, and heard Wagner's famous modern music, *Siegfried*, the opera. I couldn't even sit through one act, and rushed out like a madman, and I can't talk about it calmly even now. It's a stupid farce, not suitable for children over 7, pretentious, sham, utterly false and with no music. And several thousand people sit there and admire it. At this limit of music I agree with you. I merely extend the limits. Perhaps it's because I was spoilt in my youth, but still, the

---

[425] 1. S. N. Tolstoy's eldest daughter. 2. S. N. Tolstoy's eldest son.

musician who rejects even Beethoven, is incomparably greater than the one who accepts Wagner. Goodbye.

I meant to destroy this letter, I dislike it so much, and I would do, if you hadn't destroyed yours.

We're moving in a week's time. I kiss Marya Mikhaylovna and the girls.

426. To A. M. KALMYKOVA

The following letter is in reply to one from three members of the former Petersburg Literacy Committee, A. M. Kalmykova, V. V. Devel and N. A. Rubakin, asking what Tolstoy's attitude was towards the government's educational policy. The committee, which had recently been suppressed (along with its opposite number in Moscow) because of government opposition, had been concerned with rethinking educational theory, publishing cheap educational books for workers and peasants, building public libraries and opening reading rooms. There are six versions of the letter extant; the sixth and last one has been translated here, with Tolstoy's footnotes omitted.

Yasnaya Polyana, 31 August 1896

Dear Alexandra Mikhaylovna,

I would be very glad to join you and your associates, Devel and Rubakin—whose work I know and appreciate—in standing up for the rights of the Literacy Committee and fighting against the enemies of popular education; but I can't see any means of counteracting them in the field in which you are working.

I only console myself with the fact that I am ceaselessly occupied with this same struggle against these same enemies of education, although in a different field.

As to the particular question which is occupying you, I think that in place of the Literacy Committee which has been suppressed, one should set up many other literacy societies with the same tasks, independently of the government, without requesting censorship permission and letting the government, if it likes, persecute these literacy societies, punish their members, exile them, etc. If the government does this, it can only lend special importance to good books and to libraries, and will strengthen the movement towards education.

It seems to me that it's especially important now to do good quietly and unflaggingly, not only without asking the government, but consciously avoiding its participation. The strength of the government rests on the ignorance of the people, and it knows this, and therefore will always fight against education. It's time for us to understand this. But to give the government the opportunity of pretending that it is busy with popular education, while disseminating darkness, as all types of pseudo-educational institutions controlled by it do—primary schools, grammar schools, universities, academies, all types of committees and conferences—is extremely harmful.

426. To A. M. Kalmykova

Good is good, and education is education, only when it is absolute good and absolute education, and not *made to conform* to the circulars of Delyanov[1] and Durnovo.[2] But the main thing is that I am always sorry that such valuable, disinterested, self-sacrificing strength is wasted so unproductively. Sometimes I simply find it funny to watch good and intelligent people wasting their strength on struggling against the government on the basis of those laws which the government itself makes quite arbitrarily.

The position, it seems to me, is as follows:

There are people, and we are among them, who know that our government is very bad and who struggle against it. From the time of Radishchev and the Decembrists there have been two methods of struggle used: one method is that of Stenka Razin, Pugachov, The Decembrists, the revolutionaries of the 60s, the 1 March terrorists[3] and others; the other method is that which is preached and practised by you—the method of the 'gradualists'—which consists in waging the struggle on legal grounds, without violence, winning rights bit by bit. Within my memory both methods have been constantly used now for more than half a century, and the situation is becoming worse and worse: if the situation does improve, it isn't thanks to one or other of these activities, but in spite of the harmfulness of these activities (for other reasons which I will speak of later) and the power which they are struggling against becomes greater, stronger and more insolent. The last gleams of self-government: the zemstvo, the courts, your committees and so on—are all being extinguished, like 'foolish day-dreams'.[4]

Now that both these methods have been used in vain for such a long time, it is possible, I think, to see clearly that neither the one nor the other is any good, and why. To me, at least, who have always felt revulsion for our government, but who have never resorted either to the one or the other method of fighting it, the defects of both these methods are obvious.

The first method is no good, primarily because even if a change in the existing order were brought about by means of violence, nothing would guarantee that the newly established order would be durable, and that the enemies of this new order would not triumph in favourable circumstances, and by use of the same violence, as has happened over and over again in France and wherever else revolutions have occurred. And therefore the new order of things established by violence would have to be constantly supported by that same violence, i.e. by illegality and, consequently, it would inevitably and very quickly be corrupted just like the order it replaced. But in case of failure, as has always happened with us, all the revolutionary forces—from Pugachov to 1 March—have only strengthened the order

[426] 1. I. D. Delyanov, Minister of Education 1882–97, responsible for the 1884 statute on universities (see note 7). During his tenure of office he deprived the distinguished chemist D. I. Mendeleyev of his chair at the University of Petersburg for forwarding a student petition to the Ministry.
2. I. N. Durnovo, Minister of Internal Affairs 1889–95, responsible for suppressing the Moscow and Petersburg Literacy Committees.
3. The assassins of Alexander II.
4. Nicholas II's words in reply to a request from the zemstvo representatives for liberal reforms (January 1895).

426. To A. M. Kalmykova

of things against which they were struggling, driving the enormous number of undecided, middle-of-the-road people who don't belong to either camp, into the camp of the conservatives and reactionaries. And therefore I think one may boldly say, guided both by experience and reason, that this means, besides being immoral, is irrational and ineffectual.

The second method is in my opinion even less rational and effectual. It is ineffectual and irrational because the government, holding in its hands all power (the army, the administration, the Church, the schools, the police) and itself framing these so-called laws on the basis of which liberals wish to struggle against it—this government, knowing very well what is really dangerous to it, will never allow people who are subject to it and who act under its guidance, to do anything to undermine its power. Take for instance this particular case if you like: a government such as ours (or any other) which rests on the ignorance of the people will never allow them to be truly educated. It permits all types of pseudo-educational organisations controlled by it—primary schools, grammar schools, universities, academies, all types of committees and conferences and censored publications—so long as these organisations and publications serve its purpose, that is, to stupefy the people or, at least, not to interfere with their stupefaction; but at any attempt by these institutions or publications to shake what the power of the government is founded on, i.e. the ignorance of the people, the government, without rendering any account to anyone as to why it is acting in this way and not in another, simply pronounces its veto, transforms or closes the establishments and organisations, and bans the publications. And therefore, as is clear both from reason and from experience, such an illusory, gradual winning of rights is a self-deception which suits the government very well and is therefore even encouraged by it.

But not only is this activity irrational and ineffectual, it is harmful as well. Activity of this sort is harmful, firstly, because educated, good and honest people, by entering the ranks of the government, lend it a moral authority which it would not have without them. If the whole government consisted only of those coarse men of violence, self-seekers and flatterers who form its nucleus, it couldn't continue to exist. Only the participation of educated and honest people in the affairs of the government gives the government the moral prestige which it possesses. This is one harmful thing caused by the activity of the liberals who participate in or strike a bargain with the government. Secondly, such activity is harmful because, by making compromises in order to get the opportunity to carry it on, these same educated, honest people gradually become inured to the idea that for a good end one may depart a little from the truth in word and deed. One may, for example, without acknowledging existing religion, observe its rituals; one may take an oath; one may submit addresses which are false and contrary to human dignity if this is necessary for the success of some cause; one may perform military service; one may participate in the zemstvo which no longer has any rights; one may serve as a teacher or a professor, teaching not what one considers necessary oneself, but what has been prescribed by the government; one may serve even as a Land Captain, submitting to government requirements and instructions which are

426. To A. M. Kalmykova

contrary to one's conscience; one may publish newspapers and journals, remaining silent about what needs to be said and printing what is ordered. By making these compromises, whose limits are impossible to foresee, educated and honest people who alone could constitute some kind of obstacle to the government in its encroachment on people's freedom, imperceptibly retreat further and further from the demands of their conscience, and before they know where they are, they fall into a position of total dependence on the government: they receive a salary and decorations from it and, while continuing to imagine that they are advancing liberal ideas, they become docile servants and supporters of that very order which they opposed at the beginning.

It's true that there are also better, sincere people in this camp who don't give in to the government's enticements and remain free from bribery, salaries and position. But even these people, for the most part, having been ensnared in the nets spread by the government, writhe about inside these nets as you are now doing with your Committees, without getting anywhere; or else, losing patience, they go over to the revolutionary camp, or shoot themselves, or take to drink, or abandon everything in despair, and most frequently they retreat into literature where, submitting to the demands of the censor, they say only what is allowed, and by that very silence about what is most important, convey to the public the most distorted thoughts which are just what the government wants, and they continue to imagine that by their writing, which gives them a means of subsistence, they are serving society.

And so reason and experience show me that both means of struggle against the government which have been used up to now and are still being used, are not only ineffectual, but both help to strengthen the government's power and arbitrariness.

What is to be done? Obviously not what has proved fruitless for seventy years and has only achieved the opposite results to those intended. What is to be done? Just what those people have done, to whose activity we owe all the progress towards good and light which has been achieved from time immemorial and is still being achieved. That is what needs to be done. And what is it?

The simple, quiet, truthful fulfilment of what one considers good and needful, quite independently of the government, and of whether it likes it or not. Or, in other words: standing up for one's rights not as a member of a literacy committee or as a councillor or a landowner or a merchant or even as a member of parliament, but standing up for one's rights as a rational and free man, and standing up for them, not as in the case of zemstvos and committees, with concessions and compromises, but without any concessions and compromises, in the only way in which one can stand up for moral and human dignity.

In order to defend a fortress successfully, it is necessary to burn all the houses in the suburbs and leave only what is firmly based and what we don't intend to surrender on any account. It's just the same here: we must first concede what we can surrender, and keep only what is not to be surrendered. Only then, having taken a firm stand on what is not to be surrendered, can we also win everything we need. It's true that the rights of a member of parliament or even of a zemstvo, or a

426. To A. M. Kalmykova

committee, are greater than the rights of an ordinary man, and it seems one can do a great deal by taking advantage of these rights; but the trouble is that in order to acquire the rights of a zemstvo, a parliament, or a committee, it is necessary to abandon a part of one's own rights as a man. And having abandoned even a part of one's rights as a man, there is no longer any point of support, and it's impossible to win or to retain any genuine right. In order to pull other people out of the mire, it's necessary for you yourself to stand on firm ground; but if, to make it easier to pull others out, you go into the mire yourself, you won't pull them out but will sink in yourself. It may very well be good and useful to get an eight-hour day through parliament or a liberal programme for school libraries through a committee; but if for that purpose a member of parliament must publicly raise his hand and, in taking an oath, must lie by expressing in words his respect for what he doesn't respect; if, in our case, in order to pass the most liberal programmes, we must attend church services, take oaths, wear uniforms, write false and flattering petitions, and make similar speeches etc., then by doing all these things and abandoning our human dignity we lose much more than we gain and, by striving to attain one definite goal (and usually this goal is not achieved), we deprive ourselves of the possibility of attaining other goals which are most important. Only people who have something which they would never surrender on any account or under any conditions can really restrain and oppose the government. One must have a point of support in order to have the strength to oppose the government. And the government knows this very well and is concerned above all else to force out of people what they won't surrender—human dignity. When this is forced out of them, then the government calmly does what it needs to, knowing that it will no longer encounter any real opposition. A man who has agreed to take an oath in public and pronounce the unworthy and false words of that oath, or to wait obediently for several hours in uniform to be received by a Minister, or to sign on as a special guard for the coronation, or to observe the ritual of fasting before communion for the sake of respectability etc., is no longer frightening to the government.

Alexander II said that liberals didn't frighten him because he knew that they could all be bought, if not with money, then with honours.

You know, people who participate in the government or who work under its guidance, by pretending that they are struggling against it, can deceive themselves and their sympathisers: but those against whom they are struggling know by the opposition these people make, that they aren't really pulling, but only pretending to. And our government knows this about the liberals and constantly tests to see how effective the real opposition is, and after satisfying itself that there is no opposition worth speaking of, gets on with its affairs in the full assurance that it can do what it likes with these people.

Alexander III's government knew this very well and, knowing it, quietly destroyed everything the liberals were so proud of, imagining that it was their doing; it altered and restricted trial by jury;[5] abolished the office of Justice of the

---

5. The right of every citizen to trial by jury was established in 1864, and these juries were

426. To A. M. Kalmykova

Peace;[6] abolished university rights;[7] altered the whole teaching system in the grammar schools;[8] revived the Cadet Corps, even the state-controlled sale of drink;[9] established Land Captains;[10] legalised flogging;[11] practically abolished the zemstvo;[12] gave uncontrolled power to the Provincial Governors;[13] encouraged corporal punishment; increased administrative exile[14] and imprisonment, and the execution of political prisoners; introduced new religious persecutions;[15] took the stupefaction of the people by the barbarous superstitions of Orthodoxy to the utmost degree; legalised duelling murders; established illegality in the form of a 'state of emergency'[16] with capital punishment, as the normal order of things; and

generally composed of a cross-section of society. In 1885 Pobedonostsev had strongly recommended that trial by jury be abolished so as 'to restore the integrity of the courts', but this was not done, although after 1881 these judicial safeguards were gradually eroded and juries became less heterogeneous.

6. The office of Justice of the Peace became an elective office nearly everywhere in Russia in the years following 1864. It was considered the chief link between the district zemstvos and the peasants, but by a law of 12 July 1889 it was abolished almost everywhere.

7. By a law of 13 August 1884 major administrative and academic posts in the universities were to be government-appointed posts (under the Ministry of Education) and the power of inspectors in the universities was increased. University fees were also raised and student organisations of any type forbidden.

8. The curriculum in the grammar schools was strictly supervised, and official religious and political positions were upheld with no opportunity for discussion or critical examination. The student body also became more selective after Delyanov's 1887 circular recommending that children from humble backgrounds should be discouraged from rising above their own social status, and therefore should not be admitted to the grammar schools.

9. A government monopoly on wine was introduced in 1895 under Sergey Witte, Minister of Finance.

10. The Land Captain, a new post created in 1889, was to be filled by government appointment; it partly replaced the old post of Justice of the Peace, and candidates for it had to belong to the hereditary gentry. The Land Captain had wide authority over peasant self-governing bodies, and had the right to enforce flogging.

11. Corporal punishment was only abolished in 1904. Tolstoy's article *Shame* (1895) deals with this subject.

12. The 1890 zemstvo statute modified the electoral law so as to make the zemstvo into a mainly aristocratic body; the Governor's right of supervision over its activities was increased, and the zemstvo finances were subject to some degree of government control.

13. According to a statute of 1881, the Governors-General of regions in a 'state of emergency' (see note 16) had the right to transfer certain criminal cases from the ordinary courts to the military courts. Any alleged act of terrorism was subject to this type of arbitrary transfer. While the civil courts could not return a death sentence, the military courts were obliged to do so if the defendant were found guilty, and the military courts were so structured as to prevent acquittals based on sympathy rather than on evidence—which had occurred (notably in the trial of Vera Zasulich) in the ordinary courts.

14. There were two types of administrative exile, subject to the discretion of the authorities, and generally applied when evidence to convict a suspect was lacking but when he was considered sufficiently dangerous (politically) to be dealt with in some way: (1) vysylka, and (2) ssylka. Vysylka meant simply banishing a suspect from a given area, while ssylka meant exile to a specific place where he would be under police surveillance (maximum sentence five years). Ssylka was used more frequently than vysylka.

15. A law of 1883 placed all religious sects (with the exception of the Skoptsy) on the same legal basis. This improved the position of the smaller sects, but the Dukhobors and Stundists were treated particularly harshly, regardless of this law; for instance, an 1884 decree declared the Stundists to be an especially dangerous sect and forbade their prayer meetings.

16. A 'state of emergency' was declared in certain areas, supposedly only for a temporary period, but it was widely applied and in some areas it lasted until 1917. It gave increased powers

in passing all these measures encountered no opposition except a protest from one honourable woman who boldly told the government what she considered the truth.[17] The liberals whispered among themselves that they didn't like all this, but continued to participate in the courts, in the zemstvos, in the universities, in the civil service, and in the press. In the press they hinted at what they were allowed to hint at, and were silent about what they were ordered to be silent about; but they printed everything they were ordered to print. So every reader who received a liberal newspaper and journal, but who wasn't initiated into what was being whispered in editorial offices, read an exposition without commentary or condemnation of the most cruel and irrational measures, as well as servile and flattering addresses to the instigators of these measures, and often even praise of them. Thus all the dismal activity of Alexander III's government, which destroyed all the good that had begun to take root under Alexander II, and which attempted to return Russia to the savagery of the period at the beginning of this century—all this shameful activity of hangings, floggings, persecutions, stupefaction of the people—became the subject of an insane glorification of Alexander III in all the liberal newspapers and journals, and of his elevation into a great man, a model of human virtue. The same thing is continuing in the new reign. The young man without any understanding of life who has taken the place of the former Tsar is assured by men in power, to whom it is profitable to say so, that in order to rule a hundred million people he must do exactly the same as his father did, i.e. not ask anybody what needs to be done, but do just what comes into his head or what he is advised by the first of his retinue of flatterers. And imagining that unlimited autocracy is the sacred principle of the Russian people's life, this young man begins his reign like this: instead of asking the representatives of the Russian people to help him with advice in the conduct of government (about which he, having been educated in Guards' Regiments, neither understands nor can understand anything) he rudely and impudently shouts at the representatives of the Russian people who have come to him with their congratulations, and calls the desire timidly expressed by several of them to inform the authorities about their needs 'foolish day-dreams'! And what happened? Was Russian society shocked? Did educated and honest people—the liberals—speak out about their indignation and revulsion? Did they at least refrain from praising such a government and from participating in it and encouraging it? Not in the least. From that moment there began an especially keen competition to extol the father and the son who imitated him, and not one protesting voice was heard, and the halls of the Winter Palace were filled with infamous, flattering addresses and icons carried aloft. A coronation was arranged, terrible in its absurdity and insane waste of money: the dreadful misfortune of the deaths of thousands of people resulted from the authorities' impudence and contempt for the people, and the organisers regarded it as a small cloud over the festivities which

to the Governors of the provinces where it was put into effect and seriously undermined civil rights in those areas.

17. The authoress M. K. Tsebrikova, who wrote 'An Open Letter to Alexander III', for which she was exiled.

426. To A. M. Kalmykova

should not be interrupted because of it;[18] an exhibition unnecessary to anyone except those who arranged it was set up, and millions of roubles wasted on it;[19] the Chancellery of the Synod, with previously unheard of impudence, thought up new and very silly means of stupefying the people—namely the relics of a man whom nobody knew anything about;[20] the severity of the censorship was increased, the 'state of emergency' was continued, i.e. legalised illegality, and the situation became worse and worse.

I think that none of this would have happened if those educated and honest people who are now occupied in liberal activity on the basis of legality in the zemstvos, committees, censored literature etc., had directed their energies not towards deceiving the government and making it act to its own detriment and ruin within the forms instituted by the government itself, but only towards refraining from taking any part in government, and from surrendering their personal rights as human beings in any dealings connected with it. 'You want to institute Land Captains with birch-rods instead of Justice of the Peace; that is your business, but we will not be tried by your Land Captains, nor will we ourselves be appointed to this office. You want to make trial by jury a mere formality; that is your business, but we will not serve as judges, or as lawyers, or as jurymen. You want to establish lawlessness under cover of the "state of emergency"; that is your business, but we will not participate in it and will plainly call the "state of emergency" an illegality, and the death sentences inflicted without trial—murder. You want to set up classical grammar schools with military exercises and religious instruction, or Cadet Corps; that is your business, but we will not be teachers in them, or send our children to them, but will educate them as we consider best. You want to reduce the zemstvo to a nullity; we will not participate in it. You forbid the printing of what you don't like; you can seize and burn books, and punish the printers, but you can't prevent us from writing and talking, and we shall do so. You order us to swear allegiance to the Tsar; we will not do so, because it is stupid, false and base. You order us to serve in the army; we will not do so, because we consider mass murder to be an act just as offensive to our conscience as a single murder and, above all, the promise to kill whoever a commander orders is the basest act a man can perform. You profess a religion a thousand years behind the times, with the Iverskaya icon,[21] relics and coronations; that is your business, but we not only do not acknowledge this idolatry and superstition to be religion, but we call it superstition and idolatry and are trying to rescue people from it.'

And what can the government do against such activity? It can exile or imprison a man for making a bomb or printing a proclamation to the workers, and it can transfer a Literacy Committee from one ministry to another, or close a parliament;

18. The tragedy on Khodynka Field in Petersburg in 1895 during the celebration of Nicholas II's coronation when a massive crush resulted in the deaths of over a thousand people; public sentiment was outraged when the official Ball scheduled for that evening was not cancelled.
19. An unsuccessful exhibition given at Nizhny Novgorod in 1896.
20. The relics of the Chernigov archbishop Feodosy Uglitsky discovered in 1896 and displayed as objects of reverence; the relics were widely publicised in the press as having miraculous powers.   21. The miracle-working icon in the Iverskaya Chapel in Moscow.

426. To A. M. Kalmykova

but what can a government do with a man who doesn't want to lie in public with raised hand, or who doesn't want to hand over his children to an institution which he considers bad, or who doesn't want to learn how to kill people, or who doesn't want to take part in idolatry, or who doesn't want to take part in coronations, meetings and addresses, or who writes and says what he thinks and feels? By persecuting such a man, the government makes of him a martyr who arouses general sympathy, and it undermines those foundations on which it supports itself since, by acting in this way, it destroys human rights itself instead of protecting them.

And it is only necessary for all the educated and honest people whose strength is now being wasted, to the detriment of themselves and their cause, on revolutionary, socialist, and liberal activity, to begin to act in this way, for a nucleus of honest, educated and independent people to come into being at once, and for all the ever-vacillating mass of average people to join it, and for the one force which subdues governments to make its appearance—public opinion—demanding freedom of speech, freedom of conscience, justice and humanity. And as soon as such public opinion came into being, not only would it be impossible to suppress the Literacy Committee, but all those inhuman institutions—the 'state of emergency', the secret police, the censorship, Schlüsselburg,[22] the Synod—against which the revolutionaries and liberals are now struggling, would disappear of their own accord.

So two methods of opposing the government have been tried, and both have been unsuccessful, and it now only remains to try a third which has not yet been tried and which, in my opinion, cannot fail to be successful. This method, briefly expressed, consists in all educated and honest people trying to be as good as possible, and not even good in all respects but only in one, namely in observing one of the elementary virtues—to be honest, not to lie, to act and speak so that your motives for action are understandable to your loving seven-year-old son; to act so that your son doesn't say: 'Papa, why did you say that then, but now say and do something quite different?' This method seems very feeble, but nevertheless I am convinced that this method alone has moved mankind for as long as it has. I am convinced of this because what is required by conscience—the highest presentiment of the truth which is accessible to man—is always and in all respects the most necessary and most fruitful activity. Only a man living in accordance with his conscience can have a good influence on people. And activity in accordance with the conscience of the best people in society is always the very activity which is required for the good of mankind at any given moment.

Forgive me for having written so much to you, perhaps entirely unnecessarily; but I have long wanted to express my views on this question. I even began a long article about it,[23] but I'll hardly have time to finish it before my death, and so I wanted to express my views at least to some extent. Forgive me if I am mistaken about anything.

I press your hand in friendship,
Lev Tolstoy

22. Schlüsselburg Fortress, a prison for political offenders on Lake Ladoga.
23. The article 'Foolish Daydreams' begun in 1895.

427. To V. F. KRASNOV

Vasily Filippovich Krasnov (1878–?), a worker with whom Tolstoy became acquainted in 1896 through the photographic studio where he was then employed. In 1906 he was exiled to Siberia for three years. During this period he wrote a story entitled *Khodynka. The Story of One not Trampled to Death* which Tolstoy recommended for publication, and which served as the basis of his own story *Khodynka* (1910).

Yasnaya Polyana, end of September 1896

I would very much like to answer your question in such a way as to satisfy you completely. But in order to do so, I oughtn't to talk about an individual case of deception practised this year by our government and churchmen on our unfortunate, benighted people by means of various ceremonies performed over a dessicated or artifically dried up body of some monk,[1] but I ought to talk about everything miraculous and superhuman, i.e. contrary to the laws of reason and violating them. All human knowledge is based only on the fact that man discovers the laws of natural phenomena and regards these laws as immutable. But a miracle is the name given to a violation of these laws, and so a man who believes in any miracle must inevitably renounce all human knowledge. If a blind man's sight can be restored because some monk didn't rot, then a man might lose his sight or die or fall through the floor because I remove the earth from under his feet. We have only to admit that there can be miracles, i.e. phenomena which violate the laws of nature, and we are no longer able to know anything at all. We think that the sun will rise tomorrow, and suddenly on the other side of the earth a new Joshua will hold the sun back and it won't rise in time. And if it can be held back for an hour, it can be held back for a year and for ever. We have only to accept the possibility of miracles, and it's impossible to do anything or know anything. If people who accept miracles believe in knowledge, it's only because they reason inconsistently. A man who believes in the laws of natural phenomena and reason, who takes cognisance of them, can't believe in miracles, and a man who believes in miracles can't believe in reason. And so it's necessary to choose one of two things. I chose belief in reason, not miracles, long ago, and I chose it because reason is the same for all people, while miracles are different for all people, and reason is necessary to me for living, while miracles aren't necessary to me for anything. Therefore I advise you also to choose belief in reason and not miracles. Moreover, bear in mind that if you don't believe in miracles by modern relics or the Iverskaya icon, on the same basis you shouldn't believe in the miracles of Christ, and the miracles which tell how God appeared to the people and sent down His son, and created the world in six days etc. This is what I have to say to your question. I shall be very glad if my answer satisfies you and your neighbours. I'm glad, too, that you have got fixed up.

Lev Tolstoy

[427] 1. See Letter 426, note 20.

428. To COUNTESS S. A. TOLSTAYA

Yasnaya Polyana, 23 October 1896

I wrote this *'non-letter'* to you, my dear, and meant to send it with Tanya who has gone to Tula, but I didn't manage to—she has gone, and now I'm writing a short letter which I'll take to Yasenki myself. I felt genuinely happy yesterday, seeing you off; I was only sorry that you were frightened, and I was annoyed with poor Misha, who lacks the basic human feeling of understanding the lives of other people, and is therefore ludicrously egotistical. I write this partly—not even partly, but wholly—for his sake: it's far more necessary than any trigonometry or Cicero for him to learn to understand the lives of other people, to understand what often undoubtedly poisons life for other people, but which is completely unknown to him, to understand that other people also rejoice, suffer, and want to live, just as I do. He completely lacks this sense, and he needs to cultivate it in himself, because without it a man is an animal, and not an ordinary animal, but a terrible and frightening one. I say this to him, not because he grumbled, as you put it mildly, in the carriage yesterday, but because I have never seen in him, except in major catastrophes such as your illness, so much as a spark of sympathy for, or interest in anyone else's life—his sisters' or brothers', yours or mine. True sympathy can only be expressed in everyday life, not in catastrophes; in exceptional situations, sympathy is not sympathy for the sufferer but egoism again—the fear of the destruction of a customary and agreeable way of life. This egoism terrifies me and acts on me like the sight of a terrible, suppurating, stinking wound.

I've been storing up this feeling for a long time and now I've expressed it, only it's painful for me to know in advance that all I've said will be calmly brushed aside as something disagreeable which destroys one's egotistical complacency. If not, and if you, Misha, will think about it and look into yourself and agree, and be willing to summon up in yourself something so far lacking, I shall be very glad. You have only to recognise your imperfections and all your good qualities will at once show themselves of their own accord. And they do exist in you.

These two boys make my heart ache very much. Andryusha, who didn't come to see you yesterday, came back goodness knows when. I went to bed after 1, and he wasn't back. And today he is pleased with himself and proud, and has disappeared somewhere again.

It's terribly hard to see in my family the very opposite of everything I consider good, not only now but always.

Well, that's enough. You're fretful as it is, and I keep on worrying you. I just wanted to pour out my grief. And to whom closer than you? Lyova is putting in the double frames with Dora today, I see. I'm always glad about this. Masha has been to the village to visit the sick; she's now teaching and copying the letter I wrote to the commander of the Irkutsk disciplinary battalion.[1] This morning I

---

[428] 1. A letter concerning two peasants, both conscientious objectors, who had been sentenced in 1896 to three years in a disciplinary battalion. Remembering the death two years earlier of Yevdokim Drozhzhin in a similar battalion, Tolstoy wrote to the commander in

428. To Countess S. A. Tolstaya

slept and wrote; I've recently got into a tangle with my work, and I'd be distressed if I didn't know that this happens and will pass, and things will become even clearer. Don't fret and don't despair. You said that your visit mightn't have been as pleasant for us as your last one. On the contrary I was very pleased to see you and was very happy with you, and would have liked not to have left you, both for your sake and my own in a spiritual sense.

Tanya has decided to move on the 18th; I don't argue, but I've decided, in so far as I've thought about it all, to come when it begins to snow; it's windy today and feels as if snow is on the way.

I was composing poems in the style of Fet in bed all this morning while half asleep. It's only forgivable when one's half asleep.

I kiss you and Misha and Sasha.

Another thing that's happened is that I'm reading a splendid, wonderful article by Carpenter, an Englishman, on science.[2]

429. To COUNTESS S. A. TOLSTAYA

Yasnaya Polyana, 13 November 1896

I was terribly sad, dearest darling Sonya, to get your letter yesterday to Tanya in which you complain that we don't write to you. I'm now writing my third letter. And they have written too. I'm only sad that I missed a day after you left. I ought to have reckoned on a delay. You ask whether I still love you. My feelings for you now are such that I think they can never change, because they contain everything that can possibly bind people together. No, not everything. We lack outward agreement in our beliefs—I say outward, because I think the disagreement is only outward, and I'm always certain it will be eliminated. We are bound together by the past, and the children, and the awareness of our faults, and compassion, and an irresistible attraction. In a word, we are wrapped up and tied together well and truly. And I'm glad.

Everything is fine here. We're friendly and well. I very much want to join you soon. Work is going badly, but I decided today that I oughtn't to strain myself but to rest, and today being a wonderful, sunny day, I rode to Bulygin's in the morning, with the result that I dined alone at 4. Lyova and Dora went to Tula to buy saucepans. Marya Alexandrovna Dubenskaya left today.

They are calling me for supper. Why are you still out of sorts and your letters dispirited? I very much want to be with you as soon as possible, and, without boasting, not so much for myself as for you, but since you *are* me, then for me too.

charge of the two men to plead for mercy. (Although no reply was received, the men were treated relatively well while serving their sentences.)

2. 'Modern Science' by Edward Carpenter, included in his *Civilisation: Its Cause and Cure* (London, 1889). Tolstoy later got his son Sergey to translate this chapter into Russian, and wrote an introduction himself.

I didn't like the fact that you liked Solovyov's article.[1]
Well, goodbye for now.

L.T.

430. To M. L. TOLSTAYA

Moscow, 18 December 1896

I've just read your letter to Tanya, my dear, beloved Masha. You say in it that you regret that you wrote to me about your state of mind in all its confusion. But I'm very glad, and grateful to you.

I understand it all and I've nothing to say against your intention, caused as it is by an irresistible longing, as I see it, for marriage.[1] What is worse and what is better, neither you nor I know—I'm not speaking about marrying or not marrying, but about this husband or that. But I've already said to you some time before, I remember, or not to you but to Tanya, that marriage is a worldly affair, and as a worldly affair it must be thought about in a worldly way. And judging by your life recently—more idle and luxurious than before—and by Kolya's[2] life and habits and views, you will not only not live like Marya Alexandrovna,[3] but you'll need a fair sum of money to live on at all...

One of the main motives for you apart from marriage itself, i.e. conjugal love, is children. It's very difficult and all too obviously a change from independence and peace and quiet, to very complex and painful sufferings. How have you envisaged this? What does he think about it? How and where does he want to work, and *does* he want to work? And where and how will you live? All this needs to be thought over and decided upon, and not just perfunctorily, so that you yourselves consider it right, but so that other people who love you should also consider it so. Do you intend to ask for your legacy to be given to you?[4] Does he intend to work, and where? And please drop the idea that your husband's public service might change my attitude to him, and that your going back on your intention not to accept your legacy might change my appreciation of you. I know you and love you far more deeply than that, and no weaknesses of yours can change my understanding of you and my love for you which goes with it. I was, and still am too full

[429] 1. 'The Moral Organisation of Mankind' (*Problems of Philosophy and Psychology*, 1896).

[430] 1. Masha Tolstaya, whose romance with Pavel Biryukov had been opposed by her parents, had now fallen in love with a distant cousin, Prince Nikolay Obolensky, certainly not a Tolstoyan, and reputed to be something of a playboy. Neither Tolstoy nor Sofya Andreyevna approved of the match, although the latter was probably relieved that her daughter did at least wish to marry someone of her own class. At the time of this letter the idea of marriage was only just being broached, but despite her father's warnings Masha got engaged, and was married the following year. In a fit of depression Tolstoy wrote in his diary shortly after the wedding that he was as sorry for Masha as for a thoroughbred horse being used to cart water.

2. Prince Nikolay Obolensky.
3. M. A. Schmidt.
4. Masha had originally declined her share of her father's estate when it had been distributed in 1892, but her mother had put the money on one side for her in case she should change her mind, which she did when she got married.

430. To M. L. Tolstaya

of weaknesses myself, and so I know how sometimes, even often, they get the better of one. One thing only: although the enemy is on top of me and I'm in his power, I still cry that I won't surrender, that I can deal with him and will go on fighting him again. I know that you'll do the same too. So do so. Only you must think, you must have a good think. I say to you what I wrote to Manya:[5] apart from death there is no single act so important, clear-cut, all-transforming and irreversible as marriage. Goodbye for now, darling; I kiss you, Sonya, Ilya and the children. I'm still not well; not well at heart.

431. To M. L. TOLSTAYA

[Not sent]

To be read alone   Moscow, 12 January 1897
morning

Dearest Masha,

Although I seldom talk to you when you are here, I would like your sympathy now that I feel very sick at heart. Of all the family, you alone—however exacting your personal life and its demands—you alone understand and appreciate me fully. The life around me which I take part in with my presence either from necessity or weakness—all this dissipated, repulsive life with its absence of any, not to say reasonable or loving, but simply any interests at all apart from the crudest brutish ones of dressing up, guzzling sweet things, playing all sorts of games and flinging about other people's labour in the form of money—and all this without kindness even, but on the contrary with recrimination, bitterness and the readiness to get angry at anything that rubs the wrong way—this life becomes at times so repulsive to me that it suffocates me and I want to shout and cry; but you know it's all useless and that not only will nobody understand you, but they won't even take any notice of your feelings—they'll try not to understand them, or rather they won't understand them without even trying, just as a horse doesn't understand them. Sitting at dinner yesterday, listening to those conversations without a single living word in them, with unfunny jokes and mutual unkindnesses, and to those incoherent monologues, I looked at Mlle Aubert[1] and felt that she and I were equally superfluous, and equally embarrassed because we felt so. It's terribly loathsome, actually loathsome, that I can't master myself and not suffer, and that I can't do anything to break with this false situation and live the last years or months or days of my old age peacefully and not shamefully, as I do now. I don't know which way round it is: whether I feel it so badly because I can't get absorbed in my work, or whether I can't work because I feel it so badly, but I feel miserable and I want sympathy, I want people to understand and pity me. Poor Tanya would have liked to live closer to me, but she is terribly weak and entirely caught

5. M. K. Tolstaya, the first wife of Sergey Lvovich Tolstoy.
[431] 1. A governess in the Tolstoy home.

up in this absurd maelstrom: Duse,[2] Hofmann,[3] beauty, the exhibition, old age coming on, Sukhotin[4]—it's awful. Seryozha, Ilyusha and Misha are just the same. I haven't really any children to rest on, and I haven't got Chertkov or Posha[5] either. You yourself are racked and tormented by your own affairs, and I keep showing you my sores. Let's suffer together. Tell me all about yourself. I'll keep it close to my heart, because it may mean suffering in future, but it is something important. What torments me is the strain of trivialities and petty meannesses.

432. To V. G. CHERTKOV

To be read alone

Moscow, 12 January 1897

Why don't you write to me, dear friend? Are you all right? All right at heart? I have no liking for what you are doing there.[1] I'm afraid you are doing damage to your soul. I don't believe that a good and worthwhile job needs such preparations and preliminaries. I'm afraid they're a temptation. Write to me, particularly about yourself and your soul: how it is, what it lives by, what makes it suffer or rejoice. I'm writing to you today particularly, because I'm very miserable and lonely. Masha isn't here, and there is nobody like you and Posha,[2] to whom I like to pour out my soul, complain, and ask for sympathy and compassion. The life around me is becoming more and more senseless: food, clothes, games of all sorts, frivolity, jokes, flinging money about while living amid poverty and oppression, and nothing more. And there's no possibility of stopping it, denouncing it, making people feel ashamed. The deaf would be more likely to hear than those who shout incessantly. And I'm terribly, terribly miserable. If I were to say that I'm bearing it patiently and doing what I can, I wouldn't be telling the truth. I'm losing heart, becoming embittered, praying without hope, and I'm disgusted with myself. That's the truth.

Nothing new has happened, everything is just the same; but the stupidity and depravity of this life grows worse and worse, and there's less and less resistance on my part and a closer and closer nearness to the end, and therefore a greater and greater desire for a quiet and worthy human life. And I lack what was my salvation before: intensive, absorbing, engrossing work. I'm writing about art, but the work is partly academic, especially now, and not interesting, and I haven't the energy for other works. Please don't try to comfort me, and don't write to me about this, and don't read my letter to *anyone* except Posha. I only needed to express myself to a man I love and who loves me, and I shall feel better for it. At good moments I say

2. Eleonora Duse, who was to make a Russian tour in 1897; the tour did not take place owing to her illness.
3. Joseph Hofmann, a Polish pianist who was giving concerts in Russia at the time.
4. Mikhail Sukhotin, Tanya's future husband, who was still married to his first wife.
5. P. I. Biryukov.

[432] 1. Chertkov was in Petersburg at the time, paying official visits in connection with the Dukhobors and their projected emigration, and the return of the Khilkhov children (see Letter 389, note 6, and Letter 397). 2. P. I. Biryukov.

to myself that what has happened to me is necessary for me, that I need to live like this till I die, and then again I feel anger, and longing and reproachfulness because it hasn't been granted to me, if only just before I die, if only for a year, if only for a month, to live the life that is natural to me, away from this falsehood in which I not only live, but take part and drown.

So write to me about yourself, as frankly as I write about myself, and don't write about me.

I press your hand.

L.T.

433. To COUNTESS S. A. TOLSTAYA

Nikolskoye-Obolyanovo, 1 February 1897

My dear Sonya,

Tanya has written to you about our journey here[1] and how we are, about our outer state, but I want to write to you about what interests you—my inner, spiritual state.

I was sad when I was leaving, and you felt it, and for that reason came to the station, but you didn't dispel my miserable feeling but rather made it worse. You told me to be calm and then said that you wouldn't go to the rehearsal.[2] I couldn't understand for a long time what rehearsal. I'd never even thought about it. And all this hurts me. It was unpleasant—more than unpleasant—for me to learn that in spite of the fact that you spent so much time considering when to go to Petersburg and making preparations, the result is that you are going just at the time when there was no need to go. I know you didn't do this on purpose, but that it all happened unconsciously, as is always the case with people occupied with a single thought. I know that nothing will come now of the fact that you are going, but you can't help toying with it, and exciting yourself; and my attitude to it also excites you. And your *are* toying with it. This game is terribly painful to me. You may say that you couldn't have organised the visit differently. But if you think

[433] 1. On 1 February 1897 Tolstoy left Moscow where he had joined Sofya Andreyevna and the family in November for the winter, and with Tanya went to the estate of the Olsufyev family, Nikolskoye-Obolyanovo, where they remained for about a month. (Chertkov and Biryukov were arrested in Petersburg the day after Tolstoy's departure, and he interrupted his stay in order to visit the capital.)

One reason for Tolstoy's departure was his wife's infatuation with Sergey Taneyev (1856–1915), a distinguished musician and long-standing friend of the family. This situation had come to a head by the end of 1896 and was becoming intolerable to Tolstoy. The infatuation was entirely one-sided, however, and Taneyev was as much disturbed and embarrassed by the situation—when he finally realised it—as anyone else.

At the time of this letter, Sofya Andreyevna was becoming increasingly open about her feelings, attending all Taneyev's concerts and seeing him frequently. Taneyev continued to regard himself as a family friend, however, visiting Yasnaya Polyana to see Tolstoy (they were chess partners and often discussed art and the philosophy of aesthetics); and only later did he become so discomfited by Sofya Andreyevna's attentions (after receiving a letter he termed 'absurd' and destroyed) that he temporarily broke off relations with her.

2. A rehearsal for a concert to be given by Taneyev in Petersburg on 8 February.

433. To Countess S. A. Tolstaya

about it and analyse yourself, you will see that it isn't true: firstly, there is no particular need for the journey, and secondly, you could have gone before or after—during Lent.

But you can't help doing this. It's terribly painful and humiliatingly shameful that a complete outsider, an unnecessary and quite uninteresting man,[3] rules our life and poisons the last years or year of our life; it's humiliating and painful that one has to ask when and where he is going, and when he is playing at what rehearsals.

This is terrible, terrible, shameful and repulsive. And it's happening just at the end of our life—a life spent well and purely—just at the time when we have been drawing closer and closer together in spite of everything that could divide us. This rapprochement began long ago, even before Vanichka's death, and became closer and closer, especially recently, and suddenly, instead of a natural, good and joyful conclusion to 35 years of life together, there is this repulsive vileness which has left its terrible imprint on everything. I know you are miserable and you are suffering too, because you love me and want to be good, but so far you can't, and I'm terribly sorry for you because I love you with the best kind of love—not of the body or the mind, but of the soul.

Goodbye, and forgive me, dearest.

I kiss you.

L.T.

Destroy this letter.

In any case, write to me more often.

Why am I writing? Firstly to express my thoughts and relieve myself, and secondly and chiefly to tell you or remind you of the full significance of those worthless acts which make up the thing that torments us, to help you escape from that terrible, hypnotised state in which you are living.

This can end involuntarily by the death of one or the other of us, and that will be a terrible end both for the one who dies and the one who is left; or it can end freely by a change which will take place within one of us. Such a change can't take place in me; I can't stop seeing what I see in you, because I see your condition clearly; nor can I regard it indifferently. To do so—to regard it indifferently—I should have to bury all our past life, tear out of my heart all the feelings I have for you. And not only do I not want to, but I can't. And so there is only one possibility left, that you should wake from your sleep-walking, and return to a normal, natural life. May God help you in this. I am ready to help you with all my strength, and you must teach me how.

I think it's better not to call in on your way to Petersburg. Better call in on your way back. We've seen each other recently, and I can't help experiencing an unpleasant feeling about the trip. I feel weak, and I'm afraid of myself. Better call in on your way back.[4] You always say to me: be calm; and that offends and distresses

---

3. Taneyev.
4. Sofya Andreyevna went to Petersburg on 5 February for the rehearsal, and then to Nikolskoye, from where she returned to Petersburg with Tolstoy for the concert on 8 February.

433. To Countess S. A. Tolstaya

me. I trust your integrity absolutely, and if I want to know about you, it isn't from lack of trust, but in order to make sure how involved or free you are.

434. To A. F. KONI

Anatoly Fyodorovich Koni (1844–1927), a lawyer and member of the Senate. Koni and Tolstoy met in June 1887 at Yasnaya Polyana, and at the very beginning of their friendship Koni, who often related cases from his courtroom experience, told Tolstoy the story which served as the basis for *Resurrection*. Tolstoy was immediately struck by it, and at first invited Koni to write it up for *The Intermediary*; when this was not done, he asked for permission to use the material himself as fiction. From time to time Tolstoy requested him to use his influence to improve the lot of conscientious objectors.

Koni's friendship with Tolstoy, which he wrote about in his autobiography, *On Life's Path* (Moscow, 1916), lasted until Tolstoy's death, and he frequently visited the Tolstoy family in Moscow and at Yasnaya Polyana.

Moscow, 9 March 1897

Dear Anatoly Fyodorovich,

Yesterday evening my son told me about the terrible affair that happened in the Peter and Paul fortress and about the demonstration in the Kazan cathedral.[1] I didn't altogether believe the story, particularly because I had heard that the Peter and Paul fortress doesn't contain prisoners any more. But this morning a professor who met me confirmed the whole story, saying that they, the professors, having had a meeting yesterday, had been unable to discuss anything, since they were so shaken by this terrible event. I came home with the intention of writing to you and asking you to tell me the truth about this business, since many things are often added and even invented. I hadn't had time to begin the letter when a lady arrived from Petersburg—a friend of the woman who perished—and told me about the whole business and the fact that the young woman Vetrova who took her own life was known to me and had visited me at Yasnaya Polyana.

Is there no possibility of finding out for certain the cause of the suicide and what happened to her at her interrogation, and of pacifying the terribly agitated public opinion, pacifying it by some government measure which could show that what had happened had been an exception, the fault of private individuals and not of general instructions, and that the same thing doesn't threaten all those near and dear to us, given the silent arrest and imprisonment which are practised?

You will ask: what do I want of you? Firstly, if possible, a description of what is

[434] 1. A demonstration by university students and teachers to protest at the death of M. F. Vetrova, a student-revolutionary who, while under arrest in the Peter and Paul Fortress, had committed suicide by setting fire to herself with a kerosene lamp (February 1897). The incident was at first hushed up, but eventually came out, and a demonstration took place outside the Kazan Cathedral on 4 March.

reliably known about this matter, and secondly, advice about what to do to counteract these terrible crimes being perpetrated in the name of the good of the state.

If you have no time and don't wish to reply, don't reply, but if you do reply I shall be very grateful.

I press your hand in friendship,

Yours affectionately,
Lev Tolstoy

435. To V. G. CHERTKOV

Moscow, 11 March 1897

I miss you very much, my dear Vladimir Grigoryevich. I've only had one letter from you and one from Galya.[1] Hurry up and write, and in more detail. How did you like Kenworthy's friends? And Kenworthy himself, at home? How have you settled down with all your people? What new connections and friendships have you made? What is the new rut like which your life is entering? I'm very much afraid that you will be corrupted in England. I've just received the *Review of Reviews* and read it, and I caught such a breath of that astonishing, self-satisfied English dullness, that I put myself in your place and tried to think how you would get on with them. I think that about everybody, except the small circle of free people among whom you are living or may live. When one comes across and recognises barbarity of thought and feeling in our country, one puts it down to our regime, but over there, where you are, one is nonplussed: why?...[47 lines omitted]

436. To COUNTESS S. A. TOLSTAYA

To be read alone

Yasnaya Polyana, 12–13 May 1897

How was your journey and how are you now, my dear? Your visit left such a strong, cheerful and good impression—too good, even, for me, because I miss you more keenly.

My waking up and your being there was one of the strongest, most joyful impressions I have ever experienced: and that at the age of 69, from a woman of 53.

Yesterday I sent the Molokans off with the letters and the letter.[1] I think the

---

[435] 1. Chertkov had been sentenced to administrative exile for the part he played in supporting the cause of the Dukhobors, and had chosen to go to England, where he and his wife and child at first settled in Croydon with Kenworthy's Brotherhood Community.

[436] 1. On 10 May Tolstoy wrote several letters to highly placed figures at the court of Nicholas II, as well as to the Tsar himself, pleading for the return of the children who had been forcibly taken away from their Molokan parents in Samara, under the same law which had deprived D. A. Khilkov of his children (see Letter 389, note 6). All these letters were given to the fathers of the children concerned, who had stopped *en route* to Petersburg at Yasnaya Polyana. Unfortunately the letters were destroyed by the Molokans on the advice of a servant

436. To Countess S. A. Tolstoya

letter oughtn't to offend the Emperor. I cut out the part I read to you, and which you found risky. Twice today there was a wonderful storm and cloudburst. Summer is hurrying into life—the lilac is already pale, the lime tree blossom will soon be out, there are turtle-doves and an oriole in the thick foliage deep in the garden, and a nightingale under the windows is wonderfully musical. Now it's night, the stars are bright and shining, as though washed, and after the rain there's a smell of lilac and birch leaves. Seryozha came the evening you left; he knocked under my window and I shouted joyfully 'Sonya'. No, it was Seryozha. We're all good friends, and everyone is pleased. The work is going not too badly. This evening I feel rather more cheeful and I can hardly feel my headache. Perhaps my illness is just old age. Marya Alexandrovna was here today. Masha and Tanya are going to Tula tomorrow. If Boulanger's article on the Dukhobors is in *The Russian Gazette*, please send it.

Goodbye; I kiss you, Masha and Misha—how is Misha? Has he calmed down? If he's so much loved and in love, he ought to study particularly well, because he's happy and contented.

Well, that's all. It's getting on for 1 o'clock now on the 13th.

L.T.

437. To COUNTESS S. A. TOLSTAYA

[Not sent]

Yasnaya Polyana, 19 May 1897
night

My dear, darling Sonya,

Your intimacy with Taneyev is not merely unpleasant to me, but dreadfully agonising. By continuing to live under these conditions, I am poisoning and shortening my life. For a year now I haven't been able to work, and I'm not living, but continually being tormented. You know this. I've said so to you in anger, and I've said so with entreaties, and recently I haven't said anything at all. I've tried everything and nothing has helped: the intimacy continues and even grows closer, and I can see that it will be like this to the end. I can't bear it any longer. At first, after I got your last letter, I made up my mind to go away.[1] For three days I lived with this idea, and endured it, and decided that however painful separation from you would be for me, I would nevertheless rescue myself from this terrible situation with its humiliating suspicions, agitations and heartbreaks, and be able to live and do towards the end of my life what I consider it necessary to do. And I decided to go away, but when I thought about you—not about how it would hurt me to be

in the household of the Grand Duke Georgy Mikhaylovich, where they had called in the hope of obtaining an interview. However, a copy of the letter to Nicholas II had been made by Tolstoy, and reached its destination through other channels. There was no reply to the letter, nor were the children returned to their homes.

[437] 1. Tolstoy was deeply upset by the news that Taneyev was to visit Yasnaya Polyana in June.

437. To Countess S. A. Tolstaya

without you, however much it would hurt, but about how it would grieve and torment you, and how you would suffer—I realised that I couldn't do it, couldn't go away from you without your consent.

The position is this: I am *almost* unable to continue living as we are living now. I say *almost* unable, because I feel every moment I'm capable of breaking loose and doing something bad: I can't think without horror of the continuation of the almost physical sufferings I experience and can't help experiencing.

You know this—you may have forgotten or wanted to forget—but you did know this, and you are a good woman and you love me, and yet you didn't want to—I don't want to think that you couldn't—save me and yourself from these terrible, unnecessary sufferings.

What is it to be? Decide yourself. Think it over and decide yourself how to act. The solutions to this situation seem to me to be as follows: (1) the best thing is to break off all relations, but not gradually and not out of consideration for what people might think about it, but in such a way as to free yourself once and for all from this terrible nightmare which has been oppressing us now for a year. No meetings, no letters, no young boys, no portraits, no mushroom picking at Anna Ivanovna's or Pomerantsev's,[2] but complete freedom as Masha freed herself from Zander and Tanya from Popov. This is one way, and the best one. Another solution is for me to go abroad, parting with you for ever, and for each of us to live his own life independently of the other. This is the most difficult solution, but still a possible one, and 1,000 times easier for me than continuing the life we have been leading this year.

The third solution is also to break off all relations with Taneyev and for us both to go abroad and live there until the cause of all this has passed.

The fourth, which is not a solution, but the most terrible choice, and one I can't think about without horror and despair, is to persuade oneself that this will pass and that it's not important at all, and to continue living as we have done this year: for you, without being aware of it, to seek every means of intimacy, and for me to see and observe and conjecture and be tormented—not by jealousy, although perhaps that feeling is there too, but it isn't the main one. The main thing, as I told you, is shame, both for you and for me; the very feeling I experienced in regard to Tanya, with Popov and Stakhovich, only 100 times more painful. The fifth solution is the one you suggested: for me to stop looking at it the way I do and wait for it—if it is anything—to pass, as you say. I've tried this fifth solution and I'm convinced that I can't destroy in me the feeling which torments me, as long as the pretexts for it continue to exist.

I've experienced this for a year and have tried with all my heart, but I can't and I know I can't; on the contrary, the blows falling all the time on the same place have aggravated my pain to the highest degree. You write that it hurts you

2. Anna Ivanovna Maslova, whose family owned an estate in the Oryol district. Taneyev frequently visited them in the summer.
Yury Nikolayevich Pomerantsev, a student of Taneyev's who lived in Taneyev's home for a while.

437. To Countess S. A. Tolstaya

to see Gurevich[3] in spite of the fact that the feeling you associate with her had no semblance of a foundation and lasted only a few days. But what must I feel after two years of infatuations for which there were very obvious foundations, when, after all that has happened, you arranged daily meetings in my absence—or if they weren't daily, it wasn't your fault.[4]

And in the same letter you write out a sort of programme for our future life, so that I shouldn't interfere with your occupations and pleasures, when I know what they are.

Sonya, darling, you are a good, kind, fair-minded woman. Put yourself in my position and try to understand that I can't feel otherwise than I do, i.e. feel agonising pain and shame, and try to think, darling, of the best way, not so much to save me from this, but to save yourself from still worse torments which will inevitably come in one form or another unless you change your views about all this and make an effort. This is the third letter I'm writing to you. The first was an angry one, the second was a note which I'm leaving here. You will see from it my earlier and better mood. I'm leaving for Pirogovo in order to give you and myself freedom to think things over better and not lapse into anger or a false reconciliation.

Think things over carefully in the sight of God and write to me. In any case I shall be back soon and we can try to discuss everything calmly. As long as things are not left as they are—there can be no worse hell for me than that. Perhaps I need this. But you certainly don't. True, there are two other solutions—my death or yours—but both are terrible if they should happen before we manage to absolve our sin.

I'm opening the letter to add something more. If you don't choose the first or the second or the third solution, i.e. if you don't break off all relations with him completely, don't let me go abroad so that we should end all relations or don't go abroad with me for an indefinite time, with Sasha of course, but choose the uncertain and unhappy solution that everything should stay as before and it will all pass, then I beg you not to talk to me about it. I shall keep silent as I have recently kept silent, and simply wait for death which alone can save us from this torture.

I'm also going away because, not having slept for nearly 5 nights, I feel so nervously exhausted, I only have to start to do something and I burst into tears, and I fear that I shan't be able to endure a meeting with you and all that might come of it.

I can't ascribe my condition to physical ill-health because I've felt well the whole time and I'm not suffering from stomach pains or biliousness.

3. Lyubov Yakovlevna Gurevich, editor of *The Northern Herald*, where Tolstoy had published the story *Master and Man* in 1895, causing much jealousy and anger on the part of his wife who wanted to print it first in her own edition of Tolstoy's *Collected Works*.
4. Sofya Andreyevna saw Taneyev on five occasions between 1 May and 20 May.

438. To COUNTESS S. A. TOLSTAYA

Yasnaya Polyana, 8 July 1897

Dear Sonya,

I have long been tormented by the incongruity between my life and my beliefs. I haven't been able to make you change your life or your habits to which I have myself accustomed you, and up to now I haven't been able to leave you, thinking that I should be depriving the children while they were still young of the influence, however small, which I might have over them, and should grieve you; but neither was I able to continue living any longer the way I have been living these last 16 years, now struggling and irritating you, now yielding to the temptations to which I was accustomed and by which I was surrounded, and I have now decided to do what I have long wished to do—to go away—firstly because with my advancing years this life is becoming more and more burdensome to me and I long more and more for solitude, and secondly because the children have grown up and my influence in the house is no longer necessary and all of you have more lively interests which will make my absence hardly noticeable.[1]

But the main thing is that just as the Hindus, when they are getting on for 60, retire to the forests, and every religious man wants to dedicate the last years of his life to God and not to jokes, puns, gossip and tennis, so I, who am entering my 70th year, long with all my heart and soul for this tranquillity and solitude, and if not full accord, then at least not blatant discord between my life and my beliefs and conscience.

If I did this openly, there would be entreaties, recriminations, arguments and complaints, and I would weaken, perhaps, and not carry out my decision, and it must be carried out. So please forgive me if my action causes you pain, and above all, Sonya, in your own heart, let me go freely and don't try to find me, don't complain of me, don't condemn me.

The fact that I have left you doesn't mean that I'm dissatisfied with you. I know you *couldn't*, literally couldn't and cannot see and feel as I do, and therefore you couldn't and cannot change your life and make sacrifices for the sake of something you don't acknowledge. And therefore I don't condemn you, but on the contrary

---

[438] 1. In early June Sergey Taneyev had stayed at Yasnaya Polyana for two days and now in July Sofya Andreyevna invited him back, without telling Tolstoy of the invitation. Taneyev arrived at Yasnaya Polyana on 5 July and remained for a week, during which Tolstoy wrote the above letter to his wife, announcing his decision to leave her permanently. However, it was not delivered, and the following day a temporary reconciliation took place.

The subsequent history of the letter is interesting. Tolstoy placed it under the upholstery of a chair in his study where it remained unknown to anyone until a few years later (1901 or 1902) when he was seriously ill and told Masha of its existence, instructing her to remove it and to prevent it from becoming public until fifty years after his death. As he soon recovered, however, nothing was done about it. In 1907, when his wife was planning to re-upholster the furniture in the study, Tolstoy gave the letter, together with another one, to Masha's husband, Prince Obolensky, with instructions to give them to Sofya Andreyevna after his death. This was done in 1910. (Sofya Andreyevna tore up the other letter, whose content is unknown, in the presence of Prince Obolensky.)

438. To Countess S. A. Tolstaya

I remember with love and gratitude the long 35 years of our life together, especially the first half of that time when, with maternal self-sacrifice characteristic of your nature, you bore so steadfastly and energetically what you considered you had been called to bear. You gave to me and the world what you were able to give; you gave much maternal love and self-sacrifice, and it's impossible not to appreciate you for it. But in the later period of our life, during the last 15 years, we have drifted apart. I can't think that I'm to blame, because I know that it's not for my own sake or for other people's that I've changed, but because I can't do otherwise. Nor can I blame you for not having followed me, and I thank you and remember you with love, and always shall remember you for all you have given me. Goodbye, dear Sonya.

Yours affectionately,
Lev Tolstoy

439. To V. G. CHERTKOV

[Postscript only]

Yasnaya Polyana, 13 October 1897

...My girls are in the Crimea. To me, Masha is like a person drunk. I know she will understand me, but not now. It's impossible to talk to her now until she's slept it off and got over the hangover.

How many people there are like that, whom you can't talk to at all because you know they are drunk. Some are drunk with greed, some with vanity, some with being in love and some directly with drugs. God save us from these intoxications. These intoxications put barriers between people just as much as religiosity, patriotism or aristocratism, and prevent the unity which God wants. You live together, side by side, all your life, yet you live like strangers.

That's how it is for me now with Masha and her husband. I can't tell her that her marriage is 'a failure',[1] despite the fact that he's a nice young man. I can't say this—it's left unsaid. And it's a shame to have to come to this.

Well, goodbye.

Yours,
L. Tolstoy

440. To P. A. BOULANGER

Pavel Alexandrovich Boulanger (1864–1925), a personal friend of Tolstoy and an adherent of some of his ideas. Their friendship dated from 1886 and the correspondence between them was considerable. In 1897 Boulanger was arrested for his efforts on behalf of the Dukhobors and like Chertkov, given the choice between exile in Russia or abroad. Like Chertkov, he chose to go to England, where he

---

[439] 1. In English in the original.

settled at the Purleigh Colony, worked on Chertkov's various publishing ventures, and later edited a *Brotherhood News-sheet* on his own initiative. He was allowed to return to Russia in 1899, and he soon took up employment on the Moscow–Kursk railway. At various times he was involved in newspaper and publishing ventures which either failed or were banned. He wrote many short articles about Tolstoy, his life, and the background to his writing, as well as his own memoirs. He also helped to edit several short editions of Tolstoy's works.

Yasnaya Polyana, 17 November 1897

I got your long letter from Moscow yesterday, dear Pavel Alexandrovich. I'm still in the country and want to stay here as long as possible. The advantage of life here over life in Moscow is very great. The more I live, the more convinced I am of the undoubted fact that the simplicity, poverty, loneliness and tedium of one's life are an invariable sign of the importance, seriousness and fruitfulness of that life, and on the contrary, that complexity, wealth, sociability and gaiety of life are a sign of its worthlessness. I sit here alone: I write a bit, play patience, talk to Alexander Petrovich[1] and anybody who calls, read trifling things, walk round the room alone, and know and feel that my life is leaving its mark on me and probably therefore on someone else as well. But in Moscow and London there are very interesting events, books, people to talk to, meetings, discussions, a life which is apparently full to overflowing, but it's an empty one and—God grant—only empty, and not evil as well. The life which is in us is such a great and holy thing that we mustn't destroy its holiness, mustn't sully it, must be like children—and life will be fruitful and satisfying. Thank you very much for your letter. I need to know all this about you,[2] and you have tried to tell me everything about yourself and tried not only to show me, but also to convince me that you are all right, but I feel you've been miserable and unwell. Of course the whole thing is not to think about the morrow, but there's only one way not to think about it: to think constantly about whether one has done today's work properly. And for us people with family ties, this is very difficult because union with what has become one flesh is often destroyed, and then you lose your way...[15 lines omitted]

441. To COUNTESS S. A. TOLSTAYA

Yasnaya Polyana, 26 November 1897

Tanya came yesterday and spent a day here, and left me with the happy impression of being freed from her obsession.[1] God grant that the good, free state she is in now will last, and, moreover, that she will find herself some good and congenial work. I got your letter to Dora today, from which it is obvious that you are

[440] 1. A. P. Ivanov, an amanuensis of Tolstoy's who did occasional copying work for him.
2. Boulanger's letter is not extant, but from his *Memoirs* it appears that it raised the question of divorce from his wife, who did not share his general views on life.
[441] 1. A reference to Tanya's relationship with Mikhail Sukhotin.

441. To Countess S. A. Tolstaya

miserable and unwell. This hurts me very much, especially because I can't help you. Your argument that it's far more important and necessary for me to be with you in Moscow than that such and such a thing should be a bit worse or better written astonishes me by its unfairness. Firstly, the question is not which is more important; secondly I don't live here only because some work or other might be a bit better written; thirdly, my presence in Moscow, as you know very well, can't stop Andryusha or Misha from living badly if they want to. The strictest father in the world can't stop people with sprouting beards from living the way they consider good. Fourthly, even if it were a question of which was more important—to write what I am writing and what I at least think and hope (otherwise I wouldn't work) will be read by millions and might have a good influence on millions, or to live in Moscow without anything to do in Moscow, frivolously, anxiously and unhealthily—then anyone would decide the question in favour of not going to Moscow.

This doesn't mean that I don't want to go to Moscow, don't want to do all I can to make your life better or that I simply don't wish to be with you; on the contrary, I wish it very much, but your arguments are very unfair, just like your arguments which you derived from reading Beethoven's biography that the aim of my work is fame. Fame may be the aim of a young or very empty man. But for a serious and especially an old man, the aim of work is not fame, but the best use of one's powers. We are all called on to live and to work like a horse in harness. Whether we go to the Slavonic Bazaar[2] or mine ore[3] or play the piano, we have to do something. But a man who is not stupid and has seen life—and I consider myself to be one—can't help seeing that the only good which the conscience approves of is doing work which I can do best of all and which I consider pleasing to God and useful to people. That is the motive which guides me in my work, and as for fame, I asked myself long ago whether I would work just the same if I were never to know whether my work would be approved or not by people, and I replied sincerely that of course I would work just the same. I don't say that I'm indifferent to people's approval; approval is pleasant, but it isn't the reason or the motive for my work. I write this especially in order to wish you, Sonya dear, the same sort of work, the sort of work where you would know you were doing the best thing you could do, and, in doing it, would feel at peace before God and before mankind. You used to have work like that—bringing up children—which you did so unselfishly and well, and you know this awareness of duty done, and therefore know that it certainly wasn't fame which inspired you to do this work. This is the sort of work I wish you to have—passionately wish it, and would pray for if I believed that prayer could achieve it. Exactly what this work is I don't know, and can't explain to you, but there is such work, natural to you, important and worth while, of the sort to which one's whole life can be devoted, just as there is such work for every

2. A Moscow restaurant.
3. Tolstoy's son Lev had recently discovered ore on his property; in his diary for 12 November Tolstoy noted his strong disapproval of his son's plans to derive an income from this ore, which, or course, was to be mined by the efforts of others.

man, and this work in your case is certainly not playing the piano and listening to concerts.

How I would like you, Sonya dear, to accept this letter with the disinterested love, complete self-oblivion and sole desire for your good which I feel at this moment. My work, once again, is solely correcting *Art*. I have to send it to Maude and Grot. I'm thinking over a few things. I'm quite well, and have just been skating with Lyova and the village boys. It was good! The whole big pond is like a mirror. Why don't you skate? I'm sure it would be very good for you. But going to bed at 3 o'clock is very bad. I kiss you warmly.

L.T.

442. To. V. G. CHERTKOV

Moscow, 21 January 1898

I wrote to you recently, dear friends, but I don't want to miss the opportunity to write again. Yesterday I got your letter, No. 33. I'm rather disturbed by the fact that you write about my apparently exceptional situation. My situation is the one I deserve, and it's a very good situation. Please try to understand my situation this way and don't write to me about it, and in particular don't communicate to anybody the contents of those letters of mine in which I express dissatisfaction that my life is not as I would like it to be. I sometimes allow myself to be naughty in front of you, but only in front of you. Enough of that...[21 lines omitted]

443. To G. H. GIBSON

George Howard Gibson was a member of an American community called 'Christian Commonwealth' which had just published the first issue of a journal *The Social Gospel*, which Gibson had sent to Tolstoy with a letter outlining his views. His community was one of many similar ones throughout the world which were either consciously organised on 'Tolstoyan' lines or else recognised an affinity between their own practices and Tolstoy's ideas. In a letter Tolstoy had written the previous year to a member of a Christian community in Russia, he had given some information about various communities in other countries whose activities he sympathised with. They included the colony in Essex where Chertkov was living, one in Holland consisting of a group of young ministers, and one in America, of which Ernest Crosby was a member.

[Original in English]

Moscow, 11/23 March 1898

My dear friend,

I duly received your letter and magazine, both of which afforded me great

[443] 1. George Davis Herron, a member of Gibson's communal group.

443. To G. H. Gibson

pleasure. The first number is very good and I liked all the articles in it. It is quite true, as you say it in your article *The Social Need*, and Herron[1] in his, that a Christian life is quite impossible in the present un-Christian organization of society. The contradictions between his surroundings and his convictions are very painful for a man who is sincere in his Christian faith, and therefore the organization of communities seems to such a man the only means of delivering himself from these contradictions. But this is an illusion. Every community is a small island in the midst of an ocean of un-Christian conditions of life, so that the Christian relations exist only between members of the colony but outside that must remain un-Christian, otherwise the colony would not exist for a moment. And therefore to live in community cannot save a Christian from the contradiction between his conscience and his life. I do not mean to say that I do not approve of communities such as your commonwealth, or that I do not think them to be a good thing. On the contrary, I approve of them with all my heart and am very interested in your commonwealth and wish it the greatest success.

I think that every man who can free himself from the conditions of worldly life without breaking the ties of love—love the main principle in the name of which he seeks new forms of life—I think such a man not only must, but naturally will join people who have the same beliefs and who try to live up to them. If I were free I would immediately even at my age join such a colony. I only wished to say that the mere forming of communities is not a solution for the Christian problem, but is only one of the means of its solution. The revolution that is going on for the attainment of the Christian ideal is so enormous, our life is so different from what it ought to be, that for the perfect success of this revolution, for the concordance of conscience and life, is needed the work of all men—men living in communities as well as men of the world living in the most different conditions. This ideal is not so quickly and so simply attained as we think and wish it. This ideal will be attained only when every man in the whole world will say: *Why should I sell my services and buy yours? If mine are greater than yours I owe them to you*, because if there is in the whole world one man who does not think and act by this principle, and who will take and keep by violence what he can take from others, no man can live a true Christian life, as well in a community as outside it. We cannot be saved separately, we must be saved all together. And this can be attained only through the modification of the conception of life, i.e. the faith of all men; and to this end we must work all together—men living in the world as well as men living in communities.

We must all of us remember that we are messengers from the great King—the God of Love with the message of unity and love between all living beings. And therefore we must not for a minute forget our mission, and do all what we think useful and agreeable for ourselves only so long as it is not in opposition to our mission which is to be accomplished not only by words, but by example and especially by the infection of love.

Please give my respect and love to the colonists and ask them not to be offended by me giving them advice, which may be unnecessary. I advise them to remember that all material questions of money, implements, nourishment, even the very existence of the colony itself—all those things are of little importance in comparison of the sole important object of our life: to preserve love amongst all men, which we come in contact with. If with the object of keeping the food of the colony or of protecting the thrift of it you must quarrel with a friend or with a stranger, must excite ill-feelings in somebody, it is better to give up everything, than to act against love. And let our friends not dread that the strict following of the principle will destroy the practical work. Even the practical work will flourish—not as we expect it, but in its own way, only by strict following the law of love and will perish by acting in opposition to it.

Your friend and brother,
Leo Tolstoy

I had just finished this letter, when I received from the Caucasus news from the Duchoborys ('spirit wrestlers') that they had received an authorization to leave Russia and emigrate abroad. They write to me that they have the intention of going to England or America. They are about 10,000 men. They are the most religious, moral and laborious, and very strong people. The Russian government has by all sorts of persecutions quite ruined them and they have not the means to emigrate. I will write about it to the papers in America and England. Meanwhile you will oblige me—you and your friend Herron, Crosby, and others—if you give me some suggestions about this matter.

Yours, L.T.

444. To FOREIGN NEWSPAPERS

After writing the following statement of the Dukhobors' situation to foreign newspapers, Tolstoy wrote a dozen or more letters in August and September to leading Russian industrialists, to plead the Dukhobor cause and solicit funds for their emigration. At least four replied with donations totalling 17,000 roubles (but others, including P. M. Tretyakov, refused). Tolstoy calculated that approximately 750,000 roubles would be required for the emigration of 7,500 Dukhobors and that some 400,000 roubles might be available from the sale of the Dukhobors' possessions in Russia, the Quaker fund in England and the sale of his own unpublished works. He hoped to obtain some 350,000 roubles from personal contributions.

The following letter appeared in a slightly different English translation in *The Daily Chronicle* on 29 April 1898.

Moscow, 19 March/1 April 1898

A population of 12,000 people, the World Brotherhood of Christians as the Dukhobors who live in the Caucasus call themselves, is at the present moment in a terrible situation.

Without entering into arguments about who is right: the government which acknowledges the compatibility of Christianity with prisons, executions and, most

444. To Foreign Newspapers

important, with wars and the preparations for them, or the Dukhobors who acknowledge as binding on themselves the Christian law which repudiates all violence, above all murder, and who therefore reject military service—it is impossible not to see that this contradiction is very difficult to resolve: no government can allow people to evade obligations fulfilled by everyone, and thereby to undermine the very foundations of sovereignty; but the Dukhobors, for their part, cannot reject the law which they consider to be God's and therefore binding on their lives.

Up to now, governments have found a way out of this contradiction either by forcing those who object to military service because of religious convictions to undertake heavier obligations than military service, but ones which would not be contrary to their religious convictions, as has hitherto been done and still is done with the Mennonites in Russia (they are made to spend their period of military service on government work) or by acknowledging the legitimacy of the religious objection, and punishing those who do not fulfil the common law of the state by imprisonment for the period of their service, as is done with the Nazarenes in Austria. But the present Russian government has used yet a third solution to this contradiction with the Dukhobors, which one thought had been abandoned in our time. Apart from subjecting the objectors themselves to the most severe sufferings, it makes even the fathers, mothers and children of the objectors systematically suffer, probably in order that the torture of these innocent families might shake the determination of their nonconformist members. Not to mention the floggings, detention houses, and every type of torture which the Dukhobor objectors have undergone in disciplinary battalions, from which many have died, or their exile to the worst places in Siberia, not to mention the 200 reservists who have languished in prison for two years and now are separated from their families and sent off in pairs to the wildest parts of the Caucasus where, having no earnings, they are literally dying of hunger, not to mention these punishments for those guilty of conscientious objection, the Dukhobor families are being systematically ruined and destroyed. They are deprived of the right to absent themselves from their place of residence and are heavily fined and locked up in prison for not fulfilling the strangest requirements of the authorities: for calling themselves by a different name from the one they are told to use, for a trip to the mill, for a visit by a mother to her son, for leaving the village to gather wood in the forest—so that the last resources of previously wealthy inhabitants are quickly being exhausted. Four hundred families who have been moved out of their residences and settled in Tatar and Georgian villages where they must rent homes for themselves and buy food, having neither land nor earnings, are in such a difficult situation that within 3 years of their resettlement a quarter of them, especially old people and children, have already died from want or illness.

It is difficult to think that such a systematic destruction of an entire population of 12,000 people entered into the plans of the Russian government. It is very probable that the highest authorities do not know what is actually happening, and even if they guess, they have no wish to know the details, feeling that they must not allow such a business to continue, and at the same time, that what is happening is what is necessary.

But there is no doubt that in the course of the last three years the Caucasian authorities have been systematically tormenting not only the objectors themselves but also their families, and just as systematically ruining all the Dukhobors and hounding to death those who have been resettled.

Up to now, all intercessions on behalf of the Dukhobors and any help for them have only led to the expulsion from Russia of those who have tried to help the Dukhobors. The Caucasian government has surrounded the entire unruly population by a magic circle and this population is slowly dying out. Another 3 or 4 years and none of the Dukhobors would have been left.

And so it would have been, had there not occurred a circumstance unforeseen by the Caucasian authorities. This circumstance is that last year the Dowager Empress came to the Caucasus to see her son, and the Dukhobors succeeded in submitting a petition to her in which they asked to be allowed to be resettled all together in some far-off place, and if this was impossible, then somewhere abroad. The Empress passed on this request to the highest authorities; the highest authorities acknowledged that it was possible to give permission to the Dukhobors to leave Russia.

It would seem that the question had been resolved and a solution found to a difficult situation for both sides. But it only seems so.

In the situation in which the Dukhobors now are, resettlement is impossible for them: they do not have the resources for it and, being confined to their villages, they are unable to make a start on it. They were rich, but in recent years the greater part of their resources has been taken away from them by the courts, and in fines, and has gone on feeding their resettled brothers; and to consider collectively and decide on the conditions for their emigration is totally impossible for them, as they are not allowed out of their places of residence and nobody is allowed in to them. The attached letter describes best of all the situation which they are now in.

Here is what a man who is respected amongst the Dukhobors writes to me:

I beg to inform you that we submitted a petition to Her Imperial Majesty the Dowager Empress, Marya Fyodorovna. She passed it on to the Senate, the Senate took a decision and passed it on to Prince Golitsyn to deal with. I attach a document about it herewith.

On 10 February, I travelled to Tiflis and there I saw our brother St John, but our meeting was very short—we were immediately arrested. I was imprisoned and he was immediately sent back to England.

I told the Chief of Police that I had come on business to see the Governor. He said: 'For the time being we'll put you in prison and then we'll report to the Governor.' On the 12th I was imprisoned, and on the 18th I was taken with an escort of two soldiers to the Governor. Some head of department asked me: 'What have you been arrested for?'

I replied: 'I don't know.'

'A few days ago you were in Signakh?'

'Yes, I was.'

'And why did you come here?'

444. To Foreign Newspapers

'I intended to see the Governor. We submitted a petition to the Empress Marya Fyodorovna in the summer in Abastuman; I received a reply to the petition through the district head in Signakh, I requested a copy and he refused me, saying it was impossible without the Governor—and so I came.'

He reported to the Governor; the Governor called me in; I explained how it all was to him. He said: 'You preferred to see an Englishman instead of me.' I said: 'The Englishman is also our brother.'

The Governor had a good talk with me and advised us to emigrate abroad as soon as possible and said: 'You may all emigrate; only those who belong to the present call-up cannot go, i.e. those about to be drafted.'

And he ordered me to be released and sent back to Signakh. At present we are getting together to decide whether, with the help of God, we shall attempt to emigrate to England or to America. And in this matter we ask you as a brother to come to our help.

We beg to inform you of the situation of our brothers. Pyotr Vasilyevich Verigin was told to remain where he is for another 5 years. Our brothers in the Kars province are fined each month as before, and are forbidden to leave the area, and for failure to obey are imprisoned for one to two weeks. The illnesses continue as before, but there are fewer fatal cases. Materially speaking, our brothers are in need, especially in the Signakh district, but in the other districts they live more freely.

[35 lines omitted, containing the text of a document allowing the Dukhobors to settle abroad at their own cost, and on condition that they never return]

I happen to know the details of the persecution and suffering of these people, I am in communication with them, and they ask me to help them; therefore I consider it my duty to address myself to all good people in Russian, as well as European society, to ask them to help the Dukhobors to escape from this painful situation which they are now in. I have addressed myself to Russian society in one of the Russian newspapers—I still do not know whether my statement will be printed or not—and I am now addressing myself to all good people in England and America, to ask their help, firstly with money, of which a great deal is need for the transport alone of 10,000 people over a great distance and, secondly, with simple and direct guidance in the difficulties presented by the forthcoming resettlement of people who know no foreign languages and who have never been outside Russia.

I believe that the supreme Russian government will not oppose such help, and that the excessive zeal of the Caucasian administration in not allowing any communication just now with the Dukhobors will be moderated.

Until that time, I offer my mediation to people who wish to help the Dukhobors and to enter into communication with them, since up to now my communications with them have not been severed.

My address is: Moscow, Khamovnichesky Lane, 21.

Lev Tolstoy

445. To P. I. BIRYUKOV

Moscow, 19–20(?) 1898

My dear Posha,

I'm cold from the lack of any direct contact with you. Write about your work and about yourself, old fellow. As for work: I keep thinking about your publication *Life*.[1] The first number needs to be excellent, and so do all the others too. For that to be so, this is what is needed in my opinion (probably you think the same yourself, but I'll write it down nevertheless). It is necessary:

1. that all information reported should be so accurate that no démenti will be possible. For that you need to have careful and reliable correspondents.

2. that no exclusively religious trend should be apparent, especially in the first numbers (that everything should be imbued with a religious spirit so that there should be no ill will but, on the contrary, love for people, with anger and condemnation reserved for behaviour and, especially, for un-Christian institutions) but that no religious principles should be expressed, especially to start with.

3. that there should be as much variety as possible: that bribery and Pharisaism and cruelty and dissipation and despotism and ignorance should be denounced. I know at present (a) how some merchants proposed to build a barracks for 100 Cossacks to put down strikes, and gave 50,000 for it, to keep the workers constantly afraid, (b) I know of the suborning of an important official, (c) cheating over a miracle, (d) a meeting of a committee to review legal statutes, where all the last remaining safeguards for citizens are being removed (e) censorship horrors (f) the attitude in Petersburg to the famine (g) religious persecutions. All this needs to be grouped in such a way as to embrace as many as possible of the various sides of life.

4. that in choosing subjects and throwing light on them, the point of view of the good or harm of the people, of the masses, should prevail (if possible should be the only one).

5. that everything should be expounded in serious and austere language—without jokes or abuse—and as simply as possible, without foreign or scientific expressions.

6. the sections of the journal, I imagine, could be as follows: (a) a carefully written article on some problem, by you if you like, about the historical importance of the scriptures or about Christian communities or the revolution or military service etc. I can offer an article about refusal to do military service;[2] (b) news from Russia, good and bad; (c) a political review from a Christian point of view; (d) bibliography.

I'm writing all this, of course, without having thought about it or considered it,[3]

[445] 1. The provisional name for a journal which, under the title *The Free Word*, began to appear briefly in 1898 under Biryukov's editorship, but was published by Chertkov at Purleigh, Essex, while Biryukov was still living in exile in the Baltic Provinces. After Biryukov moved to Switzerland, the journal was continued (after a break) by Chertkov at Christchurch, Hampshire, until it ceased publication in 1905.

2. 'Carthago delenda est' (*The Free Word*, no. 1).

3. The letter is carelessly written, and the translation is a little free in places in the interests of readability. (Tolstoy's wrong numbering has also been corrected.)

445. To P. I. Biryukov

but I'm writing it all the same, because something may be useful to you and provoke thoughts. The main thing is to fear inaccuracy and exaggeration, not only of facts, but of feelings, of sentimentality. These are the two main pitfalls...[6 lines omitted]

446. To COUNTESS S. A. TOLSTAYA

Grinyovka, 6 May 1898

I didn't write to you today, the 6th, Sonya dear. It's now 10 o'clock at night. Masha and Kolya have just arrived. I'm very glad to see them. Andryusha is going to Moscow tomorrow, and I'm writing this for him to take. There's been heavy rain and hail today. It's an important event, because the heat has been very oppressive. I went to the village of Kamenka only today, after the rain; the community is unfriendly, and the food kitchen is not working properly so I gave it up altogether and shall move to another village.[1] On the other hand, after I had written you a letter at the station yesterday, I went on to two poor remote villages, the Gubaryovkas, and there everything is going splendidly. I rode back through the woods of Turgenev's Spasskoye in the evening light: fresh greenery in the woods and under foot, stars in the sky, the scent of flowering willow, and wilting birch leaves, the sound of the nightingale, the hum of beetles, the cuckoo and solitude, and the pleasant, vigorous movement of the horse under you, and health of body and mind. And I thought, as I constantly think, of death. And it was so clear to me that it will be just as good, though different, on the other side of death, and it was understandable why the Jews represented Paradise as a garden. The purest joy of all is the joy of nature. It was clear to me that it will be as good there too—no, better. I tried to awaken doubt in myself about another life, as I have before—and, as before, I couldn't—but I couldn't awaken confidence either.

If you find my wish to give money for food kitchens at all disagreeable, regard the wish comme non avenu, and forget it.

I will manage with what I have.

It's good that Misha has passed his Latin. I should have been very hurt on his behalf, if he'd had to stay down again.

I'm perfectly well. You've no need to send these mountains of provisions.

The letters I've received, many of which are interesting, have taken up a lot of time. I read more than I write, and I don't regret it, because new thoughts which I think are useful to me come quite unexpectedly. Well, goodbye. I kiss you, Misha and Sasha. Tanya is at the Olsufyevs', and a good thing.

L.T.

[Postscript omitted]

[446] 1. On 22 April Tolstoy and his wife went to his son Ilya's estate of Grinyovka; his wife returned home after a few days, but Tolstoy stayed on during April and May to help to set up food kitchens in the area for the people who were threatened by another famine. His activities were viewed with suspicion by the authorities who appeared to think that he was trying to foment a peasant rebellion.

447. To V. G. CHERTKOV

Yasnaya Polyana, 14 July 1898

My dear Vladimir Girgoryevich,

I got both your letters, numbers 45 and 46. I'm replying to number 45 in part in my letter to Galya. The translation of *Christian Teaching* is very good. I'm sending 6 signed sheets of paper.[1]

Now for No. 46.

It's always unpleasant for me to think about illnesses and the approach of death. All this—where, how and when we shall die—is God's province, inaccessible to us, and it's not right to meddle in it. But you insist so much that I'll try and satisfy your wish. Of course I want to see you, and in my *desultory*[2] dreams I journey to England and live in Essex with all my friends, and cultivate my kitchen-garden.

Now for business, and the Dukhobors.

Since it is now apparent how much money is still needed for resettling the Dukhobors, I intend to do as follows. I have three stories: *Irtenev*,[3] *Resurrection* and *Father Sergey* (I've been working on this one recently and have written the end in rough). I would like to sell them on the most profitable terms to English or American newspapers (newspapers, it seems, are the most profitable), and use what they bring in for resettling the Dukhobors. These stories are written in my old manner which I now disapprove of. If I go on revising them until I'm satisfied with them I shall never finish them. Having undertaken to give them to a publisher I shall have to let them go tels quels. The same thing happened with my story *The Cossacks*. I was unable to finish it. But I had lost some money, and in order to pay my debts I gave it to the editor of *The Russian Herald*. This time, though, the occasion is a far more valid one. The stories themselves, even if they don't satisfy my present requirements of art—they are not accessible to everyone in form—are not harmful in content and might even be useful to people, and therefore I think that it's right to sell them for as much as possible and publish them now without waiting for my death, and hand the money over to the committee for resettling the Dukhobors.

What I have written between these two lines I wrote in such a way that it could be translated and published as an introduction to these stories, or in whatever form may prove necessary...[25 lines omitted]

448. To A. L. TOLSTOY

Yasnaya Polyana, 29 September 1898

I've been wanting to reply to you all day because I've been thinking about you

---

[447] 1. Signed sheets of paper in which Chertkov was to insert the text of a letter asking English newspapers to print appeals to help the Dukhobors.
2. In English in the original.   3. The original title of the story *The Devil*.

448. To A. L. Tolstoy

and feeling sad and then cheering up again.¹ Above all, my dear, don't despair. That's one thing. But the other thing I want to say to you is that it's terribly dangerous for you to live in Moscow with nothing to do. The first thing is: find an occupation—reading. I recently recalled Rousseau's *La Nouvelle Héloïse*. There's something in it similar to what has happened to you, and this made me think of it. It's a splendid book. It forces you to think. Another thing is, I advise you to go and visit families in the evenings: your grandmother's, the Meshcherinovs etc., and to keep as far away as possible from bachelors.

Don't be despondent, think more about life as a whole and not just about the present, and be as frank as possible with dear Olga. Everything except what concerns Olga refers to Misha too; I kiss him and advise him also to give way to his impulses less and to think more.

449. To V. G. CHERTKOV

Yasnaya Polyana, 15 October 1898

I've just received your letter with Maude's letters,¹ and I won't conceal from you the fact, dear friend, that it made a very painful impression on me which I'm trying to rid myself of, but can't at all.

Firstly, your request to send you at once all the money there is. I already told you that in order to collect it (which is terribly difficult for me, morally) I need to have freedom of movement and a clear idea of what it's needed for, how much and when. As I wrote to you, I need to know this in order to adapt my démarches to it. Apart from that I'm closer to the scene of action here in Russia, and I can know better than you what is needed and where. And one can transfer money anywhere in a day by telegraph. This was one unpleasant impression—unpleasant because I have to disagree with you, and that hurts me. Just now these are only theoretical considerations, because I haven't got much money: there's about 5,000 left from the famine victims but the 12,000 from Marx² hasn't yet been received. The second unpleasant impression is the letter from Maude. What stands out so unpleasantly from all his discussions with the Canadian government is this terrible, heartless practical *John Bull* who needs *hands*³ for his colony and who is trying to get all he

[448] 1. Andrey Tolstoy, who three years earlier had wanted to marry a peasant girl, had now fallen in love with Chertkov's sister-in-law, Olga Dieterichs, and was making plans to marry her. He had already obtained permission from her father. Tolstoy, although undoubtedly relieved that Andrey had found a woman who might have a good influence on him, objected to the marriage because he did not consider Andrey sufficiently mature. (Andrey was twenty at the time.) They were married three months later, but the marriage did not last.

[449] 1. A letter in which Chertkov asked for an immediate cash payment of all the money collected by Tolstoy in Russia for the Dukhobor emigration, so as to get more favourable terms with the Canadians. He also requested a first chapter and plan of *Resurrection* for his dealings with English publishers. Tolstoy was obviously unfavourably impressed by Chertkov's shrewd business sense.

2. A. F. Marx (1838–1904) owned a printing and publishing house and published the weekly magazine *The Cornfield*.

3. 'John Bull' and 'hands' are in English in the original.

can out of the bargain, demanding that he should be provided with people who are fit, and if they die anywhere over there, it's all the same to him. Of course it's bound to be like that, but still one feels sorry for these dear people, and can't help thinking: was it worth so much trouble and so many departures from the demands of Christianity in order to be transferred from one cruel and heartless master to another, no less, if not actually more, heartless one? One feels that even in Canada there cannot be harmony between the Dukhobors and the government there so long as the Dukhobors continue to put into effect, as they do now, the demands of a Christian life. The third unpleasant impression is your request to write some summaries for publishers. I found your request to give the first chapters to the publishers to read unpleasant and, I must confess, offensive. I would never agree to it, and I'm surprised that you agreed. Summaries represent something inconceivable to me. They either want it or they don't, but I'm surprised that you who love me agreed to submit it to them for approval. I remember American publishers writing several letters with offers of a very big fee, and I assumed that the matter would be handled the same way by you, but if it's necessary to display one's wares and wait for le bon plaisir of the buyers, then however much I would like to collect money for the Dukhobors I can't agree to it, because it's unpractical, and, apart from the needless humiliation, it is moreover a way of cheapening the wares.

And so I would ask you, if you haven't done anything yet, to give up this business and leave it to me. I think I shall do it better; at least I shan't be annoyed with anyone.

Well, you see, I couldn't resist it, and my bad mood came to the surface, and I'm afraid I've offended and upset you. Please forgive me for it, or reprimand me for my unfairness.

As for a summary of the story, the considerations are also theoretical, because the first part has been written and the second part can't be considered finally written until published, and I might change it, and I wish to have the possibility of changing it.

And so my indignation about summaries and advance reading is not pride, but a certain awareness of my writer's vocation which cannot subordinate the spiritual activity of writing to any other, practical considerations. There's something repulsive and degrading to the soul about all this. Generally speaking I regret I decided on this step, the more so because you don't make it easy for me, as you have done in many cases by your love for me, but on the contrary, you make me feel remorseful about it.

Well, please forgive your ever affectionately,

L. Tolstoy

450. To V. G. CHERTKOV

Yasnaya Polyana, 16 October 1898

I wrote you a letter yesterday,[1] dear friend, and I can't stop thinking about it and

[450] 1. Letter 449.

450. To V. G. Chertkov

the impression it will make on you. Please spread a veil of love over all that is bad in it. The middle point about Maude's dealings with the Canadian government causing me a painful feeling and doubt about the whole business of the resettlement, doesn't concern you, but the two points on either side about the money and the publishing of the translation may have an unpleasant effect on you, because they apparently express lack of confidence in your efficiency. Having thought carefully about my letter today I realised that this is the gist of the matter. You are very proud of your efficiency, but I frankly don't trust it. I don't say that I'm right, but am only expressing my opinion. It seems to me that you always take on too much work, more than you are capable of, and the work doesn't make progress for that reason. Because of an exaggerated thoroughness you are slow and dilatory, and then you take a lofty, grand seigneur view of everything and fail to see a lot for that reason, and besides, for physiological reasons, your mood is changeable—sometimes you are feverishly active, other times apathetic. Because of all this I think that as a result of your good qualities you are a very valuable collaborator, but on your own—an inefficient worker.

As a result I would like to know myself what is being done and how, and to take part in decisions.[2]

On the last point, perhaps there is a bad feeling of pride about it, but the point is that it's impossible, since I'm continually changing things. The main thing is, don't be angry with me, and if I'm mistaken about your efficiency, so much the better...[14 lines omitted]

451. To. V. G. CHERTKOV

Moscow, 5 December 1898

I've just read the *Free Word News-sheet*. Everything is fine except the last page—the appeal for donations. The appeal won't produce any donations, and somehow lowers the dignity of the editors. I think that if it's necessary to appeal for donations, it should be done privately, but it's wrong to appeal in the press. All the rest—the whole tone—is fine. If only there could be a bit less Tolstoy and at least some information about the general sins of the government, and not exclusively religious persecution.

You keep reading and thinking what can be done to make everyone, or as many people as possible, read it. I think—probably I'm mistaken—that reading it must make an irresistible impression on any unprejudiced person, not completely corrupted. I very much liked the letters from the Dukhobors and Škarvan, and Kropotkin's article.[1]

2. As a result of this, and other similar letters, Chertkov sent Herbert Archer, a member of the Purleigh Colony, to Russia with information about the proposed Dukhobor emigration and the English publication of *Resurrection*.

[451] 1. The first issue of *The Free Word News-sheet* (November 1898), published at Purleigh by Chertkov, included, among other things, a letter from Pyotr Verigin, an article by Albert

Now about our young folk. Andryusha has just arrived. You're surprised, Galya dear, that I'm against his settling in the country. And I'm surprised that you're surprised. Life in the country on one's own land, in one's own house, is, first of all, the most luxurious life. Household management and carriages and horses are inevitable, and before you know where you are, dogs as well; and secondly, and most important, peaceful, proud, complacent and apparently busy idleness. I can understand life in the country on a big estate and the running and improvement of the economy, or life on the land working individually, a modest life like yours at Demenka—but this will only be living in a dressing gown; it will be peaceful, there will be no wish to escape from it, and all the resources and especially all the energy of life will go into it. She will have children, and he will have hunting and neighbours and horses etc. I see this with Ilya, good, kind Ilya and his good, kind wife. Of all the ways of life they can choose, life on their own estate is the worst from the point of view of its influence. We are used to having nothing to do and therefore going to the country, but to go to the country to live there without working is a most unprofitable state of affairs. What are they to do? What they want to and can, provided they *do* something. Two young energetic people going like old people to their estate in the country to live peacefully! The main thing is that it won't be peaceful at all, but the result will be that they will get through what there is, have a lot of children and be impoverished and oppressed. You will say again, what are they to do? I can't tell another person what to do, because I don't know where his heart lies, but I know that one needs to have a job in view and not a peaceful life...[8 lines omitted]

452. To AYLMER MAUDE

Aylmer Maude (1858–1938), the best-known English translator of Tolstoy's works, and author of the standard biography of Tolstoy and of several books and articles about his ideas. For his prolific work as a translator and interpreter of Tolstoy he was awarded a civil list pension by the British Government. Born at Ipswich, of a Quaker family on his mother's side, he was educated in England to the age of 16, and for a further two years at a school in Moscow. He remained in Russia for 23 years, employed first of all as an English tutor and later in the Russian Carpet Company of which he became business manager and eventually director. In 1884 he married an English girl also resident in Russia—Louise Shanks, the daughter of a British businessman in Moscow—who later collaborated with him in many of his translations and was solely responsible for the first English version of *Resurrection*.

Maude first met Tolstoy in 1888. He was strongly attracted by the substance of many of his ideas, although he always maintained a certain detachment, and often

Škarvan about the Dutch conscientious objector Van der Veer and an article by the anarchist, Pyotr Kropotkin, 'About the Murder of the Austrian Empress'.

452. To Aylmer Maude

referred to his own practical 'Western' outlook which prevented him from going to extremes. He soon became a frequent visitor to Tolstoy's homes in Moscow and Yasnaya Polyana, while continuing a successful business career in Russia until his return to England in 1897. He and his wife then settled at the Purleigh colony in Essex until it was disbanded in 1901 (he later based much of his criticism of the practical applicability of Tolstoy's ideas on his experience of this 'failure', as he called it). His major contribution to the Tolstoyan cause at this period was the responsibility he took in arranging for the emigration of the Dukhobors to Canada, and in accompanying them on their sea voyage. He also wrote a particularly well-informed study of their movement, and their beliefs and problems: *A Peculiar People, The Doukhobors* (1905). On his return from Canada he fell out with Chertkov over the planned Free Age Press publication of *Resurrection*, and severed relations with the press. He also quarrelled with Chertkov over certain 'corrections' which Chertkov wanted him to make in his (Maude's) book *Tolstoy and His Problems* (1901), but which Maude refused to make. But apart from his personal difficulties with Chertkov, he was on good terms with most of Tolstoy's family and friends, and this fact was a great help to him as Tolstoy's 'official' biographer (the two volumes: *The First Fifty Years*, 1908 and *Later Years*, 1910, were subsequently revised and incorporated into *The Life of Tolstoy*, 1930). Between 1925 and 1937 the Maudes translated and published the famous centenary edition of Tolstoy's works in twenty-one volumes (Oxford, World's Classics) which was the culmination of a lifetime's devoted service. Aylmer Maude also wrote two books on Marie Stopes: *The Authorized Life of Marie C. Stopes* (1924) and *Marie Stopes: Her Work and Play* (1933).

Eighty-four of Tolstoy's letters to Maude have been published in the Jubilee Edition of Tolstoy's works. They include the last words he dictated as he lay dying at Astapovo (see Letter 608).

Moscow, 12 December 1898

Dear friend Maude,

I've just got your second letter from on board ship in which you tell me about Howells etc.[1] I find Howells particularly likable from all I know about him. What do you know and think about The Christian Commonwealth?[2] I'm very interested in this society. The more I live, the more convinced I am that our excessively intellectual development hampers us a lot in life. My son once asked a peasant why he had stopped living with a neighbouring landowner. The peasant replied: 'it's impossible to live with him'—'Why?'—'He's awfully clever.' I think that most of our misfortunes come from the fact that we're awfully clever. How simply and easily the Dukhobors attain what seems to us unattainable with our intelligence and learning. I'm afraid that in the Commonwealth too, this will be an obstacle to their attaining their aim. In the last number I read an argument to the effect that patriotism might be good. This is sad.

Chertkov writes that he doesn't want to, and is unable to deal any longer with

[452] 1. William Dean Howells.   2. See introduction to Letter 443.

the Dukhobor business, part of which consists of the publication and sale of the translations of my story.[3] Archer,[4] as far as I remember, is going to Canada and so we are all obliged to place our hopes on you. However ashamed we are to ask you to take on new work after you have only just finished your work for the common cause, we can't help doing so. If you agree, I'll try to save you, as far as I can, from unnecessary work, to the extent to which this is possible for me.

I think the most difficult part is over now, and that it will be downhill work. So then, dear friend, please don't refuse to help us, and reply soon to reassure us. Give my brotherly greetings to your wife.

Yours affectionately,
Lev Tolstoy

453. To ARTHUR ST JOHN

Arthur St John (?–1939), a British army officer in Burma, who gave up his career under the influence of Tolstoy's ideas, and especially the book *The Kingdom of God is Within You*, which he read on a voyage home from the East. His first personal contact with Tolstoy was in October 1894 when he wrote to him with an account of his own spiritual revolution and received an encouraging reply. He later joined the Purleigh colony and played a big part in the Dukhobor emigration. In 1897 he was sent to Russia by Chertkov to help with the emigration from that end, and he took the Quaker Dukhobor fund with him, but after being arrested in Tiflis, he was deported from Russia. When one group of Dukhobors landed in Cyprus in 1898, St John joined them in their temporary settlement (where he contracted malaria and nearly died). In 1899 he accompanied them on their journey to Canada and lived with them in their new home for a year. He later settled in Staffordshire, helped to found the Penal Reform League, served as an ambulance driver in the First World War and published a novel *Why Not Now?* in 1939. There are some twenty letters by him in the Tolstoy archives in Moscow.

[Original in English]

Moscow, 15 February 1899

I thank you very much for your letter, dear friend. I heard of your illness and am very glad to know that you are rid of it. Nathalie G. and Mascha Shanks[1] have been here yesterday and we spoke with them very much about you.

3. *Resurrection*. Maude took over the business side of the publication of the novel.
4. Herbert Archer, an English member of the Purleigh colony, settled among the Dukhobors in Canada.

[453] 1. Nataliya Jenken, a Tolstoyan. Dutch in origin, Russian by citizenship, she was a friend of Mary Shanks, Aylmer Maude's sister-in-law. She emigrated to England after undertaking the education and upbringing of a young peasant girl whom she was not allowed to adopt, taking the child with her.

Mary Shanks, a Tolstoyan and a friend of Tatyana Tolstaya, whom she knew through the Moscow Art School (Nataliya Jenken was also a fellow-artist).

St John met both of these women in England.

453. To Arthur St John

It is strange to say it, but I was glad to know of the faults of the Duchobors.² There are no shadows in the pictures that they draw of them, and they seem not to be real.

I think that it is very good for them to have such friends as you and others of our friends. You are the consciousness of their principles, and with your help they feel more vividly their faults. I think that illness has lowered their spirit. Say them, please, that I will do what I can to take them from Cyprus, and I hope that I will be successful.³ If I could write Russian, my letter would be very long because I wish to say many things to you, but as I cannot do it, I must finish my letter.

With true brotherly love,
Leo Tolstoy

Please forward my letter to Potapoff and ⟨Verigin⟩.⁴

454. To P. I. BIRYUKOV

Yasnaya Polyana, 1 August 1899

My dear Posha,

I'm entirely to blame for not writing. I'm putting all I've got into work on *Resurrection* and it leaves me weak and empty, and besides, I've had stomach trouble continually all summer. I'm not well even now. Yesterday I got your journal *Free Thought*.¹ It's very good. I liked it very much. The introduction on freedom of thought is 5+. The accompanying note on the conference: 5. The Dreyfus affair: 5. That's a very important section. All problems which interest society need to be at least briefly elucidated from our point of view. One needs simply to take the newspapers and discuss the news which is repeated many times in all of them. For example the seizure of territory in China² and Africa,³ strikes, the Emperor's journeys,⁴ Milan⁵ etc. But you know all this yourself and are doing

---

2. St John had reported several instances of lapses of principle among the Dukhobors on Cyprus, including drunkenness.

3. Some of the Dukhobors, through lack of funds to travel as far as Canada, had accepted an offer by the English Quakers to settle them on Cyprus, where they arrived in August 1898 after sailing from Batum. However, the totally unfamiliar climate brought illness in the form of malaria and cholera which decimated their numbers. Realising that they could not adjust to Cyprus physically, they wanted to leave as soon as possible but were without funds and feared that they would be abandoned by Tolstoy and the foreign organisations seeing to their emigration.

4. A letter to two representatives of the Dukhobors in Cyprus, assuring them that their group would be joining the party due to sail to Canada from Batum in the spring of 1899.

[454] 1. Biryukov, in exile in Switzerland after being allowed to leave Russia, had just published the first issue of a new periodical, *Free Thought*, under his own editorship. It replaced his *Free Word* (see Letter 445, note 1) and in three years published twenty-one issues.

2. The partition of China by the Western powers had begun in 1898 and led to the Boxer Rebellion of 1900.

3. English activity in the Transvaal, leading to the Boer War.

4. Presumably this refers to Wilhelm II's visit to England and his rumoured visit to Paris.

5. The Serbian King, Milan Obrenovich, who pursued an aggressive foreign policy and a repressive internal one.

it. I only want to say that it's very important and necessary. *The Labour Movement:* 3 (not enough). *Finland:* 5 +, but it's marred by the fact that it seems to approve of hunting down agents.[6] *The Dukhobors:* 5, the famine: 5, *University unrest:* 3. It ought to be longer. Today's papers talk about recruiting for the army, and before that it was the supervision of professors and the company they keep. They all do it on purpose to be provocative. There's also a new form of oath today. I'm itching to write about many things in article form. But I must finish *Resurrection*. When I had not artistic work to do I longed for it, but now I want to be rid of it, so much else has piled up.

An Imperial Falsehood:[7] 3. I like it, but only because I'm wicked. I oughtn't to like it: it's not good to meddle in Nicholas' intimate family life. Better take another subject, the oath for example.

On the death penalty: 5 +. *A peaceful sect:*[8] 3. Schmitt's letters:[9] 5, but I'm afraid he exaggerates.

Generally it's very good. And it has the Herzen ferment about it. That's what's needed. And great tact is needed so that there should be some ferment in it, without all the sauerkraut disappearing in froth; so that it shouldn't be insipid, or all froth, but the liquid should have some air fixe in it. It's a good and important cause; may God help you.

Do you know the book: Verus: *Vergleichende Uebersicht der vier Evangelien*, Leipzig, Van Dyk, 1897, in which it's very well argued (with as much probability *for* as *against* in my opinion) that Christ never existed? Read the book (somebody to whom I'm very grateful sent it) and do an extract from it. This supposition or probability is the destruction of the last suburbs liable to enemy attack in order to make invincible the fortress of the moral teaching of the good, which doesn't stem from any single temporal or local source, but from the totality of the whole spiritual life of mankind. Goodbye, dear friends; you and Pasha, whom I have loved for a long time, and whom Tanya has grown to love more since meeting her.

L.T.

455. To Z. M. LYUBOCHINSKAYA

Zinaida Mikhaylovna Lyubochinskaya, a lady from Kiev, wrote to Tolstoy in August 1889 describing her nervous and emotional state and asking whether she as a Christian, albeit a questioning one, had the right to take her own life. Tolstoy's reply was gratefully acknowledged and she claimed that his advice had been her salvation.

Yasnaya Polyana, 25 August 1899

Your question about whether you, and people generally, have the right to kill

---

6. The article includes some information about the methods of hunting down Russian agents who had infiltrated the Finnish independence movement.

7. Apropos of the official announcement by Nicholas II of the birth of another daughter when he was known to be hoping for a male heir.

8. On the Brotherhood Church.   9. On the Nazarene Sect.

455. To Z. M. Lyubochinskaya

themselves is wrongly framed. There can be no question of right. If you can, then you have the right. I think that the possibility of killing oneself is a safety valve. Given this possibility, a man doesn't have the right (the expression 'to have the right' is appropriate here) to say that he can't bear to live. If he can't bear to live he can kill himself, and so there will be nobody to talk to about life being unbearable. Man is given the possibility of killing himself and so he can (he has the right to) kill himself, and continually makes use of this right, whether by killing himself in a duel, in war, in a factory or by dissipation, vodka, tobacco, opium etc. The only question can be whether it is reasonable or moral (the reasonable and the moral always coincide) to kill oneself.

No, it isn't reasonable; just as unreasonable as cutting off the shoots of a plant you want to destroy: it won't die, but will only grow the wrong way. Life is indestructible, it is outside time and space, and so death can only change its form, put an end to its manifestation in this world. And having put an end to it in this world, I don't know, firstly, whether its manifestation in another world will be more pleasant for me, and secondly I deprive myself of the possibility of tasting and acquiring for my own *self* everything it might have acquired in this life. Apart from that, and most important, it's unreasonable because, by putting an end to my life because it seems unpleasant to me, I thereby show that I have a false idea of the meaning of my life in supposing that its meaning is my pleasure, while its meaning is on the one hand my striving for perfection, and on the other—service to the work which is being accomplished by the whole life of the world. By the same token, suicide is immoral: man is given a full life and the possibility of living to a natural death only on condition of his service to the life of the world, and if he takes advantage of life only to the extent to which it is pleasant for him, he renounces this service to the world as soon as it becomes unpleasant to him, while in all probability the service was just beginning at the time when life began to seem unpleasant. Any work seems unpleasant to begin with.

For more than 30 years a monk, crippled with paralysis and only having control of his left arm, lay on the floor in the Optina Monastery. The doctors said that he was bound to suffer greatly, but not only did he not complain about his situation but, crossing himself, gazing at the icons and smiling, he constantly expressed his gratitude to God and joy for the spark of life which glowed in him. Tens of thousands of visitors came to see him, and it's difficult to imagine all the good which was spread about the world by this man, deprived of all possibility of action. Probably the man did more good than thousands and thousands of healthy people who imagine that in their various institutions they are serving the world.

While there is life in a man he can improve himself and serve the world. But he can only serve the world by improving himself, and only improve himself by serving the world.

That's all that I am able to write to you in reply to your touching letter.

Forgive me if I haven't written what you expected me to.

Lev Tolstoy

456. To RAINER MARIA RILKE

Rainer Maria Rilke (1875–1926), the German lyric poet of Czech extraction, visited Russia in April 1899, together with Lou Andreas-Salomé and her husband, the Orientalist F. Andreas. While in Moscow they called on Tolstoy, and on their return to western Europe Rilke sent Tolstoy three books: his own *Zwei Prager Geschichten*, Lou Andreas-Salomé's *Menschenkinder*, and F. Andreas' *Babi's in Persien* (about a Muslim sect founded in Persia in the nineteenth century).

Yasnaya Polyana, 13/25 September 1899

Cher Monsieur,

J'ai reçu l'envoi des livres de Madame Lou Andreas Salomé, du livre sur les Babis et le vôtre. Je n'ai pas encore eu le temps de les lire, je n'ai lu que les trois premiers récits de madame Lou Andreas qui m'ont beaucoup plu. Je ne manquerais pas de lire les autres et je vous remercie pour les livres et votre lettre. Je me souviens avec plaisir de l'agréable et intéressant entretien que nous avons eu avec vous et vos amis pendant votre visite chez moi à Moscou.

Recevez, Monsieur, mes sentiments distingués.

Léon Tolstoy

457. To PRINCE N. A. CHELOKAYEV

Prince Nikolay Alexandrovich Chelokayev (1874–1918), a Georgian engineer and owner of oil wells in Baku. He was an old friend of Princess Yelena Gurieli whom Andrey Tolstoy had met in Tiflis in the summer of 1898. Tolstoy's son proposed to her and was accepted, but on his return home he fell in love with Olga Dieterichs (see Letter 448) and married her in January 1899. Princess Gurieli then tried to commit suicide by shooting herself, and although she was unsuccessful, she died the following year from the gun wound. Prince Chelokayev's letter to which Tolstoy is replying here has not survived.

Yasnaya Polyana, 16 October 1899

Dear Prince N.A.,

The news you gave me in your letter caused me a terrible, agonising feeling of awareness of an irreparable wrong done, the cause of which was a person very close to me.

I fully understand your feeling (I can imagine how much stronger the mother's feeling is), a feeling of indignation against the person responsible for your grief.

The behaviour of my son, who was genuinely infatuated and then grew cool, although not evil, was unforgivably thoughtless and wrong in as far as he bound himself by a promise which he did not keep, and there is no justification for it, particularly in view of the terrible consequences of this behaviour.

I will show him your letter and I know how cruelly he will suffer. I also know that his sufferings cannot repair or redeem the wrong done.

And so I can only say one thing, not in his defence, but in order to mollify your indignation against him: forgive him as a Christian for the terrible unhappiness of which he has been the involuntary cause.

I thank you for the moderate tone of your letter and beg you to accept the assurance of my respect and heartfelt sympathy at your family's grief.

Lev Tolstoy

458. To PRINCE G. M. VOLKONSKY

Prince Grigory Mikhaylovich Volkonsky (1864–1912), a grandson of the famous Decembrist, journalist and author of political pamphlets, who lived in the south of France for health reasons. He had sent Tolstoy several pamphlets he had written on the causes of the Boer War.

Moscow, 4/16 December 1899

I received your letter and the pamphlets, and have read them. I am so late in replying because your letter went to Yasenki while I am in Moscow, and I am not writing in my own hand because I am ill and weak.

I'm pleased to reply, because your pamphlets are very well and sincerely written with the exception of the third, about which I agree with your family. The pamphlet is weak, not because it is too severe, but because it doesn't show sufficiently clearly the repellent features of one of the most repulsive, not to say comic, representatives of emperorhood—Wilhelm II.

But however well your articles are written, I disagree with you essentially—not exactly disagree, but I can't condemn what you condemn.

If two men get drunk in an inn and fight over cards I wouldn't venture to condemn only one of them; however convincing the arguments of the other may be, the cause of the ugly behaviour of both isn't to be found in the rightness of one of them, but in the fact that, instead of working peacefully or resting, they found it necessary to drink vodka and play cards in an inn. In just the same way, when people tell me that one side is solely to blame in any war that flares up, I can never agree. You may admit that one of the sides acts worse, but an analysis of which one it is that acts worse doesn't explain even the immediate cause of the origin of such a terrible, cruel and inhuman phenomenon as war. To any man who doesn't shut his eyes to them, these causes are perfectly obvious, as they are now with the Boer War and with all wars which have happened recently. These causes are three: first —the unequal distribution of property, i.e. the robbery of some people by others; second—the existence of a military class, i.e. people brought up and intended for murder; and third—false, and for the most part deliberately deceitful religious teaching, on which young generations are forcibly brought up. And so I think that it's not only useless but harmful to see the cause of wars in the Chamberlains, the Wilhelms etc., and thereby conceal from oneself the real causes which are far more immediate and to which we ourselves are a party.

We can only be angry with the Chamberlains and the Wilhelms and abuse them; but our anger and abuse will only spoil our blood, not change the course of things: the Chamberlains and the Wilhelms are blind instruments of forces which lie a long way behind them. They act as they have to act, and can't act otherwise. All history is a series of just such acts by all politicians as the Boer War, and so it's completely useless, even impossible, to be angry with them and condemn them, when you see the true causes of their activity and when you feel that you yourself are to blame for this or that activity of theirs according to your attitude to the three basic causes I mentioned. As long as we go on enjoying exceptional wealth while the masses of the people are ground down by hard work there will always be wars for markets, goldmines etc., which we need in order to support our exceptional wealth. Wars will be all the more inevitable as long as we are a party to a military class, tolerate its existence, and don't fight against it with all our powers. We ourselves either serve in the army, or regard it as not only necessary but commendable, and then when war breaks out we condemn some Chamberlain or other for it. But the main thing is that there will be war as long as we not only preach it but tolerate without anger and indignation that perversion of Christianity which is called ecclesiastical Christianity whereby it is possible to have a Christ-loving army, the blessing of guns and the acceptance of war as an act justified by Christianity. We teach *our children* this religion, we profess it ourselves and then say—some of us that Chamberlain and others that Kruger—is to blame for the fact that people kill one another.

That is why I disagree with you and cannot reproach blind instruments of ignorance and evil, but see the causes of war in those phenomena, the evil of which I myself can help to reduce or increase. To help to share out property equally in brotherly fashion, and to enjoy as little as possible the advantages which have fallen to one's lot; not to be party to war in any aspect and to destroy the hypnosis by means of which people transform themselves into hired murderers and think they are doing a good deed by doing military service; and above all to profess a reasonable Christian doctrine, trying with all one's powers to destroy the cruel deceit of false Christianity on which young generations are forcibly brought up—this threefold activity, I think, constitutes the duty of any man wishing to serve good and rightly disturbed by the terrible war which has disturbed you too.

459. To MAXIM GORKY (A. M. PESHKOV)

Maxim Gorky (1868–1936), the distinguished novelist, playwright and journalist, was already a literary celebrity when he first met Tolstoy in January 1900, as a result of the two-volume edition of his *Sketches and Stories* published in 1898. At an early age he had thought of founding a Tolstoyan agricultural colony and had visited

459. To Maxim Gorky (A. M. Peshkov)

Moscow to see Tolstoy and ask for land. Tolstoy was not at home and the plan got no further. When he called again in 1900 he had a long conversation with Tolstoy who thought he saw in him 'a real man of the people', and questioned him closely about his way of life and his writings. Gorky reportedly referred to the occasion as being like a visit to Finland—'neither home nor abroad, and cold as well'. Nevertheless he soon wished to call again, but was prevented by illness from doing so until the autumn, when he called at Yasnaya Polyana. In 1901–2 when Tolstoy was convalescing in the Crimea, Gorky, who was also living there for health reasons, visited him several times. They last saw each other at Yasnaya Polyana in 1902. Only one letter of Tolstoy's and six of Gorky's have survived from their correspondence, but Gorky's *Recollections of Tolstoy* have much to say about their meetings, and present a unique picture of him.

Moscow, 9 February 1900

Forgive me, dear Alexey Maximych (if I have got your name wrong forgive me again), for not having replied to you for so long and not having sent a photograph.[1] I was very, very glad to get to know you, and glad that I took a liking to you. Aksakov said that there are people who are better (he said cleverer) than their books, and there are people who are worse. I always liked your writing, but I found you better than your writing. See what a compliment I am paying you, the value of which, particularly, is the fact that it is sincere. Well, goodbye; I cordially press your hand in friendship.

Lev Tolstoy

I hope my letter finds you well. How good Chekhov's story in *Life* is.[2] I was very glad to see it.

460. To M. L. OBOLENSKAYA

Moscow, 23 March 1900

Tanya's operation has been successful.[1]
Tanya's terrible operation took place this morning, the 23rd. Mama and Mikhail Sergeyevich[2] went to the clinic with her this morning. It should have begun at 10 and finished at 11. I sat at home for a bit, but couldn't stay there, and having waited till after 11, I went to the clinic in the hope of getting there for the end. One o'clock came, then two, and still no end. She was upstairs in the operating theatre surrounded by a group of doctors in white coats with mirrors on their foreheads, who were doing something over her unconscious body. Seryozha came, and Marusya and Kolechka, then Misha and Sasha. We all waited there in agony, also in white coats. Mikhail Sergeyevich and I went upstairs and looked in through the doorway; they called me and I went in: a pale yellow, lifeless corpse lay there,

[459] 1. Tolstoy sent an autographed photograph of himself.
2. *In the Ravine.*

[460] 1. Inserted above the top line.   2. Mikhail Sukhotin, Tanya's husband.

legs above head, head on one side, with a bloody hole in the skull as big as this³ and three fingers deep, and a crowd of men in white were looking on and one was poking about. It appeared that in the frontal cavity there were, unexpectedly, three partitions which they were removing and scraping out, and this explained the length of the operation—more than 2½ hours. When they carried her downstairs, she took a long time to come round—they forced open her clenched, foaming mouth with a spoon. I called: 'Tanya.' She opened one eye (the other was tied up and blood was coming under the bandage), and shut it again. She was sick, and vomited. They say the operation was successful. A tube was inserted. It's now after 10 o'clock in the evening, and I've only just left her. She's quite weak, but in good spirits; she doesn't complain and isn't afraid. Marusya is spending the night with her. My general impression is that these are traps into which doctors try to snare people. And they are terribly offensive to me. I think—and I realised this particularly clearly after the very strong feelings I experienced and the thoughts they aroused—that all this is unnecessary and wrong. We shall all always die and we shall all be ill: if we recover from one thing we shall fall ill with another. And the important thing is that a man oughtn't to be, and cannot be cured privately for 50 or 500 or 5,000 roubles. He oughtn't to be, because other people die without help and it's necessary to help everybody, and not only oneself and one's family, and he cannot be, because things are so arranged that with all these aids, there's as much danger as there would be without treatment. I often think about you and feel how I miss you both. I'm always thinking of uncle Seryozha and I still hope to see him. Write me a better letter, with more details about him and about yourself.

L.T.

461. To EDWARD GARNETT

Edward Garnett (1868–1937), English author, critic and publisher's reader; the husband of the distinguished translator of Russian literature, Constance Garnett, who had herself visited Tolstoy when she first began to make a special study of Russia. The Garnetts had many friends among Russian exiles in England, including Prince Kropotkin. Edward Garnett was the author of *Turgenev. A Study* (1917).

[Original in English]

Yasnaya Polyana, 21 June 1900

Dear Sir,

I thank you for your letter of June 6th.¹ When I read it, it seemed to me impossible that I could send any message to the American people.

3. A triangle of fairly large proportions is drawn on the left-hand side of the page.

[461] 1. Edward Garnett wrote to Tolstoy on 6 June N.S., saying that he had been asked to write an article about *Resurrection* for the American publication, *Harper's Magazine*, and that he intended to do this if Tolstoy would furnish a statement of some sort for American readers—Garnett suggested the theme of 'hypocrisy' which, he said, had reached an unparalleled degree of refinement in American and English society. Instead, Tolstoy furnished a more flattering statement in his reply.

461. To Edward Garnett

But thinking over it at night, it came to me that if I had to address the American people, I should like to thank them for the great help I have received from their writers who flourished about fifties. I would mention Garrison, Parker, Emerson, Ballou and Thoreau, not as the greatest, but as those who I think specially influenced me. Others names are: Channing, Whittier, Lowell, Walt Whitman—a bright constellation, such as is rarely to be found in the literatures of the world.

And I should like to ask the American people why they do not pay more attention to these voices (hardly to be replaced by those of Gould, Rockefeller and Carnegie) and continue the good work in which they made such hopeful progress.

My kind regards to your wife, and I take opportunity of once more thanking her for her excellent translation of *The Kingdom of God is within you*.

Yours truly,
Leo Tolstoy

462. To J. MORRISON DAVIDSON

John Morrison Davidson was a prolific English writer on economic problems (at least six of his books are in Tolstoy's private library at Yasnaya Polyana). In July 1900 he sent Tolstoy his latest book *The Annals of Toil. Being Labour History Outlines, Roman and British*, the second part of which was dedicated to Tolstoy personally. In an accompanying letter he expressed the view that history should be written from the point of view of labour and the working classes. Tolstoy made use of his book when writing *The Slavery of Our Times*.

[Original in English]

Yasnaya Polyana, 1/13 August 1900

Dear Mr Morrison Davidson,

I thank you very much for your book. I have read the first part and not only approve, but admire it very much.

Your idea that history should be the history of the toiler, is perfectly true, and I hope will very soon be admitted by every body. You have shown also the way to do it. I hope and wish that the *Annals of toil* would have the greatest success.

I admired also very much the choice that you made of your mottos.

Thanking you once more for your book and also for the mention in it of my name, I remain, with high regard and sympathy,

Yours truly,
Leo Tolstoy

463. To AYLMER MAUDE

Yasnaya Polyana, 3 August 1900

Dear Maude,

I'm not writing to you in my own hand because I've been ill for some time with my usual debilitating illness. I got your letter enclosing Percy Redfern's letter,[1] which I liked very much for its warmth and sincerity. Ask him to excuse me for not replying to him, and tell him what I desire most of my young friends: that they should use more energy on their own inner spiritual harmony, than on propaganda.

I got your pamphlet *Tolstoy's Teaching*[2] some time ago now, and very much approved of it. It's splendidly compiled, and the most important things are put across. I liked your article on *What is Art?* very much indeed, so clearly and forcefully are the basic ideas set out.

I can't tell you how sad I am about Kenworthy's incomprehensible mental state.[3] I was going to write to him, but on consideration decided that while he was in that state, no attempts at persuasion could do anything, but on the contrary, would only add fuel to the fire.

Goodbye: I press your hand in friendship; please give my regards to your wife.

Lev Tolstoy

464. To S. N. TOLSTOY

Moscow, 24 January 1901

Yes, there was a time when I hoped to visit you and was very glad about it. I feel so good at heart with you and Masha.[1] But I don't even dream about it now. Since the time I went to Kochety to Tanya's more than 3 months ago, and jammed my finger in the door of a compartment so that the nail came off and hasn't grown since, I feel I've suddenly dropped about three rungs at once on the ladder of old age; apart from minor physical ailments, the main thing is that I've no wish to write, and to my shame I occasionally find myself regretting it. I'm so used to this work. And I sometimes think there is something more I need to say. But that's all nonsense. It will all be said when I'm not here, and there's plenty of time and plenty of people still to come.

I read a lot of papers and books, but I can't recommend anything except perhaps Maupassant's *Les dimanches d'un bourgeois de Paris*. It's well written and amusing

---

[463] 1. Percy Redfern, Secretary of the short-lived Manchester Tolstoy Society (see Letter 474). The enclosed letter was about the English Tolstoyan movement and about Redfern's own evolution from socialism to Tolstoyanism.

2. *The Teaching of Tolstoy* (Manchester, 1900).

3. John Kenworthy had become even more unbalanced since returning from Russia (he had visited Tolstoy in May 1900) and Maude had broken off relations with him.

[464] 1. Masha Tolstaya, now living with her husband, Prince Obolensky, in Pirogovo, near Sergey's estate.

464. To S. N. Tolstoy

—I'll try and send it to you—and of so-called serious literature, *Buddhist Sutras* in Gerasimov's translation. I read Nietzsche to stimulate the bile.² It's worth reading him to be horrified by what people admire.

I'm glad that Verochka is with you.³ Masha writes a little bit about her. I kiss her and am very sorry we didn't manage to meet. We're expecting Tanya for the wedding, or soon after. The wedding (Misha's) will be on the 31st.⁴ I look at them and all their youthful folly and try to remember my own foolish youth so as not to condemn them.

I'm well as regards my inner life and getting better and better; learning more and more not to condemn people and to see in everything that happens a lesson for myself of trial and preparation. It's a long time till summer and I'd very much like to see you. This is one of the joys of my life.

Regards to Marya Mikhaylovna. I hope she isn't angry with me. Goodbye.

L. Tolstoy

Don't believe the newspapermen.⁵ They print news about health and illness to fill their columns and alarm good folk.

465. To AYLMER MAUDE

Moscow, 19 February 1901

Dear friend Maude,

Of course I very much regret that you and Chertkov haven't reached agreement about translating and publishing,¹ but I'm distressed most of all that such people as you and he, both living not for your own selves but to fulfil the task we are sent to do, haven't found the common principle which would unite you on this particular question. The considerations which you advance against the Free Age Press and in favour of copyright² are just, but equally just is the consideration that the very process of publishing should accord with the basic principles which are preached in the volumes published. And I think that the latter argument is more important than the former. I think that if you don't agree with that, then your and your wife's splendid translations of what has already been published and badly translated, ought to find a publisher. But if not, I am very happy all the same about what you intend to do.³

2. Tolstoy had been reading *Thus Spake Zarathustra* (in Russian) and an article by Nietzsche's sister on the genesis of the work. Tolstoy considered Nietzsche quite literally a madman.   3. Vera Tolstaya, Sergey's daughter.
4. Mikhail Tolstoy married Alexandra Glebova on 31 January 1901.
5. A reference to a newspaper report about Tolstoy's ill-health.

[465] 1. Maude was unwilling to give up the copyright of his wife's translation of *Resurrection*, which Chertkov considered an obligation on the part of any author published by the Free Age Press. Tolstoy upheld Chertkov and, although friendly relations were maintained between Tolstoy and Maude, the book was published first in serial form in *The Clarion*.
2. In English in the original.
3. Maude, in his translation of this letter, adds the gloss '[namely to try to explain his views in my own words]'.

My attitude to this business is as follows: Chertkov has expended and continues to expend such a labour of love on the correct reproduction and dissemination of my ideas which he fully and very sensitively understands, that I can only rejoice at having such an intermediary between myself and my readers. The main thing for me is that after all the labour expended by him I can't disappoint his expectations and hinder his work instead of helping him. My help in his work is limited to the fact that all my new writings (if there are any more) I distribute first of all through him, letting everybody, if they need to, make use of them afterwards as they please.

I am very sorry that I and Chertkov should be deprived of your and your wife's help, which is very valuable because of your knowledge of languages, your conscientious work and our similar understanding of life, but what grieves me most of all is the fact that I, by my inaccuracy and alterations, may have been the cause of the dislike you have taken to this work. Please forgive me for that. Above all, don't attach importance to this and don't allow dead business to disrupt living intercourse with living people. I press your own and your dear wife's hand in friendship.

Lev Tolstoy

466. To NEWSPAPER EDITORS

Moscow, middle of March 1901

Mr Editor,

Not being able to thank personally all those people, from high officials to ordinary workers, who have expressed to me personally, as well as by post and telegraph, their sympathy over the Holy Synod's decree of 20–2 February,[1] I humbly request your esteemed newspaper to thank all these people, adding moreover that I ascribe the sympathy expressed to me not so much to the importance of my activities, as to the ingenuity and timeliness of the Holy Synod's decree.

Lev Tolstoy

467. To THE COMMITTEE OF THE UNION FOR THE MUTUAL AID OF RUSSIAN WRITERS

Moscow, beginning of April 1901

To the Committee of the Union of Russian Writers.

We have learnt with genuine sympathy of the protest by Petersburg writers against the bestial behaviour of the police on 4 March and the subsequent statement from the Union of Russian Writers.[1] This statement has led to the closure of the Union. We think that this closure will be beneficial rather than harmful for the

---

[466] 1. The decree excommunicating Tolstoy from the Orthodox Church. The letter was not allowed to be published in Russia at the time, and was first printed in England by Chertkov.

[467] 1. A police attack on a demonstration in front of the Kazan Cathedral in Petersburg in protest against the victimisation of student rebels at the University of Kiev.

467. To The Committee of the Union for the Mutual Aid of Russian Writers

purposes which are dear to Russian writers. By its closure of the Union the administrative authorities have admitted their guilt, and being unable to justify their illegal behaviour, are committing yet another act of violence, thereby weakening still further their own influence and increasing the moral influence of society which is fighting against them. And so we thank you with all our heart for what you have done, and hope that your activity, despite the forcible closure of the Union, will not weaken but grow stronger, and continue in the same direction of freedom and enlightenment in which it has always manifested itself among the best Russian writers.

Lev Tolstoy and others

468. To P. I. BIRYUKOV

Moscow, 10 April–5 May 1901

I got your letter today, my dear Posha, and am very glad that you and Pasha[1] were sympathetically inclined towards my idea, that this was your idea, and...

I wrote these lines almost a month ago and since then I haven't been near my desk—I've been constantly ill with rheumatism and a fever. Now I'm better. Since then I've also had a good letter from Pasha[2] and another one from Bodyansky,[3] and now I'll try to answer everything, and most of all for my own benefit, the educational problems which have always faced, and still face me. At the basis of everything must stand what has been discarded in our schools—a religious understanding of life—and not so much in the shape of teaching, but as a guiding principle of all educational activity. The religious understanding of life, which, to my way of thinking, can and should become the foundation of life for people of our time could be expressed very briefly as follows: the meaning of our lives consists in fulfilling the will of that infinite principle of which we recognise ourselves to be a part; and this will lies in the union of all living things, above all of people—in their brotherhood, in their service to each other. From a different angle, this religious understanding of life can be expressed like this: the business of life is union with all living things—above all the brotherhood of men, their service to each other.

And this is so because we are alive only to the extent to which we recognise ourselves to be a part of the infinite; and the law of the infinite is this union.

In any case, the manifestation of this religious understanding in life—the union of everything attained by love—is above all the brotherhood of man: it is the practical, central law of life, and it should be made the basis of education, and therefore it is good and advisable to develop in children all that leads towards

---

[468] 1. Biryukov's wife.

2. A letter in which she expressed her agreement with Tolstoy's ideas about the education of children.

3. A. M. Bodyansky, a Tolstoyan imprisoned several times and then living in England (see Letter 555). His letter is unknown.

468. To P. I. Biryukov

union, and to suppress all that leads towards its opposite. Children are always—and the younger they are, the more so—in a state which doctors call the first stage of hypnosis. And children learn and are educated thanks only to this state of theirs. (Their capacity for suggestion puts them at the complete mercy of their elders, and therefore one can't be too attentive about how and what we suggest to them.) So then, people always learn and are educated only through suggestion, which operates in two ways: consciously and unconsciously. Everything that we teach children to do, from prayers and fables to dances and music, is all conscious suggestion; everything that children imitate independently of our desires, especially in our lives, in our actions, is unconscious suggestion. Conscious suggestion is teaching and instruction—unconscious suggestion is example, education in its narrow sense, or, as I shall call it, enlightenment. In our society all efforts are directed at the first type, while the second, involuntarily and as a consequence of the fact that our lives are bad, is neglected. The people who are responsible for education either hide their lives and the lives of adults in general from children, by placing them in abnormal conditions (military schools, institutes, boarding schools, etc.)—this is a most common thing—or transfer what should take place unconsciously into the sphere of the conscious: they prescribe moral rules for life, to which it is necessary to add: fais ce que je dis, mais ne fais pas ce que je fais. It is because of this that in our society instruction has gone so disproportionately far, while genuine education or enlightenment has not only lagged behind, but is absent altogether. If it does exist anywhere, it is only in poor, working families. However, of the two types of influence on children, unconscious and conscious, incomparably the more important both for individuals and for society as a whole is the first, i.e. unconscious moral enlightenment.

A family of a rentier, a landowner, a civil servant, even an artist or a writer, lives a bourgeois life; they don't get drunk or lead a dissolute life, don't quarrel or offend people, and they want to give their children a moral education. But this is just as impossible as it is to teach children a new language without speaking this language and without showing them books written in this language. Children will listen to rules about morality, about respect for people, but unconsciously they will not only imitate, but will assimilate as a rule the fact that some people's job is to clean shoes and clothing, carry water and slops, and cook meals, while the job of other people is to dirty clothing and rooms, and to eat meals, etc. If one is seriously to understand the religious basis of life—the brotherhood of man—then one can't help seeing that people who live on money taken from others and who force these others to serve them in return for that money are living an immoral life, and no sermons of theirs will save their children from this unconscious, immoral suggestion, which will either remain with them all their lives, perverting all their judgements about the phenomena of life, or will be destroyed by them with great effort and hard work, after many sufferings and mistakes. I'm not saying this for your sake because, as far as I know, you are free of this evil, and in this respect your life can only exercise a moral suggestion on children. The fact that you are far from doing everything yourselves and use the services of other people

468. To P. I. Biryukov

for money cannot have a harmful effect on the children, if they see that you are not striving to shift the work which is necessary for your daily life from your shoulders to others, but just the opposite.

Therefore education, unconscious suggestion, is the most important thing. For it to be good and moral, what is needed—strange to say—is for the whole life of the person responsible for education to be good. What do you call a good life? people will ask. The degrees of goodness are infinite, but there is one common and important feature of a good life: striving towards perfection in love. If this is there in the people resonsible for education, and if the children are infected by it, then their education will not be bad.

For children's education to be successful, it is necessary for those who educate them to educate themselves continually and to help each other to accomplish more and more of what they are striving towards. The methods of doing this, apart from the main inner method—the work of each man on his own soul (for me, with the help of solitude and prayer)—can be very many. One must search for them, think about them, apply them and discuss them. I think that criticism, which is used by the Perfectionists,[4] is a good method. I also think it is good to get together on certain days and inform each other of methods for struggling against our own weaknesses, and our own formulas for perfection, or those derived from books. It is good, I think, to seek out the most unfortunate people, who are repulsive physically or morally, and try to serve them. It is good, I think, to try to make friends with our enemies who hate us. I write this at random au courant de la plume, but I think that this is a whole and most important province of the science of educating oneself in order to influence children. If only we recognised the importance of this aspect of education, we would cultivate it ourselves.

These are hints about one side of the business—education. Now about instruction. This is what I think about instruction: science and scholarship is nothing other than the transmission of what the most intelligent people have thought. Intelligent people have always thought along three different lines, or ways of thought; they have thought (1) philosophically, religiously, about the meaning of their lives—religion and philosophy, (2) experimentally, drawing conclusions from observations organised in a certain way—the natural sciences: mechanics, physics, chemistry, and physiology, and (3) mathematically, drawing conclusions from propositions of their own thinking—mathematics and the mathematical sciences.

All these three varieties of sciences are genuine sciences. It is impossible to pretend to a knowledge of them, and there can be no half-knowledge—you know it or you don't. All these three varieties of sciences are cosmopolitan; they not only don't separate people, but they unite them. They are all accessible to all people and satisfy the criterion of the brotherhood of man.

But the theological sciences, the legal and especially the historical sciences, Russian and French, are not sciences, or else they are harmful sciences, and should

---

4. The Perfectionists, an American fundamentalist sect dating from 1831 which abolished private property among its members.

468. To P. I. Biryukov

be excluded. But apart from the fact that there exist three branches of science, there also exist three means of transmission of their knowledge (please don't think that I'm reducing everything to threes: I'd like there to be four or ten, but they've come out in threes).

The first means of transmission—the most common—is words. But words are in different languages, and so another science has appeared—languages—again conforming to the criterion of the brotherhood of man (maybe the teaching of Esperanto is needed as well, if there is time and the pupils want it). The second means is the plastic arts, drawing or modelling, the science of how to transmit what you know to another for the eye to see. And the third means—music and singing—is the science of how to transmit one's mood or feeling.

In addition to these 6 branches of teaching, a 7th should be introduced: the teaching of a trade, and again this conforms to the criterion of brotherhood, i.e. the sort of thing everybody needs—metal-working, house-painting, carpentry, sewing...

And so teaching can be broken down into 7 subjects.

The inclination of each pupil will decide what amount of time to devote to each, apart from the work required to supply one's daily needs.

I imagine it this way: the teachers arrange the hours for themselves, but the pupils are free to come or not. However strange this may seem to us who have so distorted instruction, full freedom of teaching, i.e. so that a boy or girl can come of their own accord to study when they want to, is a *conditio sine qua non* of every fruitful type of teaching, just as a *conditio sine qua non* of nourishment is that the person taking nourishment should want to eat. The only difference is that in material matters the harm of giving up one's freedom shows up at once—there will be immediate vomiting or indigestion; but in spiritual matters, the harmful consequences won't show up so quickly, perhaps years later. Only given full freedom can one take the best pupils as far as they can go and not hold them back for the sake of the weak ones; and these best students are the most necessary ones. Only given freedom can one find out what specialisation a pupil has a bent for; only freedom doesn't destroy the educational influence. Otherwise, I shall be telling the pupil that he mustn't use violence in life, while I perpetrate the most oppressive intellectual violence on him. I know this is difficult, but what can you do when you realise that every retreat from freedom is ruinous for the very cause of instruction. But it isn't so difficult once you firmly decide not to act foolishly. I think one should do it this way. A. gives lessons in mathematics from 2–3 p.m., i.e. teaching what the pupils want to know in this field. B. does the same with drawing etc. from 3–5 p.m. You will say: what about the youngest children? The youngest, if they are properly behaved, always ask for and love a regular routine, i.e. they submit to the hypnosis of imitation: yesterday there was a lesson after dinner, so today they want a lesson after dinner...

In general, I imagine the division of time and subjects roughly like this. There are 16 waking hours altogether. I suggest spending half of them, with breaks for rest and games (the younger the pupils, the longer the breaks), on education in its

468. To P. I. Biryukov

narrowest sense—enlightenment—i.e. on work for oneself, one's family and others: cleaning, carrying things, cooking, chopping wood, etc.

The other half I would give to studying. I would let the pupil choose from the 7 subjects the ones he is attracted to.

All this, as you see, is written out carelessly. I'll work it up again, God willing, but I'm sending it to you anyway as an answer. My greetings to Zoya Grigoryevna[5] and Ivan Mikhaylovich[6] whose letter I received, and I advise him not to pay any attention to what the newspapers write. They are both good workers. I send loving greetings to you and your family and all our friends.

In a practical sense and in answer to what A. M. Bodyansky suggests,[7] I would like to add that I wouldn't advise undertaking anything new like moving to another place, or any theoretical predetermination of what the school should be; I would advise you not to invite either teachers and assistants, or pupils, but to take advantage of the conditions which already exist, developing what is there, or rather, leaving it to the future to develop.

I'll add something more about drawing and music, which, especially music... [gap in text]...the letter of young Gay[8] who wrote to his father that he was being taught to play the piano, partly prompted my wish to write to you and contributed to it. Teaching the piano is a clear sign of falsely organised education. As in drawing, so in music, children should be taught by making use of the most readily accessible means (in drawing—chalk, charcoal, pencil; in music—the ability to transmit what they see or hear with their own throats). That's the beginning. If later on—which is a great pity—exceptional children should prove to have special gifts, then they can learn to paint with oils or to play expensive instruments.

I know there are good new manuals for teaching the elementary grammar of drawing and music.

As for the teaching of languages—the more, the better—I think this is what your children, in my opinion, ought to be taught: French and German without a doubt, English and Esperanto if possible.

And one should teach them by giving them a book they are familiar with in Russian, trying to make them understand its general sense, drawing attention in passing to the most necessary words, the roots of words and grammatical forms. Moreover, one should teach foreign languages first and foremost, and not one's own.

Please don't judge this letter of mine harshly, but accept it as an attempt to sketch out 'a programme of a programme'.

I've been unwell all winter and am now in a far from normal state: my arms and legs hurt from rheumatism, my liver is bad, and I'm generally weak physically,

5. Zoya Grigoryevna Ruban-Shchurovskaya, Gay's niece.
6. I. M. Tregubov, who had sent Tolstoy some reviews of his article: 'My peace I give you...'
7. A. M. Bodyansky evidently was planning to start a school on Tolstoyan lines in England.
8. The two sons of N. N. Gay junior were living with the Biryukovs in England.

but I'm beginning to live better and better, and this life is so good that death not only won't upset it, but will only make it better.

Yours,
Lev Tolstoy[9]

469. To PRINCE P. D. SVYATOPOLK-MIRSKY

Prince Pyotr Dmitriyevich Svyatopolk-Mirsky (1857–1914), deputy Minister of Internal Affairs, and subsequently Minister in 1904.

Moscow, 6 May 1901

Your Excellency,

The wife and friends of A. M. Peshkov (Gorky) have appealed to me to intercede with anybody I am able to and find it possible to, in order that he, a sick, consumptive man, should not be killed before trial or without trial by being kept in Nizhny Novgorod prison which, I am told, is dreadful because of its unhygienic conditions.[1]

I personally know and like Gorky, not only as a gifted writer respected throughout Europe, but also as a clever, kind and sympathetic person. Although I do not have the pleasure of knowing you personally, I seem to think that you will sympathise with the fate of Gorky and his family and help them in so far as is in your power.

Please do not disappoint my expectations, and accept my assurance of the utmost respect and devotion with which I have the honour to be your obedient servant,

Lev Tolstoy

470. To V. G. CHERTKOV

Moscow, 7 May 1901

Freedom of speech was not mentioned by me quite deliberately.[1] Remarks by all intellectuals that it ought to have been included only make me even more certain of the need not to mention it. All 4 points will be understood by the dullest representative of the 100 millions. But freedom of the press is not only unnecessary to

9. For the sake of consistency in this letter, the translation uses the words 'education' for *vospitaniye*, 'instruction' for *obrazovaniye*, 'teaching' for *prepodovaniye* and 'enlightenment' for *prosveshcheniye*.

[469] 1. Gorky had been arrested on 17 April in Nizhny Novgorod, and charged with possessing an illegal printing press. His health was extremely poor at the time and Tolstoy was urged to help obtain his release on medical grounds. As a result of this letter, Gorky was given a medical examination which confirmed that his health did require his release, and he was set free under police surveillance. (From November 1901 to April 1902 he lived in the Crimea for health reasons.)

[470] 1. In an article entitled 'What the majority of the Russian working people want'.

470. To V. G. Chertkov

him, but he won't even understand why it should exist, when he isn't given the books that *are* allowed. Generally speaking I think that the people's first need is not to be treated separately from everyone else, and all 4 points deal with this, with the exception of freedom of conscience which is the basis of everything and which the people know they need.

I look from below from the point of view of the 100 millions, and so it's understandable that those who look from above from the point of view of half a million liberals and revolutionaries see something different.

If you have freedom of speech, then you must have freedom of assembly, representation and the whole catechism, the implementation of which provides nothing except the illusion that people are free. At present the people can wish not to be treated separately from everyone else; later on, if they wish for anything, it can be first of all for the land to be freed from private ownership, then for freedom from taxes levied by others, then from military service, then from courts of law, but not for freedom of the press, representation, an 8-hour working day, savings banks etc.

I'm very sorry that we so misunderstood each other...[19 lines omitted]

471. To V. G. CHERTKOV

Yasnaya Polyana, 28(?) June 1901

I'm much better today. I looked through *Fruits of Philosophy*.[1] It's impossible to write about it and argue against it, just as it's impossible to argue against a man trying to prove that copulation with dead bodies is pleasant and harmless. A man who doesn't feel what elephants feel, that copulation generally is an act humiliating both to oneself and one's partner, and therefore repulsive, an act in which a man pays involuntary tribute to his animal nature and which is only redeemed by the fact that it fulfils the purpose for which the need for this repulsive and humiliating act, irresistible at certain times, is implanted in his nature—such a man, despite his ability to argue, is on the level of an animal, and it is impossible to explain and prove this to him. I don't mention the falseness of Malthusianism which makes objective (and false) considerations the basis of an act of morality which is always subjective. Nor do I mention the fact that between the killing and destruction of the foetus and this act[2] there is no qualitative difference.

Forgive me: it's shameful and offensive to talk seriously about it. We should be talking and thinking about what perversion or blunting of moral feeling could bring people to it. And we should be treating them, not arguing with them. Really, an illiterate, drunken Russian peasant who believes in 'Friday' and who would be horrified at such behaviour, and who always regards the act of copulation as a sin, is immeasurably higher than people who write beautifully and have the audacity to cite philosophy in support of their barbarity.

[471] 1. Chertkov, occupied with a pamphlet about Tolstoy's views on sex, had sent him a recent English tract defending contraception.

2. I.e. contraception.

Goodbye for now. How good that you are well in spirit. I got both your letters yesterday. I'm very, very well. I kiss Galya, Zhozya and Dimochka.

472. To A. RAMASEHAN

A. Ramasehan, an Indian journalist and reformer, and editor of the social and political journal *The Aryan* in Madras. He wrote to Tolstoy in June 1901 telling him of his popularity with the Indian reading public and raising various problems of colonialism. Tolstoy's reply was printed in *The Aryan* after Ramasehan had made some deletions in order to tone it down.

[Original in English]

Yasnaya Polyana, 25 July 1901

Dear Sir,

I thank you for your very interesting letter. I quite agree with you that your nation cannot accept the solution of the social problem which is proposed by Europe and which is no solution at all.

A society or community kept together by force is not only in a provisory state, but in a very dangerous one. The bonds that keep together such a society are always in danger of being broken and the society itself—liable to experience the greatest evils. In such a position are all the European states. The only solution of the social problem for reasonable beings endowed with the capacity of love is the abolition of violence and the organization of society based on mutual love and reasonable principles, voluntarily accepted by all. Such a state can be attained only by the development of true religion. By the words 'true religion' I mean the fundamental principles of all religions which are 1) the consciousness of the divine essence of human soul and 2) respect for its manifestation—human life.

Your religion is very old and very profound in its metaphysical definition of the relation of man to the spiritual All—the Atman; but I think it was maimed in its moral, i.e. practical application to life by the existence of caste. This practical application to life, so far as I know, has been made only by Jainism,[1] Buddhism and some of your sects, such as Kabir Panchis[2] in which the fundamental principle is the sacredness of life and consequently the prohibition to take the life of any living being, especially of man.

All the evils that you experience—the famine and what is still more important, the depravement of your people by factory life—will last as long as your people consent to kill their fellowmen and to be soldiers (Sepoys).

[472] 1. A major Indian religion, in its origins a heretical sect of the Vedic faith. Because it recognises no higher being than perfected man—self-perfection is one of its major tenets—Jainism has been called atheistic. It also emphasises the qualities of love and meekness in the individual.

2. Kabir, a fifteenth-century religious philosopher who taught the equality of all men before God and believed that union of the individual with God could be achieved by fervent personal devotion rather than by ritual observances.

472. To A. Ramasehan

Parasites feed only on unclean bodies. Your people must try to be morally clean and in so far as they are clean from murder or readiness to do it they will be free from the regime under which they labour now.

I quite agree with you that you ought to be thankful for all that has been done by the English—for your well being—and should help them in all things tending to the civilization of your people; but you should not help the English in their government by force, and never on any account take service in an organisation based on violence. Therefore, I think, the duty of all civilized Indians is to try to destroy all old superstitions, which hide from the masses the principles of true religion, i.e. consciousness of the divine essence of human soul and respect for the life of every human being, without any exception—and to spread them as far as possible. I think these principles are virtually, if not actually, contained in your ancient and profound religion and need only be developed and cleared from the veil that covers them.

I think that only such a mode of action can liberate the Indians from all the evils which now beset them and be the most efficacious means of attaining the goal which you are looking for.

Excuse me for stating my opinion in such a straightforward way, as, likewise, for my bad English, and believe me.

Yours truly,
Leo Tolstoy

473. To AYLMER MAUDE

Yasnaya Polyana, 28(?) July 1901

[9 lines omitted]...I've forgotten what I wrote to you about Ruskin; I'm afraid it was untrue.[1] I recently read an excellent book about him: *Ruskin et la Bible*, by Hugues, I think.[2] The main thing about Ruskin is that he could never entirely free himself from his ecclesiastical-Christian outlook. In the course of his early work on social problems when he was writing *Unto this Last*[3] he freed himself from dogmatic tradition, but his hazy ecclesiastical-Christian understanding of the demands of life which enabled him to combine ethical ideals with aesthetic, stayed with him to the end and weakened his preaching; it was also weakened by the artificiality and hence the obscurity of his poetic language. Don't think that I was denigrating (dénigrer) the work of this great man who has quite rightly been called a prophet; I always admired and still admire him, but I'm indicating spots,

---

[473] 1. Tolstoy had said in a previous letter, in reply to Maude's query as to why Ruskin's aesthetic ideas had not been mentioned in *What is Art?*, that Ruskin ascribed too much importance to beauty in art and, although many of the ideas in his writings were profound, they were not connected by a central, unifying idea. (The letter had actually been written by Boulanger, at Tolstoy's request, owing to his illness.)

2. H. J. Brunhes, *Ruskin et la Bible* (Paris, 1901).

3. *Unto this Last. Four Essays on the first principles of political economy* (fourth edition 1884). Lev Nikiforov, a Tolstoyan who often did translations for *The Intermediary*, translated this book in 1900.

which even the sun has. He's particularly good when a clever and similarly inclined writer makes extracts from him, as in the book *Ruskin et la Bible* (Read it—but to read all Ruskin, as I did, one after another, very much weakens the effect)...[3 lines omitted]

474. To PERCY REDFERN

Percy Redfern (1875–1958), secretary of the Manchester Tolstoy Society which had been founded in 1900. He had written to Tolstoy shortly before the first anniversary of the Society to ask what form he thought it should take in future. His works include: *Tolstoy: a study* (1907) and *The Story of the Cooperative Wholesale Society Limited, 1863–1913*. In later years he became a Quaker and a leading historian of the Cooperative movement in the twentieth century. There are several unpublished letters by him of a religious and moral nature in the Tolstoy archives in Moscow.

[Original in English]

Yasnaya Polyana, 2/15 August 1901

Dear Friend,

You were right in guessing that I must be interested in the Tolstoy Society. So I was. But I am sorry that I have enough vanity left to be interested in it. I have always held the opinion and it cannot change—that to be a member of the old Society that was started by God at the beginning of conscious humanity, is more profitable for oneself and for mankind than to be a member of limited societies which we organise for the sake of attaining the end which we are able to conceive. I think the preference we give to our own Societies is due to the fact that the part we play in our own Societies seems to us to be of much greater importance than the one we play in God's great Society.

But this is only an illusion; all the three modes of activity which you mention in your letter will be more surely attained by a man who regards himself a member of God's great Society, than by a member of Tolstoy's Society. Such a man who is earnest, as I know you are, will firstly spread as much as he can the ideas that give him peace of conscience and energy in life without minding whether they are Tolstoy's or anybody else's.

He will secondly try with all his might to induce people to speak their mind on the most important questions of life. He will, thirdly, try to give every person he comes in contact with, as much joy and happiness as it in his power to do and will also help those who get into difficulties through strictly following the teaching of Christ.

A man belonging to God's great Society, will, beside that, perform many other useful Christian acts which have neither been foreseen nor formulated by Tolstoy's or any other Society.

474. To Percy Redfern

I own there are some advantages in the union of persons of the same mind who form Societies; but, I think, the drawbacks of such organisations are much greater than their advantages. And so I think, for myself, that it would be a great loss to me to change my membership of God's great Society for the most seemingly useful participation in any human Society.

I am very sorry, dear friend, to differ from your opinion, but I cannot think otherwise.

Your friend,
Leo Tolstoy

475. To A. L. TOLSTOY

Yasnaya Polyana, 22–3(?) August 1901

When I woke up yesterday, I began to think about you again, Andryusha, and decided I would talk to you without fail and express to you everything not only of what I think and feel about you, but what we are *all* saying about you with one voice. I think it will be useful to you, even if it will be unpleasant for you to hear it. Please hear me out, Andryusha; that is, read what I have to say carefully, and above all put yourself in my place for a moment and try to understand that I'm only guided by the desire for your good, and that I'm only writing because it's my duty, and that in all probability I shall soon die and it will be a bad thing if I die without having expressed to you what I consider necessary.

Well then, when I got up yesterday, I began to go upstairs to the library to have a talk with you—you weren't there—but as soon as I set foot on the stairs I heard that idiotic whining and screeching from the gramophone—a vile and useless way of killing time—and I felt so disgusted, in contrast to the serious and kind feeling I had when I started, that I went downstairs again in the hope that you would come down to say goodbye. But you came downstairs with Olga, and I didn't want to say anything in front of her, and so it was left. But in my soul the need to express what I think about your life was so great that I'm writing to you about it now.

The fact is that your way of life, your tone, your idle, luxurious habits, your relations with your wife, your acquaintances, your intemperance over vodka—all this is very bad and it's getting worse and worse all the time. Not to mention that idiotic gramophone, an occupation in the very worst taste, your shameless treatment of Olga yesterday in front of everybody, as though she were a slut or a slave girl, was agonising for everybody. Everybody was hurt and embarrassed, but out of decency and pity for Olga they all pretended not to notice. Your cheerfulness also was such that it not only didn't infect the others, but made the others ashamed. And I'm saying this not just as my own opinion, but as the opinion of all those people I don't name so as not to provoke your ill feeling towards them. Your idle life, vodka, tobacco—especially vodka—the evil, or if not evil, the spiritually and intellectually very low company you keep, has made you lose the sensitivity and understanding for the feelings of other people of which you were capable. And now

475. To A. L. Tolstoy

your presence in our circle only makes us all shrink with fear at the possibility of every sort of gaucherie, or even rudeness, on your part. The cause of all this is your self-assurance and self-satisfaction based on your physical strength, your agility, your name and especially on the opportunity of spending money which you haven't earned and can't earn. Just imagine what you would be and what role you would play if it weren't for your money and your name—the very thing that isn't your own, but just happens to belong to you. Just imagine clearly what you would be without your name and money, and you'll be horrified. And so the main thing you need is to live as if you didn't have these things, i.e. to live so as to be at least in some way useful to others and not to be a burden to everyone except your drinking companions. In a word, I want to tell you that you're living very, very badly, and it's absolutely clear to me that you're heading for complete destruction, choking all the best human faculties in you, of which one is very precious—a kind heart—when it isn't choked with pride, the wish to dominate, or vodka. But I can't even see this now, but I see the opposite in your terrible cruelty to your splendid wife whom you don't understand at all. You don't need to teach her, as you're trying to do, but to learn from her.

I see that you're coming to grief, and not just you alone but your family too, and your only salvation lies in self-accusation, humility, recognition of the fact that you have lived and are living very badly, and that you need not just to change a few things in your life, but to change everything and begin everything again from the beginning: to give up drinking, smoking, gipsies, horses, dogs; to break off relations with idle people and to find an occupation—useful for others, not yourself. How can this be done? I can't prescribe. If you were to believe me—which is almost impossible, and which unfortunately I don't expect—you'd find a way yourself and Olga would help you. The only thing I can say is that you need to find an occupation of use to others, and not one which is pleasant or profitable to you yourself, and to devote yourself to it. And furthermore, that although it is possible to change your life while remaining in your former conditions—at Taptykovo[1]—it will be very difficult, and so I think it would be useful for you to give up Taptykovo if you want to change your life.

Generally speaking you must remember that all considerations about Taptykovo and about money are, in comparison with the question of your soul which is perishing and could be reborn, of as little importance as a fly on a coach-wheel.

Forgive me if I've said what I considered necessary with insufficient care and love. I couldn't do any better. I was guided by love of man, and not just man in a general sense, but of one man dear to my heart.

Your father,
L. Tolstoy

[475] 1. Andrey's estate, eighteen kilometres from Yasnaya Polyana.

476. To PIETRO MAZZINI

Pietro Mazzini, a journalist and Paris correspondent of various Italian newspapers, wrote to Tolstoy in August 1901, asking for his opinion, and that of 'the Russian people', on the Franco-Russian Alliance which had been in existence since 1893 and had been growing stronger, partly owing to large French loans made to the Russian government.

Yasnaya Polyana,
27 August/9 September 1901

Cher Monsieur,

Ma réponse à votre première question: *ce que pense le peuple russe de l'alliance franco-russe?* est celle-ci:

Le peuple russe, le vrai peuple n'a pas la moindre idée de l'existence de cette alliance. Si cependant cette alliance lui fut connue, je suis sûr que (tous les peuples lui étant également indifférents) son bon sens ainsi que son sentiment d'humanité lui montreraient que cette alliance exclusive avec un peuple plutôt qu'avec tout autre ne peut avoir d'autre but que de l'entraîner dans des inimités et peut-être des guerres avec d'autres peuples et lui serait à cause de cela au plus haut point désagréable.

A la question *si le peuple russe partage l'enthousiasme du peuple français?* je crois pouvoir répondre que non seulement le peuple russe ne partage pas l'enthousiasme du peuple français (si cet enthousiasme existe en effet, ce dont je doute fort), mais s'il savait tout ce qui se fait et se dit en France à propos de cette alliance, il éprouverait plutôt un sentiment de défiance et d'antipathie pour un peuple qui sans aucune raison se met tout à coup à professer pour lui un amour spontané et exceptionnel.

Quant à la question: quelle est la portée de cette alliance pour la civilisation en général, je crois être en droit de supposer que cette alliance ne pouvant avoir d'autre motif que la guerre ou la menace de la guerre dirigée contre d'autres peuples, son influence ne peut être que malfaisante. Pour ce qui est de la portée de cette alliance pour les deux nations qui la forment, il est clair qu'elle n'a produit jusqu'à présent et ne peut produire dans l'avenir que le plus grand mal aux deux peuples. Le gouvernement français, la presse ainsi que toute la partie de la société française qui acclame cette alliance, a déjà fait et sera obligée de faire encore de plus grandes concessions et compromissions dans ses traditions de peuple libre et humanitaire pour faire semblant ou d'être en effet uni d'intentions et de sentiments avec le gouvernement le plus despotique, rétrograde et cruel de toute l'Europe. Et cela a été et ce sera une grande perte pour la France. Tandis que pour la Russie cette alliance a déjà eu et aura, si elle dure, une influence encore plus pernicieuse. Depuis cette malheureuse alliance le gouvernement russe qui avait honte jadis de l'opinion européenne et comptait avec elle, ne s'en soucie plus, se sentant soutenu par cette étrange amitié d'un peuple réputé le plus civilisé du monde. Il marche à present la tête haute au milieu de ses amis les Français aux sons de la Marseillaise et de l'hymne servile du *God Save the Tsar* (qui doivent être tres étonnés de se trouver ensemble) et devient de jour en jour plus rétrograde, plus despotique et plus cruel. De sorte que cette étrange et malheureuse alliance ne peut avoir d'après mon opinion que l'influence la plus néfaste sur le bien-être des deux peuples ainsi que sur la civilisation en général.

Recevez, cher Monsieur, l'assurance de mes sentiments les plus distingués.

Leo Tolstoy

477. To S. N. TOLSTOY

[Not sent]

Gaspra, end of October 1901

[16 lines omitted]...Now I'll tell you about our outward life here.[1] Firstly, Gaspra, Panina's estate, and the house we live in, is the height of comfort and luxury, such as I've never lived in in my life. So much for the simplicity in which I wanted to live. How can I tell you about it: the entrance is through a park along an avenue lined with flowers, roses etc. still in bloom, and borders leading up to the house which has two towers and a private chapel. In front of the house is a circular patio bedecked with roses and the most strange, beautiful plants. In the middle is a marble fountain with fish, and a statue with water flowing from it. The house has high rooms and two terraces: the lower one completely covered with flowers and plants, with sliding glass doors and a fountain below it. And there's a view of the sea through the trees. Up above is a colonnaded terrace, about 40 paces long, with a tiled floor, and below it are gullies, trees, paths, houses, palaces and a tremendous view of the sea. Everything in the house is of the best quality: window catches, lavatories, beds, piped water, doors, furniture. So is the wing, so is the kitchen, so is the park with its paths and wonderful plants, and so is the vineyard with all the most tasty, edible varieties of grape.

478. To V. G. CHERTKOV

Gaspra, 6 November 1901

[37 lines omitted]...We're living in the greatest luxury here. But the luxury of the Yusupovs[1] and the grand dukes surrounding us is greater still, and we're surrounded by them on every side.

I try to avoid them, of course, but the other day your friend Nikolay Mikhaylovich[2] turned up and wanted to make my acquaintance without fail. I don't

---

[477] 1. In September 1901 Tolstoy and his family moved to the Crimea on medical advice, and stayed for nearly a year in the Countess Panina's mansion at Gaspra on the Black Sea coast.

[478] 1. A member of the extremely wealthy and well-connected Yusupov family, Prince Felix Yusupov later acquired notoriety for his part in the murder of Rasputin in 1916.

2. The Grand Duke Nikolay Mikhaylovich, grandson of the Tsar Nicholas I (see Letter 485),

478. To V. G. Chertkov

understand why he needs to. He said that Shervashidze wasn't to blame over the Dukhobors' affair[3] and cited his report in evidence. I hope I impressed upon him that he was very much mistaken. I also impressed upon him the full extent of my infectiousness. None of them, obviously, read anything except *The Moscow Gazette*. This one plays the liberal; but how little educated and enlightened they all are, hardly less so than your audience at Oxford.[4] These terrible doors which lock people's souls and through which nothing penetrates—terrible! And the cause of it all is false religion. I was reading Mikhaylovsky's *On religion* today.[5] What arbitrary, frivolous, meaningless rubbish it is, which he thinks will cease to be rubbish because Boissier, Fustel de Coulanges, Spencer etc. will confirm it.[6] It's really a case of the blind talking about various subtleties of colour...[20 lines omitted]

479. To JOHN BELLOWS

John Bellows (1831–1902), an English Quaker who twice visited Russia (in 1892–3 and 1899) to study the conditions of religious minorities. In this connection he visited Tolstoy several times and became especially interested in the Dukhobors. Chertkov, on at least one occasion (1895), appealed to the English Society of Friends, through Bellows, for money for the Dukhobor cause. In 1901 Chertkov again turned to Bellows for his opinion of *Resurrection*, an opinion which Bellows gave to Tolstoy in a letter of 14 October 1901. He disliked the novel because he considered its treatment of sex insufficiently negative, and was particularly critical of the scene describing Maslova's seduction. The following letter is Tolstoy's reply to this criticism (published in *The Athenaeum* in 1902). It will be noticed that Tolstoy's English in this letter is not as good as usual, which can perhaps be ascribed to his illness.

[Original in English]

Gaspra, 24 November/7 December 1901

Dear friend,

I received your letter and meant to answer it but the last two months I have been so weak that I could not do it. So you must excuse me for my long silence.

I read your letter twice and considered the matter as well as I could and could not arrive at a definite solution of the question. You may be right but I think not for every person which will read the book. It can have a bad influence over persons who will read not the whole book and not take in the sense of it. It might also have quite the opposite influence so as it was intended to. All what I can say in my defence

---

3. Prince Shervashidze, the Governor of Tiflis, who ordered Cossack regiments to attack the Dukhobors who publicly burnt their weapons in Tiflis in June 1895.
4. Chertkov had read a paper on Tolstoy to the Oxford Union.
5. Nikolay K. Mikhaylovsky (1842–1904), the Populist publicist and literary critic, had published an article on religion in *Russian Wealth*, 1901, Nos. 9–10.
6. The French historians Gaston Boissier (1823–1908) and Fustel de Coulanges (1830–89), and the English philosopher and sociologist Herbert Spencer.

is that when I read a book the chief interest for me is the Weltanschauung des Authors, what he likes and what he hates. And I hope that the reader which will read my book with the same view will find out what the author likes or dislikes and will be influenced with the sentiment of the author. And I can say that when I wrote the book I abhorred with all my heart the lust, and to express this abhorrence was one of the chief aims of the book.

If I have failed in it I am very sorry and I am pleading guilty if I was so inconsiderate in the scene of which you write, that I could have produced such a bad impression on your mind.

I think that we will be judged by our conscience and by God—not for the results of our deeds, which we can not know, but our intentions. And I hope that my intentions were not bad.

Yours truly
Leo Tolstoy

480. To AYLMER MAUDE

Gaspra, 23 December 1901

Dear friend Maude,

I got your letter and article.[1] I'm very sorry that you wrote it.

You caused pain by it, and not only did not strengthen the feeling of love—and this is the main concern of life—in the heart of a person close to you, Chertkov, but on the contrary aroused unkind feelings in him, not expressed in any way, but involuntarily experienced by him.

No considerations, reports or donations carry any weight compared with the breach of love. I understand that many things were unpleasant for you and that you couldn't restrain yourself, as happens to all of us, and so I don't condemn you, but because I love you I'm pointing out what seems to me to be your mistake.

Please forgive me if I've caused you unpleasantness by doing so.

I think I already wrote and told you how particularly much I liked your edition of the first volume.[2] Everything is first-class, the edition, the notes, and most important the translation, and even more important the conscientiousness with which it has all been done. I happened to open it at *Two Hussars* and read it right through as though it were something new, written in English.

My health is shaky but doesn't prevent me from working, and I'm very grateful for that. However, even apart from that, I can't help being grateful to the one who gave me the possibility of the beautiful life which I enjoy...[4 lines omitted]

[480] 1. An article about the disagreement between Maude and Chertkov over the translation and publication of *Resurrection*.
2. Leo Tolstoy, *Sevastopol and Other Military Tales*, translated by Louise and Aylmer Maude (London, 1901).

481. To L. N. ANDREYEV

Leonid Andreyev (1871–1919), dramatist and short-story writer associated with the 'Decadent' movement in Russian literature. He made his first contact with Tolstoy whom he greatly admired in December 1901, when he sent him a volume of his collected stories. (Tolstoy had already read them in periodical form.) The following letter is Tolstoy's reply. Only three letters from each author have survived.

Although Tolstoy liked some of Andreyev's stories, he was not generally attracted to his philosophy, and felt that he pandered to the public's taste for sensationalism.

Andreyev visited Tolstoy in April 1910, and stayed overnight at Yasnaya Polyana. Valentin Bulgakov has described the visit in detail in *Tolstoy in the Last Year of His Life*. Tolstoy's reaction was generally favourable and he even suggested that Andreyev should write for *The Intermediary*, but he is reported to have said: 'I feel I ought to tell him the whole truth candidly: he writes too much.'

Gaspra, 30 December 1901

Thank you, Leonid Nikolayevich, for sending me your book.[1] Before you sent it I had already read almost all the stories, many of which I liked very much. I particularly liked the story *Once Upon a Time There Lived*, but the ending, with both weeping, seems to me unnatural and unnecessary.

I hope to see you some time and then, if you are interested, I can talk in more detail about the merits of your writings and their shortcomings. It's too difficult in a letter.

I wish you all the best,
Lev Tolstoy

482. To THE EMPEROR NICHOLAS II

Gaspra, 16 January 1902

Dear Brother,

I consider this form of address to be most appropriate because I address you in this letter not so much as a tsar but as a man—a brother—and furthermore because I am writing to you as it were from the next world, since I expect to die very soon.

I did not want to die without telling you what I think of your present activity, of what it could be, of what great good it could bring to millions of people and to yourself, and of what great evil it can bring to those people and to yourself if it continues in the same direction in which it is now going.

[481] 1. A collected edition of Andreyev's stories.

482. To The Emperor Nicholas II

A third of Russia is in a state of emergency,[1] i.e. is outside the law. The army of police—open and secret—is contantly growing. Over and above the hundreds of thousands of criminals, the prisons, places of exile, and labour camps are overflowing with political prisoners, to whom workers are now being added as well. The censorship has descended to nonsensical prohibitions, which it never descended to in the worst period of the '40s. Religious persecutions were never so frequent and cruel as they are now, and they are becoming more and more cruel and frequent. Armed forces are concentrated everywhere in the cities and industrial centres and are sent out against the people with live cartridges. In many places there has already been bloodshed between brothers, and further and more cruel bloodshed is imminent everywhere and will inevitably follow.

And as a result of all this intense and cruel activity on the part of the government, the people who work on the land—those 100 million people on whom the power of Russia is based—despite the excessive growth of the state budget or, more likely, because of this growth, become more impoverished every year, so that famine has become a normal occurrence. And general discontent with the government among all classes and a hostile attitude towards it has become just as normal an occurrence.

There is one cause of all this and it is manifestly evident: namely that your aides assure you that by halting any movement of life among the people they are thereby ensuring the well-being of the people and your own peace and security. But one can far more easily halt a river's flow than halt mankind's continual progress forward as ordained by God. It is understandable that the people to whom the present order of things is advantageous and who in the depth of their souls say 'après nous le déluge', can and must assure you of this; but it is amazing that you, a free man not lacking for anything, and a reasonable and good man, can believe them and follow their terrible advice to do or allow to be done so much evil for the sake of such an impracticable purpose as halting the eternal movement of mankind from evil to goodness, from darkness to light.

Surely you cannot fail to know that as long as we have been aware of human life, the forms of this life, economic and social as well as religious and political, have constantly changed, progressing from harsh, cruel and unreasonable forms to more gentle, humane and reasonable ones.

Your advisers tell you that this is not true, that just as Orthodoxy and autocracy were once natural to the Russian people, so they are natural to them now and will be natural to them till the end of time, and that therefore for the good of the Russian people it is necessary at all costs to maintain these two interconnected forms: religious belief and the political system. But this is really a double falsehood. Firstly, it is quite impossible to say that Orthodoxy, which was once natural to the Russian people, is natural to them now. You can see from the reports of the Over-Procurator of the Synod that the most spiritually developed of the people, despite all the disadvantages and dangers which they are subject to in renouncing Orthodoxy, are going over in greater and greater numbers each year to the so-called

[482] 1. See Letter 426, note 16.

sects. Secondly, if it is true that Orthodoxy is natural to the people, then there is no reason to maintain this form of faith so forcibly, and to persecute those who reject it with such cruelty.

As for autocracy—then similarly if it was natural to the Russian people when that people still believed that the tsar was an infallible God on earth and that he governed the people by himself, it is far from natural to them now that everyone knows, or as soon as they acquire a bit of education find out, that firstly, a good tsar is only 'un heureux hasard' and that tsars can be and have been monsters and idiots, like Ivan IV or Paul, and secondly, that however good a tsar may be, he simply cannot govern 130 million people by himself, and the people are governed by the tsar's closest advisers, who are more concerned about their own position than about the good of the people. You will say: a tsar can select as his aides people who are disinterested and good. Unfortunately, a tsar cannot do this because he knows only a few dozen people who are close to him by accident or as a result of various intrigues, and who diligently fend away from him all those who might replace them. So the tsar does not choose from among those thousands of vital, energetic, genuinely enlightened, honest people who have the social cause at heart, but only from among those about whom Beaumarchais said: 'médiocre et rampant et on parvient à tout'.[2] And if many Russian people are prepared to obey the tsar, they cannot without a feeling of outrage obey people of their own circle whom they despise and who so often govern the people in the name of the tsar.

You have probably been deceived about the people's love for autocracy and its representative, the tsar, by the fact that everywhere in Moscow and in other cities where you appear, crowds of people run after you with shouts of 'Hurrah!' Don't believe that this is an expression of devotion to you—they are crowds of inquisitive people who would run just the same after any unusual spectacle. Often these people whom you take to be expressing their love for you are nothing more than a crowd gathered together and organised by the police and obliged to represent themselves as your devoted people, as happened, for example, with your grandfather in Kharkov when the cathedral was full of people, but all the people were policemen in disguise.

If you could, as I can, walk along the lines of peasants strung out behind the soldiers or along an entire railway line while the tsar passes by, and hear what these peasants were saying: village elders and peasant policemen rounded up from neighbouring villages and waiting for several days in the cold and slush, without reward and with (only) their bread, for the tsar to pass, you would hear all along the line words totally incompatible with love for autocracy and its representative from the most genuine representatives of the people, the simple peasants. If some 50 years ago in the reign of Nicholas I the prestige of the tsar's authority was still high, during the past 30 years it has continually declined and has recently fallen so low that no one from any class constrains himself any longer from boldly condemning not only the decrees of the government but also the tsar himself, and even swearing at him and laughing at him.

2. From *Le mariage de Figaro*, Act III, scene iii.

482. To The Emperor Nicholas II

Autocracy is an obsolete form of government which may suit the needs of a people somewhere in Central Africa, cut off from the whole world, but not the needs of the Russian people who are becoming more and more enlightened by the enlightenment common to the whole world. And therefore maintaining this form of government and the Orthodoxy linked with it can only be done as it is now, by means of every kind of violence: a state of emergency, administrative exile, executions, religious persecutions, the banning of books and newspapers, the perversion of education, and, in general, by bad and cruel actions of every type.

Such have been the actions of your reign up to now. Starting with your reply to the Tver deputation which aroused the indignation of all Russian society by calling the most legitimate desires of the people 'foolish day-dreams'—all your decrees about Finland[3] and the seizure of Chinese territories,[4] your Hague Conference project[5] accompanied by the strengthening of the army, your weakening of self-government and strengthening of administrative arbitrariness, your support of religious persecutions, your consent to the establishment of a monopoly on spirits, i.e. government traffic in poison for the people, and finally your obstinacy in maintaining corporal punishment despite all the representations made to you for the abolition of this senseless and entirely useless measure, humiliating to the Russian people—all these are actions which you could have avoided taking, had you not set yourself, on the advice of your frivolous aides, an impossible goal—not only to halt the people's life, but to return it to a former obsolete state.

The people can be oppressed by violent measures, but they cannot be governed by them. The only means of effectively governing the people in our time is to head the people's movement from evil to goodness, from darkness to light, and to lead them to the attainment of the goals nearest to it. In order to be able to do this, it is necessary first of all to give the people the opportunity to express their wishes and needs and, having heard these wishes and needs, to fulfil those of them which will answer the needs, not of one class or estate but of the majority, the mass of the working people.

And these wishes which the Russian people will now express, if given the opportunity to do so, will be, in my opinion, the following:

Above all, the working people will say that they wish to be rid of those exclusive laws which place them in the situation of pariahs who do not enjoy the rights of all other citizens; then they will say that they want freedom of movement, freedom of instruction and freedom to profess the religious faith natural to their spiritual needs; and most important, the whole 100 million people will say with one voice that they want freedom to use the land, i.e. the abolition of the right to the private ownership of land.

3. A reference to a manifesto of June 1901 on the obligation of the Finns to do military service in the Russian army.
4. Russia was a party to the partition of China into spheres of influence by the Western powers.
5. A peace conference of the Western powers at The Hague in 1899, called by Russia, but with no tangible results. Tolstoy saw it as an attempt to disguise what he considered to be the militarism of Russian foreign policy.

482. To The Emperor Nicholas II

And this abolition of the right to the private ownership of land is, in my opinion, the nearest goal, the attainment of which the Russian government should set as its task in our time.

In every period of the life of mankind there is a step, appropriate to the time, which comes very close to realising the best forms of life towards which mankind is striving. For Russia fifty years ago the abolition of slavery was such a step. In our time such a step is the liberation of the working masses from the minority which wields power over them—what is called the labour question.

In Western Europe the attainment of this goal is considered possible through the transfer of the factories and workshops to the general use of the workers. Whether such a solution of the question is right or wrong, and whether it is attainable or not by the Western peoples—it is obviously not applicable to Russia as it now is. In Russia, where an enormous part of the population lives on the land and is totally dependent on large-scale landowners, the liberation of the workers obviously cannot be achieved by the transfer of the factories and workshops to the general use. For the Russian people such liberation can be achieved only by abolishing the private ownership of land and by recognising the land as common property—the very thing that has for long been the heartfelt desire of the Russian people, and whose realisation by the Russian government they still look forward to.

I know that these ideas of mine will be taken by your advisers as the height of frivolity and impracticality on the part of a man who has no comprehension of all the difficulties of governing a state, especially my idea about recognising the land as the common property of the people; but I know too that in order not to be forced to perpetrate more and more cruel violence against the people, there is only one means of action, namely: to make your task the attainment of a goal in advance of the people's wishes, and without waiting for the runaway cart to hit you on the knee, to drive it yourself, i.e. to be in the forefront of achieving the best form of life. For Russia such a goal can only be the abolition of the private ownership of land. Only then can the government be the leader of its people and effectively govern them without making unworthy and forced concessions to the factory workers and students as it does now, and without fearing for its own existence.

Your advisers will tell you that freeing the land from the rights of ownership is a fantasy and an impracticable business. In their opinion, to force a living people of 130 million to cease living or manifesting signs of life, and to squeeze them back into the shell which they long ago outgrew, is not a fantasy and not only not impracticable, but the wisest and most practical course of action. But one only needs to think a bit seriously to understand what really is impracticable, although it is being done, and what on the contrary is not only practicable, but timely and necessary, although it has not yet been begun.

I personally think that in our time the private ownership of land is just as obvious and as crying an injustice as serfdom was 50 years ago. I think that its abolition will place the Russian people on a high level of independence, wellbeing, and contentment. I also think that this measure will undoubtedly get rid of all the socialist and revolutionary irritation which is now flaring up among the workers and which threatens the greatest danger both to the people and the government.

But I may be mistaken, and what is more, the solution of this question one way or the other can only be provided by the people themselves if they have an opportunity to express themselves.

In any case, the first business which now faces the government is to eliminate the oppression which prevents the people from expressing their wishes and needs. It is impossible to do good to a man whose mouth we have gagged so as not to hear what he wants for his own good. Only by learning the wishes and needs of all the people, or the majority of them, can one govern the people and do good to them.

Dear brother, you have only one life in this world, and you can waste it agonisingly on vain attempts to halt the movement of mankind, as ordained by God, from evil to goodness, from darkness to light, or you can calmly and joyfully lead it in the service of God and man, by carefully considering the wishes and needs of the people and by dedicating your life to their fulfilment.

However great your responsibility for the years of your reign during which you can do much good or much evil, your responsibility is still greater before God for your life here on which your eternal life depends and which God has given you, not so that you can order evil deeds of all kinds or even be a party to them and allow them, but so that you can carry out His will. His will is not to do evil to people, but good.

Think about this, not in the presence of people, but in the presence of God, and do what God, i.e. your conscience, tells you. And don't be troubled by the obstacles you will encounter if you enter on a new path in life. These obstacles will be eliminated of their own accord and you will not notice them, if only what you do is done not for human glory, but for your own soul, i.e. for God.

Forgive me if I have unwittingly offended or angered you by what I have written in this letter. I was only guided by a desire for the good of the Russian people and of yourself. Whether I have accomplished this will be decided by the future, which I, in all probability, will not see. I have done what I considered my duty.[6]

With sincere wishes for your true good,
Your brother,
Lev Tolstoy

483. TO A GROUP OF SWEDISH WRITERS AND SCHOLARS

Gaspra,
22 January/4 February 1902

Chers et honorés confrères,

J'ai été très content de ce que le prix Nobel ne m'a pas été décerné.[1] Primo,

6. No reply was received to the letter.

[483] 1. A reply to a letter regretting that Tolstoy had not been awarded the Nobel Prize for Literature, first given in 1901.

483. To A Group of Swedish Writers and Scholars

cela m'a delivré d'un grand embarras, celui de disposer de cet argent qui, comme l'argent en général d'après ma conviction ne peut produire que du mal et, secondo, cela m'a procuré l'honneur et le grand plaisir de recevoir l'expression de sentiments sympathiques de la part de tant de gens, hautement estimés quoique personnellement inconnus.

Recevez, chers confrères, l'assurance de ma sincère reconnaissance ainsi que de mes meilleurs sentiments.

Léon Tolstoy

484. To WILHELM VON POLENZ

Wilhelm von Polenz (1861–1903), German novelist, essayist and dramatist whose work Tolstoy generally admired. His private library contains several volumes by von Polenz in German. The religious novel referred to below was recommended for translation by Tolstoy, who compared it favourably with Mrs Ward's *Robert Elsmere*.

Gaspra, 10/23 March 1902

Lieber Herr von Polenz,

Herzlich danke ich Ihnen für die Sendung Ihrer Bücher, mit denen Sie mir eine grosse Freude bereiten. Ausser Ihrem schönen Roman «Der Büttnerbauer», den ich nicht genug lieben kann, kenne ich noch den «Grabenhäger», in welchem ich dasselbe Talent und dieselbe Wahrhaftigkeit gefunden habe, obwohl mich die Tendenz desselben nicht völlig befriedigt.

Alles was Religion anbetrifft interessiert mich lebhaft und ganz besonders hätte gewünscht Ihre Ansichten über dieselbe zu erfahren, daher bedaure sehr, dass Sie mir Ihren religiösen Roman «Der Pfarrer von Breitendorf» unserer russischen Zensur halber nicht zusenden konnten.

Indess könnte mir geholfen werden, wenn Sie so freundlich sein wollen das Buch an untenstehende Adresse zu senden, es würde dann sicher in meine Hände gelangen, da Herr von Malzoff alle Drucksachen zensurfrei aus dem Auslande bezieht.

Obwohl ich mich auf dem Wege der Besserung befinde, bin ich in Folge meiner schweren Krankheit doch noch so schwach, dass die Feder nicht führen kann, sondern mich fremder Hilfe bedienen muss.

Indem ich Ihnen besten Erfolg wünsche in Ihren fernern literarischen Bestrebungen, verbleibe mit herzlichen Grusse.

Ihr Sie werthschätzender,
Leo Tolstoy

485. To THE GRAND DUKE NIKOLAY MIKHAYLOVICH

The Grand Duke Nikolay Mikhaylovich (1859–1918), grandson of Nicholas I, and the author of numerous historical works, especially on the period of Alexander I. He took the initiative in making Tolstoy's acquaintance in the Crimea in autumn 1901, and visited him on three occasions there (the subject of a later article by him). Their extant correspondence amounts to more than 30 letters.

The Grand Duke assisted Tolstoy in various ways, delivering his letter to Nicholas II (Letter 482), obtaining historical and ethnographical material for him for *Hadji Murat*, contributing information about his grandfather Nicholas I, and using his good offices to help the Dukhobors who had stayed behind in Russia and later wished to emigrate to Canada.

Despite a somewhat negative first reaction, Tolstoy seems to have liked the Grand Duke and to have admired his historical writings (some of which survive in his private library at Yasnaya Polyana). In 1905 he suggested that they should break off relations because of the disparity between their views and their situations in life (Letter 525), but further letters were exchanged between 1906 and 1908, and Tolstoy continued to receive books and historical material from him.

The Grand Duke was murdered by the Bolsheviks in 1918.

Gaspra,
25 April–1 May 1902

Dear Nikolay Mikhaylovich,

I received your long and interesting letter the other day. I was very pleased to get it, but certain opinions made me wish to speak my mind about the things over which I disagree with you, and which are particularly dear to me.

First of all, in calling me *a great idealist* on the basis of the project I am suggesting, you are essentially doing what all the Emperor's advisers who are acquainted with my thought are bound to do, i.e. regard me as a fool who doesn't understand what he's talking about. The attitude towards me of the majority of people, even those well disposed to me, reminds me of a passage from one of Dickens' novels, *Hard Times*, I think,[1] where a clever and serious man, a mechanic, is introduced, who has made a remarkable discovery but who, precisely because he is a very remarkable inventor, is considered by his jolly, good-natured friend to be a person who understands nothing about life and who needs watching like a child in case he should do a lot of very stupid things, and whose words, if he talks about anything outside his own speciality, are received by this good-natured friend with a condescending smile at the naiveté of a person who knows nothing in life except his inventions. The funny side of the situation is that the good-natured friend didn't draw the simple inference that if the mechanic had made important discoveries, he

---

[485] 1. Actually in *Little Dorrit*, when the mechanical inventor Daniel Doyce is introduced by Mr Meagle with a tale of Doyce's woes at the hands of the Circumlocution Office.

485. To The Grand Duke Nikolay Mikhaylovich

was obviously clever. But if he was clever, it's just as obvious that he wouldn't talk about, and particularly assert, something he didn't know and hadn't thought about.

I feel all the awkwardness and immodesty of this comparison, but I can't refrain from making it, so truly does it show all the falseness of society's attitude in general to the opinions of people who are distinguished in some way from everybody else. This attitude is the more widespread because it absolves people from heeding the meaning of what such people say. 'He's a poet, a mechanic, an idealist', and so there's no point in trying to understand the meaning of what he says. That's the reason why such a strange opinion exists, and even the habit of appointing to posts which require the greatest gifts and intelligence all sorts of Ivanovs, Petrovs, Zengers, Pleves etc., whose only virtue is that they are no different from other people. That's the first point. The second point is that it seems to me—and I regret it very much—that you haven't read and don't know the essence of George's project. The peasant class not only will not oppose the realisation of this project, but will welcome it as the realisation of the wish of many generations of their own class.

The essence of the project surely is that land rent, i.e. the excess value of land as compared with land of the lowest yield, and depending not on man's labour but on nature or the whereabouts of the land, is used for taxes, i.e. for common needs; i.e. the common revenue is used for the common cause. The only effect of this project is that if you own a certain amount of land in Borzhomi and I in the Tula province, nobody takes that land away from me, and I am only obliged to pay a rent for it which is always lower than its yield. I don't know about Borzhomi, but in the Krapiva district of the Tula province the land-rent will be about 5 roubles, while the charge for renting the land is now about 10 roubles, and so the owner of 1,000 desyatins will be obliged to pay the treasury 5,000 roubles and if he is unable to do so, which will probably be the case with 9/10 of landowners, he will give up the land and the peasants, who now pay 10 roubles each to rent it, will obviously be glad to snatch it up for 5 roubles each and will hold it from generation to generation, so that the great mass of the peasantry cannot help but sympathise with this project and will always be in favour of it.

That, in crude outlines, is the essence of Henry George's project. That's the second point. The third point is that the fact that this measure hasn't been carried out either in Europe or America not only doesn't prove that it can't be carried out in Russia, but on the contrary points to the fact that it is only in Russia that it can be carried out, thanks to autocracy. Landowners in Europe and America who make up the greater part of the government will never in their own interests tolerate the freeing of land from the right of private ownership, but even there one can see a movement in this direction, while in Australia and New Zealand this measure is already being realised. Apart from that, this measure is particularly important in our time for the sake of a still agricultural Russia, despite the fact that Witte, Kovalevsky, Mendeleyev and others earnestly wish to direct her on to the path of capitalism and factory production.

That's the third point. Now the fourth point. You write that 'for the realisation

485. To The Grand Duke Nikolay Mikhaylovich

of this grandiose idea, a tsar-hero like Peter the Great would be needed, and different collaborators from those whom Nicholas II could have at his disposal'. But I think that no particular heroism is needed for the realisation of this idea, far less the drunken and debauched heroism of Peter the Great, but one only needs the reasonable and honest fulfilment of one's duty as a tsar, in this case most particularly profitable for the tsar himself, i.e. for autocracy, and it seems to me that Nicholas II with his kind heart, as everyone says, could fully realise it, if only he understood its full importance for himself and especially for all his people. As for collaborators, then of course the carrying out of this measure is unthinkable with those bureaucratic corpses, who are all the more corpses the higher they are up the hierarchical ladder of bureaucracy, and all that company such as the Pobedonostsevs, Vannovskys and Chertkovs will have to be removed from any part in the affair. But Russia is full of collaborators who are capable and honest and eager to do a real job which they can love. That's the fourth point.

As for what you say about the need for reforms in all branches of the administration, the pernicious nature of the bureaucracy, the universal passion for profit, all sorts of 'Panamas',[2] excessive militarism, the dissoluteness of morals—all these things will automatically be eliminated from the government milieu as soon as unprincipled people, seeking only their own advancement and profit, are thrown out of it, and people are summoned to the great cause who will love it. And so I not only don't agree with you that the possibility of saving autocracy lies in various patching-up jobs such as the responsibility of ministers (to whom?), or the re-formation and revitalising of the highest institutions like the Council of State, the ministries and so on, but, on the contrary, I think that this illusion of the possibility of putting things right by sewing new patches on old rags is the most pernicious of illusions, giving support to that impossible system of things under which we now live. Any such re-formation without the introduction of a higher idea in the name of which people can work with inspiration and self-sacrifice will only be bonnet blanc et blanc bonnet.[3] Generally speaking, the realisation of my idea which seems so unrealisable to you is incomparably more possible than what they are trying to do now—support an obsolete autocracy without any higher idea, but only autocracy for the sake of autocracy.

When I speak about carrying out such a measure by means of the force of authority, I am not speaking from my own point of view whereby I consider any force, even though it seems to us beneficial, to be contrary to the Christian teaching which I profess, but from the point of view of people wishing at all costs to defend an autocracy which is obsolete and pernicious for the autocrat as well as for the people, and to give it the best possible justification.

Forgive me for writing to you at such length about matters over which we can hardly agree, but your letter which touched on problems very dear to me and which have occupied me for a long time roused in me the need to speak my mind.

2. A reference to the building of the Panama Canal and the dubious financial transactions connected with it.
3. The equivalent of 'six of one and half a dozen of the other'.

485. To The Grand Duke Nikolay Mikhaylovich

Goodbye; I wish you all the best and thank you once again for carrying out my request. I am not writing to you in my own hand because I have recently had a rechute, not of pneumonia as the doctors say, but of malaria, and I am very weak again.

Yours affectionately,
Lev Tolstoy

486. To S. N. TOLSTAYA

Sofya Nikolayevna Tolstaya, *née* Filosofova, (1867–1934) the wife of Ilya Lvovich Tolstoy.

Gaspra, 15 May 1902

Dear Sonya,

I was very glad to have a serious talk with Ilyusha about the education of children. What he and I undoubtedly agree about, although it's only negative, is that children should be taught *as little as possible*. That's because if children grow up without having learned anything, it's far less dangerous than what happens with almost all children, particularly when mothers who don't know the subjects the children are studying have charge of their education—namely that they get learning indigestion,[1] and therefore a dislike of it. A child or anyone can study successfully when he has an appetite for what he is studying. Without it, harm, terrible harm, is done which makes people mental cripples. For God's sake, Sonya dear, even if you don't fully agree with me, take my word for it and believe me that I would never have written to you about it had it not been a matter of such enormous importance. Above all, believe your husband, who looks at it perfectly reasonably.

But here comes the usual objection: if children don't study, what will they occupy themselves with? Knucklebones, and all sorts of silly, nasty things with peasant children? Given our seignorial system of life, this objection makes reasonable sense. But is it necessary to accustom children to a seignorial life—i.e. to the knowledge that all their needs will somehow be satisfied by someone, without the least participation by them in this satisfaction? I think therefore that the first condition of good education is that a child should know that everything he enjoys doesn't fall ready-made from heaven, but is the product of the labour of other people. It's too much for a child to understand that everything he lives by is the labour of other people who don't know or love him (God grant he may understand it when he grows up), but he can and must understand, and he ought to feel ashamed, that the pot in which he makes water is emptied and washed without any pleasure by a nanny or a servant, and that his shoes and galoshes which he always puts on clean are brushed and washed in the same way, and that all this is not done of its own accord or out of love for him, but for some other reasons which he can't understand. But if he isn't ashamed, and continues to enjoy these advantages, that's the

[486] 1. In French in the original.

486. To S. N. Tolstaya

start of the worst education, and leaves a very deep mark for life. And it's so simple to avoid this: and this is what I—on my death-bed, to use the high style—beg you to do for your own children. Everything they are capable of doing for themselves —emptying their slops, fetching water, washing the dishes, tidying the room, cleaning their boots and clothes, laying the table etc.—let them do themselves. Believe me, however insignificant this may seem, it's hundreds of times more important for your children's happiness than a knowledge of French, history etc. Here comes the main difficulty, it's true: children only do willingly what their parents do, and so I beg you—you are such a splendid person and I know you are able to—to do the same yourself. Even if Ilya won't do it (although one may hope he will), that won't ruin everything. For goodness sake think about it carefully, for the good of your children. It achieves two goals at once: it makes it possible to study less and to fill in the time in the most useful and natural way, and it accustoms children to simplicity, hard work and independence. Please, please do this. You will be glad from the first month, and the children even more so. If to this can be added some work on the land, if only in the form of a kitchen garden, that will be good—but this usually turns out to be a plaything. The need to look after oneself and to empty one's slops has been recognised by all the best schools such as Bedales, where the headmaster himself takes part in it.

Believe me, Sonya, that without this condition there is no possibility of a moral education, a Christian education, an awareness of the fact that all people are brothers and equal to one another. A child can understand that a grown-up person, his father—a banker, turner, artist, or manager—who supports his family by his own work, may free himself from occupations which deprive him of the possibility of devoting all his time to the work which earns him his living. But how can a child who has no profession and is still unable to do a job, explain to himself the fact that other people do for him what it's natural for him to do himself?

The only explanation for him is that people are divided into two classes— masters and slaves—and however much we explain to him in words about the equality and brotherhood of people, the conditions of his entire life, from getting up to having his evening meal, indicate the opposite to him.

Not only does he cease to believe in the precepts of his elders about morality; he sees in the depth of his soul that all these precepts are false, and ceases to trust his parents and mentors and even the very necessity for any morality at all.

One more consideration: if it's impossible to do all I mention, at least you can make the children do things, the disadvantage of not doing which would be immediately felt by them: for example if their outdoor clothes and footwear aren't clean and dry they can be kept in, or if the water isn't fetched and the dishes washed, there'll be no drink to be had anywhere. The main thing here is, don't be afraid of ridicule.[2] Nine-tenths of the bad things done in the world are done because it would be ridicule not to do them.

Your father and friend,
L. Tolstoy

2. In French in the original.

487. V. G. CHERTKOV

Gaspra, 2(?) June 1902

I got your last letter, my dear Vladimir Grigoryevich in which you ask what we in Russia think about the state of affairs.[1] I at least, although I live in Russia, can't form any definite opinion about how it will all end. You say quite truly that the Russian people have woken up. That's an indisputable new fact, and our dear Bulygin told me just as truly the other day that the present government reminds him of the drunkard who says: 'if I drink, I'll die, and if I don't drink I'll die, so it's better to drink!' There are two main phenomena here: the fact that the Russian people, and even the peasantry, have woken up or are waking up and so are beginning to act; and the fact that the government is withdrawing deeper and deeper into its shell and not only wants to maintain the present state of affairs but even to go back to an older and more backward one. Something new is bound to come out of the combination of these two phenomena, but what it will be I can't even guess, and I think nobody can foresee, since history never repeats itself. The one thing we can know is that the situation is very tense, and all people who want to help the cause of doing good need more than ever to act vigorously. I feel this acutely, and, ill as I am, I'm now busy on an article: 'An Appeal to the Working People', which I've almost finished and hope to send to you in a few days. The day before yesterday I got Struve's *Liberation*[2] and the new *Life*[3] on the same day. The first is not at all bad. But *Life*, unfortunately, didn't satisfy me at all. Not to mention the lack of seriousness of tone, its main failing is the stupid and quite unjustified predetermination of the course of human life allegedly due to find its expression without fail in socialism. There's a great deal of interesting material in it; I mean the list of strikes and political punishments and exiles. But generally speaking I can't imagine who will read this journal or what influence it might have. As for the article on education—I have the first sheet and I got the third today, but I don't have the second. Don't be disturbed by the fact that I'm not writing in my own hand. I'm perfectly able to write and I do write myself, but it's now evening and I'm particularly tired today, and I don't want to leave you without a reply. I get up and spend all day in the open air, and although I'm bent up like an old man, I can walk some twenty or thirty steps.

Well, that's all. Goodbye, dear friends. Write more often. I'll tell you in secret that despite the fact that I'm recovering, I feel I shall soon depart this life. And so far from this thought not letting go of me, I never let go of this thought, et je m'en trouve très bien. Perhaps I'm mistaken, but I wanted to tell you.

L. Tolstoy

[487] 1. The assassination of Sipyagin, the Minister of the Interior, by a Socialist Revolutionary, and the subsequent riots, attributed to S.R. activity.

2. *Liberation*, a liberal journal published abroad, first in Stuttgart and then in Paris from 1902 to 1905 under the editorship of P. Struve, later a leading Cadet in the First Duma. The journal was the organ of the Union of Liberation, a society of liberals committed to the establishment of democracy in Russia without revolution.

3. *Life*, a Marxist journal published legally in Petersburg from 1899 to 1901 and later abroad. The editor, V. A. Posse, was a friend of Tolstoy's.

488. To AYLMER MAUDE

[Original in English]

Yasnaya Polyana, 13 August 1902

Dear Aylmer Maude,

La Revue Blanche of last March contained a brief statement of views attributed to me on the sex question, followed by the opinions of a number of French authors concerning those views.

The opinions there attributed to me are grotesquely absurd, and are a careless, second-hand, and incorrect summary of a collection of undated extracts and articles put together and published by my friend Vladimir Tchertkoff.

The curious thing is, that of all the authors who express themselves on the subject, not one suspected that he was being hoaxed. They all took the summary put before them as though it were a statement of my real opinions.

I am glad, therefore, to see in your preface to the 'Revised Edition' of *Resurrection* a restatement of my views on the sex-question which is as reasonable as the summary in *La Revue Blanche* is absurd.

Leo Tolstoy

489. To. P. I. BIRYUKOV

Yasnaya Polyana, 20 August 1902

My dear friend Posha,

I haven't written to you for ages and ages, and this distresses me very much; it's as if our connection with each other is getting more distant and tenuous. And this hurts me, because you are one of my closest and best friends who have given me much joy and support. So don't let our connection be broken, not for anything. I'm afraid I mistakenly encouraged you by my promise to write my reminiscences.[1] I tried to think about it, and saw what terrible difficulty there would be in avoiding the Charybdis of self-praise (by keeping silent about everything bad) and the Scylla of cynical frankness about all the vileness of my life. To write down all one's nastiness, stupidity, meanness and depravity quite truthfully—more truthfully even than Rousseau—would make a corrupting book or article. People will say: there's a man whom many people rate highly, and look what a scoundrel he was! So we ordinary people cannot be blamed for doing what he does. Seriously, when I began to recall all my life carefully and saw all its stupidity (actually stupidity) and vileness, I thought: what must other people be like, if I who am praised by many am such a stupid beast? However, I suppose, this could be explained again by the fact that I'm only more crafty than other people. I say all this to you, not for stylistic effect, but completely sincerely. I've lived through it all. One thing I

---

[489] 1. Biryukov had first broached the question of writing a *Life* of Tolstoy in a letter on 26 April 1902; Tolstoy's reply in May was that although at first he 'was afraid of the insincerity which is characteristic of every autobiography', he finally felt that he could agree to supply Biryukov with the necessary information.

489. To P. I. Biryukov

can say is that my illness helped me a lot. A lot of nonsense vanished when I faced up in earnest to God, or everything of which I am only a changing part. I saw a lot that was rotten in me which I hadn't seen before. And I began to feel a bit easier. Generally speaking, one ought to say to people one loves: I don't want you to be well, I want you to be ill.

You are getting on well, I hear, with your dear Pasha and the children, thank God. Don't change anything; only improve things and don't be discouraged. They say you have too many unnecessary people with you. That's difficult. You must struggle on lovingly.

I said that I'm afraid of a false promise about my reminiscences. I *am* afraid, but that doesn't mean that I refuse. I'll try, when I have more strength and time. I have a plan for avoiding the difficulties I spoke of by only hinting at good and bad periods. Goodbye. I kiss you.

L.T.

490. To G. P. DEGTERENKO

Grigory Petrovich Degterenko worked for the Tolstoys for nine months as a servant while they were living in Gaspra. When they returned to Yasnaya Polyana, he wrote to Tolstoy saying that he had long been sympathetic to his ideas but had been disillusioned by the discrepancy between his way of life and his beliefs after seeing him at close quarters.

Yasnaya Polyana, 20 August 1902

I very much regret, dear Grigory Pavlovich, that you didn't talk to me personally about what you have written. Perhaps I could have said something useful to you, as well as you to me. I thank you for your letter and for the denunciation it contains. I continually suffer from the discrepancy between my way of life and the truths which I profess—especially recently as a result of my illness; I try to eliminate this discrepancy and I am grateful to those who remind me about it in the way you do in your letter, and force me to try harder to make my life accord with the truths I profess.

I am not speaking about vegetarianism, which I have never consciously betrayed in the course of 20 years, and the adherence to which has never cost me the slightest effort or deprivation. (I only learned from your letter that the doctors probably deceived me during my illness by cooking meat broths for me.) I am speaking about the luxury of the life in which I find myself, and above all about the use of paid servants.

I was very glad to learn from your letter that you are a person occupied with the important problems of life, as I noticed even from my brief conversations with you.

Thank you once more for your letter, and I wish you all the best.

Lev Tolstoy

491. To THE GRAND DUKE NIKOLAY MIKHAYLOVICH

Yasnaya Polyana, 20 August 1902

Dear Nikolay Mikhaylovich,

Thank you for your sympathy. My health is improving. But despite the fact that I get pleasure from life and try to use what is left of my life in the best possible way, I can't help feeling a certain annoyance that my carriage which had got stuck in a bog which I shall inevitably have to cross—and very soon at that—has been dragged out on this side and not the other.

My strength is still weak, but I have a great deal to do. For that reason I haven't written to you. As far as the question of the abolition of the private ownership of land is concerned, I recently wrote a detailed work about it, as well as I could, which will be published, of course, not in Russia but in England. The title of the work is: *To the Working People*.[1] Every work is une lettre de l'auteur à ses amis inconnus. It may serve as an answer to your objections. And if the subject interests you, do read it. I am now busy finishing an episode from Caucasian history of the years 1851–52, which was begun a long time ago and has kept growing.[2]

I wonder if you could help me by indicating where I might find the correspondence of Nicholas I and Chernyshov with Vorontsov for those years, and also the written comments of Nicholas I on the reports and dispatches concerning the Caucasus for those years?

Goodbye; I wish you all the best in your inner spiritual life. All that is truly good belongs only to that sphere.

Lev Tolstoy

492. To THE EDITORS OF 'DIE ZEIT'

Yasnaya Polyana, 11 September 1902

More and more often in recent times I have not only seen in different quarters signs of the brutalisations of human beings, but have heard and read not only justifications, but even eulogies of such brutalisation.

The chief exponent and eulogist of this brutalisation is the half-demented, but crazily self-assured, superficial, limited, but glib-tongued Nietzsche. So going back from effects to causes, I was involuntarily attracted to Nietzsche, and read that strange writer again, although with great dislike.[1] I would very much like to express,

---

[491] 1. Published in Russian by *The Free Word*, no. 78, at Christchurch, 1902.

2. *Hadji Murat*, not finished for some years and only published posthumously in 1912. The Grand Duke furnished important background material for this story on several occasions.

[492] 1. In September 1902 the Vienna paper *Die Zeit* sent Tolstoy an article on Nietzsche with a request for his help in counteracting Nietzschean ideas. Tolstoy had read *Thus Spake Zarathustra* the previous year with considerable distaste, although he found the style 'lively'. In 1902 he confessed to being amused at reading Shestov's comparison: *The Concept of Good in the Teachings of Count Tolstoy and Friedrich Nietzsche*.

492. To The Editors of 'Die Zeit'

if only in a short article, what I got out of this reading. If I manage to do so—if my health allows it, and other occupations which are more important in my opinion—I shall be very glad to send you the article.[2] I wish your journal success.

Lev Tolstoy

493. To THE GRAND DUKE NIKOLAY MIKHAYLOVICH

Yasnaya Polyana, 12 September 1902

I am very grateful to you, dear Nikolay Mikhaylovich, for the information you sent me.[1] It is more than I expected, and I shall be very, very grateful if you should find it possible to let me have for a time (a short time) the reports, dispatches and resolutions of the Emperor concerning the administration of the Caucasus from the time of Vorontsov's appointment until 1852, and also Volume x of the *Acts of the Caucasian Archaeological Commission*. I would take care of them, read them and return them.

What you write about the activity of Stroganov in the years 1801–1805 is very interesting and important. I shall be very glad to read your book.[2]

I have written to Chertkov asking him to send you *On Religion* and *To the Working People*. The latter concerns the question of the land which we corresponded about.

I wish you all the best with all my heart.

Lev Tolstoy

494. To V. V. STASOV

Yasnaya Polyana, 20 December 1902

Thank you, Vladimir Vasilyevich, for the books.[1] I received both consignments in good condition. Now I have an impossible request: I know that the Imperial Court journal wasn't published during the years I need, but isn't it possible to get a manuscript copy in the Archives at least for five or six days at the end of 1851 and the beginning of 1852? If it is possible, commission someone to do it for a fee which I will gladly pay.

Pas encore pour cette fois.[2] I'm getting a bit better again and I still hope to see

2. Tolstoy never wrote the article.

[493] 1. Historical and ethnographical material from the Tiflis Archives on the Caucasus in the mid-nineteenth century for Tolstoy's story *Hadji Murat*.

2. Count Pavel Alexandrovich Stroganov (*1774–1817*). *A Historical Study of the Epoch of Alexander I*, (1903) by the Grand Duke Nikolay Mikhaylovich. The author sent Tolstoy a copy of the work in 1903 which Tolstoy liked.

[494] 1. Tolstoy had requested a history of Nicholas I's reign, and some Moscow and Petersburg newspapers for December 1851 and January 1852.

2. A reply to Stasov's inquiry about his health.

494. *To V. V. Stasov*

you. Oh yes, aren't there any foreign histories of Nicholas with a negative attitude to him? Is it worth reading Custine?³ Is there anything in it about Nicholas' personality? Please forgive me; I add as usual that if you throw my letter into the waste paper basket without even replying, I shall take it that that's what's necessary, and shall be grateful to you.

Lev Tolstoy

[Postscript omitted]

3. Marquis Adolphe de Custine, *La Russie en 1839* (Paris, 1843).

IX
1903-1910

In 1903 Tolstoy was actively involved in the wave of protests against the Jewish pogroms in Kishinyov, and he wrote three stories for an anthology published in Warsaw in aid of the victims of Jewish persecution. In the same year he wrote *After the Ball* (on the subject of physical violence) which, like the rest of his fiction from this time onwards, was only published after his death. In 1904 he completed his long essay *Shakespeare and the Drama* and the magnificent novel *Hadji Murat*, the theme of which took him back to his youth and to the fighting in the Caucasus, but which seemed even to him to run counter to his professed belief in the doctrine of non-resistance to evil. Among the numerous publicist articles of his last few years which were widely read abroad are the pamphlet *Bethink Yourselves* on the subject of the Russo-Japanese War and the powerful onslaught on capital punishment *I Cannot Be Silent*. In a letter to the Russian Prime Minister he forcefully advocated the Henry George solution to the land problem and the abolition of private property, and his outspokenness on almost every issue of social, political and religious importance meant that he was the focus of attention of men and women throughout the world. Yasnaya Polyana became a place of pilgrimage, where Tolstoy held reluctant court. Letters poured in from many countries, from Gandhi and Bernard Shaw as well as from hundreds of obscure sympathisers and critics. Some people came to film him, others to record his voice, others again to take down all he said. It is hard to believe that Tolstoy, despite his vanity and egoism, welcomed this world-wide publicity which made the last few years of his life so wearisome and helped to aggravate the tensions of an already difficult family life. The death of his favourite daughter and disciple, Masha, in 1906 was a grievous blow to him. His wife's increasing neuroticism and hysterical outbursts (not without provocation), and the bitter wrangling over Tolstoy's will and the problems of copyright, brought matters to a head. At the age of 82 Tolstoy found his position so intolerable that he finally took the decision he had long been contemplating and left home for good. The story of his last days and his death on the railway station at Astapovo—'a desperate old man, beyond human aid, wandering self-blinded at Colonus' in Isaiah Berlin's memorable words —is painful reading, and a tragic conclusion to his long, searching and restless life which his vast correspondence so brightly illuminates.

495. To A. A. KORGANOVA

Anna Avessalomovna Korganova (1816–190?), widow of the army officer assigned to guard the Caucasian chieftain Hadji Murat after he had gone over to the Russian government (1851–2) and in whose house Hadji Murat lived until his escape to the mountains. Her son had written to Tolstoy after reading of his plan to write a story about Hadji Murat, and had offered what information he could. Tolstoy gratefully accepted, and wrote to ask whether Hadji Murat had actually lived in the Korganov household or in a separate house, what his dress was like and whether he was carrying a rifle when he escaped. Shortly afterwards Tolstoy also wrote the following letter to Korganova herself, and sent an envoy to Tiflis to interview her.

Yasnaya Polyana, 8 January 1903

Dear Anna Avessalomovna,

Your son, Ivan Iosifovich, having learned that I am writing about Hadji Murat, was kind enough to tell me many details about him and, moreover, permitted me to turn to you with a request for more detailed information about the *naib* Shamil who lived with you at Nukha. Although Ivan Iosifovich's information is very interesting, many things might have been unknown to him or wrongly understood by him, since he was only a ten-year-old boy at the time. I am venturing therefore to turn to you, Anna Avessalomovna, with the request to answer certain questions of mine and to tell me all you remember about this man and about his escape and tragic end.

Any detail about his life during his stay with you, his appearance and his relations with your family and other people, any apparently insignificant detail which has stuck in your memory, will be very interesting and valuable to me.

My questions are as follows:

1. Did he speak even a little Russian?
2. Whose were the horses on which he tried to escape—his own, or ones given to him? And were they good horses, and what colour were they?
3. Did he limp noticeably?
4. Did the house where you lived upstairs, and he downstairs, have a garden?
5. Was he strict in observing Mohammedan rituals, the five daily prayers etc.?

Forgive me, Anna Avessalomovna, for troubling you with such trifles, and accept my sincere gratitude for everything you do to carry out my request.

I remain, with the utmost respect, at your service,

Lev Tolstoy

P.S. Another question (6) What were the murids like who were with Hadji Murat and escaped with him, and how did they differ from him?

And yet another question (7) Did they have rifles on them when they escaped?

496. To COUNTESS A. A. TOLSTAYA

Yasnaya Polyana, 26 January 1903

My dear Alexandrine,

The older I get, the more I want to address you with greater and greater tenderness. Your last dear letter with information about Nicholas I particularly moved me. I'm lying in bed ill and weak, as you see, and am not writing myself —my daughter Masha is writing for me—and being in full possession of my mind and my feelings, I feel particularly disposed to tender emotion. All this is just another way of saying that I love you very, very much.

I'm not writing a biography of Nicholas, but I need several scenes from his life for my story *Hadji Murat*. And since I like to write only about things I understand well, ayant, so to speak, les coudées franches, I need to possess completely, so far as I can, the key to his character. That's why I'm collecting and reading everything relating to his life and character. What you sent is very valuable to me, but I need even more what you gave to Shilder.[1] I hope to get this from Shubinsky who has Shilder's papers. Details of his everyday life, what is called la petite histoire—stories of intrigues struck up at masked balls, his relations with Nelidova and his wife's relations with him—are just what I need. If it's not difficult for you, please send Mandt's memoirs too.[2]

Don't condemn me, my dear, for occupying myself with such trifles when I really do have one foot in the grave. These trifles fill in my free time and afford me respite from the real, serious thoughts with which my soul is overfull...[16 lines omitted]

497. To L. L. TOLSTOY

Yasnaya Polyana, 2 February 1903

Dear Lyova,

I've just read your drama or comedy.[1] On the whole it's good: the language, the details and several of the scenes are good. You probably want to know where I see the shortcomings.

The shortcomings in my opinion are as follows. In the first act there are too many characters and the beginning of the plot isn't clearly enough defined. Then the idea about the ruinous effect of urban life is too obtrusive, without any mitigations, i.e. any indications of its advantageous side. Then in the 4th act, the appearance of the same gentlemen in the country is unnatural.

On the whole, I repeat, it's still good, and I think that the performance of the drama in a public theatre is bound to be useful.

[496] 1. A. A. Tolstaya, having learned from the press that Tolstoy was writing about Nicholas I, wrote to tell him that she had handed over her 'recollections' of Nicholas to the historian N. K. Shilder.

2. Nicholas I's physician who recorded the last minutes of his life.

[497] 1. *The Hall-Porter of the General's wife, Antonova, or Rootless.*

497. *To L. L. Tolstoy*

The latest news about dear Dora made us happy; it's high time she recovered.

I'm very weak, but I'm apparently recovering now. Goodbye: I kiss you and all your family.

Your loving father,
L.T.

498. To S. N. TOLSTOY

Yasnaya Polyana, 23 February 1903

How good that you have written at least a few words. That's also why I am writing. I always regret one thing about your letters, namely that you write too little and, in particular, too little about yourself and your own intimate affairs. Sofya Andreyevna says very truly that English women write the most boring letters of the kind: *I hope that you are*[1] this and that, but say nothing about themselves. As for myself, I either have very little to write to you or very much. If I were to write about the events in my life, there are few of them and they don't interest me, but if I were to write about my inner life, it's an inexhaustible subject. The main thing is that I am preparing for death, i.e. for another life, and this preparation consists entirely in living the rest of my time as well as possible and trying to understand what can be understood. I think that all this will be useful *there*. My health is fairly good, but I'm weak. I'm sending you *Russian Thought*; there's an article in it by N. V. Davydov,[2] under the pseudonym Vasilich; read it. And there are some stories by Kuprin: *The Night Shift* is not bad; read it.

L.T.

499. To PERCY REDFERN

[Original in English]

Yasnaya Polyana, 23 February 1903

Dear Percy Redfern,

I think your friend who is against books and reading is quite right.

Lao-Tzu says: true words are not pleasant, pleasant words are not true. The wise are not learned, the learned are not wise.

The Brahmanes say that in their books there are many predictions of times in which it will rain. But press those books as strongly as you can, you can not get out of them a drop of water. So you can not get out of all the books that contain the best precepts the smallest good deed.

Ruskin says that the best men, those which have done the greatest good to humanity, are those that we do not know of.

The chief difference between words and deeds is that words are always intended for men for their approbation, but deeds can be done only for God.

[498] 1. In English in the original.
2. 'From the Past Life of a Provincial Town'.

500. To S. N. Rabinovich (Sholom-Aleichem)

Though it is possible to utter words only with the intention to fulfil the will of God, it is very difficult not to think about the impression which they will produce on men and not to form them accordingly. But deeds you can do quite unknown to men, only for God. And such deeds are the greatest joy that a man can experience.

As to his plan to live amongst prostitutes and tramps...I can not say that I approve of it. Rather not. I think that to change one's habitual life for such a one a man must be quite sure to be proof against the new temptations that will assail him in this new life.

This refers also to your doubts about your life.

I think that the changes in our life must come from the impossibility to live otherwise than accordingly to the demands of our conscience but not from our mental resolution to try a new form of life.

I was glad to hear all what you write about your society and yourself and thank you for your letter.

Your friend Leo Tolstoy

500. To S. N. RABINOVICH (SHOLOM-ALEICHEM)

Sholom-Aleichem (Solomon Rabinovich, 1819–1916), a popular Jewish writer of short stories, novels and plays, living at the time in the Ukraine. After 1905 he spent much time abroad because of the continuing anti-Jewish pogroms in Russia, and he lived the last years of his life in New York.

Yasnaya Polyana, 6 May 1903

Solomon Naumovich,

The terrible crime perpetrated in Kishinyov made a painful impression on me. I partly expressed my attitude to this affair in a letter to a well-known Jew, a copy of which I enclose.[1] We recently sent a collective letter from Moscow to the mayor of Kishinyov, expressing our feelings about this terrible affair.

I shall be very glad to contribute to your collection and will try to write some thing appropriate to the circumstances.[2]

Unfortunately, what I have to say is this, that the culprit not only of the Kishinyov horrors but of all the discord which is rife among a certain small section—not a national one—of the Russian people, is the government alone. Unfortunately this is something I cannot say in a legal Russian publication.

Lev Tolstoy

[500] 1. After the Kishinyov pogrom of 6–8 April 1903 Tolstoy was asked by several people to lend his name to a public protest, and to help the Jewish victims in various ways. A request from Sholom-Aleichem was preceded by letters from E. Linetsky, a dentist, and D. Shor, a Moscow pianist. Tolstoy sent them identical copies of a long letter on the general problem and the specific incident at Kishinyov, which he also enclosed with this letter to Sholom-Aleichem.

2. Tolstoy contributed three short stories to the collection.

501. To SIDNEY COCKERELL

Sir Sidney Cockerell (1867–1962), secretary to William Morris 1892–8 and later Director of the Fitzwilliam Museum, Cambridge; art historian and specialist in illuminated manuscripts. He visited Tolstoy together with Robert Hunter, an American socialist and friend of Ernest Crosby, on 29 June/12 July 1903 and wrote an interesting account of the day he spent with the family at Yasnaya Polyana. Eleven letters and one postcard from him are extant in the archives in Moscow, but only four letters by Tolstoy to Cockerell are published in the Jubilee Edition.

[Original in English]

Yasnaya Polyana, 11/24 August 1903

Dear Sir,

I safely received the books you sent me as well as the portrait of More and thank you very much.[1] I have not yet had the time to read them. I postpone it for the autumn and winter if I will live till then. Your visit has left me a very agreeable impression.

With sympathy yours truly,
Leo Tolstoy

502. To OCTAVE MIRBEAU

Octave Mirbeau (1850–1917), French journalist and writer of short stories, novels and plays. His journalism carried great weight with the public—from having been a fervent royalist in his youth, he became a bitter opponent of colonialism and militarism. Mirbeau's comedy *Les affaires sont les affaires* (Paris, 1903, translated into Russian in the same year) carried a long and ardent dedication to Tolstoy as Mirbeau's literary mentor and one who, along with Dostoyevsky, had broken down traditional Latin characteristics in art and culture generally—excessive emphasis on moderation, logic, and general superficiality, which Mirbeau said made French art 'cold'.

Yasnaya Polyana,
30 September/13 October 1903

Cher confrère,

Ce n'est qu'avant hier que j'ai reçu votre lettre du 26 Mai.

Je crois que chaque nationalité emploie différents moyens pour exprimer dans l'art l'idéal commun et que c'est à cause de cela que nous éprouvons une jouissance particulière à retrouver notre idéal exprimé d'une manière nouvelle et inattendue. L'art Français m'a donné jadis ce sentiment de découverte quand j'ai lu pour la première fois Alfred de Vigny, Stendhal, Victor Hugo et surtout Rousseau. Je

---

[501] 1. The books Cockerell sent were the works of William Morris.

crois que c'est à ce sentiment qu'il faut attribuer la trop grande importance que vous attachez aux écrits de Dostoievsky et surtout aux miens. Dans tous les cas je vous remercie pour votre lettre et votre dédicace. Je me fais une fête de lire votre nouveau drame.[1]

Léon Tolstoy

503. To V. V. STASOV

Yasnaya Polyana, 9 October 1903

Dear Vladimir Vasilyevich,

I have just read your letter to Sofya Andreyevna (she is in Moscow) and was horrified. For the sake of our friendship, drop this business and save me from these phonographs and cinematography.[1] I find them very unpleasant, and I most certainly do not agree to pose and speak.

If by this refusal I put you in the position of having to refuse something you have promised, please forgive me, but do save me. I thank you very much for the books and Mr Polovtsev for the information.[2] I'm still dawdling about with Shakespeare et je ne demords pas de mon idée.[3] I expect to finish it any day. It's not a question of Shakespeare's aristocratism, but of the perversion, due to the praising of inartistic works, of aesthetic taste. Well, let them abuse me if they like. Perhaps you will too, but I had to express what has been cooped up in me for half a century. Forgive me.

Keep well, and as kind and busy as always.

L. Tolstoy

504. To P. I. BIRYUKOV

Yasnaya Polyana, 27 November 1903

[33 lines omitted]...I certainly don't remember when I met Gay in Rome. I don't even remember seeing him in Rome. There are some completely blank spots in my past life on which no mark has been left—I remember nothing at all. I was in

[502] 1. Tolstoy believed from newspaper reports that Mirbeau was writing a new play about the French Revolution, but this was not the case. The Yasnaya Polyana library contains four of Mirbeau's works, three of them personally inscribed by the author to Tolstoy.

[503] 1. During a recent visit to Yasnaya Polyana, Stasov had tried to persuade Tolstoy to record his voice on a phonograph record, and to be filmed by a cinema camera. Tolstoy disapproved of the idea, but Sofya Andreyevna wrote to Stasov to say that she had persuaded him to agree. When Stasov replied to her about the arrangements and Tolstoy learned of it, he wrote this letter of refusal. He was later filmed in 1909 and 1910, first by Pathé, without his permission, and then by the first professional Russian cinematographer, A. Drankov, at Yasnaya Polyana, Moscow and Kryokshino (Chertkov's estate).

2. Stasov had sent an 1889 almanach containing an article on the anniversary of Borodino by Polovtsev, Head of the Imperial Archives. Polovtsev also sent a letter to Tolstoy with more information about the Borodino celebrations of 1839.

3. The essay *On Shakespeare and the Drama*, begun in September 1903 and finished in January 1904.

504. To P. I. Biryukov

Rome, probably, in 1860, after my brother's death. Your wish to write my biography touches and moves me very much and I would like to help you, with all my heart. About my loves:

The first and strongest was my childhood love for Sonichka Koloshina.[1] Then, I suppose, Zinaida Molostvova.[2] That love existed in my imagination. She hardly knew anything about it. Then the Cossack girl described in *The Cossacks*. Then a society infatuation for Shcherbatova-Uvarova.[3] She hardly knew anything about it either. I was always very shy. Then the main and most serious one was Valeriya Arsenyeva.[4] She is still alive, married to Volkov and living in Paris. I was almost engaged to her (*Family Happiness*), and I have a whole bundle of my letters to her. I have asked Tanya to copy them out and send them to you.

I don't give my diaries to just anybody to copy out because their vileness is too awful. But nevertheless they are particularly interesting and I will let you have them. Amidst the abyss of filth there are signs of a yearning for clean air. I will let you have them without fail. It wasn't a woman's love which provided me with the brightest period of my life, but love of people and of children. That was a wonderful time, especially amid the gloom of what had gone before.

I would like to take up my reminiscences again, but other things keep distracting me. I've been writing an unnecessary article about the Shakespeare delusion. Now, I think, I've finished it, and I'll continue my reminiscences bit by bit between other things. It's such pleasant, easy and absorbing work. Goodbye for now; I kiss you and your wife and children as a brother.

L. Tolstoy

505. To M. A. TAUBE

Mikhail Alexandrovich Taube (1869–?), Professor of International Law at the University of Petersburg, later deputy Minister of Education and a member of the Senate.

Taube had written an article on the subject of international peace and the concept of peace in various religions, which he sent to *The Intermediary* for publication; it was sent on to Tolstoy for his opinion and Tolstoy wrote the following remarks about it to the author. The article was printed by *The Intermediary* as 'Christianity and International Peace' (Moscow 1905).

[504] 1. Sofya Koloshina, the daughter of a Decembrist, P. I. Koloshin; the character of Sonichka Volokhina in Tolstoy's *Childhood* is based on her.

2. Zinaida Molostvova, whom Tolstoy met while a student in Kazan. She was a friend of his sister's and came frequently to visit the Tolstoy home. Tolstoy met her again in 1851 when he spent a week in May in Kazan on his way to the Caucasus, and his diary contains ecstatic references to her at this time. In 1885 a mutual friend offered to reintroduce them, but she refused.

3. Praskovya Shcherbatova. Tolstoy saw her several times in Moscow in early 1858. His diary calls her 'charming', but says little else about her. In 1859 she married A. S. Uvarov, an archaeologist.

4. Valeriya Arsenyeva. See Letter 38.

506. To Countess A. A. Tolstaya

Yasnaya Polyana, 18–19 December 1903

[Postscript to letter (19 December 1903)]

I have read your article and would like to add the following observations. In my opinion your appraisal of Buddhism and Stoicism is incorrect, or rather, incomplete. Buddhism, like Stoicism, teaches that the true essence of man is not in his body, which is not free, and therefore suffers, but in his spiritual awareness, which is not subject to any constraint and therefore to any suffering. The former has as its objective, freedom from suffering, the latter—the good of the personality. And therefore asceticism is not the objective or ideal of Buddhism. But the professor's opinion about Stoicism is quite incorrect. The professor obviously poses as the main task of mankind the existence of international law, of which he is a professor and not the good of mankind.

Stoicism does indeed destroy the stones with which the edifice of the world today is built, but this destruction, if it is harmful to the existence of international law as it is now understood, is undoubtedly beneficial for mankind by destroying what divides it.

The teachings of Buddhism and Stoicism, like those of the Jewish prophets, particularly those that are known by the name of Isaiah, and also the Chinese teachings of Confucius, Lao-Tzu and the little known Mi-Ti, which all appeared almost simultaneously, about the 6th century B.C., all equally recognise the essence of man to be his spiritual nature, and this is their greatest service. But they differ from Christianity which came after them by the fact that they stop at the recognition of the spirituality of man, seeing in this recognition the salvation and the good of the personality. But Christianity makes a further conclusion. Starting from the recognition by people of their spirituality, or to use the Christian expression, the recognition of the son of God in themselves, it proclaims the possibility and necessity of establishing on earth the Kingdom of God—i.e. universal good, which embraces the concept of universal peace.

The importance of the content of your article provoked these observations of mine, for which I ask you to forgive me if they seem to you to be out of place.

I have written this postscript so badly that I have asked for it to be copied out.

Yours,
L. Tolstoy

506. To COUNTESS A. A. TOLSTAYA

Yasnaya Polyana, 22 December 1903

Alexandrine, my dear, kind, old friend,

Tanya Kuzminskaya wrote to me about you and about your illness (I thank her for it)—that you are very weak and, in our human judgement, apparently close to death. I too was very close to it, but here I am still not dead, and sometimes I regret it—it was so good to be dying—will it be like that another time?—but sometimes I'm glad because I think that our senile lives are not only not useless, as

506. To Countess A. A. Tolstaya

people often think, but on the contrary, are of the utmost importance in terms of the influence that old people can exert on others. You, with your ardent religious feeling and heart of gold, have probably experienced and are experiencing the enlightenment that illness gives, and are now more than ever before, not just probably, but certainly, spreading love and goodness round about you. I'm writing this letter only so as to tell you how often in my relations with you I have felt this love and goodness of yours, and feeling it, have become better myself. I also want to tell you that you're mistaken in thinking—if you do think—that you and I are separated by our faith. My faith and your faith and the faith of all good people (forgive me for the immodesty of including myself among them) are one and the same thing: faith in God the Father, who sent us into this world to do His will. His will is that we should love each other and do to others as we would have them do to us. And the fact that I have carried out His will badly and am still carrying it out badly now doesn't frighten me, since I know that God is love and that He knows I have tried, especially just recently, to carry out His will, and not from fear of punishment but because the more I have done His will, the better my life has always been. And I'm sure you believe exactly the same. But even if I don't believe in some details you believe in, I don't think it's important and can't separate us in view of the very important thing that unites us.

When I was very close to death, and my thoughts refused to function, and I tried to express my attitude towards the impending passage from this life to the other, I remember I found only one thought, one feeling, one appeal to God; I said to myself: *from Thee I came and unto Thee I shall return*. And this expressed everything I felt, and comforted and cheered me. I'm sure that you feel the same, and this feeling again unites us.

If they read this letter of mine to you, tell them to write me a couple of lines about how you feel and whether things are well with you.

Goodbye, for now, my dear; be assured of my sincere love for you and my gratitude for all the good you have given me during the half century of our friendship.[1]

Lev Tolstoy

507. To JAMES LEY

James William Thomas Ley (1879–?), English journalist and author of several books and articles on Dickens. He founded the Bristol and Clifton Dickens Society in 1902, and was one of the founders of the journal *The Dickensian*. He wrote to Tolstoy in 1904 to ask his opinion about Dickens.

[506] 1. A. A. Tolstaya replied to Tolstoy on 27–9 December, 1903: 'Dear Lev, whom I have loved so long, your tender, friendly letter was all the more gratifying to me because I felt in it that very, very sincere note which always rang out between us during the days of our youth. I was also pleased by your encouraging words in which we agree in thinking that even deep into old age it's possible to be of use to others.'
She died on 21 March 1904.

508. To V. G. Chertkov

[Original in English] Yasnaya Polyana,
21 January/3 February 1904

Dear Sir,

I think that Charles Dickens is the greatest novel writer of the 19th century, and that his works, impressed with the true Christian spirit, have done and will continue to do a great deal of good to mankind.

Yours truly,
Leo Tolstoy

508. To V. G. CHERTKOV

Yasnaya Polyana, 19 February 1904

My dear Vladimir Grigoryevich,

I would have been very glad to reply to your questions, but in the field of thought to which these questions refer it is impossible, or at least I am unable, to reply; I can only follow the trend of my own thought. Perhaps what has been occupying me recently in this field of thought might serve as a partial answer to your questions. I'll try and set out, at least in a rough and ready way, these thoughts which are very dear to me.

I think, to begin again from the beginning (and this is why I disliked the publication of my thoughts about consciousness),[1] that all that any man knows for certain about his own life and that of the world is that he is awakened to the life of this world by the consciousness of his own separate material existence, and it seems to him that there is himself and his body which he can control by his own thoughts, and the whole world round about—from a tiny insect to Sirius—which he can't control. On this level of consciousness (the lowest), a man doesn't usually think that he didn't exist before and has been awakened by consciousness, but it seems to him that there is himself—his physical being—and outside him the whole world. The enormous majority of people start life, live and die with this consciousness.

But apart from the consciousness of his separateness as a material being, a man, if he thinks about it, asks himself the question: what constitutes his real being, his body or that which controls his body and can change it (even to the extent of being able to destroy the consciousness in it), and inevitably, if he thinks in a strictly scientific way, he's bound to admit that what constitutes the essence of his life is his spiritual being which receives impressions not only of the external world but also of his own body. A man is only aware of his body because there is a spiritual being which is conscious of itself in his body (Berkeley's idealism). And this consciousness of self as a spiritual being, separated from other beings by boundaries represented by matter and movement, is the second stage of consciousness, higher

[508] 1. Excerpts from Tolstoy's diaries on the subject of consciousness had been published in *The Free Word* in 1903. Chertkov wrote to him in February 1904 to question him further, and Tolstoy's reply is one of several attempts by him to clarify his thoughts on the subject. (See also Letter 576.)

than the first. But just as the first stage of consciousness contained in itself an inner contradiction consisting of the fact that a material being feels and is aware of things, i.e. does something not natural to matter and incapable of being deduced from it, so does the second stage of consciousness present the same insoluble contradiction consisting of the fact that a spiritual being, i.e. something outside space and time, is confined to limits and forms a part of something. And so a thinking man inevitably comes to the third stage of consciousness consisting of the fact that in human life a separate material being is conscious of itself (the first stage), not a separate spiritual being, but an infinite, eternally-living, unified being which manifests itself in an infinite number of forms (beings), one of which is me, in the midst of forms or beings which are contiguous with me and limit me. Such, I think, is the third and highest stage of consciousness, the one which is revealed in true Brahmanism, in Buddhism and in Christianity. According to this view of the world, there is no me, but only the eternal, infinite power of God working in the world through me and through my consciousness. Life consists in the growth of consciousness: in the transition from the first to the second and third stage, and in the strengthening, purification and vitalisation of consciousness at this highest stage. In this strengthening, purification and vitalisation of consciousness, to which there is no end, is the meaning of life and the good of life and all moral teaching.

God willing, I'll try to set this out better sometime, but it was very important for me to say it and has greatly added to the good of my spirit...[10 lines omitted]

509. To T. L. SUKHOTINA

Yasnaya Polyana, 19 February 1904

Hello, Tanichka dear! I've just finished a pile of letters I had to answer. Yours turned up last, but I'm not tired and am glad to have a chat with you. I've looked through your two letters. There's nothing to answer, so I can write what comes into my head and what is closer to my heart. Like dry leaves in autumn, friends of my own age are falling thick and fast into the grave, and I have a feeling that my brother's leaf is barely holding on and my own is frailer still, although I feel well and cheerful. I'm afraid my brother Seryozha has cancer—it's getting difficult for him to swallow. Masha has written and told me, and I keep meaning to pay a visit, but I can never manage to: either it's my stomach, or the weather, or guests. Above all he's worried by Grisha who, like Balatsky, writes stupid and malevolent letters, by sorrow and shame for his daughters, by his sufferings, and, I'm afraid, by a fear of death greater than one may or should have.[1] I think about him, and am wretched. Only his love for me makes me happy. How love repairs everything! All is well at home. Sasha makes us happy, both physically and morally. Ilyusha, so I hear and

[509] 1. Grisha: Grigory Sergeyevich Tolstoy, son of Tolstoy's brother Sergey, who was in fact dying of cancer (he died seven months later). The personal lives of Sergey's two daughters, Vera and Varvara, caused their father distress. In 1889 Varvara married a peasant and a year later Vera married a Bashkir—a marriage that was not formalised and not known to the family until some time later when Vera was in an advanced stage of pregnancy.

509. To T. L. Sukhotina

have noticed, isn't well. The young generation, your generation, has no *taboo*, i.e. an area which it's as impossible to enter *morally*, as it is physically impossible to walk through a wall. With them everything is permissible, and I'm afraid there's nothing one shouldn't do. Andryusha was here yesterday. He's going to Petersburg and wants to make arrangements to go to the war under Kuropatkin.[2] He's parted company with his lady.[3] She wrote to him that she didn't love him and he immediately stopped loving her. To be angry with him for his immorality is just like being angry with a deaf mute for not answering. When you know he's a deaf mute, it's easier to deal with him. There's even something pleasant and new about your relations, as you feel with deaf mutes when you communicate with them by funny signs. Olga is going to England. I advised him in any case to say goodbye to her and part, but to do so as if there was no rupture, which there really isn't. Seryozha[4] is all aglow with interest in the war and the internal disorders. Salomon, Buturlin, Goldenweiser and his wife, and Dmitry Vasilyevich have all been here at the same time.[5] Mama has gone to Moscow and thought up the idea of a museum of 'the Russian land',[6] which is actually very immodest while I'm still alive, and therefore disagreeable to me, but it's so unimportant. What should I say about the two important people: about you and me? About you—that I don't expect anything from your pregnancy, as from Masha's, except sorrow for you, and I comfort myself with the fact that it's good for your souls. This sounds odd, but it's true. I understand your purchase very well, and although it's a luxury, I don't venture to condemn it.[7] About myself I can say that it's work, work without end, and that I'm getting something done. As for the main job of preparing myself for death calmly and, as I would wish, joyfully—I'm also doing a little of that too. I've written one little story, *The Divine and the Human*, then half finished *The False Coupon* in rough, and progressed a little with my reminiscences. Goodbye, darling; I kiss you and dear Misha and Natasha.[8]

A. Y. Balatsky, a soldier stationed in Odessa who wrote Tolstoy nearly forty accusatory and malicious letters in 1904–5. Most of these letters were finally left unopened.

2. A. N. Kuropatkin, Minister of War 1899–1904. At the outbreak of the Russo-Japanese War he was appointed Commander-in-Chief of the Russian army.

3. Andrey had been having an affair with a married woman, Anna Leonidovna Tolmachova, which had led to a separation from his wife Olga in November 1903. (They were only formally divorced in 1907 when Andrey wished to remarry.)

4. Tolstoy's son, Sergey.

5. Charles Salomon, a French writer, translator of Tolstoy's works into French, and author of several articles about him.

A. S. Buturlin, a Greek scholar and friend of the family who helped Tolstoy in his transation of the Gospels.

A. B. Goldenweiser (1875–1961), a distinguished pianist and composer, later for many years a professor at the Moscow Conservatoire, and for a time its Principal. His memoirs of Tolstoy whom he knew well were published in 1922 and 1923, and have been translated into English in abridged form as *Talks with Tolstoy*.

D. V. Nikitin, a family doctor who lived at Yasnaya Polyana from 1902 to 1904.

6. Sofya Andreyevna had in mind a 'Tolstoy Museum', to contain manuscripts and personal articles of her husband.

7. Tanya had recently bought a house in the hills near Lausanne. She and her husband travelled abroad regularly to Switzerland.

8. Mikhail Sukhotin's two children from his previous marriage.

510. To CHARLES WRIGHT

Sir Charles Theodore Hagberg Wright (1862–1940), Secretary and Librarian of the London Library. He had been educated privately abroad, in Russia as well as in France and Germany, and translated several of Tolstoy's works into English (including *Father Sergey*, *The False Coupon* and *Hadji Murat*). He also wrote several articles about Tolstoy for English journals and newspapers.

Yasnaya Polyana, 22 April–7 May 1904

Dear Charles Wright,[1]

You know Russian so well that I hope that a letter in that language won't cause you any difficulty.

I'm very grateful to you for the excellent book which I have now received.[2] Les grandes pensées viennent du coeur. I think Spencer had too little of it and for that reason no grandes pensées. And so I'm not an admirer of Spencer, but I shall read his autobiography, and I thank you for it. Psychological facts of the highest degree of importance are often revealed in autobiographies, quite independently of their authors' will. Such facts, I remember, impressed me in Mill's autobiography. I remember you not as a relative of my daughter-in-law, but as a very agreeable friend, and I am glad of the opportunity of contact with you.

Yours truly,
Leo Tolstoy[3]

511. To ALLEN CLARKE

Charles Allen Clarke (1863–1935), Lancashire journalist, author and editor. Clarke worked in a cotton factory as a boy and was later a schoolteacher. He published many books, one of which, *The Effects of the Factory System* (London, 1899) was sent to Tolstoy by Aylmer Maude at Tolstoy's request. Tolstoy had it translated into Russian for *The Intermediary* as *Factory Life in England* (1904). Clarke was best known for his *Weekly* which he wrote under the pseudonym of Teddy Ashton, and many of his books deal with Lancashire life and customs and Lancashire folklore.

[Original in English]

Yasnaya Polyana,
30 April/13 May 1904

Dear friend Allen Clarke,

I was glad to have news from you. I wish success to your scheme.[1] It is the beginning of a great and very important work which will be done sooner or later.

[510] 1. In English in the original.
    2. Herbert Spencer's *An Autobiography* (London, 1904).
    3. In English in the original.

[511] 1. Clarke's idea of founding agricultural communities in England.

Your book translated in Russian is very much appreciated. Now I will try to translate one of your novels.² I have not yet read them but judging by the opinions of the press and my own based on the book what I know—they must have the same merits as the *Factory System*.

Your friend,
Leo Tolstoy

512. To A. F. KONI

Yasnaya Polyana, 1 May 1904

I received your letter and the offprints, dear Anatoly Fyodorovich, and I thank you.

I was especially touched by your concern over such trifles as the details of clothing in Nicholas' time.¹ My wife maintains that she remembers plumes in the 50s. Perhaps generals still had them, but the Emperor no longer wore them. If I get the chance I'll try to check up from portraits of Nicholas in the 50s. I read your court ethics,² and although I think that these thoughts, coming from such an authority as yourself, are bound to be of use to young court officers, I personally cannot, however much I wish, give up the idea that once the highest moral and religious law, Kant's categorical imperative, is accepted, the court itself will disappear in the face of its demands. Perhaps we shall manage to see each other again, and talk about it then.

I press your hand in friendship,
Lev Tolstoy

513. To V. V. STASOV

Yasnaya Polyana, 8 May 1904

Thank you for sending the books,¹ Vladimir Vasilyevich, and for the long letter.

I don't despair of seeing you. It will be very nice. I haven't yet read your Shylock,² but I shall certainly read it. I've completely given up Shakespeare now, and am busy with other things. I've just finished an article about war³ and am busy with Nicholas I and despotism in general, the psychology of despotism, which I would like to portray artistically in connection with the Decembrists...[6 lines omitted]

2. Tolstoy's intention was never fulfilled.

[512] 1. While staying at Yasnaya Polyana, Koni had read *Hadji Murat* in manuscript, and wrote some comments on his return about chapter 15 which dealt with Nicholas I.
2. 'General Aspects of Judicial Ethics'.

[513] 1. Memoirs of three Decembrists, all published abroad.
2. Shakespeare's '*Merchant of Venice*' (Petersburg, 1904).
3. *Bethink Yourselves!*

514. To V. G. CHERTKOV

Yasnaya Polyana, 13/26 May 1904

My dear Vladimir Grigoryevich,

In 1895 I wrote a will of sorts,[1] i.e. I expressed my wishes to those nearest to me about what to do with the things that survived me. I wrote in that note that I asked my wife, Strakhov and you to sort out and look through all my papers. I asked you to do this because I knew your great love for me and your moral sensibility which would indicate to you what to throw away, what to keep, and when, where, and in what form to publish it. I might have added moreover that I trusted you particularly because I also know your thoroughness and conscientiousness in this sort of work and especially our complete agreement over a religious understanding of life.

At the time I didn't write to you about this, but now, nine years later, when Strakhov is no more and my death is in any case not far away, I consider it necessary to correct my omission and to tell you personally what was said about you in that note, namely that I asked you to undertake the task of looking through and sorting out the papers that survived me, and, together with my wife, to dispose of them as you found necessary.

Apart from the papers which you have, I'm sure that my wife or (in the event of her dying before you) my children will not refuse, in carrying out my wishes, will not refuse [sic] to hand over to you the papers which you don't have, and to decide, together with you, how to dispose of them.

To be frank, I attach no importance to all these papers, except for my diaries of recent years, and I am completely indifferent to what use is made of them. But the diaries, if I'm unable to express more clearly and precisely what I have jotted down in them, might have some importance, if only for the fragmentary thoughts expounded there. And so if you cut out from them all that is incidental, unclear

---

[514] 1. This first 'will' was a note in Tolstoy's diary for 27 March 1895. This letter may be regarded as the second, and a third will was made in September 1909, apparently prompted by Sofya Andreyevna's increasingly unbalanced behaviour. This will reaffirmed what Tolstoy said in his public announcement of 1891: that all his works written since 1 January 1881 and those yet unpublished should be public property after his death. However, this will had no legal validity, as property had to be willed to some person in particular, and so Chertkov, who knew about it, arranged to have yet another one drawn up. He prudently chose to have Tolstoy's literary property left to a member of the family rather than to himself, and Alexandra, the youngest daughter and most fervent Tolstoyan in the family, was chosen. According to the terms of the will, Tolstoy left her *all* his works, including those written before 1881, with private instructions for those which Sofya Andreyevna considered to be her own property. The proceeds from *Hadji Murat*, as yet unpublished, he wished to be used for purchasing land for the Yasnaya Polyana peasants. The last will, in July 1910, (again at Chertkov's request) was exactly the same as the third, with provision for Tatyana to replace Alexandra should the latter predecease her father. Chertkov protected his own rights through a special memorandum (drawn up by himself) which Tolstoy signed in pencil and added to the will, saying that Chertkov was to be given all 'manuscripts and papers' to publish in accordance with Tolstoy's principles. The various legal wrangles after Tolstoy's death about his literary property came about when Alexandra felt that Chertkov was not fulfilling the terms of the memorandum—legally, of course, all the papers belonged to her.

514. To V. G. Chertkov

and superfluous, their publication might be useful to people, and I hope you will do this as well as you have done the extracts so far from my unpublished writings, and this I beg of you.

Thank you for all your work in the past on my writings and thank you in advance for what you will do with the papers which survive me. Union with you has been one of the great joys of the last years of my life.

Lev Tolstoy

[Attached to Tolstoy's letter are the following typewritten questions by Chertkov and Tolstoy's replies to them in his own hand.]

1. Do you wish your statement in *The Russian Gazette* of 16 September 1891 to remain in force both now and after your death?

I wish that all my works written since 1881 as well as those [unpublished works] which survive me should not be the private property of any individual, but that anyone who so desires should be able to reprint and publish them.

2. Who do you wish should have the final decision about problems connected with the editing and publishing of your posthumous writings, over which complete agreement should prove to be for some reason impossible?

I think that my wife and V. G. Chertkov, to whom I have entrusted the task of sorting out papers which survive me, will reach agreement about what to keep, what to throw away, what to publish and how.

3. Do you wish that the written authority given to me by you as your only foreign representative should remain in force even after your death if I survive you?

I wish that V. G. Chertkov alone should handle the publication and translation of my works abroad even after my death.

4. Do you put at my complete disposal even after your death all your manuscripts and papers which I have received and shall receive from you before your death, both for the purpose of publishing them in my life-time at my own discretion and of handing them on to a person empowered by me after my death?

I put at the disposal of V. G. Chertkov all my manuscripts and papers which are in his possession. In the event of his death, I think that it would be better to hand over these papers and manuscripts to my wife or to some Russian institution—a public library or academy.

5. Do you wish that I should be given the opportunity of looking through in the original all your manuscripts without any exception whatsoever, which may be in the hands of Sofya Andreyevna or members of your family after your death?

I would very much wish V. G. Chertkov to look through all the manuscripts which survive me and to copy out from them what he should find necessary for publication.

Yasnaya Polyana, 13 May 1904   Lev Tolstoy

515. To THE GRAND DUKE NIKOLAY MIKHAYLOVICH

Yasnaya Polyana, 1 June 1904

Thank you, dear Nikolay Mikhaylovich, for your intercession on behalf of the old Dukhobors[1] and for informing me of its success. I got a very stupid letter from Golitsyn[2] a long time ago, and the other day I got a letter of gratitude from the old people in Canada. This gratitude belongs more to you, and I pass it on to you.

I am very glad for your sake that you have a good and useful literary occupation which distracts you, at least a little, from an awareness of the difficult conditions in which we live. I never thought that this terrible war would have such an effect on me as it has had. I couldn't help speaking my mind about it, and sent an article abroad which will appear in a few days, and will probably be very much disapproved of in higher circles.[3]

In your last letter but one you wrote that you would perhaps visit me some time at Yasnaya Polyana. However pleasant it would be for me to see you at our house, I think that I am such a *persona non grata* with the government—and I shall be particularly so now after my article on the war—that your visiting me might be unpleasant for you, and so I think it necessary to warn you about it. In any case your attitude towards me has been so good, and has left such pleasant memories for me, that I can quite sincerely sign this letter with the words

Yours affectionately,
Lev Tolstoy

516. To G. A. RUSANOV

Yasnaya Polyana, 24 September 1904

[48 lines omitted]...I have been busy recently compiling, not so much a calendar but a Circle of Reading for each day, compiled from the best thoughts of the best writers. While reading all this time not only Marcus Aurelius, Epictetus, Xenophon, Socrates, Brahmin, Chinese and Buddhist wisdom, but also Seneca, Plutarch, Cicero and the moderns—Montesquieu, Rousseau, Voltaire, Lessing, Kant, Lichtenberg, Schopenhauer, Emerson, Channing, Parker, Ruskin, Amiel etc. (and moreover not reading newspapers or magazines for more than a month now), I am more and more surprised and horrified not so much at the ignorance but at the 'cultural' barbarity in which our society is immersed. Surely education and en-

---

[515] 1. Three Dukhobors who had been in exile when their families emigrated to Canada, and therefore remained behind but now wanted to leave, and had enlisted Tolstoy's support in raising their fare and in obtaining permission. On the last point Tolstoy had turned to the Grand Duke, who called the local Governor's attention to the case.

2. G. S. Golitsyn, the civil governor of the Caucasus.

3. *Bethink Yourselves!*

lightenment mean taking advantage of and assimilating all the spiritual heritage which our ancestors have left us, whereas we only know the newspapers, Zola, Maeterlinck, Ibsen, Rozanov etc. How I would like to be of use, at least to some extent, in this terrible calamity which is worse than war, because all terrible things, including war, breed on this terrible *cultural*, and therefore self-satisfied barbarity...
[3 lines omitted]

517. To ISO-ABÉ

Iso-Abé, editor of a Japanese socialist newspaper, *Heimin Shimbun Sha*, which was closed down by the government in 1904. Its issue of 14 August 1904 N.S. carried an article on 'Tolstoy's Influence in Japan' which Iso-Abé sent to Tolstoy with a letter on 4 September 1904 N.S. The article, the letter from Iso-Abé and Tolstoy's reply (translated into Russian) were all published in *The Free Word* in 1905.

[Original in English]   Yasnaya Polyana,
23 October/5 November 1904

Dear friend Iso Abé,

It was a great pleasure for me to receive your letter and your paper with the English article. I thank you heartily for both.

Though I never doubted that there are in Japan a great many reasonable, moral and religious men, who are opposed to the horrible crime of war which is now perpetrated by both betrayed and stupefied nations, I was very glad to get the proof of it.

It is a great joy for me to know that I have friends and coworkers in Japan with which I can be in friendly intercourse.

Wishing to be quite sincere with you, as I wish to be with every esteemed friend, I must tell you that I do not approve of socialism and am sorry to know that the most spiritually advanced part of your, so clever and energetic people, has taken from Europe the very feeble, illusory and fallacious theory of socialism, which in Europe is beginning to be abandoned.

Socialism has for its aim the satisfaction of the meanest part of human nature: his material wellbeing, and by the means it proposes can never attain them.

The true wellbeing of humanity is spiritual, i.e. moral, and includes the material wellbeing. And this higher goal can be attained only by religious, i.e. moral perfection of all the units which compose nations and humanity.

By religion I understand the reasonable belief in a (general for all humanity) law of God which practically is exposed in the precept of loving every man and doing to everybody what one wishes to be done to you.

I know that this method seems to be less expedient than socialism and other frail theories, but it is the sole true one. And all the efforts we use in trying to realize false and not reaching their aims theories only hinder us to employ the sole true means to attain the degree of happiness of mankind and of every individual which are so proper to our time.

Excuse me for the liberty I take to discuss your creed and for my bad English and believe me to be your true friend

Leo Tolstoy

I will be always glad to have news from you.

518. To L. N. ANDREYEV

Yasnaya Polyana, 17 November 1904

I have read your story,[1] dear Leonid Nikolayevich, and in answer to the question your brother passed on to me, namely whether you should revise and polish up this story, I reply that the more work and criticism goes into writing, the better it always is. But even in the state in which it now is, I think the story may be of use.

There are very many powerful scenes and details in the story, but its faults lie in its great artificiality and lack of definition.

At the present time I am intensely busy and not quite well, and so I would be glad to see you and talk to you, not just now, but when I am more free. Please believe the kind feelings with which I remain at your service.

Lev Tolstoy

519. To L. O. PASTERNAK

Leonid Osipovich Pasternak (1862–1945), a well-known Moscow artist and the father of Boris Pasternak. Like Serov and Levitan, he belonged to the Moscow school of painting and was a distinguished teacher at the Moscow College of Painting, Sculpture and Architecture where he first met Tolstoy at the Wanderers' Exhibition of 1893. Pasternak's first of many studies of Tolstoy was made from memory shortly after this meeting, and later that year he showed Tolstoy the illustrations he had done for *War and Peace*. The Tolstoys used to visit Pasternak's home in Moscow for private concerts given by his wife Rosalia Kaufmann, a former concert pianist, and Pasternak frequently visited Tolstoy both in Moscow and at Yasnaya Polyana, where he painted *Tolstoy Mowing*, *Tolstoy in his Vaulted Study* and many other works. He was commissioned to illustrate *Resurrection* for the Russian journal *The Cornfield*, and these illustrations were subsequently included in the first edition of Louise Maude's English translation of the novel. Pasternak exhibited both with *The Wanderers* and the *World of Art* groups, and later with The Union of Russian Artists of which he was a member. In 1921 he and his wife moved to Berlin and in 1938 to London. The last years of his life were

[518] 1. *The Red Laugh*.

spent in Oxford, where the Ashmolean Museum owns some eighteen of his sketches, water-colours and drawings.

Yasnaya Polyana, 22 November 1904

Thank you, dear Leonid Osipovich, for the drawings you sent.[1] I particularly liked two of them; at supper, and particularly the woman's face—they are 5 +. A 5 also for the last drawing of the woman with the two young girls.

The gentleman is good too—the effort with which he stretches out his leg.[2]

The first drawing didn't satisfy me because the angel's body is too much like a body. True, it's an impossible task—an angel with a body. The same is true of the drawing of the cobbler—he has too much body. But generally it's excellent, like all your drawings, and I'm grateful to you for them.

Regards to your dear wife. I hope the children are well and growing.

Yours,
L. Tolstoy

520. To M. M. MOLCHANOV

Mikhail Mikhaylovich Molchanov (1883–?), a law student at the University of Moscow, who became acquainted with Tolstoy in 1903. Molchanov had prepared a paper entitled 'Crime and Punishment (About the So-Called New Tendencies in Criminal Law)' to be read in the Law Faculty, and had sent a copy to Tolstoy for comment.

Yasnaya Polyana, 19 December 1904

I didn't reply to your previous letters, dear Mikhail Mikhaylovich, because in my old age my strength decreases and my work increases in inverse proportion. I only write when it's necessary. I've read your article. It's written in a lively, very lively manner, but not seriously. It's author has no firm, definite outlook on the world. And without it, it's better not to touch on psychological problems.

You give a negative answer to the problem of free will with great facility, and cite Gorky, Chekhov, Liszt, Lombroso and Ferri. But if you had read Plato, Descartes, Spinoza, Kant and Lichtenberg thoroughly, you would have realised that the authorities you cite are pathetic, microscopic insects in comparison with those elephants of thought you deal with so lightly. I would advise you to write only for yourself, to clarify your thoughts for yourself. Don't be angry, and believe me that I say this out of love for you.

Lev Tolstoy

[519] 1. Illustrations for Tolstoy's story *What Men Live By*.
2. In the story a large and well-fed gentleman visits a poor shoemaker's hut to order a pair of boots and 'stretches out his leg' for measurements to be taken.

521. To AYLMER MAUDE

Yasnaya Polyana, 31 January 1905

Dear Alexey Frantsevich,

I received your excellent book about the Dukhobors and am very grateful.[1] I have only glanced at it, not read it yet.

Yesterday and today I was reading a book which has only just come into my hands, Edward Carpenter's *Civilisation, its Cause and Cure*, and was delighted with it. The only part I knew of it was Modern Science.

You would oblige me very much by sending me a copy of the book. Please tell me also what you know about Carpenter himself. In my opinion he is a worthy successor to Carlyle and Ruskin.

When I've read your book I'll write to you. Please give my regards to your wife.

Yours,
L. Tolstoy

522. To BERNARD BOUVIER

Bernard Bouvier (1861–?), a Professor at the University of Geneva, a Rousseau scholar, and the founder of the Société Jean-Jacques Rousseau. He wrote to Tolstoy on 6 March 1905 N.S. asking if he would like to join the Society.

Yasnaya Polyana, 7/20 March 1905

Monsieur,

C'est avec le plus grand plaisir, que je me souscris membre de votre société.

Je fais les voeux les plus sincères pour le succès de votre oeuvre.

Rousseau a été mon maître depuis l'âge de 15 ans.

Rousseau et l'évangile ont été les deux grandes et bienfaisantes influences de ma vie.

Rousseau ne vieillit pas. Tout dernièrement il m'est arrivé de relire quelques unes de ses oeuvres et j'ai éprouvé le même sentiment d'élévation d'âme et d'admiration, que j'ai éprouvé en le lisant dans ma première jeunesse.

Je vous remercie donc, Monsieur, pour l'honneur que vous me faites de m'inscrire membre de votre société et vous prie d'accepter l'assurance de mes sentiments distingués.

Léon Tolstoy

523. To ERNEST CROSBY

[Original in English]

Yasnaya Polyana, 6/19 July 1905

Dear Crosby,

I have written long ago a preface to your article on Shakespeare which has

---

[521] 1. *A Peculiar People: The Doukhobors* (New York, 1904).

grown in a whole book.¹ I think that I will publish it when it is translated. So that it will answer your wishes.

The crimes and cruelties which are committed in Russia are dreadful, but I am firmly convinced that this revolution will have greater and more beneficent results for humanity than the great French revolution had.

Yours truly,
Leo Tolstoy

524. To WILLIAM STEAD

William Thomas Stead (1849–1912), a distinguished English journalist who founded the *Review of Reviews* in 1890 and was well known for his liberal and pacifist views. He spent a week at Yasnaya Polyana in 1888, and a part of his book *The Truth about Russia* was devoted to his meetings with Tolstoy. He continued to correspond with Tolstoy and seventeen of his letters for the period 1890–1906 are in the Moscow archives. Five of Stead's books are in Tolstoy's library at Yasnaya Polyana. In 1905 he told Tolstoy of his intention to devote a special issue of the *Review of Reviews* to him, and sent him his own article 'Count Tolstoy' and a preface, which appeared in the issue the following year together with articles by Aylmer Maude and others, and extracts from Tolstoys' works.

[Original in English]

Yasnaya Polyana, 4/17 September 1905

Dear Mr Stead,

I have received your letter and the preface to your article. I was glad to receive your letter, but your preface did not please me at all. It is not serious, and we, old men, at our time of life wish to be serious.

I am sorry not to be able to comply with your wish about writing something for your readers.

I am very busy and have little time left. But I will be glad to see you.

Leo Tolstoy

525. To THE GRAND DUKE NIKOLAY MIKHAYLOVICH

Yasnaya Polyana, 14 September 1905

Just before receiving your good letter,¹ dear Nikolay Mikhaylovich, I was thinking

---

[523] 1. What had begun as an introduction to Crosby's *Shakespeare's Attitude Towards the Working Classes* grew into Tolstoy's long article *On Shakespeare and the Drama* (published in English translation in 1906).

[525] 1. The Grand Duke's letter of 28 August 1905 expressed agreement with the ideas in a recent article of Tolstoy's *The Great Sin*, in which Tolstoy said that political reforms were of no avail while the fundamental problem—private ownership of land—was left untouched.

526. To The Grand Duke Nikolay Mikhaylovich

about you and about my relations with you, and was intending to write to you about the fact that there is something unnatural in our relations and to ask whether it wouldn't be better for us to break them off.

You are a Grand Duke, a wealthy man, a close relation of the Emperor; I am a man who rejects and condemns the whole existing régime and its power, and declares so frankly. And there is something embarrassing about my relations with you because of this contradiction which we somehow deliberately skirt around.

I hasten to add that you have always been particularly kind to me and that I can only be grateful to you. But all the same there is something unnatural, and in my old age it is always particularly painful to me not to be straightforward.

And so allow me to thank you for your kindness towards me, and to press your hand in friendship in farewell.[2]

Lev Tolstoy

526. To THE GRAND DUKE NIKOLAY MIKHAYLOVICH

Yasnaya Polyana, 6 October 1905

I received your letter,[1] dear Nikolay Mikhaylovich—actually 'dear' in the sense of inspiring love.[2]

I was very glad to learn from your good letter that you entirely understand me and retain your kind feelings towards me. I don't forget that although vous avez beau être grand duc, you are a human being, and for me the most important thing is to have kind, loving relations with all people, and I was glad to keep such relations with you despite breaking off contacts.

I'm very grateful indeed to you for your kind letter.

Lev Tolstoy

527. To M. L. OBOLENSKAYA

Yasnaya Polyana, 15 October 1905

You thank me for my letters, but I thank you very, very much for your last one. It's sad, but it's good that you write. May God give you strength. With other people I'm afraid to use the word 'God', but with you I know you will understand that I mean the highest spiritual thing which alone exists, and with which we can

---

2. The Grand Duke agreed to Tolstoy's suggestion in his next letter, but their relations were not entirely broken off. There were five more letters from Tolstoy to the Grand Duke, in one of which he took the initiative in praising a historical work of his. Tolstoy's last letter to him in February 1908 (Letter 554) expressed regret that he ever wrote this letter of 14 September 1905.

[526] 1. A letter in which he agreed to Tolstoy's suggestion that they should break off relations. In fact they did not do so (see Letter 525, note 2).

2. The root of the two words is the same in Russian.

527. To M. L. Obolenskaya

enter into contact through awareness of it in ourselves. This word or concept is absolutely necessary. We can't live without it. Just now I'm sad. I don't want to say so to anybody except you. One can be with God, even when one is sad, and one's sadness is good, and one can be with God when one is happy, and when cheerful, and when bored, and when hurt, and when ashamed—and then all is well. The further you advance in life, the more necessary it is. You write and say that you're dissatisfied with your past life. It was all necessary that way, and has brought you closer to this state. I meant to write simply about myself and you, and here I am writing something quite different. About you I would say that you're wrong to reproach yourself. In my eyes you have lived a good and kind life, without any hostility to people, but with love for them, and have given them joy, especially me. But if you're dissatisfied and want to be better, then God grant it. Our main trouble is the fact that we are bogged down in luxury and physical idleness, and hence in unbrotherly relations with other people. It's impossible to feel it or try to rectify it, too much. And I know you feel it, and in this respect we are all—you as well—a long way away from what should be and from what we want. About your confinement, I sometimes think that the Shakers are right. They say, let bricks be made by brickmakers, by people who can't do anything better, but we, they say about themselves, are building a temple with the bricks. Motherhood is a good thing, but it can hardly be combined with the spiritual life. The bad thing in your case is that there's neither one thing nor the other: pretensions towards motherhood, and sensuality, which is the most difficult thing in the world for the young to struggle against. But still, everything is improving and getting better. About myself I would say I've been unwell for about 5 days—my liver; I haven't been working—I've been reading a history of Alexander I and making plans for writing.[1] Then I got the proofs of *The Divine and the Human* from Chertkov and disliked it very much, and decided to revise it all. But so far it hasn't worked out.

I thought I'd finished *The End of an Age*, but I've begun to correct it again, and I think it will work out all right. You know about the railway strike and the disturbances arising from it. I think, and truly believe, that this is the beginning, not of a political revolution, but of the great inner one which I'm writing about in *The End of an Age*.[2]

Seryozha is stuck here because of the strike and, thank God, I don't quarrel with him, but live amicably. Tanya is near her time, and I'm very afraid for her, poor dear. I kiss my dear friends Lizanka and Kolya.

L.T.

I've been reading Kuprin,[3] and am sending it back—it's Tanya's book. What a good writer he would be if he didn't live in a time of mass frivolity, ignorance and madness.

[527] 1. Tolstoy was contemplating a story about Fyodor Kuzmich, allegedly Alexander I in another guise.
2. The strike by the Moscow railwaymen was the first major disturbance in the autumn of 1905, which quickly led to a general strike in the cause of political reform in Russia.
3. *The Duel.*

529. To Chan Chin-Tun

What a loathsome thing Nazansky's speech is.[4] I don't normally read such nasty things, but I made an exception and am sorry.

It's quite different with Herzen, Dickens and Kant.

528. To V. V. STASOV

Yasnaya Polyana, 18 October 1905

I was very glad to get your letter, Vladimir Vasilyevich. It would be good if you could come and see us. But I'm afraid that won't be possible in present times. This is the second week we've been sitting here without any news of what's going on in the centres. I'm afraid that a lot that's foolish and bad is going on, as always happens when passions flare up. Your mention of Herzen prompted me to re-read *From the Other Shore*, and I was grateful to you for reminding me of it. Throughout this revolution I occupy the status, gladly and voluntarily assumed by me, of advocate for the 100 million people who work on the land. I rejoice at everything that makes for, or might make for their good, and I don't sympathise with anything which doesn't have this main aim or which distracts from it. But I look with loathing on all acts of violence and all murders, on whatever side they happen. So far there is more cause to grieve than to rejoice. I am shortly returning the library books,[1] with the exception of two volumes on Catherine and Elizabeth[2] which I would like, if possible, to keep a bit longer. Do you have a book or books about the murder of Paul? If so, and if you can send them, please do. Forgive me for my request to you about the person who refused military service.

I've tried in various places. In one, I think, I've been successful.[3]

Don't fret about your illness. It's a good thing. Otherwise without illnesses dying would be too difficult.

All my family send you their regards, and I embrace my dear old friend.

Lev Tolstoy

529. To CHAN CHIN-TUN

Chan Chin-Tun, a Chinaman who had studied in Russia from 1889–96 and was still living there in 1905, but returned to China and became a noted lawyer and publicist. His experiences in Russia served as the subject of his book, *Impressions of a Visit to Russia*. He also translated several of Tolstoy's shorter works into Chinese in an effort to popularise his ideas in China.

4. Nazansky is a minor character in *The Duel*, an alcoholic infantry officer stationed in a small provincial town.

[528] 1. The Marquis de Custine's *La Russie en 1839* and D. I. Zavalishin's *Memoirs of a Decembrist*.

2. Two studies by K. Waliszewski: *Autour d'un trône, Catherine II de Russie*, and *La Dernière des Romanoffs, Elizabeth I*.

3. A reference to a certain Y. Goncharenko, sentenced to a disciplinary battalion for refusal to do military service. The case was reviewed as a result of Koni's intervention.

529. *To Chan Chin-Tun*

Yasnaya Polyana, 4 December 1905

Dear Sir,

The sending of your book and especially your letter gave me great pleasure.[1] Throughout my long life I have met several Japanese people, but I have never once met or had occasion to have dealings with a single Chinaman, a thing which I have always wanted to very much, since for a long time I have known quite well —although probably very inadequately as is natural for a European—Chinese religious teaching and philosophy, not to mention Confucius, Mencius, Lao-Tzu and commentaries on them (I was particularly impressed by the teachings of Mi-Ti, rejected by Mencius). The deep respect I have always felt for the Chinese people has been further increased in the highest degree by the events of the terrible Russo-Japanese war. In this war the Chinese people have performed a great heroic feat before which not only is the importance of the Japanese victories nullified, but all the madness and cruelty of both the Russian and the Japanese governments are revealed in their true, revolting light. The heroic feat of the Chinese people is that it has shown that the valour of a people doesn't consist in violence and murders, but in maintaining to the end, in spite of all irritations, insults and sufferings, a spirit of patience, a retreat from evil, and a preference for enduring violence to causing it. The Chinese people, in spite of all the cruelties perpetrated against it both in previous foul attacks on it by European, so-called Christian peoples, and in this latest war, has shown that it is far more imbued with the true spirit of Christianity, or rather the awareness of the universal and eternal truth which lies at the basis of all religious teachings, Christianity as well, than the Christian peoples and the Russian government. (I recall your just remark about the difference between government and people.)

I haven't read your book yet—I only received it today. But judging from your letter I'm afraid that I shan't agree with its general trend. It seems to me from your letter that you react favourably (I assume also in your book) to the changes in the governmental and social structure of China now being proposed. Changes in the sense of growth, development and improvement one is bound to sympathise with, but imitative changes, the transfer to China of forms which have proved their utter worthlessness in Europe and America to people of perspicacity, would be a

[529] 1. Chan Chin-Tun wrote to Tolstoy in December 1905, at the same time sending him a translation done by himself and a Russian scholar of Chinese of Lian Tsi-Chao's *A Political History of China During the Last Forty Years*. The letter outlined Chan Chin-Tun's belief that Russia and China had a great deal in common, and that their peoples should try to achieve a deeper understanding of each other in the future. He based his argument on the fact that both Russia and China had lagged behind Western Europe in their political and economic development, but China more so than Russia, and therefore the Chinese had more to learn from Russian experiences in development (he meant the reforms granted after the 1905 Revolution) than from Western Europe. Rapport between their two countries had particular importance, he pointed out, in the light of the Russo-Japanese War and the imperialist complications in the Far East which had preceded it. Chan Chin-Tun thought that knowledge of the Russian cultural heritage would do a great deal to promote understanding, and for that reason he had undertaken to translate some of Tolstoy's works into Chinese, as he considered Tolstoy to hold the most humanitarian beliefs of any Russian writer.

529. To Chan Chin-Tun

great and fateful mistake. Changes must grow of their own accord from the characteristics of a people, and be completely new and unlike the forms of other peoples. The stagnation of China, for which she has been so often blamed, is, if we compare it with the results achieved by Christian mankind, a thousand times better than the state of malice, irritability and incessant conflict in which Christian mankind lives. I make an exception only for Russia, for the enormous majority of its agricultural population. I expect new forms of life from it, as well as from the enormous majority of the Chinese agricultural population. God save China from going the way of Japan. The Chinese, like all people, need to develop their own spiritual powers, and not technical refinements which are only destructive when spiritual powers are warped. I fully agree with you that there is an inner, spiritual link between the two great peoples, the Russian and the Chinese, and that they need to go hand in hand, but not in the form of diplomatic alliances and government coalitions. They need, especially their agricultural population, to evolve new forms of social life independent of governments; to evolve, not various freedoms of conscience, speech, representation etc., but true, genuine freedom which consists in living without the need for a government and obeying nobody, only the supreme moral law.

I repeat that I am very glad to be in contact with you, and I shall be very glad if you find the translation of my works into Chinese worth the trouble.

Lev Tolstoy

530. To V. V. STASOV

Yasnaya Polyana, 24 December 1905

I'm sending you the Decembrists' papers, Vladimir Vasilyevich. Please pass on my thanks to their owner.[1] Chaadayev's letters are very interesting, and the passage you copied out is very close to my heart.[2] He viewed Greek art so correctly because he was a religious man. If I view Greek art in the same way, I think it's for the same reason. I had a friend, Urusov, a Sevastopol veteran and a chess player; a mathematician and a very religious man, he viewed all Greek art, both plastic and verbal, with horror and disgust. And I shared his view. But for people who are not religious, who believe that this world of ours, as we know it, is true and real and actually exists as we see it, and that there is not and cannot be any other world, for such people like Goethe and like our dear Herzen and all the people of that time and that circle, Greek art was a manifestation of the greatest and finest beauty, and so they were bound to value it. But if you don't like this art and don't recognise it in that way, vous aurez beau dire vous faîtes de la religion

[530] 1. N. Pavlov-Silvansky, a historian who worked in the State Archives in Petersburg, specialising in the Decembrist period.

2. An extract from Chaadayev's third 'philosophical letter'. P. Y. Chaadayev (1794–1856) wrote a number of 'philosophical letters' on the meaning of history, the first of which appeared in *The Telescope* in 1836 and was considered so heretical that the journal was suppressed and Chaadayev declared insane.

sans le savoir. You require art to have a spiritual content and this is the essence of religion, to see and look for spiritual content in everything.

I congratulate you on your 83rd year. However much I try, I can't catch you up. And I am trying, because the older I get the better I get.

Goodbye, then; I press your hand in friendship.

Lev Tolstoy

[Postscript omitted]

531. To THE GRAND DUKE NIKOLAY MIKHAYLOVICH

Yasnaya Polyana, 29 January 1906

Dear Nikolay Mikhaylovich,

I have only just finished looking through and reading the texts of your edition of the portraits and I can't thank you enough for sending me this magnificent edition.[1] I was particularly fascinated by the texts: they are so beautifully, cleverly and skilfully composed. In general the whole edition is valuable material for the history, not only de la petite histoire, but for the real history of the time. I felt this, because I am now working on the time between the 1780s and the 1820s.[2] For the same reason I have just read The Dolgorukys[3] and Stroganov,[4] and was also very pleased and grateful to you. Stroganov especially is underestimated for the history of Alexander I. I wish that you may continue with the same success your excellent and useful researches and publications, and I thank you once more for the use I have so far made of them.

I think that you have suffered and are suffering much that is painful during these recent times; I also think that these painful conditions, if we regard them as we should without irritation and with compassion for people's delusions, mightn't be so painful, and might even be useful for our inner, spiritual life, something I wish you with all my heart.

Yours affectionately,
Lev Tolstoy

532. To A. S. MAROV

A certain Afanasy Stepanovich Marov had sent Tolstoy a clipping of a newspaper article, 'Count Tolstoy's Workers (The Story of One)', which alleged that the

[531] 1. The Yasnaya Polyana library contains a copy of Nikolay Mikhaylovich's six-volume *Russian Portraits of the XIXth and XXth Centuries* (Petersburg, 1905–9).

2. For Tolstoy's story, *The Posthumous Memoirs of Fyodor Kuzmich*.

3. Nikolay Mikhaylovich, *The Dolgoruky Princes, Associates of the Emperor Alexander I in the First Years of his Reign* (Petersburg, 1901).

4. Nikolay Mikhaylovich, *Count Pavel Alexandrovich Stroganov (1774–1807). Historical Studies of the Era of the Emperor Alexander I* (Petersburg, 1903, 3 vols.).

532. To A. S. Marov

Tolstoys had called in Cossack troops to deal with peasants who chopped down trees for timber on his estate.

Yasnaya Polyana, 22 March 1906

Afanasy Stepanovich,

I never reply to the sort of libels like the one printed in the cutting you sent me. You can't say 'God bless you' every time someone sneezes. And very many libels of different sorts are written about me. But I am replying to you because I see from your letter that you are disturbed by the idea that a person who writes and talks so well about the sin of land ownership doesn't really believe it since he acts differently, and so, contrary to my usual silence, I shall reply to you. My attitude not only to landed property but to any property at all is this, that no Christian should consider anything his own and so should not defend his property by force even when this property is the product of his labour, and more especially should not consider his own, or defend by force, land to which all people have equal rights. Having come to this conclusion about 25 years ago I took this attitude to any property in so far as I could. In order to rid myself of landed property which was reckoned to be mine, I decided to act as though I were dead. I won't say why I acted like this, and I didn't give the land away to the peasants (which ones?). The fact is that about 20 years ago my heirs each took what was due to him by law, and I kept nothing myself, and since then I have neither owned nor had control of any property except my own clothes.

What the correspondent writes about the Cossacks being called in is completely untrue. There has never been any talk of this by my wife who owns and is in charge of Yasnaya Polyana, and I am absolutely sure that even if there were any pretext for this, she would never do so.

One can only be sorry for people who need for some reason to invent lies and disturb other people.

Since I see from your letter that you have thought a lot about the land question and have the right opinion about it, I am sending you some books by George on this question, and my books *On Life* and *What We Live For*, of a general content, which may be of interest to you.

I wish you all the best.

Lev Tolstoy

533. To M. L. OBOLENSKAYA

Yasnaya Polyana, 22 March 1906

Thank you for your letter, Mashenka dear. You speak in your letter to Yuliya Ivanovna about homesickness and your wish to be back home. I always try to drive everybody away to Mamadysh, but when people go somewhere other than Mamadysh I always advise them, having gone so far, to stay where they have gone. And the same with you: I advise you to make use of everything you can take from Europe. I personally wouldn't want to take anything, despite it all being washed

534. To Ernest Crosby

and ironed. Unfortunately, I see we are collecting all the drips: parties, pre-election campaigns, blocs etc. It's disgusting—a sort of debauchery into which they are dragging the peasants and debauching *them*. Perhaps it's inevitable and the peasants also need to go through this debauchery in order to understand all its pointlessness and perniciousness. But sometimes I can't help thinking that it isn't necessary. And the proof of its being unnecessary I see in the fact that I, for example, and many people with me, see that all these constitutions can't lead to anything else except to other people exploiting the majority—changing places—as is happening in England, France, America and everywhere, and everyone anxiously endeavouring to exploit everyone else and abandoning more and more the only sensible, moral life, the agricultural one, and laying this drab burden on slaves in India, Africa, Asia and Europe wherever possible. This European life is very clean materially, but terribly dirty spiritually. And so I sometimes doubt whether the Russian people needs to go through this debauchery and reach the dead end to which Western peoples have already come. I think this because, when Western peoples took this path, all advanced people were calling on them to take it, whereas now, not only I, but many of us, see that it means destruction. In warning people away from this path we are not saying, as earlier opponents of progress said, go backwards or stand still, but we are saying: go forwards, only not in the direction you are going because that direction leads backwards; we say: go boldly forwards towards emancipation from authority. I'm writing and thinking about this, and so I've written about it to you.

I was thinking about you yesterday as I was walking over the ice crust. (The ice crust was wonderful! You could walk where you liked over a marble floor; today it's begun to deteriorate.) I was thinking that you are weaker now and rightly dissatisfied with yourself, which is very good. But remember how much good you have done to me, how much to Sasha and many others, and the others will forgive you everything, only don't forgive yourself. But you won't do that. Goodbye darling; I kiss you and Kolya.

L.T.

534. To ERNEST CROSBY

[Original in English]

Yasnaya Polyana, 12/25 April 1906

Dear friend,

I am sorry that I gave you so much trouble with the Independent.[1] Let him alone. I regret that I have written to you about this matter. I have received your *Garrison*.[2] I like it. Lately his son[3] wrote to me that he thinks that the greatest

---

[534] 1. *The Independent*, an American weekly published in New York. The 'trouble' to which Tolstoy refers is not known.

2. Ernest Crosby, *Garrison: The Non-Resistant* (Chicago, 1905).

3. Lloyd Garrison had recently sent Tolstoy a letter (28 September), together with a one-volume selection of his father's works.

534. To Ernest Crosby

thing that his father accomplished was his proclamation of Non-resistance. I was very glad to hear it. Your *Tolstoy as Schoolmaster*[4] has been translated in Russian which is a proof that it is good.

I think that though your lecturing may be very useful, your energy can be better employed in bookwriting; I read always with great pleasure your articles in *The Crank*,[5] a very good publication.

I am sorry for the Americans, not for Adin Balou,[6] that his name and work are unknown to them.

Do not wait to come to Russia till our revolution is settled. It will not be so soon. As to the disturbances that are going on now, they are only the precursors of the great revolution which I hope will begin at once everywhere and will consist in the annihilation of state power.

You are still a young man and can have the opportunity to see the great change. Not so I. Therefore the sooner you come the more chances I will have to see you again before my great voyage.

Your friend
Leo Tolstoy

535. To M. L. OBOLENSKAYA

Yasnaya Polyana, 14(?) July 1906

Well, Masha dear, I've missed you, especially recently. It was very painful. Now things are better. A couple of days ago I went so far as to lose my temper as a result of a conversation with Andrey and Lev, who argued that the death penalty is a good thing and that Samarin who supports the death penalty is consistent and I'm not. I told them that they didn't respect me, that they hated me, and I slammed the doors as I left the room, and for a couple of days I couldn't come to my senses. Today, thanks to a prayer of St Francis of Assisi (Frère Léon) and St John—'he who does not love his brother does not know God'—I collected myself and decided to tell them that I considered myself very much to blame (and I am very much to blame since I'm 80 and they are 30), and asked them to forgive me. Andrey went off somewhere at night so I couldn't tell him, but I told Lev when I met him that I was to blame and asked him to forgive me. He didn't say a word in reply and went off to read the papers and have a pleasant chat, taking my words as his due. It's difficult. But the more difficult the better. Sasha makes us happy by her love, so I'm ashamed to complain. And there is you. I kiss you.

L.T.

4. Ernest Crosby, *Tolstoy as a Schoolmaster* (Chicago, 1904), translated into Russian and published by *The Intermediary* in 1906.

5. *The Crank*, a monthly journal, with a religious and moral tendency, published in London. The Yasnaya Polyana library has several issues from the period 1903–7.

6. Adin Ballou (1803–90), an American pastor, opponent of slavery and advocate of Christian non-resistance.

536. To V. V. STASOV

Yasnaya Polyana, 20 September 1906

Thank you for your good long letter, Vladimir Vasilyevich. Don't complain about old age. How much good it has brought me that was unexpected and beautiful. I concluded from that that the end of old age and of life will be just as unexpectedly beautiful. I know you won't agree with this. But I say what I think. I don't agree either with the role you ascribe to me in our revolution: either that I'm to blame for it, or still less that I don't acknowledge it and would like to suppress it. My attitude to the revolution is that I can't help suffering when I look at what is being done, especially if I admit that I have even the smallest degree of participation in its origin. My attitude is the same as a man's might be if, having advised people not to put their heads into an iron collar which would fasten them to a chain, found that these people, instead of not putting the collar on themselves, decided that they ought to recast the collar into irons and manacles, in order to be more comfortable than if they were wearing a collar. Not only are people forging chains for themselves, they are doing all sorts of nasty things as well and are as pleased as twopence with themselves, because they imagine that by slavishly imitating what has been done by very foolish and bad people in Europe, they are doing something very useful and important. What is going on now among the people (not the proletariat) is very important and, of course, good, but what is being done by all these comic parties and committees is not important and not good. The Herzen you love so much would probably have agreed with me. Du train que cela va, unless the people, the real people, the hundred million peasants who work on the land, by their passive non-participation in violence make all this frivolous, noisy, irritable and touchy crowd harmless and unnecessary, we shall certainly arrive at a military dictatorship, and arrive at it by way of the great crimes and corruption which have already begun. In order to replace an obsolete system by another one, it is necessary to set up an ideal which is lofty, universal and accessible to all the people. But the intelligentsia and the proletariat who are goaded on by them have nothing like that—they have only words, and not their own, but other people's. So this is what I think: I rejoice for the revolution, but grieve for those who, imagining that they are making it, are destroying it. The violence of the old regime will only be destroyed by non-participation in violence, and not at all by the new and foolish acts of violence which are now being committed.

I was glad of the chance to talk to you. My wife got your letter and thanks you for it. She is recovering.

L.T.

537. To A. Y. ALIPOV

Alexander Yegorovich Alipov (1868–1929), a peasant stove-setter and amateur sculptor. After 1917 he became a professional sculptor and his work is exhibited in

537. To A. Y. Alipov

several museums in Moscow. Alipov's statuette of Tolstoy which he sent to him in September 1906 has not survived.

Yasnaya Polyana, 22 September 1906

I received your statuette and I won't conceal from you the fact that it is very bad, but I thank you for it, and for the expression of kindness which you imparted to it. I am writing a letter at the same time to Vladimir Vasilyevich Stasov about you. You will find him every day in the Public Library. Go and see him. He will advise you what to do. And do trust him.

Lev Tolstoy

538. To A. A. JÄRNEFELT

Arvid Järnefelt (1861–1933), a Finnish writer and translator of some of Tolstoy's works into Finnish (*Resurrection, Posthumous Works*, and various articles). A sympathiser with Tolstoy's views, Järnefelt corresponded with him intermittently between 1895 and 1910, sent him a copy of his book *My Awakening*, and visited him in 1899 and 1910. He sent a translation of Tolstoy's letter to the Nobel Prize committee in Sweden.

Yasnaya Polyana, 25 September 1906

I've a big request to make of you, dear Arvid. First of all I want nobody to know that I'm writing to you. The request is this: Biryukov told me that according to Koni it may happen that I shall be awarded the Nobel prize. If this should happen, it would be very unpleasant for me to refuse, and so I earnestly beg you, if, as I think, you have any connections in Sweden, to try to prevent this prize being awarded to me. Perhaps you know one of the members, or perhaps you can write to the president asking him not to mention it publicly, so that nothing should be done about it.

Of course I could find out his address myself and write to the president, asking him to keep it a secret, but it's embarrassing for me to refuse in advance something which they are perhaps not intending to offer me. For this reason I earnestly beg you to do what you can to prevent them offering me the prize and putting me in the very unpleasant position of refusing it.

I have some news of you, not at all full, through Nazhivin. I would like to have fuller news about the outward circumstances of your life. About your inner world I can judge from my own: more and more brightness and joy.

Yours affectionately,
Lev Tolstoy

539. To I. F. NAZHIVIN

Ivan Fyodorovich Nazhivin (1874–1940), a writer of peasant extraction; he sympathised at first with Tolstoy's moral and religious views, but later reacted against them. He first visited Tolstoy at Yasnaya Polyana in September 1901, and wrote several articles and a book about him—*From the Life of L. N. Tolstoy*. He subsequently emigrated and died in Brussels. His prolific writings include a three-volume historical novel *Rasputin*, several religious novels and volumes of memoirs.

Yasnaya Polyana, 25 September 1906

Thank you, dear Ivan Fyodorovich, for your letter and the touching news about Kurtysh.[1] I can't be sorry for him. I can only rejoice and be afraid. I sent an extract from your letter to the soldiers who questioned me about how they should act when they are sent to suppress a rising.[2]

The fact that you are dissatisfied with your life is only to the good. When you truly wish to walk along a straight road and you see you are straying off it, you inevitably get back on to it. Your novel[3] has probably hindered you a lot, and I'm glad that you've finished it. I've long thought that this form is obsolete—not obsolete generally, but obsolete as something important. If I have anything to say, I won't describe a drawing room or a sunset etc.

As a pastime of no harm to myself or other people—yes. I like this pastime. But previously I used to regard it as something important. That's over and done with.

Regards to your good wife.

Lev Tolstoy

540. To V. G. CHERTKOV

Yasnaya Polyana, 26 November 1906

Dear friend,

I was just meaning to send a telegram asking about your health when I received your letter, and I can now write with an easy mind about you. But I've another cause for alarm: Masha's illness. She has had lobar pneumonia for 8 days now, and she is very, very ill. For me, selfishly, her death is neither terrible nor pitiful, although she is my best friend of all those who are near to me—I won't have long to live without her—but just contrary to reason it hurts me and I pity her—at her age she must have wanted to live—and I just pity her sufferings and those of her near ones. These vain endeavours to prolong her life by medical treatment are pitiful and unpleasant. And more and more of late death has become so close to me—not terrible, but natural and necessary, not opposed to life but just as connected with it as the continuation of life—that to struggle against it is natural only to the animal instinct, not to reason. And so any rational, or rather not rational,

---

[539] 1. Ivan Kurtysh, a Moldavian peasant and conscientious objector, sentenced to a period in a disciplinary battalion for his beliefs.

2. Sent in reply to a letter from Yakov Raygorodsky, writing in the name of several soldiers who visited Tolstoy at Yasnaya Polyana in the summer of 1906 and were given several of his ethical-religious works to take away and read. Afterwards they wrote to ask how to reconcile Tolstoy's ideas, with which they sympathised, with their duties as soldiers.

3. *Mene, Mene, Tekel, Upharsin.*

540. To V. G. Chertkov

but clever struggle against it, like medicine, is unpleasant and bad...[48 lines omitted]

I wrote this letter in the morning and now at 1.00 a.m. Masha has died. I haven't yet been able to appreciate the full loss.

541. To H. G. WELLS

H. G. Wells (1866–1946), had written to Tolstoy on 21 November 1906 and sent him *Love and Mr Lewisham*, *The War of the Worlds* and *A Modern Utopia*. He told him that his friend Aylmer Maude had warned him that he would not like *A Modern Utopia* but that he (Wells) thought it better for Tolstoy to know all that was bad about him. Wells claimed to have read all Tolstoy's works available in English, some 80 in all, and to have particularly liked *War and Peace* and *Anna Karenina*.

[Original in English]

Yasnaya Polyana, 2/15 December 1906

Dear sir,

   I have received your letter and your books and thank you for both.
   I expect great pleasure in reading them.

Yours truly,
Leo Tolstoy

542. To E. W. ELLIS

Two letters from a Mr Ellis addressed from Southwold, Suffolk, have survived in the archives in Moscow, in one of which he claims to have been interested in the Russian famine as a young boy, and in the other recording his opinion that Shelley was the greatest poet and asking for Tolstoy's views.

[Original in English]

Yasnaya Polyana, 3/16 December 1906

Dear Sir,

   I quite agree with you about Shelley. He has not given all what he could and certainly would have given to the world. He had the highest aspirations and was always bold and true.
   I was glad to know that you agree with my opinion of the merit of Shakespeare's work.

Yours truly,
Leo Tolstoy

543. To I. L. TOLSTOY

Yasnaya Polyana, 21 December 1906

Poor, pitiful Ilya,

I don't know of any undertaking by the Dukhobors in which they could offer you a job with a salary. I think one should leave well alone, and that you have no reason to seek anything better than the position which you are now being offered.[1]

Illness, as a condition that keeps us away from temptations and brings us nearer to death, is a very useful condition. I advise you to make the best possible use of it.

I'm very sad that with you, as with all my sons, I can't communicate sincerely. Probably I'm also to blame for this, but nevertheless this lack of communication which will probably never change before I die makes me very sad.

Goodbye, I wish you a longer and more productive illness.

Your loving father,
L.T.

544. To C. W. DANIEL

C. W. Daniel, one of the editors, with his wife Florence Daniel (who wrote under the name of F. W. Worland), of the London monthly religious journal, *The Crank*, of which there are several issues in the Yasnaya Polyana library. C. W. Daniel wrote in the journal as 'The Odd Man'; Ernest Crosby also wrote for *The Crank*, and Tolstoy had a high opinion of it. The Daniels were actively associated with the Tolstoy Society in London.

[Original in English]

Yasnaya Polyana,
22 December 1906/4 January 1907

To the odd man of the Crank.
Dear sir,

I thank you very much for the *Crank* Magazine, which I enjoy very much. To-day I have read the last article of Worland: 'The earth for all'; it is very good, especially his criticism of Malthus's theory, which notwithstanding its weakness has had such a large spreading. I think that true Christianity with its ideal of chastity is the best remedy of the imaginary future excess of the population. I will take care that it should be translated in Russian, if he will allow it. I liked it very much, also your answer to Shaw, as I like all the pages signed by 'Odd Man'. I would be very glad to know your name and be in direct intercourse with you.

[543] 1. Ilya Tolstoy, who at this time was in financial difficulties through the failure of various journalistic ventures, had written to his father to ask if there was any paid job he could take with the Dukhobors in Canada. He had recently been offered a job with the Peasant Bank and was debating whether to take it.

544. To C. W. Daniel

Have you many subscribers to your magazine? I wish the greatest success to your work, so very necessary in our time.

Yours truly,
Leo Tolstoy

P.S. Reading your very good note to the word 'anarchism' I remembered on the same matter the saying of Lao-Tze; he says: when great sages have power over the people, the people do not notice them; if the power is in the hands of sages (not great ones), the people like them and praise them; if those who govern are less sage the people are afraid of them and where those who govern are still less sage, the people despise them.

L. Tolstoy

545. To EUGEN REICHEL

Eugen Reichel (1853–?), German author of a book *Literature about Shakespeare* (1887) challenging the authorship of Shakespeare's plays and sonnets and Francis Bacon's authorship of *Novum Organum*. Reichel had read Tolstoy's attack on Shakespeare's plays, *On Shakespeare and the Drama*, and sent a copy of his book to Tolstoy with the suggestion that he might support his theory in print. Tolstoy's reply disappointed him and he wrote a second letter in an injured tone.

Yasnaya Polyana, 2/15 March 1907

Dear Sir,

I have read your book with great interest. Your arguments that *Novum Organum* was not written by Bacon and also that the dramas attributed to Shakespeare were not written by him are very convincing, but I am not sufficiently competent in this matter ein entscheidenden Urtheil zu fällen. One thing I know for certain is that not only the majority of dramas attributed to Shakespeare, but all of them, not excluding *Hamlet* and others, not only don't deserve the praise with which critics are accustomed to judge them, but are in an artistic sense unter aller Kritik. So it is only in a recognition of the merits of those few dramas which you single out from all the rest that I don't agree with you.

Your criticism of those much-vaunted dramas, *Lear*, *Macbeth* and others, is so well-founded and just that one ought to be surprised how people who have read your book can continue to enthuse over the apparent beauties of Shakespeare if one didn't bear in mind the nature of the crowd, whereby it always follows in its opinions the opinion of the majority, quite irrespective of its own judgement. We are not surprised that people who have been hypnotised look at white and say, as they have been prompted to, that they can see black; why then should we be surprised that when they try to apprehend a work of art, for an understanding of which they have no judgement of their own, they stubbornly say what the majority of voices has prompted them to say. I wrote—a long time ago now—my article on

545. To Eugen Reichel

Shakespeare with the certainty that I wouldn't convince anyone, but I only wanted to state that I wasn't the victim of general hypnosis. And therefore I think that neither your excellent book nor mine nor many articles, whether the proofs of Theodor Eichhoff[1] which were recently sent to me or other articles on the same theme in English newspapers which I have also recently received, will convince the public at large.

Having looked carefully into the process of establishing public opinion given the present circulation of the press whereby, thanks to the papers, people read and pass judgement on the most important matters when they themselves have no idea about these matters and because of their education don't even have the right to pass judgement on them, while daily newspapermen just as little qualified to pass judgement on these matters write and publish their judgements about them—given this sort of press circulation one should be surprised, not at the false judgements rooted in the masses, but only at the fact that correct judgements about these matters are sometimes encountered, if only very rarely. This particularly concerns the evaluation of works of poetry.

Any person can pass judgement on tasty dishes, pleasant smells or pleasant sensations generally (although there are people devoid of the faculty of sensing a smell and seeing all colours), but to pass judgements on works of art one needs an artistic sense which is very unevenly distributed. The merit of works of art is determined by the publishing and reading multitude. But the multitude always contains more people both stupid and unreceptive to art, and so public opinion about art is always very crude and false. It has always been like this and is particularly so in our time when the influence of the press more and more unites people who are unreceptive both to thought and art. And so in art nowadays—in literature, music and painting—the result has been staggering examples of success and praise for works which have nothing artistic about them, still less any common sense. I don't want to name names, but if you look at those barbaric manifestations of the mental illness which in our time is called art, you yourself will be able to name names and works.

And therefore I not only don't expect that the false reputation of Shakespeare and the ancients (I don't want to name them in order not to irritate people) can be destroyed, but I expect and can see the establishment of just the same sort of reputation for new Shakespeares, based only on the stupidity and unreceptiveness of the people of the press and the public at large. I also expect that this decline in the general level of reasonableness will become greater and greater, not only in art but in all other spheres too; in science and in politics and especially in philosophy (nobody knows Kant any longer, they know Nietzsche), and will end in a general collapse, the fall of the civilisation in which we live, a fall of the same kind as that of the Egyptian, Babylonian, Greek and Roman civilisations.

[545] 1. Theodor Eichhoff, author of several Shakespeare studies. He also questioned the authenticity of some of Shakespeare's work, but believed that seven plays and sixteen sonnets were definitely his, while the others (including *Macbeth* and *King Lear*) were not. Eichhoff had sent Tolstoy the proofs of his study of *Hamlet* in January 1907.

545. To Eugen Reichel

Psychiatrists know that when a man begins to talk a lot, to talk non-stop about everything on earth without thinking, and only rushing to say as many words as possible in the shortest time—they know that this is a bad and sure sign of incipient or already advanced mental illness. But when in addition to this the patient is fully convinced that he knows everything better than anyone else and that he can and must teach everyone his wisdom, the signs of mental illness are indisputable. Our so-called civilised world is in this dangerous and sorry position—and I think it is already close to the destruction to which earlier civilisations were subjected. The distortion of ideas of the people of our time, expressed not only in the overrating of Shakespeare but in their whole attitude to politics and science and philosophy and art, is the principal and most significant indication of this.

Lev Tolstoy

546. To A. A. ŠKARVAN

Albert Škarvan (1870–1926), a Slovak doctor who sympathised with Tolstoy's views and was imprisoned and deprived of his medical diploma for refusing to serve as a military doctor. He wrote an account of this in *My Refusal to Do Military Service: Diary of an Army Doctor* (Christchurch, 1898).

Yasnaya Polyana, 15 March 1907

[16 lines omitted]...My opinion—I'll tell you in secret—about those other immortal exemplars of poetry, the *Divina Comedia* and *Paradise Lost* is that I read them with great difficulty and then immediately forgot everything I had read...[2 lines omitted]

547. To M. V. ARTSIMOVICH

Mikhail Viktorovich Artsimovich (1859–?), Governor of Tula from 1905 to 1907 and subsequently a member of the Senate. Andrey Tolstoy worked for him in 1907, had an affair with his wife, Yekaterina Vasilyevna, and wished to marry her. With this in mind, he went to England to visit his wife, from whom he had been separated for several years, to discuss divorce, and Artsimovich's wife also raised the question with her husband who had known about the affair for some time, but did not want a divorce. Andrey Tolstoy did in fact marry her in November 1907, despite his father's disapproval, and a daughter was born to them three months later.

Yasnaya Polyana, 2 June 1907

Dear Mikhail Viktorovich,

Although I don't suffer as much as you from my son's disgusting behaviour, I regard it with no less—I won't say condemnation—but horror and loathing.

548. To Y. V. Artsimovich

I only received your letter today, 2 June, and before it arrived I saw my son today and spoke to him and expressed my views about his behaviour and its disastrous consequences whatever happens, especially if he intends to legalise it by lying before God. I sympathise with you with all my heart and suffer for you, but I am less sorry for you than for him and her, i.e. the perpetrators of the crime, and I cannot think about their future without a sense of horror. I firmly believe that people are punished, *not for their sins but by their sins*. And the mitigation of any sin, if not escape from punishment, is only achieved by one means,—by repentance and by stopping sinning, and not by the imagined legalisation of it, i.e. by making the sin worse. I said all this to my son, but young people generally imagine that because old people are free of passion (the very condition which gives value to their judgements), they cannot understand them for that reason, while they themselves lack the faculty of judging their behaviour in particular, and a firm moral criterion in general. And so my words could have had, and did have, no effect.

When I received your letter, he had already gone.

It occurred to me to write to your wife. Whether or not I shall be able to express to her all the madness and criminal nature of the action she is taking (divorce) and evoke in her higher human moral feelings, I want to try to do so. It will lighten the moral burden of a shameful act which I feel has been committed by me. In any case I shall try. It will depend on you whether or not to pass the letter on, if I am able to write it.

Your decision to ask for a 6 months' delay I consider very reasonable. Everything that can be done on my part and on the part of my wife (she is not here, she is in Moscow) to see that your wish is respected we shall do, although our influence is very weak, or rather completely insignificant.

With deep sympathy for your misfortune and with sincere and equally deep respect for the way you have acted in these very difficult circumstances and also for you as a person, I remain yours affectionately,

Lev Tolstoy

548. To Y. V. ARTSIMOVICH

Yasnaya Polyana, 2 June 1907

Dear Yekaterina Vasilyevna,

Andrey came to see me today and told me everything about your relations and your intentions.

Don't be angry with me, my dear unfortunate sister, if my words seem harsh to you; the matter I shall speak about is so enormously important that it is necessary to disregard all external considerations in order to be able to express clearly what I have to say.

You have committed one of the most serious and at the same time odious crimes that a wife and mother can commit, and having committed this crime you are not doing what is natural to any, I don't say Christian, but perfectly ordinary woman

548. To Y. V. Artsimovich

who has not lost all conscience—you are not shocked at your sin, you don't repent of it, you don't acknowledge your fall and humiliation, you don't try to save yourself from the possibility of repeating your sin, but on the contrary you wish by some deceitful means (divorce) to make it possible for the sin to continue, to make the sin cease to be a sin and become something permitted.

Dear sister, you are ill, you don't understand the full meaning of what you have done and intend to do. When you recover, you will be shocked at yourself as you now are, and at the persistence with which you go on sinning. Come to your senses and try to understand all the baseness of your behaviour and all the cruelty of the sin you intend to commit by imagining that a new crime—desertion of your husband and children—will somehow make amends for an earlier one. Come to your senses, dear sister, and try to understand that a sin once done, like a flower once picked, can never be undone. And sin inevitably brings punishment after it not only from without, but more important, and assuredly, from within. And there is only one remedy for sin: repentance and renunciation of that sin—but certainly not what you are intending to do: desertion of your husband and children, divorce, and union with your accomplice in sin. This will only increase your distress an infinite number of times: torture at heart and torture in your outward life.

Today, as I said goodbye to Andrey who has been to see me and who left behind in me a painful impression of complete moral obtuseness and lack of understanding of the meaning of his behaviour, I said to him quite sincerely that I was very sorry for him. I am also sorry for you. However sorry I am for your husband, I wouldn't stop to think for a moment, if it were possible, and if I were asked whose soul I should wish to transfer to—yours or Andrey's or your husband's. Your husband's, of course. He suffers cruelly, but his sufferings elevate and purify his soul. But your sufferings are odious and base, and humiliate and defile your soul more and more. I am sorry for him and you for your spiritual fall, but I am sorry for him and you particularly for the future which awaits you. And I can see this future just as clearly as I can see the inkwell in front of me. And this future is terrible. An especially close cohabitation as a result of an exceptional family situation, with a man of idle, luxurious and dissipated habits, self-assured, unrestrained and lacking any moral principles whatsoever, and at the same time poverty, when both are accustomed to luxury, abandoned families on both sides, and either a choked-up conscience, or everlasting suffering.

Forgive me, dear sister, for writing to you so harshly. I am truly sorry for you and him: more sorry for you. If you break it all off and return to the past, not only may your soul be regenerated, but there is every likelihood that this regeneration will come to pass as soon as you acknowledge your sin; but if your foolish and criminal plan is carried out, which God forbid, you will certainly perish both spiritually and materially.

I have been ill for about a month and am now very weak, and hence my letter is so muddled and incoherent. But in spite of its incoherence, I hope you will sense in it the feeling of true love and pity for you which guided me.

Forget that I am an old man, that I am a writer, that I am Andrey's father, and read this letter as if it were nobody's, and please, for goodness sake, think about what is written in it, think about it alone with your conscience, before God, having dismissed at least for a time all memories of Andrey, your husband and me, and think only of one thing, namely what you should do before God, what you would do if you knew you were to die tomorrow.

Forgive me, yes, actually forgive me, and believe in my sincere love and pity for you.[1]

Lev Tolstoy

549. To A. L. TOLSTOY

Yasnaya Polyana, 10 July 1907

I tore up your letter of some time ago, Andryusha, as soon as I received it. It was unpleasant for me, but I felt more sorry for you, and I destroyed it and said nothing to anybody about it. Even the feeling of unpleasantness caused by the letter was less than the feeling of pity and love for you, but now the unpleasant feeling has been eliminated, has completely disappeared, and all that remains is the wish to help you, and ease your difficult position. Mama is wrong to write that I have unkind feelings towards Yekaterina Vasilyevna. I'm just as sorry for her as for you, even more so than for you. Don't think that there is any condemnation or disrespect about this feeling. I am too old, and have thought too much not to understand that if the same thing didn't happen to me in my youth, worse things might have happened and did happen, and so I can't condemn you. But the main thing is that when I recall you and her—and I often do recall you—my heart sinks and I think: how difficult it is for him now, isolated from us all. (And if this isolation isn't difficult for him, so much the worse for him.)

I advise you not to shun us, but to come and tell us everything, and to listen patiently to everything that mama says (her irritation is understandable), and take from it what is justified—and it is mainly justified.

Most of all I advise you to overcome your pride and self-assurance—not to consider yourself always right (that's your main fault), but recognise that you are to blame and try not to present yourself as being right in everything but to make amends as much as possible for the bad you have done, and sincerely repent. I hope to see you soon.[1] I kiss you.

L.T.

[548] 1. No reply was received to this letter.

[549] 1. Despite the disapproval of Andrey's actions shown in this letter, Tolstoy made a move towards reconciliation with his son and his new daughter-in-law after Andrey's remarriage in November 1907 by inviting them to Yasnaya Polyana, though warning them that Sofya Andreyevna might prove difficult, and that they would have to be extremely careful. Andrey and his wife came to Yasnaya Polyana on 6 December, Andrey's birthday, and stayed for three days. Tolstoy was unable to discuss with them their marriage (Yekaterina was seven months pregnant by then), but gave them a letter upon their departure, warning them that they would have to exculpate their guilt by good behaviour in the future.

550. To THE EDITORS OF 'THE RUSSIAN GAZETTE' AND 'NEW TIMES'

Yasnaya Polyana, 17(?) September 1907

More than 20 years ago I renounced the ownership of property for certain personal considerations. The real estate that belonged to me I handed over to my heirs as though I had died. I also renounced the right of ownership of my works, and those written after 1881 became public property.

The only sums which I still have at my disposal are the monies which I sometimes receive, primarily from abroad, for starving people in particular areas, and the small sums which certain people provide for me to distribute at my own discretion. I distribute them in the immediate neighbourhood for the benefit of widows, orphans, the victims of fires etc.

However, this distribution by me of these small sums and frivolous newspaper contributions about me have misled and continue to mislead very many people who approach me more and more often and on a bigger and bigger scale for financial help. The pretexts for these requests are very varied, from the most frivolous to the most reasonable and moving. The most usual ones are requests for financial help to enable somebody to complete his education, i.e. to receive a diploma; the most moving are requests to help families left in a state of poverty.

Not having any possibility of satisfying these demands, I tried to answer them by short, written refusals, expressing regret at the impossibility of fulfilling the request. But generally I would get back new letters, angry and reproachful. I tried not replying, and again I would get angry letters reproaching me for not replying. But what is important is not these reproaches, but the painful feeling which the writers are bound to feel.

In view of this I consider it necessary now to ask all people in need of financial help not to approach me, since I have absolutely no property at my disposal for this purpose. I, less than anyone else, can satisfy such requests, since if I have really done as I say, i.e. ceased to own property, I cannot help those who approach me with money; and if I am deceiving people by saying that I have renounced property while continuing to own it, it is even less possible to expect help from such a person.

I earnestly beg other papers also to reprint this letter.[1]

Lev Tolstoy

551. To HENRYK SIENKIEWICZ

Henryk Sienkiewicz (1846–1916), Polish novelist (born in Russian Poland) and Nobel prize winner for literature in 1905, after which he came to be regarded as the

[550] 1. The letter was printed in nearly all the main Russian newspapers, and called forth bitter attacks on Tolstoy in the press, where he was pilloried as 'The Great Bankrupt of Russia', and in anonymous letters addressed to him. The declaration had no practical effect, as begging letters continued to arrive at the same rate as before: 180 letters in October, November and December 1907.

551. To Henryk Sienkiewicz

unofficial spokesman on Polish political and social problems. During the First World War Sienkiewicz worked assiduously for Polish independence and organised relief for Polish war veterans, but he died in 1916 without seeing an independent Poland. He is best known to English readers for his novel of Rome under Nero, *Quo Vadis*, and for his trilogy of seventeenth-century Poland, *With Fire and Sword*, *The Deluge* and *Pan Wolodyjowski*.

Yasnaya Polyana, 27 December 1907

Dear Henryk Sienkiewicz,

This strange form of address is caused by my wish to avoid the unpleasant and cold to the point of hostility 'Dear Sir', and the equally offputting 'Monsieur', and to enter into the close, friendly relations in this letter to you which I have felt towards you since I read your works: *The Polaniecki Family*, *Without Dogma*, etc., for which I thank you. The same reason prompts me to write to you in my own language in which it is easier for me to express myself clearly and precisely.

The matter you write to me about[1] is known to me and caused me no surprise or even indignation, but was only confirmation of the, for me, undoubted truth—however paradoxical it might seem to people who have fallen under the hypnosis of the state—that the existence of aggressive governments has outlived its time, and that in our time those who govern—emperors, kings, ministers, military leaders, even influential members of parliament—can only be people on the lowest level of moral development. These people find themselves in these positions because they are morally degenerate people. People engaged in plundering the property of the working people in the guise of taxation, in making preparations for murder and committing murder, in putting people to death and in continually lying to themselves and to others—such people cannot be any different. In the pagan world there could be a virtuous potentate like Marcus Aurelius, but in our Christian world even the rulers of past centuries—all the French Louis and Napoleons, all our Catherine the Seconds and Nicholas the Firsts, all the Fredericks, Henrys and Elizabeths, German and English—in spite of all the endeavours of their eulogisers can inspire nothing in our time except disgust. The present potentates, the instigators of every sort of act of violence and murder, are now so far below the moral demands of the majority that it is impossible even to be angry with them. They are only odious and pathetic. One should be angry with—or rather not angry with, but one should struggle against—not these creatures who are devoid of any human consciousness, but with that terrible, backward institution of a state system based on violence which is the main source of the sufferings of mankind. One should not struggle against people, but against the superstition of the necessity for state violence which is so incompatible with the present moral consciousness of people of the Christian world and does most to impede the people

[551] 1. Sienkiewicz wrote to Tolstoy in French on 16 December 1907 N.S. about German policy in Poznan where new appropriations of land from Polish landlords were under consideration. He hoped that Tolstoy would launch a protest against such an action.

551. To Henryk Sienkiewicz

of our time from taking the step for which it has long been ready. And it is only possible to fight against this evil by the one very simple, natural and at the same time powerful means which unfortunately has not yet been used, which consists only of living without the need for government violence and without participating in it.

As far as the details of the matter you write about are concerned: the preparations by the Prussian government to plunder the Polish land-owning peasants—I am more sorry in this matter for the people who are organising this plunder and will carry it out, than for those they will plunder. The latter ont le beau rôle. On other soil and in other conditions they will remain the same as they were, but I am sorry for the plunderers, sorry for those who belong to a nation or state of plunderers and feel solidarity with them. I think that even now, for any morally sensitive person, there can be no doubt about the choice: to be a Prussian in solidarity with his government, or to be a Pole driven out of his nest.

That is my opinion about what is being done or about to be done in Poznan now, or if not an opinion about the matter itself, then the thoughts which it aroused in me.

Forgive me if my letter is not the answer you wanted from me. If the letter is no use, throw it in the waste-paper basket or make whatever use of it you find necessary.

In any case I was glad to establish contact with you.

Your affectionate fellow writer,
Lev Tolstoy

552. To M. M. DOKSHITSKY

Moisey Mendelevich Dokshitsky, the seventeen-year-old son of a watchmaker, wrote to Tolstoy about his inability to decide between a Christian way of life and 'Saninism'. (Sanin was the amoral hero of a popular, sensational novel of the same name by M. P. Artsybashev, recently published in *The Contemporary World*, 1907.) Dokshitsky asked for Tolstoy's opinion on 'Saninism', and there was some correspondence between the two men which ended with Dokshitsky thanking Tolstoy for making him aware of the truth.

Yasnaya Polyana, 10–11 February 1908

I received your letter and was very surprised at your mention of a certain Sanin, whom I had not the faintest idea about. By chance it happened that there was a person in the house who had read the novel. I got hold of the issues of the journal in which it was published and read through all the arguments of Sanin himself and was shocked not so much at the odiousness, as at the stupidity and ignorance, and the self-assurance which goes with these two characteristics, of the author. Although at heart I wanted to pity the author, I couldn't suppress an unkind feeling towards him for the evil he has done to many people, including yourself. The author obviously not only does not know, but has not even the faintest conception of all the work of the best souls and minds of mankind in solving the problems of life which he not only does not solve himself, but has no conception of how to solve. He has no conception of the Eastern, Chinese sages, Confucius and Lao-Tzu, or of the Indian, Greek and Roman sages, or of true Christianity or of those thinkers closer to us: Rousseau, Voltaire, Kant, Lichtenberg, Schopenhauer, Emerson and others. He has artistic ability, but no true feeling (awareness) or true intelligence, so that there is no description of a single true human feeling, but only descriptions of the basest animal instincts; nor is there a single new thought of his own but only what Turgenev calls 'reversed commonplaces':[1] a person says the reverse of what everyone considers the truth, for example that water is dry, that coal is white, that incest is good, that fighting is good etc. I try to pity the poor deluded author, but his self-assurance prevents it. But I pity you with all my heart for the confusion which the reading of books has produced in your soul. And so, forgive me, I am not sending you my own books, but am sending *A Circle of Reading* which I compiled from the thoughts of various writers. I think that reading it, if you do read it and think carefully about what you read, will help you and rescue you from that terrible confusion of thought in which you can ask the question which would be funny if it were not so shocking: which is better: Saninism or Christianity? I advise you also to read the Gospels. May God help you, the God who lives in you and who is so stifled that you are hardly conscious or perhaps not even conscious at all of Him. Write, and I will reply if your questions are serious. How old are you?

Lev Tolstoy

553. To M. A. STAKHOVICH

Mikhail Alexandrovich Stakhovich (1861–1923), a liberal politician, landowner and friend of Tolstoy for nearly 30 years. When Tolstoy made his famous walk from Moscow to Tula in April 1886, Stakhovich and N. N. Gay junior accompanied him. He was a frequent visitor to Yasnaya Polyana and to the Tolstoy home in Moscow, and was a good friend of Tolstoy's son Lev Lvovich also. Tolstoy's story *Strider* (1885) was dedicated to him.

Stakhovich had a law degree and held various government posts from the 1890s onwards. In 1906 and 1907 he was a member of the First and Second Dumas, in which he participated actively while stressing his allegiance to the Tsar. In the Kerensky government he was first appointed Military Governor of Finland and then Ambassador to Spain, where he was in post when the Bolshevik revolution took place. He stayed on in Western Europe and died in Aix-en-Provence in 1923.

[552] 1. Bazarov uses this expression in a conversation with Arkady Kirsanov in *Fathers and Sons*, chapter 21.

553. To M. A. Stakhovich

Yasnaya Polyana, 28 February 1908

Dear Mikhail Alexandrovich,

I know that you do love me, and love me not only as a writer but also as a man, and, moreover, that you are a sensitive man and will understand me. For that reason I turn to you with a very big request. My request is this, that you should put a stop to the preparations for this jubilee[1] which will cause me nothing but suffering, and worse than suffering, bad behaviour on my part. You know that at all times, but especially at my age when I am so near to death—you will find this out when you grow old—there is nothing more precious than people's love. And it is precisely this love which will be destroyed, I'm afraid, by this jubilee. I got a letter yesterday from Princess Dondukova-Korsakova who writes that all Orthodox people will be offended by this jubilee. I never thought about this, but what she writes is completely true. It will create an unkind feeling towards me, not only among these people, but among many others. And that is the most painful thing for me. Those who love me I know, and they know me, and no external forms are necessary for them to express their feelings. So this is my great request to you: do what you can to cancel this jubilee and set me free. I shall be very, very grateful to you for all time.

Yours affectionately,
Lev Tolstoy

554. To THE GRAND DUKE NIKOLAY MIKHAYLOVICH

Yasnaya Polyana, 28 February 1908

Thank you very much, dear Nikolay Mikhaylovich, for your kind letter. I am now ashamed to recall my letter of 1906.[1] It was prompted by the fact that I wrote something harsh and unkind about the royal family.[2] And I thought to myself: contact with you—and such an unkind attitude to people near to you! That prompted my letter. I would not have written it now. You cannot imagine how life alters as one approaches old age, i.e. death. I actually feel that spiritual growth is in inverse proportion to the square of the distance from death; one gets better and better. I hope you will live to see this and feel it. What is most precious of all to me now is loving contact with all people, regardless of who they are: tsars or beggars. And so your kind letter which cancelled out the bad relations which mine caused was particularly precious to me. I thank you most sincerely. If you wish

---

[553] 1. A committee had been set up under Professor M. M. Kovalevsky, with Stakhovich as its secretary, to celebrate Tolstoy's forthcoming eightieth birthday on a world-wide scale. When Tolstoy's views were known, the committee was disbanded, but a Tolstoy Society was formed instead, and a Tolstoy Museum was opened three years later in Petersburg.

[554] 1. Letter 525.
2. *The One Thing Needful* (1905), which contains criticisms of the Russian monarchy.

555. *To A. M. Bodyansky*

to send me the exceptionally interesting materials you write about, I shall be very grateful.[3]

I can vouch for my discrétion and that of my daughter who is the only one who copies my letters.

Goodbye; I press your hand in friendship.

Yours affectionately,
Lev Tolstoy

555. To A. M. BODYANSKY

Alexander Mikhaylovich Bodyansky (1842–1916), a Russian landowner who renounced the ownership of his land and emigrated to Canada in 1899 to live with the Dukhobors. He returned to Russia in 1905, and wrote a book about the Dukhobors (*The Dukhobors. A Collection of Stories, Letters, Documents and Articles on Religious Questions*, Kharkov, 1907) which, owing to its hostile comments on the Russian government, had been confiscated, and Bodyansky himself arrested, although he was later released after an appeal on his behalf from Tolstoy to Pyotr Stolypin, Minister of Internal Affairs. In 1907 Bodyansky began a Tolstoyan newspaper which was closed down by the censor after a few issues; he then took to distributing Tolstoy's banned works, for which he was again arrested and sentenced to six months' imprisonment. The following letter from Tolstoy was written in reply to a letter from Bodyansky to Gusev (Tolstoy's secretary) suggesting that Tolstoy should celebrate his birthday by spending the day in prison in place of those who had been imprisoned for distributing works he had written. (Bodyansky had not yet begun his prison sentence; he eventually served two-and-a-half months.)

Yasnaya Polyana, 12–13 March 1908

Dear Alexander Mikhaylovich,

I read your letter to Gusev in which you expressed so splendidly the best and only method of celebrating my jubilee, i.e. of doing something really pleasant and completely satisfying to me, namely putting me in prison for writing those works, for distributing which you will have to spend six months in prison, and for which so many, many people are now in prison. This idea will seem to many people a joke or a paradox, but it is, however, the most simple and undoubted truth. Really, nothing would satisfy me so much and give me so much joy, as actually being put in prison—a really good prison, stinking, cold and short of food. You expressed clearly what I only dimly and vaguely wished for. I've been feeling so happy recently that I have often stopped to think, is there anything I could wish for?—and I could find nothing at all. But now I can't refrain from wishing with all my

3. Nikolay Mikhaylovich, hearing that Tolstoy needed information about a tsar's daily routine, offered to send him relevant material, as well as some extracts from Nicholas I's correspondence at the time of the trial and execution of the Decembrists.

555. To A. M. Bodyansky

heart that what you propose might be accepted, not as a joke but as an act really capable of pacifying all those to whom my writings and their distribution have caused unpleasantness, and, on the other hand, one which would cause me true joy in my old age, just before my death, and at the same time would spare me all the burden which I foresee from the impending jubilee.

I press your hand in friendship,
Lev Tolstoy

556. To N. V. DAVYDOV

Nikolay Vasilyevich Davydov (1848–1920), an eminent lawyer who held many important administrative posts in the judicial system and wrote many articles (under pseudonyms) on legal and social questions. He also lectured at the University of Moscow, and was for a time President of the Moscow Tolstoy Society. He first met Tolstoy in 1878, and they remained good friends for the rest of their lives. Tolstoy occasionally turned to Davydov for advice and legal assistance, and he was a source of inspiration for Tolstoy's plays *The Power of Darkness*, *The Fruits of Enlightenment* and *A Living Corpse*. He also made a contribution to *Resurrection* (like Tolstoy's other close friend in the legal profession, Anatoly Koni), by enabling Tolstoy to visit prisons, question prisoners and observe the courts at work. He wrote in his memoirs that although his life was very different from Tolstoy's in many external respects, he nevertheless considered himself to have been greatly influenced by Tolstoy's beliefs in fundamental questions of religious faith and human relationships.

Yasnaya Polyana, 9 April 1908

Dear Nikolay Vasilyevich,

I'm very grateful to you for your work in your committee.[1] You have obviously said everything just as well, and everything has been arranged just as well, as I could have wished. I thank you very much. I have a request to make to you: if it's a nuisance for you to fulfil it, don't do it, but if you can fulfil it I'll be very grateful. I need to know details about capital punishment, the trial, the sentences and the whole procedure;[2] if you can provide me with the fullest details you will greatly oblige me. My questions are these: who institutes proceedings, how are they conducted, who confirms them, how, where and by whom is the action carried out; how are the gallows constructed, how is the executioner dressed, who is present at the execution... I can't tell you all the questions, but the more details there are, the more necessary they are to me.

[556] 1. Davydov had been President of the Moscow committee for the Tolstoy jubilee—disbanded in March.

2. Tolstoy was gathering material for a work on the subject of capital punishment, provoked by the recent courts martial in the wake of the 1905 'revolution' (according to official sources, 683 death sentences were carried out by these courts up to April 1907). Tolstoy originally planned to write a story, but wrote an article instead, *I Cannot be Silent* (1908).

557. To Bernard Shaw

I hope to see you again: you promised to visit me, I think. Just in case, I'll say: till I see you! I press your hand in friendship; I was very glad to see you.

Truly yours affectionately,
Lev Tolstoy

557. To BERNARD SHAW

George Bernard Shaw (1856–1950) had sent his play *Man and Superman* (including an appendix, *The Revolutionist's Handbook and Pocket Companion by John Tanner, M.I.R.C.* (*Member of the Idle Rich Class*) to Tolstoy in December 1906. Tolstoy's first reading of it in January 1907 made a bad impression on him, but on re-reading it in August 1908 and making notes, Tolstoy decided to write the following letter to Shaw with a criticism of his play.

In September 1909 Tolstoy remarked to Aylmer Maude during Maude's last visit to Yasnaya Polyana that he had been reading Shaw's plays and liked them, but thought Shaw suffered from the defect of wanting to be original. Maude told him the plot of *The Shewing-up of Blanco Posnet* (as yet unpublished) and as Tolstoy was interested, Maude asked Shaw to send the play to Tolstoy. Later that year, Tolstoy reportedly said that there were very few good writers left 'except, perhaps, Shaw'. (See Letter 585 for Tolstoy's reaction to Shaw's only letter to him, accompanying Blanco Posnet.) There are several plays by Shaw in Tolstoy's private library at Yasnaya Polyana, with numerous marginal comments and markings.

Shaw's comments on Tolstoy and his works include the following: On *What is Art?* (letter to Henry Arthur Jones, May 1898)—'It is beyond all comparison the best treatise on art that has been done by a literary man (I bar Wagner) in these times.' On Tolstoyism (letter to R. Ellis Roberts in February 1900)—'Even if we embrace it, we cannot live for ever afterwards on one another's charity. We may simplify our lives and become vegetarians; but even the minimum of material life will involve the industrial problems of its production and distribution, and will defy Anarchism...Anarchism in industry, as far as it is practicable, produces exactly the civilization that we have today, and...the first thing a Tolstoyan community would have to do would be to get rid of it.'

Shaw once included Tolstoy in a list of five men in 'the Grand School—the people who are building up the intellectual consciousness of the race' (the others being Nietzsche, Wagner, Schopenhauer and Ibsen).

Yasnaya Polyana, 17 August 1908

Dear Mr Shaw,

Please excuse me for not having thanked you before this for the book you sent through Mr Maude.

Now on re-reading it and paying special attention to the passages you indicated, I particularly appreciate Don Juan's speeches in the Interlude[1] (although I think

[557] 1. In English in the original.

557. To Bernard Shaw

that the subject would have gained greatly from a more serious approach to it, rather than its being a casual insertion in a comedy) and *The Revolutionist's Handbook*.[2]

In the first I could without any effort agree fully with Don Juan's words that a hero is 'he who seeks in contemplation to discover the inner will of the world... [and] in action to do that will by the so-discovered means'[3]—the very thing which is expressed in my language by the words: 'to recognise the will of God in oneself and to fulfil it'.

In the second I particularly liked your attitude to civilisation and progress, and the very true thought that however long both may continue, they cannot improve the state of mankind unless people themselves change.

The difference in our views only amounts to this that in your opinion the improvement of mankind will be accomplished when ordinary people become supermen or new supermen are born, while in my opinion it will come about when people divest true religions, including Christianity, of all the excrescences which deform them and when all people, uniting in that one understanding of life which lies at the base of all religions, establish a reasonable attitude of their own towards the world's infinite first principle, and follow the guidance for life which stems from it.

The practical advantage which my way of freeing people from evil has over yours is that one can easily imagine that very large masses of even poorly educated or quite uneducated people will be able to accept true religion and follow it, whereas to evolve supermen from the people who now exist or to give birth to new ones would need the sort of exceptional conditions which are as little capable of being attained as the improvement of mankind through progress and civilisation.

Dear Mr Shaw,[4] life is a great and serious matter, and all of us generally, in this short interval of time granted to us, must try to find our appointed task and fulfil it as well as possible. This applies to all people, and especially to you with your great talents, your original powers of thought and your penetration into the essence of any question.

And so in the confident hope of not offending you, I will tell you what seem to me to be the defects of your book.

Its first defect is that you are not sufficiently serious. One should not speak jokingly about such a subject as the purpose of human life or the causes of its perversion and of the evil that fills the life of all of us mankind. I would prefer the speeches of Don Juan to be not the speeches of an apparition, but the speeches of Shaw, and similarly that *The Revolutionist's Handbook* should be attributed not to the non-existent Tanner but to the living Bernard Shaw, responsible for his own words.

A second reproach is that the questions you deal with are of such enormous importance that, for people with such a deep understanding of the evils of our life and such a brilliant aptitude for exposition as yourself, to make them only the

2. In English in the original.   3. In English in the original.   4. In English in the original.

object of satire may often harm rather than help the solution of these important problems.

I see in your book a desire to surprise and astonish the reader by your great erudition, talent and intelligence. And yet all this is not only not necessary for the solution of the problems you deal with, but very often distracts the reader's attention from the essence of the subject, attracting it by the brilliance of the exposition.

In any case I think that this book of yours expresses your views not in their full and clear development, but only in their embryonic state. I think that these views as they develop more and more will arrive at the one truth which we all seek and which we are all gradually approaching.

I hope you will forgive me if you find anything unpleasant in what I have said to you. I said what I did only because I recognise in you very great gifts, and have for you personally the most friendly feelings, with which I remain,

Lev Tolstoy

558. To M. P. NOVIKOV

Mikhail Petrovich Novikov (1871–1939), a peasant who first became acquainted with Tolstoy in 1894 when he called on him in Moscow. Novikov was then an army clerk; he later wrote several stories and articles on peasant life which Tolstoy liked. They remained friends, and in October 1910, a few days before Tolstoy left Yasnaya Polyana for good, he wrote to Novikov asking if he might take refuge in Novikov's village, should he leave home (see Letter 597). Novikov wrote about his relations with Tolstoy in an article entitled 'A Peasant's Letter'.

Yasnaya Polyana, 17–20 August 1908

Your request,[1] dear Mikhail Petrovich, could only be welcome to me, if I foresaw any possibility of its being fulfilled. But I think that when you wrote the letter you yourself knew in advance that your wish and mine could not be fulfilled. But the main thing I want to write to you about is the mood which permeates your letter, and the feeling which was very painful to me. Believe me—it's not for my sake, but for yours.

I remember that nice, tall handsome soldier who came to the low room upstairs in my Moscow house with questions which impressed me by their depth and sincerity. At the time you were occupied with problems of your own soul and therefore universal problems. I not only fear, but I see from your letters that it isn't so now. The main feeling which now permeates almost every word of your letter is

[558] 1. Novikov sent Tolstoy a letter early in August suggesting that Tolstoy should spend his eightieth birthday (28 August) with Novikov's family in their modest home. The letter included a strong attack on the wealthy classes (to whom, Novikov said, Tolstoy's ideas served only as a subject for theoretical argument and pleasant conversation), and on the liberal intelligentsia whose lives were blatantly hypocritical.

558. To M. P. Novikov

the feeling—forgive me—of envy and, as a consequence of it, hatred of the well-to-do classes. You say, for example, that my thoughts—not mine, but the everlasting thoughts of God which perhaps pass through me—can have no effect on people of well-to-do circles, apparently supposing that they all lack the most elementary human characteristic—a striving for improvement. It would hardly be possible to find among this milieu, which, as you know, is a corrupt one in my opinion, a single person who would take the sort of attitude to an entire class of people, admitting nothing good about them, which you take towards people of the well-to-do classes. As an old man to a young one, as one who loves to one who is loved, I say to you: look hard at yourself and think about this, dear Mikhail Petrovich. The state of a man's soul who hates even one of his brothers is terrible; but what must be the state of the soul of a man who hates an entire class? I will tell you frankly that if I were offered the choice of two situations: either the one I am in now, i.e. a life of corrupting and unlawful luxury, although condemning it as I do—which many people naturally don't believe—or even the life of a man living in this corrupt and corrupting milieu of the rich who exploit the labours of downtrodden and oppressed people at every step of their lives, and who doesn't feel this and enjoys himself in a good-natured way in his familiar conditions—or the life of a hard-working man eating the bread of his own labours and not only not exploiting the labours of others, but putting his own at the service of other people, while at the same time being filled with envy and hatred aroused in him by frequent contact with the people who oppress him—I wouldn't hesitate a moment to choose the first. It's good to be exploited, not an exploiter, but it's good when this happens in the name of obedience to the will of God and of love for other people; but when it happens in disregard of obedience to the will of God in the name of hatred of other people, restrained only by the impossibility of applying it, then the position of the exploited is a thousand times worse...[8 lines omitted]

559. To L. N. ANDREYEV

Yasnaya Polyana, 2 September 1908

I received your good letter, dear Leonid Nikolayevich.[1] I've never known what a dedication means, although I think I have dedicated something to someone myself.[2] All I know is that your dedication to me signifies your kind feelings towards me—something I saw in your letter as well—and this is very welcome to me.

In your letter you are so truly modest in your judgement about your writings

[559] 1. Andreyev's letter of 18 August 1908, asking Tolstoy's permission to dedicate to him his story *The Seven Who Were Hanged*. Tolstoy's opinion of the story was very low, and in this letter he neither gives nor refuses permission, but speaks about the writer's obligations in general. The dedication nevertheless appeared from the second edition onwards.

2. Tolstoy's story *The Wood-felling* (1855) was dedicated to Turgenev and the later story *Strider* (1885) was dedicated to M. A. Stakhovich.

that I won't venture to express my opinion about your writings in particular, but rather my ideas about writing generally, which may be of use to you.

I think first of all that one should only write when an idea which one wants to express is so obsessive that until you do express it as best you can it will never leave you in peace. Any other motives for writing, motives of vanity and especially disgusting pecuniary ones, even though additional to the main one, the need for expression, can only harm the sincerity and quality of the writing. This is very much to be feared. The second thing that is often encountered, and which I think modern writers today are often guilty of (it's the basis of the whole Decadent movement) is the wish to be unusual and original, to surprise and astonish the reader. This is even more harmful than the secondary considerations I spoke about in my first point. It excludes simplicity. And simplicity is the necessary condition of the beautiful. What is simple and free of artificiality might be bad, but what is not simple and is artificial cannot be good. The third thing is—speed of writing. It is both harmful and, apart from that, a sign of the lack of a true need to express one's thoughts, because a writer, if he has a true need, won't spare the time or the effort to bring his thoughts to a state of complete clarity and definition. The fourth thing is the wish to respond to the tastes and demands of the majority of the reading public at a given time. This is particularly harmful and destroys in advance all the importance of what is written. For the importance of any work of literature is that it isn't edifying in the direct sense, like a sermon, but that it reveals to people something new, unknown and for the most part contrary to what is considered indubitable by the public at large. But in this case it's a necessary condition that this shouldn't be so.

Perhaps something of all this will be of use to you. You write that the merit of your works is sincerity. I not only recognise this, but also that their purpose is a good one: the wish to contribute to the good of other people. I think you are sincere also in your modest opinion about your works. This is all the better for your part, in that the success they enjoy might have made you, on the contrary, exaggerate their importance. I have read too little by you, and that inattentively, as I generally read little fiction and take little interest in it, but from what I know and remember of your writings I would advise you to do more work on them and bring your thoughts to the last degree of clarity and precision.

I repeat that your letter was very welcome to me. If you are in our parts I shall be glad to see you.

Yours affectionately,
Lev Tolstoy

560. To THE 'OTTOMAN' TOBACCO FACTORY

On Tolstoy's eightieth birthday, the Ottoman Tobacco Factory in Petersburg sent him a box of cigarettes, each one bearing his name and portrait.

560. To The 'Ottoman' Tobacco Factory

Yasnaya Polyana, 3 September 1908

I received your kind letter and present. I'm very sorry that I can't accept it since, from the time more than 20 years ago when I gave up smoking as something harmful, I have always warned people off this bad habit both in speech and writing. Please believe me that my refusal to accept the present in no way diminishes my gratitude to you for your kind feelings towards me. To remind me of you, I shall keep the beautiful box you sent me with the cigarette packets in it, for storing my papers, but the cigarettes themselves I am returning. My wife has taken one packet of cigarettes to put in the museum where she collects all objects which have to do with me. I repeat my request not to take my refusal in bad part.

561. To THE PEOPLE AND INSTITUTIONS WHICH SENT CONGRATULATIONS ON MY EIGHTIETH BIRTHDAY

Although Tolstoy had put a stop to the jubilee celebrations planned for his eightieth birthday on 28 August 1908, nevertheless on that day, and for a week afterwards, Yasnaya Polyana was inundated with telegrams and letters of congratulations from all sides. Six hundred telegrams and one hundred letters arrived on 28 August alone, and a week later the number had risen to two thousand telegrams and several hundred letters (altogether the signatories numbered about fifty thousand including Bernard Shaw, Edward Carpenter, George Meredith, Rudyard Kipling, Thomas Hardy, H. G. Wells and Gerhard Hauptmann). In keeping with Tolstoy's wishes, no delegations called at Yasnaya Polyana, although a great many private well-wishers came and were treated to an outdoor banquet and a few words from Tolstoy who dined inside with his family. Photographers and reporters were also present (but kept outside). Tolstoy who was recovering from a serious illness spent the day with his family and reportedly never stirred from his armchair. As usual, he worked.

In September Tolstoy wrote the following letter of thanks (five drafts exist) which was published on 8 October 1908 in many Russian newspapers, and also sent to various institutions and individuals.

Yasnaya Polyana, 5 October 1908

When I heard a few months ago of the intention of my friends to celebrate my eightieth birthday, I stated in the press that I very much wished they would do nothing about it. I hoped my statement would be heeded and that there would be no celebration.

But what happened was something I never expected, namely that from the end of August up to the present day I have received and continue to receive such flattering greetings from so many different quarters that I feel the need to express my sincere gratitude to all those people and institutions which have behaved in such a kind and friendly way towards me.

I thank all universities, town councils, zemstvo councils, various academic institutions, societies, unions, groups of people, clubs, associations, and editorial boards of newspapers and journals which have sent me addresses and greetings. I also thank all my friends and acquaintances, both in Russia and abroad, who remembered me on this day. I thank all the people who are unknown to me of every kind of social status including prisoners and forced labourers who greeted me with equal friendliness. I thank the young men and women and children who sent me their congratulations. I also thank the clergy—although very few in number, their greetings were all the more dear to me—for their good wishes. I also thank those people who, as well as their congratulations, sent me touching presents.

I warmly thank all those who sent their greetings, and especially those of them (the majority of those who wrote to me) who, quite unexpectedly and to my great joy, expressed in their letters to me their complete agreement, not with me, but with the eternal truths which I have tried to express as best I could in my writings. Among these people there was a majority of peasants and workers, which was particularly welcome to me.

I apologise for not being able to answer each person and institution separately, and I ask you to accept my statement as the expression of my sincere gratitude to all the people who have expressed their good feelings to me at this time, for the joy they have given me.

Lev Tolstoy

562. To V. I. PANFILOV

Vladimir Ivanovich Panfilov, a topographer in the army. He wrote to Tolstoy to challenge his opinion, expressed in the recently published second volume of Biryukov's biography of him, about the practice of certain professions—specifically the military and legal professions—being incompatible with Christianity.

Yasnaya Polyana, 11 January 1909

[15 lines omitted]...As I said above, the true demands of morality are bound to be simple, and the demand for explanations and complex arguments, and the involvement of people in the circumstances of the life of the state, besides concealing from them the essence of true morality, do the further damage, also very serious, that they falsely define and evaluate the criminal nature and immorality of their acts, whereas a true evaluation of what is more and what is less moral is necessary for the lives of people under existing conditions. There is now an established public opinion, the very one which you express yourself, that all situations in which a man is placed in the service of the state are equally permissible; whereas in these situations, as in all the circumstances of our life, there is an inevitable gradation

562. To V. I. Panfilov

and differentiation, an awareness of which is not only important but essential to make possible a life which is reasonable, just, and approximating to the greatest degree of morality.

This mistake is made not only by people who serve the state, but also by people who, one would think, are hostile to it, such as the majority of socialists. And this mistake by advanced people—the socialists—is also inherited by people who don't share their views, but in this case make use of their arguments. The socialists maintain quite correctly that the life of people today with its division into the non-workers, the capitalists of various sorts, and the working masses, is completely wrong and immoral as regards those who, while not working themselves, make use of the labours of the working class. Any landowner, capitalist or politician who receives a big salary—all alike are thieves and robbers—that's all completely true. But the mistake is that they lump together in one category the people who compel the workers to serve the rich by means of violence of any kind (and any violence inevitably leads, if opposed, to murder), and those who, while not committing violence, make use of it. (Moreover, the socialists even direct their main attention to those who make use of violence (the capitalists), and not to those who are the cause of it). However, for the man for whom the moral question is uppermost, this evaluation is completely the wrong way round, and the man who is the cause of violence is undoubtedly more immoral than the man who makes use of it. Notice that I certainly don't mean that people who make use of violence are not immoral or shouldn't strive to put an end to its use, but that they are less immoral than the former, and that every man, in his own private life, should first of all stop committing violence himself, and then try to free himself from using it in the circumstances in which he finds himself...[25 lines omitted]

563. To V. G. CHERTKOV

Yasnaya Polyana, 30 January 1909

Vladimir Grigoryevich,

In view of the fact that you are preparing to edit all my writings, and for this purpose would like to have the right to make free use of my private letters to various people also, I hereby certify that if you or those to whom you entrust the continuation of this task in my lifetime or after my death should find it desirable to include in editions of my writings various of my private letters to any person whomsoever, copies of which are in your possession or will be received by you from me or by other means, then I give you and those who continue your task the full right to do so, at your and their discretion.[1]

I give you this permission also because, in supposing that some of my letters might have general significance, I am certain that both you and those who will be left by you to continue your work will know how to make use of them in the most

[563] 1. This statement was superseded by the will of September 1909 referred to in the footnote to Letter 514.

expedient manner; and furthermore because, as I do not recognise literary property, I would not want my letters to become the property of the people to whom they are addressed.

Lev Tolstoy

564. To M. A. STAKHOVICH

Yasnaya Polyana, 5 February 1909

Thank you, dear Mikhail Alexandrovich, for the mittens and the book.[1] Your opinion about Artsybashev's story *Blood* is a new confirmation of the correctness of your artistic taste; the other stories *Gololobov*, *Laughter* and *Rebellion* are also good except for the general shortcomings of all new writers: carelessness of language and self-assurance. But in any case, this man is very talented and an original thinker, although his great self-assurance hampers the proper working of his thoughts.

I was completely forgetting the most important matter. In Kharkov prison there's a certain Alexander Mikhaylovich Bodyansky, who has been sentenced to six months' imprisonment for distributing my works. I know him and respect him, although he doesn't fully share my views and is of a semi-revolutionary disposition. He's a sick old man and finds himself in the most painful circumstances which have further deteriorated as a result of a strange general order by the Minister of Internal Affairs that the term of those imprisoned in communal cells but sentenced to solitary confinement should be increased by one third. He was not transferred to a communal cell, but a criminal was put in his cell because, as a result of crowded conditions, there's a shortage of single rooms. If you can help in this matter you will do me a great favour and a truly good deed besides[2]...(2 lines omitted)

565. To I. I. PERPER

Iosif Iosifovich Perper (1886–?), a teacher and editor of *The Vegetarian Review* from 1909–15. He met Tolstoy in June 1909 and wrote several articles about him.

Yasnaya Polyana, 5 February 1909

Although not directly, I'm keeping my promise and my wish to contribute to your journal.[1]

I've read Artsybashev's magnificent story *Blood*, which by its artistic merit is better able than any arguments to influence people in the sense of attracting them

[564] 1. The first volume of Artsybashev's stories (1908).
2. Stakhovich intervened successfully, and Bodyansky's sentence was not increased (see Letter 555).

[565] 1. A promise made in a letter to Perper of 26 January 1909 after he had sent Tolstoy a specimen copy of the journal.

565. To I. I. Perper

to vegetarianism, or rather freeing them from the superstition of the necessity for eating living creatures. I won't tell you the content of this excellent story so as not to spoil it, but I strongly advise you to get the author's permission to print it, and to publish it in full or in part in your journal.[2]

With the utmost respect,
Lev Tolstoy

566. To V. G. CHERTKOV

Yasnaya Polyana, 27 April 1909

[Letter omitted. Postscript translated]

I'll write to you, dear friend, about what has happened very recently to L. N. Tolstoy. What has happened is that as well as Tolstoy, somebody else has appeared who has completely taken possession of Tolstoy and allows him no freedom of movement. As soon as Tolstoy states a willingness or, on the contrary, an unwillingness to do something, this somebody, whom I call '*I*', decides the matter for himself and sometimes agrees, but usually, on the contrary, refuses permission to do what Tolstoy wants or tells him to do what Tolstoy doesn't want. If Tolstoy wants to recall the bad qualities of a man he dislikes or to condemn him, or wants to think about how people praise him, or doesn't want to talk to a dull-witted man, or doesn't want to abandon his plans and go and see a person who wants to see him, then the *I* tells him not to think about other people's bad qualities, tells him not to condemn, tells him to abandon his work and go and see the person who needs him. And the surprising thing is that ever since I've clearly understood that this *I* is far more important than Tolstoy and that it's necessary to listen to him and that good will come of it, I immediately listen to him as soon as I hear his voice.

567. To S. A. TOLSTAYA

Yasnaya Polyana, 13 May 1909

[Draft letter. Not sent]

This letter will be given to you when I'm no longer here.[1] I write to you from beyond the grave in order to tell you what I wanted to tell you so many times and for so many years for your own good, but was unable to tell you while I was alive. I know that if I had been better and kinder I would have been able to tell you during my lifetime in such a way that you would have listened to me, but I was unable to. Forgive me for this and forgive me for everything in which I was to blame throughout the whole time of our life together and especially the early time.

2. The story was published in *The Vegetarian Review*, 1909, No. 4.

[567] 1. This letter was the result of a quarrel between Tolstoy and his wife at breakfast that morning over his story *The Devil*. The letter was written in the garden where Tolstov went to cool down. Tolstoy evidently thought better of it, and it was never sent.

I have nothing to forgive you for; you were what your mother made you; a kind and faithful wife and a good mother. But just because you were what your mother made you and stayed like that and didn't want to change, didn't want to work on yourself, to progress towards goodness and truth, but on the contrary clung with such obstinacy to all that was most evil and the opposite of all that was dear to me, you did a lot of evil to other people and sank lower and lower yourself and reached the pathetic condition you are now in.

568. To T. L. SUKHOTINA

Yasnaya Polyana, 20 May 1909

[12 lines omitted]...I'm writing in the garden now, where I jot down thoughts as they occur. Instead of writing it down in my notebook I'll write what I mean to jot down in this letter to you, particularly since it concerns women, namely: women flirt primarily with their bodies, men primarily with their minds. A woman who flirts with her mind is funny, as is a man who flirts with his body...[4 lines omitted]

569. To THEODOR WEICHER

Theodor Weicher, a Leipzig publisher who sent Tolstoy a copy of the *Goethe Kalendar auf das Jahr 1909* published by his firm, and asked for his opinion on Goethe's significance as a writer.

Yasnaya Polyana, 27 May/9 June 1909

Geehrter Herr,

Danke sehr für die Sendung Ihres Goethe-Kalenders auf 1909. Ich habe ihn mit grossem Interesse durchgesehen. Was mich besonders interessiert hat sind Goethes Gespräche mit verschiedenen Personen. Ich habe in diesen Gesprächen vieles für mich neues und wertvolles gefunden, so wie z. B. was er mit Falk über die Wissenschaften, die zu weitsichtig geworden sind, äussert, oder mit Riemer über die vegetabilen Geister und die ἐλεύθεροι, oder dass die Natur eine Orgelist, auf der unser Herrgott spielt, und der Teufel tritt die Bälge dazu.

Besonders bemerkenswert ist sein Gespräch mit Müller 1823, 3 Febr. Auch was er von den Schäden, die die Journale und Kritiken beibringen, schon im Jahre 1824 sagte, und was besonders in unserer Zeit so wahr ist.

Aber es wäre zu lang alles tiefsinnige und geistvolle, was ich in dem Buche gefunden habe, aufzuzählen.

Nehmen Sie es mir nicht übel dass ich Ihren Wunsch, mich über Goethes Werke zu äussern, wegen meinen vielen Beschäftigungen nicht erfüllen kann.

Danke noch einmal für das Buch das mir so wertvoll war.

Leo Tolstoy

570. To THE ORGANISING COMMITTEE OF THE XVIII INTERNATIONAL PEACE CONGRESS

Yasnaya Polyana, 12/25 July 1909

Au Président du XVIII Congrès de la Paix, Stockholm.
Monsieur le Président,

La question traitée par le congrès est de la plus grande importance et occupe mes pensées dépuis longues années. Je tâcherai de profiter de l'honneur que vous m'avez fait par mon éléction,[1] en tâchant d'emettre ce que j'ai à dire devant un auditoire aussi exceptionnel comme celui qui va se rassembler au congrès. Si mes forces me le permettent je ferai mon possible pour me rendre à Stockholm à la date indiquée, sinon, je vous ferai parvenir ce que j'ai à dire dans l'espoir que les membres du congrès voudront bien prendre connaissance de mes opinions.

Veuillez, Monsieur, agréer l'assurance de mes sentiments les plus distingués.

571. To N. POPKOV

Nikolay Popkov, a village schoolteacher interested in joining a Tolstoyan colony, had written to ask if there were any such colonies in the south of Russia. Tolstoy's reply is somewhat surprising as he had previously lent at least moral support to the various colonies.

Yasnaya Polyana, 22 July 1909

I don't know any Tolstoyan colonies. In general I consider the setting up of colonies and communities with separate rules useless, or rather harmful, for the cause of moral improvement.

Lev Tolstoy

572. To N. SCHMIDT

Nikolay Schmidt (1899–?) had written to Tolstoy to ask whether he considered it morally permissible to do evil to a few for the good of the many.

[570] 1. Tolstoy was elected an honorary member of the committee of the XVIII International Peace Congress to be held in Stockholm in August 1909 and invited to attend and deliver an address. However, Sofya Andreyevna's fears for his health eventually forced him to give up the idea of going himself, but he began to prepare an address to be taken and read by the Finnish writer Arvid Järnefelt. In early August Tolstoy was informed that the Congress had been put off until 1910, which was officially explained in the press as the result of strikes in Sweden. There was, however, some conjecture (which Tolstoy shared) that the cancelling of the Congress was due to fear of what Tolstoy might say in his address. When in 1910 Tolstoy was again asked to participate in the Congress he refused.

573. To P. A. Stolypin

Yasnaya Polyana, 22 July 1909

I think it ought to be clear to anybody that one should not do evil to some people with the greater good of others in view because an evil done in the present is an evil for certain, while the good which is foreseen in the future is not only doubtful, but hardly ever achieved. Moreover, the answer to what constitutes the good of the many in the name of whom the good of the few may be sacrificed is understood in completely different ways by different people. An example of this could be, if you like, the present situation in Russia where the government, for the sake of the good of the many, tortures and hangs a relatively few people, and the revolutionaries, if they don't kill many people, would nevertheless like to do evil to very many people in the name of the good of a still greater number of people. You wouldn't have asked me such questions if you had read even a few serious books by Kant, Emerson, Channing, Rousseau, Pascal, Ruskin and others about what constitutes true morality.

573. To P. A. STOLYPIN

Pyotr Arkadyevich Stolypin (1862–1911), Minister of Internal Affairs and President of the Council of Ministers, Nicholas II's most influential adviser. Hugh Seton-Watson has written of him in *The Russian Empire 1801–1917*:

After more than half a century, Stolypin remains a controversial figure. He was hated by the moderate left as a man who had dissolved the two Dumas and changed the electoral law. To the revolutionaries, he was the butcher who had set up field courts martial to shoot peasants and workers. The extreme right hated and intrigued against him, because he consented to play the prime minister, thereby diminishing the status of the rightful autocrat, the Tsar. Historical literature has usually represented him either as a blood-thirsty oppressor of the people or as a Russian Bismarck who would have made Russia great by peaceful reforms if the assassin's bullet had not laid him low.

In the following letter it is primarily Stolypin's agrarian and peasant policy which Tolstoy objects to. A law of 5 October 1906 had extended the personal freedom of the peasants. The Land Commandants were divested of some of their arbitrary authority over the peasants and the peasant voters themselves were allowed to choose their zemstvo representatives. The law of 9 November was more radical, and it is this that Tolstoy takes issue with. This law gave peasants the right to purchase land formerly owned by the commune, thereby breaking up the traditional obshchina with its strong economic and social ties. During 1908–9 the government had been applying its peasant policy with particular brutality, prompting Tolstoy's protest to Stolypin. However, Tolstoy neither finished nor sent the letter, deciding that all his appeals to the government had been and always would be futile.

573. To P. A. Stolypin

Yasnaya Polyana, 30 August 1909

[Draft letter. Not sent]

I am writing to you about a very pitiable man, the most pitiable of all those I know in Russia today. You know this man and, strange to say, you love him, but you don't understand the full degree of his misfortune and you don't pity him as his situation deserves. This man is—you. I have been meaning to write to you for a long time, and I even began to write a letter to you, not only as a fellow human being, but as a person exceptionally close to me, the son of a dear friend of mine.[1] But before I could manage to finish the letter, your activities which got worse and worse and more and more criminal, prevented me more and more from finishing the letter I had begun to you with genuine love. I can't understand the blindness with which you can continue your terrible activities—activities which threaten your material well-being (because people want to kill you and may do so any moment)[2] and ruin your good name, because you have already earned by your present activities a terrible reputation with which your name will always be coupled as long as history lasts, as an example of coarseness, cruelty and falsehood. But principally, and most important of all, your activities will ruin your soul. You know, it would still be possible to use force, as is always done in the name of a goal which brings good to a great number of people, to appease them or to change the organisation of their lives for the better, but you do neither the one thing nor the other, but just the reverse. Instead of appeasement, you provoke the anger and bitterness of people to the highest degree of tension by all these terrible acts of arbitrariness, execution, imprisonment, exile and prohibition of various sorts, and not only do you not introduce any new organisation which might improve the people's general condition, but you introduce to the single most important problem of people's lives—their relation to the land—the most crude and foolish consolidation of something whose evil is already felt by the whole world and which must inevitably be destroyed—the ownership of land. Surely what is now being done with this foolish law of 9 November[3] whose purpose is to justify the ownership of land and which has no reasonable argument to support it except that the same thing exists in Europe (it should be time for us to think with our minds)—surely what is now being done with the law of 9 November is like the measures which were being taken by the government in the 50s, not to destroy serfdom but to consolidate it.

It is so clear to me, standing as I do with one foot in the grave and seeing all the horrors now being perpetrated in Russia, that the attainment of the goal of appease-

[573] 1. Stolypin's father, Arkady Dmitriyevich Stolypin, a Tula landowner and infantry general, had served with Tolstoy in the Crimean War.

2. There had been an assassination attempt on Stolypin in 1906 by a Socialist-Revolutionary: Stolypin's house was blown up, causing the deaths of twenty-seven people and injury to Stolypin's daughter. Stolypin himself was not injured in this attempt, but he was assassinated at the theatre in Kiev by a man who was both a Socialist-Revolutionary and a police agent.

3. Tolstoy described the effects of this law in a letter of 11 November 1909 as leading to the acquisition of still more land by the landowners, who until then had been unable to buy communal land, and as promoting envy and hatred between the peasants.

ment towards which you and your accomplices are allegedly striving is only possible along a completely opposite path to the one you are taking: firstly by putting a stop to acts of violence and cruelty, in particular the death penalty which seemed an impossibility in Russia scores of years ago, and secondly by satisfying the demands on the one hand of all truly thinking and enlightened people and on the other hand of the enormous mass of the people who have never recognised and do not recognise the right to private ownership of land.

Yes, think about your activities, think about your fate, especially about your soul, and either change the whole direction of your activities or, if you can't do that, recognise them to be false and unjust and abandon them.

I am writing this letter to you alone, and it will remain unknown to anybody for, say, a month if you like. But if there has been no change in your activities by 1 October, this letter will be published abroad.[4]

574. To MOHANDAS GANDHI

Mohandas Gandhi (1869–1948), an Indian barrister educated in England, had gone to the Transvaal in 1893 where he set up a law practice. In 1894 he founded the Natal Indian Congress Party and in 1904 became the first editor of a Transvaal newspaper, *Indian Opinion*. His initiative in both cases was aimed at winning equal social and political rights for Indians in the Transvaal. In the early 1900s he became increasingly religious, and increasingly hostile to Western civilisation—at the time he was much influenced by Ruskin's *Unto This Last* and Tolstoy's ethical works. In 1908 Gandhi gave up his practice to lead an Indian campaign for equal rights in South Africa, an activity which led to his imprisonment on several occasions. He founded a 'Tolstoyan' farm in the Transvaal in 1910, but his ideas differed somewhat from Tolstoy's; he disliked the term 'passive resistance' and was an advocate of *satyagraha*, 'a force which is born of truth and love of non-violence'. Tolstoy was particularly interested in the application of *satyagraha* as a method of protest in South Africa.

While in London in 1909, Gandhi had written to Tolstoy in some detail about the condition of the Indians in the Transvaal, and had asked permission to publish a 'letter-essay' written by Tolstoy to Tarakuatta Das (*Letter to a Hindu*, 1908), sending him a copy of a new translation of the letter into English (it had been translated by Chertkov for Tarakuatta Das) for his approval. The letter was a rebuttal of Das's suggestion that passive resistance was not effective in dealing with the British in India and suggested instead that the main cause of 'the enslavement of the Indian peoples by the English' was the lack of any true religious awareness by the Indians, and that if they had been enslaved by violence, it was because they had themselves lived by violence and not by love.

Chertkov's translation was not published by Tarakuatta Das's newspaper (*The*

---

4. The letter was neither sent to Stolypin nor published.

574. To Mohandas Gandhi

Free Hindustan), so the first publication in English of the *Letter to a Hindu* was in Gandhi's *Indian Opinion* (March 1910). It had previously circulated in hectographed form, which is how Gandhi had become acquainted with it.

[Original in English]

Yasnaya Polyana,
25 September/8 October 1909

I have just received your most interesting letter which has given me great pleasure. God helps our dear brothers and coworkers in the Transvaal. That same struggle of the tender against the harsh, of meekness and love against pride and violence, is every year making itself more and more felt here among us also, especially in one of the very sharpest of the conflicts of the religious law with the worldly laws—in refusals of military service. Such refusals are becoming ever more and more frequent.

The letter to a Hindu was written by me,[1] and the translation is a very good one. The title of the book about Krishna shall be sent you from Moscow.[2]

As to the word reincarnation, I should not myself like to omit it,[3] for, in my opinion, belief in reincarnation can never be as firm as belief in the soul's immortality and in God's justice and love. You may, however, do as you like about omitting it. The translation into, and circulation of my letter in the Hindoo language, can only be a pleasure for me.

A competition,[4] i.e. an offer of monetary inducement, in connection with a religious matter, would, I think, be out of place. If I can assist your publication, I shall be very glad.

I greet you fraternally, and am glad to have intercourse with you.

575. To K. I. MUTSENEK

K. I. Mutsenek had written to Tolstoy after reading an article in *The Stock Exchange News* ('Two Days at Yasnaya Polyana') to point out the inconsistency between Tolstoy's vegetarianism and the wearing of clothing made from leather and fur.

Yasnaya Polyana, 6 November 1909

You are quite right that since I renounce the deliberate killing of living creatures, I ought not to use parts of their body for clothing, such as leather and fur.

The fact that I wear a leather belt and leather boots and even a fur hat in no

[574] 1. Gandhi had asked Tolstoy to verify his authorship of the *Letter to a Hindu*.
2. Gandhi had asked the source for quotations from Krishna which Tolstoy had used as epigraphs in the 'letter-essay'. It was *Shri Krishna. The Lord of Love* (New York, 1904) by Baha Premanand Bharati.
3. Gandhi had asked Tolstoy if he could omit Tolstoy's criticism of the concept of reincarnation from the letter.
4. Gandhi was considering an essay competition on the theme 'The morality and efficacy of passive resistance'. He decided against it in the end.

way proves that I consider this necessary or good, but only that in spite of the fact that I consider it would be better not to wear leather or fur, I am so far away from perfection in my own life, not only in the matter of not using the bodies of creatures that have been killed but in many, many other far more important things too, that the efforts which I can direct towards improving my life in a moral sense, first of all, I find it more expedient to direct towards correcting my many other failings, which are more serious than using leather and fur objects for my clothing.

Lev Tolstoy

576. To V. G. CHERTKOV

Yasnaya Polyana, 15 November 1909

I was thinking last night about what you wrote to me, and I to you, yesterday. Forget what I wrote yesterday.[1] I'm clear about what I'm writing now, namely: the consciousness of myself as a separate being is something non-spatial, immaterial, atemporal and above all immovable; and this immovable something is inseparably united with my present, movable, material body and all its perceptions and all its activities. However much this 80-year-old physical being of mine with all its perceptions and all its activities differs from my 8-year-old physical being with its perceptions and activities of that time, my consciousness of *me*, separate from everything else, is completely and absolutely identical. I, with my consciousness and body, am like a water mill for grinding flour. If I say that I am a mill without mentioning the river which drives the mill, I shall be wrong; if I say that I am the river without mentioning the mill I shall also be wrong. *I am a separate being, conscious of myself.* But consciousness is something immovable, immaterial—what we call spiritual. And just as there is a mill only because there is a river, so there is something immaterial and immovable only because there is matter and movement —what we call life. And as the main thing about the mill is the river, so the main thing about my life is consciousness. And as the river, apart from turning the millwheel, does many other things too, so consciousness, apart from giving me life, gives me knowledge of other beings like myself, and of the whole world.

My consciousness of *me*, connected in the first place with my own separate being alone, transfers its consciousness to other beings by means of what we call love and, with the end of my life, is released altogether from the material, moving being with which it is united.

To the question what happens to consciousness after its release from the body there can be no answer, since the question is about the future, the temporal, what *will be* after death.

And consciousness is outside time. It only is, not was or will be...[6 lines omitted]

[576] 1. In a letter to Chertkov the day before, Tolstoy had referred to Pascal's criticism of materialist philosophy—in the opinion of a materialist, *la matière est consciente d'elle-même*—and had tried to apply it to the body/soul dichotomy: '...matter (the human "I") is conscious of itself as spiritual, and the spirit (in man) is conscious of itself as material'.

577. To A. A. ŠKARVAN

Yasnaya Polyana, 9 January 1910

[61 lines omitted]...And so I not only think, but know from reasoning and experience that a religious man with the crudest religious ideas nevertheless stands incomparably higher in his ability to perceive the truth than the scientific man of superstition. The first knows that there is something which cannot be known; but the second is certain that there is nothing which cannot be known and that everything that he knows is true knowledge. The first only needs to get rid of the excrescences of superstition on what he regards as incomprehensible and there will be no obstacles between him and the truth. But the second cannot perceive the truth because he is completely full of the falsehood which he takes for the truth, and there is no room for him to receive the truth.

The most important thing about knowledge is not to imagine that you know what you don't know, but to know that you don't know what you don't know. Religious people have this quality, although their religion is expressed in the most crude form; but scientific people are completely devoid of it.

578. To V. F. KRASNOV

Yasnaya Polyana, 14 January 1910

I'm sorry that I didn't cross out what was bad.[1] What was bad were the comparisons and descriptions of something which the author couldn't have seen, and particularly the decadent manner of attributing consciousness to inanimate objects. Descriptions are good and affect the reader when the reader's soul blends with the object being described, and this only happens when the reader can transfer to himself the feelings and impressions being described.

Don't despair, and don't model your writing on the moderns, but on Pushkin and Gogol.

Lev Tolstoy

579. To P. MELNIKOV

Pyotr Melnikov, a worker from Baku, had written to Tolstoy and received some books in reply which, as Tolstoy says in the omitted portion of the following letter, must have been misleading and unclear, to judge from Melnikov's next

[578] 1. Although Tolstoy had recommended Krasnov's story *Khodynka* for publication in *Russian Wealth*, he had severely criticised the style of the story in a letter to Krasnov on 8 January 1910. Krasnov then asked him if he should go on writing, and regretted that Tolstoy had not crossed out what was bad in the story.

579. To P. Melnikov

letter. The main source of confusion, Tolstoy wrote, was Melnikov's belief in the infallibility of the Scriptures.

Yasnaya Polyana, 22 January 1910

[18 lines omitted]...As I understand it you are chiefly interested in two questions: God—what is God?—and the soul. What relation can God have to people, and what sort of life can the soul have after death?

In answer to the first question—what is God and what relation does He have to people—a great deal has been written in the Bible about how He created the world and what relation He has to people, rewarding them with heaven and punishing them with hell. All this is nonsense and you need to forget it completely and put it right out of your head. God is the beginning of everything, without whom there would not be anything, and a small part of whom we feel in ourselves as our life, and which is manifested in us by love (for that reason only we say that God is love). But all argument about how He created the world and man and how He will punish and chastise people, I repeat once again, you must try to forget completely in order to understand the meaning of your own life.

That is all that we know and can know about God.

As for the soul, we only know that what we call our life is a divine principle, without which nothing would exist for us, and something which animates the body, and since it has nothing bodily about it, it cannot die when the body dies.

You also ask, like many other people, whether the soul is immortal and whether it will live after the body is dead.

So that you should understand my answer to your question, I ask you to pay very careful attention to what I am going to write now.

For the human body, and for the body only, time exists, i.e. hours, days, months and years go by; and for the human body only, there also exist the material and the bodily—what can be seen and felt with the hands, what is big or little, hard or soft, tough or flimsy. But for the soul there is no time: it is always in the human body alone; just as I said 'I' about myself 70 years ago, so I feel myself the same 'I' today. Nor for the soul is there anything material: wherever I am, whatever happens to me, my soul, my 'I', is always just the same and is everywhere immaterial. And so for the body only there is time, i.e. the question what has been and what will be, and there is place where it may be located, and there is matter of which it consists, but for the soul there is no time or place or matter. And therefore we cannot ask what will happen to the soul and where it will be after death, because the words *will be* denote time, and the word *where* denotes place, and there can be neither time nor place for the soul after the death of the body.

How superficial and wrong are arguments about a future life and about heaven and hell, can be seen from the fact that if the soul is going to live after death and live somewhere, it ought to have lived somewhere before birth, but nobody mentions that.

My opinion is that the soul in us cannot die because only our body dies, but that we do not know and cannot know what will happen to the soul and where it will be, although we know that it cannot die. About rewards and punishments, I think that our life here is good and peaceful only when we live in accordance with the law of loving one another, and that it is bad and troubled and distressing when we deviate from this law. And so our life is so arranged that here, in this life (and we know no other), we already receive our reward and punishment for our deeds.

580. To V. F. TOTOMIANTS

Vakhan Fomich Totomiants (1871–?), a sociologist and theoretician of the cooperative movement. He taught in higher educational institutes in Moscow and Petersburg, as well as writing widely on cooperative principles. He had written to Tolstoy to explain the ethical and economic basis of cooperative ventures, and to ask for his opinions with a view to publication.

Yasnaya Polyana, 23 January 1910

Vakhan Fomich,

You are quite right to suppose that the cooperative movement is bound to have my sympathy. Although I continue to, and will never cease to think and say that the only radical method capable of eliminating the existing evil of struggle and violence, and the oppression of the majority of the people by the non-working classes is the revival of the religious consciousness of the people, I am bound to admit that cooperative activity, the founding of cooperatives and participation in them is the only social activity which a moral, self-respecting person who doesn't wish to be a party to violence can take part in in our time.

I also admit that cooperatives can relieve the needs of the working people which have reached a critical degree in recent times. I don't think, however, as some people think, that the cooperative movement can promote or establish a religious attitude on the part of people to the problems of life. I think, on the contrary, that only an upsurge of religious consciousness can give a lasting and fruitful character to the cooperative movement.

In any case, I think that in our time this is one of the best activities which people can devote themselves to—young people who are seeking an application for their powers and wishing to serve the people—and there are many of them. If I were young I would take up this task, and even now I don't despair of doing what I can among the peasantry who are near and dear to me.

Yours respectfully,
Lev Tolstoy

I don't think this letter deserves to be published. But if, contrary to expectations, you should find this desirable, I am prepared to give it to V. A. Posse's *Life for All*; he is very interested in this question.

581. To B. MANDZHOS

Boris Mandzhos was a student at the University of Kiev when he wrote to Tolstoy advising him to renounce everything—his title, worldly goods and family—and to lead the life of a beggar. Tolstoy took the letter very seriously and his reply was not typed in the normal way, but copied out in longhand by his secretary, Bulgakov, and only the draft kept. However, despite Tolstoy's wishes, the letter was published in the newspaper *Kiev Thought* shortly after his death.

Yasnaya Polyana, 17 February 1910

Your letter moved me deeply. What you advise me to do constitutes my cherished dream, but so far I have been unable to do it. There are many reasons for this (certainly not that I was sorry for myself), but the main one is that I certainly ought not to do it in order to influence other people. This is not in our power and should not govern our activities. One can and should do it only when it is necessary, not for hypothetical, external ends, but for the satisfaction of the inner demands of the spirit, when it is just as morally impossible to remain in one's former situation as it is physically impossible to cough when you have no breath. And I am close to that situation, and become closer and closer each day.

What you advise me to do: renounce my social status and property and distribute it to those who considered themselves entitled to count on it after my death, I did more than 25 years ago. But the one fact that I live in my family with my wife and daughter in terrible, shameful conditions of luxury in the midst of surrounding poverty, continually torments me more and more, and there is not a day when I don't think about following your advice.

I am very, very grateful to you for your letter. This letter of mine will be known to one person only. I ask you likewise not to show it to anybody.

Yours affectionately,
L. Tolstoy

582. To K. P. SLAVNIN

Kelsy Porfiryevich Slavnin, editor of a short-lived newspaper, *The New Russia*, which was published for a few months in Petersburg in 1910, and closed down in May for publishing an extract from Tolstoy's collection of thoughts *For Each Day*. Slavnin wrote to Tolstoy to ask if there was anything 'criminal' in the words objected to. He left the country before receiving a reply, and was sentenced to eighteen months' imprisonment in his absence.

Yasnaya Polyana, 27 February 1910

In order to answer your question, I need to know what you understand by the word 'crime'. If you understand what is regarded as such by our government, then I neither know nor wish to know that stupid, dirty and criminal nonsense which

582. To K. P. Slavnin

the government calls laws, and the failure to obey which is called a crime. But if you ask whether the conscience and common sense of all thinking people see 'evidence of criminality' in the words of mine which you published, defining the essence of the activity of all church theologians not only in Russia but throughout the world, then I answer that no crime was committed by me or by you, but is going to be committed by all that venal horde of bureaucrats who are prepared, because of the salary they receive, not only to put you in prison together with thousands of people languishing there, but are always ready to torture, kill and hang anyone at all, as long as they punctually receive their monthly salary, plundered from the people.

Excuse me if, perhaps, I answer your question inaccurately, but my unbridled indignation and horror at the activity of the Genghis Khan with telephones and aeroplanes who rules in our time and cloaks his infamies in the form of legality—this indignation comes to the surface with every case such as yours.

With the utmost respect,
Lev Tolstoy

583. To I. I. PERPER

Yasnaya Polyana, 10 March 1910

I'm sending you a book translated from the German under the title *Horrors of Christian Civilisation*,[1] compiled by a Tibetan lama who spent several years in the universities of Germany. The title of the book tells you about its content. Although I don't know whether it was actually written by a real Buddhist, or whether this is only a form the author chose, like Montesquieu's famous book *Persian Letters*, to express his thoughts, the book itself is very interesting and instructive.

In recent times Buddhism has been becoming more and more free of the excrescences covering it, the Christian world is getting to know its true essence more and more, and in recent times people who have gone over from Christianity to Buddhism are being encountered more and more often in both Europe and America.

Not to mention the metaphysical depth of its teaching, so well explained by Schopenhauer, the moral efficacy of this teaching with its five basic commandments for all who believe in Buddhism is particularly attractive: (1) Do not deliberately kill any living creature; (2) do not appropriate to yourself what is considered by others to be their property; (3) do not give way to sexual lust; (4) do not lie; (5) do not stupefy yourself by alcoholic drinks or smoking.

One cannot help thinking what an enormous change would take place in life if people knew these commandments and considered them at least as binding as the fulfilment of external rituals.

Lev Tolstoy

[583] 1. *Die Schrecken Civilisation* by Bruno Freidank. It was translated by A. A. Goldenweiser under the title 'Letters of a Buddhist to a Christian', and published in *The Vegetarian Review*, 1910, Nos. 5–10.

584. To V. G. KOROLENKO

Vladimir Galaktionovich Korolenko (1853–1921), a prolific author and journalist, best known for his Siberian stories, the product of his years of exile in the 1880s, and for his work as editor of the influential journal *Russian Wealth*. His monumental *History of My Contemporary*, despite its title, is primarily an autobiography. Korolenko first visited Tolstoy in Moscow in 1896 and again in the Crimea in 1902. Their last meeting took place at Yasnaya Polyana in 1910. Their correspondence is slight (four letters by each author have survived), but they respected each other highly both as writers and as men. Korolenko wrote two substantial articles entitled 'Lev Nikolayevich Tolstoy', and there are frequent references to Tolstoy and his work in his correspondence.

Yasnaya Polyana, 26–7 March 1910

Vladimir Galaktionovich,

I've just listened to your article on the death penalty[1] and hard as I tried while it was being read, I couldn't refrain—not just from a tear, but from sobbing. I can't find words to express to you my gratitude and love for this article which in its expression, its thought, and principally its feeling is outstanding.

It ought to be reprinted and distributed in millions of copies. No speeches in the Duma, no tracts, no dramas or novels could have one thousandth part of the salutary influence which this article ought to have.

It ought to have this influence because it arouses such a feeling of compassion for what these victims of human madness have suffered and are suffering that you can't help forgiving them whatever their deeds may have been, and can't, however much you wish, forgive those responsible for these horrors. As well as this feeling, your article arouses bewilderment at the self-confident blindness of the people who perpetrate these terrible deeds, and their futility, since it's clear that all these cruel and stupid deeds have the reverse effect to the purpose intended, as you admirably demonstrate; apart from all these feelings your article can't help but arouse yet another feeling which I experience to a high degree—a feeling of pity, not only for those murdered, but also for those deceived, simple, perverted people—the guards, gaolers, hangmen and soldiers—who perpetrate these horrors without understanding what they are doing.

One thing that gladdens me is the fact that an article like yours unites many, many living people who are not perverted, by a single common ideal of goodness and truth, which blazes out brighter and brighter whatever its enemies may do.

Lev Tolstoy

[584] 1. 'An Everyday Occurrence' (*Russian Wealth*, 1910, No. 3). Having written on the same subject himself recently (*I Cannot be Silent*), Tolstoy was particularly interested in the similarity of his and Korolenko's ideas.

585. To BERNARD SHAW

[Original in English]

Yasnaya Polyana, 9 May 1910

My dear Mr Bernard Shaw,

I have received your play and your witty letter.[1] I have read your play with pleasure. I am in full sympathy with its subject.

Your remark that the preaching of righteousness has generally little influence on people and that young men regard as laudable that which is contrary to righteousness is quite correct. It does not however follow that such preaching is unnecessary. The reason of the failure is that those who preach do not fulfil what they preach, i.e. hypocrisy.

I also cannot agree with what you call your theology. You enter into controversy with that which no thinking person of our time believes or can believe: with a God-creator. And yet you seem to recognise a God who has got definite aims comprehensible to you. 'To my mind', you write, 'unless we conceive God engaged in a continual struggle to surpass himself as striving at every birth to make a better man than before, we are conceiving nothing better than an omnipotent snob.'

Concerning the rest of what you say about God and about evil, I will repeat the words I said, as you write, about your *Man and Superman*, namely that the problem about God and evil is too important to be spoken of in jest. And therefore I tell you frankly that I received a very painful impression from the concluding words of your letter: 'Suppose the world were only one of God's jokes, would you work any the less to make it a good joke instead of a bad one?'

Yours sincerely,
Leo Tolstoy

586. To COUNTESS S. A. TOLSTAYA

Yasnaya Polyana, 14 July 1910

1. I shan't give my present diary to anyone; I'll keep it myself.
2. I'll take back the old diaries from Chertkov and will keep them myself, probably in a bank.[1]

[585] 1. George Bernard Shaw had sent Tolstoy his play *The Shewing-Up of Blanco Posnet*, together with a letter in which he quoted Blake's poem 'The Tyger', saying that God had created evil beings as well as good ones, and had made mistakes in creation. He ended by saying, 'Supposing the world were only one of God's jokes, would you work any the less to make it a good joke instead of a bad one?', to which Tolstoy took objection because of its flippancy. The letter was written in Russian, translated into English by Chertkov, and returned to Tolstoy to sign and forward. Chertkov's translation is retained here with very minor changes.

[586] 1. Sofya Andreyevna had given Tolstoy's diaries for 1847–1900 to the Rumyantsev Museum in Moscow, and the originals of the diaries for the past ten years were in a Moscow bank in the possession of A. B. Goldenweiser. However, Chertkov had copies of these diaries and Sofya Andreyevna wanted them safely out of his hands. After writing this letter Sasha was sent to Chertkov to collect the copies and bring them back for her mother. They were then to be put in a Tula bank under the care of Mikhail Sukhotin. After getting her way, Sofya Andreyevna, who had been highly distraught, temporarily calmed down.

586. To Countess S. A. Tolstaya

3. If you are troubled by the thought that my diaries, or those passages in which I wrote, under the impression of the moment, about our disagreements and conflicts—that those passages might be used by future biographers ill-disposed towards you, then, not to mention the fact that such expressions of temporary feelings both in my diaries and in yours can in no way give a correct idea of our true relations, I am glad of the opportunity, if you are afraid of this, to express in my diary, or simply in this letter, my attitude towards you and my appreciation of your life.

My attitude towards you and my appreciation of you are as follows: just as I loved you when you were young, so I have never ceased to love you and still love you despite the various causes of coolness between us. The causes of this coolness were (I don't mention the cessation of conjugal relations—such a cessation could only remove deceptive expressions of what is not true love)—the causes were, firstly, my greater and greater alienation from the interests of worldly life and my revulsion towards them, whereas you didn't wish to and weren't able to part with them, not having in your soul those principles that led me to my convictions, which was very natural and for which I don't reproach you. That's the first thing. Secondly (forgive me if what I shall say is disagreeable to you, but what is now happening between us is so important that we shouldn't be afraid to express and to hear the whole truth)—secondly, your character over these last years has become more and more irritable, despotic and uncontrollable. The manifestations of these traits of character couldn't help but cool, not my feeling itself, but the expression of it. That's the second thing. Thirdly, the chief cause was that fateful one for which neither you nor I are to blame—namely our completely contrary understanding of the meaning and purpose of life. Everything about our understanding of life was completely contrary: our way of life, our attitude to people and our means of livelihood—property—which I considered a sin and you—a necessary condition of life. In our way of life, so as not to part from you, I submitted to conditions of life which were painful for me, but you took this as a concession to your views, and the misunderstanding between us grew greater and greater. There were other causes of coolness as well, for which we were both to blame, but I won't mention them because they are not to the point. The point is that despite all our past misunderstandings, I have never ceased to love you and appreciate you.

My appreciation of your life with me is as follows: I, a dissolute and profoundly depraved man sexually, and no longer in the prime of youth, married you, a pure, good and intelligent girl of 18, and despite my filthy and depraved past, you have lived with me and loved me for nearly 50 years, living a difficult and laborious life, bearing children, nursing them, bringing them up, looking after them and after me, without yielding to the temptations which might so easily have overtaken any woman in your position, strong, healthy and beautiful. But you have lived in such a way that I have nothing to reproach you with. As for the fact that you didn't follow me in my exceptional spiritual journey, I cannot and do not reproach you, because the spiritual life of every man is a secret between that man and God, and

586. To Countess S. A. Tolstaya

other people shouldn't demand anything of him. And if I did demand anything of you, I was wrong and was to blame for it.

This is a true description of my attitude to you and my appreciation of you. As for what may turn up in the diaries, I only know that nothing harsh or contrary to what I write now will be found there.

So this is the third point, namely what may, but oughtn't to trouble you about the diaries.

Fourthly, if my relations with Chertkov at this time are painful for you, I'm prepared not to see him, although I must say that this would be not so much unpleasant for me as for him, knowing how painful it would be for him. But if you wish, I'll do so.

Now, fifthly, if you don't accept these conditions of mine for a good and peaceful life, I shall take back my promise not to leave you. I shall go away. I'll certainly not go to Chertkov. I shall even make it an absolute condition that he shouldn't come to live near me, but I'll certainly go away, because it's impossible to go on living as we are doing now.

I could continue to live like this if I could endure your sufferings calmly, but I can't. Yesterday you went away, agitated and suffering. I wanted to go to sleep, but I began not so much to think of you as to feel you, and I couldn't sleep, but listened till one o'clock, then two—and I woke up again and listened and then I saw you in a dream, or almost a dream. Try to think calmly, dearest, try to listen to your heart, try to feel, and you will decide everything in the right way. As for myself, I must say that I have decided everything for my part in such a way that *I cannot, cannot* decide otherwise. Stop torturing yourself, darling—not others, but yourself—because you are suffering a hundred times worse than anyone. That's all.

Lev Tolstoy

587. To AYLMER MAUDE

Yasnaya Polyana, 23 July 1910

Mr Maude,

Sofya Andreyevna read me a passage from your biography about some words of my late daughter Masha who expressed to you her unkind feeling towards Chertkov and, apparently, her astonishment at my liking for this man.[1] I think that such a definition of her attitude to Chertkov is completely wrong, since, if there may have been, and actually were, misunderstandings between them at times, her attitude in general towards my best friend was always one of love and respect,

---

[587] 1. Volume II of Aylmer Maude's *The Life of Tolstoy* (*Later Years*, London, 1910) had just been published and Sofya Andreyevna had been reading extracts from it to Tolstoy. In fact the first edition of the biography was more restrained in its criticisms of Chertkov than the revised edition published in 1930. Maude's more hostile attitude here was due not only to freedom from Tolstoy's surveillance of the finished product, but also to the prolonged and unpleasant wranglings over Tolstoy's papers which took place after Tolstoy's death and in which Chertkov played a prominent part.

and it could not have been otherwise with a daughter who loved me dearly, towards the man who has been for many years my best helper and friend. And so I would ask you to exclude this passage from your biography.

Generally speaking, I very much regret your unkind attitude towards Chertkov, since such an attitude is unnatural and wrong for a biographer, and is bound to mislead the reader.

I shall be very grateful if you will pay attention to these remarks of mine.

Lev Tolstoy

588. To V. G. CHERTKOV

Yasnaya Polyana, 31 July 1910

I've signed the statement.[1] Everything you are doing is good and I feel only gratitude towards you. Sofya Andreyevna is very calm and kindly, and I'm afraid of anything that might upset this condition and so I'm doing nothing for the time being about resuming meetings with you. We'll wait, and if only we ourselves (I) don't spoil things, everything will be as it should be, i.e. well.

I'm sure we shall see each other soon.

L. Tolstoy

589. To V. G. CHERTKOV

Yasnaya Polyana, 2 August 1910

I spoke to Posha[1] yesterday, and he told me very rightly that I was to blame for having made the will secretly. I ought either to have done it openly and told those whom it concerned, or else left everything as it was *and done nothing*. He is absolutely right, I behaved badly and now I regret it. It was bad that I acted secretly, assuming bad things about my heirs and, most important, I undoubtedly acted badly in making use of the institutions of the government I renounce in drawing up the will properly. Now I see clearly that only I myself am to blame for all that is going on now. I ought to have left everything as it was and done nothing. And the general availability of my writings will hardly compensate for the lack of trust in them, which the inconsistency of my behaviour is bound to cause.

It's easier for me to know that I only have myself to blame for behaving badly. But I think meanwhile that the best thing now is still to do nothing, although it's hard.

This is what I noted to myself this morning, 2 August, and I'm telling you, dear Vladimir Grigoryevich, in the knowledge that everything that's important to me is important to you.

L.T.

[588] 1. The statement, written by Chertkov and signed by Tolstoy, which was added to his will, clarifying points of detail to do with the disposition of his writings after his death.
[589] 1. Biryukov.

590. To V. G. CHERTKOV

Yasnaya Polyana, 12 August 1910

I'm writing on loose sheets, because I'm writing on a walk in the woods. Yesterday evening and this morning I've been thinking about your letter of yesterday.[1] Your letter aroused two main feelings in me: disgust at the manifestations of gross cupidity and insensibility which I either hadn't seen, or had seen and forgotten; and sorrow and repentance for having caused you pain by my letter in which I expressed regret for what had happened.[2] The conclusion I drew from your letter is that Pavel Ivanovich[3] was wrong, and I was also wrong to agree with him, and that I fully approve of your activity but am nevertheless dissatisfied with my own: I feel I could have acted better, although I don't know how. But now I don't repent of what I did, i.e. of having written the will which was written, and I can only be grateful to you for the part you took in this matter.

I'll tell Tanya about it all today, and it will give me great pleasure.

Lev Tolstoy

591. To V. G. CHERTKOV

Yasnaya Polyana, 14 August 1910

Thank you, dear friend, for your letter.[1] I'm moved and touched by this concern of yours just for me. When I was out walking today I thought up a note which I could write to Sofya Andreyevna, instead of talking to her, to say that I was going to see you to say goodbye, but when I got back home I saw her in such a pathetic, angry, but obviously sick and suffering condition, that I decided to take advantage of your suggestion and not try to obtain her consent to visit you. Even a visit by me alone can hardly take place now (if I go, it will be with Sofya Andreyevna, as Tanya suggests).

I know that today's particularly sick condition might seem feigned and deliberately put on (it is partly), but the main thing is that it is an illness all the same, a quite obvious illness, which deprives her of will-power and control over herself. If I say that she herself is to blame for this weakness of will, this indulgence in egoism, which began a long time ago, the blame goes back a long time and belongs to the past, but now she is completely irresponsible, and one can feel nothing but pity for her, and I at least cannot, I simply *cannot contrecarrer* her, and thereby

---

[590] 1. Chertkov had written a letter on 11 August which outlined the whole story of the difficulties over the will and stressed the necessity for making one, no matter how unpleasant to Tolstoy.

2. Letter 589.   3. Biryukov.

[591] 1. A conciliatory letter from Chertkov on 13 August, in which he said that it was perhaps better for Tolstoy not to come to Telyatinki to say goodbye (Tolstoy had promised his wife not to see Chertkov for the time being) because it would upset his wife and perhaps prevent Tolstoy from making a projected visit to Tanya and Mikhail Sukhotin at Kochety.

obviously increase her sufferings. I don't believe that a firm insistence on my demands, contrary to her wishes, would be of any help to her, and if I did believe it, I still couldn't do it. The main thing is that apart from the fact that I think I ought to act in this way, I know from experience that when I insist, it's painful for me, but when I give way, I'm not only relieved but even glad.

I'm relieved because she still more or less tries to hold herself in check with me, but it is difficult for poor Sasha, young and hot-tempered, whom she constantly and cruelly attacks with that special venom peculiar to people in her condition. And Sasha considers herself insulted and tries to get even with her, and that makes it particularly difficult for her.

I'm very, very sorry that so far I haven't managed to see you and Galya and Lizaveta Ivanovna,[2] whom I particularly wanted to see, especially since this will probably be the last chance to see her. Give her my thanks for her kind attitude towards me and my family.

I've been unwell these last few days, but I'm much better today, and I'm particularly glad of it today, because there are fewer risks of doing or saying something bad when I feel physically fresh.

I still do nothing except letters, but I very much want to write, and to write something artistic. And when I think about it, I want to even more, because I know it will give you pleasure. Perhaps a real egg will emerge, but if it's addled, it can't be helped.

I was just meaning to write to dear Galya to say that I unfortunately saw signs in her letter of unwonted irritation when my daughters told me that she had got over it. Give her my love.

L.T.

Let's write to each other more often.

592. To V. G. CHERTKOV

Kochety, 25 August 1910

[14 lines omitted]...As for myself, I can say that I'm very well here. Even my health, on which spiritual anxieties have also had their effect, is much better. I try to be as gentle and firm as possible towards Sofya Andreyevna and, I think, I am more or less achieving my object—her peace and quiet—although the main point—her attitude to you—remains the same. She doesn't express it to me. I know this seems strange to you, but I'm very often terribly sorry for her. When you think what it's like for her alone at nights, more than half of which she spends awake with the vague, but painful awareness that she isn't loved and is a burden to everyone except the children, you can't help being sorry for her.

I'm not writing anything new. I jot down in my diary thoughts and even plans for imaginary works of art, but all the mornings go on correspondence, and

---

2. Chertkov's wife and mother, respectively.

592. To V. G. Chertkov

recently on correcting Ivan Ivanovich's proofs.[1] I like some of the booklets very much.

My daughters love me, and I them, with a precious love—a bit exclusive, but not too much so, and I'm very glad to be with them. I'm oppressed as always, and especially here, by the luxury of life amidst the poverty of the people. The peasants here say: in heaven is the Kingdom of the Lord, and on earth the kingdom of the lords. And the luxury here is particularly great, and this saying sticks in my head and increases my awareness of the shameful nature of my life.

Well, that's all about myself, dear old fellow. Regards to Galya, Dimochka and all your and our friends.

I'm going to have dinner.

L.T.

593. To MOHANDAS GANDHI

Kochety, 7 September 1910

I got your journal *Indian Opinion*, and was glad to learn all that was written there about those who practise non-resistance.[1] I also wanted to tell you the thoughts that reading it aroused in me.

The longer I live, and especially now when I feel keenly the nearness of death, I want to tell others what I feel so particularly keenly about, and what in my opinion is of enormous importance, namely what is called non-resistance, but what is essentially nothing other than the teaching of love undistorted by false interpretations. The fact that love, i.e. the striving of human souls towards unity and the activity resulting from such striving, is the highest and only law of human life is felt and known by every person in the depth of his soul (as we see most clearly of all with children)—known by him until he is ensnared by the false teachings of the world. This law has been proclaimed by all the world's sages, Indian, Chinese, Jewish, Greek and Roman. I think it has been expressed most clearly of all by Christ who even said frankly that on this alone hang all the Law and the prophets. Furthermore, foreseeing the distortion to which this law is subject or may be subject, he pointed frankly to the danger of its distortion which comes naturally to people who live by worldly interests, namely the danger of allowing themselves to defend these interests by force, i.e. as he said, returning blow for blow, taking back by force objects which have been appropriated, etc., etc. He knows, as every reasonable person is bound to know, that the use of violence is incompatible with love as the basic law of life, that once violence is tolerated in any cases whatsoever, the inadequacy of the law of love is recognised and therefore the law itself is

---

[592] 1. Tolstoy's *The Path of Life*, a collection of thoughts which Ivan Ivanovich Gorbunov-Posadov was seeing through the press for publication by *The Intermediary*. The thoughts are grouped in sections which Tolstoy terms 'booklets'.

[593] 1. This letter was published in Gandhi's Transvaal newspaper *Indian Opinion* on 26 November 1910 (English translation by Chertkov).

593. To Mohandas Gandhi

repudiated. The whole of Christian civilisation, so brilliant on the surface, grew up on this obvious, strange, sometimes conscious but for the most part unconscious misunderstanding and contradiction.

Essentially speaking, once resistance was tolerated, side by side with love, there no longer was or could be love as a law of life, and there was no law of love except violence, i.e. the power of the stronger. For 19 centuries Christian mankind has lived in this way. True, people at all times have been guided by violence alone in organising their lives. The difference between the lives of Christian peoples and all others is merely the fact that in the Christian world, the law of love was expressed so clearly and definitely, as it hasn't been expressed in any other religious teaching, and that people in the Christian world solemnly accepted this law but at the same time allowed themselves to use violence and built their lives on violence. And so the whole life of Christian peoples is an outright contradiction between what they profess and what they build their lives on; a contradiction between love, recognised as the law of life, and violence recognised even as a necessity in various forms such as the power of rulers, courts and armies—recognised and extolled. This contradiction kept growing with the advancement of the peoples of the Christian world and has recently reached the ultimate degree. The question now obviously amounts to one of two things—either we recognise that we don't recognise any religious and moral teaching and are guided in the organisation of our lives only by the power of the strong, or that all our taxes collected by force, our judicial and police institutions and above all our armies must be abolished.

This spring, at a scripture examination at one of the women's institutes in Moscow, the scripture teacher, and then a bishop who was present, asked the girls about the commandments and particularly the sixth one. When the correct answer was given about the commandment, the bishop usually asked a further question: is killing always and in all cases forbidden by the scriptures, and the unfortunate girls, corrupted by their mentors, had to answer and did answer—not always; that killing is permitted in war and in executing criminals. However, when one of these unfortunate girls (what I am telling you is not fiction but a fact, reported to me by an eyewitness), after giving her answer, was asked the usual question: is killing always sinful? She blushed nervously and gave the firm answer that it always was, and she answered all the bishop's usual sophisms with the firm conviction that killing was always forbidden, that killing was forbidden even in the Old Testament and that not only was killing forbidden by Christ but also any evil against one's brother. And despite all his grandeur and art of eloquence, the bishop fell silent and the girl went away victorious.

Yes, we may talk in our papers about the successes of aviation, about complicated diplomatic relations, about various clubs, discoveries, alliances of every kind, or so-called works of art, and still pass over in silence what this girl said; but we oughtn't to do so, because every person in the Christian world feels it—feels it more or less vaguely, but still feels it. Socialism, communism, anarchism, the Salvation Army, the growth of crime, unemployment among the population, the growth of the insane luxury of the rich and the destitution of the poor, the terrible growth

593. To Mohandas Gandhi

in the number of suicides—all these things are signs of this internal contradiction which ought to and must be solved—and, of course, solved in the sense of recognising the law of love and renouncing all violence. And so your work in the Transvaal, at the other end of the world as it seems to us, is the most central and most important of all tasks now being done in the world, and not only Christian peoples, but peoples of the whole world will inevitably take part in it. I think you will be pleased to know that this work is also rapidly developing in Russia in the form of refusals to do military service, of which there are more and more every year. However insignificant may be the number of your people who practise non-resistance and of our people in Russia who refuse military service, both can boldly say that God is with them. And God is more powerful than men.

In recognising Christianity, even in the distorted form in which it is professed among Christian peoples, and in recognising at the same time the necessity for armies and arms to kill in wars on the most enormous scale, there is such an obvious and crying contradiction that sooner or later, probably very soon, it will be exposed and will put an end either to the acceptance of the Christian religion which is necessary to maintain power, or to the existence of an army and any violence supported by it, which is no less necessary to maintain power. This contradiction is felt by all governments, your British as well as our Russian, and from a natural feeling of self-preservation is prosecuted more vigorously than any other anti-government activity, as we see in Russia and as is seen from the articles in your journals. Governments know where their main danger lies, and in this question are keeping a careful eye not only on their own interests, but on the question: to be or not to be.

With the utmost respect,
Leo Tolstoy[2]

594. To V. G. CHERTKOV

Yasnaya Polyana, 25 September 1910

Your letter, my dear Vladimir Grigoryevich, made a very painful impression on me.[1] I fully agree with what you write that I made a mistake and ought to correct it, but the point is that all this appears to me in a form that is far more complicated and difficult to resolve than it can possibly appear even to a very close friend like you. I must decide the question alone, in my own soul, before God, and I am trying to do so, and anybody else's concern makes this task more difficult. I was hurt by your letter; I felt I was being torn in two directions, probably because, rightly or wrongly, I felt a personal note in your letter. If you wish to do good to me—and I know you wish to with all your soul—please let us say no more about this letter and let us *for the time being* correspond as before, as though it had never existed,

2. Signed in English in the original.

[594] 1. Chertkov's letter of 24 September 1910, in which he criticised Tolstoy for allowing his wife to interfere with relations between the two men.

about my ordeal and about our common spiritual and practical—especially spiritual—affairs...[14 lines omitted]

595. To T. L. SUKHOTINA

Yasnaya Polyana, 12 October 1910

Here I am writing to you, Tanichka dear. And how my conscience troubles me for not having written before. Are things all right at home? I hope so. I can't boast about things here: everything is just as difficult. It's nothing particular, but every day there are reproaches and tears. Yesterday and today have been particularly bad. It's the 12th of the month and 12 o'clock at night. There has just been talk and threats about a will given to Chertkov which, she says, she found out about from somewhere. I said nothing and we parted. This morning I thought I would announce that I was going off to Kochety, and would go. But then I changed my mind. Yes, it's strange; you who love me must wish me not to come to you. I hope I shan't come. Otherwise all is well, although I can't boast about my work.[1] And so much the better. I've dirtied enough paper already. Among my visitors recently was Nazhivin whom I like. I'm expecting Ivan Ivanovich.[2] Sofya Andreyevna has just interrupted me to ask me to read out extracts from my diaries when I was in love with her. There were tears again and then she came back just now, and again there were tears and requests not to write to you about her. Greetings to Misha, Tanichka and all the family.

Your father,
L.T.

596. To A. K. CHERTKOVA

Yasnaya Polyana, 23 October 1910

Thank you, my dear Galya, for Gusev's letter.[1] I've just read it and was delighted. What a clever man. What intelligence and what a heart! I always feel this heart of his in all his letters. A strange coincidence has happened. I—having forgotten everything—wanted to recall Dostoyevsky, whom I had also forgotten, and I started to read *The Brothers Karamazov* (I was told it was very good). I began to read it and I can't get over my dislike of its anti-artistic nature, its frivolity, affectation, and unseemly attitude to important subjects.[2] And now Nikolay Nikolayevich writes something which explains it all to me.

[595] 1. Tolstoy was writing an article *On Socialism*.
2. Gorbunov-Posadov.

[596] 1. Gusev had written to Anna Chertkova expressing his disapproval of Dostoyevsky's *A Writer's Diary* and his support for the Russo-Turkish war, as a 'sacred cause'. He was also critical of Dostoyevsky's review of *Anna Karenina* and his alleged distortion of the religious beliefs of the peasantry.
2. Tolstoy also said some very positive things about the novel in his notebooks and diaries, and it was one of the books which he asked to be sent on to him after he left home for good.

596. To A. K. Chertkova

You can't imagine how good for the soul it is to forget everything, as I have done. God grant that you may learn the blessing of oblivion. How glad one is to take advantage of what has been done in the past but without remembering it, to transfer all the force of one's life to the present.

I congratulate you and Dima on the addition of a year. God grant that you may both know the joy of old age. I thank you for your love and indulgence towards me, which I need very much.

L.T.

597. To M. P. NOVIKOV

Yasnaya Polyana, 24 October 1910

Mikhail Petrovich,

In connection with what I said to you before you left, I'm turning to you again with the following request:[1] if it should actually happen that I were to come to you, would you be able to find me a little hut in your village, even a very small one, as long as it's warm and on its own—so that I should only have to inconvenience you and your family for a very short time? I'm also letting you know that if I should have to telegraph you, I shall do so not in my own name, but in that of T. Nikolayev.

I look forward to your reply and press your hand in friendship.

Don't forget that all this must be known to nobody but yourself.

L.T.

598. To COUNTESS S. A. TOLSTAYA

Yasnaya Polyana, 28 October 1910

My departure will distress you.[1] I'm sorry about this, but do understand and believe that I couldn't do otherwise. My position in the house is becoming, or has become unbearable. Apart from everything else, I can't live any longer in these conditions of luxury in which I have been living, and I'm doing what old men of my age

[597] 1. Novikov had recently visited Yasnaya Polyana and Tolstoy had told him how much he wanted to leave home and live somewhere quietly and simply. Novikov had tried to dissuade him.

[598] 1. During the night of 27-8 October Tolstoy was awakened at 3 a.m. by the sound of Sofya Andreyevna in his study, going through his personal papers. This was not the first time it had happened, but this time it disturbed him so much that he got out of bed, wrote this letter to Sofya Andreyevna and prepared to leave, having first wakened Dushan Makovitsky and Tolstoy's daughter Sasha. They packed his things, ordered a carriage to take Tolstoy and Dushan Makovitsky to the station, and left—Tolstoy fearful that his wife would wake up and there would be another terrible scene. Sasha was told to remain behind to give the news to her mother, try to reconcile her to the situation, and report to her father. She alone among those in the house knew her father's destination. Sofya Andreyevna did not wake up until 11 a.m. and Sasha handed her this letter then.

commonly do: leaving this worldly life in order to live the last days of my life in peace and solitude.

Please understand this and don't come after me, even if you find out where I am. Your coming would only make your position and mine worse and wouldn't alter my decision. I thank you for your honourable 48 years of life with me, and I beg you to forgive me for everything for which I am to blame towards you, just as I forgive you with all my soul for everything for which you may have been to blame towards me. I advise you to reconcile yourself to this new situation which my departure puts you in, and to have no unkind feelings towards me. If you want to let me know anything, tell Sasha; she will know where I am and will send on what is necessary; but she can't tell you where I am because I have made her promise not to tell anyone.

Lev Tolstoy

599. To A. L. TOLSTAYA

Alexandra Lvovna Tolstaya (b. 1884), Tolstoy's youngest daughter. Like Marya she was a close friend of her father's, and like Marya she was usually inclined to take his side in domestic disputes, to her mother's chagrin. It was she who accompanied him on his last journey, and she was with him when he died. After his death she continued to teach at the Yasnaya Polyana school. Her experiences in Russia after the Bolshevik Revolution are recounted in her book *I Worked for the Soviet*, 1934. She is also the author of *The Tragedy of Tolstoy* (translated by E. Varneck, 1934) and *My Father*, published in Russian by the Chekhov Publishing House in New York in 1953. After first emigrating to Japan, she eventually settled in America, where she is at present President of the Tolstoy Foundation which has proved among other things an invaluable source of help to Russian refugees.

Shchokino, 28 October 1910
6 a.m.

Arrived safely. We'll probably go to Optina.[1] Read my letters. Tell Chertkov that if by the end of a week, by the 4th, I haven't revoked it, he should send my statement to the papers.[2] Please, darling, as soon as you know where I am—and you'll know this very soon—tell me about everything: how the news about my departure was received and everything else, the more detail the better.

[599] 1. When Tolstoy left home, he intended to go first of all to visit his sister Marya in the Shamordino Convent, and he and Dushan Makovitsky went to the nearest railway station, Shchokino, to catch an early train. They arrived at the station at about 6 a.m. when Tolstoy wrote this note to Sasha and sent it back to Yasnaya Polyana with the coachman who had driven them to the station. In the meantime, he had decided to stop briefly at the Optina Monastery which was near the Convent.

2. A statement, prompted by lucrative offers to his wife from private publishers, reaffirming that all he had written since 1881 was public property.

600. To A. L. TOLSTAYA

Kozelsk,[1] 28 October 1910
7.30 p.m.

We've arrived safely, Sasha darling—I only hope that things aren't too bad with you. It's now half past seven. We'll spend the night here and go on to Shamordino tomorrow, if we're still alive. I try to be calm, though I must admit that I feel the same agitation I always feel when anticipating anything difficult, but I don't feel the shame, the embarrassment or the lack of freedom which I always felt at home. We had to travel 3rd class from Gorbachovo; it was uncomfortable, but mentally very agreeable and instructive. We had a good meal on the journey and at Belyov, and we're now going to have a drink of tea and a sleep, or try to. I'm hardly tired at all, even less so than usual. I won't decide anything about you until I get news from you. Write to Shamordino and send telegrams there too if there's anything urgent. Tell Batya[2] to write, and tell him I read the passage marked in his article, but in a hurry, and would like to read it again—let him send it if he will. Tell Varya[3] that I thank her as always for her love for you, and I beg and hope that she will look after you and restrain your impulses.[4] Please darling—few words, but gentle and firm ones.

Send me or bring me the thing for filling my pen (we've taken the ink), and the books I've begun—Montaigne, Nikolayev, the 2nd volume of Dostoyevsky and *Une Vie*.[5]

Read all my letters and send on the necessary ones to: Podborki, Shamordino.

Tell Vladimir Grigoryevich that I'm very glad and very afraid about what I've done. I'll try and write down the subjects of my dreams and the stories that are on the tip of my pen. I consider it better for the time being to refrain from seeing him. He will understand me, as always.

Goodbye, darling; I kiss you, despite your runny nose.

L.T.

Send me as well my small scissors, pencils and dressing gown.

601. To A. L. TOLSTAYA

Optina Monastery, 29 October 1910

Sergeyenko[1] will tell you everything about me, my dear Sasha. It's difficult. I can't

---

[600] 1. Kozelsk, the nearest railway station to the Optina Monastery.
2. Chertkov.
3. V. M. Feokritova, a copyist at Yasnaya Polyana and a friend of Sasha's.
4. I.e. when Alexandra is talking to her mother.
5. Montaigne's *Essais*, P. P. Nikolayev's *The Concept of God as the Perfect Foundation of Life*, Dostoyevsky's *The Brothers Karamazov* and Maupassant's *Une Vie*.

[601] 1. Alexey Petrovich Sergeyenko was Chertkov's secretary and was sent by him to Optina on 29 October to inform Tolstoy what was happening at Yasnaya. He returned to Chertkov later that day with this letter for Sasha.

help feeling a great burden. The main thing is not to sin, and that's the difficulty. Of course I've sinned and will sin, but may it be as little as possible!

And that's what I wish you above all, especially as I know that a terrible task has fallen to your lot, beyond your strength and youth. I haven't decided anything and don't want to. I try to do only what I can't help doing, and not to do what I can help. You'll see from my letter to Chertkov how I feel, if not how I regard things. I'm relying very much on the good influence of Tanya and Seryozha. The main thing is for them to understand and to try to make her understand that life with all this spying and eavesdropping, these everlasting reproaches, this ordering me about at her own sweet will, this everlasting checking up on me, this simulated hatred of the man who is closest and most necessary to me, this obvious hatred of me, but pretence of love—that such a life is not simply disagreeable to me but utterly impossible, and that if somebody has to drown himself, it is I and not she, and I only want one thing—to be free of her, and of the falsehood, pretence and malice which permeate her whole being. Of course they can't make her understand this, but they can make her understand that her whole behaviour towards me not only does not express love, but seems to have the obvious object of killing me, and that she will succeed in doing so, since I hope by the third attack which is threatening me, to release her and myself from that terrible situation we have been living in and to which I have no wish to return.

You see, darling, how ill I am: I don't conceal it from you.

I'm not sending for you yet, but I will once it's possible, and that very soon. Write and tell me how you are. I kiss you. We're going to Shamordino.

L. Tolstoy

Dushan never lets up, and I'm fine physically.

602. To COUNTESS S. A. TOLSTAYA

Shamordino, 30–1 October 1910

A meeting between us, and still more my return *now*, is completely impossible.[1] For you it would be harmful in the highest degree, so everyone says, and for me it would be terrible, since my present position, as a result of your excited state, irritability and morbid condition, is even worse than before, if that's possible. I advise you to reconcile yourself to what has happened, to adjust yourself to what is temporarily a new position, and above all to have treatment.

If you—I won't say love, but don't hate me—you must put yourself in my position at least a little bit. And if you were to do so, you would not only not condemn me, but would try to help me to find tranquillity and the possibility of some human life, help me by making an effort to control yourself, and you would

[602] 1. This letter is in reply to Sofya Andreyevna's letter of 28 October begging her husband to return to save her from suffering and suicide. Tolstoy had written a short and blunt reply on 30 October which he did not send, preferring a more sympathetic letter—which was to be his last to his wife before his death.

602. To Countess S. A. Tolstaya

not wish for my return just now. But your mood now, your wish for, and your attempts at suicide which show more than anything else your loss of self-control, make my return just now unthinkable for me. No one except yourself can save all those near to you, myself, and especially yourself, from the sufferings we are experiencing. Try to direct all your energy, not towards getting what you desire—my return now—but towards pacifying yourself and your soul, and then you will obtain what you desire.

I have spent two days at Shamordino and Optina, and am now leaving. I'll post this letter on the way. I'm not saying where I'm going because I consider separation to be essential both for you and for me. Don't think that I left you because I don't love you. I love you and pity you with all my soul, but I can't do otherwise than I am doing. Your letter, I know, was written sincerely, but it isn't in your power to do as you would wish. And it isn't a matter of fulfilling any wishes and demands of mine, but only of your mental stability and a calm, reasonable attitude to life. As long as that is lacking, life with you is unthinkable for me. To return to you when you are in this state would mean for me to renounce life, and I don't consider myself entitled to do so. Goodbye, Sonya dear; may God help you. Life isn't a joke and we have no right to throw it away at will, and to measure it by length of time is also unreasonable. Perhaps the months that are left to us to live are more important than all the years we have lived already, and we must live them well.

L.T.

603. To S. L. TOLSTOY and T. L. SUKHOTINA

Shamordino, 31 October 1910
4 a.m.

I thank you very much dear friends—true friends—Seryozha and Tanya for your sympathy in my grief and for your letters. I was particularly glad to get your letter, Seryozha: short, clear, interesting, and above all, kind. I can't help being afraid of everything and I can't rid myself of responsibility, but I couldn't manage to act otherwise. I wrote to Sasha, care of Chertkov, to say that I had asked him to let you—the children—know. Read the letter through. I wrote what I felt, and I feel that I can't act otherwise. I am writing to her—Mama. She will also show it to you. I wrote after careful thought, and I wrote all I could. We're leaving now, we still don't know where for...[1] We can always be reached through Chertkov.

Goodbye and thank you, dear children, and forgive me for being nevertheless the cause of your suffering—especially you, my dear darling Tanya. Well, that's all. I'm in a hurry to leave in case Mama should find me, as I'm afraid she might. A meeting with her now would be terrible. Goodbye, then.

L.N.

[603] 1. Some time after 3 a.m. on 31 October Tolstoy suddenly felt that he could not safely remain at Shamordino, so he roused Dushan Makovitsky and Sasha, who had now joined him, and prepared to leave. Before leaving, he wrote this and the following two letters.

604. To M. N. TOLSTAYA and Y. V. OBOLENSKAYA

Shamordino, 31 October 1910
4 a.m.

My dear Mashenka and Lizanka,[1]

Don't be surprised and don't condemn me for leaving without saying goodbye to you properly. I can't express to you both, especially you, Mashenka darling, my gratitude for your love and sympathy in my ordeal. Although I have always loved you, I don't remember feeling such tenderness for you as I have during these few days, and as I feel as I leave you. We're leaving unexpectedly, because I'm afraid Sofya Andreyevna will find me here. And there's only one train, before 8.00. Forgive me for taking your books and *A Circle of Reading*. I'm writing to Chertkov asking him to send you *A Circle of Reading* and *For Each Day*, but the books I'll return myself. I kiss you, dear friends, and love you with such joy.

L.T.

605. To V. G. CHERTKOV

Shamordino, 31 October 1910
4 a.m.

Thank you, dear friend, for your help, both from me and from Sasha. We're afraid of everything and have decided to leave at once, 4.00 a.m. on the 31st. Where for—we don't yet know. I'll let you know on the way. I rely on your help and I need a lot of help.

1. Please let those of my children who are in Yasnaya know about my letter to Sasha which was sent care of you. They can decide themselves whether to let Sofya Andreyevna know about the contents of the letter. I'm writing to Sofya Andreyevna, not refusing to return, but making it a first condition that she should work on herself and calm down.
2. Get all my correspondence and send it on.
3. Most important of all, keep a watch through somebody on what is happening at Yasnaya, and let me know if she finds out where I am, and inform me by telegram so that I can leave. A meeting with her would be terrible for me.
4. Trivialities: get Bulgakov to find my article on Socialism and send it to me, and send *A Circle of Reading* and *For Each Day* to my sister M. N. Tolstaya, a nun at Shamordino, Podborki station, Kaluga Province. That's the main thing. I'll write if I need anything else. May Galya love me as before. I value love particularly just now, and respond to it in a painfully touching way. Greetings to Dimochka and all friends, and thank dear Alyosha[1] for his efforts. How was his journey? Well, that's all.

L.T.

[604] 1. Tolstoy's sister and her daughter.
[605] 1. Sergeyenko.

605. To V. G. Chertkov

I'm adding a few more words in the train. We were afraid that Sofya Andreyevna might come to the monastery, and decided to leave at once. We're going south, probably to the Caucasus. Since it's all the same to me where I am, I decided to choose the south, particularly as Sasha is coughing. Of course we'll inform you of where we are. If you want to telegraph, do so to Rostov, to Frolova.[2] I would very much like to know what is happening there. If it's just as before, drop me a line.

L.T.

31st. 12 o'clock noon.
I'm well, and glad to be with Sasha.

606. To V. G. CHERTKOV

Astapovo, 1 November 1910

Took ill yesterday. Passengers saw me leave train in weak condition. Afraid of publicity. Better today. Going on. Take measures. Keep me informed.[1]

Nikolayev

607. To S. L. TOLSTOY and T. L. SUKHOTINA

Astapovo, 1 November 1910

My dear children, Seryozha and Tanya,[1]

I hope and trust that you won't reproach me for not having asked you to come. To have asked you and not Mama would have caused her great distress, as well as your other brothers. You will both understand that Chertkov, whom I did ask to come, occupies a special position in relation to me. He has devoted his whole life to the service of the cause which I have also served for the last 40 years of my life. It's not so much that this cause is dear to me as that I recognise its importance—rightly or wrongly—for all people, including yourselves. I thank you for your kind relations towards me. I don't know whether I'm saying goodbye or not, but I felt the need to express what I have expressed. I also wanted to add some advice to you, Seryozha, that you should think about your own life, who you are, what you are, what is the meaning of a man's life and how every reasonable man should live it.

    2. I.e. Sasha. In order to keep Sofya Andreyevna off their trail, Tolstoy, Chertkov and Sasha had adopted the pseudonyms of Nikolayev, Batya and Frolova respectively.

[606] 1. At approximately 8 a.m. on 31 October Tolstoy boarded a train in Kozelsk with the three people accompanying him, intending to go south to the Caucasus: they purchased tickets to Rostov-on-Don. However, towards evening, between 4 p.m. and 5 p.m., Tolstoy began to shiver, and proved to have a high temperature. They decided to leave the train at the next station, which was Astapovo, about 140 miles south-east of Tula. The station master offered them space in his home at the station and Tolstoy was installed there. The next day he sent this telegram to Chertkov and also asked Sasha to send for him. Chertkov arrived at Astapovo at 9 a.m. on 2 November with Sergeyenko.

[607] 1. This last letter to Tolstoy's children was dictated to Sasha, as he was now too weak to write himself.

607. To S. L. Tolstoy and T. L. Sukhotina

The views you have acquired about Darwinism, evolution and the struggle for existence won't explain to you the meaning of your life and won't give you guidance in your actions, and a life without an explanation of its meaning and importance, and without the unfailing guidance that stems from it is a pitiful existence. Think about it. I say it, probably on the eve of my death, because I love you.

Goodbye; try to calm your mother, for whom I have the most genuine feeling of compassion and love.

Your loving father,
L. Tolstoy

608. To AYLMER MAUDE

[Original in English]

Astapovo, 3 November 1910

On my way to the place where I wished to be alone I was taken ill...[1]

[608] 1. Tolstoy's last letter, dictated to Chertkov and written in English, but unfinished owing to Tolstoy's extreme fatigue. It is a reply to a letter he received from Maude before his departure from Yasnaya, asking about Tolstoy's health, promising to send his new biography of Tolstoy, and asking what to do with fifty pounds remaining from the Dukhobor fund.

Tolstoy lost consciousness at about 5 a.m. on 7 November and died an hour later.

INDEX

I am most grateful to Mrs Sheila Bentley for compiling the index for me. It includes specific references to all Tolstoy's works and to his views on a number of important problems, but excludes items of purely biographical interest. Numbers in italics are page references to letters received. Personal titles and ranks have normally been omitted, except in the case of royalty. The references to *Yasnaya Polyana* are to the journal of that name, and not to Tolstoy's estate. R.F.C.

Aesop, 231, 245
Akhmatova, Yelizaveta Nikolayevna, *171*
Akhsharumov, Nikolay Dmitriyevich, 194
Aksakov, Ivan Sergeyevich, 91, 92, 175, 200–202, 349, 360
Aksakov, Konstantin Sergeyevich, 91, 92, 113
Aksakov, Sergey Timofeyevich, 91, 113, 114, 320, 586; *A Family Chronicle*, 92, 158; *Years of Childhood*, 92
Alexander I, Emperor, 157, 185, 188, 207, 217, 329, 615, 624, 651, 655
Alexander II, Emperor, 56, 58, 63, 84, 103, 160, 162, *163*, 200, 205–6, 232, 307, 333–4, 337, 340, 347, 351, 380, 389, 540, 543, 545
Alexander III, Emperor, 167, 337, *340*, 347, 348, 367, 397, 405, 467, 477–8, 499, 503–4, 511, 543, 545
Alexandrovka, 136
Alexeyev, Nikita Petrovich, 9, 15
Alexeyev, Pyotr Semyonovich, *On Drunkenness*, 436, 460
Alexeyev, Vasily Ivanovich, 310, 352, *353*, *359*, 397, *445*
Alexeyeva, Yelizaveta Alexandrovna, 352, 354, 359
Alfred, Duke of Edinburgh, 103, 267
Alipov, Alexander Yegorovich, *659*
Alma, Battle of the, 46–7
Alyokhin, Alexey Vasilyevich, 479
Alyokhin, Arkady Vasilyevich, 445, 448, *470*, 479
Alyokhin, Mitrofan Vasilyevich, 445, *536*
Amiel, Henri Frédéric, 500, 644
Andreas, Friedrich Carl, 583
Andreas-Salomé, Lou, 583
Andreyev, Leonid Nikolayevich, *608*, *646*, *680*; *Once Upon a Time There Lived*, 608;
The Red Laugh, 646; *The Seven Who Were Hanged*, 680
Anna Ioannovna, Empress, 333
Annenkov, Pavel Vasilyevich, 53, 61, 88, 90–91, *98*, 107, 111–12, 277, 280, 318
Annenkova, Leonila Fominichna, 509
Apraksins (family), 255
Arbuzov, Sergey Petrovich, 306
Archer, Herbert, 576, 579
Aristophanes, 206
Aristotle, 106, 428, 440, 449
Arnold, Matthew, 143, 373, 382; *Literature and Dogma*, 370
Arsenyev, Nikolay Vladimirovich (Shmigaro), 63, 68, 70–1, 73
Arsenyev, Vladimir Mikhaylovich, 63
Arsenyeva, Olga Vladimirovna, 63, 70, 77, 79–80, 87
Arsenyeva, Valeriya Vladimirovna, 55, *63*, *67*, *68*, *70*, *71*, *73*, *78*, *80*, *84*, *86*, 88, *89*, 161, 634
Arsenyeva, Yevgeniya Vladimirovna, 63, 70, 71, 74, 80, 86
Arsenyevs (family; 'the guests'), 83, 87–8
Artsimovich, Mikhail Viktorovich, *666*, 668–669
Artsimovich, Yekaterina Vasilyevna, 666, *667*, 669
Artsybashev, Mikhail Petrovich, 672, 685; *Sanin*, 672; *Blood*, 685; *Gololobov*, 685; *Laughter*, 685; *Rebellion*, 685
Aryan, The, 599
Astapovo, 515, 627, 716, 717
Athenaeum, The, 606
Aubert, Mlle, 552
Aulard, François, 494
Austerlitz, Battle of, 191, 194

719

Index

Averkiyev, Dmitry Vasilyevich, 278
Avseyenko, Vasily Grigoryevich, 299–300
Avvakum, Life of the Archpriest, 317

Babst, Ivan Kondratyevich, 117
Bagration, Pyotr Ivanovich, 11, 16
Bacon, Francis, *Novum Organum*, 664
Balaklava, Battle of, 42
Balatsky, Andrey Yakovlevich, 638–9
Ballou, Adin, 588, 658
Baratynsky, Yevgeny Abramovich, 300–1
Barclay, Robert, *An Apology for the True Christian Divinity*, 493
Barsheva, Olga Alexeyevna, *478*
Bartenev, Pyotr Ivanovich, *188*, *213*, *214*, *216*, *217*
Baryatinsky, Alexander Ivanovich, 16, 19
Baryatinsky, Alexander Petrovich, 317
Bashilov, Mikhail Sergeyevich, *203*, 206, *207*, *208*, *212*
Beaumarchais, Pierre Augustin Caron, 610
Bedales School, 619
Beethoven, Ludwig van, 58, 81, 106, 301, 436, 539, 564
Behrs, Alexander Andreyevich, 170, 176, *184*, 190, 269
Behrs, Andrey Yevstafyevich, 157, 165, 170, 176, 181, 185–8, 204–5, 207, 209, 215
Behrs, Lyubov Alexandrovna, 165, 170, 172, 187, 189–90, 574
Behrs, Pyotr Andreyevich, 170, 187, 189, 190, 259, 262–3, 278, 329, 444
Behrs, Sofya Andreyevna, *see* Tolstaya, S. A.
Behrs, Stepan Andreyevich, 170, 190, 234–6, 306, 312, 318, 324, 389, 427
Behrs, Tatyana Andreyevna, *see* Kuzminskaya, T. A.
Behrs, Vladimir Andreyevich, 170, 187, 190
Behrs, Vyacheslav Andreyevich, 170, 190
Behrs, Yelizaveta Andreyevna, 165, 168, *169*, 170, 185–6, 189; *Luther*, 170
Belinsky, Vissarion Grigoryevich, 51, 60, 90, 98, 155, 362, 364
Bell, The, 144–6, 158
Bellows, John, 493, *606*
Belyaev, Alexander Petrovich, 316–17
Béranger, Pierre Jean, 230, 298; *Le Bonheur*, 230
Béraud, Jean, 507
Berg, Fyodor Nikolayevich, *Memoirs of a Sevastopol Veteran*, 215
Berkeley, George, 448, 637
Berlin, Isaiah, 627

Berlioz, Hector, 301
Bernardin de St Pierre, Jean Henri, 412
Bervi, Vasily Vasilyevich, *In the Backwoods*, 59
Bessonov, Pyotr Alexeyevich, 240
Bestuzhev, Mikhail Alexandrovich, 317
Bestuzhev, Nikolay Alexandrovich, 317
Bibikov, Alexey Alexeyevich, 310, 352, 359, 366
Bibikov, Alexander Nikolayevich, 256, 358, 524
Bibikov, Vladimir Alexandrovich, 524
Bible, Scriptures etc., 159, 161, 413, 426, 481, 695; *Apocrypha*, 335; *New Testament*, 97, 124, 126, 161, 248, 319, 322, 338, 342, 345, 361–2, 397, 418–19, 421, 424, 440, 442, 485–486, 499, 512, 516, 523, 673; *Old Testament*, 248, 335, 357, 361, 440, 442, 485–6
Biryukov, Pavel Ivanovich, 412, *413*, 419, *427*, 429, 431, *435*, 443, 445, *447*, 551, 553–554, *571*, 580, *592*, *621*, *633*, 660, 683, 703–4; *Persecution of Christians in Russia in 1895*, 522
Biryukova, Pavla Nikolayevna (Pasha), 581, 592, 622, 634
Bismarck, Otto E. L. von, 211, 520
Björnson, Björnstjerne, 483; *The New System*, 482; *In God's Way*, 483
'Black Hundred' organisation, 524, 526
Boborykin, Pyotr Dmitriyevich, *196*; *The Forces of the Zemstvo*, 196; *Setting Forth*, 196
Bobrinskoy, Vladimir Alexeyevich, 91
Bobrinsky, Alexey Pavlovich, 294
Bobrishchev-Pushkin, Pavel Sergeyevich, 317
Bodyansky, Alexander Mikhaylovich, 592, 596, *675*, 685
Boer War, The, 580, 584–5
Bogdanovich, Modest Ivanovich, 331
Bogolyubov, *see* Yemelyanov, A. P.
Bogoyavlensky, Nikolay Yefimovich, 487
Boissier, Gaston, 606
Bondarev, Timofey Mikhaylovich, *518*
Books of the Week, 400, 470
Borel, Edouard, 470, 488
Borisov, Ivan Petrovich, 130–1, 138, 148, 180, 195, 205, 214, 231
Borodino, Battle of, 175, 215–16, 262, 329, 465, 633
Botkin, Vasily Petrovich, 61, 68, 88, *90*, *92*, *93*, *95*, 98, *100*, *102*, 107, *111*, *115*, *127*, 135, *153*, *154*, 195, 230, 302; 'The Poetry of A. A. Fet', 91

720

Index

Boulanger, Pavel Alexandrovich, 558, *562*, 600
Bouvier, Bernard, *648*
Boxer Rebellion, 580
Brahmanism, Brahmin, etc., 405, 424–5, 440, 496, 630, 638, 644
Braddon, Mary Elizabeth, 189; *Aurora Floyd*, 189; *John Marchmont's Legacy*, 189; *Lady Audley's Secret*, 189
Brotherhood Church, 534, 581
Brotherhood Community, 557
Brotherhood News-Sheet, 563
Brotherhood Publishing Company, 534
Brunetière, Ferdinand, 502
Brunhes, H. J., *Ruskin et la Bible*, 600–1
Buddha, Buddhism, 298, 310, 336, 401, 405, 424, 440, 442, 450, 486, 490, 496, 590, 599, 635, 638, 644, 698
Bulgakov, Valentin Fyodorovich, 368, 608, 697, 715
Bulgarin, Faddey Venediktovich, 137
Bulygin, Mikhail Vasilyevich, 479, 620
Bunin, Ivan Alexeyevich, *501*
Burnouf, Eugène, 290, 309
Butlerov, Alexander Mikhaylovich, 454–5
Buturlin, Alexander Sergeyevich, 639
Buyemsky, Nikolay Ivanovich, 9
byliny, 223, 244, 260, 485–6
Byron, George Gordon, 206

Campbell, Hamilton, *474*
Carlyle, Thomas, 648; *Sartor Resartus*, 307
Carnegie, Andrew, 588
Carpenter, Edward, 648, 682; *Civilisation: Its Cause and Cure*, 550, 648
Catherine II, Empress, 652, 671
Caucasus, Caucasian, etc., 1, 8, 9, 12–13, 16–17, 19, 23, 32–3, 36, 51, 55, 58, 61–2, 77, 84, 95, 99, 117, 125, 130, 269, 281, 292, 457, 491, 493, 522, 567–70, 623–4, 627–8, 634, 644, 716
Century Illustrated Monthly Magazine, The, 466, 467
Cervantes, Saavedra Miguel de, *Don Quixote*, 206, 412
Chaadayev, Pyotr Yakovlevich, *Philosophical Letters*, 654
Chamberlain, Joseph, 584
Chan, Chin-Tun, *652*
Channing, William Ellery, 588, 644, 689
Chechnya, Chechen, etc., 9, 17, 19, 21, 25
Chekhov, Anton Pavlovich, 497, 519, 647; *In the Ravine*, 586

Chelokayev, Nikolay Alexandrovich, *583*
Chénier, André, 95
Cherbuliez, Victor, *Prosper Randoce*, 259
Chernyayev, Mikhail Grigoryevich, 306
Chernyshevsky, Nikolay Gavrilovich, 30, 57, 59–61, 88, 90, *154*, 156, 364; *Cavaignac*, 118
Chertkov, Vladimir Grigoryevich, 2, 166–7, 337, *367*, *369*, *370*, *374*, *381*, *383*, *385*, 388, 390, *391*, *400*, *404*, 411, *412*, 413–14, 417, *420*, *430*, *438*, 442, *448*, 450, *451*, *458*, *461*, 472, *478*, 483, *510*, 512, *517*, 524, 534, *553*, *554*, *557*, *562*, 563, *565*, 571, *573*, *574*, *575*, *576*, 578–9, *590*–1, *597*, *598*, *605*, *606*–7, *620*, 621, *624*, *637*, *642*, 651, *661*, *684*, *686*, 691, *693*, 700, 702, *703*, *704*, *705*, 706, *708*, 709, 711–15, *715*, *716*, 717
Chertkova, Anna Konstantinovna (Galya), *née* Dieterichs, 402–3, 452, *709*
Chicherin, Boris Nikolayevich, 92, 124, *132*, *133*, *150*, *152*, 153, 310, *465*; 'From my Reminiscences: About the Diary of N. I. Krivtsov', 465; *Science and Religion*, 310; 'Le système des éléments chimiques', 465
Christ, Christian, Christianity, etc., 9, 121–2, 126, 132, 145–6, 166, 198, 223, 228, 251, 261, 265, 290, 296, 300, 309, 314, 322–3, 336, 338, 342–3, 345–8, 350, 354–5, 360–2, 371, 380–2, 384, 391, 401–2, 404–5, 407, 418, 428, 431, 440, 442, 444, 446, 449, 456–463, 468–9, 472, 474–5, 478–9, 482, 492–6, 498–9, 501–3, 506–8, 520–2, 532, 548, 565–568, 571, 575, 581, 584–5, 600–1, 617, 619, 635, 637–8, 653–4, 656, 663, 667, 671–3, 678, 683, 698, 706–8
'Christian Commonwealth' Community, 565–566, 578
Christian Science, 435
Cicero, 549, 644
Citizen, The, 237, 300, 303, 310
Clarion, The, 590
Clarke, Charles Allen, *640*; *The Effects of the Factory System*, 640–1
Cockerell, Sidney, *632*
Committee of the Union for the Mutual Aid of Russian Writers, *591*
Comte, Auguste, 401
Confucius, 401, 405, 439–40, 442, 486, 635, 653, 673
Contemporary, The, 30, 32–3, 35, 37–8, 51, 57, 59, 61–2, 78, 88, 90–2, 94, 98, 107, 112, 114, 117–19, *154*, 156, 389
Contemporary World, The, 672

721

Index

Cornfield, The, 574, 646
Coulanges, Fustel de, 606
Crank, The, 658, 663
Crimea, Crimean, etc., 19, 42–3, 47, 58, 232, 260, 337, 378, 382, 443, 508, 513, 562, 586, 597, 605, 615, 699
Crimean War, The, 16, 46, 52, 135, 138, 231–232, 306, 378, 690
Crosby, Ernest H., *511*, 565, 567, 632, *648*, *657*, 663; *Shakespeare's Attitude Towards the Working Classes*, 649; *Garrison: The Non-Resistant*, 657; *Tolstoy as Schoolmaster*, 658
Custine, Adolphe de, *La Russie en 1839*, 625, 652

Dahl, Vladimir Ivanovich, *Proverbs of the Russian People*, 307, 338
Daily Chronicle, The, 567
Damien, Father Joseph, 481
Daniel, C. W., *663*
Danilevsky, Nikolay Yakovlevich, 226, 244, 307
Dante Alighieri, *La Divina Commedia*, 666
Danube, 19, 39–41
Darwin, Charles, Darwinism, etc., 225, 242, 266, 284, 452, 717
Das, Tarakuatta, 691
Daudet, Alphonse, 96; *Le Petit Chose*, 259
Davidson, John Morrison, 515, *588*; *The Annals of Toil*, 588
Davydov, Alexey Ivanovich, 84, 124, 143, 150
Davydov, Nikolay Vasilyevich, 630
Dawn, The, 237, 242, 244
Day, The, 201
Decembrists, 99, 145–6, 311, 315–17, 324, 329, 331, 333, 465, 540, 584, 634, 641, 654, 675
Defoe, Daniel, *Robinson Crusoe*, 157
Degterenko, Grigory Petrovich, *622*
Delyanov, Ivan Davydovich, 540
Descartes, René, 284, 289, 426, 440, 647
Desjardins, Paul, 494
Dickens, Charles, 56, 86, 143, 400, 636–7, 652; *Bleak House*, 388; *David Copperfield*, 39, 485; *Little Dorrit*, 61, 400, 615; *Nicholas Nickleby*, 70; *Oliver Twist*, 388; *Our Mutual Friend*, 400; *A Tale of Two Cities*, 400
Diderot, Denis, 476; 'De l'interprétation de la nature', 476
Dieterichs, Anna Konstantinovna, *see* Chertkova, A. K.

Dieterichs, Olga Konstantinovna (m. A. L. Tolstoy), 524, 574, 583, 602–3, 639
Dmitriyev, Fyodor Mikhaylovich, 151
Dokshitsky, Moisey Mendelevich, *672*
Dolgorukov, Vasily Andreyevich, 58, 157, 163
Doré, Gustave, 463
Dostoyevsky, Fyodor Mikhaylovich, 154, 225–6, 237, 312, 338, 340, 347, 360, 363–4, 492, 495, 632–3; *The Brothers Karamazov*, 347, 382, 709, 712; *The Devils*, 354; *The Insulted and Injured*, 340; *Notes from the House of the Dead*, 155, 338, 340; *Notes from Underground*, 154; *A Writer's Diary*, 709
Drankov, Alexander Iosifovich, 633
Droz, Antoine-Gustave, 259, 377
Drozhzhin, Yevdokim Nikitich, 491, 501, 549
Drummond, Henry, *The Greatest Thing in the World*, 464
Druzhinin, Alexander Vasilyevich, 57, 59, *61*, 68, 78, 88, 90–1, 94, 98, 100, 107, 111–12, *124*, *129*; 'Count L. N. Tolstoy's Military Stories; M. Shchedrin's Provincial Sketches', 112; *Polinka Sachs*, 61, 485
Dukhobors, 414, 452, 457, 491, 493, 513, 522, 534, 544, 553, 557–8, 562, 568–70, 573–6, 578–81, 606, 615, 644, 648, 663, 675, 717
Dumas, Alexandre (fils), 496
Dumas, Alexandre (père), 324
Dunayev, Alexander Nikiforovich, *479*
Durnovo, Ivan Nikolayevich, 540
Duse, Eleonora, 553
Dyakov, Dmitry Alexeyevich, 16, 63, 143, 184, 187, 216, 301
Dyakov, Dmitry Dmitriyevich, 532

Eckermann, Johann, 481
Eichenbaum, Boris, 179, 232
Eichhoff, Theodor, 665
Eliot, George, 223, 486; *Felix Holt*, 377; *Scenes of Clerical Life*, 128
Elizabeth I, Empress, 333, 469, 652
Ellis, E. W., *662*
Emerson, Ralph Waldo, 588, 644, 673, 689
Engelhardt, Mikhail Alexandrovich, *360*
Epictetus, 440, 442, 486, 644
Ertel, Alexander Ivanovich, 414, 438, *449*
Esperanto, 446–7, 595–6
Euripides, 225

Family and School, The, 242
Family Evenings, 329
Feinermann, Isaac Borisovich, 385, 405, *489*

722

Feokritova, Varvara Mikhaylovna, 712
Fet, Afanasy Afanasyevich, 12, 102, 111, 116–118, 130–1, *135*, *141*, *148*, *152*, 153, 165, 175, *180*, *193*, *195*, 205, 207, 213, 220, 221, 224, 227, 229, 230, 246, 255, 277, *281*, 298, 300, *304*, 312, *316*, *319*, 326, 329, *331*, *333*, *334*, *335*, 339, 359, 452, 486, 550
Fet, Marya Petrovna (née Botkina), 117, 138, 148, 180, 193, 195, 206, 208, 214, 221, 225, 230, 231, 255, 277, 282, 298, 304, 319, 332, 334–5
Feuerbach, Ludwig, 382, 486
Fichte, Johann Gottlieb, 284, 431
Filosofova, Natalya Nikolayevna, 487
Filosofova, Sofya Nikolayevna (m. I. L. Tolstoy), 432, 437, 487, 552, 577, *618*
Flaubert, Gustave, 96; *La Légende de Saint Julien l'Hospitalier*, 305
Foreign newspapers, *567*
Fontenelle, Bernard le Bovier de, 311
Foss, Johann Friedrich, 231
Foundations, 357
Franklin, Benjamin, *Autobiography*, 412
Free Age Press, The, 368, 534, 578, 590
Free Thought, 414, 580
Free Word, The, 368, 571, 576, 580, 623, 637, 645
Freidank, Bruno, *Die Schrecken Civilisation*, 698
Frey, William, 385, *401*
Froebel, Julius, 56
Fruits of Philosophy, 598
Fyodorov, Nikolay Fyodorovich, 353–4

Gandhi, Mohandas, 627, *691*, *706*
Garnett, Edward, *587*
Garnett, Constance, 587–8
Garrison, William Lloyd (junior), 657
Garrison, William Lloyd (senior), 588, 657–8
Garshin, Vsevolod Mikhaylovich, 377
Gaskell, Elizabeth, *Life of Charlotte Brontë*, 103
Gaulois, 496
Gay, Nikolay Nikolayevich (junior) (Kolechka), 403, 414, 437, 445, *482*, 499, 504, 596, 673
Gay, Nikolay Nikolayevich (senior) *366*, *419*, *437*, 444, 460, 468–9, 473, *498*, *503*, 507–8, 633; *Christ in the Garden of Gethsemane*, 419; *The Crucifixion*, 498, 503; *The Heralds of the Resurrection*, 462; *Judas (Conscience, The Traitor)*, 499; *The Last Supper*, 366, 419, 444, 462; *Mercy*, 463; *The Verdict of the Sanhedrin*, 498; *What is Truth?*, 451, 460, 462, 467, 508
George, Henry, 509, 511–12, *536*, 616, 627, 656; *The Irish Land Question*, 512; *The Perplexed Philosopher*, 512; *Progress and Poverty*, 486; *Protection or Free Trade*, 512; *The Science of Political Economy*, 537
Getz, Faivel-Meyer Bentzelovich, *458*
Gibson, George Howard, 565; *The Social Need*, 566
Glebova, Alexandra Vladimirovna (m. M. L. Tolstoy), 590
Glinka, Mikhail Ivanovich, *A Life for the Tsar*, 189
Goethe, Johann Wolfgang von, 112, 206, 223–5, 232, 481, 654, 687; *Faust*, 118, 339; *Hermann und Dorothea*, 486; *Iphigenia*, 80; *Werther*, 82, 265
Gogol, Nikolay Vasilyevich, 60, 97–8, 137, 154, 224, 226, 243, 376, 396, 694; *Dead Souls*, 98, 485; *Nevsky Prospect*, 485; *The Overcoat*, 485; *Selected Passages from Correspondence with Friends*, 427–8; *The Two Ivans*, 485; *Viy*, 485
Goldenweiser, Alexander Borisovich, 639, 700
Goldsmith, Oliver, *The Vicar of Wakefield*, 412
Golitsyn, Grigory Sergeyevich, 569, 644
Golokhvastov, Pavel Dmitriyevich, *254*, *259*, *292*, 300, 312
Golovachov, Alexey Adrianovich, *Ten Years of Reforms*, 307
Goltsev, Viktor Alexandrovich, 473
Goncharenko, Yevtikhy Yegorovich, 652
Goncharov, Ivan Alexandrovich, 57, 68, 99, 112, 130, 461, 482; *Oblomov*, 112, 124; *An Ordinary Story*, 86
Gorbunov-Posadov, Ivan Ivanovich, 706, 709
Gorchakovs (family), 2, 8, 330
Gorchakov, Alexey Ivanovich, 8, 330
Gorchakov, Alexander Mikhaylovich, 58
Gorchakov, Alexander Nikolayevich, 330
Gorchakov, Mikhail Dmitriyevich, 40, 41, 45, 47, 50, 52
Gorchakov, Mikhail Nikolayevich, 330
Gorchakov, Nikolay Ivanovich, 330
Gorchakov, Sergey Dmitriyevich, 8, 38, 40
Gorchakov, Vasily Nikolayevich, 330
Gorchakova, Yekaterina Vasilyevna, 330–1
Gordon, Charles George, 481
Gorky, Maxim (A. M. Peshkov), *585*, 597, 647

Index

Gould, Jay, 588
Greeks, Greek, etc., 223, 230–1, 233, 235–6, 239, 246, 261, 335, 654, 665, 673, 706
Gribovsky, Vyacheslav Mikhaylovich, 381, 383, 404–5
Griboyedov, Alexander Sergeyevich, *The Misfortune of Being Clever*, 92, 203
Grigorovich, Dmitry Vasilyevich, 57, 62, 92, 117, 119, 241, 358, 412; *Cat and Mouse*, 117; *The Hapless Anton*, 485; *The Ploughman*, 57; *Relations in the Capital*, 91
Grigoryev, Apollon Alexandrovich, 68, 91, 130, 225–6, 238, 295, 297, 299; 'T. N. Granovsky and his Professorship in Moscow', 91
Grinyovka, 572
Grot, Nikolay Yakovlevich, *428*, 431, 476, 489, 565; 'On Free Will', 429
Grunsky, Karl, 515
Gurevich, Lyubov Yakovlevna, 514, 560
Gurieli, Yelena Konstantinovna, 583
Gusev, Nikolay Nikolayevich, 675, 709
Guyau, Marie Jean, *L'art au point de vue sociologique*, *Les problèmes de l'aesthétique contemporaine*, 502

Hadji Murat, 21, 628
Hansen, Peter Gottfriedovich, 451, *482*
Hapgood, Isabel Florence, 451, 460, 464
Hardy, Thomas, 682
Harper's Magazine, 587
Hauptmann, Gerhard, 682
Hawthorne, Nathaniel, 464
Haydn, Franz Joseph, 121, 301, 509
Hegel, Georg Wilhelm Friedrich, 226, 284–5, 381, 431; Hegelian, 272
Herald of Europe, The, 305, 408
Herodotus, 223, 236
Herron, George Davis, 565–7
Herzen, Alexander Ivanovich, 56, 94, 132, *143*, *146*, 158, 160–1, 225, 349, 356, 437, 465, 581, 652, 654, 659; *From the Other Shore*, 652; 'A Letter to the Emperor Alexander II', 465
Hinduism, 310, 561
Hofmann, Joseph, 553
Homer, 112, 223, 231, 260, 499; *The Iliad*, 106, 223, 486, 499; *The Odyssey*, 223, 231, 486
Horace, 208
Howells, William Dean, 464, 578; *The Rise of Silas Lapham*, 464; *The Undiscovered Country*, 464

Hugo, Victor, 206, 305, 632; *L'Abîme*, 305; *Les Misérables*, 223, 486; *Notre Dame de Paris*, 486
Hume, David, 430
Hunter, Robert, 632

Ibsen, Henrik, 483, 645; *Brand*, 483; *Hedda Gabler*, 482
Independent, The, 657
Indian Opinion, 691–2, 706
Inkerman Heights, Battle of, 44, 47
Intermediary, The, 337, 368, 377, 379, 381–2, 384–5, 387, 390, 400, 404, 408, 412, 414–15, 417–18, 420, 428, 435, 439, 450, 464, 469, 501, 514, 556, 600, 608, 634, 640, 658, 706
International Intermediary, The, 515
Islam, 457
Islavin, Konstantin Alexandrovich (Kostenka), 8, 69, 81
Islavin, Vladimir Alexandrovich, 110
Islavina, Lyubov Alexandrovna, *see* Behrs, L. A.
Islavins (family), 5, 165
Islenyev, Alexander Mikhaylovich, 5, 8, 165, 168, 189, 191
Iso-Abé, *645*
Ivakin, Ivan Mikhaylovich, 338
Ivanov, Alexander Andreyevich, *The Appearance of Christ to the People*, 462
Ivanov, Alexander Petrovich, 388, 563
Ivanov, Nikolay Nikitich, 413, 415, *438*; *Sin*, 413
Ivashov, Vasily Petrovich, 324

Jainism, 599
Jarnëfelt, Arvid, 515, *660*, 688
Jenken, Nataliya, 579
Jews, Judaism, 185, 223, 339, 382, 457–9, 463, 468, 489, 572, 627, 631, 635, 706
Journal de St Petersbourg, Le, 327

Kabir Panchis, 599
Kalmykova, Alexandra Mikhaylovna, 381, *539*
Kant, Emmanuel, 221, 223, 283–4, 287, 431, 440, 449, 492, 641, 644, 647, 652, 665, 673, 689; *Critique of Practical Reason*, 309, 429–430; *Critique of Pure Reason*, 283, 430–1
Kantor, William L. (Chaim-Wolf Kantor), *456*
Karakozov, Dmitry Vladimirovich, 205
Karamzin, Nikolay Mikhaylovich, 238, 325, 443; *Poor Liza*, 244

724

Index

Karl Ivanovich, 202
Katkov, Mikhail Nikiforovich, 91, 117, 128, 153, *155*, *185*, 187, 189, *190*, 198, 206, 225, 259, 263, 266, 272, *274*, 301, 402
Kavelin, Konstantin Dmitriyevich, 117, 325
Kazan, University of, 1, 4, 12, 59
Keller, Gustav, 149
Kennan, George, 460, *466*, 482
Kenworthy, John Coleman, 515, 522, *533*, 557, 589
Khilkov, Dmitry Alexandrovich, *457*, *490*, *491*, *492*, *493*, 499, 501, *506*, *515*, 553, 557
Khilkovsky, 9
Kholevinskaya, Marya Mikhaylovna, *535*
Khomyakov, Alexey Stepanovich, 201
Kierkegaard, Sören Aaby, 483
Kiesewetter, Johann Gottfried Karl Christian, 93, 95
Kiev Monastery, 223
Kiev Thought, 697
Kipling, Rudyard, 682
Kireyevsky, Nikolay Vasilyevich, 66, 73
Kirillov, Ivan, *Statistics*, 254
Kleen, Victor-Hector de, 53, 181
Knight, William Angus, *The Philosophy of the Beautiful*, 502
Kochety, 589, 704, 709
Kokhanovskaya, Nadezhda Stepanovna, 125
Kokorev, Vasily Alexandrovich, 117–18
Kolbasin, Dmitry Yakovlevich, *94*, 107, 108
Koloshin, Dmitry Pavlovich, 268
Koloshin, Pavel Ivanovich, 634
Koloshin, Sergey Pavlovich, 8
Koloshin, Valentin Pavlovich, 52
Koloshina, Sofya Pavlovna (Sonichka), 634
Koltsov, Alexey Vasilyevich, 486
Komissarov, Osip Ivanovich, 205–6
Koni, Anatoly Fyodorovich, 448, 515, *556*, *641*, 652, 660, 676; 'General Aspects of Judicial Ethics', 641
Korb, Johann Georg, 254
Korganov, Ivan Iosifovich, 628
Korganova, Anna Avessalomovna, *628*
Kornilov, Vladimir Alexeyevich, 44
Korolenko, Vladimir Galaktionovich, *699*
Kovalevsky, Maxim Maximovich, 616, 674
Kovalevsky, Yegor Petrovich, 62, 112, *138*
Kovalevsky, Yevgraf Petrovich, 140
Kramskoy, Ivan Nikolayevich, 220, 265, 367, 379, 460, 462; *Christ in the Wilderness*, 462
Krasnov, Vasily Filippovich, *548*, *694*; *Khodynka*, 548, 694

Krayevsky, Andrey Alexandrovich, 61, 78, 125
Krishna, 692
Krivtsov, Nikolay Ivanovich, 465
Kropotkin, Pyotr Alexeyevich, 576–7, 587
Kruger, Paul, 585
Krylov, Ivan Andreyevich, 313
Kryokshino, 633
Küchelbecker, Vilgelm Karlovich, 318
Kugler, Franz Theodor, *Handbuch der Kunstgeschichte*, 445
Kupferschmidt, Alexander Mikhaylovich (Sasha), 176, 187
Kuprin, Alexander Ivanovich, *The Duel*, 651–652; *The Night Shift*, 630
Kuropatkin, Alexey Nikolayevich, 639
Kurtysh, Ivan Markovich, 661
Kuzminskaya, Tatyana Andreyevna (née Behrs), 4, 5, 165–6, *169*, *176*, *177*, *183*, 186–7, 189–90, 195, 208–9, 216, 235, 262, *269*, 326, 388–9, 393, 635
Kuzminsky, Alexander Mikhaylovich, 169, 176, 269, 405, 453

Laborde, Mme, 177
Labour Prophet, The, 512
Lachinov, Nikolay Alexandrovich, 218
Lacroix, Paul, 308
Lao-Tzu, 310, 401, 405, 428, 440, 442, 486, 494–5, 500, 630, 635, 653, 664, 673
Laptevs (family), 5
La Rochefoucauld, François de, 200
Las Cases, Emmanuel, *Mémorial de Ste Hélène*, 450
Lavisse, Ernest, 494
Le Dantu, Camille, 324
Lederle, Mikhail Mikhaylovich, *484*
Leibnitz, Gottfried Wilhelm, 440
Lelewel, Joachim, 146
Leonid, Archimandrite (Lev Alexandrovich Kavelin), *278*
Leopardi, Giacomo, 442
Lermontov, Mikhail Yuryevich, 243, 289; *A Hero of our Time*, 485
Leskov, Nikolay Semyonovich, 241, 412, 472, *480*, *505*; *The Hour of God's Will*, 472
Lessing, Gotthold Ephraim, 644; *Nathan der Weise*, 412
Ley, James, *636*
Liberation, 620
Lichtenberg, Georg Christof, 644, 647, 673
Life, 586, 620
Life for All, 696

Index

Linetsky, Emmanuil Grigoryevich, 631
Liprandi, Pavel Petrovich, 42, 43
Longinov, Mikhail Nikolayevich, 60–1, 153, 200
Lowell, James Russell, 588
Lubbock, John, 484
Lully, Jean Baptiste, 423
Lunin, Mikhail Sergeyevich, 329
Lunina, Yekaterina Sergeyevna, 329
Lvov, Yevgeny Vladimirovich, 291
Lvova, Alexandra Vladimirovna, 98, 106
Lyall, Edna, *Donovan*, 464; *We Two*, 464
Lyubochinskaya, Zinaida Mikhaylovna, 581

Maeterlinck, Maurice, 645
Maistre, Joseph de, 188, 292
Makarova, Akulina, 520, 524
Makovitsky, Dushan Petrovich, 515, 710–11, 713–14
Malaya Vorotynka, 7
Malikov, Alexander Kapitonovich, 310, 347
Malikova, Yelizaveta Alexandrovna (Liza), 352, 354, 359
Malthus, Thomas Robert, 663; Malthusianism, 598
Maltsov, Ivan Sergeyevich, 614
Maltsov, Sergey Ivanovich, 378–9
Mandt, Mikhail I., 629
Mandzhos, Boris Semyonovich, 697
Marakuyev, Vladimir Nikolayevich, 484
Marcus Aurelius, 440, 442, 644, 671
Marov, Afanasy Stepanovich, 655
Marx, Adolf Fyodorovich, 574
Marya Alexandrovna, Empress, 201, 333
Marya Alexandrovna, Grand Duchess, 103, 200, 267–8, 271
Marya Fyodorovna, Empress, 569–70
Marya Nikolayevna, Grand Duchess, 103, 105, 107
Maslova, Anna Ivanovna, 559
Maude, Aylmer, 167, 175, 368, 414, 522, 524, 534, 565, 574, 576, *577*, 589, 590, 600, 607, 621, 640, 648, 649, 662, 677, 702, 717; *The Life of Tolstoy (Later Years)*, 702; *A Peculiar People. The Doukhobors*, 648; *The Teaching of Tolstoy*, 589
Maude, Louise (*née* Shanks), 577, 579, 589–591, 607, 646, 648
Maupassant, Henri de, 411, 464, 497, 500, 502; *Les dimanches d'un bourgeois de Paris*, 589; *Mont-Oriol*, 498; *Pierre et Jean*, 498; *Sur l'eau*, 498; *Une Vie*, 712
Maydel, Yegor Ivanovich, 320

Maykov, Apollon Nikolayevich, 112, 114, 243, 367, 499
Maynov, Vladimir Vladimirovich, 446
Mazzini, Pietro, 464, 604
Melnikov, Pyotr, 694
Melnikov-Pechersky, Pavel Ivanovich, 112
Mencius, 439–40, 442, 486, 653
Mendeleyev, Dmitry Ivanovich, 540, 616
Mengden, Yelizaveta Ivanovna, 93, 275, 327
Mennonites, 568
Menshikov, Alexander Sergeyevich, 40, 47
Menshikov, Mikhail Osipovich, 520
Meredith, George, 682
Meshchersky, Vladimir Petrovich, 237; 'Russia from the Pen of a Remarkable Man. Contemporary Letters', 238
Meyerbeer, Giacomo, *The Huguenots*, 77
Michelet, Jules, 229
Mikhail Nikolayevich, Grand Duke, 42
Mikhaylov, Mikhail Illarionovich, 151
Mikhaylov, Nikolay Vasilyevich, 439
Mikhaylovsky, Nikolay Konstantinovich, *On Religion*, 606
Mikhaylovsky-Danilevsky, Alexander Ivanovich, *The Military Gallery of the Winter Palace*, 188
Miklukho-Maklay, Nikolay Nikolayevich, 406
Milan Obrenovich, King of Serbia, 580
Mill, John Stuart, 225, 227–8, 356, 640
Milton, John, *Paradise Lost*, 666
Milyukov, Pavel Nikolayevich, 496
Milyutin, Vladimir Alexeyevich, 5
Minsky, Nikolay Maximovich (N. M. Vilenkin), 449; *By the Light of Conscience*, 448–9
Mirbeau, Octave, 632
Mirsky, Dmitry Petrovich, *see* Svyatopolk-Mirsky, D. P.
Miserbiyev, Sado, 21–2
Mi-Ti, 635, 653
Molchanov, Mikhail Mikhaylovich, 647
Molière (Jean Baptiste Poquelin), 223–4, 429
Molokans, 417, 508, 557
Molostvova, Zinaida Modestovna, 634
Montaigne, Michel de, *Essais*, 712
Montesquieu, Charles Louis de Secondat, 644; *Persian Letters*, 698
More, Thomas, 632
Morris, William, 632
Mortier de Fontaine, Louis Henri Stanislav, 64, 67–8, 80–2, 117
Moscow, University of, 12
Moscow Gazette, The, 152, 206, 211, 263, 606
Moscow Literacy Committee, 270, 540

Moscow Musical Society, 55, 117
Mozart, Wolfgang Amadeus, 58, 301; *Don Giovanni*, 58, 503
Müller, Friedrich Max, 290, 309, 440, 462
Musin-Pushkin, Alexey Ivanovich (Alyosha), 6
Musin-Pushkin, Mikhail Nikolayevich, 5–6
Mutsenek, K. I., *692*

Napoleon I, 139, 145, 185, 217, 232, 273, 450, 469, 671
Napoleon III, 96
Nazarenes, 568, 581
Nazaryev, Valeryan Nikanorovich, *Life and People of the Past*, 470
Nazhivin, Ivan Fyodorovich, *660*, 709; *Mene, Mene, Tekel, Upharsin*, 661
Neave, Joseph, 493
Nechayev, Sergey Gennadiyevich, 354, 463–4
Nekrasov, Nikolay Alexeyevich, 5, *29, 31, 33, 34, 36, 38, 48,* 51, 53–4, 57–8, *59*, 88, 90, 93, 100, *107*, 112, *114, 118, 119*, 156, 196, 258, 310, 312, 389, 415
Nekrasova, Yekaterina Stepanovna, *Yulianiya Lazarevskaya*, 400
Nesselrode, Karl Vasilyevich, 58
New Jerusalem Monastery, 278, 312
New Russia, The, 432, 697
New Times, *305, 483,* 495, *670*
New York Herald, The, 477
Newspaper Editors, *591*
Newton, William Wilberforce, 284
Nicholas I, Emperor, 2, 42, 103, 137, 280, 308, 315, 318, 324, 331, 420, 605, 610, 615, 623–625, 629, 641, 671, 675
Nicholas II, Emperor, 347, 512–13, 540, 546, 557–8, 581, *608*, 615, 617, 650, 689
Nietzsche, Friedrich, 590, 623, 665; *Thus Spake Zarathustra*, 590, 623
Nikiforov, Lev Pavlovich, *463, 498,* 520–1, 600
Nikitin, Dmitry Vasilyevich, 639
Nikolay Mikhaylovich, Grand Duke, 605, *615, 623, 624, 644, 649, 650, 655, 674*; *Count Pavel Alexandrovich Stroganov (1774–1817)*, 624, 655; *The Dolgoruky Princes*, 655; *Russian Portraits of the XIXth and XXth Centuries*, 655
Nikolay Nikolayevich, Grand Duke, 42
Nikolayev, Pyotr Petrovich, *The Concept of God as the Perfect Foundation of Life*, 712
Nikolskoye-Vyazemskoye, 12, 36, 180, 195, 229, 330, 452

Nineteenth Century, 328
Nobel Prize, 613, 660
Northern Bee, The, 137
Northern Herald, The, 497, 500, 503, 514, 560
Notes of the Fatherland, 51, 61, 78, 84, 88, 90, 98, 124–5, 196, 389–90
Novosiltsev, Pyotr Petrovich, 130
Novikov, Alexey Mitrofanovich, 487
Novikov, Mikhail Petrovich, *679, 710*
Novosyolov, Mikhail Alexandrovich, *420*, 435

Obolenskaya, Marya Lvovna, *see* Tolstaya, M. L.
Obolenskaya, Yelizaveta Valeryanovna (*née* Tolstaya), 185, 192, 195, *715*
Obolensky, Dmitry Alexandrovich, 5–6, 118, 175, 237, 330
Obolensky, Leonid Dmitriyevich, 437
Obolensky, Leonid Yegorovich, *380, 384,* 400
Obolensky, Nikolay Leonidovich (Kolya), 508, 551, 561, 572, 589, 651, 657
Ogaryov, Nikolay Platonovich, 145; *Caucasian Waters*, 146
Ogaryov, Vladimir Ivanovich, 22
Okhotnitskaya, Natalya Petrovna, 57, 70, 176, 179, 224, 380
Old Believers, 317, 333
Olsufyev, Mikhail Adamovich, 447
Olsufyevs (family), 554, 572
O'Meara, Barry, *Napoleon in Exile, or a Voice from Ste Hélène*, 450
Optina Monastery, 53, 280, 303–4, 352, 455, 582, *711–12*, 714
Orekhov, Alexey Stepanovich, 77, 187, 189, 357
Organising Committee of the XVIII International Peace Congress, 688
Orlov, Alexander Ivanovich, 428
Orlov, Nikolay Alexeyevich, 98
Orlov, Vladimir Fyodorovich, 353–4, 400, 403
Orthodoxy, 201, 233, 347, 349–50, 377, 384, 420, 446, 457, 489, 495, 513, 528, 544, 591, 609–11
Osinsky, Valeryan Andreyevich, 351
Osten-Saken, Alexandra Ilinichna (Aunt Alexandra), 1, 3, 52
Osten-Saken, Dmitry Yerofeyevich, 46
Ostrovsky, Alexander Nikolayevich, 57, 61–62, 68, 73, 91, 112, 118, 137, 199, 226, 278, *403, 412*; *Among Friends One Always*

727

Index

Ostrovsky, Alexander Nikolayevich (*cont.*) *Comes to Terms*, 92; *A Lucrative Situation*, 91–2; *Minin*, 278; *Poverty is No Crime*, 404; *The Storm*, 137; *A Warm Heart*, 220
Ottoman Tobacco Factory, *681*
Ovsyannikova, 509
Owen, Robert, 144
Ozmidov, Nikolay Lukich, 400, 404–5, 419, *431*
Ozmidova, Olga Nikolayevna, 402–3

Paine, Thomas, *The Age of Reason*, 477
Pall Mall Gazette, The, 484
Palmerston, Henry John Temple, 56, 143
Panayev, Ivan Ivanovich, 29–30, *51*, 62, 68, 90–1, 102, 107–8, 112, 114, 156
Panayeva, Avdotya Yakovlevna, *Domestic Hell*, 107
Panfilov, Vladimir Ivanovich, *683*
Panina, Sofya Vladimirovna, 513, 605
Parfeny, Abbot, *Travels*, 317, 323
Parker, Theodore, 588, 644; *A Discourse of Matters Pertaining to Religion*, 486
Partition, The, 418
Pascal, Blaise, 223, 294–5, 335, 428, 442, 490, 689, 693; *Pensées*, 294, 486
Pashkov, Vasily Alexandrovich, 384, 438
Paskevich, Ivan Fyodorovich, 40–1
Pasternak, Leonid Osipovich, *646*
Paul I, Emperor, 213, 652
Pauthier, Jean Pierre Guillaume, *Les livres sacrés de l'Orient*, 440
Pavlov, Nikolay Filippovich, 117
Pavlov-Silvansky, Nikolay Pavlovich, 654
Pellico, Silvio, 412
'People and Institutions which sent Congratulations on my Eightieth Birthday', *682*
Perfectionists, 594
Perfilyev, Vasily Stepanovich, 16, 42, 216, 242, 444
Perfilyevs (family), 16, 170, 216, 241
Perovskaya, Sofya Lvovna, 341
Perovskaya, Yekaterina Vasilyevna, *see* Gorchakova, Y. V.
Perovsky, Boris Alexeyevich, 147, 149, 160, 331
Perovsky, Lev Alexeyevich, 330–1
Perovsky, Vasily Alexeyevich, 310–11, 315, 331
Perper, Iosif Iosifovich, *685*, *698*
Peter I, Emperor, 5, 223, 230, 240, 242, 246, 252, 254, 258, 261, 333, 374, 617

Petersburg, Military Academy, 47
Petersburg, University of, 1
Petersburg Gazette, The, 59, 107
Petersburg Literacy Committee, 484, 539–40
Petrov, A., 104
Petrov, Ivan Ivanovich, 412
Petrov, M. A., 129–30; *The Elections*, 129; *Sargin's Grave*, 124
Philo of Alexandria, 339–40
Pilate, Pontius, 395, 468
Pirogovo, 4, 15, 27, 36, 44, 89, 510, 560, 589
Pisarev, Rafail Alexeyevich, 487
Pisemsky, Alexey Feofilaktovich, 91, 112–13, 130, 156, 197, *241*; *In the Whirlpool*, 241
Plato, 106, 231, 239, 285, 440, 647; *Phaedo*, 486; *Symposium*, 486
Plekhanov, Georgy Valentinovich, 312
Pletnyov, Pyotr Alexandrovich, *156*
Plutarch, 412, 644
Pobedonostsev, Konstantin Petrovich, 341, *347*, 544, 617
Pogodin, Mikhail Petrovich, 117, 175, *217*, *219*, 254; *Historical Aphorisms*, 218–19
Pogorelsky, Antony, *The Little Black Hen*, 485
Pokrovskoye, 33, 53, 165
Polar Star, The, 144–6
Polenov, Vasily Dmitriyevich, 463
Polenz, Wilhelm von, *614*; *Der Büttnerbauer*, 614; *Der Grabenhäger*, 614; *Der Pfarrer von Breitendorf*, 614
Polonsky, Yakov Petrovich, 68, 130, 180, 299, 352
Polovtsev, Anatoly Viktorovich, 633
Pomerantsev, Yury Nikolayevich, 559
Popkov, Nikolay, *688*
Popov, Alexander Nikolayevich, 308
Popov, Yevgeny Ivanovich, 448, *469*, 491, 500, 504, 559
Posse, Vladimir Alexandrovich, 620, 696
Potapenko, Ignaty Nikolayevich, *A Family Story*, 497
Potekhin, Alexey Antipovich, *In the Peasant Commune*, 305, 412; *The Sick Woman*, 412
Praskovya Isayevna, 24
Prescott, William Hickling, *The Conquest of Mexico*, 485
Pressensé, Edmond de, 363–4
Problems of Philosophy and Psychology, 477, 489, 495–6, 523, 551
Proudhon, Pierre Joseph, 56
Pugachov, Yemelyan Ivanovich, 540
Pulley, H. W., *The Ground Ash*, 374

Purleigh Colony, 457, 534, 563, 571, 576, 578, 579
Pushchin, Mikhail Ivanovich, 105
Pushchins (family), 99, 105
Pushkin, Alexander Sergeyevich, 30, 60, 67, 98–9, 117, 156, 172, 206, 224, 239, 243–4, 252, 258, 260–1, 267, 279, 301, 338, 362, 452, 485, 498, 694; *The Captain's Daughter*, 258; *The Guests were arriving at the country house*, 258; *Egyptian Nights*, 258; *The Shot*, 258; *The Tales of Belkin*, 258–60; *The Stone Guest*, 58; *Yevgeny Onegin*, 485
Pypin, Alexander Nikolayevich, 267, *364*
Pythagoras, 401, 413

Quakers, 493, 567, 577, 579–80, 601, 606

Rabinovich, Solomon Naumovich (Sholom-Aleichem), *631*
Rachinskaya, Marya Konstantinovna (m. S. L. Tolstoy), 452, 552
Rachinskaya, Varvara Alexandrovna, 151, 159
Rachinsky, Konstantin Alexandrovich, 151
Rachinsky, Sergey Alexandrovich, 151, *158, 311*
Radishchev, Alexander Nikolayevich, 540
Radstock, Lord, 294, 384
Ralston, William Sheddon, 327, *328*
Ramasehan, A., *599*
Raphael, Sanzio, *Sistine Madonna*, 121
Rayevsky, Ivan Ivanovich, 487
Raygorodsky, Yakov, 661
Razin, Stepan Timofeyevich (Stenka Razin), 540
Reader's Library, 61–2, 84, 88, 112, 124, 129, 156, 171, 196
Rebinder, Konstantin Grigoryevich, 107
Redfern, Percy, 589, *601, 630*
Rees, Fyodor Fyodorovich, 213, 216, 220, 242
Reichel, Eugen, *664*
Renan, Ernest, 136, 225–6, 309, 332–3, 356; *L'avenir de la science*, 473; *La vie de Jésus*, 322
Repin, Ilya Yefimovich, *379*, 381, 385, 387, 436, 444, 461; *Ivan the Terrible and his Son*, 380; *Saint Nicholas Saves Three Men Unjustly Condemned to Death in Myra in Lycia*, 444; *The Scourging of Christ*, 381
Review of Reviews, The, 467, 472, 557, 649
Revue Blanche, La, 621
Revue de Famille, La, 496
Revue des deux Mondes, La, 224, 355
Revue Etrangère, La, 355

Ribot, Théodule, 431
Richau, Daniel Carl, 204–5
Richet, Charles, 502
Rilke, Rainer Maria, *583*
Robertson, Frederick William, 486
Rockefeller, John, 588
Rod, Eduard, *441*, 502; *Le Sens de la Vie*, 441
Rolland, Romain, 414, *421*
Rostovtsev, Nikolay Yakovlevich, 45, 51, 132
Rousseau, Jean-Jacques, 100, 181, 412, 492, 498, 574, 621, 632, 644, 673, 689; *Confessions*, 485; *Emile*, 485; *La Nouvelle Héloïse*, 100, 485, 574
Rozanov, Vasily Vasilyevich, 226–7, 492, 495, 645
Ruban-Shchurovskaya, Zoya Grigoryevna, 596
Rubinstein, Nikolay Grigoryevich, 301–2
Rusanov, Gavriil Andreyevich, *442*, *499*, *644*
Ruskin, John, 464, 533, 600–1, 630, 644, 648, 689; *Unto this Last*, 600, 691; see also Brunhes, H. J., *Ruskin et la Bible*
Russia, 349, 360
Russian, The, 219
Russian Antiquities, 317
Russian Archives, The, 188, 213, 215, 217, 254, 465
Russian Conversation, 59–60, 210, 237
Russian Gazette, The, *483*, 487–8, 494, 503, 558, 643, *670*
Russian Herald, The, 91, 102, 118, 125, 127, 132, 155–8, 158, 185, 187, 191, 206, 214, 224, 238, 273–4, 277, 298, 305–7, 492, 573
Russian Invalid, The, 48, *218*
Russian Library, The, 326–7
Russian News, 414
Russian Review, The, 480, 495
Russian Survey, The, 470
Russian Thought, 220, 464, 473, 630
Russian Wealth, 409, 606, 699
Russian Word, The, 130, 432, 495
Russian Worker, The, 275, 438
Ryleyev, Kondraty Fyodorovich, 145

Sadler, Percy, *Sadler's English Dictionary*, 39
Sado, see Miserbiyev
Sadovnikov, Dmitry Nikolayevich, *Riddles of the Russian People*, 338
Saillens, Ruben, *438*
St Francis of Assissi, 658
St John, 658
St John, Arthur, *579*
Sakharov, Ivan Ivanovich, 68, 70, 77, 80

Index

Salomon, Charles, 639
Saltykov-Shchedrin, Mikhail Yevgrafovich, 112, *389*; *Provincial Sketches*, 112, 203
Samara, 157, 223, 234, 236, 249, 262–4, 269, 271–80, 352, 420, 432, 452
Samarin, Yury Fyodorovich, *210*, 220, 232, 266–7, 658
Sand, George, 96
Savikhin-Ivanov, Vasily Ivanovich, 414–15; *Uncle Sofron*, 385, 418
Schelling, Friedrich Wilhelm, 284, 431
Schiller, Johann Friedrich von, 69; *Die Räuber*, 412, 485
Schmidt, Marya Alexandrovna, 404, 419, *478*, 551, 558
Schmidt, Nikolay, *688*
Schmitt, Eugen Heinrich, 515, 581
Schöngraben, Battle of, 191
Schopenhauer, Arthur, 135, 221, 223, 239, 284–6, 298, 334–5, 339, 430, 441, 644, 673, 698; *Parerga und Paralipomena*, 477; *Die Welt als Wille und Vorstellung*, 221, 332, 335
Schroeder, Félix, 502
Schumann, Robert, 301
Schuyler, Eugene, 327
Scott, Walter, 112, 206
Semyonov, Nikolay Petrovich, 330
Semyonov, Sergey Terentyevich, 437; *The Butuzov Brothers*, 479; *Into the City*, 412
Semyovsky, Mikhail Ivanovich, 317
Seneca, 440, 644
Sergeyenko, Alexey Petrovich, 712, 715
Serzhputovsky, Adam Osipovich, 40
Seton-Watson, Hugh, 689
Sevastopol, 19, 43–7, 49, 51–2, 54, 77, 84, 138, 234, 293, 378, 654
Shakers, 651
Shakespeare, William, 223–5, 533, 633–4, 641, 648, 662, 664–6; *Hamlet*, 533, 664–5; *Julius Caesar*, 533; *King Lear*, 533, 664–5; *Macbeth*, 366, 664–5; *Othello*, 533; *Romeo and Juliet*, 533
Shamil, 17, 628
Shamordino Convent, 53–4, 711–14
Shanks, Mary, 579
Shatilov, Iosif Nikolayevich, 260
Shaw, George Bernard, 627, 663, *677*, 682, *700*; *Man and Superman*, 677, 700; *The Revolutionist's Handbook*, 678; *The Shewing-up of Blanco Posnet*, 677, 700
Shcherbacheva (aunt of V. V. Arsenyeva), 67, 79

Shcherbatova, Praskovya Sergeyevna, 634
Shelley, Percy Bysshe, 662
Shenshin, Pyotr Afanasyevich, 229, 277, 282, 319
Shenshina, Nadezhda Afanasyevna, 130–1
Sheremetev, Sergey Alexandrovich, 163
Sheremetevs (family), 255
Shervashidze, Georgy Dmitriyevich, 606
Shestov, Lev Isaakovich, *The Concept of Good in the Teachings of Count Tolstoy and Friedrich Nietzsche*, 623
Shilder, Nikolay Karlovich, 629
Shishkina, Marya Mikhaylovna (Masha), 4, *14*, 183–4, 187, 539, 590
Sholom-Aleichem, *see* Rabinovich, S. N.
Shor, David Solomonovich, 631
Shostak, Yekaterina Nikolayevna (*née* Islenyeva), 106, 110, 130
Sibiryakov, Konstantin Mikhaylovich, 384
Sienkiewicz, Henryk, *670*
Silistria, 39, 40–1, 44, 46, 77
Silvester, 279
Simon, G. Eugène, *La cité chinoise*, 435
Sipyagin, Dmitry Sergeyevich, 620
Škarvan, Albert Albertovich, 516, 576–7, *666*, *694*
Skoptsy, 544
Slavnin, Kelsy Porfiryevich, *697*
Slavophilism, 56, 58–9, 91–2, 113, 115, 117, 138, 200–1, 210, 217, 225–6, 232, 237, 240, 244, 270, 349, 427, 495–6
Smirnov, Nikolay Mikhaylovich, 211
Sobolev, Andrey Ilich, 6, 7, 27
Social Gospel, The, 565
Society for Public Education, 140
Socrates, 381, 442, 644
Sokhanskaya, Nadezhda Stepanovna, *From a Provincial Gallery of Portraits*, 125
Solovyov, Vladimir Sergeyevich, 281, 318, 322, 354, 360; *The Crisis of Western Philosophy*, 272, 281; *Faith, Reason and Experience*, 310; 'The Moral Organisation of Mankind', 551
Son of the Fatherland, The, 94
Sophocles, 225
Sopotsko, Mikhail Arkedyevich, *526*
Sosnovsky, Mikhail Ivanovich, 405–6
Spasskoye, 148, 352, 358, 443, 572
Spectator, The, 203
Spencer, Herbert, 381, 512, 606, 640; *An Autobiography*, 640; *Principles of Biology*, 476
Spinoza, Benedict de, 166, 284, 492, 647

730

Spring, The, 479
Stakhovich, Mikhail Alexandrovich, 388–9, 448–9, 559, *673*, 680, *685*
Stanitsky, N., *see* Panayeva, A. Y.
Stankevich, Alexander Vladimirovich, 117
Stankevich, Nikolay Vladimirovich, 155
Starogladovskaya, 9, 14–15, 17, 19, 25, 29–38
Stary Yurt, 10, 15, 21–2
Stasov, Vladimir Vasilyevich, 318, *323*, *496*, *624*, *633*, *641*, *652*, *654*, *659*, 660; *Shakespeare's 'Merchant of Venice'*, 641
Stasova, Nadezhda Vasilyevna, *518*
Stead, William Thomas, 484, *649*
Stendhal (Beyle, M. H.), 632
Sterne, Laurence, *Sentimental Journey*, 1, 485
Stock Exchange News, The, 692
Stoics, Stoicism, 424, 440, 635
Stolypin, Arkady Dmitriyevich, 45, 690
Stolypin, Pyotr Arkadyevich, 675, *689*
Storozhenko, Nikolay Ilich, 450–1
Stowe, Harriet Beecher, *Uncle Tom's Cabin*, 118
Stoy, Karl Volkmar, 159
Strakhov, Nikolay Nikolayevich, 225, 233, 237, *238*, 242, 243, 257, *260*, 261, 263, 265, 266, 270, 272, 274, 277, 279, 280, 282, 283, 293, 295, 296, 299, 302, 303, 304, 306, 307, 308, 309, 312, 317, 321, 325, 326, 329, 334–5, *335*, *338*, *339*, 340, 341, 348, 349, 350, 356, 363, 387, 430, 445, 448, 473, 474, 475, 476, 477, 492, 495, 514, 523, 533, 642; *The Biography, Letters, and Extracts from the Notebooks of F. M. Dostoyevsky*, 363; *The Course and Nature of Modern Natural Science*, 492; *The Last of the Idealists*, 280; *Letters about Nihilism*, 349–50; *On the Basic Concepts of Psychology*, 305, 307, 310, 325; *On the Growth of Organisms*, 266; *Philosophical Essays*, 514; *The Revolution in Science*, 242; *The Struggle with the West in our Literature*, 225, 356; *Three Letters on Spiritualism*, 303; *A Trip to Italy*, 293; *The Woman Question*, 227; *The World as a Whole*, 239, 258
Strauss, David Friedrich, 136, 225, 309
Stroganov, Grigory Alexandrovich, 192
Stroganov, Pavel Alexandrovich, 624
Struve, Pyotr Berngardovich, 620
Stundists, 504, 544
Sudakovo, 63–4, 77, 80–1, 88
Sukhotin, Mikhail Sergeyevich, 387, 553, 563, 586, 700, 704, 709
Sukhotin, Sergey Mikhaylovich, 187
Sukhotina, Tatyana Lvovna, *see* Tolstaya, T. L.
Sukin, Alexander Yakovlevich, 317
Sumarokov, P. P., 'Country Letters', 124–5
Surikov, Vasily Ivanovich, *The Boyarynya Morozova*, 415
Suslova, Apollinariya (Polina) Prokofyevna, 495
Suvorina, Anna Ivanovna, 265
Suvorov, Ivan Vasilyevich, 13, 25
Svistunov, Pyotr Nikolayevich, *316*, 324–5, 329
Svobodin, Pavel Matveyevich, *415*
Svyatopolk-Mirsky, Dmitry Petrovich, 389
Svyatopolk-Mirsky, Pyotr Dmitriyevich, *597*
Swedish Writers and Scholars, *613*
Swift, Jonathan, *Gulliver's Travels*, 412, 467
Syutayev, Vasily Kirillovich, 354, 362
Sytin, Ivan Dmitriyevich, 409, 412, 447

Taine, Hippolyte Adolphe, 166, 225–6
Taneyev, Sergey Ivanovich, 167, 513, 554–5, 558–61
Taptykovo, 524, 603
Taube, Mikhail Alexandrovich, *634*
Tchaikovsky, Pyotr Ilich, *301*, 502; *Yevgeny Onegin*, 328
Telescope, The, 654
Temps, Le, 277
Tessié du Motay, Marie-Edmond, 145
Thackeray, William Makepeace, 86; *The Newcomes*, 61; *Vanity Fair*, 70
Theuriet, André, 464
Thoreau, Henry David, 588
Thousand and One Nights, The, 335, 485
Time, 180, 225
Times, The, 522
Tishchenko, Fyodor Fyodorovich, *407*, *416*; *The Sinner*, 409; *The Unfortunate Ones*, 408, 416
Tolmachova, Anna Leonidovna, 639
Tolstaya, Alexandra Andreyevna (Granny), 12, 55, 97–8, 102, *103*, *105*, *108*, *120*, *121*, *123*, *125*, *128*, *130*, *146*, *149*, *155*, *157*, *160*, *164*, *169*, *172*, *181*, *191*, *197*, *200*, 227, 233, 240, 245, *247*, 248, 250, *251*, 256, *263*, 267, 270, *271*, *273*, *293*, *295*, *303*, *310*, *315*, 318, *319*, *330*, *332*, *355*, *376*, *481*, *516*, *629*, *635*
Tolstaya, Alexandra Lvovna (Sasha; Tolstoy's daughter), 509, 516, 550, 560, 572, 586, 638, 642, 657–8, 700, 705, 710–11, *711*, *712*, 714–16

Index

Tolstaya, Dora Fyodorovna, *see* Westerlund, D. F.

Tolstaya, Marya Konstantinovna, *see* Rachinskaya, M. K.

Tolstaya, Marya Lvovna (Masha; Tolstoy's daughter), 236, 254, 359, 403, 446–8, 451, 479, 482–3, 485, 499–500, 504, *508*, 509–511, 523, 549, *551*, 552, 553, 558–9, 561–2, 572, *586*, 589–90, 627, 629, 638–9, *650*, *656*, *658*, 661–2, 702, 711

Tolstaya, Marya Nikolayevna (Tolstoy's mother), 1

Tolstaya, Marya Nikolayevna (Marie, Masha; Tolstoy's sister), 14–15, 24, 32–3, 37, 47, 52, *53*, *57*, *58*, 88, 111, 123, 127, 134, 143, 158, 161, 163, *181*, 185, 192, 195, 197–8, 224, 241, 250, 364, 393, 437, 517, 711, *715*

Tolstaya, Olga Konstantinovna, *see* Dieterichs, O. K.

Tolstaya, Pelageya, Nikolayevna (Tolstoy's grandmother), 2

Tolstaya, Praskovya Vasilyevna, 331

Tolstaya, Sofya Andreyevna, *née* Behrs (Tolstoy's wife), 4, 56, 164, *165*, 169–70, 172–3, 176–9, *180*, 183–5, *186*, *188*, 200–1, 203–8, *215*, 220, 222, 224, 230, *234*, *235*, 246–8, 253–4, 262–3, 267–8, 277, 300, 302–4, 316, 320, 324, 327–8, 332–3, 337, 340, 352, *352*, 353, *355*, *357*, *366*, 368, 373, *374*, *377*, *378*, 383, *386*, 389, 392, *393*, 400, *402*, 411, 419, 436, *443*, 447, 451, 458, 465, 470, 477–478, 482, 484, *486*, 489, *492*, *497*, *509*, 514, 516–17, 525, 533, *549*, *550*, 551, *554*, *557*, 558, 561, *563*, 572, 586, 627, 630, 633, 639, 642–3, 656, 659, 667, 669, 682, *686*, 688, *700*, 702–5, 709, *710*, *713*, 715–717

Tolstaya, Sofya Nikolayevna (m. I. L. Tolstoy), *see* Filosofova, S. N.

Tolstaya, Tatyana Lvovna (Tanya; Tolstoy's daughter), 175, 192, 198, 216, 253, 304, 359, 377, 379, 386, 402–3, 405, 413, 433, 444, 447, 451, 464, 469, 484, 487, *502*, *504*, 508–510, *523*, 535, 549–52, 554, 558, 559, 563, 572, 579, 586–7, 589–90, 634, *638*, 642, 651, *687*, 704, *709*, 713, *714*, *716*

Tolstaya, Varvara Sergeyevna, 638

Tolstaya, Varvara Valeryanovna, 47, 58, 185, 192, 195, 241

Tolstaya, Vera Sergeyevna, 435, 538, 590, 638

Tolstaya, Yelizaveta Alexandrovna, (*née* Yergolskaya), 4

Tolstaya, Yelizaveta Andreyevna, 55, 97, 102, 105, 107, 147, 169, 198

Tolstaya, Yelizaveta Valeryanovna, *see* Obolenskaya, Y. V.

Tolstoy, Alexey Konstantinovich, 159–60, 200, 300–1, 452

Tolstoy, Alexander Petrovich, 159

Tolstoy, Andrey Lvovich (Andryusha; Tolstoy's son), 447, 470, 509–10, 520, 523, *524*, 527, 532, 549, 564, 572, *573*, 577, 583, 602, 639, 658, 666–8, *669*

Tolstoy, Dmitry Andreyevich, 271

Tolstoy, Dmitry Nikolayevich (Mitya; Tolstoy's brother), 6–7, 16, 39, 55, 76, 359

Tolstoy, Fyodor Ivanovich ('American'), 202

Tolstoy, Grigory Sergeyevich, 638

Tolstoy, Ilya Andreyevich, 16, 330–1

Tolstoy, Ilya Lvovich (Tolstoy's son), 175, 207, 252–3, 359, 373, 386, 403, *432*, 437, 447, 479, 487, 552–3, 572, 577, 618–19, 638, *663*

Tolstoy, Ivan Lvovich (Vanichka; Tolstoy's son), 437, 447, 509, 516, 555

Tolstoy, Lev Lvovich (Lyova; Tolstoy's son), 175, 253–4, 359, *375*, 389, 392, 403, 414, 447, *470*, 479, 488, 496–7, *502*, *519*, *537*, 549–50, 564–5, *629*, 658, 673; *The Age of Majority*, 503; *The Hall-Porter of the General's Wife*, 629; *Love*, 470, 479; *Montecristo*, 479

Tolstoy, Lev Nikolayevich, views on:

Art; the arts, literature, etc. (general comments), 116–17, 133–4, 142, 197, 237, 243–4, 260, 279, 295, 297, 299–300, 301, 325, 357, 380, 415, 417–18, 419, 423–6, 439–40, 442–3, 444, 460–1, 462–3, 468–469, 498, 502–3, 503–4, 507–8, 526–7, 632, 654–5, 661, 665–6

Education, 138–41, 149–53, 159–61, 171, 182, 199, 202–3, 240–1, 271, 273, 321, 375–6, 404, 413, 439–40, 446–7, 532–3, 539–40, 592–6, 618–19

Literature (his own), 12, 26, 33–5, 37, 45, 48–9, 62, 78, 99, 113, 129, 133, 194, 205, 208, 214, 218, 221, 230, 237, 238–9, 244, 257, 266, 267, 278, 296–7, 311, 315, 324, 328, 390, 477, 483–4, 510–11, 523, 534, 564, 607, 642–3, 660, 674, 684–5, 700–1

Literature (other people's, excluding works indexed separately), 60, 96, 196–7, 225, 242–4, 266, 304, 326–7, 340, 365, 408–9, 461–2, 470, 471–2, 485–6, 492, 497, 505–

Tolstoy, L. N., views on (cont.)
  506, 571, 588–9, 644–5, 647, 672–3, 678–679, 681, 694
Organised government, 84, 95–6, 117–18, 157–8, 160–4, 198–9, 247–52, 341–7, 349–50, 356, 467, 493, 512, 535–6, 540–7, 556–7, 567–70, 574–5, 591–2, 599, 604–605, 608–13, 617, 653–4, 657, 671–2, 684, 689, 690–1, 697–8, 699, 703, 708
Peasantry, 58, 106, 114–15, 145–7, 149, 155, 160, 211, 264, 275–6, 369–70, 402, 465, 467, 480–1, 486–7, 523, 597–8, 610–613, 657, 690–1
Philosophy of life, 6, 17, 23, 26, 66, 69–70, 74–5, 108–10, 113–14, 261, 283–91, 299, 321, 334, 353, 359, 374–5, 380–1, 383, 386–7, 388, 393–400, 402–3, 409–10, 420, 422–7, 428–9, 430–1, 437–8, 441–2, 445–6, 449, 453–4, 482, 493–4, 496–7, 500–1, 505–6, 520–1, 525–6, 527–32, 549, 561–2, 563, 566–7, 601–2, 602–3, 621–2, 630–1, 637–8, 645, 651, 655, 675–676, 678, 679–80, 683–4, 686, 688, 689, 693, 696, 697, 698, 710–11
Private property and economic problems, 115, 195, 246, 269, 369–70, 382–3, 383–4, 391–3, 402–3, 420, 483–4, 489, 496, 512, 518, 534, 536, 611–12, 616, 622, 623, 637–8, 656, 670, 684
Religion, 20–3, 26, 83, 120–1, 121–2, 123–124, 125–6, 141–2, 198, 251, 255–6, 261, 280, 289–90, 291, 294, 295–6, 298, 303, 312–15, 322–3, 332–3, 336, 339, 354, 360–3, 367, 370–3, 376–7, 380–1, 382, 383–4, 401–2, 425–6, 435, 455–6, 458, 458–9, 461, 474–5, 490–1, 492, 494–5, 496, 503–4, 516–17, 520–1, 548, 572, 581–2, 599–600, 601–2, 635, 636, 645, 650–1, 693, 694, 695–6, 700
Revolution and anarchy, 144–5, 159, 161, 205–6, 320–1, 334, 341–7, 349, 350–1, 405, 502, 540, 547, 556–7, 620, 652, 658, 659, 664, 707
Science and Materialism, 284–7, 290, 325–6, 356 (positivists), 423–6, 465, 473–4, 476, 494, 594–5, 694
Sex, marriage and the family, 23–4, 71–2, 75–7, 78–9, 82, 83, 84–5, 120, 172, 177–9, 192, 198, 227–9, 250, 369, 419–20, 430 (note), 433–5, 469, 479, 504–5, 506–7, 518–19, 524–5, 529–30, 536, 537–8, 551–552, 598, 663, 666–9, 687
Socialism, 310, 620, 645, 684, 707

War and pacifism, 7, 14, 29, 32, 39–42, 44–47, 49–50, 52, 180, 185, 211, 233–4, 306, 360–3, 406–7, 456–7, 482–3, 584–5, 644, 645, 653, 688, 692, 706–8

Tolstoy, Lev Nikolayevich, works:
After the Ball, 5, 627
Albert, 55, 93, 95, 114, 119
All's Well that Ends Well, 206
Anna Karenina, 16, 156, 187, 223, 226, 258, 260, 266, 268–9, 271, 277–80, 283, 296–8, 300–2, 305–7, 311, 433, 442, 662, 709
Appeal to the Working People, An, 620
Bethink Yourselves, 627, 641, 644
Boyhood, 3, 5, 19, 24, 30, 35, 51, 54, 60, 84, 94, 97, 101, 202, 451
Captive in the Caucasus, A, 223, 237, 244
Carthago delenda est, 571
Childhood, 1, 3, 5–6, 8, 13, 19, 24, 26, 30–5, 38, 54, 60, 62, 84, 88, 94, 97, 154, 159, 202, 634
Christian Catechism, 308
Christian Teaching, 509, 511, 515, 573
Christianity and Patriotism, 411, 500
Circle of Reading, A, 367, 644, 673, 715
Confession, A, 5, 223, 337, 381, 394, 442
Cossacks, The, 9, 13, 56, 93, 99, 117, 119, 155–6, 180, 327, 573, 634
Criticism of Dogmatic Theology, A, 337
Death of Ivan Ilich, The, 337, 383, 472
Decembrists, The, 145, 182, 223, 308, 313, 317, 324, 337
Destruction of Hell and its Rebuilding, The, 515
Devil, The, 573, 686
Diary of a Mother, The, 515
Divine and the Human, The, 639, 651
Dream, A, 115
Early Manhood, 35
Eighteen Hundred and Five, 156, 182, 185, 190, 192–4, 207
End of an Age, The, 651
False Coupon, The, 515, 639–40
Family Happiness, 55, 125, 127, 129, 299, 634
Father and Son, 57
Father Sergey, 513, 515, 573, 640
Few Words About the Book 'War and Peace', A, 217
Final Report on Help for the Famine-Stricken, A, 496
First Russian Reader, A, 230
First Stage, The, 483
First Step, The, 411, 483

733

Index

Tolstoy, Lev Nikolayevich, works (*cont.*)
  Foolish Daydreams, 547
  For Each Day, 697, 715
  Four periods of growth, 30
  Fruits of Enlightenment, The, 411, 443, 445, 451, 454–5, 482, 676
  God Sees the Truth but Waits, 223, 237
  Great Sin, The, 649
  Hadji Murat, 17, 21, 281, 513, 615, 623–4, 627, 629, 640–2
  History of My Childhood, A, 33–5
  History of Yesterday, A, 1, 194
  How I first killed a hare, 230
  I Cannot Be Silent, 627, 676, 699
  'In a village there lived a righteous man ...', 405
  Infected Family, An, 199
  Interlocutors, 313
  Introduction to *The Flower Garden*, 418
  Irtenev, 573
  Journey to Mamakay Yurt, A, 62
  Khodynka, 548
  Kiesewetter, 93
  Kingdom of God is Within You, The, 411, 483, 493, 500, 579, 588
  Kreutzer Sonata, The, 167, 411, 427, 436, 442, 448, 450–1, 477–8, 482
  Labour of Men and Women, The, 409
  Landowner's Morning, A, 32, 55, 61, 76, 78, 83–4, 94, 101
  Letter from the Caucasus, A, 35
  Letter to a Hindu, 691–2
  Light Shineth in Darkness, The, 513, 515
  Living Corpse, A, 676
  Lucerne, 55, 101–2, 107–8
  Master and Man, 513–14, 520, 560
  Meeting a Moscow Acquaintance in the Detachment, 55, 62
  Memoirs of a Billiard Marker, The, 38
  Memoirs of a Madman, The, 222
  Military Tales, 84, 88
  New Primer, A, 195, 274
  Nicholas Stick, 420
  Non-Action, 494
  Novel of a Russian Landowner, The, 32, 35
  On a Future Life outside Space and Time, 283
  On Art, 445, 565
  On Life, 167, 419, 428, 438, 451, 475, 656
  On Public Education, 152, 195
  On Religion, 624
  On Shakespeare and the Drama, 533, 627, 633, 634, 649, 664
  On Socialism, 709, 715
  On the Importance of the Christian Religion, 283
  On the Means for Helping the Famine-Stricken Population, 488
  On the Moscow Census, 337
  On the Soul and its Life outside the Life that We Know and Understand, 294
  One Hundred Years, 332
  One Thing Needful, The, 674
  Path of Life, The, 706
  Polikushka, 56, 180, 412
  Posthumous Memoirs of Fyodor Kuzmich, The, 515, 655
  Power of Darkness, The, 412, 415, 676
  Primer, 195, 223, 226, 240–2, 244, 246, 249, 252–3, 257, 259, 262–3, 272, 275, 278, 292, 412–13
  Prince Fyodor Shchetinin, 311
  Raid, The, 9, 13, 16, 19, 35–6, 38, 84
  Reduced to the Ranks, 62, 78, 84, 94
  Reminiscences of Childhood, 4, 13
  Reply to the Holy Synod's Edict, A, 513
  Resurrection, 175, 320, 433, 466, 511, 513, 515, 519, 523, 534, 556, 573–4, 576–81, 587, 590, 606–7, 621, 646, 660, 676
  Russian Readers, 385
  Settlers and the Bashkirs, The, 515
  Sevastopol in August, 19, 52, 55
  Sevastopol in December, 19
  Sevastopol in May, 5, 19
  Sevastopol Stories, 30, 84, 451, 607
  Shame, 544
  Short Exposition of the Gospels, A, 354
  Slavery of Our Times, The, 588
  Snowstorm, The, 55, 57
  Spark Neglected Burns the House, A, 381
  Statute on Village Schools, A, 151
  Story of a Cadet, The, 51–2
  Story of a Russian Landowner, The, 9
  Strider, 180, 680
  Tale of Ivan the Fool, The, 387
  Terrible Question, A, 487
  Those who Labour and are Heavy Laden, 330–1
  Three Deaths, 119, 122
  Time to Come to Our Senses, 436–7
  To the Working People, 623–4
  To Young People, 436
  Translation and Harmony of the Four Gospels, A, 337–9, 414
  Two Hussars, 55, 57, 202, 277, 453, 607
  Two Old Men, 387

Upbringing and Education, 164
War and Peace, 3, 5, 8, 13, 56, 99, 156, 169, 175, 182, 185, 188, 190, 194, 199, 203, 206, 210, 213–15, 217–20, 223, 226, 231–233, 238, 257–8, 261–3, 265, 295, 297, 450, 472, 646, 662
What I Believe, 365, 367, 382, 535
What is Art?, 155, 400, 502, 513, 589, 600, 677
What is Religion?, 513
What Men Live By, 366, 647
What the majority of the Russian working people want, 597
What Then Must We Do?, 227, 337, 369, 383, 388, 393, 400, 422, 441, 451
What We Live For, 656
Where Love is, God is, 337, 381, 438–9
Who is Right?, 505, 515
Why Do Men Stupefy Themselves?, 411
Wood-felling, The, 19, 51, 62, 84, 680
Youth, 5, 8, 16, 30, 35, 54, 60, 62, 80, 84, 88, 90, 94, 101, 451

Tolstoy, Mikhail Lvovich (Misha; Tolstoy's son), 355, 378, 447, 470, 509–10, 523, *527*, 549–50, 553, 558, 564, 572, 574, 586, 590
Tolstoy, Nikolay Ilyich (Tolstoy's father), 1, 2
Tolstoy, Nikolay Lvovich (Tolstoy's son), 268, 271
Tolstoy, Nikolay Nikolayevich (Nikolenka; Tolstoy's brother), 1, 4, 8–11, *12*, 16, 20–7, 29, 31–2, 35, 38, 40–2, 44, 46–7, 52–4, 56, 92, 111, 118, 123, 125, 134, 141, 143, 147, 634; *Hunting in the Caucasus*, 12–13, 92
Tolstoy, Nikolay Sergeyevich, 112
Tolstoy, Pyotr Ivanovich, 4
Tolstoy, Pyotr Lvovich (Tolstoy's son), 254, 268
Tolstoy, Sergey Lvovich (Tolstoy's son), 4, 53, 166, 175, 181–3, 188, 190, 192, 198, 205, 230, 252–3, 258, 304–5, 326, 352–3, 392, 405, 447, *452*, 465, 550, 553, 558, 586, 639, 651, 713, *714*, *716*
Tolstoy, Sergey Nikolayevich (Tolstoy's brother), 1, 4, *7*, 10, *14*, 22, 27–9, 32, *35*, *37*, *38*, 42, *43*, 47, *52*, 66, *83*, *87*, *88*, 137, *142*, 147, 169, 181, 183, 186–7, 256, 320, 356, 377, 502–3, *538*, *587*, *589*, *605*, *630*, 638
Tolstoy, Valeryan Petrovich, 4, 8–9, 32–3, 37, 42–3, 45, 47, 50, 52–4, 57–8, 111, 192–3, 198

Tolstoy Foundation, 711
Tolstoy Museums, 387 (Rome), 436, 639 (Moscow), 674 (Petersburg)
Tolstoy Societies, 663 (London), 589, 601 (Manchester), 674, 676 (Moscow)
Tolstoyanism, 381, 402, 404–5, 413, 420, 457, 469, 471–2, 479, 482, 501, 511, 515, 522, 526, 533–4, 536, 551, 565, 578–9, 585, 589, 592, 596, 600, 677, 688, 691
Totomiants, Vakhan Fomich, *696*
Tredyakovsky, Vasily Kirillovich, 362
Tregubov, Ivan Mikhaylovich, 596
Trepov, Fyodor Fyodorovich, 320
Tretyakov, Pavel Mikhaylovich, 220, 265, 419, *460*, *462*, 468, *507*, 567
Tri-Pitaka, The, 310
Troitse-Sergiyev Monastery (Troitsa), 128, 165, 223, 278
Trollope, Anthony, 223, 486
Trutovskaya, Vera Konstantinovna, *The Evil Disease, or Syphilis*, 436
Tsebrikova, Marya Konstantinovna, 545; *L'Assommoir* retold, 386; *The Weaver and the Baker*, 386
Tsertelev, Dmitry Nikolayevich, 470
Turgenev, Ivan Sergeyevich, 12, 13, 38, 47, 52–4, 56, 58, 62, 91, 93–6, *96*, 99–100, 102–103, *111*, 114–18, 125, 130–1, 137, 143, 145–6, *148*, *150*, 151–4, 157, 193, 205, 223, 241, 255, 277, 302, 305, *318*, 326, *327*, 338, 352, *358*, 364, 365, 572, 673, 680; *Asya*, 114, 118; *Enough*, 365; *Fathers and Sons*, 96, 148, 157, 673; *Faust*, 53, 91; *Hamlet and Don Quixote*, 365; *A Hamlet of the Shchigrov Province*, 280; *A Nest of Gentlefolk*, 96, 137; *On the Eve*, 96, 137; *Phantoms*, 91; *Smoke*, 70, 214; *A Sportsman's Sketches*, 94, 96, 485; *Tales and Stories*, 69–71, 94; *The Watch*, 295; *Virgin Soil*, 303–4
Turgeneva, Olga Alexandrovna, 70, 75, 81
Tyutchev, Fyodor Ivanovich, 122, 135, 157, 239, 255, 257, 300, 413, 452, 486
Tyutcheva, Anna Fyodorovna, 200–1
Tyutcheva, Yekaterina Fyodorovna, 147, 187, 267–8

Uhde, Fritz, 507
Union against Drunkenness, 436
Unwin, T. Fisher, *488*
Urusov, Leonid Dmitriyevich, 378–9, *382*, 386
Urusov, Sergey Semyonovich, 175, 210, 220,

Index

Urusov, Sergey Semyonovich (cont.) 227, 231, 291, 293–4, 303, 337, 443–4, 654; *A Guide to the Study of Geometry*, 233; *A Survey of the Campaigns of 1812–13*, 219, 232
Ustryalov, Nikolay Gerasimovich, 254
Uvarov, Alexander, 215
Uvarov, Alexey Sergeyevich, 188, 634
Uvarov, Dmitry Petrovich, 330–1
Uvarov, Fyodor Alexandrovich, 329
Uvarov, Fyodor Petrovich, 188, 215
Uvarova, Yekaterina Sergeyevna, *see* Lunina, Y. S.
Uvarova, Yekaterina Vasilyevna, *see* Gorchakova, Y. V.

Vasnetsov, Viktor Mikhaylovich, 507–8
Vedas, Vedic faith, 310, 440, 599
Vegetarianism, 166, 385, 399, 401, 411, 492, 508, 622, 686, 692
Vegetarian Review, The, 685–6, 698
Vengerov, Semyon Afanasyevich, 356
Vereshchagin, Vasily Vasilyevich, 462
Vergani, Jenny, 9, 66, 70, 73, 75, 77, 80–2, 85–86, 90
Verigin, Pyotr Vasilyevich, 522, 570, 576, 580
Verne, Jules, 332; *Les enfants du capitaine Grant*, 509
Verus, S. E. (P. van Dyk), *Vergleichende Uebersicht der vier Evangelien*, 581
Vetrova, Marya Fedoseyevna, 556
Viardot, Louis, 277
Viardot, Pauline, 53, 96, 277
Vigny, Alfred de, 632
Vogt, Karl Christoph, 186; *Altes und neues aus Thier- und Menschenleben*, 185
Vogüé, Melchior de, 451
Voice, The, 61
Voice of Tolstoy and Unity, The, 369
Voices from Russia, 132
Volkonskaya, Louisa Ivanovna, 194
Volkonsky, Alexander Alexeyevich, 8, 194
Volkonsky, Grigory Mikhaylovich, 584
Volkonsky, Nikolay Sergeyevich (Tolstoy's grandfather), 43, 213
Volkonskys (family), 8
Voltaire, François Marie Arouet de, 412, 644, 673
Voyeykov, Alexander Sergeyevich, 9
Voyeykova, Alexandra Alexandrovna, 105

Wagner, Nikolay Petrovich, 454
Wagner, Wilhelm Richard, 539; *Siegfried*, 538

Waliszewski, Kazimierz, *Autour d'un trône, Catherine II de Russie, La Dernière des Romanoffs, Elizabeth I*, 652
Ward, Mrs Humphry, 223; *Robert Elsmere*, 614
Weber, Georg, 431
Week, The, 464, 479, 520
Weicher, Theodor, 687
Wells, Herbert George, 662, 682
Welsh, Hannah, 509–10
Westerlund, Dora Fyodorovna (m. L. L. Tolstoy), 537–8, 549–50, 563, 630
Westernism, Westerners, 56, 96, 115, 225, 427
Whitman, Walt, 588; *Leaves of Grass*, 464
Whittier, John Greenleaf, 588
Wilhelm II, Emperor, 580, 584–5
Witte, Sergey Yulyevich, 544, 616
Wood, Mrs Henry, 486
Works which made an Impression, List of, 485–6
World's Advance Thought, 456
World Brotherhood of Christians, *see* Dukhobors
Wright, Charles, 640
Wundt, Wilhelm Max, 283

Xenophon, 223, 231, 644; *Anabasis*, 223, 486

Yanzhul, Ivan Ivanovich, 502
Yaroshenko, Nikolay Alexandrovich, 452
Yasnaya Polyana, 56, 141, 143, 147, 151–2, 154, 159, 169–70, 188, 195
Yemelyanov, Arkhip Petrovich, 320
Yergolskaya, Tatyana Alexandrovna (tante Toinette), 1, 2, 3, 6, 8, 9, 11, 15, 17, 20, 23, 25, 28, 31, 32, 39, 42, 44, 46, 49, 52, 53, 63, 71, 79, 83, 88, 100, 108, 121, 123, 127, 133–4, 138, 147, 157–8, 160–3, 169, 177, 179–81, 183, 199, 203, 224–5, 270
Yesipov, Grigory Vasilyevich, 254
Young Ladies of Tiflis, The, 409
Yurkevich, Pamfil Danilovich, 220
Yuryev, Sergey Andreyevich, 220, 232, 450–1
Yushkova, Pelageya Ilinichna (Aunt Polina), 1, 2, 4, 27, 50
Yusupov, Felix, 605

Zagoskin, Mikhail Nikolayevich, *Roslavlev*, 186–7; *Yury Miloslavsky*, 258
Zalyubovsky, Andrey Petrovich, 419
Zasulich, Vera Ivanovna, 320–1, 544
Zavalishin, Dmitry Irinarkhovich, *Memoirs of a Decembrist*, 652

Zeit, Die, 623
Zend-Avesta, 310, 440
Zheltov, Fyodor Alexeyevich, *417*, *532*; *The Quagmire*, 418; *A Village Festival*, 418
Zhikharyov, Stepan Petrovich, *Memoirs of a Contemporary*, 215
Zhirkevich, Alexander Vladimirovich, *461*

Zhukovsky, Vasily Andreyevich, 231, 311, 315
Zola, Emile, 494, 496–7, 645; *L'Assommoir*, 386
Zubova, Marya Nikolayevna (m. S. L. Tolstoy), 452
Zutphen, A. D., *500*

Southern Methodist Univ.
PG 3379.A2E5 1978 v.2
Correspondence.

3 2177 00932 5612

br